Seasons of Marriage and Family Life

*F*or everything there is a season,
    And a time for every matter under heaven:

A time to be born, and a time to die;

A time to plant, and a time to pluck up what is planted;

A time to kill, and a time to heal;

A time to break down, and a time to build up;

A time to weep, and a time to laugh;

A time to mourn, and a time to dance;

A time to cast away stones, and a time to gather stones together;

A time to embrace, and a time to refrain from embracing;

A time to seek, and a time to lose;

A time to keep, and a time to cast away;

A time to rend, and a time to sew;

A time to keep silence, and a time to speak;

A time to love, and a time to hate;

A time for war, and a time for peace.

Ecclesiastes 3:1–8

SEASONS OF MARRIAGE AND FAMILY LIFE

WILLIAM R. GARRETT

St. Michael's College
Winooski, Vermont

Holt, Rinehart and Winston

New York   Chicago   San Francisco
Philadelphia   Montreal   Toronto
London   Sydney   Tokyo
Mexico City   Rio de Janeiro   Madrid

Credits for part opening photographs: Part 1, Woodfin Camp & Associates. Rick Winsor, photographer; Part 2, Copyright © by Stock, Boston, Inc., 1978. Peter Simon, photographer; Part 3, Courtesy of William Garrett; Part 4, Copyright © by Stock, Boston, Inc., 1978. Gabor Demjen, photographer. Part 5, Editorial Photocolor Archives. Marian Bernstein, photographer; Part 6, Monkmeyer Press Photo Service. David Strickler, photographer; Part 7, Courtesy of Roz Sackoff; Part 8, Woodfin Camp & Associates. Rick Winsor, photographer. Cover photograph courtesy of Robert M. Vogel.

Publisher: *David P. Boynton*
Acquiring Editor: *Marie Schappert*
Developmental Editor: *Rosalind Sackoff*
Administrative Editor: *Jeanette Ninas Johnson*
Project Editor: *Harriet Sigerman*
Design Supervisor: *Robert Kopelman*
Production Manager: *Annette Mayeski*

Library of Congress Cataloging in Publication Data

Garrett, William R.
  Seasons of the family.

  Bibliography: p.
  Includes index.
    1. Marriage—United States.   2. Family—United States.
  3. Life cycle, Human.   I. Title.
  HQ536.G36   306.8   81-7240
  ISBN 0-03-057281-9   AACR2

CBS COLLEGE PUBLISHING
Holt, Rinehart and Winston
The Dryden Press
Saunders College Publishing

To Linda

whose charismatic charm has defied Weber's law of routinization through more than twenty years of marriage

PREFACE

The academic field commonly known as marriage and the family is already well stocked with a wide variety of textbooks. The present array of introductions reflects, in part, the differing orientations to marriage and family life that instructors design into their courses offered in sociology, home economics, human development, and education departments. Potential users of this text from all these areas deserve to know, therefore, why this text was written and what it has to offer.

Let me say at the outset that this book includes almost everything that I would like to have imparted to my own students in class lectures—if there had been enough time during a given semester. Indeed, few comments have struck me as more curious over the years than the assertions by textbook writers that the ideas they have presented are "fully classroom tested." How, I wondered, is such a feat possible? With only two to three contact hours per week a course, lecture presentations must necessarily be selective in their coverage of topics, research findings, and major trends. This book has afforded me the opportunity of discussing the material that I would have given to my students—had we enjoyed the luxury of spending fifteen hours a week together. Since I am sure my frustration with time constraints is not unique, I look upon this book as a vehicle whereby all of us who wrestle with the demands of teaching a course like marriage and the family can complement our lectures with a larger repository of important information than can be communicated through the medium of the spoken word. Thus, this book has been consciously designed as a tool for enhancing the classroom experience by remaining as sensitive as possible to the needs of instructors for reliable data and competent interpretation as well as to the questions that students typically bring to the study of marriage and family life.

Toward these goals, then, several specific features of this book are worthy of note. First, the organization of the subject matter is geared to the life cycle of individual family units. This approach not only allows the presentation to unfold according to the internal logic of the subject matter, but it also encourages students to locate their own family experience within the larger framework of the life-cycle stages. Clarity and relevance are the twin benefits that arise from this organizational feature. Thus, with the exception of Part I—which introduces the background materials for studying marriage and the family—each Part division tends to correspond to a particular stage in the family life-cycle. Part II, for example, treats the dynamics of courtship and mating. This segment of the narrative includes one chapter each on sex-role socialization (which forms the basis for heterosexual courtship), the social patterns of dating, and the process of mating. Part III opens with a chapter devoted to the decision to marry, followed by a chapter on the early adjustment to marriage, and closes with a discussion of the alternatives to traditional marriage. Part IV is concerned with the parent-child relationship. The first chapter of this unit considers the choice of parenthood, while the second chapter deals with the socialization of children. Part V examines the crucial dynamics between a husband and wife in a full family household. Accordingly, the interactions between a mature husband and wife are dealt with before turning to a full chapter-length discussion of the processes of separation and divorce. Part VI represents a brief interlude in the life-cycle sequence. Two chapters are devoted here to a consideration of the family's relationship to other basic institutions as well as to the ethnic and class variations in family life. Part VII addresses the issues of growing old. One chapter treats the problems of launching children and retirement, while the other considers the inevitable movement toward widowhood, widowerhood, and death. The final Part evaluates the status of marriage and the family in contemporary America through an assessment of recent trends and the articulation of several modest forecasts for what the future holds in store.

This summary should make clear that my aim has been to develop a complete coverage of the family life cycle. Many other texts concentrate on the early experience of couples in dating and marriage by examining sex-role socialization, dating, marriage and its adjustments, the coming of children, and then conclude with a discussion of marital disruption in separation and divorce. Accordingly, they fail to discuss the full family household very extensively and give almost no mention to the postparental family or the dynamics of aging as this affects family life. Particularly as the American population ages and as the problems of older people become more prominent in public debate, the elimination of these critical periods in family development appeared to be an unwarranted and unwholesome omission. Even though most students who use this text will undoubtedly be young, they will just as surely be the offspring of aging parents and persons who must eventually have to confront the process of growing old or the loss of a spouse. Thus, a text that discusses the latter stages of the family life cycle is not only more intellectually honest, but it is also more relevant to the real-life issues that students will encounter in their own personal experience.

A second major feature of this book is a concerted effort to balance applied and institutional concerns in the course of its development. Implicit in this decision, of course, has been the recognition that some instructors may well elect to omit certain chapters and highlight the material presented in others. For example, a course oriented toward the practical dynamics of marital interaction and family problem-solving may not need to cover Chapter 2 (with its discussion of family types and its brief history of Western family development), Chapter 13 (with its sociological description of the interrelation of the familial institution with the economy, polity, religion, and education), or Chapter 14 (with its depiction of ethnic and class variations in family life). Also, for such applied courses, several appendices have been included at the end of the book dealing with such topics as the means of birth control, the biological basis of human development, and family finances. Additional sections of a practical nature have been deliberately incorporated into those chapters treating sex-role socialization, dating, early marriage adjustment, socialization and child rearing, parental adjustment in a full family household, and the dynamics of aging. Conversely, instructors who focus on the family as a social institution may wish to avoid the appendices as well as the applied sections just mentioned, and concentrate on those chapters—such as 2, 13, and 14—with a pronounced sociological thrust.

A third feature is the eclectic nature of those analytical perspectives undergirding this introduction to marriage and family life. As I point out in the first chapter, marital dynamics and family processes are too complex to be analyzed with reference to one theoretical tradition alone. The three dominant perspectives integrated into this survey include the symbolic interactionist, the developmental, and the structural functional approaches. I have attempted to bring each one into the discussion where the topic under consideration called for a particular perspective. Because of the sheer amount of research inspired by the structural functional tradition, any report that surveys the available research cannot avoid the appearance of concentrating on structural functional investigations, if an evenhanded sampling of work in the field is to be presented.

Similarly, because I respect the vital nature of those normative questions pertaining to family behavior and structure, I have not tried to impose my own normative biases on the reader. My responsibility as a social scientist is to provide reliable information and sound interpretation—not moral pronouncements or normative prescriptions for conduct. Objectivity is never absolutely achieved, however, even with the best of intentions. Thus, in spite of my earnest desire to control them, my personal convictions might have cropped up from time to time as this narrative unfolds. What I do wish to assure the reader is that I have not premised this introduction on a consciously held hidden agenda for the reform of marriage and family life. Whatever changes are or need to be made in these institutions must ultimately be the responsibility of family participants, and not the personal designs of textbook authors. Hopefully, this book will contribute to a deeper understanding of these institutions, and in that limited way aid in the collective decision-making process that will determine the future of marriage and family affairs.

In addition to the text commentary, several teaching aids have been developed for both the student and the instructor. Students will find study questions at the end of each chapter. Boxes incorporating high interest materials on specific aspects of marriage and the family and "Test Yourself" items have been scattered throughout the text. An instructors' manual has also been developed to provide faculty with further suggestions as to how this text may be used more successfully.

In the course of writing any book, an author invariably acquires a number of personal debts. I am pleased to have the opportunity to acknowledge and thank those special people who have enhanced the quality of this book in innumerable ways. Patrick Powers, the Acquisitions Editor at Holt, Rinehart and Winston, first stunned me with an invitation to write this book over two years ago. Measuring up to his confidence and expectations has been a tall order. I hope the final outcome approximates what he initially envisioned. Before this project was completed, Patrick accepted a management position in the CBS Corporation. His former responsibilities were assumed by Marie Schappert who fulfilled them with skill and single-mindedness of purpose. Her input has come at a critical time in this project, and I am pleased she was there to provide her expertise in such a capable fashion. No one has worked closer, longer, and harder with me in writing this manuscript than Rosalind Sackoff, the Developmental Editor. When this endeavor began, Roz and I were little more than acquaintances, but now I regard her as a dear friend—apparently not always the relationship that develops between editor and author. Indeed, she is the only editor I have met who possessed the remarkable skill of demanding something and apologizing for it in the same sentence. Her skilled professionalism is reflected on virtually every page. Moreover, Roz has helped transform the hard work of writing into a thoroughly enjoyable experience. In the production stage, Harriet Sigerman, the Project Editor, has masterfully handled those technical procedures without which an author's work would never see the light of day. Her patience has been exceeded only by her sound judgment. I am also endebted to Mrs. Patricia Allard who typed the final draft of this manuscript with her usual skill and good-natured tolerance in correcting those words I consistently spelled in a creative fashion.

A number of academic colleagues have given unsparingly of their time to review, criticize, and recommend changes in earlier drafts. Two deserve special mention. Professor Thomas Yacovone of Los Angeles Valley College offered invaluable counsel during the preparatory and early stages of the writing. Professor David Klein, University of Notre Dame, provided exceptionally detailed, erudite, and perceptive reviews. My only regret is that I could not follow up every lead in the relevant literature that he suggested. Other reviewers who evaluated the manuscript at various stages include in alphabetical order: Luther Baker, Central Washington State College; George Britton, Lenoir Community College; Kathleen Campbell, Bowling Green State University; Mark Hutter, Glassboro State College; Jay Mancini, Virginia Polytechnic Institute; Isaac Nicholson, Mesa College, Grand Junction, Colorado; Thomas Ramsbey, Rhode Island College; Fred Stultz, California Polytechnic Institute, San Luis, Obispo; Carolyn Warren, Central Missouri State University; and Jane Wedemeyer, Santa Fe Community College.

Although these reviewers have helped spot faulty citations or interpretations, whatever errors may remain as this manuscript moves toward that awesomely irrevocable form of a published book must remain my responsibility alone.

A book on the family is, no doubt, subtly shaped by an author's own experience, perhaps more so than in other less emotionally-charged areas of social scientific analysis. Looking back, I am increasingly grateful to my parents for providing me with an unusually warm and supportive family of orientation where my initial commitment to family life was formed. This commitment has continued in my own family of procreation. Unfortunately, the long hours that went into the preparation of this book meant less free time to spend with my wife, Linda, to whom this book is fondly dedicated, and our two teen-age sons, Brent and Todd. When I became too engrossed in the writing, however, they happily intervened with diversions that introduced a sense of balance and brought me back to the reality of the importance of family participation. For all these interruptions as well as the daily expressions of love, support, and patience, I find words inadequate to express the depth of my appreciation. Indeed, they have each taught me a great deal about the deeper meanings of family life, both in terms of the enduring marital satisfactions arising from a companionate partnership and the pleasures bound up in that phrase, "the joys of parenthood." It is out of these experiences that I have reached my present and resolutely held conviction that the story of marriage and family life is so eminently worth telling.

William R. Garrett

CONTENTS

Seasons of Marriage and Family Life

PART ONE

"For everything there is a season, and a time for every matter under heaven."

Ecclesiastes 3:1

The couplet quoted above suggested the title Seasons of the Family *for this introduction to the study of marriage and the family. Originally penned by the ancient Hebrew sage who wrote the Old Testament book of Ecclesiastes, the couplet, and this book, clearly use "seasons" metaphorically. We often use metaphors to describe social groups or institutions; for example, we speak of "a healthy economy," or "our dying cities," "a sick society," and "the heartbeat of the nation."*

Social scientists, however, use metaphors reluctantly and for good reason. In social science, empirical accuracy and descriptive clarity are critical. And metaphors tend to evoke suggestive rather than exact images. Nonetheless, they can be useful in certain situations.

Our title, Seasons of the Family, *calls attention to the fact that, just as nature moves through a cycle of seasons, so too does a married couple move through a developmental cycle. Generally speaking, this process begins with the preparation for marriage which occurs in each partner's early sex-role socialization. The cycle proceeds to the creation of a new family in marriage, enters a period of full family involvement after the children's birth, and eventually ends when the last partner dies. By this time, however, the children usually have already married and renewed the cyclical process. Thus, the seasonal imagery of nature roughly describes the family's developmental cycle as well.*

Of course, the "seasonal" metaphor does not describe every family's experience. Some families are disrupted by divorce or the premature death of a spouse. Other marriage partners decide against having children. Some individuals never marry—although the percentage of these persons has been declining since the turn of the century in the United States. Then, too, the seasonal metaphor may not apply in some cases because various class, religious, ethnic, and cultural groups shape family life in ways that are clearly different from the usual family cycle. Such differing family patterns are profoundly important, and we shall consider several major variations as this presentation unfolds.

An Introduction to the Seasons of Marriage and the Family

While the major topics in our table of contents are titled "A Season For . . .," several of these seasons overlap in time. For example, "A Season for Parents and Children," "A Season for Husbands and Wives," and "A Season for Family Interaction With the Wider Society," all occur at about the same time in most families. One does not cease being husband or wife once one becomes a parent. Similarly, community involvement begins in family life with the marriage ceremony. Therefore, the seasonal metaphor in this book, like any metaphor, should not be taken too literally.

Part One of this book introduces certain terms, concepts, and historical information that are needed to understand marriage and the family in contemporary American society. Chapter 1 opens with two contrasting viewpoints of marriage and family life in America. It goes on to define terms, to survey briefly the concepts that help one to understand marriage and the family, and to identify major questions about these institutions.

As Part One makes clear, the terms for marriage forms and family types come primarily from the anthropological branch of the social science community. In the past, historians, aided by sociologists, have gathered most of the data on marriage and family life. Accordingly, while Chapter 1 of Part One sets forth the dominant sociological orientation to marriage and family life, the second chapter reveals that the methods of other social science disciplines have been generously drawn upon. A similar pattern persists in later chapters. Consequently, the book's analysis actually includes a broad range of perspectives in an effort to understand marriage and family life as fully as possible.

Seasons of the Family has not been written with a hidden agenda for the reform of the American family. Rather, the author hopes that this book will help students understand better the factors that make up and affect marriage and family life. The author's role as social scientist, however, is strictly limited to describing what is going on and the effects of current behavior patterns. What ought to be happening in these institutions is the responsibility of all who belong to marital units and family groups. If Seasons of the Family contributes to this decision-making process, the author will consider this "labor of love" highly worthwhile.

Basic Perspectives on Marriage and the Family

Contrasting Viewpoints on the Status of Marriage and the Family Today

Toward a Definition of the Family
    Definitions Based on Family Activities
    Definitions Based on Family Organization
    A Working Definition of the Family

Conceptual Approaches to the Study of Marriage and Family Life
    The Symbolic Interactional Approach
    The Developmental, or Life-Cycle, Approach
    The Structural Functional Approach
    The Conceptual Perspectives Employed in this Survey

Are Marriage and the Family Indispensable to Society?
    The Family's Universal Presence
    The Family's Unique Contributions to Social Life
        Legitimate Procreation
        Socialization of Children
        The companionship Role of Marriage Partners
    Can the Family Be Replaced?
    Three Explanations for the Existence of Family Groupings
        The Family as a Product of Biological Necessity
        The Family as a Product of Natural Law
        The Family as a Product of Social Convention

The Difference between Family Participation and Family Analysis
    Family Privacy and the Public Character of Social Research
    Can Scientific Knowledge Improve Family Life?

The Benefits of Family Living
   Marriage and Personal Fulfillment
   The Family and Societal Needs
   The Strain Between Personal Fulfillment and Societal Needs

Summary

In fact, the family has been slowly coming apart for more than a hundred years. The divorce crisis, feminism, and revolt of youth originated in the nineteenth century, and they have been the subject of controversy ever since.

Christopher Lasch,
Haven in Heartless World

Yet, as I delved further into the data that describe what Americans do and how they live, I became less sure that the family was in trouble. Surprising stabilities showed up, and surprising evidence of the persistence of commitments to family life . . . I became convinced that the time has not yet come to write obituaries for the American family or to divide up its estate.

Mary Jo Bane
Here to Stay

The study of marriage and the **family** holds a special fascination for virtually everyone. In part, this interest is highly personal. People wonder, Will I find happiness in marriage? Is my marriage likely to become a divorce statistic? Are my children being reared properly? Will my marriage grow stale after a few years? Will old age bring loneliness and despair? For many persons today, then, interest in marriage and the family expresses a legitimate concern about their own futures as marriage partners, parents, and family members.

This is, however, but one side of the coin. Bound up with these personal concerns is the broader social issue about the family's status. In America, our society's well-being is widely believed to be closely related to family stability. Erosion of family bonds is generally regarded as a threat to the nation's social fabric. People sense that their fates are linked with the future of marriage and the family as social institutions. Thus, the important questions for many who embark upon a study of marriage and the family often are: What is the status of the American family? Does marriage have a future in this society? Do social scientists agree on these issues?

In one sense, this book is a response to the first two questions. Certainly by its final pages, readers should understand the current strengths and weaknesses of these two institutions. By that time, too, readers should be able to answer those questions on their own. The final question—Do social scientists agree on these issues?—is addressed frankly in the next section. While the answer may be unsatisfying, it is interesting to reflect that if social scientists were of one mind on the current status of marriage and the family, the issue probably would never have been raised in the first place.

Contrasting Viewpoints on the Status of Marriage and the Family Today

When Charles Dickens began his novel, *A Tale of Two Cities*, with the classic sentence, "It was the best of times, it was the worst of times," he could also have been describing contemporary evaluations of American family life. Indeed, the quotations that open this chapter are almost as opposed to each other as the two statements in the Dickens sentence. Christopher Lasch speaks for those who doubt the family's ability to withstand contemporary attacks on its basic structure and activities. Mary Jo Bane, by contrast, is convinced that the American family is basically stable, effective, and well equipped for the near future. Most other interpreters of contemporary family life take a stand between these two extremes.

Such differences of opinion can hardly surprise us. Who is not familiar with such mass media reports as, "What's happening to our families?" As these programs make clear, many family experts and members of the public often disagree. The media regularly reminds us, for example, that murder is more common between family members than between total strangers, and that child abuse and wife beating occur regularly. In addition, our presidents of the last half-century, from Franklin D. Roosevelt to Ronald Reagan, have used the media to express their concern over the erosion of family bonds and to warn of the harmful effects that the family's decline will have on society.

Of course, media coverage is not entirely negative. We often read or hear moving human interest stories about the heroic efforts of persons to preserve their families in crises or against the winds of social change. Indeed, media coverage typically alternates between expressing concern for, and confidence in, the future of the American family. And media personnel are not alone in their displays of deep concern. Politicians, social analysts, and the public all share an interest in fostering the stability of marriage and the family.

How can we mesh contrasting expressions of concern and optimism about the family? Are perceptions so different because family patterns themselves are so disorganized? Or, does the confusion exist in the mind of the public, mass-media communicators, and the experts who try to interpret the family's current status? In other words, do we have enough information about the family to decide whether it is healthy?

These questions deserve direct responses. And social scientists are in a good position to provide them. In recent years, social scientists have produced many excellent studies on marriage and family life. However, this broader knowledge has not silenced the controversy, which is not based so much on a lack of data, as on the lack of a universal conceptual framework that can be used to interpret the data. In short, social scientists disagree about the *meaning* of family patterns and behaviors they have examined. Consider this brief example.

Everyone now acknowledges that more unmarried couples are living together, sharing bedroom and budget. Some observers believe this pattern

An Introduction to the Seasons of Marriage and the Family

indicates the increased sexual maturity of American youth. They view living together before marriage as an emerging courtship pattern which prepares young men and women to adjust to marriage later on. Other analysts see living together as evidence that the American family's moral foundations are eroding. To them, this pattern of premarital sexual relations is a dramatic turn toward greater pleasure-seeking and rejection of society's authority to impose sexual norms.

Significantly, people holding either point of view appeal to the same statistics in making their judgments. They agree about what is happening, but they part company over the meaning of this widely recognized change in social conduct. From this situation we can conclude that reaching an informed understanding of the status of marriage and the family is a complex operation that demands more than data alone. It entails both the collection of reliable facts and their evaluation in a general conceptual framework.

Students who try to analyze family life may be dismayed at social scientists' many, and often conflicting, explanations of this subject. Though making this discovery can be bewildering, an important benefit arises from the perception of contrasting viewpoints. We can understand family problems and resources much better through alternative viewpoints, even when they span as wide a range as the current perspectives of the "family in crisis" and the "family as a stable institution." Each extreme, as well as the views in between, can accent and bring into focus particular aspects of marriage and family life which otherwise might have gone unobserved. Thus, the variety of perspectives fosters a more comprehensive analysis of marriage and family life than would a single conceptual approach. As this presentation unfolds, the benefits arising from different interpretations should become increasingly apparent.

Toward a Definition of the Family

Before we can proceed with our investigation of the family, we need to define this institution as exactly as we can. Generally speaking, social scientists divide into two camps when they define the family. The **functional** camp defines the family by what the group *does*, while the **substantive** camp focuses on what the family *is*, in organizational terms.

Definitions Based on Family Activities

Families come in more varieties than the legendary Heinz soups—a fact that makes them very hard to define. Social scientists seek a definition which will cover typical as well as extreme family types. The functional approach to defining the family concentrates on essential family activities which distinguish this social institution from others. Once a unique set of activities is identified, all groups carrying on these functions can be defined as families.

George P. Murdock was one of the early leaders in developing the functional definition of the family. In his (1949) classic study, *Social Structure,* he listed four universal functions of nuclear families: procreation, sexual relations between marriage partners, cooperative economic activities, and the socialization of children. More recently, Ira Reiss eliminated the first three functions as unique to the family, and laid greater stress on the last item, the socialization of children. Accordingly, Reiss (1980:29) defined the family institution as ". . . a small kinship structured group with the key function of nurturant socialization of the newborn." The organization of this "kinship structured group" is open-ended, emphasizing the socialization function. A single mother and child, a single father and child, as well as several generations living together, would all qualify as families as long as the group participated in the nurturant socialization of the newborn.

Definitions Based on Family Organization

Substantive definitions of the family focus on patterns of social organization and the roles existing within this organization. Thus, the family is seen as a specialized social group, and its corresponding social roles are fixed to positions created by its unique organization. One definition typical of the substantive approach has been proposed by Bell and Vogel (1968:2): "A family system exists in any society in which the related positions of mother, father, and children are recognized and shared notions."

Note that this definition does not mention group activities. Instead, it emphasizes several interlocking social positions. These positions—mother, father, and children—form the organization. They are its necessary characteristics. Of course, behind this emphasis on social organization, may stand the assumption that certain activities logically follow from these role patterns. The roles of mother and father, for example, imply certain types of social conduct toward children such as discipline, love, and moral training. However, because friends, neighbors, teachers, and other persons outside the family also can engage in these activities, many social scientists believe that organizational categories provide a better basis for defining the family. A group constituted on the parental role will remain a family, whether or not similar functions are performed by other individuals or social groups (Zelditch, 1964).

A Working Definition of the Family

Few definitions of the family are purely functional or substantive. Rather, they combine aspects of both. As one classical theorist of functionalism observed long ago, activities require an organizational structure, just as an organizational structure gives rise to a related set of social activities (Malinowski, 1960:114). Structure and function, organization and activity, cannot be radically separated. Thus, in our definition of the family we are trying to provide some balance between functional and substantive traits to avoid the one-sidedness which often distorts definitions. As a basic working definition, then, *the family may be regarded as a kinship-structured institution, found in many different forms, but normally composed of an adult male and female, along with their children, who live together in a more or less permanent relationship approved by society as marriage, the minimal functions of which entail procreation, affectional intimacy including sexual relations, status placement, and the socialization of children.*

Conceptual Approaches to the Study of Marriage and Family Life

Definitions do not stand alone. They represent important elements set within broader theoretical perspectives. Every field of study must create a conceptual framework in which to interpret the bits of information gathered in its research. Such a conceptual framework draws together a discipline's major ideas and organizes them into a rational system which shows how the parts relate to each other. Each social science includes a number of conceptual or theoretical approaches. We will discuss only three conceptual schemes in this chapter. They are important for the study of marriage and the family, as well as for organizing the viewpoints we shall examine later in this book. These conceptual schemes are: the symbolic interactional, the developmental, and the structural functional.

The Symbolic Interactional Approach

Symbolic interactionism originated from ideas first introduced by George Herbert Mead (1934) at the University of Chicago. Mead's point of departure was the explanation of socialization—that is, how personality develops in everyday life. Since Mead's pioneering efforts, symbolic interactionists have tended to concentrate on the micro-social, or person-to-person, level of interpretive analysis (Stryker, 1964:133–43; Goffman, 1959).

Three concepts are prominent in the analysis of the symbolic interactionists: symbolic meaning, role, and reference group. According to Herbert Blumer (1969), a leading figure in the symbolic interactionist school, people relate to social objects and events largely in terms of the meanings of those objects or events. Rather than being fixed, however, meaning is constructed and reconstructed in the daily interactions of persons. Language is the means people use to share meanings in social situations. As we learn to use language correctly, we can understand the attitudes attached to words and perform the behaviors others expect of us in our **social roles.**

Symbolic interactionists use the term social role to mean a mutually recognized set of behavioral expectations for a person of a particular status. For example, mother and father are two status positions within the family's social organization. People behave in these roles according to generally accepted norms and expectations and in response to others who are affected by their behavior. Nonetheless, social roles are not rigid prescriptions for social conduct, which people must obey willy-nilly. Interaction also includes an interpretive process through which people modify their role performance to fit particular situations (Coser, 1977:564–5). Therefore, despite certain generalized role expectations, no two individuals who assume the role of mother should be expected to conduct themselves in exactly the same manner.

People acquire their individual role behavior through their contact with others in various reference groups. **A reference group** is any group which helps us define one or more of our social roles, and which helps us evaluate ourselves or form attitudes. In principle the number of potential reference groups is unlimited. They may be large—such as class, ethnic, or regional groups—or they may be more intimate groups, such as neighborhood cliques, nuclear families, local clubs, or religious organizations. Familiarity with a reference group's point of view is critical for individual conduct, for it allows us to adopt the group's perspective, modify our own behavior, and "see ourselves as others see us."

Symbolic interactionism is particularly well suited to the analysis of marriage and the family. These institutions are small groups suitable to the microsocial focus of this conceptual framework. Moreover, the family is the group in which we acquire our initial social roles, experience socialization, and form strong emotional ties. The insights of symbolic interactionism will be significant in later chapters when we explore the topics of sex roles, socialization, and marital dynamics.

The Developmental, or Life-Cycle, Approach

Unlike the other two conceptual frameworks, the **developmental approach** applies almost solely to the study of marriage and family life. Basically, the idea of the developmental approach is to organize researchers' materials in terms of the life cycle of events. Although developmental theorists have paid considerable attention to interaction among family members, they have also emphasized the stages of a family's life cycle as the critical variables (Christiansen, 1964:22).

The developmental approach is a relatively recent way to study family life, having emerged in the 1930s (Hill and Rodgers, 1964:171). Since then, the developmental approach has enjoyed increasing popularity among family analysts. Most textbooks on marriage and the family, including this one, are usually organized around the major events of the life cycle (Miller and Klein, 1981:13). Among scholars who use this approach, the major point of disagreement is the exact number of stages that are distinct levels in the life history of a marriage or family.

In her presentation of the developmental approach, Evelyn M. Duvall (1967) identified eight stages through which a family typically progresses (Figure 1–1). These stages relate to the birth of the first child, since in her view,

Figure 1-1
The Family Life Cycle by Length of Time in Each of Eight Stages. *(Source: Evelyn Duvall, 1967:13)*

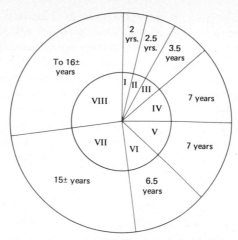

I   BEGINNING FAMILIES (Married couple without children).
II   CHILDBEARING FAMILIES (Oldest child birth–30 months).
III   FAMILIES WITH PRESCHOOL CHILDREN (Oldest child 30 months–6 years).
IV   FAMILIES WITH SCHOOL CHILDREN (Oldest child 6–13 years).
V   FAMILIES WITH TEENAGERS (Oldest child 13–20 years).
VI   FAMILIES AS LAUNCHING CENTERS (First child gone to last child leaving home).
VII   FAMILIES IN THE MIDDLE YEARS (Empty nest to retirement).
VIII   AGING FAMILIES (Retirement to death of both spouses).

the first child's arrival starts the parents' critical period of adjustment. Others have disagreed sharply with her assumption. Rodgers (1962), for example, has insisted that later children also must be incorporated into the developmental stages. Consequently, he produced a far more complex series of stages than Duvall. This debate is likely to persist as different researchers concentrate on separate phases of the life cycle. For our purposes, it is enough to note that the developmental approach is an illuminating way to organize information about marriage and family life. Beyond this, the central assumption of the life-cycle approach—certain developmental tasks occur at crucial points in the family's history—has considerable merit. A failure at a critical point may not destroy a family, but it may undermine its efficiency or its members' self-regard.

The Structural Functional Approach

Structural functional theory has been the dominant school of sociological analysis for most of this century (Goode, 1973:18–22). Contemporary functionalism builds upon the work of the French classical theorists, Auguste Comte and especially Emile Durkheim (1933;1965), and is today presented most extensively in the writings of Talcott Parsons (1951, 1954, 1960, and 1977) and Robert K. Merton (1968). Functional analysis assumes that social facts or events should be examined in terms of their effects on society (Turner and Maryanski, 1979:xi). Functionalists would typically ask: What does the family do for society? How do sexual norms affect our collective social life? What are the results, for society and individuals, of our kinship system? These questions clearly aim to determine how social life is influenced by such factors as cultural norms, organizational structures, and social processes.

Moreover, functional analysts tend to view society as a system made up of many parts that depend upon each other. Change in one segment of the social order may profoundly affect other units of society. Integrating such actions is viewed as a major system problem which citizens and leaders of social institutions must continually confront. Functionalists believe that the sources of social solidarity are the cultural norms and values of a national group. Norms not only shape basic social order, but also motivate individuals to fulfill social roles essential to a stable society. Broadly speaking, functionalists view norms and rules as external social limits imposed on individuals. On the other hand, symbolic interactionists usually contend that social norms are guides that people themselves construct and reconstruct during their daily social transactions.

The question of social norms reveals an important feature of functionalism. Its focus is on collective social life and the beliefs, structures, and social processes that define the situation in which an individual acts. To be sure, people are not seen as mere pawns moved about by more powerful social forces. Change can be undertaken by individuals. However, functionalists insist that society has impressive ways of exercising social control and that people usually conform to the norms and roles within the social order.

Is the idea of social control a conservative bias built into functionalism, or is it simply a realistic picture of social life? This question has fueled a heated controversy for well over a decade. Regardless of its outcome, we should note that much of the research on marriage and family life is based on functional assumptions. Functionalism has penetrated so deeply into the social sciences that one must include this body of research to produce a comprehensive survey of the subfield of marriage and the family. At certain points in this book, functionalism will play a larger part in our discussion. This will occur primarily when we treat macro-social issues, family roles performed for society, and the interchange between the family and other social institutions, such as the economy, community, and the society's value system.

The Conceptual Perspectives Employed in This Survey

We shall use all three of the major conceptual approaches we have described. Indeed, we have tried to balance each approach with the other two to present a fuller picture of marriage and family life. Occasionally, we also have introduced the studies of phenomenological, critical, and exchange theorists. The strategy of presenting many points of view is based on two assumptions. The first is that family affairs are too complex to be covered fully by any single conceptual approach. The second is that narrowing our focus to one conceptual approach would eliminate a number of excellent studies whose insights we ought to consider as we frame a general interpretation of marriage and family life today.

Citizens of various cultures knew the importance of marriage and the family long before social science came into being. People everywhere have taken for granted that these institutions enrich individual and social life. But are they indispensable? Can individuals and societies survive without some form of marriage and family system? In exploring that issue in this section, we shall discuss the universal presence of the family, the family's unique contributions to social life, and the possibility that the family can be replaced by other social groups.

The Family's Universal Presence

As far as can be determined, every society has included some type of family system. Indeed, apart from religion, the family is the only other truly universal institution (Goode, 1964:4). Family life began in prehistory. While we cannot reconstruct the earliest types of family system, we probably can assume that the family was important even then. Indeed, the anthropologist, Clifford Geertz (1973:43), has argued that the family was in part responsible for the very development of our species, *Homo sapiens*. Cultural organizations like the family and cultural tools like language, Geertz suggests, helped stimulate our small-brained, prehuman ancestors to develop into large-brained, fully developed human beings. If Geertz is correct, then the family played a major role in the evolution of the species. It also would follow that the family is as old as the human race.

Perhaps as important as the family's influence on the development of the race is the fact that societies apparently have not outgrown their need for family systems. Although many ancient and modern thinkers have dreamed up societies without families, nothing ever came of their schemes. The family remains the institution charged with bringing new members into society and with socializing them to assume adult obligations.

The importance of family life is evident in the fact that no society leaves family arrangements to chance or treats the quality of family affairs with indifference. Through custom and law, societies directly regulate the family's activities and organizational patterns (Bell and Vogel, 1968:1). Nowhere can individuals follow their whims in the conduct of family affairs. Thus, the family is not only a universal institution, but also a universal object of intense social interest. Accordingly, societies have historically paid close attention to its proper order and its social maintenance.

The Family's Unique Contributions to Social Life

Society is composed of five basic institutions: politics, economics, religion, education, and the family. Each institution carries out specific activities on

The Chinese Family System: A Case Study in Arranged Marriages and Family Interests

Few family systems are so sharply different from the American norm of the nuclear family as that of the classical Chinese before the Communist Revolution. In the following excerpt, the sociologist, C. K. Yang, describes three variations on the theme of arranged marriages which were practiced in China. These include taking a child bride and two more extreme practices—"marrying the spirit" and taking a "daughter-in-law-in-anticipation." Each of these variations illustrates how marriage was regarded as a family affair rather than an institution designed for individual fulfillment of the interests of the spouses.

Families that could not afford an elaborate wedding as required by custom commonly resorted to the practice of taking a "child bride." A very young girl, sometimes even an infant, was purchased by a poor family which would raise her along with the young son. When they both reached marriageable age, they were married with a simple ceremony. While the ritualistic function was not outstanding in such a situation, the economic bondage of the couple to the parents was strong, for the parents had not merely raised the son but also the girl. The subordination of the child bride was even greater than that of brides normally married into the family, for she owed directly to the parents-in-law the efforts and expense of bringing her up. Consequently, the parents-in-law's treatment of a child bride was frequently more tyrannical than normally. It is obvious that in such circumstances the son or the wife could not consider their marriage as an affair that they themselves had sponsored or entertain the moral possibility of leaving the parents' household and setting up an independent family unit by themselves.

Taking a child bride as a form of marriage was still common in many rural sections throughout China proper in the early years of Communist rule. While more will be said about this subject later, the following case serves to indicate the current character of this practice. In the immediate vicinity of the county seat of Yi-shi county, Shansi Province, Kao Chuan-wah, was taken as a child bride at the age of twelve. On the day of her betrothal, when the bridal chair was already at her door, she was still playing with other children on the street, blissfully ignorant of what was taking place. At last, crying and kicking, she was dragged into the bridal chair by her parents and carried away "to suffer inhuman treatment under the cruel hands of the parents-in-law."

Similarly, weird but rare forms of marriage, such as "marrying the spirit" and taking a "daughter-in-law-in-anticipation," which were occasionally practiced in some parts of China, particularly in the South, were products of the same situation. When a woman was betrothed to a man and the man died before the marriage, "marrying the spirit" in full wedding ceremony was sometimes arranged with the consent of the parents of both families, and the bride went through all the ceremonies next to a wooden tablet with the dead man's name and dates of birth and death written on it. Taking a "daughter-in-law-in-anticipation" was a practice in which a couple, having no son as yet, took in a bride in anticipation of the birth of a son. When the right of divorce was emphatically asserted by the Communist Marriage Law in 1950, a twenty-eight-year-old woman in Hupeh Province brought her eight-year-old husband in her arms to the court for a divorce. She had been a "daughter-in-law-in-anticipation." While the economic factor played a part in these practices, they were primarily a product of an institution which considered marriage an affair of the family and dictated by the parents for the purpose of perpetuating and operating the traditional family organization. They illustrate the extreme to which marriage could be carried, even without a male spouse in actual existence, all for the purpose of completing this link in the cycle of events in the family in order that the organization of the family could at least symbolically approach the traditional ideal form.

Source: C. K. Yang, *Chinese Communist Society: The Family and the Village* (Cambridge, Mass.: M.I.T. Press, 1965), pp. 26–7.

society's behalf. For example, the political institution maintains social order and the educational institution transmits society's cultural heritage to a new generation. The family also performs tasks for its members and society at large. Some of the family's specialized functions are legitimate procreation, the socialization of youth, status placement of family members within the stratification system, companionship for adult partners, and social control.

We can fairly ask whether other social groups could not carry out these family activities. If the answer is yes, the family could be permanently set aside, and its functions transferred to other social groups. Many social scientists, however, believe the family is uniquely qualified to perform its social tasks. And while other social groups *might* assume family activities, they could not discharge them as well as the family. To explore the family's special qualifications, we shall consider three of its major functions: legitimate procreation, the socialization of children, and the companionship role shared by marriage partners.

Legitimate Procreation   Rules governing sexual relations vary widely among societies. Yet all societies set firm limits on who may procreate. Random reproduction simply is not tolerated, even among societies which allow far more casual sexual relations than American society (Rodman, 1969:94–107). A family consisting of husband and wife is typically designated as the **legitimate procreative** unit. The key term is legitimate. No matter how a social order may define marriage, wedlock indicates the "legitimacy" of parenthood and the status rights of children born to that union (Parsons, 1964:58–9). By the same token, illegitimacy applies to all births in which the parents did not meet the basic condition of marriage.

The rules of legitimacy define a child's location within society's organizational structures. From the social placement of an offspring one can determine who is accountable for the child's care. Social placement also identifies which adults are responsible for the socialization of each child. Thus, by making a husband and wife the legitimate procreative unit, society assures an infant of a specific "place" in society with a set of adults who are responsible for the nurturance of the child. Society's concern with legitimacy is not an effort to brand or embarrass children born out of wedlock, but a well-intentioned attempt to ensure the welfare of the children in each new generation.

Socialization of Children   Parents have the major responsibility for the social training, or **socialization,** of children. The logic for this arrangement is simple. In the first place, children need to be fed, loved, cuddled, and nursed back

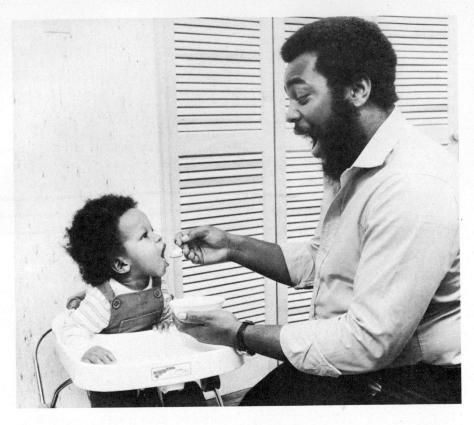

to health when they fall sick. Infants must be instructed how to behave, speak, and avoid the many dangers in the household and community. Teaching children to act in a socially acceptable fashion requires an enormous amount of adult time and patience. The ties of blood and affection between parents and children make it more likely that young people will receive quality care from their parents than from other adults.

Socialization also has usually been allocated to the family because it is uniquely fitted for the task. The family's relatively small size allows infants and older children to receive a great deal of individual attention. Moreover, the family includes both female and male leaders, providing the children with models for gender identification. In addition, the family is a domestic unit. The home is the hub of most of the young people's routine, daily activities. For these reasons, then, most societies have found the family better suited than any other group for the socialization of children.

Nonetheless, various schemes have been proposed that would reassign socialization to other social organizations. A few plans actually have been adopted. One famous experiment can be found in the Israeli commune called a **kibbutz.** To mold a new character structure among its youth, commune members collectivized the socialization process (Spiro, 1965). Children were placed in dormitories according to their age group. Nurses and teachers supervised child rearing. During daily visits of about one hour, parents were

An Introduction to the Seasons of Marriage and the Family

Figure 1-3
Collectivized social-
ization in a kibbutz is
under the direction of
an adult, such as the
woman being hugged
by the child above.
The socializing person
in daily activities is
usually not the child's
parents. (© F. B. Grunz-
weig. Photo Researchers,
Inc.)

restricted to cuddling and playing with their children. To all appearances, young people who grew up in this system made the normal emotional adjust-ments. Moreover, most kibbutz youth seemed to approve of the child-rearing method. Yet, even in Israel, only a small minority use the kibbutz's collectiv-ized socialization. Most young Israelis live with their parents in nuclear fam-ilies similar to those in the United States. The kibbutz experience demon-strates that socialization can succeed outside the nuclear family, but the option has not been very attractive.

The Companionship Role of Marriage Partners The family's third contribu-tion to social life is the companionship role binding marriage partners. The rise of companionship is surprisingly recent. Prior to the Industrial Rev-olution, when arranged marriages were the norm, companionship was not considered a necessary part of the husband-wife relationship, especially among the lower classes in the West. Each mate was expected to perform his or her assigned tasks. But love, intimacy, and mutual caring simply were not part of the ties binding marriage partners. Now, however, husband and wife consider companionship marriage's most significant goal, outranking children and economic success (Blood and Wolfe, 1965:150). Several factors account for this dramatic change.

In the modern world, most of our daily contacts with others are imper-sonal. We relate to others in clearly defined and formal roles, including such interactions as teacher-student, doctor-patient, employer-employee, and clerk-customer. One person must play the appropriate role in relation to the other. You do not act the same way, for example, toward a teacher as you do toward a physician, boss, or clerk in the grocery store. Moreover, most of these instances require rather careful role management. One doesn't want to appear stupid to a teacher, incompetent to a boss, or guilty to a police officer. Thus, we devote a great deal of psychological energy to our "performance" so that we put our best foot forward.

We often escape from these tension-producing situations by withdrawing into the privacy of the nuclear family. There, husband and wife can "blow off steam." They can relax away from public view, away from the anxieties and everyday problems of the outside world. The companionship nurtured in this private setting assures spouses that they are accepted, understood, and loved. Given this psychological support through thick and thin, marital partners can feel free to express their deepest feelings of triumph and failure without fear of rejection or loss of face. Companionate marriages help husbands and wives cope with the normal psychological tensions of social life.

Since the companionship ideal arose so recently, it seems that in the past friends outside the family may have performed the role of psychologically balancing adult personalities. Certainly, too, in non-Western cultures, husband and wife have not typically enjoyed this sort of intimate relationship (Vogel, 1971). In any case, the companionable relationship is important now in American marriages. Indeed, the older sources of companionship—the extended family, the close-knit community peer group, and the occupational or guild association—have all largely disappeared along with the village culture to which they belonged. Today, we seek our greatest intimacy in marriage. Perhaps we seek companionship in marriage not so much because other groups cannot provide intimate relationships, but mainly because they currently do not. In any event, before companionship could be removed from marriage, people would have to be convinced that such a basic change was desirable, and another social group or groups would have to take on the deeply personal companionship role. Since neither of these conditions seems likely to be met in the forseeable future, we expect companionship will remain an important link between marriage partners.

Can the Family Be Replaced?

Our quick summary of the familial functions of legitimate procreation, socialization of children, and companionship between spouses presses toward the conclusion that, while other institutions might possibly assume these functions, little popular demand exists for such alternative arrangements. Moreover, firm evidence that other institutions could perform these activities better is hard to find. Thus, hypothetically, the family *can* be replaced. But is it likely to be replaced any time soon? The answer is a firm no. Social forecasters periodically predict, of course, that the family, politics, or religion may well become obsolete and disappear from social life. Such projections may prove correct in the long run. But for the immediate future, the three functions we have examined seem firmly implanted in the family. This would appear to give the family a strong lease on life. It also would help account for the family's universal presence in all societies.

Three Explanations for the Existence of Family Groupings

Throughout history social theorists have attempted to account for the prevalence of family systems. They have advanced three major explanations of family life, which view the family as a product of: biological necessity, natural law, and social convention. Social scientists have generally favored social convention, but the other two also deserve a brief discussion to flesh out the available alternatives.

The Family As a Product of Biological Necessity Peter Berger (1967:5) recently observed that human infants are remarkably "unfinished" at birth. While many of the lower animals are determined by inborn drives and biological natures which help them survive, human offspring cannot fend for themselves. The result is a long period of dependency on parents, an insight that was not lost on early social scientists. Many regarded the family as a social necessity, a response to the biological needs to protect and nurture the young until they became self-sufficient.

The sexual drive is another biological force that often is thought to have been an important cause for the establishment of the family. Among the lower animals, the sexual drive varies considerably, as do mating practices. In many species, sexual arousal is confined to a specific season. And mating is frequently limited to one brief encounter—as in the case of the honey bee, in which the queen kills the male drone immediately after she mates with him. The human species, by contrast, experiences sexual desire throughout the year. This fact has led George Homans (1950:232–3) to remark that, if we were endowed with a different sexual makeup, a married man and woman might not have to live together permanently. In fact, however, our sexual drive is an important biological factor behind the human tendency to form enduring family groups (Homans, 1950:233).

Pierre van den Berghe (1978:87–105; 1979) places even more emphasis on the biological bases of marriage and family life. The institutions of kinship and marriage, he claims, do not result entirely from cultural and social learning, as many anthropologists insist. Rather, the biological processes of mating and reproduction, partly determine these institutions. This argument follows the sociobiology approach pioneered by Edward Wilson (1975). The sociobiologists urged that genes determine much of our social behavior, such as aggression, love, and parental care. Because favoritism toward relatives appears in other animals, not just humans, van den Berghe contends that such partiality results from gene similarity. We are thought to hold a special affection for those who share a number of our genes. This response springs from our inner desire to pass on our genes and see them reproduced in offspring. However, since mating with someone whose genetic structure is too close to our own would weaken the genetic structure we pass on, inbreeding with relatives is almost universally forbidden. Moreover, once adults mate, strong biogenetic interests hold the parents and their children together in the family group. Children are a genetic investment which parents strive to protect. But toward the outer boundaries of the kinship system, genetic similarities decrease, and so does affection and a sense of social responsibility.

Kinship and marriage, according to the sociobiologists, are not the only aspects of family life sustained by our genetic inheritance. Gender roles, age, and sex hierarchies also are rooted in our biology. With striking consistency, van den Berghe (1978:94–5) notes, adults dominate children and males dominate females. Only the degree of subordination varies among cultures. This claim, as one might suspect, has not made sociobiologists many friends in the women's liberation movement. Feminists claim sociobiology is trying to justify male sexism. Sociobiologists typically reply that they are merely reporting on biology's implications for family and social life, letting the chips fall where they may. Thus, they say, feminists and others disturbed by their findings should attack our genetic structure, not the scientists reporting on our biologically rooted tendencies.

The debate over sociobiology is likely to remain heated for some time (Caplan, 1978). At stake is the amount of influence our genes and biology exert on marriage and family patterns. The novelty of sociobiology is its claim that far more of our cultural patterns are biologically grounded than we previously suspected. For if marriage and family patterns result from our genetic constitution, they probably are not as changeable as many social scientists have believed. Reform movements, from women's liberation to utopian communes as a substitute for the nuclear family, are doomed to fail because they are at odds with our genes. About all we can say is that, while the sociobiology debate touches on important issues, the contest's outcome remains uncertain. This is one controversy we shall watch with great interest over the next few years.

The Family as a Product of Natural Law   We find a rather different understanding of the "cause" of family life in the natural law tradition. Natural law theory arose in ancient times. The Stoic philosophers of ancient Rome presided over the first full flowering of its ideas (Hatch, 1957:142–70). They described a natural moral order, understood through reason alone, which would structure human social relations (Buchanan, 1966:97–9). Accordingly, natural law embraces both a method (human reason) and a content (norms for social relations). Among other things, these laws specify individual rights, family structures and obligations, property rights, inheritance rules, and a theory of the state.

Natural law might have had little impact on Western civilization if Christianity had not taken these ideas as a basis for its social ethic (Troeltsch, 1931:142–61). From the early Church Fathers until our time, Roman Catholic theologians have recognized two types of knowledge: supernatural knowledge attained through revelation and knowledge of the natural law attained through reason. Furthermore, since the New Testament contains no theory of the state, family life, individual rights, or other social relations, natural law is a great help to the Church in stating its position on these issues. Thus, for example, Pope Paul VI in *Humanae Vitae* (1968), the encyclical letter opposing birth control, founded his appeal almost solely on natural law arguments. This understanding of the source of family structures, therefore, remains enormously significant for large segments of society.

Because of its philosophical nature, we can neither prove nor deny natural law theory with social scientific evidence. Final judgments on natural law must be left to philosophers and theologians. Yet, this position does present another explanation for the development of marriage bonds and family patterns, for the natural law theory clearly declares that the family is more than a consequence of biological drives (Thomas, 1965:59). The family, in this view, is a central feature of the metaphysical structure of reality.

The Family as a Product of Social Convention Social scientists are most comfortable with this third approach to analyzing the cause of family patterns. This interpretation recognizes the importance of biological needs and drives. The need for sexual gratification, love, psychological support, and other drives provides the human motivation for clustering into small, kin-related groups. However, by themselves, these needs cannot account for the exact patterns which family and marriage systems assume in a society. Rather, it is the values, norms, and historical experiences that shape the family arrangements which a society endorses. In other words, the family is a specialized social institution that was created by societies to meet universal biological needs. Yet, the accent here falls on cultural influences on family life, not on biological factors.

For example, young people through the ages have shared common needs, whether they lived in ancient Greece or contemporary America. They have required food, shelter, protection, and social training. But the family units designed to satisfy these basic wants have been structured in drastically different ways. Since the basic needs vary little among societies, sociologists have reasoned that the cultural tradition must specify whether families in a given society will be monogamous or polygamous and whether some families will be adult centered and others child centered. This approach has the advantage of explaining both the family's universal presence and the wide variation in marriage and family patterns. The family is universal because the needs to which it responds are universal. Meanwhile, family structures differ because cultural values vary from one society to another (Parsons, 1951, 1964; Parsons and Bales, 1955).

Each of these three efforts to account for the cause of family systems is independent of the other two. None of them can be proved right or wrong on strictly scientific grounds, for each is based on different assumptions. The sociobiologists, for example, develop a natural-science argument. The natural-law theorists construct a philosophical reply. And the advocates of a social-convention interpretation give a sociological answer. Each approach has its own important results which relate only to that one approach.

The Difference between Family Participation and Family Analysis

Many students who enroll in a course on the family are convinced that they already know a great deal about the topic because they have lived in families all their lives. Family participation, however, is altogether different from family analysis. In the first place, our participation is usually limited to just two families—the one we are born into and the one we create in marriage. This is hardly a large enough sample from which to draw conclusions about family life. Also, our personal experience tends to be confined by strict cultural, ethnic, racial, religious, and class practices. We do not learn much about lower-class families in middle-class households, or about Christian homes in Jewish households. Nor does one become familiar with the joint family of India or the Australian aborigine family by growing up in an Irish Catholic family in Boston or a black family in Watts or a white farm family in Iowa.

Family participation and scientific observation differ in another important way. Observers ask different questions than participants. Persons engaged in family living need certain kinds of information. They are concerned with solving immediate problems or making practical plans. Family analysts, by contrast, focus not only on why and how problems arise, but also on the forces shaping family processes. The research orientation fosters an interest in describing and interpreting forms of marriage and family activities set in specific historical periods and cultural contexts. These broader goals can have practical outcomes, however. People can better grasp the implications of their own family conduct when they see it in the framework of scientific family analysis. Such an analysis is also a more valid basis for general conclusions about family life than our own personal experience.

Family Privacy and the Public Character of Social Research

Over the last several decades, the family has become an increasingly private institution. Family members value a haven from public exposure. Consequently, many individuals—social scientists as well as family members—have asked whether it is right to probe deeply into the private lives of human subjects, even if such investigation serves valid scientific interests. No easy answer exists about how far one may press the search for information without violating the rights of family members. The major, if not the sole, justification for gathering data on this private sphere is our need to improve our understanding of the interpersonal dynamics of family members. For example, many myths about sexual behavior were shattered by the pioneering, and still controversial, research undertaken first by Kinsey and later by Masters and Johnson. Family research also holds forth the promise of revolutionary findings.

We do not mean to imply, of course, that our need for data justifies any way of gathering it. Ethical standards must be observed. But we are suggesting that the trade-off for social scientific probing into family affairs is a deeper understanding of the tensions and strengths, the weaknesses and problem-solving resources present in this institution. As a team of television producers discovered in making a documentary called "Six American Families," the research experience often can be as illuminating for the subjects as it is for the audience (Wilkes, 1977).

Given our justification of research even on sensitive family issues, we probably are inclined to answer "yes" to our heading's question. But matters of this sort are often not so simple as they first appear. A good deal of scientific evidence already exists to improve our lives. Yet we systematically ignore it. We know, for example, the increased danger of lung cancer from smoking tobacco, but millions of us light up every day. We are aware of the statistics on drinking and driving, yet alcohol-related highway deaths occur every day. Why should additional data on family life make possible a more humane world?

Sheer information cannot, of course. Only when individuals apply that knowledge can we begin to fashion a social order more conducive to human growth and fulfillment. Social science merely provides the raw materials for making intelligent decisions. Science cannot control people's motivations or compel us to act in our own best interests. Science is, after all, only a methodology, a technique for gathering and interpreting information. The responsibility for the data's use remains with individuals. If it were not left with them, the responsibility would be granted to the government. It would have the power to determine on the basis of social needs and scientific calculations, who should marry, how many children they should produce, and how these children should be raised. This sort of Big Brother approach to family life does not appeal to many Americans.

In a more positive vein, however, scientific information can help persons cope with a wide range of problems they may encounter in marriage and family life. For instance, we know that teenage marriages have a high failure rate. Wide circulation of this fact along with the reasons for such marriage failures can alert young people to the special problems they are likely to face. Scientific information also can help produce better public policy on marriage and family affairs. Although no one wants government to be our Big Brother, governmental policies can strengthen family life. Minimal family incomes, insurance against serious illness, and fair income tax structures could help reduce the financial worries which often cause family discord. Furthermore, educational policies, the commitment to child-care centers, as well as regulations on divorce procedures, abortion, children's rights, and other issues, directly affect family life. While social research cannot dictate what ought to be done in each of these areas, it can identify some of the possible results of policy options. In recent years, government has shown a greater interest in such scientific data. During the years ahead, social science will probably play an even larger role in policy formation for family affairs.

Social science clearly is a potential resource for the improvement of family life. Yet, we would be wrong to assume that science can conquer all the troublesome issues confronting family members. While scientific medicine can tackle diseases like polio and develop a vaccine, no such breakthrough is likely to be forthcoming to prevent divorce, child abuse, or adultery. Family problems are basically people problems, which are much more complex psychosocially than problems which pit man against nature. Social science can bring about a fuller understanding of family dynamics. It can expose some of the myths which might lead us astray in formulating family policy. But social science cannot save the family, even with its most sophisticated research findings. In the final analysis, family members themselves must make marriages succeed and see that family life is a source of mutual satisfaction.

The Benefits of Family Living

Most Americans regard being a family member and a marriage partner as rewarding experiences. However, such positive attitudes toward these institutions cannot be taken for granted. If family life offered no benefits, the nation's marriage rate undoubtedly would decline rather quickly. One also might witness a withering of societal support for the family. Like all social institutions, the family must perform effectively to retain public confidence. Moreover, the family is evaluated for its ability to meet both individual and societal needs. This double demand can create social strains as the family strives to gratify individual wants and societal expectations simultaneously.

Figure 1-4
Satisfaction with Selected Life Domains: 1973–1980. Note in this figure that family life is more satisfying for Americans than other life domains. *(Source: Social Indicators 1980, p. xxxviii.)*

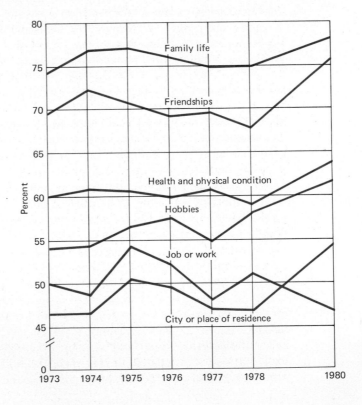

An Introduction to the Seasons of Marriage and the Family

Marriage and Personal Fulfillment

In American society, marriage has long been understood to satisfy a number of the spouses' personal needs. Mates, for example, have looked to one another for sexual gratification, love, respect, psychological support, and economic security. Wife and husband assume their marital vows, expecting that each will help the other meet life's joys and sorrows and fulfill their mutual hopes. Yet, personal growth is only one important goal of marriage. As partners fashion their own style of marriage, societal norms and obligations to children and relatives also must be met.

During the 1970s, however, "personal fulfillment in marriage" acquired a new meaning. The phrase became a slogan for the social phenomenon that writer Tom Wolfe characterized as the "me-generation." Several textbooks (Schultz and Rodgers, 1975, for example) and best-selling books on marriage (such as O'Neill and O'Neill, 1972a) advocated that individual satisfaction is the major goal of marriage. Traditional marriage often was dismissed as a set of arbitrary social rules imposed by an abstract society, whose demands retarded, rather than encouraged, individual growth. Couples were urged to experiment with new forms of married life-styles, sexual techniques, group marriage, communal living, and other exceptions to the monogamous, nuclear family. Furthermore, if one's marriage was not exciting and fulfilling, an individual had grounds for dissolving the marriage.

The underlying assumption was that marriage should be designed for people, not people for marriage. The personal fulfillment ideology suggested that husbands and wives needed to kick the "togetherness habit" (Lasch, 1979) and create their own personal identities other than wife-mother or husband-father. Marriage vows, it was recommended, should be understood as agreements that were binding as long as each partner felt the relationship was rewarding. The O'Neills even suggested that marriage be a "non-binding commitment." By this peculiar, apparently contradictory phrase, they meant that neither partner should make excessive demands on the other. Nor should either partner be treated as a possession over whom the other spouse had exclusive sexual, emotional, or protective rights.

The novelty of this ideology was not the discovery of personal fulfillment as an important aspect of marriage. Rather, it was the elevation of personal fulfillment to the status of the *major* goal of marriage. Few marriages could survive very long if they responded only to individual needs. Indeed, some social scientists have particularly blamed today's rising divorce rate on the "personal fulfillment" ideology. Research in the 1980s will surely help clarify whether this viewpoint was a significant factor.

The Family and Societal Needs

Just as individuals rely on marriage to meet certain of their basic needs, society depends on the family to carry out several functions on behalf of society. We already have spoken of the importance of procreation and socialization as

The More Things Change . . .

Recently a young woman we know, armed with a newly acquired higher degree in the behavioral sciences, went looking for a job. One of her interviews was with a consulting firm. Her discussion with a partner in the firm was pleasant and relaxed; in fact, it went on for most of the afternoon without specific reference to the position to be filled. Finally, out of frustration, the woman asked the partner to describe the job he had in mind.

There was no opening, he told her. Taken aback, she asked him why he had responded to her résumé. The rest of the exchange went like this:

"Some of the partners think it's time we had a woman in the firm."

"How do *you* feel about hiring a woman?" she asked.

"Well, my own feeling is that we have enough problems already. But maybe they're right," he answered.

Trying to conceal her anger, she asked him, "What happens now?"

"I was thinking about talking to an acquaintance of mine in Chicago. His firm hired a woman a few months ago, and I'd like to ask him how she worked out."

When this young woman tells the story of her interview, she very often gets laughter—from men. Some men can't conceive of such stupidity or insensitivity or rudeness—or all three. But there are many women who can empathize with this job hunter's experience in humiliation (only one of several, she reports, in her search for a job). They know there is often a vast difference between the way a woman is interviewed and considered for a responsible position and the treatment a man receives.

Equality of opportunity and pay for women is the law. There are harsh penalties for denying this equality, as AT&T, Northwest Airlines, and others are learning. In 1973, a survey of 111 organizations by *Industrial Relations News* and *Recruiting Trends*, two weekly newsletters, revealed that almost 80 percent of those organizations were feeling pressure to provide more opportunities for female employees, and that that pressure was coming from government agencies such as the Equal Employment Opportunity Commission and the Office of Federal Contract Compliance of the Department of Labor. "EEOC's docket of complaints keeps growing," the survey reports, "indicating increasing willingness on the part of women to press a case."

Women's groups such as the National Organization for Women (NOW) have become potent forces. There are employment agencies; search firms that specialize in placing women (one, Catalyst, has a nationwide computerized system to match women and jobs); women's counseling services; women's political, social, and professional groups; women's publications, such as periodicals and directories; and most of these are developments of the last few years to help women find careers.

Source: Margaret V. Higginson and Thomas L. Quick, *The Woman's Guide to a Successful Career* (New York: Harper & Row, Publishers, 1976), pp. 1–2.

means of assuring a society's existence. These functions are so crucial that, to paraphrase an old adage, if the family did not exist, then societies would have to invent it to survive.

Individualistic Americans may not see readily how and why the family works on behalf of society. Members of traditional societies would understand this immediately. In cultures untouched by modernization, people promptly recognize the priority of collective needs over individual interests. For example, they accept arranged marriages, which form unions that have advantages for the extended family, clan, or tribe, but not for the individual marriage partners. The idea of placing an individual's preference above group needs is rare indeed.

Modern individuals tend to reject traditional societies whose family organization blocks individual self-expression. Yet, such societies can teach us a major truth about the social obligations of the family and its members. The lesson is that the family can draw persons from their self-centered concerns into a lively participation in community affairs. Social life requires the contributions of its individual members as a basic condition for its survival. The family remains perhaps the most important institution for orienting individuals to assure their contribution (Goode, 1964:4–5). This occurs in two ways. First, the family functions as an agent of society by instilling a sense of responsibility for group goals. And second, the family oversees our conduct to ensure that we behave in a socially acceptable manner.

The family's supervisory role is somewhat more obvious in traditional societies. Family members rarely escape the extended family's surveillance. Yet, similar processes are at work in modern nuclear families. Moreover, the family's supervision is not to be viewed as repressive social control. The family tries to impart to its young members the role behavior they will need in social life generally. For example, unless families instill self-discipline in their offspring, they will have difficulty mastering the study skills required in acquiring an education, holding a job, or taking part responsibly in the political process. All the basic institutions, in fact, depend on the family to teach individuals the role behaviors and basic social skills they need to function within those institutions. If the family fails to train the individual socially, the economy, the educational system, or the community in general can do little to offset this basic shortcoming.

Thus, we can see that societal norms governing family behavior are not arbitrary social rules. These norms help attain societal goals and provide social support for the family. Implicit in this support is the recognition of the interdependence linking the society, family, and individuals. Balancing societal needs against individual interests is a delicate process. Traditional societies tend to stress group needs while modern societies emphasize individual interests. But neither type of society can ever simultaneously disregard the demands arising from both group and individual needs.

The Strain Between Personal Fulfillment and Societal Needs

Every group in society experiences some social strain. The family is no exception. As an interlocking institution relating people to the wider social order, the family often is caught between two opposing sets of expectations when individual demands on the family work against societal interests, and vice versa. In India, for example, parents prefer large families. More children means more hands to work the land and better care of parents in their old age. However, India's huge population puts enormous pressures on its food supplies, employment, and public services. In this situation, that which benefits parents harms society, and what benefits society endangers the well-being of individual parents (Berger, 1976:204–6). In India, parents usually have won out over society. But in other instances, individual needs have suffered at the expense of societal interests.

To a greater or lesser degree, such social strain affects family life everywhere. Moreover, each new generation must work out the compromise between individual and societal needs. Because no solution is ever perfect, some tension, social strain, and public conflict over the proper orientation of family life is normal. Calls for family reform will probably cease only when societal members conclude that the family is no longer important. Today's heated controversy about family patterns leaves little doubt, however, that the family is still considered crucial to our social life.

Summary

In this opening chapter we presented a number of conceptual perspectives and raised a series of critical issues about marriage and family life. Our working definition of the family describes it as a kinship-structured institution, found in many different forms, but normally composed of an adult male and female along with their children who live together in a more or less permanent relationship approved by society as marriage, the basic functions of which entail procreation, affectional intimacy including sexual relations, status placement, and the socialization of children.

We also introduced three conceptual approaches—symbolic interactionism, developmentalism, and structural functionalism—which will be employed at certain points throughout this book. The symbolic interactional approach is especially well suited to the analysis of micro-social dynamics of marriage and the family. It will be important in later chapters on sex roles, socialization, and husband-wife interactions. The developmental approach, which provides this book's basic organization, focuses on the life cycle of family units. The structural functional approach highlights the interchange between the family and other institutional structures, such as the economy, community, and societal value systems. Thus, the conceptual approaches employed in this book are consciously pluralistic because they bring to bear several views on contemporary marriage and family life.

The first major "issue" we addressed in this chapter was: Are marriage and the family indispensable institutions in society? We explored three related issues, namely, the family's universal presence, its unique contributions to social life, and whether other social institutions can replace the family and carry on its functions.

Discussing these issues led to a consideration of the underlying "cause" of families. We examined three explanations which view the family as a product of biological necessity, natural law, and social convention. The latter position, of course, is most common among social scientists.

Finally, we considered a series of more practical issues. The first, contrasting family participation and family analysis, suggests that living in a family does not make one an expert in family affairs. Next, we posed the issue of whether scientific knowledge can improve family life. In the concluding section, we analyzed the benefits of family living. We concluded that society expects the family to respond to both individual and societal needs, which can cause the family some social strain.

STUDY QUESTIONS

1. How do the functional and substantive definitions of the family differ from each other?
2. How does the developmental approach to the study of the family differ from the symbolic interactional and structural functional approaches?
3. In what ways can one account for the fact that the institution of the family is found in all societies?
4. Can the family be replaced as a social institution without endangering society?
5. Why is participation in a family not sufficient for analyzing family dynamics and processes?
6. What are the benefits and liabilities of living in family groupings?

The Family in Various Times and Places: A Typological and Historical Overview of Marriage and Family Patterns

Major Family Types
    Family Types Based on Kinship Structures: Nuclear and Extended Families
    Family Types Based on Life-Cycle Functions: Families of Orientation and Procreation

Major Marriage Forms
    Monogamous and Polygamous Marriage Systems
    Patriarchal, Equalitarian, and Matriarchal Marriage Systems
    Marriage and the Reckoning of Descent
    Marriage Arrangements and Authority Within the Family

The Historical Development of the Western Family
    The Hebrew Family of Old Testament Times
    The Family in Greco-Roman Culture
    The Early Christian Outlook on Marriage and the Family
    The Family in the Teaching of Medieval and Reformation Churchmen
    The Industrial Revolution and the Rise of the Modern Family

The Historical Development of the American Family
    The Puritan Family
    Family Life on the American Frontier
    The Rise of the Modern Middle-Class Family in American Life
    Toward the Postmodern American Family

Summary

If "variety is the spice of life," as the old saying goes, then family life is certainly well seasoned, for its variety is more than generous. Few institutions are as diverse as family patterns when they are compared across cultures and through history. We must be familiar with several major forms and family types to appreciate how present-day families differ from those of other societies, past and present. Accordingly, this chapter opens with the terms sociologists use for identifying organizational patterns in family and marriage systems. Next, the chapter outlines family development in Western civilization, emphasizing the changes in the American family experience.

Major Family Types

Although the family is universal, domestic life does not assume a uniform pattern of social organization in all societies. Family types differ as much as the separate cultures in which they exist. As products of Western culture we can scarcely imagine life in the polygamous families of the Australian aborigines, in the arranged-marriage system of classical China, or in the patriarchal pattern of Old Testament families. Each pattern, however, met its society's needs, probably much better than they could have been met by our nuclear family pattern. While examining these types of domestic life, we must remember that the family participates in a wider societal framework, in which it performs specialized tasks. Domestic labor patterns, sex roles, kinship structures, and marital arrangements that are right in one society might well be unworkable in another. Thus, these variations are not accidental. They are adaptations of family structures to a social order's particular needs and cultural traditions.

In the following discussion, we describe family types from a number of vantage points. Each view discloses an important aspect of family organization. We begin by examining family patterns based on structural differences before discussing family types based on life-cycle functions. In the following section, we explore marriage forms, household arrangements, descent systems, and authority roles. As you will see, American family practices are not typical of families elsewhere.

Family Types Based on Kinship Structures: Nuclear and Extended Families

A **kinship system** includes all of one's relatives, whether by marriage (**affinal** relations—"in-laws" in American society) or descent from a common ancestor (**consanguineal** kin). A kinship system also includes rules governing such related issues as inheritance, succession, sexual relations, and place of residence (Freedman, 1964:336). Quite clearly the kinship system is much broader than the immediate family. The varying numbers of kinsfolk in the operational family unit has given rise to two domestic arrangements—extended and nuclear families.

As the name suggests, the **extended family** unites two or more generations—the parents and at least one of their married children (Nimkoff, 1965:19)—into a functional social unit. Generally, the fully extended family embraces three generations living together in one house or in immediately adjacent houses. More importantly, an extended family functions as an economic unit. A prime example is the joint family of India, an unusually close-knit extended family whose married sons reside, work, and hold property in common with their parents (Mandelbaum, 1972:36).

The counterpart to the extended family is the **nuclear family.** It is far less complex, consisting of a married couple and their offspring. This basic building block for most kinship systems usually remains intact, even when it is integrated into an extended family pattern. In Western societies, the nuclear family usually is the residential, economic, and social unit that carries out the routine family functions. Monogamous marriage is the basic social relationship underlying the nuclear family. This marital relationship is expected to be continuous, with exclusive sexual and residential rights for the partners. Husband and wife contribute to the nuclear family's household management, economic support, and child rearing.

Family Types Based on Life-Cycle Functions: Families of Orientation and Procreation

Family rights and obligations differ significantly, depending on whether a family member is a child or parent. Two categories help distinguish families in relation to one's own position in the life cycle. The **family of orientation** is the one into which an individual is born and which socializes the person. In this family we acquire our first role patterns, our basic identity, and our knowledge of language and cultural symbols. Our family of orientation nurtures us so that we can later participate in society outside of our immediate family circle.

A **family of procreation** is established when a person gets married and has children. Thus, a family of procreation for parents is a family of orientation for their children. Most people participate in both types during their lives. Yet, our rights, obligations, and social responsibilities differ markedly with our placement in either type of family

Major Marriage Forms

As Clayton (1979:55) quite rightly points out, with only two sexes, a limited number of **marriage** combinations are possible. Nevertheless, humankind has devised more forms of marriage and household arrangement than this book could ever examine in great detail. We will focus on the more popular patterns. But first we need a common understanding of marriage. Social scientists generally affirm that, everywhere in the world, marriage involves a stable

An Introduction to the Seasons of Marriage and the Family

set of socially recognized husband-wife relationships which includes, but is not limited to, sexual relations. A more technical definition might say that marriage is a contract between spouses of the opposite sex which makes children born to them legitimate. The legitimacy, of course, is bestowed by society, not by the parents.

Several aspects of this definition deserve additional comment. First, marriage's contractual character needs to be underscored. Marriage is a legally approved and public agreement between two (and sometimes more people) for an exchange of goods and/or services. Americans may well take offense at this unromantic definition. Most of the world's population, however, would not object to emphasizing the economic aspect. For them, marriage has little or nothing to do with romance. They assume that marriage is basically an economic exchange involving the payment of a bride price or the transfer of a dowry. The bride, in return, constitutes an asset by virtue of her labor or the fusion of her family's holdings with those of her husband's family. Yet, even in our romantically based marriage system, the economic imagery of negotiation and striking bargains is not out of character with the actual dynamics of married life. Love does not miraculously eliminate vested interests or differences in points of view. Quarrels still erupt between loving spouses— over expenditures, for example. Should the wife buy another dress or the husband a better set of golf clubs? Who should take out the garbage, feed the dog, or do the family bookkeeping? Does Dad need to cut the lawn or take the kids fishing? And—perhaps worst of all—is going to a PTA meeting more important than watching the Monday night football game? Such common questions always involve a certain amount of negotiation and compromise.

We also should note that our definition says marriage is a contract between at least two spouses. Because more than two persons might be united in the same marriage, we must distinguish between two basic forms of marriage—monogamy and polygamy.

Monogamous and Polygamous Marriage Systems

Monogamy is the marriage of one man to one woman. It is the most common marital form throughout the world. In industrialized societies, supported both by custom and law, monogamy is virtually the universal norm for marriage. Polygamy is a general term describing the marriage of three or more persons. Though the word polygamy commonly is used to refer to the marriage of one man to several women, the term also includes polygyny and polyandry, which we shall discuss shortly. Kenkel (1966:30) has observed that more societies favor polygamy than monogamy. His observation seems to contradict our contention that most people practice monogamy. However, one must recognize that even in societies that permit polygamy the vast majority of marriages are monogamous. Ironically, the cultural ideal of multiple marriage partners tends to prevail in poorer traditional societies in which additional spouses usually mean additional costs; few members of such societies can afford this. Moreover, as long as the ratio of men to women remains relatively equal, polygamous marriage on a large scale is impossible for lack of partners. By design and by default, monogamy is far more common than polygamy.

Each basic marital form has several possible subtypes. For example, a monogamous society may allow *serial monogamy*, in which individuals are permitted to remarry after an earlier marriage has been terminated by death or divorce. This is also the pattern in the United States. A society also may follow the custom of *straight-life monogamy*, which does not permit remarriage. Few societies, and no modern social orders, invoke this rather harsh rule.

The variations of polygamy are: **polygyny,** the marriage of one man to two or more women, which is the most common polygamous marriage; **polyandry,** the marriage of one woman to two or more men, which usually occurs when few women are available; and **group marriage,** the marriage of several men to several women, with all members of either sex regarding all members of the opposite sex as spouses. Polygyny and polyandry have seldom been practiced throughout history, but both persist in some societies. For instance, Islamic law permits a man to marry as many as four women (Koran, 1974:366), provided he adequately supports them and treats each wife and her offspring equally (Hodgson, 1974:181–2). These two conditions apparently were intended to limit male freedom, which in ancient Arabic tradition allowed a man to take as many wives as he wanted (Andre, 1960:189). In nineteenth-century America, Mormons also practiced polygyny, until the Supreme Court ruled it illegal in 1890, clearing the way for Utah's admission to the Union in 1896 (Ahlstrom, 1972:507).

Social scientists have long debated whether group marriage ever flourished as a legitimate arrangement among preliterate peoples. Although some early anthropologists believed they had found instances of it, later scholars have doubted these reports. Nimkoff (1965:18) expressed the primary viewpoint among social scientists today when he proposed that group marriage was

Figure 2-1
Monogamy and Polygamy. *(Source: After Dushkin, 1977:151.)*

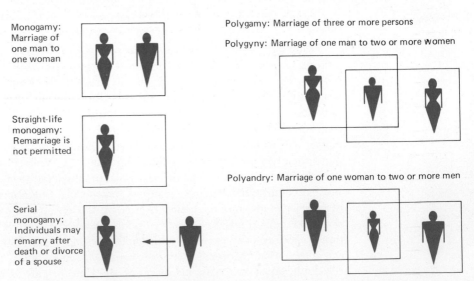

Monogamy: Marriage of one man to one woman

Straight-life monogamy: Remarriage is not permitted

Serial monogamy: Individuals may remarry after death or divorce of a spouse

Polygamy: Marriage of three or more persons

Polygyny: Marriage of one man to two or more women

Polyandry: Marriage of one woman to two or more men

An Introduction to the Seasons of Marriage and the Family

a theoretical possibility that probably never existed as a norm within a society. No society today recognizes group marriage. Its enormous built-in difficulties suggest that it would not work well or last long. Nonetheless, the American press occasionally reports on informal experiments with group marriages, which often are developed in communal living arrangements. Larry and Joan Constantine (1973) conducted the most widely discussed study on multiple marriages in America, many of which were polygynous rather than true group marriages. Of course, none of these "marriages" are legal in the United States.

Patriarchal, Equalitarian, and Matriarchal Marriage Systems

The leadership role identifies the marriage systems we shall discuss next. Each type gives different decision-making powers and other prerogatives to the parent-leaders. The major types of leadership range from patriarchy at one extreme, through two types of equalitarianism, to matriarchy.

Patriarchy is the most extreme form of male dominance. The male head of the family has authority and power over all family members. He also has a number of important legal rights, such as total claim to the family's property and assets. Some early anthropologists claimed that patriarchy is to be found today only in small tribal groups or in history in such extinct civilizations as those of ancient Greece and Rome.

A more common and less extreme pattern is the **husband-dominant** type. In this case, the male spouse makes the major decisions affecting the household, but his power arises from cultural traditions rather than legal statutes. This pattern was common in American society from the Puritan era through the nineteenth century (Morgan, 1966). Reinforced by massive waves of immigrants entering American society, the husband-dominant marriage persists among some working-class groups, particularly those with strong ethnic identities (Komarvsky, 1967:222–5; Rubin, 1976).

Among the middle classes in America, the leading form of family government is **equalitarian**. Partners share power and decisions are reached through mutual agreement. If they use the **syncratic** pattern of equalitarian governance, both spouses share all major decisions equally. This pattern is difficult to follow in actual practice, since marriage partners rarely possess equal interests, expertise, and creativity. The other equalitarian variation, the **autonomic** pattern, gives greater influence to each spouse in that person's area of experience or competence. The autonomic arrangement is far more common for equalitarian marriages, and probably more efficient.

The **wife-dominant** leadership structure is similar to the husband-dominant type, except that the female makes the major decisions. Very few societies embrace this pattern. In America, the wife-dominant structure usually appears only when the husband is weak, ineffective, or absent. The strong negative image of the "henpecked husband" indicates that this pattern deviates from the norm. Of course, households in which the male is absent due to death, divorce, or desertion are wife-dominant by default.

Matriarchy is the final type in this series. The opposite of patriarchy, it is woman dominance a leadership system in which women reign supreme, holding all legal rights, property, and decision-making power. We have presented the matriarchal type primarily to be sure we had included all of the possible leadership types. No pure form of matriarchy is known to exist today (Goode, 1964:14).

Generally, societies throughout the world tend to encourage greater equality between male and female parents. This pattern is not simply a response to the women's liberation movement in industrialized societies. Women have been gaining decision-making power for a long time. Modernization appears to be a major factor promoting women's fuller participation in both family life and societal affairs. However, economic development alone does not always translate into more opportunities for women (Laslett, 1977). Frequently, political action is also necessary to ensure sexual equality. Certainly, this was true for societies as different as Communist China (Schurmann, 1966:395–6) and the United States. Whatever the social causes, however, the evolutionary course for leadership roles is clearly away from patriarchal or even husband-dominant types and toward equalitarianism.

Marriage and the Reckoning of Descent

The issue of descent refers to who will be recognized as related to whom and in what manner. Americans often regard it as a relatively simple matter. Our kinfolk are those who share in our lineage through a blood relationship or through marriage. Our simplified kinship system is not like descent patterns followed elsewhere, however. Primitive societies, in particular, often develop enormously complex kinship structures.

In the main, three different systems determine descent: **matriliny** (tracing kinship through the female line); **patriliny** (tracing kinship through the male line); and **bilaterality** (tracing kinship through male and female lines). We use a bilateral system in the United States, which means that we see ourselves as descended from, and related to, the families of both of our parents. The only favoritism still shown the male line is the custom that the wife take her husband's last name at marriage and their children receive it at birth. This practice may not last much longer. More and more wives are retaining their maiden names or joining their last names to their husbands' with a hyphen.

Descent systems, therefore, vary considerably, from the highly complex structures usually found in primitive societies to rather simple systems typical of economically advanced societies. It also should be clear that descent is a social, not biological, relationship, even though Americans tend to link blood relationships with kinship.

Marriage Arrangements and Authority Within the Family

Marriage and the family are integrated institutions whose various components must function together. Once a society's authority system for family life has been established, the other key elements of the marriage and family structure tend to fall into place. For example, a patriarchal family system normally occurs in societies which have the extended family structure, allow polygynous

An Introduction to the Seasons of Marriage and the Family

marriages, and trace their lineage through a patrilineal scheme. Equalitarian forms are associated with modern societies with a nuclear family structure, monogamous marriages, and a bilateral lineage system. Matriarchal families—if any could be discovered—probably would occur in primitive cultures that perhaps permit polyandrous marriage and certainly have a matrilineal descent system.

Such a clustering of variables suggests that there is a built-in reason why specific family types occur with their related marriage forms. As more and more societies modernize, we can safely predict a gradual shift in world family systems toward the nuclear family structure, monogamous marriages, and a bilateral descent system. We also could expect to see more equalitarianism and less male dominance. For now, however, striking differences remain in family structures and their related marriage arrangements.

CLOSE-UP

Family Life in the Religious Community of the Shakers

The religious community known as the Shakers—one of the most unusual cult groups to flourish in 19th century America—had its roots in a French peasant Protestant uprising in the year of 1688. Eventually forced out of France, a small group migrated to England where a part of their doctrines and rituals were taken up by a cell of Quakers. First called the Shaker Quakers, this group converted Ann Lee, a pious woman of meager means, who was later to become "Mother Ann," the leader of the Shakers in America. Mother Ann along with eight of her followers came to the New World in 1774. Her husband immediately deserted her for another woman, and Mother Ann settled with her flock along the Hudson in upper New York State. From here, the group established a number of farming communities modeled after the original settlement.

The name, Shakers, derived from an unusual ritual dance in which men and women moved about a large assembly room in two circles with their hands held before them, fingers pointing down, so that sin could fall from the body through the finger tips. This ritual dance was probably inherited from the French peasant cult. Mother Ann added to this dance a number of distinctive doctrines. For example, she believed that God was a dual personality composed of a masculine and feminine principle. Jesus was the incarnation of the masculine side of the Divine Spirit, while she represented the feminine element. Mother Ann saw her church, therefore, as a fulfillment of the community established by Jesus. Indeed, the Shakers regarded themselves as the spiritual vanguard of a "new order" of religious life. The goal of the Shaker church was to help persons attain true spiritual perfection, for they believed that the end of the world was coming soon. Consequently, they set aside worldly concerns—like continuing the human race through procreating children—and dedicated their lives to realizing a heavenly existence on earth. Toward this end, they embraced strict chastity—sexual relations between husbands and wives was even forbidden—and sought after purity and pious spirituality.

As a means to attaining their spiritual life, the Shakers lived by twelve virtues which included: faith, hope, charity, chastity, honesty, simplicity, meekness, prudence, innocence, humility, patience, and thanksgiving. The community kept

(continued)

close surveillance over its individual members to assure that they did not slip back into earthly behavior. For those who could live separated from the world, use simple language, follow complete chastity, own property in common, and perform one's proper duty to God and man, then the resurrection and participation in heaven could begin on earth.

The Shakers recognized that only a very few persons could accept the stern discipline which they required. For this reason, they counseled potential members not to make a hasty decision. Everyone who entered the community had to do so voluntarily, and one was free to leave whenever he or she chose. For those who remained, however, daily life was strictly organized. The basic structure of the community was to divide the group into "families" comprised of 25 to 100 persons. The "families" were housed in their own homes. Separate entrances for men and women led to separate sleeping quarters. Everyone ate together in a common dining room, but men and women were fed at separate tables. Leadership in the group was radically equalitarian between the sexes. Each house had a female and male minister, called an Eder and Eldress. In addition, Deacons—an equal number from each sex—were assigned the task of overseeing the labor force of the community. Trustees acted to handle property negotiations, since a radical communism and joint ownership of property prevailed. The Shakers wore simple clothing, made furniture of stark simplicity, avoided placing pictures, curtains, or unnecessary decorations on the walls (these collected dust), and worked at farming or small scale production, often selling their products through their own stores to members of the outside community. Many were extremely creative when it came to labor-saving devices, and they invented numerous items from the clothes pin to a threshing machine.

The Shaker communities reached their high point of development during the nineteenth century. Their peculiar family life, however, which organized individuals into spiritual rather than conjugal families and their insistence on chastity had the effect of retarding growth. All increase in numbers could only come through conversion to the sect. When this ceased, the days of the group were numbered. By 1950, the Shakers were reduced to a small handful of elderly persons, and today the community is a historical memory. The Shaker community was an experiment which ultimately foundered on the decision that total chastity was required of a pious, spiritual life. Their vision of a "spiritual family" may have been a noble ideal, but it finally proved no substitute for physical families in which a new generation is produced to perpetuate a way of life.

The Historical Development of the Western Family

Americans tend to treat family lineage and tradition lightly (Williams, 1970:57–8). Black families in American life are not the only ones to lose their roots, a phenomenon that author Alex Haley dramatized in the later 1970s. Virtually all families, with the possible exception of certain "blue-blooded" New England and Southern families, have little sense of their family past. Just as we are largely ignorant of our own family trees, so too are we relatively uninformed about the history of the family as an institution. Our "information" is often more mythical than factual. As a rule, the history of the family is approached nostalgically. The past was the "good old days," when families were close-knit, self-reliant, and far more stable than they are today. Unfortunately, much of the historical record flatly contradicts this image. In the following survey of family development in the West, we can discover what family life really was like in "the good old days."

The Hebrew Family of Old Testament Times

The two most important "seed bed" societies for the later development of Western civilization were the Hebrew and Greco-Roman cultures. Most of our knowledge of the Hebrew tradition comes from the Old Testament. Its independent books were written between about 1400 B.C. and 100 A.D. (Oesterley and Robinson, 1962:7–12). In addition to religious reflections, these books contain references to changes occurring in the wider culture of the time.

Originally, the Hebrews were a nomadic people who lived in extended, patriarchal families which allowed both the practice of polygyny and the use of concubines who were women kept for the sexual pleasure of certain designated males (de Vaux, 1965:20–1). Wives held a higher status than concubines, however, and the children of wives could inherit property. Family relations constituted social ties of great importance in ancient Israel. The Ten Commandments required children to honor their parents and prohibited adultery (Deuteronomy 5:6–12); both were efforts to increase family solidarity. Moreover, kinship bonds furnished the basis for one's social placement in the community. Religious, political, and other status rights were based on these kinship ties.

The male heads of the household had sweeping powers. Although the patriarch could not sell his wife into slavery, he could arrange his sons' marriages, sell his daughters into slavery, and start divorce proceedings against his wife (Kenkel, 1966:41–2). The wife's primary duties were to produce many children, preferably sons, oversee their early training, and carry out other household tasks. Hard as this kind of marriage sounds, companionship was encouraged repeatedly in the sacred texts and many spouses did love each other.

Kinship's importance in the Hebrew community led the tribes of Israel to the practice of endogamy, or marrying within one's own group. Individuals were instructed to select mates from "within the family of the tribe of their fathers" (Numbers 36:6–7). Such marriages protected the right of inheritance and kept a family's property from falling into the hands of someone outside the tribe. More important was the rule that young Hebrews not marry outside the nation of Israel, a restriction designed to safeguard the Hebrew character as the chosen people of God. One peculiar marriage custom was the **Levirate duty** which required that a woman widowed without children was to marry her dead husband's brother. This step enabled the wife to produce children in her dead husband's lineage and thus insure that his name "not be put out of Israel" (Weber, 1952:72–3). Rather than the welfare of the widow, the basic concern was that heirs be produced to assume title to the deceased husband's property and that his lineage be continued.

On balance, therefore, the Hebrew family responded throughout its history to individual and group demands. Personal needs were met through the family's provision for companionship, children, and a supportive network of social relations on which individuals could rely in times of distress. In addition, the family performed a number of economic, religious, and communal tasks. For example membership in the family virtually ensured participation in the Hebrew religio-political order of social experience. The family was, in short, the crucial pillar supporting ancient Israel's society.

The Family in Greco-Roman Culture

Family systems in ancient Greece and Rome shared many similarities, even though they were not identical. Family life centered around its members' ancestors, who were worshipped daily around the family hearth (Nilsson, 1940:72–83). The male head of the household, the **pater familias,** offered prayers, sacrifices, and tended the hearth fire, for it was allowed to go out only after the last family member died (Coulanges, 1873:25–39).

Religious acts performed by the male household head symbolized his far-reaching dominance over family members. The Greco-Roman family leader was a patriarch who enjoyed more authority over family members than even his Hebrew counterpart. Although Greco-Roman culture never approved of polygyny or concubinage, the patriarch almost totally controlled the lives of all family members under his rule. He could decide, for example, whether a newborn child would be abandoned, sold into slavery, or accepted into the family circle (Greenleaf, 1979:17–21). The *pater familias* arranged marriages for his children, and a wife caught in adultery could be put to death by her husband—although divorce required the consent of other clan patriarchs (Queen and Habenstein, 1967:163–9).

While the law permitted such grim punishment, our best evidence indicates that husband-and-wife relationships usually grew into close-knit social bonds. Women had considerable respect and could attend the theater, sports events, banquets, or other festivities. As more and more slaves were introduced into the Empire, women also assumed more responsibility in household management, as their husbands were drawn away into affairs of state, economic activities, and the pursuit of philosophy or the arts. Wives also could inherit their husbands' estates.

The Greco-Roman family, therefore, was the bedrock institution of society. Under its supervision, religious, economic, legal, and educational tasks were carried out. Persons outside the family literally had no place in society. Foreigners had to join a family circle as clients, as did persons of low status and rural members of society. A patron of a client looked after the inferior's welfare, and the client joined in the domestic worship around the hearth (Coulanges, 1873:255–69). Thus, the family was an all-inclusive institution. It

CLOSE-UP The Characteristics of Family Systems in Traditional, Modern, and Postmodern Societies

I. *TRADITIONAL SOCIETIES*
 1. Courtships are under strict community controls
 2. Parents arrange marriages with mate selection based on economic concerns
 3. Little intimacy is present in the husband-wife relationship
 4. Family members enjoy limited privacy from community surveillance
 5. High death rate among infants—often caused by parental neglect
 6. High birth rate is necessary to offset infant mortality
 7. Family life is adult centered—interests and needs of children receive low priority in family affairs
 8. Life expectancy for adults is short; life is hard
 9. Economy is dominated by agrarian activities and social life is village oriented

II. *MODERN SOCIETIES*
 1. Courtship is couple controlled
 2. Romantic attachment is the basis for mate selection
 3. Intimacy is prevalent in husband-wife relations
 4. Family members maintain privacy from community surveillance
 5. Death rate for infants and adults declines sharply
 6. Birth rate is low
 7. Family life is child-centered—interests and needs of children have high priority in parental decision making
 8. Life expectancy increases; the standard of living improves
 9. Economy is dominated by industry and social life is urban oriented

III. *POSTMODERN SOCIETIES**
 1. Courtship is strongly influenced by the youth peer group
 2. Romantic attachment is the basis for mate selection, but marriages are less stable
 3. Husband and wife relations reflect greater eroticism
 4. Children gain freedom from parental influence by moving into the youth peer culture at an earlier age
 5. Relations with kinfolk decline
 6. Birth rate decreases, creating smaller families
 7. Family life is oriented more toward personal fulfillment—whether the person is adult or child
 8. Affluence increases, with more family income devoted to leisure activities
 9. Postindustrial economy is dominated by the growth of the professions and service sector

*As as emerging social order, the traits for the postindustrial society are somewhat more speculative than those of the other two types.

based unions, and a decline in the number of offspring. Taken together, these changes ushered in a new era in family affairs.

Karl Marx (1974:83–4) and Frederick Engels (1942) were two of the first thinkers to connect the rise of the modern family with the Industrial Revolution. Yet, they regarded the modern, bourgeois family as a corrupt social form. In miniature, the husband-father's power over his wife and children resembled to their minds, the economic power that capitalist owners and bosses used to exploit workers. Whatever the validity of this political claim, they were right in their further observation that urban industrial jobs pulled many young people out of the country villages. Free from community and parental supervision, they entered into romantic relationships. One swift result was a dramatic rise in the illegitimacy rate (Shorter, 1973:48, 84). An even more important change was modern youth's growing demand that love be the basis of the marriage contract.

The "birth of romance," as Shorter (1977) calls this revolution in expectations, is credited with triggering other major changes in family practices. An increase in maternal care and the rise of domesticity were two such practices. Increasing maternal care (Shorter, 1977:168–204) meant that mothers devoted more time to their offspring and supervised their early social training. Previously, a mother had sent her infants to a wet nurse in a nearby village for the first two years. One wet nurse might take in as many as a dozen children. Since her milk supply was inadequate, she substituted pap, a mixture of flour, water, and sugar. Pap's low nutritional value left children easy victims to disease. Children also were **swaddled,** or wrapped in cloth strips to restrict movements, during this time. As a result of these practices and outright neglect, the death rate for children two years or younger ranged from 40 to 70 percent in many parts of eighteenth- and early nineteenth-century Europe. Moreover, foundling hospitals also contributed significantly to infant deaths. These hospitals received children abandoned by their parents or unwed mothers. Shorter (1977:173–5) shows that 15 to 20 percent of the children were unwanted but legitimate offspring. In mid-nineteenth-century France, some 33,000 children were abandoned every year. Death rates soared as high as 80 percent for children left in the foundling hospitals (Greenleaf, 1979:72).

The increase in maternal care drastically changed this situation. As love became the basis for marriage, the parents' love seems to have included their children as well. Parents became concerned for their welfare. Breastfeeding by mothers became a symbol of a greater interest in the child's physical-social development. With better maternal care, the infant survival rate rose well beyond the level attributable to advances in medical science alone.

The bond of romantic love between spouses and their renewed concern for their children triggered another important change, which Philippe Aries (1962:400–1) described as the **rise of domesticity.** The house became a modern home, that is, a private living space in which family members could develop intimacy and affection for each other. The workplace was set off from the family living quarters, kinsfolk moved into their own homes, community surveillance declined as families went behind closed doors, and except for formal schooling, parents took charge of their children's social training. Privacy permitted the free expression of love, not only between husband and wife but also between parents and children.

Together, these three changes—the growth of romance, the increase in maternal care, and the rise of domesticity—largely reshaped the traditional village family into the modern nuclear family. Some scholars regard the Industrial Revolution as the critical factor in this social change, for it brought youth out of the countryside and freed them from rigid communal-family norms. Attracted to the city by the promise of jobs and new wealth, young people also could modify the cultural norms regulating family life. Wage earners had the financial independence to select mates they loved, to allow their wives to give their children better care, and to afford a private residence. In these ways, the Industrial Revolution is understood to have helped to transform domestic relations and give rise to the modern family.

Alongside this interpretation, however, we find alternative points of view about the existence of a nuclear family before the Industrial Revolution and the degree of isolation today's nuclear family has from relatives. Peter Laslett (1965), for example, has compiled historical data from as early as 1600 to show

Figure 2-2.
These two theologians, Luther and Calvin (upper left and right), helped lay the moral foundations for the modern family. The two social theorists, Marx and Engels (lower left and right), examined the dynamics of the modern family and pronounced it immoral, exploitive, and a major cause of human misery and alienation in the 19th century. *(Courtesy of Culver Pictures and of Bettman Archives.)*

The Family in Various Times and Places

that an English villager, his wife, and their children, normally lived together under one roof without other relatives. Thus, Laslett maintains, the nuclear structure also marked the premodern family. Another historian, Lawrence Stone (1979), also claims that industrialization could not have been the "cause" of the modern family, for in some social classes the shift to the affection-based, child-centered family began well before the Industrial Revolution.

From other quarters, social scientists have questioned whether today's nuclear family is quite as isolated as family analysts had once assumed. Litwak (1960), Hereven (1978), Smelser and Halpern (1978), and others have suggested that the extended family still serves as an important resource to the nuclear family unit. Relatives often help nuclear family members find jobs; they provide loans in financial crises; they babysit and give technical advice on child-raising; and they provide comfort, sympathy, and encouragement through letters, telephone calls, and visits. According to these views, the nuclear family is still linked to the extended family.

Thus, it is clear that several unresolved issues surround the topic of industrialization and the modern family. In later chapters, we shall discuss several studies that relate to these topics. Even if we can reach no final judgment, you will gain some insight into the issues at stake in this controversy.

The Historical Development of the American Family

The American family experience must be seen against the European backdrop. When the first colonists reached these shores, they carried with them Old World cultural norms. Yet, the unique natural and social environments of the Puritans and the frontiersmen and the experience of the urban-dwellers during the rapid industrialization of the late nineteenth and early twentieth centuries have given our family life its own distinctive character. In the following historical survey, we shall identify some of these special features.

The Puritan Family

Puritanism entered American life with the Pilgrims who landed at Plymouth Rock in 1620 and with a larger body of Puritans who founded Massachusetts Bay Colony in 1630 (Miller, 1961, 1970). Although religious differences divided these two groups, they shared a simlar outlook on family life. Each regarded the family as a pillar of society, the primary institution for molding people into responsible citizens. In this effort, the family was supported by the moral teachings of the Church and the legal power of the state.

Many Puritan goals have been thoroughly misunderstood by Americans. Puritanism has often been criticized for its stern moralism. Actually, critics are usually reacting against the repressive Victorian morality of the nineteenth century, not Puritanism. The Puritans were highly moral, yet not prudes. It was, after all, the Victorians, not the Puritans, who put skirts on piano legs in the interest of sexual modesty. Of course, the Puritans could be serious and they hated improper behavior. Yet, they also retained a sense of proportion, practicality, and even humor—traits which the Victorians frequently lacked.

The Puritan family, in particular, was a blend of morality and common sense. This was evident from the outset when Puritans in Massachusetts required everyone to live within a family. Unattached persons who had made no other living arrangements were assigned to a family by the court, for all persons were to be ruled by family discipline (Morgan, 1966:142–8). Otherwise, single persons might encounter temptations they could not resist. On the other hand, the family was a bulwark of proper social order, from which all could benefit and none should be excluded.

The standard family pattern in Puritan society was the nuclear form (Demos, 1971:180–1), despite the court's action on behalf of single persons. Kinsfolk seldom resided with the nuclear family, except in cases of economic or physical hardship. Servants or apprentices were sometimes added to the household, but usually only in the wealthier classes. Common folk lived in humble, single-family dwellings. Kinsfolk often lived nearby, but they did not interfere in their relatives' domestic affairs. The nuclear family's independence was established as a norm early in American social experience.

The Puritan family was not so modern in other respects, however. Arranged marriages flourished in seventeenth-century New England just as it did in Europe. Parents typically negotiated long and hard for the best financial arrangements they could secure for their offspring. But Puritan society did not grant parents absolute power to select mates. Children retained an implicit veto power over their parent's choice, for spouses were morally obligated to love one another (Morgan, 1966:80–6). Over time, Puritan youth took full charge of their own mate selection, but they still sought their parents' advice in making this vital decision.

Once a marriage partner was selected, a civil magistrate rather than a clergyman, usually performed the ceremony. The newly created family moved into its own house. Here, the husband's authority reigned supreme, but wives were not repressed as they were in the traditional family. The commandment that spouses love one another went a long way toward preventing the wife from becoming a household slave. Indeed, wives quite regularly advised their husbands on all manner of subjects and they held considerable power, if not official authority, over many of his decisions (Morgan, 1958:22–4). Thus, Puritan women in America were, in practice, far more liberated than most of their contemporaries in the Old World.

Although Puritans strongly supported marriage, they also recognized several grounds for divorce. The major factors justifying the ending of a marriage were adultery, impotence, desertion, or "providential absence." The court which granted a divorce in such instances frequently urged remarriage as soon as possible. More often, a marriage ended because of the death of a spouse. On these occasions, too, relatives and the community favored remarriage. Remarriage, however, did not result in the loss of one's in-laws by a former marriage. The Puritans reasoned that "once the two had become one flesh" even death did not destroy those affinal bonds and the responsibilities that went with them.

The relationship between Puritan parents and children is noteworthy. Parents enjoyed an intimacy with their children largely absent from European households. Parents also were very interested in their children's social training, health, and vocational preparation. However, Puritan parents laid the greatest stress on the molding of a child's moral conscience. Children had to be instructed to honor their father and mother, for this was the beginning of their obedience to God (Greven, 1977:25–55).

On balance, the Puritan family was a curious blend of traditional and modern elements. The nuclear family's separation from other relatives, the relative equality between husband and wife, as well as the concern and affection parents lavished on their children—these were tendencies toward modern family life. In contrast, the Puritan acceptance of arranged marriages, communal supervision of family conduct, and the use of the apprenticeship system of training in the crafts were traditional Old World customs. Thus, while the Puritan family was not fully modern, it was already producing several modern patterns on American soil.

Family Life on the American Frontier

Few aspects of American social experience have been more thoroughly romanticized than life on the frontier (Boatright, 1968:43–5). Popular mythology has portrayed the frontier as an environment promoting individualism, self-reliance, freedom, and close-knit family life. Unfortunately, the reality was a far cry from the homespun piety of such television programs as "Daniel Boone" or "The Little House on the Prairie."

Life in the frontier family lacked gentleness or romantic emotion. Mates often were selected haphazardly. A frontiersman was generally willing to take any available woman as a wife, since she probably would die rather soon of disease, malnutrition, childbirth, or Indian attack. A rugged (and lucky) husband could easily outlive three or four wives. Thus, romance was not an important factor in mate selection. Other family links also were not close. Fathers frequently communicated with their children through slaps and grunts rather than complete sentences. Children ate their meals after the father and older male children had taken their portion, and table manners were at best uncouth. Children who could contribute their labor to family survival were a valuable asset, but physical coercion, not love and moral training, controlled their actions. Life in the frontier family was brutish and frequently short (Hofstader, 1963:76–80).

After the frontiersmen came the second wave of settlers, the pioneer farmers who finished clearing the land. They brought some cultural sophistication and a generally more civil level of behavior. The pioneer farmer's life was hard, but his family interactions were more stable and wholesome. Parents tended to love one another and their children. They also were profoundly concerned about their children's moral training and social development. The stability of the pioneer farmer supported a settled community life.

The third wave of newcomers to the frontier consisted of merchants, professionals, and others who would supply the needs of the farm families. This third group brought responsible social order, supporting strict family solidarity. Members of the merchant-professional class saw that their children were dependable, adept at the social graces, and fairly well schooled. They also were expected to put off marriage until they had begun their careers. With this group, middle-class life found its way to the frontier (Lipset, 1963:101–69).

On the whole, the frontier was probably one of the most destructive forces American families have ever confronted. The isolation, cultural breakdown, and hostile natural environment thrust enormous burdens on family members, often pushing them beyond their endurance. Above all, the frontier experience shows how much the family depends on other social institutions. When the government, economy, religion, and education are strong, the family is likely to thrive. But when they are weak, the family may suffer. The frontier family's mere survival speaks well for the family's ability to withstand serious threats.

The Rise of the Modern Middle-Class Family in American Life

During the nineteenth century, the middle-class family arose to displace the traditional farm family as the normative domestic unit. Like the modern family in Europe, its central features were the separation of the workplace from the home (Berger and Berger, 1972:84–5), the increase in privacy for nuclear family members (Strong, *et al.*, 1979:45–7), the emergence of a companionship and equality between husband and wife (Shorter, 1977:227–8), and the development of a child-centered ethos (Seeley, Sim, and Loosley, 1963:4–5, 159–223). Thus, the modern family achieved an emotional solidarity which set it apart from previous familial systems in the American social experience (Blood and Wolfe, 1965:156–74).

A major result of these changes was the emergence of adolescence as a distinct period in the life cycle of individuals (Eisenstadt, 1965:26). In traditional societies, children often were treated as miniature adults, or they passed quickly from child to adult, due to early marriage or early entry into the work force. Modern families no longer need child labor on the farm or around the house. Hence, youth are freed to take part in the youth peer group during their teens and the early adult years. Modern parents typically regard this activity as an important part of maturation. Adolescence is a period during which a young person enjoys considerable financial and psychological support from the family and can experiment with new life-styles, independence, and creative self-expression. Predictably, the youth culture alternates between conformity to adult patterns and rebellion against the social controls of society (Parsons, 1964:173). Through it all, however, the youth culture has managed to establish itself as a permanent aspect of modern societies. Moreover, young people often are torn between following the behavioral norms of their peer culture and adhering to the guidelines of the nuclear family (Larkin, 1979). Tension between the family and the youth peer group intensifies as we move into the era of the postmodern family.

Toward the Postmodern American Family

The concept of **postindustrial**, or **postmodern**, society developed quite recently. Daniel Bell (1976, 1978) has been largely responsible for introducing this term to describe the emerging new social order. Not all social scientists are convinced that America has entered the postmodern era. Moreover, information on both the postindustrial society and the postmodern family is relatively incomplete. Thus, the trends we will describe are only attempts to assess developments in societal and family life. With these cautions, then, we present the major features of postindustrial society as including: economically, a growth in the service and technological sector; politically, an increase in citizen participation and a demand for social justice; and culturally, an emphasis on self-expression, pleasure-seeking, and creativity in the realm of values and meaning. The danger inherent in postindustrial society, Bell warns, is that the economy is moving in a collective direction. This situation requires individual discipline, high educational achievement, and the ability to work cooperatively in specialized corporate groups. On the other hand, the culture is moving in the opposite direction by encouraging more indulgent, liberated, and even antisocial patterns of self-expression. The tug-of-war between economic collectivism and cultural individualism, Bell contends, is the fundamental contradiction of postindustrial society.

The familial institution, meanwhile, may well be trapped in a virtual no-man's-land created by such social strains. The family is expected to respond to societal needs by producing disciplined people who can acquire technical education and enter smoothly into the complex work groups of a corporate economy. At the same time, the family is expected to produce individuals whose drive for self-fulfillment will attain the cultural norms of creativity and find authentic meaning in their private sphere of experience. Whether the family can nurture individuals sensitive to two such different orientations remains a question.

To complicate matters further, Shorter (1977) has marshalled evidence which indicates that the mid-1960s were a critical watershed period, marking the appearance of the postmodern family. The first sign of change was the "second sexual revolution of modern times." The revolution's cause was the transformation of the youth peer culture into a counterculture (Roszak, 1969). The most important result was a swift institutionalizing of values, norms, and social behaviors generally opposed by the middle-class family. They included greater experimentation with premarital sex, widespread use of drugs, a rejection of the work ethic, dropping out of school, radical politics, the use of profanity and obscenity in everyday conversation, and a profound distaste for corporate capitalism, organized religion, and even the middle-class family itself.

When the tumultuous 1960s gave way to the "me-generation" of the 1970s, the youth peer group lost many of its more radical and aggressive patterns. Yet, certain features remained, such as drug use, premarital sexual experimentation, living together, a skeptical attitude toward the work ethic and achievement, and a desire for personal pleasure and self-gratification (Larkin, 1979). Meanwhile, adolescence grew longer. The peer culture eventually embraced the "sophisticated preteen of eleven," as well as the advanced graduate student dependent on financial support from home (Greenleaf, 1979:141).

The situation also may have changed for many adult members of the postmodern family. Some features introduced by the youth culture have found their way into adult life-styles and family practices. The sexual revolution, to cite one example, gave rise to greater marital and perhaps extramarital sexual activity. Divorce increased sharply, and the pleasure-seeking, self-fulfillment concept of marriage gained popularity. "Women's liberation," coming on top of these other changes, merely increased pressure on the nuclear family. More and more women sought freedom from household duties and child care. Their entry into the work force, the classrooms of higher education, and other types of community involvement often left the family nest unattended. For the most part, however, the nest had already been emptied by the withdrawal of youth into the activities of the peer culture (Shorter, 1977:279-80).

On balance, the most decisive change in postmodern family life may be the decline in domesticity. The family's influence on youth seems to have been drastically curtailed by children's adoption of the peer culture's attitudes and behaviors. As erotic attachment has joined older norms of companionship and love, marriage may have become more fragile. Furthermore, the changing role of women is creating a new climate for domestic relations.

These changes may permanently alter family practices as we enter into the postindustrial era. Or, they may be merely short-term trends. Perhaps by the end of this decade we will have a more definite answer. Whatever that answer is, it seems unlikely that the long history of family development will end with the proverbial whimper in the postmodern age.

Summary

Families come in many shapes and sizes. This chapter reports on some of the major types of marriage and family systems which social scientists have classified. It also surveys the history of the Western family, and devotes special attention to the changes in American family life.

The first family type is based on kinship structures and includes nuclear and extended families. A nuclear family is a married pair and their offspring who form a household unit. An extended family encompasses the parents, their married children, and their grandchildren, all of whom make up a residential and economic unit. Hence, the extended family often contains three generations. Nuclear families represent the norm in modern, industrialized societies, whereas extended families are more typically found in traditional, agrarian societies.

A second set of family types is based on life-cycle functions and includes families of orientation and procreation. The family of orientation is the one into which we are born and from which we receive our primary socialization. By contrast, the family of procreation is one in which we are the parents and leaders. Most of us take part in both of these family types during our life cycle.

If we classify families by marriage systems, we emerge with two types of family— one based on the monogamous marriage and the second on the polygamous union. Monogamy is the marriage of one man to one woman, the pattern in the United States and most modern societies. Polygamy refers to three types of marriage involving multiple partners. Polygyny is the marriage of one man to two or more women. Polyandry is the marriage of one woman to two or more men. A group marriage weds two or more men to two or more women; each person regards all others of the opposite sex as legitimate partners. We have no evidence of group marriage anywhere as a legitimate form of domestic life.

Marriage systems also can be distinguished by their leadership patterns. Patriarchy, the first type, gives the male head of the household complete power, authority, and legal rights over family possessions and decision making. The husband-dominant pattern is a milder form of male dominance supported by custom, rather than law. The next major type is equalitarianism; husband and wife jointly share decision-making power. The wife-dominant pattern grants the female most decision-making power. This often arises by default when the husband is ineffectual or absent from the family circle. Matriarchy, the final type of leadership, gives the female head of the family supreme legal, economic, and decision-making powers. So far as we know, no matriarchal societies exist today; and they may never have existed.

Rules governing descent are a final means of identifying family types. Three descent systems are the most popular forms for reckoning kinship. They are: matriliny (tracing descent through the female line); patriliny (tracing descent through the male line); and bilaterality (tracing descent through both the male and female lines).

These various types and patterns actually appear together rather regularly in historical family systems. For example, traditional societies supporting patriarchal norms usually have extended, polygynous, and patrilineal patterns. Modern societies, like our own, typically endorse monogamous, nuclear, equalitarian, and bilateral norms for family life.

Our analysis by type of family is complemented by an historical approach to family experience. We focused first on the development of the Western family. Two cultures, the ancient Hebrew and Greco-Roman, laid the foundations for family life in the West. The first Christians blended aspects of each culture to support monogamous families, marital fidelity, and parental concern for the moral rearing of their children. The early Church Fathers more strictly stressed the need for sexual purity and the wife's subservience to her husband. Through it all, however, the early Church was highly supportive of both marriage and the family.

Medieval churchmen from Augustine to Aquinas transformed marriage into a sacrament of the Church and brought family life under the Church's full moral supervision. Protestant reformers rejected the sacramental character of marriage, but they did not deny marriage's religious importance. Indeed, Calvin regarded the responsible performance of one's marital and familial obligations as a means of glorifying God.

Few events appear to have affected family life more than the Industrial Revolution, according to one school of thought. Traditional village life placed the family under rigid community controls. The Industrial Revolution attracted large numbers of peasant youth to the cities, where they escaped repressive community supervision. An almost immediate result was the birth of romance; couples began to select mates on the basis of love. Maternal care increased when spouses generalized their love to include their children. Out of these changes arose a new pattern of domesticity in which the nuclear family found refuge in a home of its own. Other students of family life,

An Introduction to the Seasons of Marriage and the Family

however, suggest that the nuclear family already had appeared before industrialization and that extended kin relationships have persisted since industrialization.

In the New World, the Puritans had already established a beachhead for the American family. They took strong steps to assure that the family could function properly. Although marriages were still arranged, Puritan equalitarianism, concern for the children's welfare, and the tendency for nuclear families to live alone, all foreshadowed the modern pattern that later developed more fully in the West.

Life on the American frontier very nearly defeated efforts to establish a stable family system. The family was the only basic institution on the cutting edge of the frontier. Without the support of the Church, government, and the civilizing effect of cultural norms, family life deteriorated seriously. Arriving pioneer farmers and the merchant-professional classes helped restore family stability. However, the American family hardly seems to have gained strength from its ordeal on the frontier.

The rise of the middle-class family in the nineteenth century represented the triumph of urban, industrial society. Out of this atmosphere came the modern, American family. Founded on an equalitarian, companionate marriage system, it permitted mate selection on the basis of romantic attachment; children emerged as the objects of love and concern. During this time, too, adolescence arose as a distinct period separating childhood from adulthood. The central feature of adolescence soon came to be youth peer-culture participation.

Several commentators have recently argued that the postmodern family began to emerge in the mid-1960s. For the first time, the peer culture also became a counter-culture. The result was youth's earlier escape from family controls as young people accepted their peer culture's view of behavioral and moral norms. Changes in adult relations also have been suggested. It is still too early to tell if the postmodern era has, in fact, begun. But it is clear that the Western and American family systems have undergone a long process of evolution. In retrospect, the nuclear family of today is really a very recent development in the social history of family life.

STUDY QUESTIONS

1. In a family containing parents and children, for which members is this unit a family of procreation and for which is it a family of orientation?
2. Why is there such a wide variation in marriage forms and family types in differing societies?
3. What is the dominant trend in family authority as you move from traditional to modern social orders?
4. How does the attitude toward children differ between Roman culture and the contemporary industrialized nations of the Western world?
5. Was Puritan society more traditional or modern in terms of its family system?
6. What are the emerging characteristics of the postmodern American family?

PART TWO

A Season for Courtship

"A Season for Courtship" deals with the general theme of the development of romantic attachment between two members of the opposite sex. Chapter 3 examines the social process by which males and females (biological distinction) acquire a gender identity (psychological orientation) and internalize the sex-role patterns of masculinity and femininity (culturally defined modes of conduct). Chapter 4 explores the attitudes and behaviors associated with the dynamics of dating. In Chapter 5, we shall discuss mating, the process of selecting a marriage partner.

Each of these three chapters builds logically upon the preceding one. Sex-role socialization prepares an individual for dating. Similarly, dating is a prelude to mate selection. Each chapter also describes the patterns of social behavior involved in courtship, which eventually culminates in marriage.

3

Sex, Gender Identity, and Sex Roles

What are little boys made of?
Snips and snails and puppy dog tails.
And what are little girls made of?
Sugar and spice and everything nice.

Remember this nursery rhyme? No doubt, most readers will think it is an example of medieval sex-role stereotyping. The rhyme appears to imply that boys like creepy-crawly things while girls work at being sweet and nice. However, the jingle's original message was altogether different. It reflected the mistaken premodern belief that a mother's diet during pregnancy determined her child's sex (Greenleaf, 1979:48). Women who ate meat and potatoes could expect boys, while those who indulged in richer foods filled with sugar and spice would deliver girls. Today we recognize diet as an important factor contributing to healthy prenatal development. But we know that our sex results only from the chromosomes we inherit from our parents.

Other misconceptions about sex and the sexes are plentiful. For example, American culture tends to represent males as the first sex, and females as a deviation from nature's basic design. This folklore may well arise from the biblical story of creation, in which Eve was made from one of Adam's ribs. Flattering as this notion is to the male ego, it conflicts with biological fact. Modern research on prenatal development has revealed a different sequence. A fetus's first tendency is to develop into a female of its species. It takes the introduction of the Y, or male, chromosome to signal the fetus to change its growth pattern and take on male physical characteristics (Weitz, 1977:19). The Y chromosome triggers the production of the hormone, androgen, which prompts the formation of male genital organs and other physically distinctive male traits.

The chromosome structure—XX for females and XY for males—is the biological foundation on which we base gender identity and sex roles. (Appendix I presents the biological aspects of reproduction and physiological development in more detail.) However, biology does not account for all the differences which divide the sexes. Every culture overlays the biological features of the two sexes with many learned behaviors appropriate for men and women. Determining which behaviors are genetically inspired and which are culturally acquired is not easy. Indeed, this subject has become quite controversial, especially since the emergence of the women's movement (Mason, Czajka, and Arber, 1976).

A Definition of Terms

The failure to define basic terms precisely has created much of the confusion over human sexuality. Since we shall use the three terms, **sex, gender iden-**

tity, and **sex roles** frequently, we must establish a clear meaning for each of them.

Sex   Of the three terms, sex is the easiest to define. Sex refers to the biological differences between males and females (Oakley, 1972:16). Among the contrasting features included in this term are the XY and XX chromosome pairs, the hormones androgen and estrogen, the external genitalia of penis and vulva, the internal genitalia of testes and ovaries, and such secondary sex characteristics as voice pitch, physical size, and the different distributions of body hair. Each sex can perform certain biological functions. Only the female, for example, experiences a menstrual cycle, can give birth, and nurse the young. The male alone can produce sperm. Although the menstrual cycle in women seems to produce more dramatic chemical and mood changes than those that men experience, this belief may simply reflect our lack of knowledge about male body chemistry (Bohannan, 1970:27–34). Thus, as we define the term, sex (biological) is sharply distinguished from sexuality (behavioral).

Gender Identity   Male and female are biological categories. Gender, by contrast, refers to a person's psychological identification with one of the biological sexes. By viewing oneself as masculine or feminine, which are gender categories, one lays the foundation for acquiring the behavioral traits associated with that sex. Gender identity and biological sex are usually the same. However, a person's gender identity can differ from his or her genetically determined sex. This abnormal pairing usually disturbs the individual severely, and it often motivates these people to seek sex-change operations. **Transsexualism** is identification with the gender opposite to one's biological sex. Unlike homosexuals, transsexuals genuinely believe they are trapped in bodies with the wrong sexual makeup (Weitz, 1977:52–4). Because one's gender identity does not always coincide with one's physical sexual structure, cultural training and social experience are thought to strongly influence the person's awareness of being masculine or feminine (Gagnon and Henderson, 1980:50–1).

Sex Roles   Sex roles are the expectations that members of society share about behavior appropriate to men and women. All societies have relatively distinct guidelines on the attitudes and behaviors that are "right" for the sexes. In American society, for example, traditional sex roles for women require that they are dependent, passive, empathetic, intuitive, nurturing, supportive, and interpersonally oriented. Men, on the other hand, are expected to be independent, aggressive, prone to assuming leadership roles, task-oriented, rational, analytic, confident, and emotionally controlled (Bardwich and Douvan, 1972:225). Of course, no one member of either sex ever has all of these ideal features. But these traits do specify each sex's basic orientation. In recent years, members of the feminist movement have challenged many traditional sex-role characteristics as degrading (David and Brannon, 1976:41–2; Thompson, 1970). Women's rights advocates point out that the content of sex-role patterns varies a great deal among cultures. One culture's masculine traits are regarded as strictly feminine in another cultural system. Thus, sex roles are not biologically inherited. They are social patterns that we learn from our society as the appropriate ways for the sexes to behave. For this reason, sex roles can be redefined whenever sufficient social support exists for such changes (Duberman, 1975a).

Forming Sex Roles Through the Socialization Process

We are born male or female; we learn to become masculine or feminine. Socialization is the learning process through which we internalize the behavior patterns considered proper for each gender. We begin learning almost immediately after birth. Acquiring sex roles and performing them adequately is not as simple as learning to ride a bicycle or memorizing the alphabet. Moreover, sex roles are critically important because they touch almost every aspect of our lives. They help shape one's attitudes, interests, emotions, the way one walks and talks, and one's expectations from life. In modern societies, the norms of sex-role behavior are broader and more changeable than those of traditional societies. Today, people in a modern society are often somewhat confused about others' expectations for their sex-role performance. We shall examine this issue more fully after we have described the processes of acquiring gender identity and sex-role patterns.

Figure 3–1
Little girls are traditionally socialized to want to be like "mommy." (© Joanne Leonard, 1978/Woodfin Camp & Associates.)

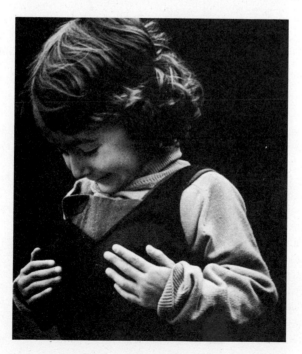

Learning to Be Feminine or Masculine: Content and Process

Feminine and masculine roles cannot be described in absolute terms. No universal model for sex roles is recognized by all societies. In America, women are typically expected to be emotional, sympathetic, and to appreciate poetry and the fine arts more than men. In classical China, men alone were considered capable of these sentiments. In her classic study of three New Guinea tribes, Margaret Mead (1963) found a remarkable degree of variation in sex-role norms. Members of the Arapesh tribe encourage men and women to behave as American culture expects women to act. Both Arapesh sexes are mild-mannered, nurturing, responsive, and docile. Mundugumor tribe members display the opposite traits. Both sexes are fiercely competitive, violent, and belligerent. They carry to the extreme the aggressiveness that American society regards as normal for males. The third tribe, the Tchambuli, distinguishes sharply between the sex roles of men and women, but they reverse our culture's patterns. Males are more interested in art and esthetics; they wear curls and jewelry; they gossip and are "catty" to one another. By contrast, the women are competent, domineering, energetic managers. They handle all the important affairs of society, both political and economical. These cross-cultural examples show clearly that learning to be feminine or masculine means mastering the behavior your society attributes to either sex role. Thus, femininity and masculinity are social roles determined by our society.

Infancy and the Beginning of Gender-Identity and Sex-Role Formation

Society prescribes gender identity and sex roles on the basis of a person's anatomical sex. From the time the delivery room doctor makes a hasty examination and announces, "It's a girl" or "It's a boy," each baby is treated differently according to his or her sex. One of the first acts for prescribing a gender identity is naming the child, since first names tend to be sharply segregated by sex—a point that was made humorously a few years ago in a Johnny Cash song about a boy who spent his whole youth fighting because his father named him Sue. Parents further help others recognize their child's gender by dressing girls in pink and boys in blue. This custom came about because all fully clothed babies look alike.

Does it really matter whether male and female babies are distinguishable? Apparently, yes. Not only do parents tend to get highly insulted when others mistake their child's gender, but adults generally want to know an infant's sex so that they can relate to the child properly. All who come in contact with the newborn—parents, relatives, nurses, friends—tend to relate to the infant by admiring one set of sex-typed traits in girls and another in boys. Girls are complimented for their curly hair and delicate features, while boys are praised for their larger size, robust features, and vigorous activity. For example, one group of researchers (Rubin, Provenzano, and Luria, 1974) interested in sex-role typing interviewed thirty first-time parents on the day after their children were born. Although the hospital physicians reported no striking differences among these babies, who were equally divided by sex, parents—and especially fathers—expressed contrasting impressions of their child on the basis of the offspring's sex. Girls were typically perceived as smaller, less alert, and softer, while boys were viewed as stronger, larger, and more active. Clearly, sex-role stereotypes had molded parental perceptions.

Moreover, differing perceptions lead to differing treatment of infants. Adults are far more inclined to speak softly, handle gently, and be more tender toward female babies, while boys usually are more vigorously treated (Stockard and Johnson, 1980:181). Infants do respond to the sexually differentiated attention they receive from their parents and other socializing agents hovering around them, although we do not know exactly when they begin to respond.

Certainly by the toddler stage, children have ample reminders that they belong to only one sex and that they ought to take on the proper gender orientation. Money and Ehrhardt (1972) insist that gender identity is firmly implanted by 18 months of age, and that changing a child's gender identification is quite difficult after that age. Similarly, Jerome Kagan (1964) has shown that by age three children know the basic cultural norms for masculinity and femininity. They can specify that fathers are strong, big people who "go to work," while mothers are smaller, pretty people who take care of the house. By school age, boys and girls have learned the basic sex types and relate somewhat differently to traditional sex-role definitions. In a study of youngsters in grades one through six, Gloria M. Nemerowicz (1979) and her colleagues discovered that girls are much more inclined than boys to break with traditional sex roles. This is due partly to the fact that boys tend to see the man as worker and the woman as homemaker. Girls are much less likely to see work as the point of difference between the sexes. Moreover, as both boys and girls grow older, their views on proper male and female sex-role behavior clearly become broader.

Before these differences can emerge, however, each sex must internalize his or her expected gender orientation. Young children, especially, make some mistakes along the way. On these occasions, adults and peers remind them that they must "act like young ladies" or like "little men." Gender identification and sex-role performance are reinforced in many other ways. For example, when little girls are dressed in frills and lace that evoke adults' compliments, the girls are subtly being told that prettiness is feminine. Girls also are encouraged to stay clean, to play quietly, and to enjoy games rather than try to win them.

Boys are urged to behave in just the opposite way. The socialization of a boy into "manliness" means above all that he must not grow up like a girl and become a "sissy." Avoiding all the attitudes and actions labeled sissy is not easy. A little boy must learn, when he skins his knee or is frightened, that "little boys don't cry, only girls cry." Boys also are expected to get dirty and not be afraid of frogs, snakes, and worms. Boys soon learn to like pocket knives, toy guns, and tackle football. Boys do not like dolls, playing house, or girls—at least not until adolescence.

Play time is an important opportunity to try out future feminine and masculine roles, as George Herbert Mead (1962:364–5) and other classical theorists of social roles so clearly understood. Because of play's importance, children's toys often are sexually segregated. To see how distinctly toys are grouped by sex, consult a recent Sears Roebuck or J. C. Penney Christmas catalog. Approach these "wish books" with a sensitive eye for what Erving Goffman (1979) calls "gender advertisements," and you will find them everywhere. Roller skates for schoolchildren must be ordered in boy's or girl's style. Sleeping bags are available in Wonder Woman and Superman designs. In the pages devoted to such toys as dolls, play kitchens, and baby carriages, boys are in the background watching the girls. Similarly, when trucks, erector sets, and racing cars are pictured, girls stand at a distance watching the boys at work.

Figure 3–2
Play is a time when boys and girls try on adult roles. (© *Stock, Boston, Inc., 1981. All rights reserved.*)

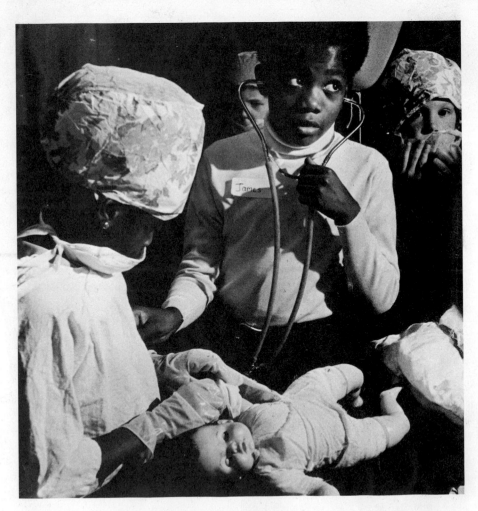

Wristwatches come in boy's or girl's styles and few unisex watches are displayed. Big Wheels, the modified tricycle, comes in two designs for three-year-olds. The Mini Sweetheart is "decorated specially for little girls . . . featuring a daisy squeeze horn." No girls are shown on the pages advertising microscopes, chemistry sets, or telescopes in recent catalogs of both companies. While both catalogs depict girls using exercise equipment, including barbells in one book, the overall impression is that toys are segregated by sex.

Children's books often reinforce the sexual stereotypes found in toys and observed in play (Weitzman, 1972). Girls see that the female in a book cares for the home and children while the father goes off to work. From time to time, women are depicted in the work force. However, such women usually are set in established "female occupations" that relate to domestic or nurturing roles, such as those of nurse, schoolteacher, waitress, or secretary. Only quite recently have children's book authors tried to break this stereotype by showing women in a much wider variety of occupations.

How children use toys and books shows that play is not only a time for fun. Children discover important social facts as they entertain themselves. They try on social roles and acquire attitudes which will be invaluable in their adult roles as family members. Merton (1968:438–40) refers to this as "anticipatory socialization." Play during childhood prepares one to assume the future roles of wife or husband, mother or father, as well as the mature sex roles of woman or man in society.

Friendship Networks and the Games Children Play

In part, children's play encourages gender identification and sex-role internalization through the different friendships and games played by boys·and girls. These pattens arise very early. One study found variations in play as early as 13 months of age (Goldberg and Lewis, 1969). Girls spend more time "mothering" stuffed toys, dolls, and even their playmates. Moreover, they tend to develop stronger social relationships with fewer playmates and exhibit more cooperative behavior in their play (Eder and Hallihan, 1979).

Another study revealed that girls prefer less complex games than boys. The girls' object in play was to enjoy others' company rather than to win (Lever, 1968). Accordingly, a girl's game usually has fewer rules, fewer players, and no fixed end. Boys engage more in games with recognized goals, such as a touchdown, a run, or a field goal. Even when boys and girls perform the same activity, they often relate to it differently. For example, riding bicycles for girls is usually a form of play; boys turn bike-riding into a race.

No one ever directly teaches youngsters these differential preferences for the two sexes. Children pick them up simply because they live within a culture. Boys know without being told that the basketball goal which mysteriously appears above the garage door is only for them. No one tells girls they should play mostly leaderless games like jump rope or hopscotch. Yet these patterns prevail in girls' play styles from an early age. By the same token, boys are not told that in their games they will scrape more elbows, rip more shirts, and wear out more sneakers than their sisters, but they manage to do so all the same.

Boys also relate to their peers and playmates differently than girls. Boys do not value their friendships with other boys quite as highly as girls regard their friendships. Boys tend to see the game as most important. Accordingly, boys move in and out of friendship groups with relative ease as they search out the play activity that interests them most at the moment. Companionship and socializing take second place. Boys are somewhat less apt to be jealous when a group member does something else which appears more exciting. In short, boys' play style is oriented more to activities than to persons.

Differing play patterns have convinced many social scientists that play experience is closely linked to sex-role mastery. Each reinforces the other. Sex roles shape play activities, while play styles help children internalize masculinity or femininity. While girls learn to be pretty, boys learn to be tough. Girls learn that being emotional is permissible; boys learn not to cry. As girls learn to cooperate, boys learn to win. The socialization that occurs during play may well increase women's ability to assume their nurturing role as mothers. But on the negative side, young girls' nonaggressive play experience could create behavior patterns which later would work against them in highly competitive occupations which are comparable to boys' "game" experiences.

Learning Sex Roles Through Imitation

While overt instruction in sex-role performance and the covert lessons of play are important ways to learn to be masculine or feminine, children also learn in other ways. Imitation, or **modeling** (Stockard and Johnson, 1980:188–91), is a common method. Girls watch their mothers, and other female role models, for clues to correct behavior. Boys relate to their fathers similarly. This is not really self-conscious activity. Children internalize their mother's or father's attitudes, interests, likes, and expectations in the imitative-identification process. However, all little girls are not exact copies of their mothers, nor are all little boys mirror images of their fathers. But in general, children do first become aware of the content of feminine and masculine orientations by copying their parents' attitudes and behavior patterns. Once the child has grasped the basic gender orientation, the other role models acquired from the mass media and from peers of the same sex can provide additional social behaviors with which to experiment. However, a girl's mother and a boy's father usually will remain their most important role models. Their influence is especially notable during early childhood dependency when a youngster's emotional attachment and social interaction with his or her parents is stronger and more persistent than other social relationships.

The Adolescent Peer Group and Sex-Role Performance

With adolescence, adopting sex roles takes on a new urgency (Weitz, 1977: 88–90). Parents become concerned about a "tomboy" daughter who is not

64   *A Season for Courtship*

thoroughly feminine, or a son who is "too nice." Parents may gently encourage their daughter to act more "like a young lady," or their son "to stand up for himself." The peer group's response to inappropriate behavior will, no doubt, be more direct, and sometimes even cruel. Girls who walk with a masculine stride, boast that they can throw a baseball farther than a boy, or show other "male" traits usually can expect to become the butt of ridicule. Boys, too, may be pressured to exhibit "macho" traits. Hair style, dress, language, and a thousand and one other characteristics must conform to the current fads or a price may be paid. Adolescence is no time to be different and the school is no place to challenge conventional sex-role behavior. One must get the details of sex-role performance right, or be subjected to schoolmates' lethal humor (David and Brannon, 1976:8). Teenagers feel enormous pressure to be accepted by the group. The code of conduct allows few compromises with "normal behavior patterns for the sexes." Variations in behavior are tolerated when they are linked to a separate subculture within the youth peer group. Basically, each subculture is organized around a different means of acquiring status among one's peers. The more common subcultures involve athletics, beauty, popularity, or brains (Coleman, 1961; Larkin, 1979).

For most adolescent females, the preferred sex role requires that the girl be attractive, vivacious, personable, and above all, skilled in interpersonal relationships (Shorter, 1977:275). Boys can be "loners" and yet survive in the youth subculture. A girl is pressured considerably more to develop friendship networks, to excel in the dating game, and to become a leader in extracurricular activities. In his pioneering study of the adolescent subculture in American high schools, James Coleman (1961) discovered that girls seek status mostly through popularity. When adolescent girls were asked whether they would rather be remembered for their "beauty" or their "brains," beauty won hands down. However, physical appearance was not really the objective. Beauty did not count for much unless it brought popularity. Besides being attractive to boys and dating the most desirable males, popularity also meant being "in" with the leading crowd, getting elected to leadership positions, and being seen as friendly by others. Most high school girls saw the role of cheerleader as having the highest status. This one social role combined beauty, popularity, and leadership. Cheerleaders are very visible. They date athletic stars who usually hold the highest status among the male students. And they are the guardians of the school spirit, charged with creating an emotional climate that unifies their school against other schools.

Of course, not all girls can become cheerleaders. But almost every girl can attain some of the other aspects of the feminine role model. Most girls can learn to wear makeup, dress according to fashions, master the latest dance steps, cry at athletic defeats, and flirt. At the same time, almost every girl can avoid having her femininity questioned. For example, whatever her native intelligence, a girl soon learns not to appear "smarter" than boys, especially a boy she wishes to date. Komarovsky (1976:52–9) uncovered several strategies whereby girls sought to offset their intellectual abilities by developing compensating "weaknesses." For example, girls encouraged in their dates a feeling that they were emotionally dependent on the boys; hinted that they had spent more time studying than they actually had, and often simply "played dumb"—especially in regard to the rules and strategies of sports. Curiously, these charades were approved by boys and girls. Apparently, female peers were no more willing than their male counterparts to tolerate deviance from the norms of femininity.

Adolescent males, Coleman (1961) found, had three ways to gain recognition—by being an athlete, a scholar, or a "ladies' man." Coleman (1961: 146–63) discovered that the males preferred to gain attention through athletics; being the "ladies' man" ran second, and the least attractive route was scholarship.

The "rugged individual" image for males, stressing control of objects and physical power, has always been part of American folklore. "Doers" rather than thinkers have provided boys' role models from the frontier days of Daniel Boone to the he-man movie image of James Bond to Terry Bradshaw's exploits on the football field. Lately, however, Edward Shorter (1977:275) believes, the peer culture has redoubled the stress on heroic exploits, from athletic prowess to sexual conquest to drinking more beer than the other guys. Curiously, in this era of women's liberation, the peer-group definition of masculinity seems to stress even more being macho.

Such role demands can create serious strain for adolescent males. Not all young men excel in sports, nor can they all play the "ladies' man." In addition, the sex roles that males are trained to adopt may create problems later in their roles as husbands and fathers. Male behavior within the family is not based on strength, power, and aggressiveness. Instead, this role requires tact, understanding, and firm guidance. Therefore, traits that ensure success in the adolescent peer culture could prevent success in family life.

Feminine Roles in the College and Young-Adult Years

Beginning with the college, or young-adult years, women have a chance to break away from the strict feminine role patterns of childhood and especially those of the high school years. While few young women can, or want to, suddenly shed all feminine characteristics, they are now more free to pursue careers and develop life-styles which they, rather than society, can choose.

TEST YOURSELF

On How Sex Roles Relate to Work Roles
The questions below have been selected from a number of sample surveys which social scientists have used to gather opinions on the way in which people relate sex-role attitudes toward work roles. After each statement, circle whether you agree strongly (AS), agree mildly (AM), disagree mildly (DM), or disagree strongly (DS). Under each choice is a number. Add up all your number scores when you have completed the self-test (note that sometimes the scores range from 1 to 4, while on other questions the scores are from 4 to 1). If your score is close to 10, then you hold a traditional outlook on the relation of sex roles to work roles. A score close to 40 will indicate a more liberal and equalitarian viewpoint.

A Season for Courtship

Men are better at economics and business than women.

AS	AM	DM	DS
1	2	3	4

There are some professions and types of businesses that are more suitable for men than women.

AS	AM	DM	DS
1	2	3	4

Women have as much to contribute to business and public life as men and should be given a better chance.

AS	AM	DM	DS
4	3	2	1

Women don't work as hard on their jobs as men do.

AS	AM	DM	DS
1	2	3	4

Women are usually less reliable on the job than men, because they tend to be absent more and quit more often.

AS	AM	DM	DS
1	2	3	4

In general, men are more qualified than women for jobs that have great responsibility.

AS	AM	DM	DS
1	2	3	4

Women have as much chance to get big and important jobs; they just aren't interested.

AS	AM	DM	DS
1	2	3	4

Women are hired for certain types of "helping" jobs (such as nurses, teachers, secretaries, and the like), and are usually content being right where they are.

AS	AM	DM	DS
1	2	3	4

Men tend to discriminate against women in hiring, firing, and promotion.

AS	AM	DM	DS
4	3	2	1

It's more natural for men to have the top responsible jobs in a country.

AS	AM	DM	DS
1	2	3	4

Source: Karen Oppenheim Mason, with the assistance of Daniel R. Denison and Anita J. Schacht. *Sex-Role Attitude Items and Scales from U. S. Sample Surveys.* Rockville, MD: National Institute of Mental Health. 1975, pp. 24–6.

Some women prefer marriage, and the homemaker-mother role to a career in the marketplace. Others avoid the homemaker-mother role; even if they marry, they see themselves as professional career women. Most married women today actually carve out two vocations—in the home and the marketplace. The majority of women now launch a career, marry, have children, and return to a career once the children are established in school (Lowenthal. 1975).

Indeed, the rapid increase in working mothers and **dual-career families** (Rapoport and Rapoport, 1978; McLaughlin, 1978: 909; Oppenheimer, 1977) has posed the question of whether feminine socialization creates disadvantages for women as they later compete with men in business careers. Since women are taught to be dependent, nonaggressive, people-oriented, and emotional, how can they survive, much less succeed, in the object-oriented, conflict-ridden environment of business life?

A serious drawback to answering such questions—apart from the general lack of pertinent studies—is the limited number of women who have reached high positions in business. Sex discrimination in hiring and promoting women has tended to restrict them to "female occupations." A recent study of 163 large U.S. companies (Kanter, 1977:17–8) revealed that 96 percent of all managers and administrators earning more than $30,000 were men. In half the companies, women held only 2 percent of the lowest supervisory jobs and 2 percent or less of the middle-management jobs. Three out of four companies had no women in top management. Such low numbers make it difficult to study women executives and draw reliable conclusions.

However, in her in-depth investigation of one major corporation, Kanter (1977) concluded that women managers performed as well as their male counterparts. Sex differences, she argued, had virtually no impact on work behavior (1977:262). Women could exercise power, make decisions, and cope with the tensions of business life as readily as men. From her point of view, the corporation's structural characteristics, such as the rewards for skill and efficiency and the freedom to exercise power, most directly influence its managers' behavior, whether they are men or women.

How do Kanter's findings correlate with the differing sex-role socialization of men and women? Should women not behave differently at work because of their feminine role orientation? Social scientists once thought so, accepting the logic that a warm, loving mother would find it very difficult to be a tough-minded business manager or an objective decision-maker in the political sphere. Apparently, however, this is not true. Indeed, several recent studies have disclosed that women can switch roles fairly easily to match institutional contexts (Rapoport and Rapoport, 1977). **Multiple roles** is the term sociologists apply when persons simultaneously occupy several social positions, each in a different institution and each requiring a different role performance (Merton, 1968:423). Just as a male lawyer can switch to his fathering role in the family, women can switch from mother to lawyer, teacher, or politician as they move among institutional positions. Some strain usually does arise when we change roles. For example, teachers who have been talking with students all day are likely to speak in the same manner to their own children at home. But such role carry-over occurs whether a teacher is male or female. For both sexes, **role strain** results from multiple roles.

Does the feminine or masculine orientation entail more than mere role taking? Sex roles also prescribe male and female temperamental dispositions. Thus, even if persons can switch roles, can they readily control acquired characteristics of temperament? Again, the answer apparently is yes. An interesting piece of research on male dispositions and behavior (Balswick and Peek, 1971) shows that while men were trained to repress their emotions generally, the companionate relationship in marriage was an exception to this practice. In marriage, a man is expected to be emotionally expressive toward his wife and children. This finding dovetails with those of Kanter who discovered that some situations give free rein to feminine or masculine temperaments, while others require that one's learned sexual temperament be restrained. Generally speaking, the learned feminine temperament as expressed in gentleness, intimacy, and responsiveness is fully appropriate in family situations but inappropriate in job-related, academic, or political spheres. Accordingly, women must adjust the expression of their sex-related temperament to their immediate social situation.

The Problem of Feminine Role Ambiguity

Women today are bombarded with conflicting advice on femininity, a drastic change from only a few generations ago. Then, every young girl knew almost exactly what part she was to play in life—wife, homemaker, mother. Her major decisions were made first by her parents and later by her husband. Meanwhile, societal norms allowed little leeway in these decisions. Early in this century, woman's greater economic independence and the more balanced allocation of decision-making power between spouses (Bernard, 1975:111–30) brought about a radical transformation which greatly increased role options for women (Chafe, 1972:245–54).

A major consequence of these changes was an increase in women's **role ambiguity** (Bardwich and Douvan, 1972). Many feminists argue that women can only find satisfaction in work outside the home, while traditionalists say that only the homemaker-mother role can yield true fulfillment. The upshot is a "no-win" situation for women. Whichever option they choose, someone is standing on the sidelines offering an opinion that makes them feel guilty about their choices. Even so-called feminine advertisements can reflect this sex-role ambiguity. For example, a cigarette slogan declares, "You've come a long way, baby." Supposedly, women have now attained the equality they need to smoke what men smoke. Instead, however, women are offered a "feminine" cigarette. If you've come a long way, baby, why can't you smoke what the cowboys smoke in Marlboro country? And why, too, are you still called "baby"?

These illustrations reveal a peculiar irony. As women have achieved more freedom from the household social roles and found new opportunities for personal growth, they have become more anxious over the meaning of the feminine sex role (Scanzoni, 1975:198–9). Sociologists can explain why this debate over femininity has occurred. Role ambiguity, the lack of clear, behavior guidelines for persons of a certain status, is extremely frustrating (Turner, 1970:304–6). People who dislike a well-defined role can reject or modify a role. However, when role expectations are unclear, people face a more perplexing problem. They do not know how they *ought* to act. Frustration, discontent, and anxiety arise from such ambiguity. Therefore, women's current dilemma focuses on whether a woman can play the feminine sex role without choosing a life-style centered on a husband, children, and home. We shall explore this issue in greater depth later in this chapter when we discuss social equality and sex roles.

The Masculine Role in Adulthood

During adolescence, male sex-role behavior is strictly enforced, and not, usually, by adults. Instead, the peer group imposes the pattern of behavior on its youthful members. Men gain more freedom when they enter adult economic and familial roles. At this stage, most husbands and fathers can perform many household tasks and engage in other behaviors that the peer-group culture would never have permitted when they were adolescents. By this time, most men also have discovered that the macho image exalted in their youth does not fit their roles as husbands and fathers. Certain aspects of the traditional masculine sex role can, of course, directly reinforce a man's ability to perform effectively in business. The emphasis on achievement, rationality, and meeting the world head-on can enhance one's career opportunities. Yet, these same attributes can be unsuitable when set within the context of family life (Balswick and Peck, 1971). In the highly successful film, *Kramer v. Kramer,* the behavior of the lead character, played by Dustin Hoffman, made this clear. The behavior that made Hoffman a successful advertising executive, such as working relentlessly for the company, undermined his domestic life. His effort to learn to be a good father tapped personality skills, resources, and behavior patterns radically different from those he used on the job. Thus, men, like women, must differentiate between home-based and work-based attitudes and patterns of behavior.

Working-class men typically have the most difficulty moving from work to home behavior with ease, according to various studies (Komarovsky, 1967; Rubin, 1976). Working-class men tend to adhere to traditional male and female sex-role patterns. At the same time, more and more middle-class men are willing to perform household tasks. These husbands can be found cooking meals, making suggestions for home decor, and spending more of their time raising the children (Lopata, 1972:104–22). This behavior has not appeared to diminish their own masculine gender identity. Nor does any firm evidence suggest that the overall importance of the masculine sex role is declining in America today.

Men in their adult years may manifest their masculinity through a broad range of sterotypical roles. David and Brannon (1976) compiled a partial list of the masculine sex role's central themes. Briefly, they are:

1. No sissy stuff. Avoid the stigma of all feminine characteristics and qualities.
2. The big wheel. A man must mold success, status, and competence into a personal image others respect and admire.
3. The sturdy oak. The real man exudes an air of confidence and self-reliance.
4. A "give 'em hell" approach. The male must sustain an image of aggressiveness and daring.

70

Each theme is an idealized aspect of masculinity which real individuals may modify to suit their own personalities. Taken together, however, these traits set off men's attitudes, temperament, and behavior from women's.

Those who urge radical changes in the feminine role are matched by those who want to redefine American masculinity (Bem, 1978; Filene, 1975:212–18; *Newsweek*, 1979). Advocates of female rights generally assume they cannot achieve their aims without also changing the concept of masculinity. However, few concrete suggestions as to how the masculine sex role should be changed have been offered (Osmond and Martin, 1975:745). More often, lingering macho traits and the inability to be more emotionally expressive are regarded as the problems. Without question, some aspects of the traditional male sex role have the potential to produce antisocial behavior. For this reason and others, there appears to be a trend toward abandoning the more macho aspects of the adult male sex role. It is still a bit too early, however, to specify precisely just how the meaning of masculinity will change in the next few years.

Social Equality and Sex Roles

Today's controversy about sex roles is a debate over the social equality of men and women in American society. Although women make up 51 percent of the U.S. population, they are still discriminated against in many aspects of our

Figure 3–3
More and more today, traditional male and female roles are becoming interchangeable. (© *Vivienne della Grotta, 1980/Photo Researchers, Inc.*; © *Robert A. Isaacs, 1980/Photo Researchers, Inc.*)

TABLE 3-1
Earned Academic
Degrees in 1980

Type of Degree	Percent Earned by Males	Percent Earned by Females
Bachelor's	56	44
Master's	54	46
Ph.D.	77	23
Medicine	84	16
Law	81	19
Dentistry	96	4

social life (Abramson, 1979). For example, in higher education, women are defined as a minority for hiring purposes, according to the federal government's affirmative action guidelines. Curiously, Jews, who constitute less than 3 percent of the population (Sklare; 1971:37–9), are *not* considered a minority by the same program because of their heavy concentration in college and university faculties.

In the economic sphere, meanwhile, slightly more than half of America's female population works outside the home. However, because women are clustered in low-paying jobs, their median income is 59 percent of that of the male worker (U.S. Bureau of the Census, 1977). Also when education, type of job, experience, and time in the labor force are constant, women earn only 73 percent as much as men (Suter and Miller, 1973:965). In addition, McLaughlin (1978) found that male-dominated occupations had higher pay scales than did female-dominated occupations. Indeed, the more women employed in a field, the lower the field's overall pay. Women also encounter discrimination when they seek mortgages, credit cards, or try to establish credit ratings independent of their husbands or as single persons.

Women's economic woes are not confined to jobs outside the home. Their domestic role also has special disadvantages. For instance, full-time homemakers do not receive their own social security benefits. They are excluded because they do not receive payment for their services and because they have no fixed point of retirement. Indeed, labor statistics treat homemakers as economically inactive, even though they may spend 80 hours a week performing such services as cooking, cleaning the house, washing clothes, ironing, and supervising children (Oakely, 1976). Moreover, the homemaker's role is assigned solely on the basis of sex. Our culture has no established role of "househusband." Likewise, when women, especially those from blue-collar households, work outside the home, they frequently find themselves working two jobs—the nine-to-five job plus their usual tasks as homemaker. More and more women regard their automatic assignment to household duties as unfair.

We could extend this catalog of sexual inequalities indefinitely. Media reports relate countless stories of sexual discrimination—not all against women, we should point out. For example, a wife can choose whether to stay home or seek a job outside the home. Her husband, by contrast, can be sued for nonsupport if he stays home and his wife does not assume the "breadwinner" role. Some observers say this situation constitutes sexist discrimination against men because they are denied a choice available to their wives. Furthermore, when a couple divorces, the children are still awarded to the mother's custody. Fathers very frequently claim this is unfair, feeling they are being denied access to their children.

These problems point up the central issue of whether sex roles are by their nature unequal. Can a society establish masculine and feminine roles without making either one inferior? Such questions are extremely important since equality, along with achievement, is a central value in our society (Lipset, 1963). Yet, like almost all major issues demanding public attention, both sides can marshal sound arguments.

Contemporary Opposition to Sex Roles

Critics of current sex roles do not form one unified front. They range, instead, from those who would blend several masculine-feminine traits, to those who seek one social role for men and women. Among those seeking some homogenization of sex roles, Mary Jo Bane's position (1976) may be the least demanding. She calls for a greater sharing of household tasks, child-rearing, and decision making between husband and wife. Eliminating masculine and feminine ideals is not her aim; she seeks only a more equalitarian husband-wife relationship. She wants to see women freed from undesired homemaker tasks and elevated from second-class citizenship.

Jessie Bernard (1975a) takes a stronger stand. She focuses on motherhood, claiming that mothering is too important a social function to be left to women alone. Fathers should also learn to be emotional, involved with their children's social development, and prepared to assume their fair share of the household's workload. Bernard recognizes that this change may require substantive modifications in the masculine role image. Yet, to her mind, stronger families, healthier children, and happier women would result from such changes.

A more radical and sweeping change is the objective of those social scientists and feminine activists who champion **androgyny**, a single social role applicable to both men and women. The term derives from two Greek words, *andro,* which means man, and *gyne,* which means woman (Forisha, 1978:29). Androgynous individuals can exercise the full range of human emotions and behaviors, not simply those usually reserved for their sex. Fusing masculine and feminine traits into this new gender identity, its supporters claim, would allow individuals to respond appropriately to social stiuations as they arise in daily life. Men would no longer have to react aggressively and women passively. People attracted to the androgynous alternative know that its full-scale use would change the way we socialize young people. Moreover, a change of this scope could not be accomplished quickly or without social resistance. In the long run, however, its backers believe androgyny offers a more humane role structure that will ultimately eliminate sexual inequality (Singer, 1977).

Androgyny is not simply a political ideology. Sandra Bem (1974) has attempted to develop a way to measure androgynous characteristics. In her view, masculine and feminine are opposite poles. Using 60 traits, "players"

Professing Androgyny

In the following quotes excerpted from an article by Connie Bruck in *Human Behavior*, psychologist, wife, and mother Sandra Bem outlines some of her feeling and ideas about the difference between the sexes, which she regards as comprising burdensome and restrictive roles that stand in the way of living a fulfilled life.

" . . . [My] interest in sex roles 'is and has always been frankly political,' [and my] major purpose is 'a feminist one: to help free the human personality from the restricting prison of sex-role stereotyping and to develop a conception of mental health which is free from culturally imposed definitions of masculinity and feminity.' "

"I think it's very important to realize that social scientists, like everyone else, have very strongly rooted assumptions that it doesn't even occur to them to question," . . . "It's just like we've now come to be aware that Freud was a product of his culture, that many of his theories about women were much like any other person's, living there at that time. Sometimes, social scientists learn to question assumptions in some little area and manage to make an innovation there, but in general, they have the same mindsets, and the same blind spots that everyone else does."

"Bem's first technical step was to develop the *Bem Sex-Role Inventory (BSRI)*, which treated masculinity and femininity as two independent dimensions rather than as opposite, either-or, ends of a single continuum, as most previous inventories had done. 'What the other inventories all had in common was this assumption that masculinity and femininity must be opposites,' Bem explains. 'So, for example, a typical question is: do you like to take showers? On the average, males prefer showers, females prefer baths—so none of the tests give you a way of saying you like showers *and* baths, I wanted to say, surely you can like or be both of these things, whether you're talking about showers or baths or personality characteristics.' "

" . . . traditional sex roles do produce an unnecessary and perhaps even dysfunctional pattern of avoidance for many people."

" . . . femininity may be what produces nurturant feelings in women, but at least a threshold level of masculinity is required to provide the initiative and perhaps even the daring to translate those nurturant feelings into action."

"The real moral of androgyny . . . is that behavior should have no gender." Androgyny as it's been defined in the research challenges a not very core assumption—that instead of people being just one way, they should be both. Well, that's something . . . but it doesn't go very deep. One measure of the fact that it doesn't is how easily it's been accepted."

"I feel that most people see the two sexes as forever going to be different in some basic, maybe metaphysical, way that's going to be reflected always in how we view them. And I'm really saying that maybe the big emphasis we put on gender, as a core of distinction, is purely arbitrary. Because I can picture a world where people are different . . . but the sexes aren't."

'Today, we grow up learning to relate differently depending on whether we're interacting with our own sex or the other. One of the most striking—actually, horrifying and depressing—things to me when I look at children, that from the ages of three and four, they're primarily playing with same-sex peers. Except for the specific acts of dating in adolescence and marriage in adulthood, by and large the world is a same-sex, sex-segregated world. Those are really the people you know well, those are the people you play with; the only thing you don't generally do is have sex with them. That bothers me a lot.

In my utopian world . . . a person's gender wouldn't be the key factor in terms of how you spoke to them. All your interactions would be a function of the characteristics of the *individual person* rather than that person's gender— and that would extend to sex as well. . . . A kind of sex that I've always found very appealing—conceptually, in the abstract—is sex between friends. And I think it would be part of living in a world where gender wasn't that central"

"My mother was a model of 'women work and are competent and speak their mind.' My father—well, he never made me into a 'daddy's little girl.' He never made me into anything."

"I can remember tingling at 14, when boys walked by—but I have the feeling that people should outgrow that. I see it as a kind of immaturity that keeps people from relating to each other as people."

can rate their personalities to find whether they score high on masculine or feminine dimensions. A score which falls in between the two poles, representing a balance between them, is regarded as androgynous. Actually, the Bem Sex-Role Inventory (BSRI) measures the number of sterotypical traits in one's personality. Bem does not formally define the androgynous sex role, with its rights and obligations.

A final alternative, designed to challenge current sex-role patterns and to further the emancipation of women, was proposed by Ann Oakley (1972, 1976). She recommends the elimination of gender roles, the homemaker role, and the family as a social institution, because, she claims, the family sustains both of the other role patterns. Her agenda's net effect would be very similar to androgyny. That is to say, Oakley (1976:239–40) wants to see women liberated and elevated to full legal, economic, cultural, and political equality. Piecemeal reforms, she says, leave intact gender identifications which perpetuate inequality between the sexes. Thus, resolving the sexes' social rights and responsibilities requires that masculine and feminine gender roles be eliminated entirely.

We have outlined four positions on sex roles. The conservative stance of mild reformism (Bane) lies at one end, while the radical perspective (Oakley) lies at the other. In between fall the positions of Bernard and the concept of androgyny. Linking these positions is a basic conviction that current sex roles foster some feminine repression. Accordingly, each position recommends a way to bring masculine and feminine sex roles closer or to unite them in a single role. Oakley may be correct in asserting that a radical homogenization of sex roles can be obtained only by dismantling the family. Meanwhile, many people would probably regard the loss of family life as too high a price to pay, even for complete sexual equality. Others would argue as vehemently that asking people to choose between the family and sex-role equality is not a proper way to state the alternatives. Still others would view sex-role inequalities as a natural and necessary pattern which cannot or should not be changed. In the following section, we shall examine several of the points of view which, for a variety of reasons, support the retention of sex-role differences.

Contemporary Support of Sex Roles

Those who want to maintain male-female sex-role distinctions are as diverse in their views as those who argue for sex-role homogenization. At the conservative extreme stand those who regard masculine superiority as natural, necessary, and humanly unalterable. This group includes "male chauvinists" as well as many social scientists who read the data differently than their liberal colleagues. A chief archconservative on this issue is Steven Goldberg (1973), who asserts that the biological differences between men and women always produce male domination. In his view, patriarchy inevitably results from such male-female relations. Sociobiologists are not quite as adamant about that point but they do tend to agree that male dominance results from biologically based forces (van den Berghe, 1978). To their mind, all efforts to counteract nature by equalizing sex roles are doomed to failure.

A far larger group of social scientists who deplore discrimination against women stand to the left of, and are clearly distinguishable from, the sociobiologists. While they support efforts to gain more rights for women, they are not yet prepared to scrap sex roles altogether (Weitz, 1977:247; Chafe, 1972). One of the more important defenders of sex roles—although perhaps not intentionally and certainly without any motive to perpetuate feminine subordination—was the late Talcott Parsons.

Parsons (1955, 1964) saw sex roles as intimately tied to the nuclear family's leadership roles. Sex-role socialization was understood to prepare men and women for leadership roles within the family. Men's objective, rational, task-oriented style fitted them for the family's instrumental leadership role, while women's nurturing, supportive, emotionally oriented behavior suited them for the role of the household's expressive leader. These two leaders complement each other, and they do so because their behaviors are different. The family, Parsons maintained, requires both leadership types. If our socialization patterns were reversed, men might be the expressive leaders and women the instrumental leaders. However, each leadership type would still be assigned to one sex. Of course neither leadership role is necessarily superior to the other. Their functions are simply different, to meet the varying social demands impinging on the nuclear family.

If Parsons is correct, tampering with sex roles might undercut the family leaders' ability to do their jobs well. Thus, Parsons insists that any proposal to modify sex roles results in serious changes in family structures and processes. Parsons' implied warning somewhat resembles the view of his most radical opponent, Ann Oakley. Both recognize that sex roles and family roles are indivisible. Yet, while Parsons urges that sex roles be kept to sustain the family, Oakley demands the family's destruction to free individuals from sex roles.

Those who are concerned with the family's vitality and sexual equality must confront the issue that divides Parsons and Oakley. Namely, can a family sustain itself while retaining different but equal sex roles? The most troublesome feature of this dilemma is that most people do, indeed, favor the attainment of these dual aims. However, if both are not possible, predicting the likely winner—the family or sexual equality—would be difficult, precisely because our culture values both.

Summary

We introduced three basic terms: sex, gender identity, and sex roles. Sex, a biological term, signifies the physical differences between males and females. Gender identity is a person's psychological identification with a given sex. Sex roles, by contrast, are the attitudes and behaviors the public expects of men and women. Sex roles are cultural definitions of masculinity and femininity which can and do vary among societies. Sex, gender identity, and sex roles are related, but each is a distinct aspect of the biosocial differences between the sexes.

Sociologists tend to focus their attention on sex roles, since social factors influence these patterns most strongly. Both the process by which we internalize sex roles and the content of masculinity and femininity are studied. Our parents and other socializing agents impose our first sex-role behavior on us shortly after birth. Young girls soon learn they should appear emotional, attractive, nurturing, expressive, and person oriented. Boys try to be strong, objective, aggressive, unemotional, and object oriented. Toys and play styles reinforce sex-role differences.

In adolescence, the peer group also enforces distinct behaviors for the sexes. Girls are encouraged to prefer beauty over brains, to seek popularity, and to develop a vivacious personality and skill in subtly controlling relationships. Adolescent males are offered a macho ideal which stresses athletic prowess and sexual conquest over intellectual achievement. In their collegiate and adult years, both men and women enjoy more latitude in their sex-role behavior. Though young women do not suddenly shed feminine traits, they are freer to pursue careers and develop life-styles which they choose rather than simply accept. Some women still prefer the role of wife, homemaker, and mother. Others opt for single careers, with marriage an eventual possibility. In practice, most women today combine both roles by launching a career, marrying, having children, and returning to work once the children are in school. One cost of greater freedom, however, has been an increased ambiguity in regard to the woman's role. As adults, men also feel freer to express emotions and do household jobs, two functions almost unthinkable in adolescence.

Today's central controversy about sex roles in America is really about men and women's social equality. Reformers want to slightly modify sex-role patterns to provide women with greater opportunities in the home, economy, and social life. Radicals believe sex roles are inherently unequal. To make them equal, we must destroy all gender roles and eliminate the family, because it perpetuates sex-role patterns. A similar position suggests a single role for men and women called androgyny.

Conservatives believe sex roles are biologically determined and cannot be erased by social engineering. Most social scientists take a less absolute stance. They support women's economic, political, and social rights, but they do not believe sex roles must be eliminated to achieve these other political goals. Parsons for example, warns that fusing sex roles may stop the family from functioning. He believes sex roles are linked to leadership roles in the nuclear family. Tampering with sex roles to introduce drastic changes may well destroy the family.

The present debate over sex roles focuses on whether we can have a strong family, sex-role differences, and gender equality. How we resolve this question will profoundly affect marriage and family life in the year 2000 and beyond.

STUDY QUESTIONS

1. In the realm of social science, how are the terms sex and sex roles distinguished from one another?
2. What are some of the ways in which infants are encouraged to make the correct gender identification?
3. Why is a child's play so important in learning social roles and proper sex-role behaviors?
4. How significant is the adolescent peer group in overseeing sex-role performance?
5. What are the factors that contribute to feminine role ambiguity?
6. How is the contemporary debate over social equality between men and women related to the issue of sex roles?

The Social Patterns of Dating

4

Like the *Wide World of Sports*, dating today is filled with the thrill of victory and the agony of defeat. Yet, without these two extremes—the exhilaration of forming a new relationship and the melancholy when it falls apart—dating would lose much of its fascination. From puppy love to deep involvment, dating and falling in love is an extraordinary human experience, an almost endless source of inspiration for popular songs, and a primary activity among young people, which most staid adults recall with fond memories, while preferring not to live through it again.

Of course, to speak at all about dating and romantic love is distinctly modern. Generations before us did not link romance with mate choice. In a traditional society, courtship was rare or conducted in groups under strict community controls (Shorter, 1977:44–78). Parents, who kept a close watch over property and finance, commonly arranged marriages. Far more important than love was the opportunity marriage presented to preserve or increase family assets; the rich were especially careful for they had fortunes to preserve (Stone, 1979:181–216). As William Goode (1973:245–60) has pointed out, love had to be strictly controlled so that it did not interfere with such important matters as lineage, inheritance, and power relations. In traditional societies, love and marriage did *not* "go together like a horse and carriage." Indeed, they were almost as foreign to social life as a horseless carriage.

European youth broke away from family and community controls by moving to the cities in great numbers. New patterns of courtship arose almost immediately. In America, attitudes toward courtship behaviors were more flexible. Consequently, couples in the New World enjoyed at least some independence in selecting a marriage partner (Kett, 1977:11–61).

Changing Patterns of Courtship in America

Dating in Colonial times reflected the limitations imposed by time, distance, and transportation. Perhaps the most famous and novel of courtship customs was "bundling," which was popular in snowy New England. Bundling originated in northern European countries (Tomasson, 1970; Stone, 1979: 384–5) where long winter nights, great distances between the homes of courting persons, and inadequate heating systems made courting difficult. Young men could not return home after visiting a girlfriend because traveling at night in harsh weather was too dangerous. The couple could not sit up late at night talking because fuel was too expensive to heat the house just for them. Bundling was the compromise. A young man and woman shared the same bed for the evening, allowing them to converse privately, to keep warm, and to avoid night travel by the young man. Of course, couples were strictly forbidden any sort of sexual activity—and some apparently obeyed. The court records indicate a significant number of illegitimate births and trials for sexual offenses involving single persons (Demos, 1971:152). Bundling may have contributed to the illegitimacy rate, at least during the winter months. Later in the eighteenth century, the girl's parents often placed a board between the boy and girl, hoping to minimize physical contact. Obviously, even this device would not thwart an ardent pair, and some found the opportunities more than they could resist. On balance, however, bundling was a practical way for young people to get acquainted before they decided to marry and spend their lives together.

As the population moved westward during the nineteenth century, bundling died out and courtship turned toward more conventional practices. Young people met at dances, barn or house raisings, and church meetings. For the lower classes, engagements were often short, and couples knew relatively little about each other before they married. Wealthy families enjoyed many more activities, ranging from sheer recreation to courting. Young women practiced music, learned to dance, mastered the domestic arts, and

Figure 4–1
Dating in the nineteenth century allowed little privacy for a young couple. Here, a suitor reads to his love, while the chaperon sleeps nearby. *(The Bettman Archive.)*

generally prepared themselves for roles as wives and household managers. They also went to endless parties, dances, picnics, and outings, which eligible young men also attended (Grevin, 1977:289–95). Courting lasted much longer and included many more pleasant diversions than did courtship among the common folk.

Today's dating practices did not really appear on the social scene until the turn of the century. Young people generally were not afforded a leisurely adolescence until the 1920s. In the next several decades—despite both the Great Depression and World War II—the number of young people entering colleges steadily increased. With this change came greater freedom of action, especially in courting habits (Parsons, 1965:132–3). The casual date became an everyday event. Gradually, dating patterns worked out by college students and other young adults filtered down to change the behavior of students in high school and junior high (Handlin and Handlin, 1971:226–35).

Few innovations more drastically affected the dating habits and sexual conduct of American youth than the automobile (Cummins, 1978; Bettelheim, 1965:99). Cars not only afforded greater mobility to search out recreation or entertainment, but they also provided considerable privacy. From the 1940s on, more and more young people found the automobile a convenient place for petting and lovemaking. Many dates began with a movie, a school dance, or a private party, and ended by parking on lover's lane (Hollingshead, 1975:310–23). Teenagers also needed cars to reach favorite hangouts, many of which were drive-in restaurants, and to provide a place to talk privately.

Over time, dating rituals also evolved. The nature of a date varied with the nature of the pair's relationship. Certain dates required a formal invitation, usually from the male partner. This pattern was also common when the two knew each other only slightly. Once they became better acquainted and developed a bond of affection, steady dating often resulted. A "steady date" involved a declaration by the girl and boy not to date anyone else. During the 1950s and early 1960s, high school couples often exchanged class rings to seal a steady relationship.

Courtship patterns that were followed from the mid 1960s to the early 1980s were far less oriented toward marriage than ever before. Even the terminology changed. The steady date became "going with someone." Fewer and fewer couples made formal dates, or expected the boy to call for the girl at a particular time or place, or to accompany him to a specific event. Larkin (1979) reports that while some of the elitist "jock/rah-rah" crowd (including athletes, cheerleaders, and prom goers) as well as some less glamorous high school students continued to date in the 1970s, most young people mingled in groups with little pairing off. The greater informality gave individual members of the youth group more latitude and freed the male particularly from some financial burdens that earlier dating styles had imposed. As we move farther into the 1980s, however, the pendulum may be swinging back toward more formal dating. Dating practices probably will not return to the elaborate ground rules of the 1950s, but we may see some pressure for clearer guidelines about daters' mutual obligations.

Figure 4-2
Over the last decade,
dating has become
less formal and more
of a group rather than
a paired activity. (©
*Christa Armstrong, 1977/
Photo Researchers, Inc.*)

CLOSE-UP

Dating Rituals: A Comparison of the 1950s and 1980s

Dating rituals gradually evolve from one decade to the next, as youth set many of their own standards for how the dating game will be played. Perhaps the most distinguishing characteristic which separates dating practices in the 1950s from those current now is the extent to which dating behavior was highly regimented for the early generation. For example, high school couples in the fifties often sealed their relationship of "going steady" by exchanging senior class rings. The collegiate group during the fifties developed a somewhat more elaborate system of dating rituals. The stages in this system were highly formalized—at least in comparison to dating practices today. The stages popular in the fifties included the following:

(1) The initial stage was simply called "dating around." This meant that both the boy and girl were free to date whomever they pleased, with no special ties or obligations to any one partner.

(2) The second stage entailed "going steady." This was a verbal agreement between the dating couple not to go out with anyone else. Movement into this status involved no symbolic gestures other than a declaration made by the couple of their "going steady" status.

(3) Getting "lavaliered" was the third step. A lavaliere was a necklace given to the girl which held the Greek letters of the boy's fraternity.

(4) Next came being "pinned." This was a far more serious step than being lavaliered, for the boy gave the girl his fraternity pin which she would wear everyday as a symbol of their commitment to one another—whether it matched her outfit or not.

(5) Engagement represented the next plateau. An engagement ring—then as now—symbolized the couple's intention to marry.

(continued)

The Social Patterns of Dating

(6) Marriage constituted the final stage.

At each level in this graduated model, the relationship between the couple became more serious and personally binding. Going steady or being lavaliered, for example, were far less indicative of the fact that the couple was contemplating marriage than being pinned or engaged. Moreover, at any stage prior to marriage, the relationship could be voluntarily terminated by either the girl or boy. Breaking off the relationship at the lavaliered stage, however, was far easier emotionally than breaking an engagement.

During the late 1960s, this structured pattern was rejected by college youth in favor of a more informal system of dating. By the early 1980s, college youth were far less oriented toward dating as a process leading to the selection of a marriage partner than in the 1950s. Accordingly, fewer and fewer couples made formal arrangements for dates or expected the boy to pick up the girl he was dating to accompany him to a particular event. Rather, the word was usually passed through informal channels that one member of the dating couple would be somewhere with a group of friends, so the other member could arrange to be there at approximately the same time. In this way, contact could be made and the couple could spend some time together, but neither was really answerable to the other or responsible for a fixed commitment to meet together. The notion of a "steady date" also dropped out of vogue, and a young person who went out with no one else spoke of "going with someone." Pairing off into an isolated couple apart from the group normally occurred only after the relationship had become "serious," or on special occasions like a formal dance.

The greater informality of the 1980s has offered more latitude to dating partners and released the male, in particular, from some of the financial burdens earlier styles of dating imposed on him. Some commentators are suggesting, however, that, as we move further into the 1980s, we should expect a pendulum swing back toward more formalized dating rituals. Yet, it does seem unlikely that dating practices will return to stages as elaborate as those operative in the 1950s.

Another significant change among serious dating couples is the introduction of **cohabitation**, or living together, before marriage. In face of the rising divorce statistics, many young people fear the permanence of marriage. They see living together before marriage as the ultimate in steady dating. If they discover they are compatible, marriage is the next logical step. However, if they have trouble getting along, they may rule out marriage because of the likelihood of divorce, if they were to make their arrangement permanent.

Living together may not be the ideal solution to the mate-selection problem. Social scientists do not have much data on couples who cohabit before they marry. Glick and Norton (1977:36) estimate that because of moral opposition the number of young Americans who live together will never reach the 12 percent mark now prevalent in Sweden. Furthermore, from a logical point of view, living together is not the same as marriage. Cohabiting couples can split up at the first sign of trouble. No external constraints pressure them to resolve their problems. Marriage, by contrast, is both a legal contract and a personal commitment which each partner is urged to honor and work at seriously. One does not walk away from a marriage as one might from cohabitation—although the recent *Marvin v. Marvin* decision (see further discussion on *Marvin v. Marvin* in Chapter 8, page 205) makes even cohabitation almost as legally binding as marriage (Belkin and Goodman, 1980:248). Indeed, the legal implications of cohabitation are just now being worked out in several states (Newcomb, 1979). Couples may discover that their informal arrangement has actually involved each partner in binding legal obligations. Whatever the outcome of these legal issues, however, cohabitation has now emerged as an integral aspect of the courtship process, which we shall discuss more fully in Chapter 8.

On balance, then, the dating process in America, from bundling to cohabitation, has beeen an evolving social phenomenon. Sociologists tend to view the changes as continuing adjustments to people's needs and interests. Particularly in a personal area like dating, people like to believe they are acting independently rather than responding to social pressures. Nonetheless, dating, like almost any social process, can be fully understood only when it is viewed as a cultural pattern. Throughout this chapter, we shall explore some of the more important social variables shaping contemporary dating practices.

Casual and Serious Dating: Forms and Functions of Courtship

Should social scientists seriously study the dating process? What can be gained by exploring why people date, who dates most, and how people play the dating game? Can we not rely on common sense to tell us that people date because they think it is fun? What more does one really need to know?

Actually, a great deal more remains to be examined, for dating is not simply an idle pastime. Courtship does not flourish apart from other facets of the social order. Our dating practices relate directly to America's family system, economic order, class structure, and cultural norms. Thus, a simple description of dating hardly scratches the surface of this important social process.

Why Do People Date?

Dating is necessary in American society because people are free to choose their marriage partners. Selecting a mate assumes some familiarity and ease in relating to the opposite sex. Dating provides this experience. Males and females can gain social skills by playing their sex roles against their dating partners. Long before they are ready to select a permanent marriage partner, young people use **casual dating** to build their experience in ways of establishing social relationships with members of the opposite sex. Cross-gender interaction allows young people to overcome the awkwardness which typifies boy-girl relations as dating begins. Dating also can be a way for individuals to fit into their peer group. Going with someone clearly defines one's social position within the larger context of the youth culture.

Furthermore, casual dating also can enhance one's status within the peer group. Frequent dating symbolizes popularity, at least among certian youth subcultures (Larkin, 1979). Yet, frequency is only half the story in terms of status. Although young people from the higher socioeconomic classes date more often than lower-class youths, the choice of a date does make a difference. Beyond the class system, the youth culture has its own status groups and ranking methods (Havighurst and Taba, 1963; Coleman, 1961). For example, dating a star athlete generally confers a higher status upon girls than dating a nonathletic scholar or the school orchestra's first violinist. Similarly, dating a cheerleader or the student association's social chairman increases a boy's status in the athletic or popularity subcultures more than dating a studious girl who is outside the party circuit. Thus, being able to date someone from the "leading crowd" can improve or sustain a high-status position.

The reasons for dating, then, are many and varied. Young people and single adults see casual dating as a pleasant activity which provides companionship without the social obligations involved in marriage. Dating also gives the two partners the opportunity to clarify their sex roles, especially during various recreational activities. Achieving intimacy with another person and some sexual experimentation are also both common features of dating. Underlying all other motivations, however, is dating's role as a prelude to mate selection. To be sure, not all dating is immediately oriented toward marriage. But marriage eventually results from a relationship which began as a casual date.

Who Dates Whom?

In principle, American society places few restrictions on who may date whom. People who date should be single and old enough to handle the dating relationship. Generally, one dates a member of the opposite sex—although homosexual dating is clearly on the rise. Certain laws forbid adults to date minors, which in several states constitutes statutory rape. Such laws reinforce the normative expectation that people should date within their own age groups. However, "May and December" dating by adults is subject only to the constraints of custom, not law. Apart from these relatively modest restrictions, American dating thrives in a free-market atmosphere. Every eligible person is free to negotiate for the best dating partner he or she can get.

In practice, however, several factors limit date selection. Some are relatively obvious. Most people, for example, want to date someone physically attractive rather than plain, someone intelligent rather than dull, interesting rather than boring, or sophisticated rather than uncouth. Beyond these preferences, which everyone develops with experience, lie more subtle, hidden factors that may be equally important in choosing a dating partner. Perhaps most significant is social-class standing.

Our knowledge of the impact of social-class standing on dating behavior results from a long series of independent studies. They reveal a steady refinement in our understanding of how social class and status influence dating practices. Willard Waller (1937) conducted the pioneering study as he explored a new pattern of casual dating among college students, which led to his discovery of a practice he called the "rating and dating complex." No longer was dating a prelude to marriage, he observed; it had become a means of gaining prestige on campus. The overriding goal was to date the highest ranking member of the opposite sex. Qualities meriting a high rating were often materialistic and pleasure-oriented, such as membership in a certain fraternity, a pleasant personality, money, easy access to a car, skill in the latest dances, and fashionable dress. Waller derided the rating and dating complex as an exploitative, hedonistic system which degraded romantic love and fostered antagonism between men and women.

Waller's research in the 1930s was an opening wedge in the drive to explode the myth that an individual's own choice was the primary factor in that person's selection of dates. Individuals were not choosing dates for their character attributes or their potential in an eventual love relationship. Rather, in his eyes, a rating system imposed by a peer group without humane interests was simply victimizing daters. Subsequent studies aimed at replicating Waller's findings failed to reveal the strong rating-dating complex found in his original study. For instance, Blood (1955) found that in the 1950s rating was based on an entirely different set of factors than those discerned by Waller. The new rating system was based primarily on personality traits, such as friendliness, a sense of humor, and thoughtfulness. More significant, however, than the rating factors themselves was the discovery that the practice of rating itself continues and that the peer group, rather than individuals outside the youth culture, established the rating criteria.

In a new study on campus dating, Ira Reiss (summarized in 1980: 94–9) sought to reinterpret earlier findings about the rating complex. Reiss proposed that the differing rating systems were actually variables which reflected the dating individuals' class backgrounds. Indeed, Reiss gathered data to show that rating factors, which would help students select partners from a similar social class, influenced casual and serious dating. Similarity of backgrounds encompassed both the campus status system and the standing of the daters' parents. Reiss does not contend, of course, that biological and psychological factors are irrelevant to choosing a dating partner, but he does stress the importance of social class and other collective forces in explaining dating behavior.

How Do We Play the Dating Game?

In our brief discussion of courtship practices earlier in this chapter, we noted several changes in the rules governing dating behavior. In this section, we are concentrating on the activities of dating couples. For a casual dating couple, the date's activity, whether it is a movie or a basketball game, may be far more important than it would be to serious dating partners, who are very likely to consider their time together more important than the particular activity.

Most dates involve "going to" something. Couples may go to a movie, a party, a restaurant—the most common activities. Or, they may decide to go to the beach, a rock concert, the library, a coffeehouse, to the mountains for

Figure 4–3
During these inflationary times, many dates involve activities that do not cost much money. (*© David Rosenfeld, Photo Researchers, Inc.*)

a day of skiing, or simply out for an evening of bowling. The activity's intensity may range from a quiet evening watching television to the senior prom.

Dates are occasions for communicating and building relationships. Few experiences are more boring than being with someone who says very little all evening. Particularly when people first start to date, talking is a crucial aspect of the experience. Couples talk primarily about themselves. They describe their likes and dislikes, dreams and fears, their mutual acquaintances, and similar experiences. Or they talk about school, their parents, and the future (Rubin, 1973:160–72). From such sharing, intimacy grows. Indeed, psychologist Erik Erikson (1968:135–41) has written that without the cultivation of intimacy and the ability to share one's feelings, the young adult's psychosocial development may well be arrested or malformed. Thus, the relationships and the social skills that are refined through dating yield important consequences for the dating couple, even when they do not marry. Without this acquired sensitivity, establishing a companionate marriage would be much more difficult. Time spent communicating is, therefore, excellent preparation for the move from dating to marriage.

Not all dates of course, are spent sedately watching a movie or just talking. An awakening interest in the opposite sex corresponds to an awakening interest in sexual activity itself. From the early Kinsey reports (1948, 1953) until now, ample data confirm that sexual experimentation is an integral part of the dating process. Because the next two sections deal with sexual attitudes, norms, and behavior, we need only point out here that the sheer press of circumstances requires dating couples to confront sexual intimacy earlier than previous generations. The sexual revolution of the 1960s drastically changed both attitudes and behavior related to premarital sexual activity (Yankelovich, 1974: 86–102). Men, in particular, are more apt to expect sexual intimacy if they are to continue dating a girl (Komarovsky, 1976). Evidence also demonstrates that males are more likely to be the aggressors in premarital sexual relationships (Reiss, 1960: 107–48; Kaats and Davis, 1975: 37–9). However, over the last 15 years, the major change in sexual attitudes and behaviors has been women's willingness to accept male advances and engage more freely in premarital intercourse (Moneymaker and Montanino, 1978: 32–5). In one sense, then, the sexual revolution really has been a transformation of female attitudes and conduct. Generally, men have always been the partners who have wanted more intense sexual relationships.

Despite greater sexual intimacy on dates today, most youths do not believe they are promiscuous. Having sex simply for its thrill and pleasure, without affection for your partner, is seldom condoned by the youth culture's sexual norms. However, as Burgess-Kohn (1979:24) accurately observes, most youth "today believe that if two people are in love, it is all right for them to engage in sexual intercourse outside of marriage." The key phrase, of course, is "if two people are in love." The feeling of affection is regarded as the factor that makes sexual intercourse more than merely a physical exploitation of one's partner. At the same time, the youth culture concedes that this affection may not be strong enough to sustain a marriage. Thus, some social scientists suspect that the insistence on love before sexual intercourse may be a subtle deception which youths use to justify their erotic adventures. Erich Fromm (1956:54) long ago voiced the reservations of many social scientists: "Because sexual desire is in the minds of most people coupled with the idea of love, they are easily misled to conclude that they love each other when they want each other physically."

Whether the sexual activity associated with dating results from lust or love is not a topic for discussion now. But we should point out that sexual intimacy is a far more central part of dating than it was only twenty years ago. Today, feelings and behavior correspond more closely. Young people who feel a mutual love attraction are much more likely to express themselves physically than their parents were two decades ago. Indeed, the deeper the emotional bond between dating partners, the greater the likelihood that they will indulge in sexual experimentation during the dating process.

Another dating activity introduced during cultural revolution in the 60s was the use of drugs (Carey, 1968:122–44). For a while, drugs challenged alcohol as the "icebreaker" which seemingly dispelled the tensions of girl-boy relations. During the late 1970s, drinking rebounded somewhat on college campuses, especially when hallucinogenic drugs fell from popularity because they may do permanent physiological damage. Apparently, daters also have used alcohol and "pot," or marijuana, to lower their sexual inhibitions (Burgess-Kohn, 1979:50–51). Many marijuana smokers insist that being high increases one's capacity for sexual stimulation (McCary, 1979:118). While clinical evidence indicates clearly that marijuana does not increase the sex drive, it may alter sense and time perceptions temporarily and thereby prolong or intensify the pleasurable feelings of sex (Pierson and D'Antonio, 1974:54, 70). Large intakes of drugs, including alcohol, also clearly lower the sex drive and often create temporary impotence. Nonetheless, smoking pot is now almost as common among many dating high school and college students as drinking beer.

Thus, we have seen that dating encompasses almost every activity people enjoy doing together. By the same token, all those tedious tasks no one really enjoys, are usually excluded from dating. For example, few couples make a date to clean one partner's apartment or dormitory room. Much of dating's attraction is the chance to do something interesting with someone you like. In this regard, dating differs drastically from marriage, in which the couple cannot avoid many mundane tasks, many of which they must perform together.

The Problems of Dating

Dating is fun if one is involved in pleasurable activities with a compatible partner. However, not all dates unfold according to our fantasy scripts. Almost everyone who has dated has had promising dates which turned out badly. We shall explore several areas in which difficulties may arise.

Making a Date The first major hurdle in dating is, of course, getting a date. The two sexes have different anxieties about this first step. Girls usually fear that no one will ask them out, while boys are afraid of being rejected. Accordingly, people who want to date each other usually exchange social signals that say they would be willing to go out (Larkin, 1979:108–11). For such an exchange to take place, potential daters must meet where they can converse. In his study of 200 university students, Knox (1979:178) found that dating couples most frequently identified the places they met their partners as "in class," "at a party," "at work," "at church," or "through a friend." Clearly, the immediate environment is important. Consequently, high school students whose families move to another community, people who leave home for a job elsewhere, or students away at college will all have a limited social life until they develop a new network of friends. Shy people who do not come into contact often with other young people may have an especially difficult time getting dates. The growth of computer dating services indicates how isolated some people feel from potential dating partners. These services bring together persons who want to date by matching partners according to several similar background traits. Of course such services cannot guarantee that their matchmaking will bring together persons who will genuinely like one another.

Suzanne Gordon (1976:243–4) reports the services promise much more than they actually deliver. Most people still prefer to make dates without the aid of modern technology.

Enjoying a Date   Once a date has been set, the next goal is to have a good time. Any number of problems can arise. One's partner may be boring, self-centered, obnoxious, sexually aggressive, or too interested in drinking or drugs. Dates also may fail because the partners discover they have radically different interests and tastes. Without some common interests, one or both partners are likely to write off a particular date as a bad experience. The old saying, "opposites attract," applies only to magnets, not to enjoyable dates.

Taking Advantage of One's Date   "How shall I exploit thee? Let me count the ways." Unfortunately, many people of both sexes play the dating game selfishly. Each gender uses the other in its own way. Males are much more inclined to press for sexual favors (Hettlinger, 1974:71–82). Because females often insist on a sign of love before giving in to male advances, men sometimes exaggerate their love to gain physical satisfaction. In Kirkendall's (1961:97) study of premarital relations, for example, his subjects typically admitted:

> "She simply wouldn't go ahead until I told her I loved her . . . She knew as well as I did there wasn't a word of truth in it, but she had to hear it."

> "I told her I loved her, and all that baloney."

> "I said that I was sure intercourse would strengthen our relationship."

Such obvious deceptions are not uncommon for men who see dating only as a way to satisfy their own sexual desires.

Women, by contrast, are more likely to engage in economic exploitation. If a partner will pay for the movies, restaurant meals, or other entertainments, some women will pretend they find them appealing. Typically, a woman who seriously exploits partners will insinuate that she may consider a permanent relationship, even though she has no such intention (Gordon, 1976:232–4).

Exploitation in dating is often more subtle. "I date Judy because she owns an incredible sports car." Or, "Jim is a dreadful bore, but we go out occasionally because his father is president of the bank where I hope to get a job after graduation." Or again, "Janice is great in math, so I always arrange a date with her when I don't understand something or final exam season rolls around." In each instance, a partner uses a date to achieve a goal outside of a dater's normal expectations. Each one's self-serving deception degrades the partner's—and their—integrity.

Despite such problems as getting and enjoying a date, and exploiting one's partner, dating persists. Thus, most young people must feel that its advantages outweigh its disadvantages. Dating practices have changed over time, but interest in going out with the opposite sex shows no evidence of waning. An important change in the dating game is the modification of sexual attitudes and behaviors, topics we discuss in the next two sections.

People's attitudes and social behaviors do not always correspond, as behavioral scientists have known for a long time. For example, research on civil rights issues has demonstrated that persons who express strong prejudicial attitudes toward minority groups often behave in nondiscriminatory ways when they meet members of minority groups. Similar discrepancies exist between sexual attitudes and sexual practices.

What Are Premarital Sexual Attitudes and Standards?

Society expects unmarried men and women to follow certain ideal norms in their daily sexual conduct. These norms generally are called premarital sexual attitudes and standards. Of course, no society's members can live up to the group's ideals fully. Moreover, the absolute ideals governing sexuality are changing norms. Over time, they shift with almost every other aspect of our cultural life. Certainly, change has occurred in the sexual norms of American society over the last few decades.

The Traditional Norms for Sexual Relations

The Judeo-Christian tradition is without doubt the major source of traditional norms informing sexual relations in American society. The Puritans, as we noted in Chapter 2, stood against loose morals, including sexual relations prior to, or outside of, marriage. In Hawthorne's novel, *The Scarlet Letter*, the conjugal intimacy between Hester Prynne and the Reverend Mr. Dimmesdale revealed the difficulties Puritans encountered in controlling their sexual behavior. Yet, to the Puritan mind, failure to lead a chaste life in no way called into question the ideals of chastity and marital fidelity.

Some years later, Benjamin Franklin affirmed, on pragmatic grounds, his commitment to a similar sexual code. In his *Autobiography*, Franklin (1950:93–5) listed 13 values which he considered both necessary and desirable for a morally responsible person. Number 12 reads: "Chastity. Rarely use venery but for health or offspring, never to dulness (sic), weakness, or the injury of your own or another's peace or reputation." His own good counsel, notwithstanding, Franklin acquired a widespread reputation as a "lady's man" in the salons of Paris, even in his old age.

Despite such influences, it was the Victorian era which actually introduced the attitudes that shaped many of America's traditional norms. The Victorians dominated the nineteenth century with their extremely conservative stance toward all expressions of sexuality (Smith-Rosenberg, 1978). Premarital and extramarital sexual intercourse were roundly condemned. Indeed, many Victorians believed that coitus for any purpose other than procreation was immoral. Women were held to be insensitive to sexual stimulation and incapable of a climax comparable to those that men achieved. Consequently, many women did not achieve sexual climax. Masturbation was considered the cardinal sin of childhood (Greenleaf, 1978:82). Heavy petting between a dating couple was taboo, and even among engaged couples kissing was considered extremely intimate behavior. Girls, in particular, were expected to be virgins at marriage. Male virginity was to be expected, but was less important than the purity of the Victorian bride. Clearly, Victorian sexual standards were moralistic and repressive.

Middle-class sexual standards in early twentieth-century America were not quite so rigid. Intercourse was deemed appropriate only between marriage partners, who could enjoy it as long as they did not talk too much about it. Premarital and extramarital sexual relations, of course, were still deviations from the norm, although their frequency was clearly on the rise (Moneymaker and Montanino, 1978:29–30). Heavy petting occurred more often, but usually only between partners who had gone together for a long time or who were engaged. Masturbation was still labeled as "self-abuse" by the majority of adults, the medical community, and moral leaders in the popular culture. A typical expression of the attitude toward masturbation appeared in a very early edition of the official handbook of the Boy Scouts of American which informed its young readers that:

> In the body of every boy who has reached his teens, the Creator of the universe has sown a very important fluid. This fluid is the most wonderful material in all the physical world. Some parts of it find their way into the blood, and through the blood give tone to the muscles, power to the brain, and strength to the nerves. This fluid is the sex fluid . . . Any habit which a boy has that causes this fluid to be discharged from his body tends to weaken his strength, to make him less able to resist disease, and often unfortunately fastens upon him habits which later in life can be broken off only with great difficulty (quoted in Hettlinger, 1974:17).

Traditional sexual standards also permitted modest forms of lovemaking, such as kissing and hand holding, as long as couples did not "carry on" in public. Although some religious groups opposed mixed-couple dancing because it promoted sexual arousal, the "roaring twenties" and the swing era of the big bands in the 1930s thoroughly established dancing as a conventional dating practice. Public attitudes toward homosexuality remained staunchly negative, with typical descriptions labeling it "perverse" or "unnatural" (Levitt and Klassen, 1979:20–25). Likewise, traditional norms governing sexuality in its broader social context strongly opposed illegitimacy, prostitution, pornography, abortion, and divorce (Vincent, 1969; Rosen, 1967).

On the whole, middle-class attitudes and standards gradually moderated from 1900 to 1960. At the turn of the century, traditional sexual norms were clearly presented by teachers, parents, clergy, and civic guardians of public morality, but human sexuality was seldom discussed either in public or in the home. However, one source of information that became more popular over the decades was the marriage manual. By analyzing this literature, Michael Gordon (1978:59–83) documented several major shifts in attitude toward premarital and postmarital sexuality. To his mind, the most important change was the growing emphasis on the legitimacy of marital sexuality. Especially during the decade following World War I and extending into the early 1930s, Gordon notes a dramatic revolution in sexual mores, with the goals of sexual satisfaction and mutual orgasm emerging as predominant themes. In the 1940s, we see a more frank discussion of sexual techniques and a more permissive stance toward premarital and extramarital relationships. None of these changes, with the possible exception of the sexual revolution of the 1920s, ushered in as thorough an attitude change as American society experienced in the 1960s.

Contemporary Sexual Attitudes and Standards

The decade of the 1960s was a period of almost unprecedented turmoil in American society. From the civil rights movement, to urban riots, the Vietnam War, the student revolution, and the emergence of the counterculture, one disruptive social change followed hard upon the heels of another. Amid these interlocking crises, society witnessed an upheaval in sexual attitudes and standards that had a far-reaching importance. Edward Shorter (1977) described the revolution of the 1960s as an "explosion of sexuality," with increased eroticism manifested in premarital, marital, and extramarital relations. Other observers spoke of the "new morality" (Duvall, 1969), sexual liberation (Hettlinger, 1974), a sexual renaissance (Kirkendall and Libby, 1966), the "cult of free love," and the coming of a "sexually permissive society." Whatever their own stance on sexual norms, almost everyone agreed that a major change in sexual values was underway.

The sexual revolution's persistence into the 1970s and 1980s has distinguished it from other social movements launched in the 1960s. While the civil rights movement faded, opposition to the Vietnam War died out completely, and the radical features of the counterculture withered away, the pressures for sexual freedom steadily intensified, bolstered by the campaigns for women's and gay's rights (Humphreys, 1979:134–47). The data for the last seven decades in American social experience indicates a growing permissiveness in the social code regulating sexual relations. A major indicator of attitudinal change is the extent to which society in various times opposed or allowed premarital sexual relations.

Attitudinal Trends in Premarital Permissiveness

The traditional sexual code clearly forbade premarital intercourse. But engaged couples or persons who were deeply in love were less censured for violating the chastity norm. And what is the public attitude today about sex before marriage? A look at the number of people condoning premarital sex should give us a rough index to attitudes on sexuality in general. To assess such attitudes, Ira Reiss (1960) devised an instrument for measuring premarital sexual permissiveness. The scale he created included four premarital sex-

Reiss Male and Female Premarital Sexual-Permissiveness Scale

Ira Reiss developed this scale to determine how people feel about premarital sexual behavior. You can answer these questions yourself and keep your own score. If you strongly agree with most of the views expressed, then you fall on the liberal side of the permissiveness scale. If you strongly disagree with most statements, then you probably hold conservative views on premarital sexual behavior.

The words below mean just what they do to most people, but some may need definition:

Love means the emotional state which is more intense than strong affection and which you would define as love.
Strong affection means affection which is stronger than physical attraction, average fondness, or "liking"—but less strong than love.
Petting means sexually stimulating behavior more intimate than kissing and simple hugging, but not including full sexual relations.

Male Standards (Both Men and Women Check This Section)

1. I believe that kissing is acceptable for the male before marriage when he is engaged to be married.

Agree:	(a) Strong	(b) Medium	(c) Slight
Disagree	(d) Strong	(e) Medium	(f) Slight

2. I believe that kissing is acceptable for the male before marriage when he is in love. (The same six-way choice found in Question 1 follows every question.)

3. I believe that kissing is acceptable for the male before marriage when he feels strong affection for his partner.

4. I believe that kissing is acceptable for the male before marriage even if he does not feel particularly affectionate toward his partner.

5. I believe that petting is acceptable for the male before marriage when he is engaged to be married.

6. I believe that petting is acceptable for the male before marriage when he is in love.

7. I believe that petting is acceptable for the male before marriage when he feels strong affection for his partner.

8. I believe that petting is acceptable for the male before marriage even if he does not feel particularly affectionate toward his partner.

9. I believe that full sexual relations are acceptable for the male before marriage when he is engaged to be married.

10. I believe that full sexual relations are acceptable for the male before marriage when he is in love.

11. I believe that full sexual relations are acceptable for the male before marriage when he feels strong affection for his partner.

12. I believe that full sexual relations are acceptable for the male before marriage even if he does not feel particularly affectionate toward his partner.

(The 12 female questions are the same except the gender reference is changed.)

Source: Reiss (1980:80).

ual standards: abstinence, the double standard, permissiveness with affection, and permissiveness without affection.

Abstinence   *Premarital sexual intercourse is considered wrong for both men and women, regardless of the circumstances.* This, of course, is the formal standard of all the major religious traditions—Protestant, Catholic, and Jewish—in Western culture. However, the secularization of religion, and its decline in moral authority, should be expected to weaken the commitment to abstinence (Cox, 1966:167–89). Of course, the commitment has not been wholly grounded in the teachings of the various religions. Three constant fears have also reinforced chastity—the fear of detection, the fear of pregnancy, and the fear of contracting veneral disease. Modern technology, in the form of the automobile, the pill, and penicillin, has lessened those fears, and thereby forced couples to decide for or against abstinence on other grounds. A final remaining reason why some people choose abstinence is their desire to enter marriage with their virginity intact. As one respondent put it: "Virginity's the greatest gift a girl can give to her husband. I've always felt that way and I'm not changing" (Mallowe, 1978:155). We should not conclude from this quote that only women feel this way. Although fewer males than females are virgins, significant numbers of both sexes apparently feel they should not engage in sexual experimentation and intercourse before marriage. The sexual revolution has not rendered virginity obsolete, only rarer than in previous generations.

The Double Standard   *Premarital intercourse is more acceptable for men than for women.* Women are likely to take offense at this attitude, though some may agree. This category reflects the age-old discrepancy between the ways that sexual norms are applied to men and women. Reiss refers to it as an "informal standard." That is to say, many cultures have tolerated male promiscuity, while severely punishing females who are sexually active before marriage. Quite obviously, a logical contradiction, not to mention a logistical problem, is bound up in this attitude. With whom are men to gain sexual experience, if all women are to remain virgins before marriage and presumably faithful wives after marriage? The double standard, however, does explain why more men than women enter marriage as nonvirgins. A major consequence of the sexual revolution of the 1960s, however, was to bring the attitudes of men and women into greater alignment. Today, men and women are much more likely to agree that if premarital sexual activity is proper for men, it is also proper for women (Carns, 1973). In a study involving students at a southern university, King, Balswick, and Robinson (1977:457) discovered that between 1965 and 1975, students had so clearly moved away from the double standard that they saw no important difference between the immorality of premarital sexual activity of men and women. The more striking change was in the attitude of women. While 70 percent of the 1965 female sample felt premarital sexual intercourse was immoral, only 20.7 percent held that view in 1975. Similarly, while 70 percent of the 1965 female respondents believed that a woman who has had sexual intercourse with many men is sinful, only 37.2 percent agreed in 1975. Among males in 1975, 33.6 percent agreed that such a woman was sinful. Other studies tend to confirm a general drift toward equality between the sexes regarding sexual standards (Hunt, 1974; Berger and Wenger, 1973; Vener and Stewart, 1974).

Permissiveness with Affection *Premarital intercourse is considered right for both men and women when a stable relationship with love or strong affection is present.* Ever since romantic love became the basis for marriage, premarital sexual relations between seriously dating or engaged couples have steadily increased. Generally, Western societies have not set aside the rules against premarital relations for couples in love, but they have been considerably more understanding of such intimacy. In Puritan New England, for instance, the penalty for premarital relations between engaged partners was usually about half as severe as the punishment imposed on persons who were not engaged (Queen and Habenstein, 1967:286–7). If, in such a strict culture, love can lessen the seriousness of the norm violation, it is easier to understand why our freer social environment leads to even more permissiveness with affection.

Does the fact that couples in love have always expressed their affection through sexual intimacy mean that this attitudinal standard has changed little in recent times? Not really. Indeed, during the last twenty years that Reiss has been sampling attitudes, no single standard has changed more than permissiveness with affection. The data also reveal that attitude change has occurred in two separate ways. The first is simply the more widespread belief now than twenty years ago that couples who are deeply in love or engaged may have premarital intercourse (Reiss, 1960, 1967, 1980; King, Balswick, and Robinson, 1977). The second type of attitude change relates to the substantial reduction in the degree of love which now justifies sexual intimacy among unmarried couples. Young people, far more than the adults sampled by Reiss (1980:182), felt that sexual intercourse was a way to develop a relationship which might eventually lead to marriage. This represents a rather important shift away from the earlier view that it was a couple's intent to marry which justified sexual relations between them.

The second change creates something of a puzzle for young people. Without the public declaration of their intent to marry, which engagement signifies, when do sexual relations become acceptable for them? How does one distinguish among the fine shades of simply liking, being strongly affectionate toward, and being truly in love with your partner? Is liking sufficient for sexual relations or should one wait for love to develop? And how can you be sure your partner really loves you and is not avowing affection simply to make you a willing sexual partner? Such questions are deeply troubling for young people, as is amply indicated by many responses from high school and college students reported to Jane Burgess-Kohn. One college student, for example, suggested that "(I)f you have been going steady and are really in love, you can improve your relationship with a sexual relationship. It ensures more love, trust, and respect in one another. Certainly there is no harm in sexual intercourse if you are going steady and planning to marry. Until then, know your limits" (Burgess-Kohn, 1979:31).

This advice, however, leaves hanging the crucial question of your limits. For surely the "limits" involve more than just personal discretion; they should also entail what is socially acceptable, not simply by the peer group, but by the wider society. Another college male speaks about discerning the real feelings of one's partner. He comments (Burgess-Kohn, 1979:37): "There is no way to tell if the guy really loves you or is using you to satisfy his sex drive . . . You will just have to play it by the emotions exchanged. I know many guys that play a woman for a sucker, but I also know just as many who are sincere in their relationships. I say that she had better not have premarital sex unless she knows without a doubt that he loves her for real. If she can't see how she could know, then she should know that this is reason enough *not* to have sex. If a guy does love you, he will wait until you are ready."

Such counsel wins high marks for honesty, but low marks on practicality. This college student is really saying that half his male peers cannot be trusted with their professions of love when sexual conquest rewards their deception. Unfortunately, too, social science is not likely to be too helpful to persons facing these questions. No one yet has devised a reliable instrument for telling whether a person who claims to be in love really means it. Nor should we hold our breath until someone clever enough to do this comes along. Thus, one need not be hypermoralistic to recognize that the changing attitude toward permissiveness with affection simply invites sexual exploitation. Moreover, with the decline of the double standard, very nearly as many women as men are likely to mislead their partners with the sole aim of sexual gratification. Gathering hard, statistical data on how many young lovers are seduced into sexual liaisons by unscrupulous partners is an extremely difficult, if not altogether impossible, research task. However, a substantial amount of "soft" data in the form of case studies suggests that the problem is real, and perhaps growing (Kirkendall, 1961; Komarovsky, 1976; Burgess-Kohn, 1979). Indeed, anyone who cares about the quality of interpersonal relationships cannot help but be concerned about this attitude change and the potential for abuse that it affords.

Permissiveness Without Affection *Premarital intercourse is considered right for both men and women if they are so inclined, regardless of the amount or stability of affection present.* This final attitudinal stance encompasses what is often called *recreational sex.* Persons who hold this view do not require or even expect a declaration of love. One engages in sexual relations with whomever one pleases for the sheer enjoyment of the experience. Like the other attitudes included in the permissiveness scale, this one is really not new. Usually, however, only men have been allowed to pursue "fun sex" without obligation, at least in Western culture. Donald Marchall (1971:103–62) does describe a culture in Magaia, a southern Cook Island in Polynesia, where extensive premarital and extramarital sexual experience is regarded as normal, but this is quite atypical when compared to American and other Western societies.

However, perhaps the most curious finding of many studies on sexual attitudes undertaken after the erotic revolution of the 1960s is the number of

A Season for Courtship

young people who reject sex without affection. Mass media coverage during that decade tended to create the impression that this country was entering an era of "anything goes" in sexual behavior among the young. Yet, the studies of Reiss and others (Hunt, 1973; Erhmann, 1964) clearly confirm that only a small minority of young people actually regard recreational sex as acceptable behavior. The emphasis on close personal relations which justifies permissiveness with affection works against legitimizing impersonal sex. Thus far, the sexual revolution has not made pleasure-centered sex more important than person-centered sexual relations, an effect many social scientists had feared. Most young people today regard sexual intimacy as a way to show love, but they stop well short of condoning orgies of promiscuity when love is not present.

An Overview of the Premarital Sexual Permissiveness Scale Findings

Few research instruments have been employed as widely in recent social research as Reiss' Premarital Sexual Permissiveness Scale. Apart from specific details, perhaps the most interesting finding is that no single standard fits all Americans. Indeed, virtually all of the published studies reflect an extremely wide variance in attitudes. Not even in the ranks of college students does a consistent pattern exist. The sexual life-styles of college students in one region of the country often were rejected by college students in another region. Everywhere, however, the question of sexual permissiveness is now publicly discussed.

Generally speaking, the relative rankings of groups that stand high or low on the permissiveness scale have been rather clearly established. The data indicate that males remain more permissive than females. Yet, the variance between the sexes is rapidly narrowing as the double standard fades. In mid-1977, for example, King, Balswick, and Robinson (1977:458) predicted the emergence of a single standard of premarital permissiveness for men and women by the early 1980s. Tabulated responses also indicate that blacks are more permissive than whites. Class factors are clearly at work here, for lower-class blacks have notably higher rates of premarital coitus than other blacks (Reiss, 1960:119–20). Futhermore, college students generally score higher on the permissiveness scale than adults, which is not at all surprising. Indeed, if any study had shown adults more permissive than college youth, it would have recorded one of the most startling turnabouts in the history of social research. Few studies examined the attitudes of noncollege youth and compared them to the college population. One remarkable exception was Yankelovich. He (1974:23–5) discovered that, while noncollege youth were less permissive with respect to condoning casual premarital sexual relations in 1969, by 1975 almost no difference existed between the two groups. And finally, evidence from a number of studies shows that permissiveness varies by region of the country. The South was the least permissive region, while California, followed closely by the Northeast, was the most permissive.

Taken together, then, the general trend shown in these studies is a movement toward greater premarital permissiveness with affection. Clearly, the sexual revolution has succeeded in undermining commitment to the traditional standard of sexual abstinence before marriage. Yet, the opposite extreme of a completely pleasure-oriented standard for sexual behavior also has not been accepted by the youth culture or by adults. Love, to some degree at least, must be present to justify sexual relations in the minds of most Americans. Otherwise, the relationship declines into sheer exploitation.

Premarital Sexual Behavior

Our discussion has focused largely on attitudes toward premarital sexual relations. In this section, reports on premarital sexual behavior itself will be examined. Acquiring valid information on this sensitive issue is considerably more difficult than sampling attitudes. Persons who respond to questionnaires or interviews are usually more forthcoming when they are asked how they feel about this subject than when they are asked how they behave. Accordingly, many people answer in the way they think the researcher expects or in a fashion that makes their behavior appear to conform to the prevailing norms. Consequently, descriptions of behavior are somewhat more subject to error than reports of attitudes. This variance can be partly offset by indirect measures of other aspects of sexual relations, such as the use of contraceptives, abortion, or the rate of pregnancy before marriage. Data on these rates give a rough index to the degree of premarital intimacy.

Correlations Between Attitudes and Behavior

The Kinsey Studies The famous Kinsey studies on sexual behavior in the human male (1948) and the human female (1953) were not only landmark pieces of social research, but they also exploded the myth that the young American's actual behavior closely followed traditional standards for premarital sexual relations. Kinsey revealed much higher rates of sexual intimacy than most citizens would have believed likely. For male college graduates, for example, Kinsey (1948:552) reported that 67 percent had premarital intercourse. Of males who had earned only high school diplomas, 84 percent had sexual intercourse before marriage. Boys who did not pursue their education beyond grade school were the most likely to have had premarital sex; a remarkable 98 percent of this group were found to have done so. Although Kinsey's sample did not truly represent the whole nation, his findings were broad based enough to send shock waves through American society. The incidence of premarital intercourse was substantially lower for women, but they too were far more active sexually than most people had imagined (Kinsey, 1953:282–345). It seemed to many Americans that the sexual revolution had already occurred. The truth of the matter was that it lay ahead in the 1960s.

The Second Sexual Revolution in American Social Experience The first sexual revolution in American life occurred in the 1920s; the second emerged in the 1960s. Whereas Kinsey disclosed a tremendous gulf between actual behavior and traditional attitudes, the 1960s were a time when attitudes more nearly matched behavior. Hypocrisy of every kind was bitterly criticized during this convulsive decade. One consequence was that as sexual attitudes moved toward greater permissiveness, youth became more forthright in revealing the extent of their sexual activities. However, not only honesty in reporting premarital relations, but also the rate of premarital experience itself was changing. According to Reiss (1980:173), the rate of change in premarital intercourse was relatively moderate between 1925 and 1965. Thereafter, the rate of premarital sexual behavior sharply increased in American society.

Using the data of Kinsey and his associates as a base line, we can document the following tendencies in premarital behavior patterns. Kinsey (1953:333) found that 20 percent of his female sample had engaged in premarital intercourse by age 20. In 1971 and 1976, Zelnick and Kantner (1977) conducted research on never-married women between 15 and 19 years of age, using national samples. In the first study, 27 percent of their sample group had experienced premarital intercourse. The second study, five years later, revealed that 35 percent had engaged in premarital intercourse—a 30 percent rise in the frequency rate in just half a decade. If we examine only one age group—19-year-old women—we discover that 55 percent had premarital coitus in 1976, whereas only 47 percent in the same age group had done so in 1971. When we recall that the Kinsey study of female behavior reported only 20 percent premarital coitus by age 20, then the 55 percent figure for 19-year-old women in Zelnick and Kantner's sample clearly shows a marked increase in premarital sexual intercourse. These data confirm that the sexual revolution was occurring in sexual behavior as well as in attitudes toward permissiveness.

Between the years of the two Zelnick and Kantner studies, Morton Hunt sampled premarital sexual behavior in a research project undertaken for the Playboy Foundation. His findings are of interest because they include data for both men and women. Responses tabulated for a 1972 nationwide study showed that of young married people 18 to 25 years old, 95 percent of the men and 81 percent of the women had engaged in sexual intercourse prior to marriage (Hunt, 1974:15). These figures also indicate a narrowing of the gap between the sexes relative to premarital sexual behavior. Indeed, the increased sexual activity of females accounts for much of the difference between rates of premarital sexual intercourse now and, say, 25 years ago.

Premarital Sexual Behavior in the Near Future The general trend in sexual behavior before marriage over the last 15 years is unmistakably clear. Fewer young people today are virgins when they marry; sexual experience is being acquired at a younger age; and women are now almost as active sexually as men. Some might look at these facts and conclude that the sexual revolution has gone about as far as it can go. After all, if only 5 percent of the men and 19 percent of the young women today refrain from premarital intercourse—assuming Hunt's figures are accurate—how can premarital sexual behavior increase significantly in the near future? The answer, of course, is that sexual relations among young people can still intensify quite dramatically. Most individuals with premarital experience confine their relations to only one or two partners. Moreover, many people eventually marry the partners with whom they are most sexually active. If this trend were to change decisively and young people were to begin experimenting with more sexual partners, then the sexual revolution could be elevated to a new level of premarital activity.

Is this likely to become the new pattern of behavior in the years just ahead? Ira Reiss, one of the most sophisticated observers of the sexual behavior of young people, answers in the negative. He believes the period of rapid social change in premarital relations is now behind us. We are entering, he suggests, a period of consolidation similar to the years between 1925–1965. Thus, neither a sharp decline in sexual activity nor a rapid increase in the sexual revolution appears near at hand. Unfortunately, we will have to wait until the end of the 1980s to determine whether Reiss' educated hunch proves accurate.

The Peer Group and Dating Behavior

Thus far, this chapter has reviewed a number of striking changes in the dating practices and sexual behavior of young Americans. Naturally, the new meanings assigned to dating and sex did not arise in a social vacuum. Instead, they are a response to a whole new set of social circumstances in the postindustrial era of American society. No single feature of the current social scene is more important for understanding the changes described earlier than the youth peer culture. In this section, then, we shall examine the role of the peer group in shaping the attitudes and behavior of youth. The areas of social strain between the family and the youth peer culture are also identified.

The Emergence of the Youth Peer Culture

As we noted in Chapter 2, in regard to the history of the American family, the youth peer culture emerged as a relatively autonomous social group in American life during the early decades of this century. At first, membership was confined to the sons and daughters of the affluent, who could afford to allow their children to remain in high school or attend college rather than enter the work force. The youth culture grew in size and influence in direct relation to the time young people spent in school. The educational institution provided the necessary social context for youth to congregate in large numbers, share a common set of experiences, and organize those experiences into a cultural life-style with its own distinctive norms, values, attitudes, and behaviors. It was not by accident that, during the 1960s, when college enrollments doubled in the United States, the youth peer culture also assumed a much greater autonomy from adult social controls.

Social scientists have identified a number of important functions performed by the youth peer culture (Parsons, 1964; Keniston, 1968; Erikson, 1965). It permits the teenage generation to identify itself socially; it allows youth the freedom to experiment with alternative life-styles; it facilitates the expression of new ideas for youth to test out; and it allows youth to take responsibility for their own actions. However, with respect to dating and sexual behavior, in which we are primarily interested, the youth culture accomplished a good deal more. It placed these matters firmly under the control of youth themselves. While parents and the adult community had previously exercised considerable influence over the attitudes and behavior of youth, the peer group now intervened to provide an alternative standard of conduct. The sexual revolution, for example, was almost exclusively a creation of the youth peer culture. Adults generally, and parents in particular, tended to raise a strong voice of protest against increased sexual liberties. Youth who participated in the sexual liberation launched in the 1960s found their major source of social support in members of their own age group, that is to say, in the youth peer culture.

The Prevailing Norms of the Contemporary Youth Culture

During the 1960s, the youth peer group went through a major cultural re-orientation. It became, in a word, a *counter-culture*. Some analysts, like Roszak (1969), viewed the counter-culture motifs as a radical critique of technocratic society. Perhaps they were, but in retrospect they also appear to have been a good deal more. The counterculture opposed the norms of middle-class life in American society. Yet, before an alternative cultural pattern could be set for youth to follow, another model beyond the standards of middle-class parents was needed. An analysis of the norms embraced by the youth culture in the 1960s and beyond suggests that the new cultural formula was not wholly an original creation, formed of belief and action patterns never before seen in American life. They were only new to the middle class. Previously, however, these norms had been typical of the cultural perspective shared by the lower classes in the United States. Consider, for example, these cases in point:

1. Drug use. Prior to the 1960s, the middle class condemned the use of drugs more strongly than almost any other form of deviance. Narcotics use was a problem confined to the lower class, with the exception of certain highly specific professsions like medicine or the music industry.
2. Living together before marriage. Cohabitation was not invented in the 1960s by the youth culture. "Shacking up" was, however, predominantly a lower-class practice almost unknown in middle-class circles.
3. Clothing styles. The youth culture in the 1960s appropriated the dress code of the working class. Suddenly, blue jeans, blue-collar work shirts, painter's overalls, and other typical forms of clothing for the lower class became the required uniform of middle-class college students.
4. Language. Middle-class mores sternly opposed profanity and obscenity.

Figure 4–4
A generation ago, drugs were a lower-class phenomenon. Today, however, most middle-class adolescents have at least sampled marijuana in their peer-group activities. (© *Ira Berger, 1981/Woodfin Camp & Associates.*)

Before the 1960s, only sailors "cussed like sailors." The use of four-letter words was a lower-class characteristic. The counterculture institutionalized the use of profanity and obscenity, at first no doubt for the sheer shock value these words carried. Under the influence of the peer group, junior high school girls now use language which their male teachers never even heard in an army barracks.

5. Orientation to the present and hedonism. Historically, achievement, in accord with the Protestant work ethic, has characterized the American middle class, while orientation to the present has just as surely identified the lower class. Oscar Lewis (1961) and Edward Banfield (1974) led the way in convincing the social scientific community that the need for immediate gratification was the central feature of the culture of poverty. Beginning with the hippies of the 1960s, the middle-class achievement orientation was soundly rejected in favor of an orientation to the present. The stress on self-gratification so thoroughly permeated the youth culture in the 1970s that the novelist, Tom Wolfe, christened the decade as the era of the "me-generation."

6. Religion. The counterculture dismissed organized religion as the last bastion of middle-class morality. However, in the late 1960s and early 1970s, many young people, alienated from politics, shifted to religion as an institutional focus. They did not return to the major religions, but to radical,

pentecostal groups. The result was the "Jesus freaks," or what is now more commonly called the "new religions" (Needleman and Baker, 1978). The practices associated with these religious groups were not really new. But is was new to have middle-class folk engaged in such activities as speaking in tongues, healing, witnessing, and other enthusiastic forms of religious expression, which were formerly the marks of lower-class religiosity.

7. Education. Few institutions were more deeply affected by the cultural revolution in the youth peer group than education. Far more important in the long run than the student unrest and campus takeovers of the 1960s was the revolution in student attitudes. It was manifested in the loss of discipline, the rejection of academic achievement, and a pursuit of what Edward Shorter (1977:275) called "educational certification," rather than knowledge or academic skills.

8. Sports. The youth culture has evinced an increasing interest in violent physical, contact sports. The popularity of aggressive games like football, hockey, soccer, and even basketball has soared in the last 15 years, while baseball, the all-American sport, has had some difficulty holding its own.

9. Music. Rock music has been the favorite of the counterculture. The beat was strong, loud, sensual, and performed by musicians whom many adults regarded as ungifted and incompetent. Perhaps the judgment was unfair, but the popular varieties of rock music played over the radio made little pretense of sophistication by existing musical standards. The instrumentation was largely an electronic version of the country-western guitar, long associated with lower-class musical tastes, but the rock musicians sang with a distinctly urban accent. Indeed, from the Beatles on, many musicians were recruited from the urban lower classes and possessed little formal musical training.

10. Mass media. The counterculture turned a critical corner in mass-media consumption. Capitalizing on counterculture themes, the mass media introduced a stronger emphasis on sex, brutality, the sensual; and in television, a good deal more shallow and silly entertainment appeared. The media reflected the youth culture's changing standards of taste and propriety.

11. Sexual relations. The youth culture endorsed a much more liberal social code for sexual relations. As we have just seen, both attitudes and behavior relative to sexual intimacy were affected dramatically. While Kinsey found the lower classes the most active sexually during the 1940s and 1950s, middle-class youth closed the gap during the sexual revolution. Increased sexual activity also brought a sudden upsurge in the rate of illegitimate births. During the first half of this century, illegitimacy was confined largely to the lower classes. After the revolution of the counterculture, illegitimacy became a serious problem for the middle class as well (Glick and Norton, 1977:24).

When we consider all these areas of change together, a distinct pattern begins to emerge. As the youth culture tried to disassociate itself from the middle-class culture typical of the parental generation, young people took on the values, norms, and behavioral styles of lower-class groups. Many practices that the middle class had formerly regarded as deviant became normal for their children. Yet, the influence of the counterculture did not stop there. Once new behavior and value patterns were introduced into middle-class life through the youth peer culture, they tended to "percolate up" into adult life-styles as well. Soon, some parents also were growing long hair, "smoking pot," using four-letter words, engaging more frequently in extramarital sex, and pursuing a pleasure-oriented life-style much like their adolescent off-spring.

The counterculture's impact on adult parental life-styles has not been as thoroughly researched as the changes in the behavior of youth. Thus, the apparent influence of child on parent should be recognized as an interpretation of broad trends, for which hard evidence is still limited at several critical points. Moreover, the counterculture did not affect all young people in the same way. Those caught up in the "new religions," for example, tended to avoid sexual permissiveness and the profanity and obscenity which other elements of the youth peer culture embraced. Although Daniel Bell (1976, 1978) has begun to explore several of these issues, no systematic investigation of these themes has been undertaken. Nor have we been able to follow the attitudes and behaviors of those youths who have left the peer group for adult life. It would be quite interesting to know, for example, whether leaving the youth peer culture for a job, marriage, and adult responsibilities returns a person to more traditionally conservative and middle-class attitudes and values. Regardless of such individual reactions, substantial evidence suggests that the changes introduced in the 1960s will not be reversed and that the counterculture has accomplished a permanent revolution whose basic norms are likely to be with us for a long time.

Social Strains between the Family and the Peer Group

Parent opposition to the peer culture was most vehement during the radical days of the 1960s. In those years, the ever-present evidence of free love, use of marijuana, four-letter words, long hair, campus unrest, and the protest movement created a cultural shock which sent many members of the older generations reeling. As quiet settled over the youth culture in the 1970s, young people and their parents began a period of accommodation. However, a number of peer-group practices remained, and many parents continued to resolutely oppose them. Drug use, excessive drinking, premarital sex, poor school performance, and living together surfaced as the major sources of conflict between parents and their children (Larkin, 1979).

A major consequence of the cultural revolution, however, was a dramatic decline in parental authority and the ability of parents to exercise social control over much of their adolescent children's behavior. The loss of parental control has created a new freedom for youth, but this has proved to be a mixed blessing. Now more than ever, young people find themselves torn between fulfilling parental expectations and adhering to peer-group guidelines. This tension would be lessened if young people felt little affection for their

Figure 4–5
A mother and her adolescent son do not always see eye to eye.
(© Sepp Seitz, 1981/ Woodfin Camp &Associates.)

parents or were completely indifferent to their views. However, the bulk of recent research (Reiss, 1961; Kenniston, 1965; Yankelovich, 1974; Bane, 1976; Komarovsky, 1976) indicates a remarkably strong bond of affection linking parents and children. Moreover, young people do seem to care what their parents think about their life-styles and attitudes. This makes the social strain between the family and the peer group a matter of deep concern for many young people in contemporary society.

Furthermore, some evidence indicates a mounting opposition and perhaps even a counterattack on society's permissiveness toward the youth peer culture. Criticism from social conservatives have been made all along. Today, however, more and more liberals and intellectuals are beginning to express reservations about the dangers that can arise from peer-group norms. Christopher Lasch (1979), a supporter of leftist politics, has recently published a stirring defense of the bourgeois family, parental authority, the inculcation of discipline in children, premarital abstinence, and achievement. This may well be the opening round in a major social campaign to come to the aid of beleaguered parents who feel outnumbered by the collective forces of the youth peer group. Thus, one should not expect any swift resolution to the clash of views between parents and the peer culture.

Summary

This chapter deals with three major topics associated with dating behavior: dating practices, premarital sexual attitudes and behavior, and the influence of the peer culture, especially on the sexual standards and the conduct of youth.

The lack of an arranged marriage system in American society makes the social practice of dating a necessity. However, dating is more than a mere prelude to eventual mating. It also allows couples to develop skills in cross-gender relations, provides a recreational outlet, improves one's status, and reinforces sex roles. Over the course of American history, dating practices have changed a great deal. The overriding trend is toward greater freedom and intimacy for dating couples.

Sexual attitudes and behaviors for young people also have varied. The sexual revolution launched in the 1960s greatly altered premarital norms and conduct. Insofar as attitudes are concerned, the largest transformation was in the commitment to the ideal of premarital abstinence. Yet, youth did not embrace a pattern of permissiveness without affection. During the last 15 years, an attitude emerged which considers sexual relations acceptable before marriage, if the two people are in love. Couples themselves must decide whether they have enough affection for each other to justify sexual relations and intimacy.

Permissive attitudes toward premarital intercourse increase the probability that sexual activity will accelerate. The data confirm a revolution in sexual behavior among the youth. Sharply increased rates of sexual activity became apparent in the mid-1960s and they continued into the 1980s. While the Kinsey study of female sexual behavior in the late 1940s revealed that 20 percent of the women in a sample group of 19-year-olds were not virgins, a national study conducted by Morton Hunt, found that 95 percent of the men and 81 percent of the women reported that they had engaged in premarital sexual relations. These data support two important conclusions. The sexual revolution in premarital relations is not only an accomplished fact, but the double standard—allowing men freedom to engage in sexual relations yet condemning women for the same conduct—has apparently declined substantially, so that women today are almost as active sexually before marriage as men.

The sexual revolution did not occur in a social vacuum. It was inspired by the tremendous cultural changes taking place in the youth peer group during the 1960s. For reasons we do not yet fully understand, the youth peer group assumed the posture of a counterculture in the late 1960s. It opposed the norms of middle-class life with a set of values, attitudes, and behavior patterns derived primarily from the cultural perspective of the lower classes in American society. Practices which had formerly been taboo in middle-class life—such as drug use, living together, orientation to the present, premarital sex, and pentecostal religion—suddenly were endorsed by the youth peer group and elevated to a position as the norm for middle-class young people.

Predictably, the changes in normative standards for the peer culture created major social strains as young people were torn between their parents' expectations and the peer-group's guidelines. These tensions are severe since most youth still seek approval from their parents and their peers, yet both groups usually are committed to different standards. Accordingly, youth today are thrust into an exceptionally difficult situation. Their decisions on sexual attitudes and dating behavior must straddle the conflicting views of their parents and their peer culture without, if possible, alienating either one.

STUDY QUESTIONS

1. What were the justifications for accepting the courtship practice of bundling?
2. What are the social functions served by the practice of casual and serious dating?
3. How would one describe the major trends in sexual attitudes over the course of twentieth-century America?

A Season for Courtship

4. What is the "double standard" in attitudes toward sexual behavior? Is the double standard growing stronger or weaker today?
5. What is the evidence for and against a revolution in sexual behavior among American youth since the mid-1960s?
6. Would it be accurate to suggest that social strain now exists between the norms of the traditional American family and the youth peer culture?

5

Selecting A Mate

Mating as a Social Process
    The Structural Limitations on the Mating Process
    The Normative Guidelines for the Mating Process

Prescribed and Preferential Mating
    The Endogamy Rule in Preferential Mating
    The Exogamy Rule in Preferential Mating

Homogamy and Heterogamy in Mate Selection
    The Social Filters of Homogamous Mating
    The Homogamy of Age
    The Homogamy of Residential Propinquity
    The Homogamy of Religion
    The Homogamy of Race and Ethnicity
    The Homogamy of Social Class
    The Homogamy of Education
    The Homogamy of Attitudes, Values, and Social Outlooks
    The Filtering Influence of these Background Factors

The Mating Process and the Development of Love
    The Complementary-Needs Theory
    The Stages of Mate Selection
    From Liking to Loving
    The Wheel Theory of Love
        Rapport
        Self-Revelation
        Mutual Dependency
        Intimacy and Need Fulfillment

Summary

During the 1950s, the commonly held view of romantic love was aptly expressed in the lyrics of "Some Enchanted Evening," a song from the hit musical comedy and movie of that decade, *South Pacific*. According to this popular mythology, true love was to be recognized as an overwhelming emotional experience which could strike without warning. A person would know that he or she had met the "right" woman or man almost instantly, even though they might just glance at one another "across a crowded room." But once this initial contact had been made, once one had found the person that fate had chosen for you, then he or she was to throw all other cares away, fly to his or her lover's side, and never let the lover go.

This romanticized view of falling in love makes for pleasant entertainment. The theme recurs in almost every culture, from Ovid in ancient Rome, to the "blue willow-plate" legend of classical China with its two lovers depicted as doves, to *Romeo and Juliet*, to Erich Segal's *Love Story*, and Neil Simon's *Chapter Two*. Of course, these romantic tales of falling in love bear little resemblance to the way the process of selecting a mate actually occurs.

The *mating* process does not generally begin with romance. Indeed, it is far more accurate to view romantic love as one of the last "crystallizing" factors which enter into the process of mate selection. The sociological notion of redefining the role of love in mating does have a "debunking" quality about it. Peter Berger (1963:38–41) long ago described sociology as a debunking enterprise, that is, one which takes a professional interest in unmasking the taken-for-granted assumptions of society. Certainly, on the issue of love in mating, the sociological perspective almost directly contradicts the popular culture's view that marriage partners are selected primarily on the basis of a strong love attachment. From one vantage point, of course, this claim contains a measure of truth. Americans do expect marriages to be founded on a love relationship between spouses. Moreover, to consider marrying someone whom one does not love is regarded as a shameful, almost dishonest practice in our culture. However, sociologists stress that love develops between most partners only after other filtering factors have narrowed the field of eligible partners and helped bring the two lovers together.

For this reason, then, this chapter is organized somewhat differently than one might expect. A swift glance at the order of the headings will show that love is introduced at the end of the chapter. The social process of mating is examined first from the sociological perspective; then the various social factors which influence mate selection are explored. Against this backdrop, the issue of romantic love, its dynamics and consequences, is finally taken up. In this way, the topic coverage will nearly parallel the order of our social experience.

Mating as a Social Process

Selecting a mate is one of life's major decisions. In many cultures, it is regarded as much too important to be left entirely in the hands of the couple involved. Youth, inexperience, and an excessive concern with physical attractiveness might all combine to cloud young people's judgment. Accordingly, in many premodern societies, parents or elder kinsfolk make the selection for young people. Among a group of Algerian immigrants living today in Paris, for example, Michel (1974:15) found that one of three women and one of five men had never so much as seen their mates before they married. Few expressed any displeasure with this arrangement. To their minds, the adults were in a far better position than they to make the right choice.

In other cultures, such as our own, the selection of a mate is regarded as too important a decision to be made by anyone other than the couple moving toward marriage. They, after all, have the greatest vested interest in the outcome of the decision-making process. They alone will, quite literally, have to live with their decision. Given parental concern for a son or daughter's welfare and happiness, most mothers and fathers are willing to offer advice on selecting a mate. Most children still do seek parental approval, although the formal practice of a young man asking the father for permission to marry his daughter has now passed out of vogue, to the general relief of all young men. However, final responsibility for finding a compatible mate now rests squarely on the shoulders of eligible partners. Before we express too much concern for mating couples, however, we should remember that they are not thrust out entirely on their own resources. Certain social conventions and structures aid them in the decision-making process. These guidelines arise from two social patterns. They include, in the first instance, the structural conditions under which mating takes place and, in the second instance, the norms of behavior for mate selection.

The Structural Limitations on the Mating Process

American society adheres to a "free-choice" system of mate selection. This does not mean, however, that an individual is free to mate with literally anyone she or he chooses. "Every society controls to some extend who may mate with whom . . . " (Goode, 1964:20). Laws against incest prohibit marriages between persons more closely related than first cousins, and in 29 states first-cousin marriages are forbidden (Williams, 1970:56). Since these laws are very limited in their scope, what a "free-choice" system signifies is that structural limitations on the mating process are essentially institutionalized social practices and customs rather than legal statutes. One may, therefore, marry across racial, class, age, ethnic, and religious lines. However, persons who do so will often encounter some social stigma as a consequence. Interracial marriages undoubtedly still trigger the most violent opposition, even though the practice is becoming more common in American society since the Supreme Court ruled in 1967 that laws against racial intermarriage were unconstitutional (Aldridge, 1973:64). Thus, the formal openness of the "free-choice" system is qualified by the informal limitations established by social custom and normative guidelines.

Of course, the "free-choice" system makes little sense, unless it operates in an open marriage market which provides ample opportunity for eligible partners to meet (Rosenblatt and Cozby, 1972). Whether the sexes are allowed to intermingle in informal social settings or are kept apart by parents, the community, or school officials directly affects the ability of the "free-choice" system to function effectively. American society now erects few barriers curtailing contact between the sexes. Indeed, schools, community recreational programs, religious groups, and the business community provide a diverse array of activities that enables young people to meet eligible partners.

Closely related to the freedom of interaction is the structural fact of living or going to school near a potential mate. One does not meet the vast majority of potential mates in the total population simply because sheer distance keeps a young woman's and a young man's paths from crossing. It is extremely difficult to be attracted toward and fall in love with someone you've never met. In fact, since the start of social scientific research on mating processes, physical closeness has consistently been a very significant structural factor affecting mate selection (Katz and Hill, 1958). Much of this early work was done prior to the widespread availability of the family car as a means of overcoming geographical distances. However, parental choice of a residential community still indirectly, but very decisively, affects the mate selection of their marriage-age children. The same principle also applies to the decision to send their children to a residential college. Students are not only grouped together geographically, sorted by age and other social factors, but they are also provided opportunities to meet in class, on campus, at parties, and through other campus activities. The recent trend toward delaying marriage may well cause a sharp decline in the influence exerted on mate selection by parental residence and the college environment (Glick and Norton, 1977:5–7).

The Normative Guidelines for the Mating Process

The most basic norm governing mate selection in American society holds that couples should only marry for love. Romantic love, however, is a notoriously volatile and subjective emotion. Moreover, as Lucile Duberman (1977:83) points out, each culture "exerts different pressures on people to fall in love for different reasons and in different ways." During the socialization process, we learn not only how to love, but whom to love. The popular expression for the normative viewpoint is that we should marry "the right person." Generally speaking, we all understand this to mean we should select a mate from that pool of eligible people with whom we share a similar background, class rank, religious heritage, and age compatibility. Social conventions tend to bring together persons who share several social characteristics. This is not simply a matter of in-group prejudice, although sometimes it may be involved. In a society which lays heavy stress on a companionate relationship between marriage partners—and American society certainly falls within this category—similar interests, experiences, and social expectations are decided advantages. They dramatically increase the statistical probability that a marriage will succeed (Goode, 1965).

Most persons engaged in the mating process recognize the social logic of these normative guidelines—just as partners who deviate from them often try harder to make their marriages successful because they know they are battling the odds. The underlying message of the social conventions related to mate selection is that love often is not enough to sustain a marriage partnership through thick and thin. In addition, spouses very frequently need the security that arises from complementary backgrounds, social perspectives, and life experiences. Of course, nothing guarantees that similar backgrounds will automatically produce marital compatibility. Idiosyncratic personality traits of matched couples also can disrupt a marriage. However, a couple's chances generally are much better if the range of social differences is steadily narrowed (Burgess and Wallin, 1965:176–82).

Sociologists are trained to expect that where social norms exist one should also find penalties for those who violate the rules, as well as persons with the power to enforce those penalties. In a "free-choice" system operating in an open-marriage market, who enforces the rules for mate selection? And what are the social penalties which encourage persons to marry "one of their own kind?" As noted earlier, relatively few legal constraints exist, and they pertain almost exclusively to incest and marriage to minors. The informal social constraints are quite varied and range widely in their intensity. The once-powerful norms of religious and ethnic subcultures, which ostracized anyone who married outside the group, have now largely faded from view because the subcultures have moved into the mainstream of American culture and gained upward social mobility (Gordon, 1964). Many young people still tend to select mates from within the ranks of their religious or ethnic groups, but the penalties for not doing so are usually no more than mild parental disapproval or perhaps an occasional rebuff from a religious leader.

The most effective enforcement of the normative rules for mate selection arises from three relatively independent sources: the community reference group, parents, and the individual partners who are seeking mates. The community reference group holds the power to approve or disapprove a particular match. Most individuals care what others think about their choice of a mate, and hence the opinion of the reference group often can be quite influential. Gossip is one of the more conventional ways to express reference-group displeasure. For example, a May-December couple contemplating marriage is likely to be subject to such comments as, "Can you imagine a young girl in her thirties marrying Fred Astaire when he's in his eighties?" Or, if a steady dating couple includes an upper-class male and a physically attractive, but lower-class female, they are likely to be subjected to such leading questions as, "Can you believe that an intellectual like Arthur Miller ever married a sex-symbol like Marilyn Monroe?" In both instances, the message is plain. Those around the couple do not really approve of the match. They are urged to break if off while they can. Of course, the vast majority of couples never place themselves under this sort of social pressure. They adhere from the outset to the reference-group norm that "like marries like"—in part, just to avoid such situations.

Parental acceptance of a mate choice is usually as important as the reference group's approval. However, because the parents were responsible for

Figure 5–1
May-December marriages pose unique, but not insurmountable, problems for partners with wide age differences. *(© Stan Goldblatt, 1981/ Photo Researchers, Inc.)*

the socialization of their child to a particular set of values, the young person's choice of a mate is likely to be acceptable to them. Mate selection is one area in which the generations agree most emphatically—at least on the desirable attributes of a prospective marriage partner.

Strangely enough, however, the individuals who are selecting their mates are usually most concerned with following the normative guidelines. Of course, they do not act in this way because they are familiar with the socio-logical finding that spouses with similar backgrounds are more likely to suc-ceed in their marriages. Instead, they pick such mates because they find they are more comfortable with partners who share their interests—and who are therefore more attractive as potential mates. In this instance, then, the nor-mative expectations of community reference groups coincide with the per-sonal interests of mating couples. Often without anyone's conscious reflection, the social filtering process continues to narrow the field of eligible partners.

People tend to fall in love with people they see frequently, and people tend to get together with persons they enjoy because those individuals resemble them in many social respects. When our choice of a marriage partner is a member of this select group, our parents and members of the community are very likely to agree that this is "the right person" for us.

Prescribed and Preferential Mating

Two sociological principles help us identify the polar extremes among mating systems. These are the principles of *prescribed* and *preferential mating.* Prescribed systems of mate selection refer to marriages that are arranged by someone other than the nuptial couple. In a pure prescribed system, mates have no voice in the selection of their husband or wife. One of the more effective forms of prescribed marriage was the child-bride system practiced in India before modernization (Mandelbaum, 1972:110–112). This arrangement allowed children to marry well before puberty and move into the household of the husband's father. Under these circumstances, neither partner could really resist the marriage. However, the marriage could not be sexually consummated until after the female's first menstrual cycle.

Arranged-marriage systems which delayed mate selection until the partners were older sometimes encountered opposition from one or both of the partners. Frequently, youths who had passed through adolescence had gained some experience by interacting with members of the opposite sex. If they did not have a partner to whom they were devoted, they often did have an image of their ideal mate. Elders making the arrangement, however, were responding to an entirely different set of concerns. To them, marriage was a means of linking or preserving kinship lines, protecting property, or acquiring power (Good, 1973:254).

CLOSE-UP

Couple's Suicide over "Bride Price" Shocks Turks
Ali Eski and Nuran Aydogmus were young and very much in love and wanted to get married, but their families could not agree on the "bride price," so they committed suicide.

This Turkish love story has shocked the public. The traditionalists could not understand how the couple could rebel against the age-old custom of paying for a bride, while modernists and intellectuals expressed concern that the custom was still so strong.

There is growing controversy over the practice of paying the bride price. While many city-bred young people consider the custom degrading for women, their elders, at least in the countryside, insist that it is a guarantee of virginity.

The National Security Council, the governing military junta, recently established a special commission to study the economic and psychosocial aspects of the custom. Its report, excerpts from which have been made public, was heavily weighted in favor of maintaining the custom.

According to the report, the principal negative reaction comes from people with insufficient buying power, the result of an unfair distribution of income. The implication was clear: Once there is a better distribution of wealth, a young man will be able to afford the bride of his choice and the problem will resolve itself.

The tragic love affair of 22-year-old Ali and 16-year-old Nuran, published on the front page of the widely circulated Istanbul newspaper *Hurriyet*, has fanned controversy over the practice. After they fell in love a year ago, word of their passion spread quickly in the town of Mihaliccik. The sweethearts told their families that they wanted to marry, so negotiations began.

The girl's father, Ali Ihsan Aydogmus, a photographer, set a price on his daughter's head that was high for that farming area. He was quoted by *Hurriyet* as saying: "I give no girl to anyone without getting 100,000 liras [$1,100] in bride money." Disheartened, the couple ran away but were caught and brought back. Nuran obtained a doctor's certificate confirming that her virginity was unimpaired.

The village headman intervened in favor of the sweethearts but the girl's father was adamant in his demand for "ready cash" and refused an offer from the boy's family of 30,000 liras in advance and 70,000 on a promissory note, an increasingly common procedure.

In desperation Nuran slashed her wrists and Ali took an overdose of pills, but they were found in time and saved.

Neighbors pleaded their cause in vain. Deciding again that suicide was the only solution, they succeeded. Shepherds supposedly found their bodies lying arm in arm in the fields.

The tradition of bride price is still widespread, particularly in rural eastern Anatolia, where old values are strong, according to the report to the National Security Council. The custom is not prevalent in western Anatolia and Thrace, where, the report stressed, people of "individualist and modern conscience observe the civil laws."

The tradition's advantages were listed in a summary of the report: Virginity is protected since the money is paid for virgins; the economic interests of the bride and her family are considered; the bride gains in value according to the amount paid; the financial burden prevents a second marriage except for the very rich; a husband is likely to treat his wife well because he knows that if he does not she will go home to her parents and he will not get the money back; and the money ties the woman to her house, protecting the paternal family structure.

The findings listed three main disadvantages: A woman with a bride price is regarded as goods for sale; marriage is made increasingly difficult to seek; and serious economic problems are created for the man's side.

—Marvine Howe,
adapted from an article
in *The New York Times*

Several more recent and modernizing societies have retained aspects of the arranged-marriage system. Eastern European Jews who came to America before 1920 typically used the services of a "matchmaker," especially to find proper mates for their daughters (Hurvitz, 1975). Indeed, this practice inspired the popular tune, "Matchmaker, Matchmaker, Make Me a Match," from the musical comedy *Fiddler on the Roof*. Similar practices exist in Korea (Kim, 1974) and in contemporary Japan (Vogel, 1971:174–8), where the matchmaker is called a "go-between." However, modernization has greatly eroded popular support for the services of the "go-between," and youth have begun to take greater control over the selection of their mates.

The preferential principle of mate selection allows greater decision-making latitude to the marrying individuals. But even here, as we have seen, the field is not left entirely open. The preferential system defines the pool of eligibles from which one may select a mate. Every society sets an elemental precondition that one's mate must be a person of the opposite sex. This heterosexual requirement effectively narrows the field by 50 percent for everyone. Marriage, by apparently universal definition, must provide the possibility of parenthood, and this clearly demands a heterosexual union.

The Endogamy Rule in Preferential Mating

Social scientists divide preferential mating systems into two groups—those that endorse the rules of *endogamy* and those that endorse the rules of *exogamy*. The endogamy rule prohibits marriage outside of an individual's social group, assuring that marriage partners will be similar in most of their social characteristics. Perhaps the most famous endogamy rule—partly because it was a classic violation of the incest taboo—was the ancient Egyptian requirement that a pharaoh marry his sister to qualify as a legitimate heir to the throne. This practice arose from the claim of divinity for the ruling family (Lewinsohn, 1958:24); according to the religious-political tradition of ancient Egypt, marriage outside the ranks of royalty would have jeopardized the divine nature of the king and queen.

Most endogamous systems are far less sensational. Some primitive tribes prescribe intra-clan or tribal marriages to perpetuate their kinship structures and preserve their solidarity. Somewhat more common are the expectations of leaders within religious or ethnic subcultures that young people should not marry "outsiders." Endogamous marriage clearly contributes to the maintenance of subcultural distinctiveness and prevents its merger with other groups (Cavan, 1964:553). The general trend among youth in American society, however, is toward an ideological stance allowing intermarriage across religious and ethnic lines. But, in practice, strong evidence suggests that endogamy in mate selection continues with respect to such factors as race, religion, age, education, and social class.

The Exogamy Rule in Preferential Mating

The exogamy rule requires an individual to select a mate from a social group outside his or her own group. The *incest taboo* is one example of an exogamous rule; it forces persons to look beyond the nuclear family and close relatives in their search for a marriage partner. Primitive cultures often institutionalize exogamy by developing a cross-clan marriage system. In these instances, eligible marriage partners must be members of different clans (Warner, 1964a:16). Although exogamy is frequently practiced in American society, no fixed requirements dictate that one must select a mate from outside any of one's major social groups—except, of course, the laws against incestuous unions. Individuals strongly motivated toward achievement may feel some pressure to improve their socioeconomic standing by "marrying up," which is a form of class exogamy. Most Americans would look askance at such a cold, calculating approach to mate selection.

Homogamy and Heterogamy in Mate Selection

Social scientists have long been interested in discovering with greater accuracy just what kinds of people are drawn to each other and marry. Do most persons involved in the mating process seek out partners who share similar social or personality characteristics? Or, is a person more often attracted to someone whose social profile and personality traits differ decidedly from his or her own? Literally hundreds of research reports on these questions fill the pages of scholarly journals—and they are still coming. Thus far, two basic definitions have been established in this area. Homogamy, for example, refers to the tendency for like to marry like. By contrast, heterogamy is the tendency to be attracted to another person who differs in certain social aspects or in personality type.

However, once one moves from the relatively clear-cut realm of definitions to the rather untidy realm of concrete research findings, the question of whether the homogamous or heterogamous pattern prevails in American society becomes tremendously complex. One can say in the most sweeping of generalizations that the findings, taken collectively, do indicate that homogamy is much more obvious in mate selection in the United States than heterogamy (Eckland, 1980). Yet, as soon as one begins to press for more exact details on the extent of homogamy, that grand generalization must immediately be qualified. Before examining some of the refinements to the theory of homogamy, we can review several social characteristics that are commonly shared by couples who fall in love and eventually marry.

The Social Filters of Homogamous Mating

One person can be "like" another in several ways. The series of variables we shall consider are the background characteristics relevant to the mate-selection process. Sociologists typically describe these traits as filters which gradually narrow the field of eligible marriage partners. The rule of thumb is that the more of these traits a couple shares, the more likely they will be to move through the courtship process to marriage. These factors include age, propinquity, religion, race and ethnicity, social class, and attitudes, values, and social perspectives.

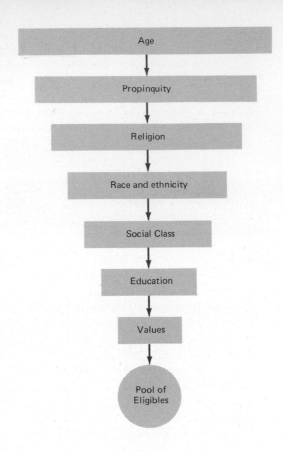

The Homogamy of Age

Age homogamy refers to couples who are nearly, but not exactly, the same age. Only about 10 percent of all brides and grooms are the same age at marriage. In fact, the average bride is about 2.5 years younger than her husband. The usual age for first marriage for women is between 18 and 24, while the usual age for men is between 20 and 26 (Glick and Norton, 1977:6). The custom in the United States is for girls to date older boys. A male college senior can date a freshman girl without anyone raising an eyebrow. However, if the situation were reversed, and a senior girl dated a freshman boy, the campus gossips would be working overtime. One consequence of this traditional pattern is that only about 10 percent of all American women marry younger men, but about 80 percent of the men marry younger women. It would be far more rational, of course, to reverse this pattern so that older women married younger men. As it now stands, a woman's life expectancy lasts approximately 7.7 years longer than that of a man born in the same year (U.S. Bureau of the Census, 1977:144). When the average 2.5-year differential in age between husband and wife at the time of their first marriage is added, a majority of married women are almost guaranteed to be widows for

A Season for Courtship

about the last decade of their lives. However no one has ever suggested that mate selection is guided by rational considerations.

Age homogamy also fits into a kind of sliding scale. As they grow older, people are less concerned about wide variation in partners' ages. For example, most people would consider a 37-year-old man who marries a 31-year-old woman to be well within the normative guidelines for marriage partners. However, if a college sophomore proposed marriage to a freshman girl in high school, one can safely predict widespread protest, even though the age gap between the two students equaled the age gap between the 37- and 31-year-old partners.

Quite clearly, these two cases are drastically different because in the first couple both partners have reached maturity, whereas in the second the freshman girl is still several years away from adulthood. Indeed, as a general rule, the younger the dating couple, the closer the ages of the boy and girl. But when people grow older, the age gaps gradually widen. By the time men reach 60 years of age, their brides are typically 10 years younger than them (Glick and Landau, 1950).

Thus far, the focus has been on the age of persons in first marriages. Partners entering a second marriage are predictably older and the age spans between them are somewhat wider. This is true partly because many second marriages involve fully mature widows or widowers. But it is also true that age at first marriage is a prime sign of the likely success of a union. Couples who marry in their teenage years experience much higher rates of marital disruption (Schoen, 1975), and they usually score lower in terms of marital happiness. These problems are due to a number of factors. Many teenage brides are already pregnant before they marry (Furstenberg, 1976); both part-

Figure 5–3
In second marriages involving older couples, it is often parents who seek the approval of their grown children and frequently the participation of their children in the marriage ceremony itself. (© *Stock, Boston, Inc., 1978. All rights reserved. Mike Mazzaschi, photographer.*)

ners are typically less mature than older couples; they have far more severe economic problems; and often they are not as well educated. With all these factors working against such young partners, age homogamy alone is not likely to ensure marital success.

The Homogamy of Residential Propinquity

Propinquity is the term sociologists use to describe the fact that couples live geographically close to one another. Such proximity was one of the first background traits that sociologists proved to be a major factor in mate selection. Studies begun in the 1930s found that courting couples usually resided within a few city blocks of each other, almost always within easy walking distance (Leslie, 1979:410–411). The first theoretical explanations for this finding contained more common sense than sociological sophistication. The theorists reasoned that physical closeness simply provided the opportunity for couples to contact one another, while geographical separation prevented interaction. Later students offered another interpretation. Neighborhoods in American society tend to be segregated by class, race, ethnic type, and religion (Stein, 1964; Eckland, 1980:140). Thus, the home of the family of orientation is a rough index to other background traits as well. When dating couples live in the same neighborhood, the chances are quite good that they will be members of the same social-class stratum, enjoy similar educational opportunities, belong to the same race, and probably the same religion, be it Protestant, Catholic, or Jewish.

In recent years, the concept of proximity has been broadened to encompass other types of physical nearness encouraging interaction. As more and more young people go away to college, move into apartments as single working adults, and delay their first marriages, proximity also has come to include interactions at school, at work, in a new neighborhood, and in the recreational gathering places of young people. Such proximity provides more opportunities to meet persons of more varied backgrounds than did the family neighborhood with its built-in controls for such social variables as race, religion, and class. Thus, in the years ahead, residential homogamy may well become less important as a predictor of mate selection.

The Homogamy of Religion

No religious community encourages its young people to marry outside its faith. To do so would be an act of institutional suicide. However, pressure from church and synagogue leaders to marry within the faith has declined notably in recent years. This results partly from a more lively ecumenical spirit of toleration among religious groups. But it is also an accommodation to the rise in interfaith marriages which has continued almost without interuption since the 1930s (Wilson, 1978:242).

Historically, both Roman Catholics and Protestants have reserved their strongest opposition for intermarriage with members of the Jewish faith (Glock and Stark, 1969:147–9). The recent relaxation of opposition to intermarriage with Jews has not yet overcome the long historical tradition against such unions. Indeed, it undoubtedly helps explain why Jews have the lowest rates of intermarriage for all three of the major religious communities in American life. But discrimination by Christian groups does not fully explain the high rate of homogamy for American Jews. Sklare (1971:191) reports that not until the 1960s did intermarriage surface as an important topic in the Jewish community. Many liberals of the Jewish community found it difficult to oppose the practice forthrightly, even though they did apparently harbor some reservations. Parents and many of the official religious leaders tried more vigorously to discourage intermarriage. They believed that their children's happiness and the survival of the Jewish identity (Sklare, 1971:191–206) were at stake. Together, then, in-group commitment and out-group opposition have conspired to promote a high level of marital endogamy for American's Jewish population.

While Protestants are the most likely of the three major groups to marry across religious lines, they are much more likely to marry a Protestant of a different denomination than they are to marry a Roman Catholic or a Jew (Greeley, 1972a:244–7). One curious finding reported by Stark and Glock (1970:192) is that "in marriages which cross Protestant-Catholic or Christian-Jewish lines many couples retain their original faiths, (while) in marriages of persons from different Protestant denominations both persons tend to end up in the same denomination." Thus, though most Protestants marry within their own denominations, those who do not formally adhere to the principle of homogamy in their marriages usually do achieve homogamy shortly after marriage when one partner switches to the other's denomination.

Until the Second Vatican Council of the 1960s, Roman Catholic canon law placed several serious barriers in the way of interfaith marriages. The non-Catholic partner was required to agree to a marriage ceremony performed by a priest. In a prenuptial agreement, the couple promised to avoid birth-control practices contrary to Catholic teaching, which meant that they could abstain from sexual relations or use the rhythm method. Also, all children born to the union must be baptized and reared in the Catholic faith. Without such an agreement, the Church would not recognize the legitimacy of the marriage (McKenzie, 1971:219). Almost all of these requirements have now been severely reduced. The non-Catholic partner in a mixed marriage no longer must agree to the baptism and rearing of children in the Church, although some bishops still do encourage the practice in their diocese. With a dispensation from the bishop or a qualified Church official, a Catholic now can be married by a civil official or a clergyman from another religious tradition. How much these changes have affected the intermarriage rate of Roman Catholics is hard to say. Probably, other social factors have been more significant. Upwardly mobile Catholics, for example, are still the most likely to marry outside their faith, while lower-class Catholics, where ethnic considerations remain strong, are the most reluctant to enter mixed marriages (Wilson, 1978:249).

The Homogamy of Race and Ethnicity

For no single background factor is homogamy more pronounced than it is for race. Consider these figures: 99.7 percent of white husbands are married to white wives; 99.2 percent of black husbands are married to black wives; 87.8 percent of Chinese husbands are married to Chinese wives; and 66.8 percent of Japanese husbands are married to Japanese wives (Reiss, 1980:334). How does one account for such high rates of racial homogamy?

The high white-white and black-black, and correspondingly low black-white marriage rates reflect the racial antagonism which has long been an important feature in American society. Laws against racially mixed marriages, as noted earlier, were not struck down by the Supreme Court until 1967. Discriminatory practices in the marketplace, education, and housing have also confined many blacks to segregated residential areas, low-paying jobs, and noncollege school programs. The upshot was to reduce the opportunity for interaction between members of the two races (Jencks, 1973:16–41). With greater upward mobility, and with more blacks in colleges, professional schools, and high-salaried jobs, one can expect to find more blacks in previously all-white neighborhoods, businesses, social clubs, religious groups,

Figure 5–4
The strongest background factor related to homogamy is race. 99.2 percent of all black husbands are married to black wives. (© *Stock, Boston, Inc., 1978. All rights reserved. Ellis Herwig, photographer.*)

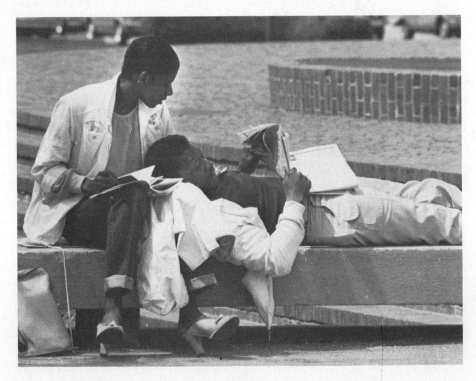

A Season for Courtship

schools, and political organizations. Duberman (1977:91) predicts that as young blacks and whites intermingle, the rate of intermarriage is likely to increase.

The data have already begun to confirm her hunch. In an analysis of the 1960 and 1970 census materials, David Heer (1974) compared the prevalence of black-white marriages over the decade and found an increase of 26 percent (one must remember, however, that these large percentage increases actually refer to rather low *actual* rates of intermarriage). The largest gains were registered in the North and West, with the South actually declining in interracial marriages by the substantial margin of 35 percent. A breakdown of the data by marriage partner and race also revealed that the sharpest rise (62 percent) involved the marriage of a black man to a white woman. The opposite pattern of a white man marrying a black woman actually declined 9 percent over the decade. One important trait of the black-white marriage in comparison to the racially homogamous union is its greater instability. Over the decade, the proportions of marriages still intact were: black husband and white wife, 63.4 percent; white husband and black wife, 46.7 percent; black husband and wife, 77.8 percent; and white husband and wife, 89.8 percent. Examined comparatively, the white husband-black wife marriage had a failure rate almost five times higher than that for marriages in which both partners were white. These data suggest the enormous difficulties interracial couples face in trying to make their marriages succeed in contemporary American life.

Although ethnic homogamy is not as strong as racial homogamy in mate selection, ethnic ties are somewhat more binding than most Americans believe. Such well-known students of ethnic subcultures in our society, as Warner (1963, 1964b) and Herberg (1960) predicted some years ago that full assimilation was near at hand. Free intermarriage of ethnic group members probably would be one clear signal that assimilation had, indeed, occurred. However, recent studies suggest that while rates of intermarriage among ethnic groups have risen, ethnicity remains important in both the social structure and the marriage market (Glazer and Moynihan, 1971). Indeed, Andrew Greeley (1972:108–26) argues that ethnicity now operates in conjunction with religious affiliation, so that one reinforces the other. Thus, intermarriage between an Irish Catholic and a German Catholic is far more likely than intermarriage between an Irish Catholic and a German Lutheran. The scant information available on ethnic groups today does seem to confirm Greeley's interpretation. This means that ethnicity combined with religious affiliation produces extremely high rates of homogamy in mate selection.

The Homogamy of Social Class

Social-class standing affects behavior, values, and attitudes more directly than almost any other aspect of the social structure does. Thus, the critical importance of social-class influences in determining mate selection should come as no great surprise. All individuals seek spouses who possess desirable qualities. Stratification systems, among other things, are structures of evaluation. They are arranged to indicate that those who possess more income, prestige, social sophistication, education, possessions, and social power are generally regarded as more desirable marriage partners. Both individuals and their families are typically eager to negotiate the best arrangement possible on the open marriage market.

William Goode (1973:258–9) suggests that the upper classes make a more concerted effort to control the mate choice of their offspring, presumably because the upper classes have the most to lose if their children marry social inferiors. Actually, of course, even in an open-class system such as our own, most persons marry someone at about the same class level as themselves. One should not necessarily read this as overwhelming support for social equality between mates. The simple truth is that most people refuse to marry someone of a lower class standing and cannot find a partner in a class above their own. The inevitable result is not only marriage homogamy, but also a class system which remains relatively stable over several generations (Goode, 1964:82).

While social-class homogamy is generally reported to exist in the sociological literature on the subject, agreement on how to measure class and status differences is relatively rare (Otto, 1975). Some researchers rely almost exclusively on economic criteria, such as family income, while others employ a composite of measures, such as income, father's occupation, and mother's education. Still other investigators use other subjective, self-evaluation instruments with varying levels of specified alternatives. The result is a body of findings whose results are difficult to correlate with other reliable measurements. In spite of the methodology, which complicates this research, one can say that, generally speaking, persons of the same social class associate more easily with one another because they share similar interests, forms of thought, behavioral expectations, reference groups, and background experiences. Moreover, persons who are more comfortable with one another are more likely to advance through the courtship phase and marry. The end result is homogamy of social class between marriage partners.

The Homogamy of Education

The historical tendency across several generations of American marriages has been toward a high degree of educational homogamy between marriage partners. Although men once proceeded to slightly higher levels of education than women, husbands and wives now typically achieve relatively equal levels. Thus, someone with only a high school diploma usually marries another person who also has not gone beyond the secondary level. Similarly, college graduates marry other individuals with college degrees. The typical explanation of this phenomenon is that persons with the same educational levels usually share the same interests, social perspectives, and values.

As with measures of social class, however, the problems of measuring educational achievement are not only complex, but increasingly troublesome. The difficulty arises primarily from the tendency today for people to remain in the educational system longer and to return after a period of work to pursue advanced degrees.

Moreover, the degree of educational homogamy, while still significant, is lower than was reported earlier in the century (Rockwell, 1976). Does this signal the decline of education as a filtering factor in mate selection? Perhaps, but not necessarily. Differences between levels of educational achievement for mating couples began to manifest themselves in the data during the 1960s when the marriage age was still going down. Thus, one can conclude that, although partners have attained different educational levels when they marry, one or both of them may plan to pursue a degree later. Early in this century, the pattern for both men and women was to complete formal education before marrying. For couples today, this arrangement often is neither feasible nor desirable. Moreover, with some persons waiting until middle age or later to complete their schooling, sociologists would really need to have data covering couples' whole life course to determine the final extent of their educational homogamy. These data are just now beginning to emerge. Dennis Hogan (1978, 1980), for example, has gathered evidence which shows that men who change the normal life-cycle transition of schooling, followed by the first job and then marriage, have a higher divorce rate than normal. Specifically, he (1978:585) found that men who finish school and then marry before taking their first job have a 17 percent higher divorce rate, while men who marry before finishing school have a 29 percent higher divorce rate than those who follow the normal sequence of school, first job, and marriage. Thus, it would appear that educational homogamy and the proper sequencing of life-cycle events are important factors in mating *and* in holding the partnership together.

The Homogamy of Attitudes, Values, and Social Outlooks

While this final filtering factor merits separate consideration in regard to mate selection, this type of homogamy does relate subtly to several other characteristics, such as religious affiliation, social standing, educational level, and racial or ethnic identification. Persons who are alike in certain important areas, such as religion, social class, and education do not always possess compatible value standards, attitudes, and social perspectives.

Several social and personal influences may account for differing social outlooks in otherwise well-matched partners. The region of the country in which one is reared does affect one's cultural orientation. Broadly speaking, each section of the country subtly influences the thinking patterns of its residents. Partners who come from the same region can be expected to understand and communicate better with each other than mates from highly different regions.

Intelligence also affects the value and attitudinal compatibility of mates. Two people who are far apart in native intelligence are likely to discover they hold few interests in common. Their reading habits, recreation interests, esthetic tastes, and life-styles may move in opposite directions. Therefore, a companionable relationship is much more likely to develop when both mates have similar intellectual abilities. Despite the social wisdom of seeking intellectual homogamy, some males persist in feeling threatened by a female partner who is equally intelligent. Komarovsky's (1976:49) sample of male college seniors, for example, contained a surprisingly large number who responded in this fashion:

> A brilliant girl would give me an inferiority complex; the girls I date are less smart than I.

> I enjoy talking to more intelligent girls, but I have no desire for a deep relationship with them. I guess I still believe that the man should be more intelligent.

> I may be a little frightened of a man who is superior to me in some field of knowledge, but if a girl knows more than I do, I resent her.

More often than not, of course, males who voice these sentiments actually end up marrying women who are at least as intelligent as they. Komarovsky also discovered that many college women reinforce this male expectation by "playing dumb," partly in deference to their dates' egos. However, many women seem to prefer to believe their mates are more intelligent. Believing this may give them the secure feeling that he can adequately provide for their future. Behind all this well-meaning deception, meanwhile, the truth is that intellectual homogamy is not only the norm, but also the reality of mate selection in American society.

Whether a similarity of values, attitudes, and social outlooks arises from regional location, intelligence, or other factors, similar viewpoints do attract individuals to each other. The ability to appreciate another's values and attitudes is a decided advantage in forming a meaningful relationship with a person of the opposite sex. And when one agrees with, as well as understands that person, the relationship very often can develop into a lifelong partnership. Indeed, Rubin (1973:140) contends that far more important than whether a person looks, sounds, or behaves like us, is whether someone *agrees* with us. Like minds appear to be extremely important in fostering a love relationship.

The Filtering Influence of these Background Factors

Throughout this discussion, we have noted that important background factors filter out potential mates until a person is left with a limited number of eligible people who are likely marital prospects. Of course, everyone does not readily submit to this filtering process and marry a person with compatible characteristics. Romantic love is a variable which can intervene at any point to offset the influence of these social factors. Perhaps we should remind ourselves that, while homogamy of race is the strongest of all these variables, 50 percent of all interracial marriages are successful. Should we discount the importance of the social factors we have described? By no means! The possibility of marriage failure appears to increase as background variance increases. The social factors help narrow the field so that love has a better chance to work its unique magic in the hearts of mating couples. In the remainder of this chapter, we shall focus on the social dynamics of love as it begins to take hold on couples who are usually already well-matched.

Definitions of love abound, as do the types of love defined. The varieties of love range from infatuation between dating couples to the intense conjugal love of married pairs. Novelists, poets, philosophers, and theologians have all written reams on love. Social scientists, who have more recently joined the effort to describe and explain the social dynamics by which people fall in love and fall out of love, generally agree on at least three aspects of the love relationship. First, love is a complex feeling and corresponding relationship. It encompasses emotional and sexual aspects. Second, love is a process. The intensity of the love bond changes over time and in relation to the quality of the interaction between the two partners. The old adages that "familiarity breeds contempt" and "absence makes the heart grow fonder" run counter to the sociological understanding of the love process. Time together allows a couple to build up a stock of common experiences, which promotes greater understanding and commitment—assuming, of course, that the relationship is mutually satisfying. If the relationship is hostile, it usually falters.

Finally, social scientists generally agree that the feeling of love is the basis upon which one makes that critical decision about a mate. Indeed, this is a crucial distinction between dating and mating. Dating is a form of courtship undertaken for a variety of reasons, not necessarily just to select a mate. Mating, by contrast, is a lifelong process. It begins in courtship, is publicly formalized by marriage, and continues until the relationship is broken by either death or divorce. The feeling of love developed during the courtship season is the basis upon which one selects a permanent mate. This decision is invariably accompanied by doubts as to whether one really loves the other enough to make such a lasting commitment. The failure rate of marriages adds a realistic urgency to such worries. Science is not very helpful in alleviating these anxieties. No test exists for determining whether lovers are experiencing "the real thing" or simply sexual attraction and emotional infatuation. What science can do is describe the processes by which love develops so that people, young and old, can better understand the nature of their own experience in forming a mating relationship.

The Complementary-Needs Theory

Homogamy and heterogamy can arise between mates in the areas of sociological background factors and psychological personality traits. Can a person seek out a mate who is similar in social characteristics, but different in personality type? In a classic study of mate selection, Robert Winch (1958) proposed that precisely this happens in many instances. The sociologists who stressed the importance of social and cultural homogamy were not wrong, from Winch's point of view, but neither had they fully analyzed the psychological aspects of the love process. Winch's Complementary Needs Theory was designed to fill this gap.

Briefly stated, he argued that similar sociocultural traits narrowed the field of eligible partners. Out of this pool, however, individuals tend to be attracted toward those whose psychological needs differ from and complement their own. Other things being equal, a male with a strong need to actively show love may be drawn to a female with a strong need to receive love passively. Or, an extroverted person with a strong need to attract attention may be drawn to an introverted partner with a strong need to give attention. Each individual finds need gratification in the other, because their needs are exactly opposite. Moreover, their dependency on one another intensifies the love relationship and strengthens the pair bonding.

The Stages of Mate Selection

A further refinement and integration of homogamy and complementary-needs theory was accomplished by Kerckhoff and Davis (1962). In a study of seriously dating and engaged couples, they followed for several months the process of establishing a permanent relationship. Their data revealed a series of stages in mate selection, with different "filters" at work in each stage. At the early stages, homogamy of social-status variables, such as class and religion, was crucial for the relationship to become established and progress. The second stage was characterized by a high degree of agreement on various family norms between the man and the woman. This was a different type of homogamy than the similarity of social characteristics. Partners who stayed together through this stage moved on to the final stage of need complementarity. Here, they found confirmation of Winch's hypothesis that couples are drawn together by different needs which each partner can gratify for the other. The discovery that complementarity of needs emerges very late in mate selection posed an interpretive question, namely, why the delay in the appearance of complementary needs? Kerckhoff and Davis finally concluded that during the early stages of courtship, partners idealize each other. That is to say, when couples first start dating, they are often responding to an idealization of their date's personality. Over time, that stylized image is eroded and a more realistic perception of the other person emerges. At this point, which is usually late in the mating process, need complementarity begins to surface.

By dividing the mating process into a series of distinct stages, Kerckhoff and Davis included in one theoretical model the paradoxical aspects of homogamy and need complementarity, while placing the role of value consensus in a new light.

From Liking to Loving

Many of the attempts to understand how love grows and develops between a man and a woman are not very well grounded in scientific evidence. Zick Rubin set out to improve this situation by developing an instrument designed to measure "liking" and "loving." He (1973) proposed that liking entails both affection and respect. Loving, however, includes a great deal more—caring, attachment, the desire for intimacy and physical closeness, and an emotional

130

bond. Rubin suggested that the normal course of a relationship is to move from liking to loving, and he set out to discover the various factors which helps a couple progress along this path.

To gather reliable information on the degree of liking and loving which binds two people together, Rubin developed two scales, a "liking scale" and a "loving scale." Each is designed to measure the degree of affection and attachment present in a given dating or mating relationship. Out of Rubin's research have come a number of interesting results, among them his conclusion that liking and loving have a feeling *and* a cognitive or intellectual component. Love, then, is not simply an emotional response. It also entails a good deal of thinking. Thus, to properly understand love, a researcher must give as much consideration to its cognitive aspects as she or he gives to the emotional aspects of mating behavior. Love, in short, combines elements of both heart and mind.

The Wheel Theory of Love

One of the more prominent models that tries to explain how love develops is the "Wheel Theory of Love," proposed by Ira Reiss (1980). His model is comprised of four interrelated processes which include rapport, self-revelation, mutual dependency, and need fulfillment. These processes are arranged in a cycle with one leading logically to the other. Falling in love entails movement in one direction, while falling out of love involves the reverse process. Let us look at each of the four parts of this theory.

Figure 5–5
Graphic presentation of the Wheel Theory of Love. (*Source:* Ira Reiss, *Family Systems in America* [1980:129].)

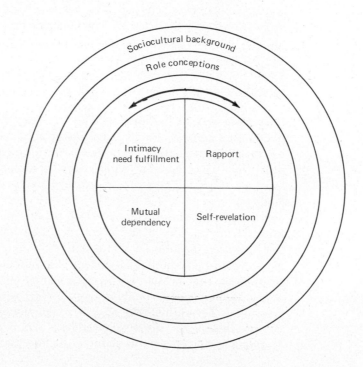

Rapport In the first stage, two young people meet and get acquainted. Their ability to relate to one another and establish an easy flow of dialogue comes under the heading of rapport. If love is to develop, Reiss maintains, a comfortable relationship must first be established between the two individuals. Moreover, the possibility of building rapport is greatly enhanced when both share a similar social and cultural background. Homogamy, in short, is a major influence on the ability of a couple to establish rapport with one another.

Self-Revelation This second process in the cycle builds upon the first. "A feeling of rapport almost inevitably leads one to feeling relaxed and therefore self-revelation can more easily occur" (Reiss, 1980:126–7). By self-revelation, Reiss means the willingness to disclose intimate information about oneself. The subjects of these disclosures may vary widely, from our attitudes about religious or political issues to our more personal fears and aspirations. Again, background characteristics and social training affect how much we choose to reveal about ourselves and how soon. Gender norms and individual personality traits also affect whether one is shy or forthcoming about one's true feelings. Before love can develop with real depth, however, a man and a woman must gain insight into the unique features of each other's personality.

Mutual Dependency Rapport stimulates self-revelation, which encourages progress toward the next major stage—mutual dependency. As two people interact over time, they nurture a desire to be with one another. They become accustomed to doing things together, having someone with whom to share a growing range of experiences and someone to talk with privately. Each looks forward to cooperative activities, even when it means some adjustment on both sides. Behavior patterns arise which cannot be fulfilled alone, and the presence of the other person becomes a kind of second nature which each begins to miss when the person is absent for a time. Clearly, the love bond is now becoming a serious relationship, as the two partners feel dependent on each other for both psychological and physical support and gratification.

Intimacy and Need Fulfillment The final stage in the development of a love relationship centers around a fulfillment of our deepest personality needs—for love, understanding, acceptance, trust, and sympathetic support. These needs have in common a requirement for intimacy, for each requires a personal closeness and privacy. Of course, human beings have many needs—for food, water, shelter, and so forth—but the need for intimacy is special. Only another person who extends love can provide the need fulfillment which intimacy requires. Moreover, only a permanent mating relationship can assure that this need for intimacy will continue to be satisfied.

Viewed as a whole, Reiss' model can show how love develops as a social relationship that bonds two people together in permanently paired dependency. A flow in one direction or the other determines whether love is increasing or decreasing. Movement around the circle toward intimacy would indicate the normal course followed by a mating couple.

Some persons marry prematurely, before the full cycle toward intimacy is

Individual Marriage Contracts: Some Hints for Writing Your Own

The practice of writing individual marriage contracts has become more popular in recent years. Couples often find this an excellent exercise for clarifying each partner's expectations as they enter into marriage. Designing a marriage contract tailored to the interests and needs of two individuals, however, can be a more difficult task than it initially appears. Here are some hints for those who want to try their hand at fashioning their own contract on which to base a marriage.

1. *Purpose and Limitations.* The purpose for an individual marriage contract is to specify clearly and explicitly what each partner expects from the marriage and from the spouse. This helps avoid surprises later, when one spouse discovers that his or her assumption about a major facet of their life together was not shared by the other. Almost everything which a couple agrees to include can be written into the contract. The limitation of individual contracts, however, is that they often cannot be enforced legally should one partner refuse to comply—especially if the contract dispute is over some issue which contradicts a state law pertaining to marital obligations. Individual marriage contracts, then, are more useful to couples in their private decision-making than they are as legal instruments for the protection of rights.

2. *Defining a Marital Style.* Individual marriage contracts also provide a couple with an opportunity to spell out the values upon which their union is based. For example, a couple may wish to indicate that their marriage is to be equalitarian. This commitment, then, would have several ramifications which they might well spell out in terms of child care, career opportunities, the sharing of household tasks, and so forth. Or again, a couple could decide to indicate in their individual contract that the personal growth and fulfillment of each partner is the basic goal of their life together. When a mutually agreed upon value commitment is considered important enough to be written into an individualized contract, it is often incorporated into the marriage ceremony as part of the couple's vows and promised to one another.

3. *Issues Most Often Included.* Although the marital style will determine, in part, the particular items covered by a personal marital contract, almost every couple will probably want to consider several common issues. These include:

(A) Whether the wife will take her husband's surname, or retain her maiden name, or whether both will use a hyphenated last name;

(B) How household tasks will be allocated and who will be responsible for what everyday activities—such as cleaning, washing, cooking, minor home repairs, and so forth;

(C) Whether or not the couple will have children, and if so, how many and at what time in the marital life cycle;

(D) What type(s) of contraception to use and who will take the responsibility for birth control measures;

(E) How child care responsibilities will be divided between the husband and wife, as well as the child-rearing techniques they will employ in raising their children;

(F) Whether they will rent or buy a place to live, and whether residential decisions will accommodate the husband's or the wife's career plans

(continued)

(will the husband, for example, be willing to move to another city so that the wife may take advantage of a better job offer?);

(G) How the breadwinner function will be divided, who will control the family finances, and how economic decisions will be made;

(H) How in-law relations will be handled, and whether vacations will be spent visiting relatives;

(I) What proportion of leisure activities will be spent apart from the spouse and what leisure activities will they spend together;

(J) How their sexual relations will be arranged and whether absolute fidelity will be preserved in their sexual relations;

(K) How they will go about the process of changing specific aspects of their marital contract as the marriage progresses over the life cycle.

4. *Potential Negative Consequences.* Not all social scientists are convinced that individual marriage contracts are superior to the traditional, unwritten agreements. Thus, it may be helpful to review briefly some of the potential negative consequences which could arise from this practice. Critics warn, for example, that couples entering marriage for the first time may not be in a very good position to anticipate the sorts of relationships which are desirable in their married life. The formal promises written into the contract, then, may actually inhibit adjustment during the first years of marriage. This is especially true if couples are not aware of the need to renegotiate provisions of the contract in an ongoing fashion. Also, partner's needs and expectations change rather markedly over the course of a marriage. Couples may outgrow the declarations of their contract well before they are aware of it. The flexibility of the unwritten contract, therefore, might sometimes be more desirable than the fixed character of a written document. And finally, since few states recognize individual contracts as legal instruments, partners may assume that they have secured more protection for their interests than actually obtains. Thus, the potential for generating hurt feelings or a sense of betrayal may be somewhat greater with an individualized contract than without it.

The upshot from these criticisms is not to recommend that individualized marriage contracts ought to be avoided. Many couples have—and still do—find them helpful in understanding the expectations and point of view held by their spouse. Rather, the appropriate lesson to be drawn is that marriage is more than a set of contractual rules; it is a living social relationship which is dynamic and changing. Couples who remind themselves of this important fact while they construct and live with individual marriage contracts may well be in the best position to find the most fulfillment in their married life.

---

completed. Others complete the cycle, marry, and then fall out of love as the cycle is reversed, producing discontent with the relationship and, more and more frequently, divorce. Clearly, the mating process is a continuous phenomenon. In one profound sense, the relationship can never be completed because the needs that prompt mating can never be fully satisfied. Thus, to view marriage as the end of the mating process would be a serious mistake. Marriage is simply a public recognition that mate bonding has occurred and that a permanent relationship of love has been legitimized. Yet, each marriage partner's need for a mate who can provide intimacy persists throughout the marriage.

Summary

Mating is a much more serious social process than dating. The courtship activity of dating may be undertaken for a variety of reasons; however, mating has one purpose; the selection of a lifelong partner. Romantic love is the basis upon which mates are selected in American society. However, not everyone is an eligible partner in the mating process, even though our free-choice system operates on an open marriage market. In a formal sense, laws against incest and marrying minors reduce the field. More important, however, are the influences of social custom and mate compatibility in narrowing the pool of eligible mates.

Mate compatibility means the similarity between a man and woman in terms of several sociological characteristics. The tendency for "like to marry like" is called homogamy. The major areas of homogamy in mate selection in American society include age, residential propinquity, religion, race or ethnicity, social class, education, attitudes, values, and social perspectives. These traits serve as social filters which group together persons who are sufficiently alike to offer at least the potential for a compatible relationship of love.

In addition to the theory of homogamy as an explanation of the mate-selection process, Winch offers an additional hypothesis which he calls the complementary-needs theory. In his view, when homogamous people have been grouped in a specific pool, people choose their mates on the basis of which person complements and gratifies their psychological needs. Thus, an extrovert who needed attention might be attracted to an introvert who needed to give attention. Kerckhoff and Davis carried this notion further. In their research, they interpreted mate selection in terms of a three-stage process. Zick Rubin also introduced a developmental model based on the movement from liking to loving. Rubin concluded that both of these interpersonal relationships involve emotional as well as cognitive elements.

A final interpretation of the mating process is the Wheel Theory of Love proposed by Ira Reiss. His model builds upon four interrelated processes, which proceed from rapport to self-revelation, mutual dependency, and intimacy. Progress through these various stages leads ultimately to the love required of a mating couple that will last through the pair's life cycle. Movement in the reverse direction, however, can lead to a falling out of love and a break in the mating relationship. Reiss's model shows that mating is a lifelong process. The needs of mates for love, understanding, trust, support, and a good deal more, persist with the same vigor throughout marriage.

STUDY QUESTIONS

1. How important is romance to the mating process in traditional societies and in contemporary American society?
2. What are the basic differences between a prescribed and a preferential mating system? Which one is normative for our culture?
3. Identify the various homogamy factors in mate selection. Which ones appear to be more important in narrowing the field of eligible partners?
4. When social scientists speak of the filtering process in mate selection, what are the social dynamics to which they refer and what is the relation of romantic love to this process?
5. How does Winch's complementary needs theory qualify the role of homogamy in mate selection?
6. What are the major stages in the wheel theory of love developed by Ira Reiss and by what progression does one fall in or out of love, according to this model?

PART THREE

A Season for Marriage

Marriage is one of the most popular institutions in American life. This is reflected in the fact that virtually everyone in our society marries at least once. The decision to marry can be viewed as an immediate result of the courtship process. Marriage is, in fact, the culminating event of courtship. Moreover, marriage also is a movement of individuals into a different stage of their life cycle. Indeed, for many, it signals nothing less than entry into full adulthood with its social roles and responsibilities.

The major topics in this section are the decision to marry, the adjustments which occur during the early stages of marriage, and finally the alternatives to traditional marriage. Each topic is covered in a separate chapter. It should become clear over the course of these three chapters that not everyone follows the same marital script, nor does everyone marry or stay married. It may well be that the popularity of marriage results from the fact that all marriages are not alike.

6

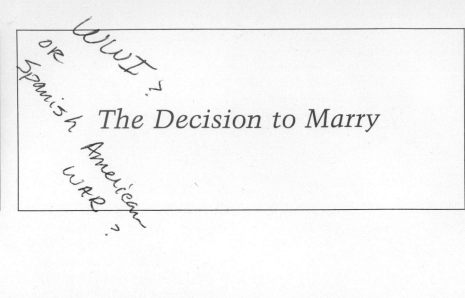

The Decision to Marry

Marriage is one of the most important decisions a person makes. Few decide lightly. The preparation for marriage begins early, when love emerges in the dating process. This leads to the selection of a mate most people regard as a permanent partner. Loving and mating, however, are subject to far less social control than marriage. The decision to marry represents a commitment which is at once more public, permanent, and far-reaching in its consequences. And in modern societies, at least, marriage requires the authorization of the state. Civil authorities must issue a license before a marriage is recognized as legally binding.

Curiously, however, the state makes little inquiry into the preparation of a couple entering the married state. A license is issued on demand to a man and a woman of legal age who have the appropriate medical documentation and normal mental capacity. No minimum courtship period is required; nor are the contracting parties informed of their rights and obligations. Indeed, the state considers it none of its business whether the man and woman love one another.

The state's limited supervision over parties entering a marriage signifies that falling in love and selecting a mate is largely a private matter. George Orwell's nightmarish 1984 vision of Big Brother regulating test-tube reproduction and banning romantic love between the sexes is a long way from being realized. Today, even the early Puritan practice of court intervention in family affairs for the purpose of increasing marital solidarity would be met with almost universal opposition. The state simply has no business meddling in the affairs of the heart. In these matters, people reserve the right to make their own decisions, and sometimes their own mistakes.

The Sociological Importance of Love as a Basis for Marriage

The development of a love relationship has been described in the two previous chapters in relation to dating and mating. Indeed, love will be important in this chapter and virtually every one which follows, since love is a pervasive element in marriage and family life today. While we have discussed love in American society as the proper basis for marriage, the sociological importance of love has not been systematically explored as it relates to the structure of marriage. That is the subject in this section. Moreover, the framework introduced here will provide the necessary background to examine the reasons for marriage, the incidence of marriage, and the symbolic events surrounding a nuptial agreement.

Toward a Sociology of Love

According to William Goode (1973:246), almost everyone has the psychological potential to experience and express love. It is a universal feature of the human experience. If this is the case, however, why is love not the universal basis of marriage and the family? Why is love repressed in some societal systems?

Social scientists seek the answer to such questions in the social structure of particular societies. Love between marriage partners would be a terribly disruptive force in certain types of family arrangements. Consider, for example, the peculiar situation of the Chinese family up until the modern period (Yang, 1965). Parents and clan patriarchs handled the matter of mate selection, with the aim of perpetuating kinship lines and increasing family fortunes. A young bride fit into the structure of the family unit as a handmaiden to her mother-in-law. A young woman was frequently subjected to severe treatment. Some women were known to beat their daughters-in-law to death in overzealous efforts to instill in the young woman a proper sense of deference and obedience. Mothers-in-law often were rebuked for such aggression because a young wife's death was a serious economic loss to the family unit. A good bride did not come cheaply, and impulsive discipline by the mother-in-law could waste a substantial amount of the family's economic resources.

If a Chinese husband truly loved his wife, his mother's treatment of her would almost certainly create social conflict. Harmony could prevail only if he felt no great affection for his spouse. This does not mean that love was wholly absent from the classical Chinese family. The five cardinal virtues derived from Confucianism clearly endorsed love and affection—as the proper bond

Figure 6-1
In our culture, romantic love is the basis for the bond of marriage. *(Photography by Jean Shapiro.)*

A Season for Marriage

of relationship between a *father and son*. The Confucian norms for husband and wife, however, merely instructed both to "attend to their separate functions" (Yang, 1965:6–7). It was universally understood that loving one another was not a duty of marital partners.

Although the Chinese case is an extreme example of repression of marital love, it does illustrate how patterns of social structure can influence the appearance of love by extending or withholding approval for various forms of its expression. This basic proposition holds true for our American marriage system. The classical Chinese were as psychologically capable of manifesting love as we are today, but our family organization encourages a strong love relationship, whereas theirs did not. Love, then, is channeled and institutionalized in different ways, given the requirements of the dominant social organization.

American Social Structure and the Role of Love Relations

American society emphasizes the nurturing of a marital love relationship. Why does our family structure, set within its wider cultural framework, make love such a critical element in marriage? We can isolate several independent factors to help us answer that question.

In the first instance, kinship for us is a relatively weak social bond in comparison, say, to traditional societies. (Parsons and Bales, 1955:10–11). The marital pair of husband and wife typically live apart from other kin. Kinship loyalty is first to one's spouse and then to the children born to that union (Parsons, 1954:186). Thus, the marriage relationship is not only more important than other kinship ties, but it also is more segregated from parents, siblings, and other relatives than it is in many other societies.

A powerful force is needed to separate a man and a woman from the love attachments, blood ties, and intimate social experiences they have built up by living for years in their families of orientation. If they are not willing to forgo their primary loyalty to their families of orientation and other kin, a new **conjugal family** probably cannot be established. Romantic love is the powerful force which induces a man and a woman to leave all else behind and strike out on their own within a marriage partnership. In one important sense, then, romantic love is not only the basis for their marriage, but also the means by which each one achieves independence from earlier family ties.

Romantic love is also encouraged by another aspect of our family structure. In extended family systems, individuals who comprise the domestic unit receive social support from a wide variety of kinsfolk. Parents, siblings, aunts and uncles, as well as clan members in some cultures, are readily available to advise, counsel, and to confirm the propriety of one's actions. In our family arrangement, this support from relatives is weakened, though not entirely lost (Delissovoy, 1973). A married pair is expected to carve out their own lifestyle, rear their own children, select their home, support themselves, and generally make their own major decisions. Most of the social support once provided by relatives is now concentrated in the spouse. A deep love attachment helps assure the partners that they will receive the social support they need. Love implies concern for the other person and a willingness to share in the burdens and pains the other feels. Without an intense love attachment, an individual might feel acutely isolated from social life generally. On the other hand, attachment to one's spouse gives life meaning and direction, and gives the partners a sense of identity and belonging. No wonder, then, that a person who loses his or her spouse often goes through a traumatic period of social disorientation (Goode, 1965).

As this analysis indicates, romantic love is strongly encouraged as a basis for marriage by the family structure institutionalized in American society. The emergence of the **"romantic love complex"** was not merely an accidental response to a set of social conditions in the wider cultural order. Rather, the stress on love resulted from the need to base family life on a powerful, solidifying force which would bind marriage partners to one another.

Some readers may feel this interpretation takes some of the romance out of falling in love. Who, after all, wants to believe their romantic passions are a product of the structure of society? Nonetheless, it is worth knowing that falling in love is a normal behavior in our society. To love and be loved in a

---

TEST YOURSELF

On Husbands' and Wives' Emotional-Sexual Responsibility to One Another
Each of the following statements was used in a social scientific survey gathering opinions about how persons perceive the responsibility of spouses to one another. Read each statement below and circle the response which best expresses your point of view. Scoring information is given at the bottom of this questionnaire.

It is alright for wives to have an occasional, casual, extramarital affair.

AS	AM	DM	DS
1	2	3	4

Women have an obligation to be faithful to their husbands.

AS	AM	DM	DS
4	3	2	1

If both husband and wife agree that sexual fidelity isn't important, there's no reason why both shouldn't have extramarital affairs if they want to.

AS	AM	DM	DS
1	2	3	4

A wife should respond to her husband's sexual overtures even when she is not interested.

AS	AM	DM	DS
4	3	2	1

A husband should respond to his wife's sexual overtures even when he is not interested.

AS	AM	DM	DS
1	2	3	4

Wifely submission is an outworn virtue.

AS	AM	DM	DS
1	2	3	4

marriage partnership is not merely a personal desire; it is a positive response to what society needs and requires from many of its members. The social necessity for love in no way diminishes the personal gratification which arises from romantic attachment. Or, put somewhat differently, sociology may not improve your love life, but it can help you understand why your love life is so important.

The Basic Reasons for the Institution of Marriage

Why marriage? This is a question that has grown in popularity in the last several years. In the last section, we presented a sociological explanation for romantic love but it does not really address many of the worries and criticisms surrounding marriage. Yet, with more and more young people living together, delaying marriage, or staying single (Stein, 1981), and with more and more adults finding their marriages "on the rocks," questioning marriage itself is neither an idle nor an irrevelant response. Moreover, the present controversy over marriage—whether it is changing, how it is changing, why it is not changing rapidly enough, or why it should not be changed at all—is a dispute in which almost everyone has an opinion. For Mary Jo Bane (1976), marriage is clearly here to stay. Mervyn Cadwallader (1975) agrees with this forecast, but still considers marriage "a wretched institution." Rustum and Della Roy (1979) regard monogamy as outmoded. Yet they can find no alternative which would better serve human needs. The social analyst, Christopher Lasch (1979), who believes marriage is now besieged by sociologists and the counseling professions, proposes a return to the conservative values and structure of the middle-class family. Morton Hunt (1975) remains convinced that marriage has a future, even though some recent developments, such as living together, group-marriage experiments, and the high divorce rate also will persist. And so the chorus of interpretation goes.

Obviously, one cannot cite all the current viewpoints on the need for marriage or formulate a critical response to each one. Furthermore, many of the arguments advanced today are far more political or ideological than social scientific. However, having raised the question, "why marriage?" we can review several major social reasons typically given for this institution.

Reason One: Societal Legitimacy for Sexual Relations

"Marriage is popular," G. B. Shaw once wrote, "because it combines the maximum of temptation with the maximum of opportunity." No doubt this quote from *The Revolutionist's Handbook and Pocket Companion* refers to the fact that marriage is the only institution, in our society at least, in which **legitimate sexual relations** can occur. Although the human sex drive is part of our biological endowment, no society tolerates indiscriminate sexual gratification; instead, it introduces controls to regulate sexual conduct. Although some nineteenth-century anthropologists speculated that our early ancestors lived in packs and practiced sexual promiscuity, no one has yet found any society of any type which does not seek to channel sexual behavior into acceptable patterns of expression (Henslin, 1978:2–3).

With remarkable uniformity across cultural lines, marriage is the institution in which sexual relations are entirely proper. Marriage, according to Morton Hunt (1975:410), appears to be a genuinely universal pattern, as common as language and religion. Furthermore, every marriage system includes some limitation on the sexual freedom of the married partners. Of course, these limitations vary considerably, and in many cultures, matrimony confines the sexual activity of women far more than that of men. Nonetheless, **conjugal rights** for partners are recognized everywhere as a benefit arising from marriage.

Discussion of legitimate sexual relations in marriage should not conclude with this mention of conjugal rights, for many feminists regard conjugal rights as shorthand for male exploitation. In our legal tradition, shaped by male legislators and attitudes, "conjugal rights" historically had come to affirm a husband's right of sexual access to his wife. Both in our culture and our legal system, this view is now being modified to recognize that, even in marriage, sexual relations must be voluntary on the part of both partners. Germaine Greer (1971:179) writes in bitter protest, for example, about sexual relations as just another "household duty" women are expected to perform. Moreover, in recent years, wives have successfully prosecuted their husbands for rape when they insisted on sexual relations. Even in marriage, therefore, legitimate sexual behavior is limited (Gelles, 1980).

The recent change from the "conjugal rights" notion to an emphasis on sexual fulfillment in marriage recognizes that sexual gratification ought to be an expectation of both husband and wife (Brisset and Lewis, 1970:46–7). The explosion in the sale of marriage manuals and how-to books devoted purely to sexual techniques is a rough index of the greater sexual activity in marriage. Indeed, a Morton Hunt survey (1974), undertaken for the Playboy Foundation, confirmed that sexual liberation in the last 15 years has had its greatest effect "within the safe confines of the ancient and established institution of monogamous marriage."

Reason Two: Societal Legitimation of Procreation

One of the major reasons societies seek to regulate sexual behavior is to control the birth of children (Goode, 1964: 20–21). Each society has a vested interest in its next generation, for its members hold the future of that social order. By the same token, collective anxiety about marital disruption and divorce is largely an expression of concern that children receive the necessary physical care and social training (Bane, 1976:3–4). Without a stable marital union which can care for its offspring, the security of children is jeopardized, their social position is made ambiguous, and their social training can become a public problem.

For all these reasons, **illegitimacy** is regarded as a more serious problem than premarital intercourse. Even societies which are far more tolerant of sexual promiscuity than ours still remain strongly opposed to the birth of children out of wedlock. Clark Vincent describes our own mores with respect to premarital permissiveness and illegitimacy as a mass of contradictions. He notes (1969:6–7), for example, that many states have heavier fines for allowing dogs in heat to run loose than they do for unmarried couples who are convicted of having sexual relations in private. Thus, while the cause of illegitimacy—namely premarital sexual intercourse—is not severely condemned, the result, a child born out of wedlock, is sternly denounced. Moreover, to further compound the contradictions, the social disapproval brought on by an illegitimate birth is still borne more often by the unwed mother than by the unwed father. Why should society disapprove more vigorously of illegitimacy than premarital sexual intercourse? The chief difficulty with illegitimacy is not really that it threatens to strip away the integrity of family life, as is often supposed. Rather, the rules of legitimacy are fundamentally designed to ensure that each new member of society is properly placed within the social order. **Social placement** refers to the assignment of a class standing to the newborn, but it also entails a good deal more. Being situated in a status position also designates which adults are responsible for the material support and social training of a child. Unless these basic social needs are met, a newborn infant would be a burden on society, and the child might never develop the necessary skills to become a productive member of that social order.

Reason Three: Meeting the Material Needs of Family Members

People of all cultures share the basic needs for food, clothing, shelter, and protection against foes, whether human or supernatural, as defined by the culture (Redfield, 1953:10–12). Failure to meet these needs can jeopardize one's very survival. Preindustrial societies tend to be organized so that material needs are met collectively through the contributions of almost all family members, except the very young and the very old (Geertz, 1973:42). Indeed, the more primitive the culture, the more difficult it is for an individual to survive without the support, guidance, and protection of extended family members. The conjugal pair, however, is the first line of defense against material deprivation. They tend to be immediately accountable for the food, clothing, and shelter necessary for themselves and their offspring. Murdock (1949) claims that, for this reason, the nuclear family is an operational unit in all societies, even those characterized by large, extended families.

Economically advanced societies offer more opportunities for single adults to manage on their own. Most individuals can secure a job whose earnings will cover the vital necessities. Yet, Americans still prefer to marry and establish a household in which these material necessities can be met. For children, of course, material support from the parents is a necessity, not simply a luxury. Young people remain dependent on their parents or guardians for a much longer time now than they did only a few generations ago. Adolescence has been so prolonged that in many cases it extends through the college years and into the period of graduate studies. One upshot of this trend has been a dramatic increase in the cost of rearing children. Espenshade (1977) estimated that, at 1977 prices, the average cost of raising a child from birth through four years of college was $65,000. This figure is steadily increasing, even within those households whose young people seek part-time or summer employment. Without some material support, youth would be thrust into the labor market long before they were equipped with the skills required by a complex, technological economic system. Thus, marriage partners take upon themselves much higher costs when they decide to have children today.

Reason Four: The Socialization of Children

Socialization is the learning process, beginning at birth, through which an individual adopts as his or her own the norms, values, and beliefs of a particular culture, and the roles appropriate to the individual's social positions. The classical sociologist, Emile Durkheim, was one of the first to recognize the family's critical role in supervising the internalization of moral norms in the next generation. Durkheim (1961) typically described this process as moral education, which also was carried on by the school, church, and ultimately, society at large. In his view, a child entered the world very nearly as a blank page (1956:124–5). As soon as possible, society must transform this asocial being into a cultured self by overlaying a social nature which enables the person to lead a moral life. The ability to take on moral norms that can effectively restrain our selfish impulses sets human beings apart from the lower animals. In other words, a child is not born a member of society. That status is attained, along with moral norms and social roles, through the socialization process.

Socialization is not accomplished overnight, of course. Our primary socialization begins at birth and continues into our adolescent years. The family unit and especially parents assume the major role in socialization until a child

146

enters school. Even when a person enters school and begins to come under the influence of the peer group, however, the family is still the dominant socializing force, shaping the individual's attitudes, values, and behavior (Turner, 1970:164–82). Much of the content of our primary socialization in the family agrees with our adult experience, and therefore is never outdated. We retain, for example, the language, symbols, and many of the attitudes and values we acquired from our parents. In fact, most of us will choose adult reference groups which match the orientation we first adopted in our families. This includes such reference groups as our religion, political party, social-class outlook, and our general cultural perspective (Hyman, 1969:52–66).

Socialization continues throughout our life cycle (Elkin and Handel, 1974:142). Entering college as a freshman requires socialization to this new status. Marriage partners are socialized to their new roles as husband and wife. When one grows old, a person is resocialized into the senior-citizen status. Much of our later socialization depends on the cultural learning acquired in our primary socialization. Even when we reject part of the cultural heritage transmitted to us by our family of orientation, we do so by using the basic cultural skills, reasoning processes, and meanings which our family first instilled in us.

Socialization is clearly critical to our social development, as we shall see even more clearly when we explore the process more thoroughly and systematically in Chapter 10. However, one might well wonder why socialization is cited as a reason for marriage. Actually, most societies leave socialization to the marriage partners for several reasons. Parents usually have a stronger emotional attachment to their children than do other adults. Parents also can oversee the socialization of their children, since the nuclear family almost always lives together as a unit. Furthermore, all parents are profoundly interested in the future of their children. Hence, they try to provide them with the necessary cultural training to ensure their success as adults. For all these reasons, most societies have entrusted to the married pair the responsibility for socializing their children. Moreover, this pattern does not appear to be changing. Actually, modernization has increased the socializing responsibility of the marital pair in the nuclear family. While members of the extended family often took a direct hand in rearing children, the nuclear family of modern society jealously guards the rights of parents to socialize their own children.

Reason Five: The Need for Status Identity

All societies are made up of complex patterns of social organization. To function as a competent member of society, each person must know exactly where he or she fits into the larger social network of societal relationships. Few situations are more frustrating, or even terrifying, than being unsure of our social status. If our social position is ambiguous, we cannot be confident about how we ought to behave and how others will relate to us.

To meet this problem, almost all societies assign children to the social position held by their parents. Some societies, such as classical India when

Saudi Men Still Hold Firm Rein, but Women Have Easier Time

Riyadh, Saudi Arabia—In public Samira al-Fawzan wears the traditional head-to-toe veil, but in her furniture store she appears in fashionable European clothing.

"If a woman in Saudi Arabia wants to work, she can," Mrs Fawzan said. "The veil won't stop you. In running a business I am contributing to the economic growth of Saudi Arabia, and I am doing so by observing all our Islamic traditions and practices."

As the Saudis race to invest their oil riches in ambitious economic-development programs, the roles played by Mrs. Fawzan and many other urban women indicate that the traditionally conservative Islamic social structure is gradually yielding to change.

Nonetheless, many restrictions remain on women in this country of perhaps 10 million people. Despite the insistence of Saudi religious leaders that women enjoy equality with men in the Islamic world, the situation is clearly weighted in favor of Saudi men.

Women are not allowed to work with men, and no one is predicting the early lifting of the prohibition. Women and men are not permitted to swim together. Socializing is frowned upon; even in private, it is said, few unmarried women will venture to mix with unattached Saudi men without the presence of a family-approved chaperone.

Most marriages are still arranged, sometimes with cousins. Women who travel are required to be accompanied by close male relatives, who have the traditional right to see them unveiled. Virtually all women feel compelled by custom to wear the veil in public.

A woman needs the approval of the senior male member of her family to start or own a business. Mrs. Fawzan had to obtain the written authorization of her husband; a commercial license was then issued by the Government.

Among educated women in such cities as Riyadh, Jidda, Taif, Dhahran and Dammam there is some grumbling about the restrictions. Some women maintain, in particular, that keeping the bans on individual travel and on driving is irrational and that it confuses tradition and religion.

The changes concerning the status of women and the opportunities available to them largely apply to urban women, whose proportion of the female population is indeterminate because of the absence of official census figures.

In the nomadic desert communities, officials say, it will be a long time before change takes place, at least partly because of pervasive illiteracy.

. . .As for the veil, in interviews across the country remarkably few women objected to it vigorously.

"The veil is protection for our bodies—it is not a prison for our minds," said Cecile I. Rouchdy, headmistress of the Dar al-Hannan girls' school in Jidda. Fatamma al-Awsiyeh, a 20-year-old resident of Jidda who has a job in a bank run by women, agreed that the veil offered "Islamic-style protection," but she added that "the way it is done here is an intrusion."

Asked whether she felt otherwise restricted, she said that life for women was generally unrestricted within the household and that she, like other affluent Saudi women, frequently traveled abroad with her family. "The freedoms I would like are to be able to drive and to travel on my own," she added.

. . . Wasisa Hakim, 23, who recently returned from Britain after earning her high school diploma, has joined the Saudi American Bank as a teller and works in the women's section. Driven to work by the family chauffeur, she wears a veil outdoors.

. . . Miss Hakim, stating that she did not feel restricted by society, said: "People ask, 'Why don't single women get to meet single men without an escort?' Well, it is not in our tradition to meet men that way. We have freedom up to a point. I don't think our women should go as far as Western women do. We don't usually discuss things like politics, for instance, but these are things that as women don't concern us."

Another Saudi woman at the bank, 20-year-old Basama al-Owssiy, who was queried about marriage, replied: "Ask God. The right person hasn't come along. I would like to build a career, and I think that is possible along with marriage responsibilities. If the right person comes along, I can reach agreement with him. I can't see him having any objections to my working. I don't want to be simply a housewife and stay at home. . . ."

—Pranay B. Gupte
from *The New York Times*

the caste system was most strong, forbade movement out of the class assigned at birth. The estate system of medieval Europe and traditional societies of today are not quite as strict as the caste system, but barriers do exist making social mobility from one stratum to the next difficult (Weber, 1958b:39–54). The social-class system in American society allows individuals relatively free movement up or down among the strata. Moreover, the boundaries of social classes are not as sharply defined as they are in either caste or estate systems (Bottomore, 1968:9–34).

The open-ended character of our stratification system does not mean that class standing is less important in American society than in other cultures. But Americans do find that, because we lack an inherited class status, it is hard to tell immediately and exactly where each person stands in the stratification system. This problem is compounded by our society's long-standing and strong orientation to achievement (Lipset, 1963:101–39). Thus, an American faces the peculiar situation of being expected to try to improve his or her class standing within vertical status ranks which are not clearly defined. This social arrangement forces us to find our status position by comparing our behavior, attitudes, and moral norms to those we believe to be our social equals. Once our social equals have been established, we can strive to attain acceptance by a higher status group. Should the higher status group admit us, then we have made some social gains in upward mobility.

Social mobility, whether upward or downward, occurs, therefore, in two steps. We inherit our initial status position from our family of orientation. Upon leaving this nuclear unit, each person's adult status hinges on individual achievement. Although our primary socialization tends to bequeath to us a set of values, attitudes, and behaviors which helps prevent downward mobility, our failure to succeed in school or work can result in a loss of status. Conversely, success in higher education, business, politics, or the performing arts can greatly increase our class standing. Again, however, our primary socialization tends to prevent too wide a shift in social position, for we usually retain the attitudes and behavior of our primary socialization even though our income or prestige may increase a great deal. In other words, our assigned status position not only results from the family's financial resources, but also reflects the cultural perspectives typical of that status group. Even if one attains considerably greater financial rewards, one is still likely to identify with the values of one's family of orientation. For this reason, dramatic shifts in upward or downward social mobility actually occur rather rarely in American social life, as Lipset and Bendix (1959) have shown.

Reason Six: Societal Pressure to Marry

Almost everyone in American society grows up expecting to marry some day. This is a realistic assumption since between 90 and 95 percent of all Americans marry at least once (Bane, 1976:22). Such a high marriage rate indicates that entering the bonds of matrimony is the norm to which all young people are expected to conform sooner or later. Our parents, our peer groups, society at large, and even our own definition of a fulfilled life, pressure us to marry. Few can resist and not many people really want to. An unmarried adult beyond the age of 30 will find herself or himself in a steadily shrinking minority. Moreover, many well-meaning individuals treat single people as objects of pity, a source of irritation for many singles who have deliberately chosen not to marry or to delay marriage.

The discrimination often practiced against single adults is a somewhat less subtle pressure to marry. Many companies, for example, prefer married women or men, because they regard people with families as more stable and dependable. According to this logic, married people with children, a mortgage, car payments, and credit card bills are more likely to be responsible employees. This is not because single persons are inherently less dependable, but because they do not always have the motivational pressures to perform that are typical of married people. Singles also encounter frequent discrimination in housing. Some landlords refuse to rent to single persons, claiming that they are more likely than married couples to throw wild parties. Another subtle pressure to marry takes the form of recreational outlets and the need for companionship. Generally speaking, the more that husbands and wives engage in the same recreational activities together, the greater their marital happiness scores (Orthner, 1975). Morever, married couples tend to socialize with other married couples. Thus, the social life of singles, even in metropolitan areas, is often more lonely than that of their married counterparts if the singles do not develop adequate friendship networks (Stein, 1981:9–18).

A final inducement to marry, which is especially strong among working-class youth, is a desire to attain adult status in the eyes of one's family and friends. In her study of working-class women, Lillian Rubin (1976) discovered that a substantial number of her subjects saw marriage as a way to achieve freedom from parental controls and move into adulthood. As long as they remained within the parental household, they were subject to many of the restrictions imposed during adolescence. But marriage swiftly established their maturity, independence, and their right to pursue their own life-style. In retrospect, many of Rubin's informants questioned the wisdom of using marriage as an escape route from childhood dependency, and they regretted their hasty judgment in selecting their marriage partners. Thus, whether or not it is undertaken for the right reasons, marriage is an important symbolic **rite of passage** which, in most societies, marks the move from youth to adult.

For all of the reasons we have discussed—from legitimate sexual relations to societal pressure to marry—marriage remains a popular institution in American life. Indeed, at no time in our history has such a large segment of our population tried marriage at least once. Furthermore, because the remarriage rate has climbed along with the divorce rate, more people are married today than ever before.

The Incidence of Marriage

The reasons people marry are the backdrop for a consideration of the actual incidence of marriage. In this section, we will survey data on who marries, when, and with what degree of marital satisfaction. These data reveal some interesting trends when compared over several generations in American life.

Who Marries?

Perhaps the most accurate response to this question is that almost everyone marries. The United States has recently achieved the highest marriage rate among the industrialized nations of the world (Glick and Norton, 1977:4). The rate reached a peak of 11 per 1,000 citizens in 1972 and then declined gradually to 9.9 per 1,000 in 1976. This compares with a 10.1 marriage rate for the USSR, 10.0 for Egypt, 8.7 for Canada, 8.5 for Israel, and 7.8 for Japan. The marriage rate in the United States is increased in part by our divorce rate, the highest among the industrialized nations (*Social Indicators*, 1976:61). The combination of first marriages with remarriages elevates the overall marriage rate. When slightly more than 80 percent of all those who divorce later remarry, as is currently true in the United States, the inevitable result is a considerable boost for the overall marriage rate.

The other side of the coin, however, is that very few people remain single all their lives. Among those in the 45-to-54 age group in 1977, only 5.6 percent of the males and 4.3 percent of the females had never married (U.S. Bureau of the Census, 1978). The percentage of persons who eventually marry has been increasing with only slight interruptions since 1900. The low point in the marriage rate for the twentieth century, however, occurred in the 1920s, when only 88 percent of males and 90.4 percent of females married. This was due primarily to the effects of the Great Depression which took place at the end of the 1920s. General economic conditions in society always have a definite effect on the rate of marriage, the age at first marriages, and the number of children a couple produces.

When Do People Get Married?

The median marriage age for both men and women declined between 1900 and 1960. At the turn of the century, men typically married at 25.9 years of age. By 1960, however, the median age of grooms was 22.8 years and 20.3 for brides. Since then, the trend has been toward delaying slightly the age of first marriages. As of 1978, men waited until they were 24.2 years of age and women were 21.8. Thus, while couples today are marrying somewhat later, they are still marrying earlier than they were at the turn of the century.

The factors which prompted the average delay of first marriages by about 18 months over the last 20 years are probably quite varied. The Vietnam War, two recessions, and social turmoil during this period certainly must have had some effect. Perhaps the most important factor, however, was a general shift in our counterculture attitudes toward young people living together. The early results from the March 1977 Current Population Survey revealed that nearly two million unrelated adults of the opposite sex were sharing the same living quarters (Glick and Norton, 1977:32)—more than double the number in 1960. While the practice of living together probably has delayed the age of first marriages (Glick and Spanier, 1980), it does not appear to have depressed the marrying rate. Living together should not be taken as a sign that young people are losing interest in marriage. Since most couples plan to marry and eventually do, cohabitation is regarded more and more as a prelude to matrimony, a trial period during which both persons seek to determine whether they are compatible and whether their relationship is stable enough to support a long-term commitment (Macklin, 1980:285–307).

The delay in the age of first marriages is not without its social consequences, even though the median delay is only about 18 months over the last two decades. Since sexual activity has not yet declined, the rate of illegitimate births has risen sharply. For example, only 5 percent of all births in 1960 were children born out of wedlock; in 1975, the figure rose to 14 percent (Glick and Norton, 1977:6). No reliable estimate can be made about how much lower the illegitimacy rate would have been without the delay in first marriage age, but we can surmise that it would have been a good deal lower. Thus, even the addition of one year to the median age of first marriages can have profound ramifications, for it drastically increases the proportion of single young people in a specific age category. Nevertheless, by age 30, slightly more than 90 percent of all young people in American society have been married at least once.

How Satisfying Is Marriage?

Measuring marital satisfaction is a much less precise art than determining the rates of marriage, divorce, and other quantifiable factors. Perceptions of happiness are, by nature, highly subjective. The National Opinion Research Center at the University of Chicago sampled the degree of happiness reported by

A Season for Marriage

married couples in 1973, 1974, and 1975. These findings are somewhat surprising. When given the choice of rating their marital satisfactions as "very happy," "pretty happy," and "not too happy," the "very-happy" category was selected by 67.4 to 69.1 of the sample couples. Only 2.6, 3.5, and 2.7 couples in each of the three successive years reported that their marriage was "not too happy." From these data we may conclude that not only is the "idea" of marriage popular among Americans, but marriage itself is also very satisfying.

If these data accurately portray marital bliss, how can we explain the very high divorce rate in American society? Surely marital unhappiness and divorce go hand in hand. Actually, the divorce rate and marital happiness are related, but probably inversely. That is, unhappy marriages tend to end in divorce, followed by remarriage, and thereby produce a second marriage which is happier than the first. Consequently, if our divorce rate were much lower, then we probably would see a sharp rise in the number of unhappy marriages. Thus, one trade-off for a high divorce rate is a general increase in marital satisfaction. The irony here is unmistakable. While almost everyone would like to see the divorce rate decline, no one really wants to see the rate of marital unhappiness increase. The challenge in working for a lower divorce rate is to try not to reduce marital satisfaction in the process.

Another important point about the scores on marital happiness is that they tend to change over the course of the family life cycle. In a major reevaluation of the research findings on this issue, Rollins and Cannon (1974) noted that contradictory results have been reported thus far. Blood and Wolfe (1965), for example, noted declining happiness for both husbands and wives over the course of the family life cycle. Other researchers had discovered a U-shaped curve as marital happiness remained high immediately after marriage, declined sharply during the family years, and then increased after middle age. Similar findings of a U-shaped curve were reported by Angus Campbell (1975) in a survey of 2,164 adults. Not only were married persons found to be happier than singles in this study, but, in addition, marital satisfaction declined during the life-cycle stage when children were part of the nuclear family unit. Therefore, it appears that it is not the stages, themselves, of the life cycle that decrease happiness, but the kinds of demands made upon marriage partners during specific periods of family development.

The Symbolic Significance of Entering a Marriage Partnership

Progress through the life cycle is periodically marked by symbolic events which are referred to as the "rites of passage." They now include such high points as birth, confirmation or Bar and Bat Mitzvah, graduation from high school or college, engagement and marriage, the birth of children, retirement, and finally, death. Among all these bench marks of life-cycle events, marriage is perhaps the most public and certainly one of the most far-reaching in its consequences. Most of our adult lives are spent in marriage and most persons will spend from 35 to 40 years with the same partner. It is not the time span of a marriage, however, which makes the wedding event so symbolically important. Rather, it is the special social bonds which marriage creates.

The Symbolic Significance of the Engagement Period

The **engagement** period is a common, but not a legally necessary, prelude to marriage. In American society, the courtship process normally culminates in a formal period of engagement. This entails a statement by the two partners of their intention to marry each other. So many of today's engagements are publicly recorded by newspaper announcements and declared by the fiancé's gift of an engagement ring to his female partner. (In recent years, jewelers have launched vigorous campaigns urging engaged women to reciprocate by giving their fiancés diamond rings too. No doubt, we may assume that jewelers are more interested in selling rings than they are incensed by the discrimination against men, who have not, in the past, received rings.)

A formal engagement conveys several public meanings. First, it signifies that the relationship between the two dating partners is serious. They are avowing their decision to become spouses. Closely related is the expectation that neither one will now accept dates from a third party. In other words, engagement is a public declaration to everyone else that the choice of an exclusive mate has been made. Occasionally, of course, one of the engaged partners may go out on a date with someone else. However, if the partner who has been "cheated on" finds out, this could readily be regarded as a serious enough breach of expectations to warrant cancelling the engagement. Doubts are likely to be raised about that person's faithfulness once the marriage has taken place. And finally, engagement is a declaration of love. While love can be asserted in the privacy of courtship, it does not carry the same force as an engagement which makes public one's intention to marry the other person.

Apart from its symbolism, an engagement serves a number of important, practical functions. Since couples typically date each other frequently and exclusively during this period, engagement gives them an opportunity to get to know each other much more thoroughly than before. Some couples find it extremely hard to maintain a satisfactory relationship during this period. Their love and irritation with the other person may fluctuate widely. This may be a signal of serious trouble ahead after marriage. Breaking off a relationship during the engagement is far easier, both legally and emotionally, than waiting for marriage to confirm the partners' incompatibility. Of course, to take readings of this sort, the couple must be engaged long enough to allow various moods and personality traits to manifest themselves.

The engagement period also can be an important time for planning toward a lifetime together. Couples need to make several major decisions which can create problems if each holds different expectations. These decisions include whether the wife will work outside the home after marriage; how many children they expect to have and when; where they will live; financial provisions adequate to support their household; whether one or both partners should seek advanced education; working out a comfortable relationship with both sets of future in-laws; and settling on a list of priorities for major purchases after marriage. The more decisions of this nature couples can resolve during their engagement, the easier their adjustment to marriage is likely to be after the honeymoon. Moreover, working through these issues can suggest how each will participate in the decision-making process in marriage. If the male partner, for example, insists on having the final word on all major issues, his fiancée could take this as a warning signal that he is not really committed to an equalitarian relationship between them. It is far better, in such instances, to agree on power relations before marriage, rather than have one partner resolve to change the other after they have become husband and wife.

Sometimes when troubles and disagreements erupt during the engagement, couples rush ahead with their marriage plans, hoping that matrimony will miraculously cure their difficulties. Especially when parents have shown some disapproval, or when one partner is beginning to doubt the relationship, or when the wife-to-be becomes pregnant, the partners may feel themselves under mounting pressure to marry quickly. Marriage counselors usually advise couples to delay until the right conditions prevail for a happy union. This is often extremely difficult for young people. Everyone likes to believe that he or she is somehow different and that their marriage will not founder on those rocky shores which have led to divorce for other couples. In some cases, couples do grow closer as they confront serious early problems. However, most people who enter a marriage in the face of financial problems, strong parental disapproval, a pregnancy, or disagreement over major decisions will simply find that their problems worsen rather than vanish. All those people who are now divorce statistics did not, after all, enter marriage expecting their union to fail.

The Marriage Ceremony

Toward the end of the engagement, a great deal of attention is likely to be devoted to planning the marriage ceremony. Today, even a small wedding is likely to be an extremely complex affair. Together, a couple must set a date for their wedding, reserve a place for the ceremony, and arrange to have a duly authorized person witness the exchange of marriage vows. In the midst of all these preparations, it is rare that someone does not express the half-hearted wish that the couple had just eloped.

To be sure, some will question whether the expenditure of time, energy, and money is fully justified for a ceremony which lasts from 15 to 60 minutes. One can only say that, if couples and their parents did not want an elaborate ceremony, they would simply plan a more private, less complex affair. However, many young women in America grow up looking forward to that romantic day when they will walk down the aisle in a long wedding dress with a flowing veil. Moreover, the elaborate preparations for the wedding ceremony do underscore the event's social importance. Let us review several of the major symbolic meanings in the marriage ceremony.

In most societies, weddings are performed under religious auspices,

Figure 6-2
The rich symbolism of a traditional religious marriage ceremony can add meaning and depth to the exchange of vows. *(Copyright © by Stock, Boston, Inc., 1978. Elizabeth Hamlin, photographer.)*

thereby invoking the sanction of supernatural forces on the marital pair (Mace and Mace, 1960). Indeed, in Sweden, the most secular of modern Western societies, 94 percent of all marriages are conducted in a church, rather than by civil authorities in a nonreligious setting (Tomasson, 1970:185). Most wedding ceremonies in the United States are performed by religious officials, usually in a church or synagogue. Thus, surrounded by clergy, religious symbols, relatives and friends, and accompanied by music and liturgical assurances of divine approval, the exchange of vows takes on a very serious air.

The service has other symbols as well. The white wedding gown is a sign of innocence and purity. The practice of the bride's father escorting her to the altar to join her future husband and the formal act of "giving the bride away" as a part of the liturgy, signifies the leaving of one household and the start of a new family unit by the bride and groom. The tradition of selecting a best man and groomsmen as well as a maid of honor and bridesmaids assures that the event will have witnesses to acknowledge the proceedings. The exchange of vows is the partners' public and formal acceptance of their marital responsibilities as husband and wife. The exchange of wedding rings is a token of the bride and groom's love for one another; the circle of the ring is also a symbol of their unending commitment to each other. The proclamation of the couple's new status as husband and wife is made under the authority of the state and, in religious ceremonies, the authority of the church or synagogue. Even the traditions of cutting the wedding cake—a practice which dates from Roman days when a newly wedded couple ate a special cake dedicated to the gods (Mace and Mace, 1960:32–3)—throwing the bridal bouquet, and showering the bride and groom with rice as they leave the wedding are all rich in the symbolic lore which this ceremony has come to possess.

The final symbolic event played out in connection with a wedding is, of course, the honeymoon. Almost every industrialized society supports the practice of a couple withdrawing from social contact with friends and relatives and traveling to a place of seclusion where the newly wedded couple can

A Season for Marriage

begin their life together in a period of rest and relaxation (Gersuny, 1970). While the level of sexual activity on a honeymoon is the subject of considerable joking, the honeymoon does symbolically express the right of individuals who are now married to engage in all the prerogatives of their new family status. Moreover, from a functional point of view, the honeymoon gives the couple a chance to adjust to one another apart from the day-to-day responsibilities they will experience when they return from the honeymoon and set up housekeeping. Thus, despite their weariness from wedding preparations and the residual tension from the ceremony itself, most couples look back upon their honeymoon as a happy way to begin their new life together.

The Marriage Contract

Marriage ceremonies come in a wide variety of forms. Traditional weddings use standard exchanges of vows in which the partners publicly promise to love and cherish each other. Some modern couples prefer to write their own vows and legally can promise whatever both agree is appropriate. For years, one

Figure 6-3
Marriage certificates can be very simple, such as one from a civil ceremony, or quite elaborate, as this Ketubah, a Hebrew marriage scroll. These scrolls are usually hand-painted on parchment. *(Rapho/ Photo Researchers, Inc.)*

New York judge used two standard questions and a quick proclamation to perform marriages: "Do you want to marry her?" "Do you want to marry him?" "You're married" (Dille, 1971:48). Despite its abbreviated form, this ceremony had all the legal force of an extravagant church wedding. The law requires little more than a statement of intentions that the two desire to be married, that they possess a marriage license, and that an official, acting on behalf of the state, pronounces them husband and wife. All marriage ceremonies, in other words, produce the same result; they create a new legal social unit. A couple leave the marriage ceremony with a different status. In a remarkably short span of time, they assume enormous responsibilities and mutual obligations. For this reason, marriage is typically described as a contract.

The legal agreement entered into by the marrying pair differs significantly from civil contracts like a mortgage or a contract between two companies. For example, the details of a **marriage contract** are not clearly spelled out in terms of what each partner promises the other. Some couples have attempted to overcome the ambiguity of the implied obligations by writing a specific contract agreement especially tailored to their marriage. These "**comprehensive marriage contracts**," as they are sometimes called, may define rights and responsibilities that others simply work out as the questions arise. In some instances, the wife promises to help support the family with an outside income. Other couples contract not to have children or to allow their partners sexual relationships outside the marriage bond. Still others specify how each marital partner will be related to kinsfolk and what obligations are binding on them, and some even define the terms of terminating the marriage. Such comprehensive contracts probably could not be enforced through legal action. No court is likely to dissolve a marriage because a husband fails to keep his promise to cook at least three evening meals a week, or because a wife decides that she wants to have children despite her contractual commitment to a childless marriage. Thus, individual marriage contracts may help partners clarify the expectations they have for their life together, but these agreements may well be legally useless.

Many spouses enter marriage equipped with **informal marriage contracts** (Sager, et al., 1971). Marriage counselors use this term to refer to an individual's assumption that his or her spouse has agreed to certain conditions simply by agreeing to marriage; meanwhile, the other partner really had no intention of agreeing to those conditions. A wife, for example, may assume that after they marry, her husband will drop out of his Friday night bowling league and spend the evening with her. Most informal contract expectations relate to role performance and social relationships. Traditionally, however, the state has maintained a strict "hands-off" policy toward husband-wife dynamics unless a partner is threatened with violence or bodily harm. Legal statutes usually pertain only to such matters as property rights, inheritance, family support, and parental liability for minor children. Thus, the critical questions of power relationships, compatibility, allocation of household tasks, and many other matters must be worked out informally and without guidance from the state. Thus, to speak of an informal marriage contract is to use the term contract very loosely. Such contracts help social scientists and marriage counselors clarify the specific content of marital partners' mutual expectations. However, this definitional use should not be confused with a legally binding set of stipulations.

Using contract language has the further advantage of implying that marital dynamics include continuous negotiation between husband and wife. Exchanging vows in a wedding ceremony grants a new status of "married" to a couple, but being married "is not so much a state as an activity" (Henslin, 1980:161). Indeed, Berger and Kellner (1977:8) captured this dynamic aspect of married life in their observation that "marriage in our society is a dramatic act in which two strangers come together and redefine themselves." The new social reality of marriage requires a sharp break with the past for both wife and husband. Now they must adjust their role performance to one another. The result is a period of bargaining as they settle into a mutually recognized pattern of interaction. A few couples develop their "marital style" (Cuber and Harroff, 1965) with relative ease. For most couples, however, the transition period is periodically marked by tears, broken dishes, and emotional reconciliations. These processes are important for working out the finer details of the informal marriage contract by which husbands and wives order their lives.

Thus, in one profound sense, a marriage relationship is "socially constructed" rather than instantaneously achieved through a ceremony. Moreover, unlike negotiations which settle a labor contract between a company and its employees, marital bargaining is a continuing process. As couples move through their life cycle, gain experience, and participate in the changing world about them, they must periodically revise and renew their informal marital contract. These dynamics tend to make marriage interesting, challenging, and a source of enduring personal fulfillment. Conversely, couples who lack the skill, willingness, or patience to bargain fairly are likely to find their marital relationship stagnating and perhaps see their initial love withering away. The question, therefore, is not so much whether a marital pair will function with an informal contract, but whether that contract will be vital, fulfilling, and supportive of mutual affection.

In concluding, we should underscore this point. The formal legal contract comprised in marriage and recognized by the state is not really the most critical aspect for making or breaking a marriage. Far more important than the legal statutes is the informal contract which couples devise to specify their mutual expectations. Marriages fail most often because partners cannot agree on the informal contract's contents, or because one partner believes the other is consistently violating these expectations. In the next chapter on marital adjustment, we shall pursue several features of the informal contract in greater depth and detail.

Marriage is a societal institution regulated by the state through its licensing authority. Marriage is also a social relationship between a wife and husband which, in the American culture, we expect will be based on love. Some cultures strive to repress romantic attachment in marriage, because it might disrupt the larger family system. In American society, however, the opposite norm prevails. Romantic love is a structural necessity within our nuclear family system. Love is the social cement which bonds husband and wife together; it is the motivating force behind the decision of a woman and man to leave their families of orientation and create a new family of procreation.

To be sure, several reasons, besides love, prompt people to enter a marital partnership. Such reasons include societal legitimacy for sexual relations, the legitimate procreation of children, meeting the material needs of family members, the socialization of children, the need for status identity, and societal pressure to marry. These basic reasons for marriage must be compelling, because almost everyone in our society marries at least once. Indeed, almost 95 percent of Americans today will enter the bonds of matrimony. Most will marry in their twenties, and 90 percent of all young people in this society will have married at least once by age 30. Moreover, the vast majority of Americans describe their marriages as "very happy" or "pretty happy." Thus, not only do Americans have one of the world's highest marriage rates, but they also report a very high rate of marital satisfaction.

Marriage is one of the major symbolic events in our life cycle. It serves as a rite of passage which marks a transition to full adulthood. Consequently, the engagement period stands as a public testimony of our love for and intent to marry a specific person. The marriage ceremony itself is filled with symbolism. All of this is designed to signify our transition to a new status and to underscore the solemnity of the vows being exchanged by a bride and groom. Most weddings, therefore, are conducted in a religious setting and in the company of friends and relatives. The verbal promises made by a couple may vary a good deal from traditional vows "to love and cherish one another," or from modern vows written by the partners themselves. But whatever the form, the end result is the same: the formation of a new legal unit comprised of husband and wife.

Marriages are actually a form of contract. In the strict legal sense, marriage is a partnership between a man and a woman recognized by a third party, namely, the state. The formal guidelines of statutory law, however, do not define many issues for family affairs beyond certain property rights, obligations for children, and rights to inheritance. The daily relationship between husband and wife is negotiated as an informal contract. This entails a mutually agreed upon approach to the roles each partner will perform, the tasks each will undertake, and the sort of relationship they will seek. The informal marriage contract is absolutely critical to a successful partnership.

STUDY QUESTIONS

1. How can love between marriage partners be disruptive in some family systems and an essential element in other family systems?
2. Why are legitimate sexual relations and legitimate procreation limited to the institution of marriage, and what benefits are afforded to children because of this concern with legitimacy?
3. Why is there strong social pressure to marry and what subtle forms does this pressure take?
4. Both in terms of who gets married and when, how have the trends related to marriage changed over the course of the twentieth century?
5. What are the symbolic and practical functions arising from the practice of an engagement period before marriage?
6. In what ways is a marriage contract different from other legal contracts? What do social scientists mean when they refer to the "informal contract expectations" in marriage?

A Season for Marriage

A Time to Adjust to Marriage: Making the Partnership Work

7

A traditional marriage ceremony includes a set of vows which are exchanged by the bride and groom in a form similar to this example:

> _____(Name)_____ In taking the (woman/man) whom you hold by the right hand to be your lawful and wedded (wife/husband), I require you to promise to love and cherish (her/him), to honor and sustain (her/him), in sickness as in health, in poverty as in wealth, in the good that may light your ways, in the bad that may darken your days, and to be true to (her/him) in all things until death alone shall part you.
>
> Do you so promise?

Few couples entering marriage for the first time can fully appreciate how difficult these promises are to keep. Newlyweds can differ over an infinite variety of issues. Each such irritation may be trivial by itself, but collectively they can affect the whole relationship between husband and wife. For example, he may like a cigar after dinner; she may discover the odor makes her nauseous. She may wear a new dress; he may fail to notice. She gets tickets for the ballet; he had planned to watch the All-Star baseball game on TV the same evening. She is tired and wants to go to sleep; he wants to watch Johnny Carson. And so it goes.

Learning to Live Together

The first year of marriage produces many surprises. Living together day after day, spouses begin to learn more about each other than when they were just dating. During the mating period, partners often engage in what social scientists describe as an "idealization" of their partners (Schulman, 1974). Bad traits are screened out of one's perception, leaving only the favorable aspects. The intimate contact of marriage has the effect, however, of forcing a more realistic appraisal of one's marriage partner. Consequently, adjustment during the first years of marriage generally means solving some problems. In this chapter, we shall examine the processes involved in establishing a stable marriage relationship. In later chapters, other marital adjustments will be explored—such as the changes that occur after the birth of children, the establishment of a full family household, and the coming of retirement.

The Cultural Shock of Marriage

Marriage brings about an abrupt and almost total social change in our lifestyle and behavior. More and more single adults are living away from home, supporting themselves, and enjoying a great deal of freedom for some time before they marry (Social Indicators, 1976:42). The carefree behavior of both the man and the woman is drastically curtailed when they exchange marital vows. Marriage requires spouses to consult each other when they plan activities.

Most people notice the change more immediately in the little decisions. No longer can you dash out to a late movie or grab a hamburger simply on a whim, especially if your spouse is not in the mood. No more can you work late without calling home to say that you will be delayed. Socializing is more and more oriented toward other couples rather than single friends. Even relationships with relatives are often subtly changed. Expenditures of money also must be made jointly. No longer is one quite as free to save or splurge according to one's own preference. The spouse also has a legitimate claim on collective financial resources and a voice in deciding how money is to be spent.

Thus, no matter how much couples may love one another and look forward to married life, the actual experience of living together, adjusting one's lifestyle, and accommodating one's routine to the needs of a spouse is almost always something of a cultural shock.

Undoubtedly, the wife still makes the most serious adjustments during the first year or so of marriage. Becoming a wife entails a number of immediate changes. The wife's last name usually changes; his doesn't. Names are a critical aspect of our identity. Now, however, the wife must use her husband's name to identify herself, write checks, sign letters, and to fill out the usual forms encountered in everyday life. After the wedding, the bride is a wife, a *homemaker* (Lopata, 1972). Moreover, because it is customary in our society for women to be employed before marriage and because most continue in their jobs until the birth of the first child (Bebbington, 1973), the wife usually performs in two jobs during the first years of marriage. One is outside the home and the other is running the household.

While the role of wife is gradually learned over time, the role of homemaker is often assumed less spontaneously. Today, young women frequently lack the training in homemaking skills which their grandmothers received. Thus, a new wife is often thrust into a social position in which she may have only a slight interest, and for which she has had little preparation. She must quickly train herself and her husband to organize the household. A helpful husband can be a decided asset, of course. Yet, he is not likely to be any more competent than she in most areas of domestic maintenance. And whatever the husband's role, it is still usually the wife who is held responsible for the condition of the home.

No one says that this allocation of responsibility is fair. It is, however, almost universal in our culture. Ann Oakley (1974:29) referred directly to this issue when she observed that, "not only is the housewife role specifically a feminine role, it is also women's major occupational role today: the responsibility for running a home is one which is shared by the majority of all adult women." Furthermore, this new set of tasks can be an enormous psychological and physical burden. As women gain more experience, they generally achieve greater competence and satisfaction from their homemaker role (Lopata, 1972). Unfortunately, that satisfaction scarcely compensates for the difficult problem of adjustment wives often encounter at the outset of their marriages.

Like the new wife, the new husband also must adjust his life-style to accommodate another person. He may feel the loss of freedom more acutely than she. In addition, most husbands feel much more pressured to perform effectively as breadwinners. Even if his wife is still employed, the husband understands that he is responsible for paying the rent, meeting the car payments, and honoring other financial obligations. This imposes on most new husbands the need for more careful economic planning than they had done before marriage. Usually, husbands are as ill prepared to make financial decisions as their wives are to assume homemaker tasks. Inexperience in both areas can breed anxiety and mistakes in judgment. However, sharing as full partners can help reduce the tensions which a newly married couple often encounters.

The Need for Compromise Between Marriage Partners

Compromise is a key word in successful marriages. Marital adjustment can be very difficult if each partner always insists on having his or her own way. Of course, some compromises can be destructive. Nothing is really gained, for example, if she wants to go out to a movie and he wants to go bowling, and they compromise by watching situation comedies on television, which interests neither of them. Such a mutually unsatisfying activity will simply produce more tension.

However, developing competence in the art of compromise requires more than a willingness to seek an adequate solution. Kiernan and Tallman (1972) isolated three major components of adaptability which contribute to successful adjustment. They were flexibility, empathy, and the motivation to accommodate to the other person's point of view. Increasing one's skills in each of these areas can help a couple adapt and move toward stable adjustment. Some marriage partners find compromise relatively easy right from the start. For others, adapting is more difficult and requires conscious effort. Couples who fail to develop these skills may not be more inclined to divorce, but their marriage may be ridden with conflicts and become less than satisfying.

CLOSE-UP

Husbands, Wives, and Rivals

Shortly after the big break in the "Son of Sam" case, two broadcasting executives—one in radio, the other in television—reached from the bed to the telephone. It was the same bed, but two phones—and one of them was dead.

"Damn," said Jo Moring, news director of the NBC Radio Network, slamming down the black phone and reaching for the white one. At that, Jerry Moring, news manager of WNBC-TV and owner of the white phone, growled, "Hands off."

"But," she said, "I must call my desk."

"Fine," he said, "after I call my desk."

Love did not fly out the window. Though their career paths have converged, veered off, and at times collided, the Morings' seven-year marriage is still on the track.

. . . What complicates life for the Morings and other ambitious couples is that their professional interests are sometimes at odds. These are couples in which he and she may be vying for the same job, in which his and her advertising agencies are making a pitch for the same account, in which both of their publishing houses are bidding on the same book.

True, working for rival businesses is not the only way for marital partners to get ahead in the same field. An increasingly popular route is to become professional partners. More and more Mom and Pop law firms, medical practices, art studios, and ad agencies are opening every day.

On the other hand, now that so many employers have scrapped old policies against hiring husbands and wives, some couples find themselves working for the same company, though generally not in the same department.

. . . Other couples compete indirectly. That is, their companies compete, whether or not they care to acknowledge the fact. As the couples tell it, their individual employers differ so in size and style that rarely do their interests clash. Still, there are moments.

For Gretchen Raker, the moment came the day she accepted an advertising job with Ogilvy & Mather Inc. Glancing around the office, Miss Raker's eye fell on a container of New Country Yogurt and, in her words, "my stomach fell."

"Are you, uh, eating it or pitching it?" she asked, pointing to the yogurt.

"Pitching it," replied the man from Ogilvy.

In ad talk, that meant Ogilvy was shooting for the account. So, oddly enough, was MCA-Graham. Miss Raker knew this because she knew MCA-Graham's managing director, John Andes. They were living together at the time.

Well, neither agency got the account, but Miss Raker and Mr. Andes got married several months ago, and since then they have pondered how to handle future rivalry between their agencies, should it arise.

"That's always unpleasant," conceded Miss Raker, an assistant account executive. "You have to either trust the other person or just not talk about it."

"It's better not to talk specifics," Mr. Andes added, "A lot of my business is confidential, as is hers."

Most competing couples would go along with that. Trade secrets, sales figures, even seemingly harmless interoffice gossip should not become "pillow talk," as several put it. In fact, Marcia Grace, a creative group head with Wells Rich Greene, and Roy Grace, creative director at Doyle Dan Bernbach, have what they call a Gentleperson's Agreement to this effect.

Said Mrs. Grace: "If something is really privy, I shred it mentally."

More often than not, said Preben Bast, fur director at Lord & Taylor, the secrets he keeps from his wife, Greta Bast, fur buyer for Henri Bendel, would probably put her to sleep.

"But if it's something about store policy," he went on, "and I have been told to tell nobody, that means nobody—not even Greta."

. . . Similarly, Sally and Stewart Richardson's publishing jobs seem fairly noncompetitive on the surface. As director of subsidiary rights for St. Martin's Press, she sells. As editor-in-chief at Doubleday, he buys.

No conflicts?

"It has happened that we were both lying in bed reading the same manuscript," Mrs. Richardson recalled. "When we found out, we agreed not to talk about it."

. . . Offsetting the competitive moments are many more harmonious hours, according to couples wedded to the same profession. When she stays after work

(continued)

to drink with a client, he understands. When he flys off on a sudden business trip, she understands. In some cases, their busy times and business trips coincide.

The Basts, for example, attend the American and European fur shows together. "In the fur business we are considered competitors," she said, laughing, "but sometimes we are seated side by side. It's kind of sweet."

The Richardsons travel each year to the Frankfurt Book Fair. "It's lovely," she said, "because we can double up and do a lot of entertaining, not the sort of parties where one partner feels like a fish out of water."

Of all the competing couples, Jo and Jerry Moring can look back on the most varied job arrangements. In the course of their high-powered careers, they have worked for several stations and she has worked in both mediums. There were times when he was her boss, when they were based in different cities, when she was with ABC, and he was with NBC, when they were slugging on rival softball teams.

Now both are part of the NBC family at 30 Rockefeller Plaza—one in radio, the other in television. The chances for competition would seem slim, but don't bet on it.

—Georgia Dullea,
excerpted from *The New York Times*

Organizing a Household

Marriage creates a new family. Since the normal pattern in America is for husband and wife to live apart from their families of orientation, a new household must be constructed once a marital union has been established. Organizing a household usually suggests certain physical activities, such as finding an apartment or house, securing the necessary furnishings, utensils, and appliances, and decorating the rooms. All these tasks are really the easy part of setting up a household. The most difficult aspect is the *social* organization of the new family unit. Spouses must learn to function within the various social roles accorded to husbands and wives; they must share power, and assign themselves certain tasks. In addition, they must learn to cooperate in the running of the household. We shall examine each of these issues briefly.

The Social Roles Associated with the Position of Husband

The traditional American role identified the husband's duties in terms of rights, powers, and privileges (Scanzoni, 1975: 35–7). He was to be head of the household, a good provider, moderate in his sexual demands and faithful to his wife, firm but affectionate toward their children, free from such disruptive habits as drunkenness, and careful not to interfere with his wife's daily running of the household. Jessie Bernard (1965: 687–8) describes these traditional role expectations for the husband as an instance of a **"parallel pat-**

A Season for Marriage

tern" of development. By this she means that the husband lives primarily in a male world sharply different from his spouse's domain. His orientation is toward his own duties, obligations, life, and recreation, rather than toward his partner's personality and companionship needs.

Since at least the turn of the century this traditional role has shifted toward a greater interaction between husbands and wives. For the husband, this change has triggered a succession of major modifications, along with a fundamental reorientation of his privileges and power. No longer is the husband the undisputed head of the household. Major decisions are now the joint responsibility of spouses (Blood and Wolfe, 1965:11–46). Nor is the husband likely to be the sole breadwinner (Waite, 1976; Oppenheimer, 1977). The growing number of working wives has increased the need for husbands to share regular household tasks. However, the most significant change has been a demand for more personal involvement between marriage partners. Such interaction helps to integrate the worlds of the spouses rather than keep them on separate, parallel tracks. The husband expects to find his most intimate, fulfilling, and intense social relationship with his wife. In short, his dominant role is that of companion to his marriage partner.

The Social Roles Associated with the Position of Wife

Changes in the husband's role prompt changes in the roles of the wife, since both are defined in relation to one another. For example, the decrease in the husband's power simultaneously increases the decision-making power allocated to his wife. In the traditional understanding of the wife's roles, women related passively to their husbands and avoided exercising power in the household. According to the norms of the traditional parallel pattern, a good wife kept a clean house, cooked reasonably well, did not nag her husband, was a willing sexual partner, and took good care of the children (Bernard, 1964:687). The wife's social life was directed primarily toward other women in the neighborhood, church or synagogue, or in the family. Above all, she was not to interfere in her husband's life so as to make him unwilling to provide for the family.

When Burgess and Locke (1953) titled their influential text on marriage and family life, *The Family: From Institution to Companionship*, they summed up what they regarded as the dominant trend reshaping the very foundations of marriage and family life in American society. Looking back, it would be hard to argue with that judgment. The introduction of affection and consensus between marital partners as the foundation of family unity effectively realigned the roles of wife and husband to conform to the norm of companionship. For modern Americans, the companionate relationship means that they seek from marriage "someone to do things with, someone to love, someone to talk to," although perhaps not always in that order (Scanzoni, 1970:26).

Another notable result of the companionate relationship is the redefinition of marital success and adequate role performance for both husband and wife. No longer is success based on such skills as cooking, cleaning, or child rearing. Of greater importance is the ability of the wife to enter into a satisfying relationship with her husband. If she can feel and express love for her mate, share his search for fulfillment and allow him to support her own aspirations, then both partners are likely to rate their marriage as happy and successful—even if she has little interest in excelling in the traditional homemaker skills. On the other hand, a spouse who fails to achieve such personal involvement may become the object of severe criticism. The hostility and frustration created by a failure to develop interpersonal intimacy is always expressed though it may be displaced (McCary, 1980:278). For example, a husband may fault his wife for slovenliness about the house or slackness with their children when he actually is angry because he suspects that she no longer feels any affection for him. Similarly, a wife may complain of her husband's failure to make enough money when her real complaint is that he does not give her his attention or he is indifferent to her need for personal fulfillment. Dirty dishes or an uncut lawn are far less likely to cause marital strife when a couple is bound by a strong affectional relationship.

Thus, the social roles of both husband and wife have shifted in recent years from a predominant concern with the performance of tasks to the quality of personal interaction between the partners. Above all else, husband and wife are expected to be loving, concerned for one another, and united in a companionate relationship. Successful adjustment to interpersonal relationships can offset poor performance in other aspects of the traditional husband and wife roles. Genuine lovers are ready to tolerate the shortcomings they may discover in their marriage partners.

Power Relations in the Family

Power is an attribute of every social group from a children's play group to a complex nation-state. All groups create power and all groups exercise power in their decision-making processes. The family is no exception. Because marriage forms two people into a new social group which must make collective decisions, the minimal conditions are set for the development of power relations. **Power** is used here to mean the ability of an individual to impose her or his will on another person, and thereby influence the behavior of other members of a social group, despite their resistance (Weber, 1958a:180). Moreover, power is fluid and subject to rapid changes. For example, the love that links the partners in a successful marriage strongly affects each partner's power and the manner in which they can wield it in the family. Therefore, love between spouses does not eliminate the need for power. But it does alter the distribution and use of power by family members.

Generally speaking, power is exercised primarily by the family's adult leaders, the wife and the husband. Basically, power can be distributed between these two adults in three ways. The husband may monopolize power, the wife may monopolize it, or it may be more or less shared equally between husband and wife. We need to examine each of these arrangements briefly, for they have quite different consequences for family relations as a whole.

A Season for Marriage

The Husband-Dominant Pattern The most extreme case of husband dominance arises in a pure patriarchal system, such as in the ancient Hebrew and
Roman cultures examined in Chapter 2. In American society, patriarchalism
was never the norm, but a milder form of husband dominance, often called
paternalism, did prevail as the basic model for power relations until roughly
1900 (Blood and Wolfe, 1965:16–7). **Paternalism** was based on a cultural
tradition in which the husband and father was viewed as the family's protector, breadwinner, disciplinarian, decision maker, and ultimate authority in all
family disputes (Sennett, 1980:54). However, from the 1920s on, a number of
factors led to the decline of male superiority in marriage. It was becoming
commonplace for women to work before marriage. Women continued to help
support their families after marriage and sometimes even after the birth of
children. Moreover, educational opportunities for women increased dramatically, providing them not only with marketable skills but also with the confidence to cope with the outside world. Gradually, too, wives' decision-making
abilities were recognized. As the myth of female dependency declined, discontent with the husband-dominant pattern became widespread. Greater participation by women in economic activities, their acquisition of voting rights,
and higher educational achievement, as well as other forces, strengthened
their position in marriage. The basic change did not occur simultaneously in
all social classes and ethnic groups (McLaughlin, 1973). The urban, educated
upper middle class was the vanguard, producing generation after generation
of women who were more independent, socially skilled, and competent in
money matters. From this group, for example, leaders emerged to fight for
the right to vote, to disseminate birth-control information, and to provide
greater employment opportunities. Moreover, as women assumed more social
power outside the household, they resisted playing a passive role in family
decisions. Liberation in the family and society mutually reinforced each other
and spread throughout the several quarters of American social life. Paternalism as an acceptable mode of defining power relations between husband and
wife gradually become obsolete. It was replaced by an equalitarian standard
for sharing power in family decision making.

The Wife-Dominant Pattern Fewer couples admit to living within a wife-
dominant system than within any other of the types. This is not really surprising, given the traditional legitimation of the husband's leading role in family decision making. Research to date has discovered several variables which
tend to increase the amount of conjugal power enjoyed by wives. Wife-dominant households, for example, are clustered in low-status families. Indeed,
the decision-making power of husbands increases with higher education, income, and social status (Blood and Wolfe, 1965:30–6). Race is another important factor prompting wife dominance in family patterns. Black families are
almost two times as likely to be led by females or dominated by wives as
white families, largely because of job discrimination, low educational level,
and the type of socialization experienced by black males (Schultz, 1969; Vincent, 1970:338–9; and Farley, 1977:199–200). An employed wife also enjoys

a far greater role in decision making than an unemployed wife, since her contribution to family resources puts her in a better bargaining position to insist that her desires are satisfied (Scanzoni, 1970:159–61). And finally, the power of wives tends to change over the course of the family life cycle. Middle age appears to be the age of peak wife dominance, a time when wives have apparently gained enough self-confidence and experience so that they can wield far more power than younger women in family affairs (Blood and Wolfe, 1965:41–44).

Wife-and-Husband Equality   Most Americans now believe that a balance of power should exist between marriage partners. Democratizing marital relations is something which Americans could not oppose without contradicting their basic social values. However, supporting decision-making equality is often easier said than done, especially for new husbands who have just mastered the finer points of the masculine sex role. Ray Baber (1953:213) recounts a still typical experience for many new husbands when he describes a young man who is proud of his fiancée's spunk and "ability to stand on her own two feet." But when she continues to act that way after the wedding, her independence suddenly loses some of its luster. She opens a charge account or agrees to go out of town for the weekend on a company business trip or makes a major purchase, all without telling him. He becomes irritated. As a man, of course, he probably would have made similar decisions without first checking with her. He also will be somewhat embarrassed when he realizes that his reaction is based on the lingering remnants of a double standard of behavior. Yet, the traditional assumption that the husband should be the head of the household is difficult to eliminate, even when a husband is himself committed to the principle of equality.

A true balance of power presents partners with other problems beyond occasional backsliding in their domestic decision making. One of the more serious issues is the meaning of equality. At first glance, the answer appears obvious. But one must remember that power is a concept which covers a wide range of perceptions and behaviors. Frequently, spouses' perceptions about the exercise of power do not coincide with their behavior (Rollins and Bahr, 1976). These discrepancies between belief and behavior also pose a thorny problem for research undertaken by social scientists. Are reports of equalitarian decision making by family participants reliable or are some respondents revealing their biased perceptions rather than their actual conduct? To control for this possibility, researchers Centers, Raven, and Rodriques (1971) constructed a study focused on a number of decisions, some traditionally made by husbands and others by wives. They discovered that their subjects actually did display a great deal of equality in the decision-making processes.

Another finding, which built upon the earlier work of Blood and Wolfe (1965), confirmed that basically equality could be achieved in two ways. Some couples adhered to a **syncratic model,** in which all major decisions were made equally by husband and wife. More common by far, however, was the **autonomic pattern.** In these cases, the husband and wife each took major responsibility for decisions in the areas in which each was deemed to possess superior skill. Both the syncratic and autonomic forms are equalitarian types of power relationships, but they use equality in rather different ways. Moreover, it is worth noting that 86 percent of the subjects in this study fell within these two types of equalitarian authority structures. The syncratic model was reported as typical of their marriages by 16 percent of the men and 20 percent of the women, while the autonomic pattern was regarded as describing the marriages of 70 percent of the men and 67 percent of the women in this group. Only 10 percent of the men and 9 percent of the women in the research population reported their marriages were husband dominant, while only 4 percent of both men and women considered their marriages wife dominant. Another study by Dyer (1979:367–8) found similar patterns of equalitarianism. In power relations, 84.5 percent of the families were strongly equalitarian and only 3 percent were traditional in their husband dominance. That is to say, 90 percent of the women held strongly equalitarian family expectations and 84.5 percent of the men were similarly inclined. These data suggest, then, that both in terms of belief and behavior the traditional pattern of male dominance has been superseded in American life by a form of equalitarianism. Even if the change has not come easily, especially for husbands who have had to relinquish some of their power and authority, the change has, nonetheless, come.

Decision Making in the Family and Task Allocation

One of the first major steps in organizing a household is assigning particular tasks to the husband or wife. In every family, certain jobs must be done to sustain the marital unit and maintain the standard of living appropriate to its status. Someone must shop for groceries, shovel snow, wash the clothes, service the car, pay the bills, fix the meals, and do dozens of other chores. To meet these responsibilities efficiently, partners divide the labor, so that each one accepts a specific group of tasks. Even in a household of only husband and wife, one partner alone cannot keep the family working smoothly. Determining how duties will be shared is a major decision-making process which is also one of the first tests of how equalitarian a couple's marriage actually will be. Fortunately, the early decisions can be changed and tasks reassigned if the first division of labor seems unfair or some tasks are clearly assigned to the wrong person.

Tasks normally are not allocated on a random basis, however. Criteria exist which can guide couples in dividing household labor. Some of the more common criteria are:

Physical Abilities In American society, women almost always marry men who are larger than they. This help assure that most husbands will be physically stronger than their wives. Consequently, men are often assigned the physically demanding tasks. The myth of male physical prowess—which is

only partially based on biological fact since many women are larger and stronger than some men—earns most husbands the dubious honor of shoveling the walk, painting the house, mowing the lawn, moving the furniture about, and performing those other jobs which require brawn. Of course, when one partner has a physical handicap, task allocation tends to take this fact into account.

Expertise Husband and wife bring to marriage unique experiences in which each has developed a separate set of skills and talents. For example, when a young woman with a degree in accounting marries a man who majored in fine arts, she is likely to be assigned the task of managing the household budget, while her husband may take the lead in selecting the artwork, picking out the color scheme, and generally assuming responsibility for decorating the house. When one partner has clearly superior skills, couples normally try to turn that expertise to their common advantage.

Natural Affinities Just as partners bring different skills to marriage, they also bring different interests. A husband may discover, for instance, that he enjoys the challenge of fixing meals, even though he has had little experience in the kitchen. If the wife finds cooking a tedious and unrewarding chore, she can be expected to willingly agree that he should pursue his innate interest as the household chef. She, on the other hand, may enjoy working with tools. Hence, a trade-off can be worked out, making her responsible for repair jobs around the house. However, natural affinity for a given task does not automatically guarantee that the interested person will perform it competently. Our hypothetical young couple may eat a number of inferior meals and put up with a few inadequate repair jobs before each partner finally masters the tasks they agreed to undertake. Usually, however, we manage to develop skills in those areas which are basically interesting to us.

Societal Conventions Particularly during the first years of marriage, tasks are frequently prescribed for one sex on the basis of expectations set by our cultural tradition. It is simply taken for granted that certain activities are female dominated, and others are male dominated. Even today, few wives really question the fact that they will be responsible for fixing the meals and their husbands will be responsible for mowing the lawn. Most husbands assume as a matter of course that buying and maintaining the family car is primarily their task. The tendency to follow societal conventions which link specific household tasks to sex-role definitions is more common among working-class households than white-collar families (Shostak, 1969:126–33). In

Figure 7-2
Many household tasks need not be divided; spouses can do them together and share the workload. (© *Suzanne Szasz, Photo Researchers, Inc.*)

contrast, college-educated couples drawn from the upper middle class are least likely to adhere to a division of labor based on traditional sex roles.

Partner Consensus Many everyday activities remain which do not clearly fall to either partner. Dropping off clothes at the dry cleaner, shopping for groceries, and paying the bills are just a few. Not one of these tasks really requires any skill or physical strength; nor does sexual stereotyping assign these tasks to one partner. Thus, couples must work out who will perform each one. Highly personal factors may weigh heavily in their decisions. A wife who does not drive may find it difficult to get to the supermarket, and so it is agreed that the husband will shop for food on his way home from work. Or again, the wife may decide she ought to know something about the family finances, so she offers to keep track of the money and pay the bills. Some tasks may be allocated simply to be fair. For example, if one does the cooking, then the other cleans up the kitchen and washes the dishes. Quite clearly,

---

TEST YOURSELF

On How Household Tasks Should Be Divided Between Husbands and Wives

Each of the statements below has actually been used in a social scientific survey. These items are designed to test how you feel tasks should be divided in the areas of child rearing, household chores, finances, and family decision making. After each statement, circle whether you agree strongly (AS), agree mildly (AM), disagree mildly (DM), or disagree strongly (DS). Under each choice is a numerical score. Add up all of your scores when you have completed the self-test (note that sometimes the scores range from 1 to 4, while on other questions the scores are from 4 to 1). If your score is between 60 and 45, you probably favor equality in the division of household tasks. A score between 15 and 30 would indicate a strongly traditional view of sex role division of tasks. A score between 30 and 45 would indicate moderate traditionalism or moderate equalitarianism.

1. Child Rearing

In general, the father should have greater authority than the mother in the bringing up of children.

AS	AM	DM	DS
1	2	3	4

Parental authority and responsibility for discipline of the children should be equally divided between husband and wife.

AS	AM	DM	DS
4	3	2	1

If a child gets sick and his wife works, the husband should be just as willing as she to stay home from work and take care of that child.

AS	AM	DM	DS
4	3	2	1

Raising children is more a mother's job than a father's.

AS	AM	DM	DS
1	2	3	4

A Season for Marriage

2. Household Chores

Men should share the work around the house with women such as doing the dishes, cleaning, and so forth.

AS	AM	DM	DS
4	3	2	1

Only when the wife works should the husband help with housework.

AS	AM	DM	DS
1	2	3	4

In general, men should leave the housework to women.

AS	AM	DM	DS
1	2	3	4

If a man is working to support the family, his wife has no right to expect him to work when he is home.

AS	AM	DM	DS
1	2	3	4

3. Finances

Married women should keep their money and spend it as they please.

AS	AM	DM	DS
4	3	2	1

As head of the household, the husband should have more responsibility for the family's financial plans than his wife.

AS	AM	DM	DS
1	2	3	4

The husband has in general no obligation to inform his wife of his financial plans.

AS	AM	DM	DS
1	2	3	4

Husbands and wives should be equal partners in planning the family budget.

AS	AM	DM	DS
4	3	2	1

4. Family Decision Making

A wife should not have equal authority with her husband in making decisions.

AS	AM	DM	DS
1	2	3	4

In marriage, the husband should make the major decisions.

AS	AM	DM	DS
1	2	3	4

In the family, both of the spouses ought to have as much say on important matters.

AS	AM	DM	DS
4	3	2	1

Source: Karen Oppenheim Mason, with the assistance of Daniel R. Denison and Anita J. Schacht. *Tax-Role Attitude Items and Scales From U.S. Sample Surveys.* Rockville, Md.: National Institute of Mental Health. 1975, pp. 16–19.

too, the distribution of tasks when no criteria apply can provoke power struggles between a husband and wife. Indeed, achieving agreement on some tasks may be an elusive goal.

Departures from the conventional division of labor are signs of increasing equality between partners. Husbands can no longer simply tell their wives which jobs they will perform around the house. Nor are couples willing to allow social conventions to prescribe their household responsibilities. Unfortunately, however, decision making in task allocation, as in other areas of family deliberations, does not always proceed harmoniously. Conflict is an inevitable result of living together. In the next section, we shall focus on typical forms of marital strife and some strategies to cope with conflict.

Major Forms of Marital Strife

No matter how compatible a couple is, no matter how deeply in love they are, disagreements will arise between them as surely as night follows day. Some institutions are predicated on violence, and hence are not surprised by its emergence. We expect politics to be a struggle for power. Business is based on competition. But the institution of marriage is founded on love. Thus, conflict in family life is often regarded as abnormal. Such a view is clearly misguided and naive. Love and hostility, attraction and antagonism are inseparable aspects of intimate human relations (Freud, 1962a:64–80; Simmel, 1964). Lewis Coser (1964:85) goes somewhat further by suggesting that the "absence of conflict" does not mean that persons have a strong and stable relationship. Closeness gives rise to social strife. It is more often those persons who view their relationship as tenuous and fragile who avoid conflict altogether. Thus, the ability to engage in mild forms of conflict is a useful index of marriage partners' trust in each other and commitment to their marital union.

Conflict becomes abnormal in family affairs only when it is not adequately controlled. Aggressive feelings must be vented periodically, if marriage partners are to maintain stable personalities. However, a large part of marital adjustment is learning how to expel these hostilities without saying or doing something which permanently damages the marital relationship. Adjustment is easier when we know the typical problems in married life. Once these causes of strife have been explored, various strategies for discharging tensions and handling marital conflict can be more fruitfully examined.

The Problem of Money

An observation recorded by the Old Testament author of Ecclesiastes applies to the problems of money. The comment has an unbiblical, yet peculiarly modern ring to it. Ecclesiastes (10:19) says: "Bread is made for laughter, and wine gladdens life, but money answers everything."

This obviously is an overstatement. Yet beneath the cynicism stirs an element of truth. A major cause of marital conflict is a lack of money. This holds true not only for newlywed couples or couples with very low incomes, but for almost all families in America. Lloyd Saxton (1980:547) estimates that perhaps 98 percent of the households in the United States never have "enough" money. As income increases, so does the perceived need for material possessions suitable to one's status. Thus, higher-income families generally carry higher levels of debt than middle or low-income families. There is always a long list of items to be purchased, if only the family income were a few thousand dollars more.

Clearly, then, identifying money as a major problem in marriage does not mean that most families lack the basic necessities of food, clothing, and shelter—although we do have a large number of citizens who suffer a level of material deprivation that is quite unnecessary in our affluent society. The material possessions a family "needs," however, vary according to their social status. In an achievement-oriented society, money represents the means to establish a standard of living at a given status position (Lipset, 1963:101–39; Coser, 1969:viii–ix). The American dream of "getting ahead" is primarily a desire to raise our status position above that of our parents. Exchange theorists suggest that this process differs for men and women. Men achieve primarily through occupational success, while most women must realize their mobility goals primarily through marriage to an upwardly mobile male (Goode, 1966:593). Not all social scientists, however, are convinced that attractive but lower-status women exchange their desirable physical features for a husband who offers occupational prestige, wealth, or high family status. Taylor and Glenn (1976), in particular, recently have suggested that this interpretation may be a bit too simplistic, but they did not have enough data to dismiss the hypothesis entirely.

Generally speaking, the dominant American value of achievement is a strong motivating force which instills a desire for upward social mobility among most members of our society. Achievement is symbolized by income which largely determines one's standard of living. When Americans complain of never having "enough money," they really are saying that their status aspirations still exceed their economic resources. As long as people's aspirations exceed the reality of their situations, money is likely to be a source of marital strife. Furthermore, while working-class couples feel the pinch of limited financial resources most acutely (Goode, 1965:69–75; Rubin, 1976:70–80), money problems certainly are not limited to this class group. Indeed, if the exchange theorists are even partially correct, a large number of women are frustrated because their husbands' occupational success has not brought them the full measure of upward mobility they had expected when they married (Jorgensen, 1977). This could easily be an enduring source of marital disappointment.

A final comment on money matters touches upon a more practical aspect. A skillful piece of research undertaken by Galligan and Bahr (1978) revealed that a family's level of income was not a very accurate predictor of marital strife and instability. The key factor in promoting marital stability was a cou-

ple's skill in using their income wisely. When money was foolishly spent so that the family had no accumulated assets to show for its labors, conflicts over money swiftly arose. These researchers concluded that money management was far more important to marital harmony than level of income. Married couples quarrel more over money when they lack a family budget, splurge irrationally on luxury items, or when one partner believes the other is making personal expenditures which are unnecessary or wasteful. This mishandling of family resources can squander the funds needed to cover basic necessities. As a result, family members may be thrust into a situation which is embarrassing, anxiety-ridden, and a full of strife. If financial planning and spending restraint are not introduced, real deprivation, despair, and, in extreme cases, divorce can result.

Of all the adjustments marriage requires, money management is probably the most important—and the least fun. Conserving one's limited financial resources is seldom a thrilling experience, particularly when newlywed couples are eager to acquire such expensive items as new furniture, a car, major appliances, or basic household necessities. Too often, couples run up an enormous debt during the first year or so of marriage while the wife is still working, and then she becomes pregnant with their first child. Suddenly, on top of their accumulated debt, they are hit with a double blow—the expenses of having a child and the loss of the wife's income. If nothing has been set aside for this situation, a couple may need years to become financially solvent again. Situations such as these are tailor-made for bitter family quarrels and years of anxiety.

Marriage makes sexual relations between husband and wife legitimate. However, a marriage license does not, as Eric Berne (1970:218) aptly observes, make a spouse a good sexual partner anymore than a driver's license makes a good driver. Sexuality is learned behavior. We are endowed with a sex drive, but the techniques of sexual performance are not automatic, inborn abilities. Moreover, marital sexual behavior is not only a physiological relationship; it embraces psychological and cultural aspects as well. Therefore, how a husband and wife adjust to one another in their sexual relations is deeply influenced by their attitudes and knowledge about sexual matters.

Most couples enter marriage with high expectations for sexual fulfillment. The transition in sexual relations from the single to the married state is seldom as easy in reality as it is in the partners' idealization of their sexual life. When society and parents attempt to control premarital sex among young people by suggesting that sex is wrong, dirty, or immoral, they may well increase the difficulties of newlywed couples who are trying to enter into legitimate sexual relations without a lingering sense of guilt that their behavior is tinged by depravity (Nixon, 1964:133). Some partners simply take longer to adjust to their new marital status and participate freely and comfortably in its sexual opportunities. It is difficult to forget the old rules about premarital sexuality the instant one says "I do" and begins to play under the new rules of married life.

Moreover, marital sexuality tends to differ markedly from premarital activity (Hunt, 1964:168–80). One function of the dating-mating process has been to link romantic love more closely to sex (Moneymaker and Montanino, 1980:29–34). Heavy petting, whether or not it ends in intercourse, is part of the new sexual mores which Reiss (1964:126–45) labeled "permissiveness with affection." After marriage, lovemaking soon evolves toward quite a different pattern. The long periods of intimacy and heavy petting are replaced with watching television, reading, or puttering around the house doing a thousand and one odd jobs. At bedtime, however, a husband may suddenly be ready for sexual activity without any warning. Because women are culturally conditioned to take longer to become sexually aroused and because they are accustomed to romantic foreplay from their dating period, a wife may quickly come to feel that her husband is taking her for granted and treating sex like a mechanical act rather than an expression of love.

The trap of an apparently dull or routine sex life can be avoided if couples will remember a few basic facts about their relationship. First, as Pierson and D'Antonio (1974:73) observe, "seduction is essential to good sex." (Seduction here is used to mean foreplay, heavy petting, and mutual expressions of affection). Second, the husband is not the only partner responsible for initiating sexual activity. Equalitarianism is as appropriate in a couple's sex life as it is in their power relations and decision making. Third, too much emphasis on technique and performance can interfere with a couple's ability to derive the pleasure they want from sex. Newlywed couples who are fresh from reading a whole stack of "how-to" manuals may become so tense about remembering all the "do's" and "don'ts" of marital sex life that it is reduced to an initial series of frustrating failures. Americans tend to approach every activity in terms of the "work ethic." For example, we cannot just play golf; we have to work on our slice. We cannot just bowl; we have to "perfect our delivery." If we take the same approach to our sex lives, it can be deadly. Love is not a performance and sex is not an activity one needs to scrutinize for possible errors like a high school quarterback who studies last Friday night's game. Above all, sexual relations are an expression of affection, commitment, and gratitude. Finally, young married couples should remember that good sexual adjustment requires a sense of humor, an ability to laugh at oneself, one's bungling efforts, and one's failures and successes. Humor is the sign of a relaxed mood without pretensions. It helps place sex in the proper perspective. Unfortunately, marriage manuals and sexual how-to books, in their zealous effort to promote marital fulfillment, tend to convey the message that, unless young couples get their sex life in order and soon, their marriage is likely to end up on the rocks. David Reuben, M.D., the author of the best-selling book, *Everything You Wanted to Know About Sex—But Were Afraid to Ask* (1969), provides a typical example of such overstatement. He claims (1971:363):

> The only way for a wife to find true sexual fulfillment in marriage is to make it her primary goal. She must be willing to cast aside everything else in life that might come between herself and her husband.

The truth of the matter is that sexual fulfillment, while an important aspect of any contemporary marriage, is still not the sum and substance of a couple's life together. Or, to be somewhat more exact, the importance of marital relations tends to vary a great deal between husband and wife, among social classes, and from one historical period to the next.

In this connection, too, some sociological data are interesting. It reveals that couples who are satisfied overall with their marriages enjoy more active and rewarding sex lives. On the other hand, couples with active sex lives generally rate their marriages as more satisfactory (Reiss, 1980:280–85). Does sex make for a good marriage, or does a good marriage make for good sex? The probability is that marital satisfaction and sexuality reinforce each other. Of course, when answering the questions of a social survey, most couples will reply that their sex life could be improved, just as most couples would agree that their families could benefit from a higher income. More important to marital adjustment is whether sexual incompatibility frequently leads to marriage failure and divorce. Unfortunately, the answer must be less clear-cut than the question, for the dissolution of a marriage is usually such a complex process that partners cannot always discern the sources of their discord. Kinsey (1948:544) perhaps put it best when he stated:

> Sexual adjustments are not the only problems involved in marriage, and often they are not even the most important factors in marital adjustments. . . . Nevertheless, sexual maladjustments contribute in perhaps three-quarters of the upper level marriages that end in separation and divorce, and in some smaller percentage of the lower level marriages that break up.

The critical phrase would appear to be that ". . . sexual maladjustments *contribute* . . ." to marriage failures, but Kinsey carefully avoids proposing that sexual incompatibility *causes* separation or divorce. In a similar fashion, even marital infidelity often seems to result from factors other than dramatically different sexual appetites (Neubeck, 1969:14–24). Thus far, then, sociological research has now shown that sexual maladjustment is a *primary* cause of marriage failure, even though it may be a *contributing* cause.

Our conclusions about sexual adjustment during the first years of marriage are that newly married couples today enjoy a more active, pleasurable, and fulfilling sex life than did, say, the generation of their grandparents (Reiss, 1980:275–85). Although the early Kinsey report (1948, 1953) revealed more sexual activity in marriage than most Americans had suspected, still, the relatively low rates of female orgasm (Kinsey, 1953:562) create the distinct impression that intercourse was regarded not so very long ago as a husband's right and a wife's duty. Many couples apparently had not recognized their sex life as an occasion for mutual pleasure and gratification. Furthermore, Kinsey's (1953:641) data showed that females were physiologically capable of reaching orgasm as quickly as males, but women were less responsive to psychological stimuli. This was largely due to female cultural training which encouraged them to show restraint in sexual matters. Kinsey believed that husbands should be more sensitive to the needs and feelings of their partners, while wives needed to take part more freely and without inhibiting restraints in sexual relations. Masters and Johnson (1966, 1970) were later to voice similar convictions.

Today, however, couples appear to be entering marriage better informed and with more realistic attitudes toward sexual relations. This is due in part to the increased number of sex education programs, marriage and family courses, as well as freer and more candid discussion of all kinds of sex-related topics. Partly, too, the change is a result of the declining, but still present, double standard. Young women entering marriage in the 1980s are far less content to engage passively in sexual relations. They believe they have as much right to a fully satisfying sex life as their husbands do. Indeed, Hunt (1974) discovered that many wives now complain that marital sex does not occur frequently enough, a complaint that was almost exclusively heard from men just a few years ago.

However, before we paint too rosy a picture of marital sexual adjustment, we must reckon very seriously with the fact that marital expectations have increased along with improved sexual performance. The net result may well be no major gain in overall sexual satisfaction. The very success of sexual therapists and marriage counselors, such as Masters and Johnson, Reuben, Ellis, and others, in sensitizing couples to the "joy of sex" may be somewhat counterproductive when it leads couples to approach marriage fully convinced that they will achieve complete sexual adjustment within a few months. Sociologist Michael Gordon (1978:68–83) warns against the danger of what he calls the "cult of mutual orgasm." He means that the heavy stress laid on simultaneous sexual climax sometimes deprives couples of the good feelings of psychological and physical intimacy associated with sexual relations. Gordon is not the only social scientist concerned that rising marital expectations may outpace sexual satisfactions and undermine the gains in sexual adjustment permitted by the recent liberalization of sexual attitudes. Perhaps the best defense against this danger is for newlywed couples to pay less attention to technique, rules, and performance, and more to mutual satisfaction and caring. In the final analysis, gaining the sexual experience that each partner needs to help gratify the other is one aspect of life together which married couples can thoroughly enjoy learning over the course of their lives.

Problems with In-laws

From the days of vaudeville, jokes about mothers-in-law have been part of the basic repertoire for all stand-up comedians. For many young couples, however, in-laws are no laughing matter. Although one or both of the parental families often provide monetary loans, psychological support, or some form of advice to young couples just starting out, nothing tends to make newlywed couples more angry than in-law "interference" in their domestic affairs. Perhaps the most optimistic feature of in-law problems is that they decline notably after the first few years of marriage (Duvall, 1954). The birth of a grandchild, in particular, tends to ease tensions and symbolizes the fact that the "kids" have now grown up.

Contrary to popular impressions, the most commonly reported conflict is not between a new husband and his mother-in-law, but between a new wife and her mother-in-law (Leslie, 1979:244–6). A mother usually has been most involved in caring for her son—doing his laundry, cooking his meals, cleaning his room, and perhaps even serving as his confidant and adviser on troubling issues. Suddenly, the new wife assumes all these functions. Many mothers are a bit relieved; and yet they feel a tinge of jealously that a new woman has displaced them. Will his new wife feed him properly and be able to cook his favorite dishes? Will she put so much bleach in the laundry that he breaks out in a rash? Will she take him to her parents' home for the holidays? Will she spend money like water so they are always in debt? And, most of all, will she make him happy? Parents today invest so much time and emotional concern in their children that they often find it difficult to let go, even after their children have married. Indeed, one drawback of intense parental affection is that parents often find it hard to accept anyone as good enough for their son or daughter.

Adjustment to in-laws is a two-way street. Not only must each partner form a relationship with another set of parents, but the parents, in turn, also must learn to adjust to a new daughter- or son-in-law. The dominant value governing in-law relations in American society, according to sociologist Robin Williams (1970:68), is equality. After marriage, a husband is constrained by normative social expectations to treat his wife's parents in a fashion equal to his own, just as she is expected not to favor her blood relatives. The same rules apply to the parental families; a set of parents is not to favor their own child against the other young spouse. For example, if a wife's parents give her an automobile and him a pen for Christmas, one could assume that strained

relations and pronounced social repercussions would result from this dispropor-
tionate display of affection. Married couples, too, must take pains to ensure that
their visits, favors, displays of affection, and gifts are balanced between the two
parental families. Otherwise, they can create problems which may take years to
overcome.

What can be done to alleviate in-law tensions? Evelyn Duvall (1967:497)
suggests that harmonious relationships with in-laws can be achieved if two
factors, acceptance and mutual respect, are present on both sides. Acceptance
may be overtly conveyed or subtly suggested by the way in-laws treat their
child's spouse. When young married persons feel close to in-laws, or when
they report that their in-laws do not try to embarrass, criticize, or demean
them in the eyes of their spouses, then acceptance can be said to prevail in
that relationship. However, if relations are to be truly effective and harmonious, mere acceptance is not enough. Young wives and husbands also want to
feel that they enjoy their in-laws' respect. A prime indicator of mutual respect
is the willingness of persons on both sides of the in-law relationship to acknowledge the other's personal integrity and distinctiveness. This requires a
great deal of emotional maturity—which may explain why in-law problems
decline as the years pass.

Problems with Communication

"What we have here is a failure to communicate." This famous line from the
movie *Cool Hand Luke* is one of the complaints heard most often by marriage
counselors, although it often is phrased in slightly different terms. Here are
some examples of couples describing their failure to communicate:

> "He never talks, he just gets mad and storms out of the house."

> "My wife believes the best way to deal with problems is just to ignore them, say
> nothing, and pretty soon they'll mysteriously go away."

> "Of course, I'm hurt when my husband doesn't even notice that I've gotten all
> fixed up for him. I just keep hoping that one day he'll realize he ought to com-
> pliment his wife once in awhile."

> "Come to think of it, I guess I never asked my wife how she felt about giving
> up her job. I just assumed every mother wanted to say home with her kids."

> "In our family, I generally do all the talking. My husband sits there with his
> eyes glued to the TV, nodding from time to time, but I know he's not listening
> to a word I say."

One subtheme of communication failures between husbands and wives is
dissatisfaction with the total relationship. Indeed, the link between good communication and marital happiness has been documented repeatedly by social
scientists (Bienvenu, 1970). It is important to understand why this is true.
Marital dialogue does more than simply exchange information. Communication helps establish a relationship; it provides feedback on expectations and it
allows for the evaluation of each spouse's role performance. Especially during
the early years of marriage, each partner is still trying to clarify what conduct
is suitable to his or her role as husband or wife. Consequently, when a wife

tells her husband, "After we've both spent a busy week, I really don't think it's right for you to run off every Friday evening to play handball with the boys and leave me home alone with nothing to do," she is saying rather directly that he is not fulfilling the companionship role in the way she expected. She could have phrased her displeasure to only hint at the problem. For example: "What do you suppose the wives of the other guys are doing while you four are playing handball?" In this instance, however, he may not have gotten the message.

Unmistakable feedback is necessary if partners are to signal each other clearly and agree on how each should adapt their husband or wife role to the other's performance (Kantor and Lehr, 1974:11–15). Thus, the give-and-take of the communication process does more than simply allow for the sharing of information between partners. This interaction permits role clarification and evaluative responses as well. Husbands and wives who know what their mates expect of them and who receive positive reinforcement that they are performing their roles suitably generally are more satisfied with their roles and happier with their overall marital relationships (Stuart, 1970).

Verbal exchanges are not the only forms of marital communication. Sometimes our actions can supersede our words, and very frequently our words and actions send contradictory signals. Recently, family therapists have begun to focus a great deal of attention on nonverbal communications and the messages they convey (Haley, 1970:199–201). Our facial expressions, body movements, and eye contact all combine with our verbal utterances to form our total communications (May, 1969:238; Scheflen, 1970). We sometimes feel freer to express in body language what we hesitate to say verbally. For example, when one partner suggests that they go out to dinner at a restaurant both had enjoyed, the other spouse may respond by turning away to do something else, while saying in a flat tone, "It's OK with me, if that's what you really want to do." Now the one who made the suggestion is confused. The verbal communication said yes, but the body language clearly said, "No, I'm not in the mood." To go out for dinner on the basis of the verbal statement alone would risk a disappointing evening. Thus, spouses need to develop their skills in reading nonverbal as well as spoken communications.

One problem with body language is that it is a much less exact communication than spoken words. If a husband comes home from work sluggish, quiet, and withdrawn, his wife might quickly conclude that he is either angry or indifferent to her. In fact, he may simply be very tired from a particularly trying day. To improve their skills in reading their spouses' nonverbal cues couples need to check their interpretations of body language signals by periodically asking if the messages they think they are receiving are correct perceptions of the other person's feelings. Just as skill in verbal communication correlates with marital satisfaction, so too does skill in nonverbal communication (Kahn, 1970). Moreover, the two forms reinforce each other. Even clear messages are better understood when we look to body language cues for confirmation of the meanings we have drawn from our partner's words. Sensitivity to the interrelationship between verbal and nonverbal forms of communication can help improve our transactions as spouses. These skills take time to develop, however, and most couples need a good deal of daily practice before they become proficient at "reading" their partners.

In the long run, the sheer volume of messages that spouses exchange matters less than the quality of their communicative relationship. Rallings (1969:290) has compiled seven basic suggestions, which, when taken together, are a practical set of rules for a marital dialogue which is relatively free from outside interference and distorted messages. Ralling's seven suggestions are:

1. Provide opportunity for communication. Married couples need a place and a time when they have privacy, are not subject to interruptions, and feel relaxed.
2. Develop good listening habits.
3. Say what you mean. According to David Mace and Eric Berne, even if it leads to overt conflict, quarreling has its merits. If quarreling is not excessive and focuses on the argument without ego slashing, it is better than cool, intellectual discussion that does not deal with feelings. Feelings are a vital part of our interaction and are absolutely necessary in this communication process.
4. Cultivate conversation with your spouse. One barrier is sex differences with regard to interests. Seek shared interests.
5. Develop your own private language. When extended to the children in the family this becomes a source of amusement and cohesion for the entire family.
6. Use fully all available means of communication, especially the nonverbal.
7. Seek professional help if needed.

While communication problems can be a serious source of marital difficulties, especially during the first few years of marriage, no one should assume that open dialogue by itself will remove all tension and strain from marital relations. Young people who have been exposed to transactional analysis, the writings of Eric Berne, or any number of other popular psychologists may be inclined to believe that communication will solve everything. Unfortunately, that is not true. Nor is total honesty always the best policy, especially when it will needlessly crush the other person without adding anything to the marital relationship. A husband struggling in his career, for example, does not need to be told that one of his wife's old boyfriends is now doing exceptionally well and probably making twice as much money as he is. Even though it may be true, such a disclosure will not make him feel good nor will it improve his career chances.

Frankness to the point of brutality violates another rule of effective communication—namely, that partners must be sensitive to each other's needs and feelings. Moreover, everyone deserves some measure of privacy. Although "the two become one" in marriage, every thought, feeling, or action does not have to be disclosed to one's partner. Everything good can be overdone, and frankness and togetherness are no exceptions.

Marriage means quite different things to different people. No two persons—even those with similar social and cultural backgrounds—enter matrimony with identical subjective expectations. Our personal histories, interests, fears, and aspirations come together into a unique developmental sequence. One brings to marriage a self-concept informed by our values, our needs, and our perceptions of the proper way to perform roles. Everyone also possesses different capacities for empathy, self-disclosure, understanding, accommodation, and expressiveness. These unique traits all but guarantee that no wife and husband ever will agree completely, at the outset, on the important matters which they will need to resolve together during the first years of marriage.

Of course, viewpoints clash less often and less vigorously within homogamous marriages (Levinger, 1970:107–25). When class positions, religious persuasions, age and educational levels, and racial backgrounds are relatively similar, fewer opportunities for bitter conflicts arise and the road to adjustment is considerably smoother. However, even persons from homogamous backgrounds are likely to find themselves saying something like this: "I've certainly learned a lot about him/her since we got married." Indeed, many people learn a great deal about themselves after they marry.

Matrimony transports couples into a different realm of reality. Never-married individuals cannot grasp the sorts of adjustments which will be required of them, even though they may have tried to anticipate how their lives would change after the wedding. Many of their images of behavior in their marital roles probably are idealized and largely unrealistic. Consequently, the sheer dynamics of married life will force upon them new ideas about who they are and what they should expect from marriage. In the early weeks of marriage, many partners play their husband or wife roles according to the traditional script, for they usually have been exposed to little else on which to model their relationships. They drift into what Cuber and Haroff (1965) describes as a passive-congenial marriage, that is, a pairing characterized by a demand to fit into a standardized routine free of conflict and with only limited demands imposed upon the other person. Gradually, however, we can expect that one partner will begin to press for adjustments which will tailor marital role performance to his or her particular needs and experience. For example, a husband may decide that a traditionally passive role for the wife is demeaning for her and puts him in a domineering position which he finds thoroughly distasteful. Or, the wife may decide after a short while that his traditionalist's allocation of cooking and house-cleaning tasks to her is too burdensome and thus they need to make basic changes in their respective role patterns. As long as they agree on the nature and degree of adjustment required in their circumstances, the change usually can be made with little domestic turmoil. However, when the need for basic realignments is perceived by only one partner, marital stress and social conflict can result.

In this regard, Ruth Cronkite (1977) has shown that mutual adjustments between marriage partners can be accomplished rather rapidly in most instances, usually within the first 18 months of marriage. Moreover, she discovered that the strongest influence shaping marital role performances was the perspective of one's spouse. In other words, husbands and wives socialize each other. Each helps to shape the other's normative behavior. Furthermore, such socialization was not confined to just the first few months of marriage. Across the family life cycle, preferences periodically change, requiring that adjustments be made in role performance. Apparently, the constant factor is the importance of the spouse's preferences in the definition of our own expectations for our role performance.

Other social factors also prompt adjustments between spouses. Not only do people change marriage relationships; marriage relationships also change people. Situational demands often arise unexpectedly to change the way one relates to duties and takes part in the marital drama. When the refrigerator breaks down, the bills exceed income, one partner becomes ill, or tempers flare over a petty issue, couples are reminded afresh of the far-reaching obligations they have assumed as a family unit and as partners.

How spouses would cope with any one of these problems is not so much the concern here as how they would cope with the *strife* such problems often generate. Of course, conflict frequently can arise from good fortune as readily as from misfortune. Consider this example. A husband is awarded an important promotion, but it entails moving to another city. The wife will be forced to resign from her job, and she was very little chance of finding a similar position near her husband's new location. Should she forfeit her own career to further his? Or, should he turn down the promotion to accommodate her career? A generation ago, the husband's career almost always took top priority. Today the situation is less clear; no "right" answer automatically appears. Since the expectations of both mates cannot be fulfilled, one solution to their dilemma might be to compensate the partner whose interests were sacrificed by giving greater weight to that partner's interests the next time a direct clash occurs. Such a strategy does not eliminate frustrated expectations; indeed, no strategy can do that. At best, it equalizes the disappointments so that one partner is not called upon to yield on more critical issues than the other. In our less than perfect world, justice in interpersonal relations is often the best for which one can hope.

Summary

A wedding confers upon the bride and groom a new status as wife and husband. Marriage, however, is not a static condition; it is better understood as an intimate social process. Making the marital partnership work requires more than love. A newly married pair also must be willing to compromise, to respect the other person's point of view, and to seek mutually acceptable patterns of adjustment as they confront the day-to-day problems which arise during their first years together. Adjustment to marriage and to one another requires effort, commitment, and skillful decision making by both wife and husband.

This chapter examines the ways in which couples cope with the initial problems of adjustment to married life. Learning to live together and dealing with the cultural shock of marriage requires some willingness to compromise. Couples who fail to master negotiating skills are likely to find the road to adjustment rocky and long. Perhaps even marriage itself will be perceived as a bitter disappointment and marital happiness as an elusive goal.

One of the first tasks of a newly married pair is the organization of their household. Marriage creates a new legal and social unit—the family. Provisions must be made to meet its material needs, such as living quarters, furniture, food, clothing, and other basic necessities. More important, however, is the social organization of the household. Spouses must learn to function within their new roles as husband and wife, power must be divided between the two partners, tasks must be assigned, and both must learn to cooperate in the successful running of the household's daily operations.

In the final section, the major causes of marital strife are discussed. Conflict is a normal result of social relations, and marriage is no exception. Marital strife becomes abnormal only when it is not adequately controlled. Many differences actually can be turned to constructive ends and thereby strengthen marital bonds. Five typical areas of conflict in early marriage explored in this chapter are: problems with money, sexual adjustment, in-laws, communication, and differing marital expectations. Although some suggestions for handling disagreements are also included, strategies for conflict management in marriage will be described in greater detail in later chapters when we discuss divorce and marriage adjustment in the full family household.

STUDY QUESTIONS

1. What are some of the typical adjustment problems a young couple encounter immediately after marriage?
2. Which social roles have traditionally been associated with the position of husband and which with that of wife?
3. What are the more common patterns for distributing power between marriage partners, and to what extent is equality becoming more and more the norm between American spouses?
4. Why is the problem of money so pervasive in American marriages, even among more affluent couples?
5. How can one account for the fact that in-law problems usually decline over the course of a marital career?
6. What are some of the factors that contribute to good communication between marriage partners, and what factors tend to frustrate the acquisition of communication skills?

Alternatives to Traditional Marriage

8

The pluralism of marital styles and family forms is an important feature of American life. The traditional model of "the American family" is generally understood to include the married pair and their children living together in a single household in which the father performs the breadwinner role and the mother manages the household and supervises the rearing of the children. This normative pattern actually describes quite a small percentage of American households at any time (see Table 8-1). Living in **dual-breadwinner nuclear families,** in childfree or **postchild-rearing marriages,** in **single-parent families,** or as single individuals (a category which includes never-married, widowed, separated, or divorced persons) is now more common than living in traditional, single-breadwinner nuclear families.

The pluralism of marital styles and family forms does not necessarily mean that the normative pattern is being rejected. Single persons, for example, may simply be postponing marriage, but will someday enter into the normative model. Young couples in childfree marriages may intend to have children later on. Postchild-rearing families have moved on to a stage in the life cycle that is beyond the normative pattern. Single-parent families created by divorce or the death of a spouse often are not the preferred pattern, but the outcome of special circumstances. Hence, many reasons account for people living in social units other than the traditional family. Some of these alternatives are deliberately chosen, while others are patterns that result from the turn of events.

TABLE 8-1
Types of Households in the United States

Heading single-parent families	16%
Other single, widowed, separated, or divorced persons	21
Living in childfree or postchild-rearing marriages	23
Living in dual-breadwinner nuclear families	16
Living in single-breadwinner nuclear families	13
Living in no-breadwinner nuclear families	1
Living in extended families	6
Living in experimental families or cohabiting	4
	100%

Source: James Ramey, "Experimental Family Forms—The Family of the Future." *Marriage and Family Review.* 1978, 1:1.

Although alternative marriage and family forms have been widely discussed in recent years, a good deal of confusion surrounds this issue (Marciano, 1975). James Ramey (1978) has suggested that much of this confusion arises from the tendency of lay people and professionals to group variations in the normative pattern together with experimental family forms. Most people living in an alternative form are variations on the norm rather than experimental family structures. Typically, participation in experimental family patterns results from a rejection of the traditional family norm. Included in this category would be such practices as cohabitation, voluntarily child-free marriages, and open marriages. Variations are merely modifications of the traditional family type which may result from any number of individuals or social factors. However, these variations do not entail a desire to redefine the normative marriage and family pattern. Among the more common variations are such types as the single-parent families created by widowhood or divorce, dual-breadwinner families, and postchild-rearing marriages.

In this chapter, both variant and experimental alternatives to the traditional family pattern will be explored. Specifically, the discussion will cover the decision to remain single, a homosexual life-style, cohabitation, childless marriage, dual-career and dual-breadwinner marriages, the open marriage and communal or group-marriage patterns.

Staying Single

Throughout our history, the American value system has provided little social support to those who prefer to remain single. Generally, opposition to singlehood has taken subtle forms of expression instead of a broadside attack. The Puritans, for example, prohibited solitary individuals from living alone by requiring, through court decree if necessary, that unmarried persons reside with established families in the community (Morgan, 1966). In the nineteenth century, American youth were socialized to expect that they would eventually marry (Greven, 1977). Women in particular had few vocational opportunities apart from the roles of wife and mother. Nonetheless, persons who failed to follow the usual script by marrying were commonly labeled bachelors or spinsters (or worse, "old maids"), designations whose negative connotations implied that something was unnatural about, or wrong with, these individuals.

Ironically, singlehood has become more acceptable socially but is still less common during the twentieth century (U.S. Bureau of the Census, 1979:40,81–3). While the never-married formerly were inclined to suffer from feelings of self-doubt and inferiority because of their deviance from the norm, Peter Stein (1976) claims that singlehood now is emerging as a legitimate life-style requiring no apology. And what of the future? "In tomorrow's world," Alvin Toffler (1970:256) assures us, "being single will be no crime." We can assume Toffler means that the ideology of singlehood will continue to flourish and people will feel freer to choose that status in the decades ahead. Many

TABLE 8.2

Women and Men Remaining Single (Never Married) 1960–1978

	(in percent)		
Women Single:	1960	1970	1978
Ages 20–24	28.4	35.8	47.6
25–29	10.5	10.5	18.0
Men Single:			
Ages 20–24	53.1	54.7	65.8
25–29	20.8	19.1	27.8

Source: U.S. Bureau of the Census, 1978, P-20, No. 327:4 and 1977, P-20, No. 306:3. Reprinted from: Reiss (1980: 223)

generally agree with Toffler's "hunch" about what the future holds for the single life (Stein, 1981).

Reasons for Choosing the Single Life

Single persons make up a diverse group. More individuals than just the never-married fit into this category. Some singles have been married but are now separated, divorced, or widowed. The single life means something different for each of these groups, especially for those who were forced into the single status by the death of a spouse or family disruption. This section will focus primarily on the never-married segment of the single population; the other forms of singlehood will be examined in a later section.

Opting for the single life may result from two quite different decision-making processes. Individuals may be pushed toward singlehood out of a desire to avoid marriage, or they may be pulled toward singlehood in positive response to certain advantages it affords. Among the "push" factors, Stein (1980:154) identifies such influences as the feeling of being trapped by marriage, suffocating one-to-one relationships, poor communication with a mate or potential mate, boredom, obstacles to self-development, sexual frustration, limits on mobility and the range of available experiences, conformity to societal expectations, isolation, and participation in the women's movement. All of these features tend to make marriage appear less attractive as a life-style than singlehood, at least to a good number of people.

Stein also enumerates a succession of "pull" factors which draw individuals toward singlehood. These include greater career opportunities, an increased variety of experiences, self-sufficiency, sexual freedom and availability, an exciting life-style, freedom to change, mobility, sustaining friendships, and women's or men's support groups. Apart from the basic attractiveness of these features, Stein's research also showed that the greatest need of single persons is a substitute network of social relationships capable of providing intimacy, companionship, and an enduring bond of social support. Indeed, being driven away from marriage does not appear to be enough in itself to sustain the single life for very long. People need social interactions with others who can boost their morale and share important experiences with them. Unless other singles can be found to satisfy these highly personal needs, the single life may become too lonely and isolated an existence to be fulfilling.

To be sure, those who choose the single life still must be willing to pay some social cost for their decision (Libby, 1979:51–9). The pressures of societal expectations, parents, relatives, and married friends to find a partner and leave the "unattached life" behind is often difficult to resist. Marriage in American society frequently is taken as a sign of adult status, while singles often are suspected of being immature, "real losers," latent homosexuals, self-centered, or simply oddballs. Jessie Bernard (1975:592–3) points out that single women in particular tend to be subjected to repressive parental dominance long after they have reached adulthood. Thus, the decision to continue in the single life is probably more difficult than choosing to get married. The obstacles to "creative singlehood" are clearly falling by the wayside, but they have by no means been entirely removed as yet.

Prolonged Singlehood through the Postponement of Marriage

Many people who plan to marry eventually are prolonging their single life through a deliberate decision to postpone marriage (Glick, 1975:17–8). The reasons for this strategy are not the same for all marriage-age persons. Some apparently enjoy the thrill of being free and are reluctant to relinquish that freedom as early as their counterparts did about a generation ago. Many are in college and want to complete their education before they think about marriage. Still others wish to launch a career and make sure that it is well established before they give any thought to finding a mate. And finally, with the relaxation of premarital sexual standards, single people can find more outlets for their sexual drive outside marriage than was previously the case (Libby, 1979:37). Thus, one major reason for marrying earlier—the desire to find a willing sexual partner—is now greatly reduced.

Singlehood, of course, has always been a premarital stage, but one with little basic social importance. The single life was generally seen as a kind of "holding pattern" until entry into a conventional monogamous marriage. However, the delay of marriage shown by current data means that the single period is now becoming more common as an institutionalized period of the individual life cycle. According to one estimate, the number of men still singles at ages 20–24 will reach 60 percent by 1990, and the number of single women in the same age category will stand at 49 percent (*U.S. News & World Report*, 1975). For the same age groups in 1960, only 53 percent of the males and 28 percent of the females were single. The trend to delay marriage also is reflected in the sharp rise of persons living alone. Between 1960 and 1978, the United States experienced an increase of over 100 percent for singles living apart from other relatives (U.S. Bureau of the Census, 1979:51). To some extent, this increase reflected the fulfillment of a fairly widespread desire to live away from home before marrying. Some individuals may have been seeking a taste of the swinging singles life, but most simply wanted the independence and sense of self-sufficiency which living alone affords.

The institutionalization of singlehood as a distinct period of premarital independence (Kobrin, 1976) has been aided by an increase in services now available to the unmarried. Only recently did the American business community discover that more than 20 million people in this society are age 18 or older and have never married, and that another 20 million are either widowed or divorced (U.S. Bureau of the Census, 1979:40). Lately, singles have come to comprise a substantial market whose unique needs require rather specialized services. Perhaps the most well-known marketing effort aimed at the unattached person is the singles bar. But, certainly, these are not the only enterprises trying to capitalize on the singles market. Other responses include singles apartment houses, weekend retreats at resort hotels, special tours for singles, books and magazines designed with singles in mind, church and civic

Figure 8.1
The discovery of "singles" by the American business community as a market population with special needs and interests has resulted in a variety of new services—many geared to recreational activities.

organizations for the unmarried, and even special courses on the single life offered by several colleges and universities (Keyes, 1975). In a reciprocal sort of fashion, these services not only address the special needs of single persons, but they also help sustain the single life. Without them, more pressure might well build up, urging singles to seek the security and social benefits of marriage.

Unchosen Singlehood

It is one thing to choose singlehood as a life-style, either temporarily or permanently, but it is quite another matter to be forced into singlehood by the loss of a spouse through death, separation, or divorce. Many in this category want to remarry, especially when the spouse is lost during the years when a person is still actively involved in economic and social affairs. Apparently, some persons can meet the challenge of unchosen singlehood in a constructive fashion, while others find it a socially disorienting experience from which recovery is often long and extremely difficult. This response tends to vary, depending on whether the singlehood was created by divorce or the death of a spouse.

In his classic study on divorce, William Goode (1965) pointed out that a person thrust back into the single life after being married typically experienced a great deal of role ambiguity. No clear definitions spell out how divorced persons should behave as unattached individuals. The trauma and discontent associated with role ambiguity, Goode argued, encouraged early remarriage and return to an established set of social expectations for individual conduct. Perhaps the greater number of divorces is causing the side effect of steadily reducing this ambiguity. At any rate, recent data indicate that divorced persons are waiting longer before remarrying (Glick and Norton, 1977:5–7). This seems to suggest that singlehood is not quite so traumatic a status for the previously married. However, because almost 80 per-

194   *A Season for Marriage*

cent of those who divorce eventually remarry, singlehood does not appear to be the preferred status of most divorced persons, at least not as a permanent life-style. Some data do indicate that remarried men and women report levels of marital happiness and satisfaction which are comparable to those of never-divorced couples (Glenn and Weaver, 1977). We might conclude then that, despite the longer period before remarriage, many couples who terminate their first marriage are not opting for the single life as such, but are searching for a new spouse.

Widowhood (or the less common **widowerhood**) differs quite profoundly from divorce because it is almost always involuntary and often occurs without much warning, except in the later years. Widowhood presents its own special problems, including loneliness, a sense of guilt for surviving, a sudden drop in social relationships, and—worst of all—serious financial problems. Indeed, Harvey and Bahr (1974) discovered that the widowed person's morale was depressed more by the poverty and financial hardship resulting from the loss of a spouse, than it was by the person's social isolation. However, even if the financial problems of widowhood can be resolved, the grief, depression, and the loss of friends and family still cloud the future of persons denied the companionship of their spouses (Lopata, 1972:42). Adjustment to the single role is somewhat more difficult for men and women under these circumstances. Men have higher rates of suicide, mental illness, and a general vulnerability to all forms of destructive influences than do women (Berarado, 1970). Yet despite these basic limits on the widow and widower status, some people develop creative single life-styles. They work, pursue hobbies, visit relatives, engage in social service projects, travel, and make important contributions to the life of their communities. These individuals demonstrate that postfamily singlehood can be socially productive and have meaning for the surviving spouse.

Homosexuality as an Alternative Life-Style

Another reason some people select an alternative to traditional marriage is their homosexual orientation. A **homosexual** may be defined as someone whose choice as a sexual partner is a person of the same sex (Gould, 1979:36). To distinguish the characteristics of homosexuality, behavioral scientists have, over the last decade especially, tended to lay as much stress on the development of a homosexual way of living, or "life-style," as they have on the sexual affinity for someone of the same sex. At the same time, a change has occurred in the interpretation of the basic cause (or causes) of homosexuality. For a long while, Freudian psychoanalysts in particular defined homosexuality as a perversion or illness (Schur, 1965:70–74). In 1973, however, the American Psychiatric Association removed homosexuality from its list of pathologies (Gould, 1979:36–44). This action coincided with a growing conviction that homosexuality is a learned sexual orientation.

Figure 8-2
As the signs indicate, this demonstration was designed to make the point that gay persons are a part of the "real" world and are represented in a wide variety of occupations. *(© Tom McHugh, Photo Researchers, Inc.)*

One myth shared by many heterosexuals is that homosexuals follow a common life-style. On the contrary, both gay men and women order their lives in a variety of ways. In one of the most extensive studies yet undertaken on homosexuality, Bell and Weinberg (1978) recently developed a five-part typology to distinguish the varieties of life-style behaviors reported in their sample of about 1,000 males and females who defined themselves as homosexuals. These five types included:

1. **Close-Coupled.** This homosexual relationship was a kind of quasi-marriage whose two partners were faithful to one another and relied on each other for sexual and interpersonal satisfactions.
2. **Open-Coupled.** Such homosexual pairs lived together, but they also sought love and sexual relationships outside this partnership.
3. **Functional.** This homosexual person lived as a "single" who organized his or her life around a wide-ranging number of sexual experiences.
4. **Dysfunctional.** These people were not only troubled by their homosexuality, but they also encountered more sexual problems that persons in the first three types.
5. **Asexual.** Persons in this category were identified as homosexuals but they had little or no sexual experience with others. Their interest and participation in sexual affairs was decidedly lower.

Since slightly more than three fourths of the study's subjects fit into one of these five categories, homosexuality is clearly not one life-style; instead, it includes a wide variety of behaviors. Moreover, Bell and Weinberg gathered data which dispelled a succession of other myths about homosexuality. They (1978:229–31) reported, for example, that heterosexuals rather than homosex-

TABLE: 8.3

Percentage of Respondents in Each Homosexual Subgroup with Certain Sexual, Social, and Psychological Characteristics

Males	Close-Coupled (N = 67)	Open-Coupled (N = 120)	Functional (N = 102)	Dysfunctional (N = 86)	Asexual (N = 110)
	%	%	%	%	%
The Homosexual-Heterosexual Continuum					
Exclusively or predominantly homosexual in behavior	94	96	95	92	83
Overtness					
Extrafamilial overtness is relatively high	21	20	27	21	8
Level of Sexual Activity					
Has homosexual sex at least twice a week	69	60	100	47	0
Sexual Partnerships					
Had at least 20 homosexual partners in past year	0	61	100	90	0
Had fewer than 6 homosexual partners in past year	69	15	0	5	46
Sex Appeal					
Rates own homosexual sex appeal as below average	12	10	2	20	30
Sexual Techniques					
Used an extensive sexual repertoire in past year	63	72	74	77	38
Level of Sexual Interest					
Thinks somewhat or quite a bit about sexual matters	84	80	89	87	69
Sexual Problems					
Reports somewhat or very much of a problem with					
—getting partner to meet his sexual requests	13	40	15	44	33
—finding a suitable sexual partner	7	34	22	80	75
—being able to meet partner's sexual requests	7	21	10	42	38
—not having sex as often as he would like	19	38	10	53	54
—worrying about his sexual adequacy	10	23	3	46	30
—maintaining affection for partner	7	27	23	47	31
—premature ejaculation	13	34	10	35	36
—being able to reach orgasm	4	12	6	30	18

[a]Items were selected for this table on the basis of their theoretical salience and, where possible, male-female comparability. In addition, they had to display statistically significant intergroup differences in regression analysis and also meet a criterion of substantive significance: for any item, at least one group that was significantly different statistically had to show a difference of at least 10 percentage points from another group.

(continued)

TABLE: 8.3 continued.

	Close-Coupled (N = 81)	Open-Coupled (N = 51)	Functional (N = 30)	Dysfunctional (N = 16)	Asexual (N = 33)
	%	%	%	%	%
Acceptance of Homosexuality					
Does not at all regret being homosexual	69	54	78	0	37
Strongly disagrees that H is an emotional disorder	48	43	52	24	44
Wishes he had been given a magic HT pill at birth	22	24	15	50	32
Would take a magic HT pill today	1	10	6	30	18
Social Adjustment					
More than three-fourths of R's men friends are H	67	77	75	66	46
Spends little or no leisure time alone	75	60	43	26	20
Spends at least 5 evenings a week at home	64	54	19	38	47
Homosexuality has harmed R's career	12	28	16	43	23
Has been arrested (for any reason) more than twice	1	7	17	8	6
Has been assaulted or robbed on account of H	21	40	33	50	38
Psychological Adjustment					
Feels fairly happy or very happy	99	88	95	71	60
Does little or no worrying	28	30	44	8	35
Seldom or never feels lonely	84	75	70	36	50
Relatively low in self-acceptance	19	41	25	56	46
Relatively depressed	12	37	24	55	47

Females

	Close-Coupled (N = 81)	Open-Coupled (N = 51)	Functional (N = 30)	Dysfunctional (N = 16)	Asexual (N = 33)
The Homosexual-Heterosexual Continuum					
Exclusively homosexual in both feelings and behavior	59	57	50	19	30
Exclusively or predominantly homosexual in behavior	96	91	80	69	69
Had heterosexual coitus in past year	9	18	37	50	33
Overtness					
Familial overtness is relatively high	20	25	6	0	12
Extrafamilial overtness is relatively high	9	20	10	0	9
Level of Sexual Activity					
Has homosexual sex at least twice a week	43	51	60	31	0
Sexual Partnerships					
Had at least 20 homosexual partners in past year	0	8	10	12	0
Had fewer than 3 homosexual partners in past year	100	53	33	50	100
Sex Appeal					
Rates own homosexual sex appeal as below average	6	10	0	19	27

	Close-Coupled (N = 81)	Open-Coupled (N = 51)	Functional (N = 30)	Dysfunctional (N = 16)	Asexual (N = 33)
	%	%	%	%	%
Sexual Techniques					
Used an extensive sexual repertoire in past year	70	84	80	81	27
Level of Sexual Interest					
Thinks somewhat or quite a bit about sexual matters	51	67	80	62	61
Sexual Problems					
Reports somewhat or very much of a problem with					
—getting partner to meet her sexual requests	7	25	7	38	24
—finding a suitable sexual partner	9	29	23	81	73
—being able to meet partner's sexual requests	6	28	0	31	27
—not having sex as often as she would like	13	31	20	69	45
—worrying about her sexual adequacy	5	21	7	50	39
—partner not being able to reach orgasm	4	12	10	31	9
—maintaining affection for partner	7	25	17	44	24
—being able to reach orgasm herself	4	14	10	62	39
Acceptance of Homosexuality					
Does not at all regret being homosexual	68	59	100	0	73
Social Adjustment					
Has at least 6 good, close friends	35	33	57	38	33
More than three-fourths of R's women friends are H	42	51	43	25	36
Spends little or no leisure time alone	72	73	53	19	21
Spends at least 5 evenings a week at home	73	59	37	12	69
Attends religious functions at least once a month	9	6	0	18	18
Psychological Adjustment					
Feels fairly happy or very happy	94	84	87	69	67
Relatively exuberant	47	39	60	19	30
Seldom or never feels lonely	84	61	63	62	27
Relatively depressed	23	45	33	56	39
Relatively paranoid	27	51	40	44	45
Has sought professional help to give up her homosexuality	9	12	3	19	27

[b]Items were selected for this table on the basis of their theoretical salience and, where possible, male-female comparability. In addition, they had to display statistically significant intergroup differences in regression analysis and also meet a criterion of substantive significance: for any item, at least one group that was significantly different statistically had to show a difference of at least 10 percentage points from another group. Because so few of the lesbians cruised, cruising variables are omitted.

The data in these two tables were gathered by Bell and Weinberg and have been arranged by their five types of homosexual experience.

Source: Bell and Weinberg (1978: 478–81).

uals, are more likely to make objectionable sexual advances; that the sexual activity of homosexuals is usually very cautious and not undertaken in places frequented by heterosexuals; that most homosexuals are indistinguishable in their nonsexual behaviors from heterosexuals; and that most homosexual activity takes place between consenting adults. Indeed, the lives of many homosexuals, especially the closed couples, open couples, and functionals, are just as happy and satisfying as many heterosexuals.

During the 1970s, gays defined themselves as a minority group and took aggressive action to wrest civil rights from the dominant heterosexual majority (Levine, 1978). The increased visibility of homosexuals as a group over the last decade results, in part, from the more vigorous stance taken by the gay-rights movement and the greater social tolerance for homosexuality. Thus far, however, the data are simply inadequate to establish whether homosexual persons are increasing in number or more people are simply "coming out" and acknowledging their sexual orientation (Karlen, 1980).

Premarital Cohabitation

Another important alternative to traditional marriage is the much-publicized practice of cohabitation. This can be defined as a nonmarital union in which two members of the opposite sex, who are unrelated and not married, consent to share the same living quarters, and thereby establish a household unit. Cohabitation usually is predicated on affection between the two partners, but couples who enter this arrangement generally are not ready, for one reason or another, to embrace full commitment to legal marriage (Peterman, Ridley, and Anderson, 1974:354).

Although cohabitation has been practiced to a limited degree in the past by persons who formed **common-law marriages,** by the elderly, and by divorced persons who felt the need for a trial period before contemplating remarriage, the upsurge in cohabiting among never-married youth over the last two decades is a drastic social change. One study by Arafat and Yorburg (1973) disclosed that almost 80 percent of their student subjects would consider cohabitation, if the right opportunity arose, while only 20 percent were unwilling to cohabit for any reason. The actual incidence of unmarried couples living together, however, is much lower than the acceptance of the practice. Clayton and Voss (1977) examined data from a random national sample of 2,150 young men and found that 16 percent of the whites and 29 percent of the blacks had cohabited for at least six months, although only 5 percent of each group were cohabiting at the time of the study. If the time span mentioned in the study's question had been shorter, undoubtedly slightly more men would have reported living with women. Some studies of college students have revealed that as many as one third of the subjects had lived together (Peterman, Ridley, and Anderson, 1974), although the figures usually are somewhat lower—25 percent is a very common estimate for college students nationwide (Knox, 1979:202).

What are we to make of increasing cohabitation? Is it a trial marriage, a substitute for marriage, a new style of courtship, or merely a convenient arrangement for sharing economic expenses and enjoying sexual relations? Since cohabitation, like marriage, means different things to different people, some cohabitants undoubtedly believe that living together holds one of these meanings. Contrary to most popular assumptions, however, most cohabiting couples do not see their relationship as a trial marriage (Henslin, 1980:106). On the basis of her research, Macklin (1972) suggests that most couples gradually drift into a cohabiting arrangement as a result of spending more and more time together, but without much conscious planning about testing the durability of their relationship. Divorced persons are somewhat more inclined than never-married college students to live together on a trial basis before remarriage, largely because they fear making another mistake (Wells, 1979:72).

TABLE 8.4
Unmarried Cross/Gender Couples Living Together: U.S., 1960 to 1978

Year	All Unmarried Couples	In 2-Person Households	In Households that Include Children
1960	439,000	242,000	197,000
1970	523,000	327,000	196,000
1977	957,000	753,000	204,000
1978	1,137,000	865,000	272,000

Source: Glick and Norton, 1977:33; and *U.S. Bureau of the Census*, P-20, No. 336:19,1979. Courtesy of the Population Reference Bureau. Reprinted from: Reiss (1980:103).

For the most part, cohabitation is not seen as an alternative to marriage. Bower and Christopherson (1977) found that their cohabitant and noncohabitant respondents were very nearly equal in their interest in eventual marriage—96 percent of the cohabitants and 99 percent of the noncohabitants felt this way. However, the sexes appear to differ on this issue. Women are more interested in transforming cohabitation into a marital relationship, while men are somewhat more interested in the immediate advantages, especially sexual outlets, that cohabitation provides. Thus, men viewed cohabitation as an alternative to marriage more often than their female partners (Lyness, Lipetz, and Davis, 1972). The difference was not big enough to suggest that the tendency to marry will be decisively influenced by the rise in cohabitation. Most likely, about all that will be affected is the age at first marriage, since cohabitation apparently delays the age at which it occurs.

Seeing cohabitation as no threat to conventional marriage norms also helps to reinforce a major view among social scientists that cohabitation is basically a new dimension of the courtship process rather than a substitute for marriage (Macklin, 1972; Henze and Hudson, 1974; Henslin, 1980; Reiss, 1980). This judgment may be somewhat premature, since the sort of nationwide random-sample studies necessary to confirm its relative accuracy are lacking today. At the same time, hard information on the prevalence of cohabitation in the general population still remains sketchy at best. However, the current data do point to the conclusion that cohabiting couples see their relationship as quite different from marriage. For example, among other things, living together lacks the permanence usually allied with conventional marriage. All of the ceremonial events surrounding the beginning of a new status position as husband and wife are missing. There is no public exchange of vows and no rings, no granting of a license by the state, no announcement in the newspaper, no showering of the couple with gifts and parties. Of course, the private character of the relationship makes it easier to terminate the arrangement. Yet, it also deprives the relationship of the kind of social approval and support that marriage enjoys. Thus, the temporary and informal character of the living-together pattern lends additional weight to the view that cohabitation is primarily a new form of courtship.

The opposite of the "trial-marriage" view of cohabitation holds that living together is merely a convenient arrangement that reduces cost while providing "easy sex," a way to enjoy one another's company, a good place to study, or a way to find out what it is like to live with a person of the opposite sex (Machlin, 1972). Men are far more inclined than women to cite sexual gratification as their major reason for cohabiting. However, neither sex said "an interest in future marriage" was a major reason for starting to live together (Arafat and Yorburg, 1973). Consequently, while most cohabiting couples believe their arrangement will enable them to develop a satisfying relationship, few expect that marriage will follow it immediately.

Although the meanings which couples attach to cohabitation vary, researchers have been able to reconstruct a social profile of persons likely to live together. Cohabiters tend to attend religious services less frequently than noncohabiters; to identify with a liberal life-style; and to have used drugs more often (Henze and Hudson, 1974). In addition, a greater percentage of males report having cohabited. The vast majority of those who have lived together believed that their parents disapproved of the practice in principle. Just over half thought their parents probably or definitely did not know of their cohabitation. About the same proportion of cohabiters and noncohabiters expected to marry eventually. But couples who live together usually marry later and desire fewer children than noncohabiters (Bowers and Christopherson, 1977). The data of Clayton and Voss (1977) also show that cohabitation is more likely among black males than white males, among divorced men than never-married men, and among men who are not in school or are high school dropouts than among college students. While Clayton and Voss also found that cohabitation related positively to urban residence in the northeastern and western regions of the country, Bower and Christopherson (1977) found no major differences in the rate of cohabitation by region.

Given this social profile, one might reasonably expect that cohabiting couples would structure their temporary households in a more equalitarian fashion than married couples. Although comparative research findings are limited, cohabitation does not appear to be any more "liberated" in household-task performance than contemporary marriage. One study contrasting cohabiting to married couples in their household division of labor (Stafford, Backman, and DiBona, 1977:54) concluded that:

not any different

> Cohabitation apparently is not the cure-all for traditional sex-role inequality. At least in terms of the division of household labor, the couples of the "now" generation, whether cohabiting or married, are still dividing the work along traditional lines with the woman bearing the brunt of the labor. The young men share the dishes and laundry more than their fathers did; but, likewise, the young women share the lawnmowing and home repairs more than their mothers did . . . This division leaves the woman most of the household duties whether or not they also are employed in the labor force.

If greater liberation from traditional sex-role stereotypes is not being gained in cohabitation arrangements, what, if any, are its benefits? Cohabitants usually mention several positive effects. For example, many couples who live together, assert that their relationships is free of the hypocrisy and role-playing which they believe often develops in marriage. In one study (Arafat and Yorburg, 1973), students rejected the need for marriage by dismissing it as a mere legality:

> "A wedding license is just a scrap of paper."

> "Marriage is just one of society's definitions."

> "I feel that if two people want to live together unmarried, they should because all the legalities in the world won't keep them together if they want out."

A recurrent theme in many such statements is a fear of being trapped in a relationship that has turned sour. Apparently, some people also feel that, since marriage sets up fixed roles and expectations, the institution actually can hamper personal growth and fulfillment.

Although cohabitation may strengthen affectional bonds, help clarify the partner's goals in marriage, increase self-confidence, build interpersonal skills, promote emotional maturity, and foster a deeper understanding of the heterosexual relationship, cohabitation is not without its drawbacks. While living together requires a process of adjustment very similar to that of marriage, cohabiting couples separate more often over these problems than do married couples. Often, too, ending an informal arrangement leaves emotional problems which are hard for former partners to resolve. This is especially common when a person leaves with strong doubts about his or her own worth, a sense of incompetence and failure, feelings of hostility toward the opposite sex, or with an unwillingness to enter another heterosexual relationship, including marriage (Ridley, Peterman, and Avery, 1978). Indeed, Macklin (1980:296) questions whether it really is easier to end a cohabitation arrangement than a marriage. She writes that the evidence suggests:

. . . the interpersonal dynamics involved in the severing of a relationship are the same whether one is married or cohabiting, with the degree of trauma dependent upon the length of time the individuals have been together and the degree of emotional involvement between them. Cohabitants can expect to experience the same process of denial, depression, anger, ambivalence, and reorientation to singlehood associated with the dissolution of any serious relationship.

In other words, if Macklin's conclusions are correct, couples who cohabit because they think the relationship will be emotionally easier to end may well be fooling themselves. Certainly, when cohabiting couples separate, little societal and parental pressure urges them to continue the relationship, and usually no court proceeding is required. This may help reduce any suggestion that the couple somehow has failed. Yet, a psychological cost still must be borne in most instances. Predictably, the psychological adjustment will be harder when one partner would like to continue the relationship.

Conflict with parents is a second negative result that may arise from living together. One common finding in almost all the research on cohabitation was the participants' belief that the overwhelming majority of parents disapproved. Undoubtedly for this reason, over 50 percent of cohabiting couples do not disclose their living arrangement to their parents (Arafat and Yorburg, 1973; Bower and Christopherson, 1977). Fear of discovery remains a constant threat for this group. Parental telephone calls and visits create anxiety; couples scurry around to conceal the partner's clothes and other possessions. Frequently, too, parents are less than eager to find out the truth about their son or daughter's "roommate." Accidental or intentional disclosure often leads to direct confrontation, which can produce strained relations and emotional distress on both sides. In extreme cases, parents may cut off the funds of their cohabiting child or ask his or her university to help terminate the relationship.

Serious negative consequences also may arise from the legal results of cohabitation. Although couples often claim that their living arrangement is strictly a private affair and no business of the state, the courts have been known to insist that cohabitants have legal obligations to one another. Technically, cohabitation is a crime in about 20 states (Macklin, 1980:300), but these statutes are rarely enforced. However the court probably will not recognize the illegality of the relationship as a defense against any claim by a partner. Indeed, today the exact legal status of cohabiting couples is difficult to define. Few precedents exist and the courts are just beginning to work out the legal implications of such arrangements. But several specific issues can give rise to complications.

The division of real estate and personal property accumulated during cohabitation are two major items that may require court litigation. Such problems can arise easily. Let us say that shortly after a couple decides to live together, they decide to pool their funds and buy a house. The man contributes $15,000 and the woman $5,000. They purchase a home for $70,000, with his name legally listed as the owner. She stops working and plays the role of homemaker. He pays the mortgage, taxes, and insurance. Three years later they decide to part company and sell the house, receiving $33,000 more than they paid. He returns her $5,000 investment along with interest. If she is not satisfied, however, she could sue him for half of the increased value of the house, plus payment for her cleaning, cooking, and other services during the three years of cohabitation. A request for a payment of $20,000 a year would not be unrealistic, and the total settlement could easily be about $75,000. Whether a settlement actually could be won on these terms would vary according to particular state laws, a jury's verdict, and the ruling of the presiding judge. Recent trends in cohabitation suits suggest that the woman in this case would be very likely to receive a favorable ruling on most of her claim (Bernstein, 1980). In the mid-1970s, the landmark decision in the case of Michelle Triola and the actor Lee Marvin laid the groundwork for subsequent cohabitation suits, and opened the door for recovery of accumulated assets.

One way to avoid, or at least reduce, the chances of court litigation is to sign a **cohabitation contract** at the beginning of the relationship; it should outline the mutual obligations and rights of each party (Stevens and Holmes, 1979). Nonetheless, because all states do not recognize these documents as legally binding contracts, couples cannot rest secure in the knowledge that

---

CLOSE-UP

Love's Labor's Arbitrated

Nearly five years ago the California Supreme Court decided that a Miss Triola was entitled to a trial on her claim that she and a Mr. Marvin had an unwritten agreement re the disposition of income and property from the time they lived together. On that day, cohabitation law was born and so, it's fair to say, was a new unease in the always touchy roommate situation.

Miss Triola was characterized by her lawyer as "the Joan of Arc of live-in women." Since her victory, her standard has been borne by women suing men, men suing men, women suing women—the many facets, that is, of human affection. But the cases one reads about are only the tip of the iceberg, newsworthy because they involve money and fame. At any given moment there are, known only to their friends and whoever lives next door, hundreds of the unfamous left to squabble without benefit of church or state over custody of the stereo and bookcases.

Some of the quarrels, or "cohabitant suits," are of a complexity that would stagger Solomon. Others, however, could be obviated by what matrimonial lawyers are calling L.T.A.'s "living together arrangements," which specify whose property is whose at the breakup.

Since, as is known by every romantic brought crashing to reality, all love affairs are predicated on an exchange of goods and services, L.T.A.'s strike us as inevitable. An L.T.A. is, after all, a variation on a classic union position— "No contract, no work." That policy did a lot for labor; perhaps it will do as much for love.

—Editorial
The New York Times

---

they have avoided possible court action. Moreover, the whole idea of "living-together contracts" runs counter to the idea of free-spirited cohabitation. Critics of cohabitation quickly point out that, when contracts become necessary, the difference between living together and marriage is minimal.

More serious than property claims are the problems of pregnancy or the birth of a child. Many couples cohabit without discussing beforehand what they would do in case a pregnancy results. Others agree that they will seek abortion, put the child up for adoption, or legally marry (Reiss, 1980:105). Cohabitation contracts typically state how a couple's children will be supported, who will be responsible for their nurture and socialization, and who will receive custody should the partners separate. Because parental obligations are spelled out in the legal codes, cohabitation contracts probably would be considered invalid if they included provisions which did not agree with the legal definitions in the codes. For example, a contract between a cohabiting couple in which they agree the man will not support any children would probably be set aside by a court—although the mother would have to sue for child support and testify that the man is the child's father—on the grounds that this arrangement contradicts the law, which makes the father responsible for the support of his child.

Of course, as long as a cohabiting couple remains together, questions about child support and custody generally do not arise. However, when such unions dissolve, some provision must be made for the daily care of the children and the sharing of the costs of child rearing. Unfortunately in these instances, parents who simply choose to disappear and escape their responsibilities altogether usually can do so with little fear of being caught (Bernstein, 1980). Of course, this situation also can arise when couples divorce, but it is somewhat easier for cohabiting males to escape since the female must prove his paternity and show that he failed to meet his legal responsibilities when the couple was living together.

One final comment about cohabitation simply points out a curious irony which has grown up with the increasing popularity of the custom. Living together is perceived by the partners as an alternative to the institution of marriage. Indeed, much of the attraction of cohabitation is its informal, less structured character. However, Jan Trost (1978) observes about the practice in Sweden—where cohabitation is far more common than in the United States—that the growing number of couples living together with clearer definitions of rights and role obligations is rapidly assuming the form of a social institution. Ironically, a practice which began as a reaction against marriage by those who wanted another alternative or were not yet ready to marry, is seemingly becoming a social institution in its own right.

However, attaining institutional status as a courtship pattern is not the same as achieving social acceptance for cohabitation. At present, Glick and Norton (1977:33) report that only about 1 percent of all people and all households in the U.S. include unmarried couples living together." Moreover, in their outlook for the future, they (1977:37) further suggest that "probably considerably less than one-tenth of unmarried adults will ever live like a man and wife without being married." [Glick and Spanier (1980) later qualified this earlier estimate in view of the 19 percent increase in cohabitation between March 1977 and March 1978.] Moreover, they see no evidence to suggest that the practice will diminish in the near future. Thus, this way of living is likely to become more accepted as a temporary or permanent alternative to traditional marriage.

Marriage without Children

The traditional American family includes a wife, husband, and their children. American cultural values have so stressed the importance of children that the alternative of a child-free marriage was not really widely discussed until the late 1960s. The National Organization for NonParents (NON) was created in 1972 to lend ideological and social support to couples who preferred not to bring children into the world (Bernard, 1975: 42–3). NON was not so much antichild as antiparenting. The group affirmed that parenthood was not a role everyone should automatically accept, for legitimate reasons exist for not pro-creating.

Basically, the major reasons that are cited for remaining childless by NON, as well as by feminist groups and population- and pollution-control groups, are:

1. The world is already overpopulated. More children will simply add to the strain on limited food resources and government services.
2. Additional children will accelerate the world's population problems.
3. The role of motherhood should be chosen, not automatically ascribed to women.
4. Couples who remain childless can spend more time together and develop a more intimate relationship than couples who are parents.
5. Childless couples can enjoy a spontaneous life-style without being tied down by the cares and responsibilities of child rearing.
6. Persons can enjoy children without being parents. (Although some child-less couples entertain the possibility of adoption, most do not pursue this avenue very vigorously out of concern for preserving their life-style. See Veerers, 1973).
7. Dual-career couples often can find greater rewards in their vocations than in child rearing.
8. A child-free marriage allows for greater financial security in one's later adult years.
9. Partners without children can devote more time to community concerns and organizations dedicated to improving the general welfare of human-ity.
10. Parenthood is a demanding role which all persons are not qualified to enter. It requires more time, patience, money, energy, and career dis-ruption than many are willing to tolerate. Thus, those who truly wish to

be parents should take on the role, but all others should be equally free to pursue a life-style without children.

Couples who find these reasons for not having children convincing are still likely to feel considerable social pressure to procreate (Rao, 1974). Parents on both sides are likely to say that they are eager to become grandparents. Friends with small children can be expected to extol the virtues of parenthood and encourage childless couples to follow their example. The most persistent source of pressure, however, is likely to emanate from the general cultural environment in which it is almost universally assumed that couples will have children, unless they physically cannot.

How do couples resist these pressures and pursue a childless life-style? Veerers (1973) uncovered two different routes by which couples arrive at the same goal. The most direct course is to agree before marriage not to have children. Occasionally, people will insist that any potential mate share this view before they ever consider marriage. A more common approach is simply to postpone childbearing until a better time. The delay may be based on a desire to launch a career, to follow a freer life-style for a while, or to amass a larger nest egg for the period when the mother will be out of the work force. After childbearing has been deferred for a number of years, a qualitative change in the couple's point of view may occur and they openly acknowledge that they probably will remain childless. In this instance, the decision for a childless marriage is a long process rather than a self-conscious conclusion reached early in the relationship.

One of the more persistent findings of the research on voluntarily childless couples is the need for a support group to reinforce this commitment (Veerers, 1973; Houseknecht, 1977; Ory, 1978). Since childlessness is a pattern that varies from the cultural norm, the presence of individuals and groups who agree with this view is all the more important to those who maintain a marriage without children. Apparently, however, these supportive "others" exist in somewhat greater number than had been suspected (Houseknecht, 1977). Moreover, when reference-group support for a childless marriage is combined with the structural and situational factors—such as the concern with overpopulation, the sheer cost of children, or the desire to pursue a career—the likelihood of childbearing is greatly reduced (Ory, 1978:538).

The greatest opposition to childbearing has been from feminist groups. While men become fathers and yet actively pursue their careers, women must go through pregnancy, childbirth, and early care of their offspring, which necessarily interrupts their careers (Espenshade, 1977:25–7). The time required to recover physically from birth, plus the years required for early child care place a much heavier burden on mothers than on fathers. Accordingly, advocates of women's rights have lobbied strongly for "elective motherhood." Margaret Movius (1978), for example, has called voluntary childlessness the ultimate liberation. Others have put the issue much more forcefully. Jeannie Binstock (1978) has asserted her position in quite unequivocal terms: "Women must be 'liberated' [from motherhood] to enjoy the fruits of other occupations, *whether they want to be or not* [italics in the original]." Despite this exaggerated rhetoric, the object of Binstock's campaign is not to prohibit mother-hood. Rather, she and her colleagues simply want to see a childless marriage accepted as an alternative for a larger proportion of the women who now suffer under the burdens of child rearing. The basic feminist assumption is that enough women will always desire the experience of motherhood to sustain the society's population. Those who currently need social support, how-ever, are the women who wish to forego motherhood to pursue other life-styles. In the following chapter, the reasons for wanting children and the actual incidence of families that have children will be discussed.

Dual-Career Marriages

In the traditional family model, the husband and father serves as the bread-winner by holding a job or pursuing a career outside the household, while the wife and mother supports this position by managing the household and taking primary responsibility for child care. The **dual-career** or **dual-worker family** realigns these basic adult roles so that both husband and wife can work outside the home. When the term dual-career marriage was first coined by Rhona and Robert Rapoport (1971:18), they specifically pointed out that dual-worker and dual-career families are not identical. As social scientists use the term, career is not just another word for a job. A career refers to work which requires a high degree of commitment and often specialized training; the ca-reer person follows a developmental sequence, moving forward through a se-ries of stages. Career development in the professions usually means that the person acquires a good deal of competence and experience, and makes a con-tribution to his or her particular field. In academic life, for example, all of these factors are part of the movement from instructor, to assistant professor, associate professor, and finally, to full professor. Careers in business involve movement upward from post to post within the management structure. A job, by contrast, refers to any form of work for which one receives pay. In a job, however, making money, not a commitment to the field of endeavor, is the motive. One does not speak, for example, of making a career as a stock clerk in a grocery store.

Clearly, dual-worker families outnumber dual-career families. Only slight-ly less than 24 percent of the working married women in 1978 were employed as managers, administrators, professional, technical, and kindred workers (U.S. Bureau of the Census, 1979:401). This means that over three fourths of all working wives were in noncareer employment. Furthermore, some career wives are married to men in noncareer occupations, so that it is unlikely that more than 20 percent of those families with two wage earners are truly dual-career marriages. Most research thus far has focused on the dual-career group. However, because the orientations and problems are different for dual-worker and dual-career families (Bernard, 1975a:182), the characteristics of each group will be examined briefly.

On Attitudes toward the Women's Movement

Here are some statements people have made about activist women's groups. For each one, indicate whether you agree strongly (AS), agree mildly (AM), disagree mildly (DM), or disagree strongly (DS) by circling the response which best represents your point of view. Scoring information can be found at the bottom of this questionnaire.

The leaders of women's organizations are trying to turn women into men, and that won't work.

AS	AM	DM	DS
1	2	3	4

It's about time women did something to protest the real injustices they've faced for years.

AS	AM	DM	DS
4	3	2	1

If women don't speak up for themselves and confront men on their real problems, nothing will be done about these problems.

AS	AM	DM	DS
4	3	2	1

Women who picket and participate in protests are setting a bad example for children. Their behavior is undignified and unwomanly.

AS	AM	DM	DS
1	2	3	4

It's women who have nothing better to do who are causing all the trouble.

AS	AM	DM	DS
1	2	3	4

Women are right to be unhappy with their role in American society, but wrong in the way they are protesting.

AS	AM	DM	DS
1	2	3	4

Scoring: Total all of your numerical scores for the questions above. A high score indicates a strong and positive support for the aims of the women's movement. A low score indicates a negative reaction to the aims and tactics of the women's movement.

Source: Karen Oppenheim Mason, with the assistance of Daniel R. Denison and Anita J. Schacht. *Sex-Role Attitude Items and Scales From U.S. Sample Surveys.* Rockville, Md.: National Institute of Mental Health. 1975, p. 54.

The Alternative of Dual-Career Couples

Dual-career couples strive toward two goals at the same time. They actively pursue career advancement in their respective fields and they seek to maintain a balanced family life (Bebbington, 1973:530). Even under the best of circumstances, this is no simple task. Dual-career couples generally have several factors working in their favor, however. Most dual-career wives—although this is apparently less often true of their husbands—come from social-class backgrounds which are higher than their noncareer counterparts (Rapoport and Rapoport, 1971:24-5). Dual-career couples also enjoy a higher educational level, including several years of university experience. Usually, this translates into greater social sophistication and more ability to understand and manipulate the external world. Finally, career couples usually earn more than dual-worker families. The scarce commodity for professional-manager couples tends to be time more than money.

These advantages seldom add up to a blissful, problem-free existence for dual-career families because they also have their own unique difficulties. Rhona and Robert Rapoport (1977:299–319) summarized them as five major dilemmas:

1. *Overload dilemmas.* In the traditional household, wives performed the "back-up" functions for the worker employed outside the home. She always saw that the house was cleaned, meals were cooked, and shopping was done. The husband took care of the intermittent jobs—home repairs, maintaining the car, and similar tasks. But when both spouses follow careers, the core of work in the household becomes an overtime job. Each partner—and often the children—must assume additional tasks and frequently relinquish a good portion of their recreation time simply to keep the household functioning. The overload on both husband and wife can produce a good deal of social strain.

2. *Normative dilemmas.* Cultural norms often change more slowly than social practices. The notion of working women, and especially working wives, still meets some opposition in certain quarters of society. The arrival of the first child is often taken as a signal that it is time for the mother to give up her career outside the home. At this point, couples must face the dilemma of whether they will follow conventional norms or agree that the wife should continue to develop her career. Resolving this question is often as difficult for the wife as it is for her husband. Not all husbands want their wives to stay home with the children. Very often, the wife's guilt at leaving her children makes her decide against a career outside the home. Since the 1960s, however, it has become somewhat easier for wives to deviate from the norm of home-based motherhood to pursue a career.

3. *Identity dilemmas.* Masculine identity is centered on the man's work and his ability to provide for his family. Feminine identity has traditionally been centered on domestic roles. When both husband and wife pursue careers, the result is frequently an identity crisis for each. Although there are signs that the traditional sex-role stereotype is decreasing for both partners, it is still embedded deeply enough in the culture to produce occasional problems.

4. *Social network dilemmas.* The time demands on both partners when each seeks to maintain a career and perform household-family functions is tremendous. Hence, friendship networks associated with work as well as kin-

Figure 8-3
Today, women are moving into many professional roles once reserved exclusively for men—such as the role of banker. (© Bettye Lane, Photo Researchers, Inc.)

ship affiliations suffer. There is simply not enough time, after occupational and immediate-family duties, to maintain the sociability networks which family and friends often expect. The result is that other contacts and important social networks often wither away.

5. *Role-cycling dilemmas.* When two people follow different careers, they often are called upon to make critical transitions at different times. The promotion of a wife, for example, may require a move to another city. Unless her husband can find a comparable job at the same time, she probably will not be able to accept the position. Of course, the same holds true for the husband. Timing the development of two careers so that they mesh smoothly is sometimes impossible, and hence partners must sacrifice some opportunities to allow their spouse's career to continue. Decisions of this sort are not made easily, however, since neither spouse really wants to hold back their mate's career.

These dilemmas are troublesome to dual-career couples, but research findings tend to indicate that they are not complete roadblocks to marital adjustment and success. Moreover, considerable gains from the dual-career pattern help offset these drawbacks. Being among the first to explore new avenues of marital organization is an exciting adventure which carries its own rewards, just as working out a new identity or enjoying the success of a challenging career produces a psychological payoff which is not to be dismissed lightly. Dual-career couples often can help promote each other's advancement, especially when the two are working in the same or closely related fields (Martin, Berry, and Jacobsen, 1975). And finally, they can be comforted by their higher standard of living. Though dual-career couples take pains to point out that they are not pursuing two careers just for the money (Rapoport and Rapoport, 1977:321), such disclaimers are easier to make when the in-

A Season for Marriage

comes combine to reach a respectable level. Yet, job satisfaction, self-esteem, and even vicarious pleasure in the success of one's spouse often are as important as the higher income. On balance, then, spouses in dual-career marriages rate their experience as a demanding yet rewarding alternative to traditional family life.

The Alternative of Dual-Worker Couples

As a general rule, the orientation to work varies considerably, between dual-worker and dual-career marriages. Working couples are more inclined to view the second income earned by the wife as an economic cushion. Most could survive on the husband's salary alone, but they could not maintain a very high standard of living. Wives in working-couple households seldom justify their employment by a simple declaration of their desire to work (Rapoport and Rapoport, 1978:76). However, Jessie Bernard (1975a:187) believes that many women give the "need for money" as the primary reason for working because this is socially acceptable in a culture which is still basically committed to the woman's place-is-in-the-home ideology. She suspects that many wives work, at least in part, to get back into the mainstream, to achieve some independence, and to escape the isolation and boredom of the household.

Working couples are also subject to two specific forms of stress created by dual employment. For the husband, the chief problem is usually a loss of self-esteem because he cannot fulfill the traditional role of supporting the family on his income alone. Indeed, one study clearly revealed that, while working wives generally were more satisfied and performed better than non-working wives, husbands of working wives were less satisfied than husbands of nonworking wives (Burke and Weir, 1976). Apparently, some traditionally oriented men still find the idea of working wives difficult to accept. This problem does not seem to be as severe for husbands in dual-career marriages.

Another source of stress is the overload responsibilities placed on working wives (Rapoport and Rapoport, 1978:15). Some husbands take the position that the wife can work outside the home as long as household chores do not suffer. In these instances, one commonly hears of the wife's "two jobs," although one rarely hears of the husband's "two jobs" unless he actually is holding down two full-time jobs. Some women accommodate themselves to this attitude by taking a job which requires little commitment. Their primary orientation is toward family life. Hence, they often are not very productive at work, nor do they derive much satisfaction from their jobs (Bailyn, 1978:159). Perhaps the greatest loss, however, is that their work never becomes an opportunity for individual achievement and self-realization.

The Future of Dual-Career and Dual-Worker Families

The number of family units in which both husband and wife are gainfully employed has steadily increased during the twentieth century. By the late

Wives primarily concerned w/family life instead of their jobs.

Figure 8-4
Being a working mother is often difficult. Sometimes the solution, as here, is to take your child to work with you. *(United Press International Photo)*

1970s, the number of married women who held a job outside the household approached 50 percent (Weingarten, 1978:147). No one has yet predicted that this trend is likely to be reversed in the foreseeable future. Indeed, more wives and mothers probably will enter the work force in the decades ahead, so that the percentage will actually increase. One reason for this belief is the changing cultural attitude toward working wives and mothers. Husbands and wives, especially among the better-educated social classes, are more willing to adjust family life to accommodate the demands placed on both spouses in the labor force. Managers and top executives sometimes still resist promoting married women to high posts when they can possibly give the position to a male competitor—usually on the assumption that married women will place family needs above job commitment. But we may expect that social pressure and legal action will decrease this sort of discriminatory behavior (Rosen, Jerdee, and Prestwich, 1975).

Internal family adjustments to the competing demands of occupation and family life will also persist in the future. However, working couples report high degrees of both job satisfaction and marital happiness. Thus, the gains and costs of dual-earner marriages appear to be slanted toward support for the practice. Although a higher family income clearly helps to make dual-worker arrangements more attractive, money takes second place in many marriages to the opportunity for wives to achieve along with their husbands. The social-psychological payoff in terms of heightened self-esteem, personal fulfillment, and a sense of accomplishment all suggest that women are not likely

money 1st place

A Season for Marriage

to return willingly to the traditional model of family life which affords them only one vocational option—the homemaker role.

Across the course of human history and in most societies, people have assumed that marital unions were created to maintain the social order, and only secondarily to satisfy individual needs. The idea that societal interests or family appearances are more important than individual growth, fulfillment, and happiness has been radically challenged in recent years. Those who are schooled in the humanistic psychological theories of Rollo May, Carl Rogers, Abraham Maslow, and the ideas of such self-help strategies as transactional analysis have insisted that the personal satisfaction of the two partners is the new rule for measuring marital success. In this view, marriages maintained for the sake of appearances, for the children, or for fear of losing one's social standing are not really worth preserving. Rather, the purpose of marriage is redefined to be a way to increase the development of an individual's potential. Meanwhile, anything which contributes to this growth process, should be certified as a legitimate aspect of the marital experience. On the other hand, anything which stifles individual fulfillment should be relegated to the rubbish heap of outmoded marital styles.

The nonconformist alternatives to traditional marriage emphasize, almost unanimously, several themes. They stress the need for a marriage process in which couples actively cultivate such aspects as openness, gaining new experiences, honest communication, escape from role playing, supportive caring, the frank expression of needs, intimate and satisfying interpersonal relationships, the development of trust, the acquisition of a deeper self-knowledge, freedom from sexual hang-ups, companionship without a sense of jealous possessiveness, and living for the present rather than being bound by past failures or by future materialistic goals. The interest in achieving these aims has generated a variety of new options. They include the alternatives of open marriage, swinging, and communal or group marriage.

Open Marriage

The notion of **open marriage** was first made popular by Nena and George O'Neill (1972a). Open marriage was contrasted to what they defined as the conventional "closed marriage" of American culture in which couples related to their mates in a possessive fashion—speaking, for example, of "*my* wife" or "*my* husband"—and thus frustrated both partners' personal growth so that marriage became a monotonous grind. The remedy was a new model for marriage, which they conceived in these terms (O'Neill and O'Neill, 1972b):

> Open marriage can then be defined as a relationship in which the partners are committed to their own and to each other's growth. Supportive caring and in-

creasing security in individual identities makes possible the sharing of self-growth with a meaningful other who encourages and anticipates his own and his mate's growth. It is a relationship which is flexible enough to allow for change, which is constantly being renegotiated in the light of changing needs, consensus in decision making, in tolerance of individual growth, and in openness to new possibilities for growth. Obviously following this model often involves a departure, sometimes radical, from rigid conformity to the established husband-wife roles and is not easy to effect.

According to the O'Neills, the most serious difficulty couples encounter while trying the open-marriage approach in developing honest and open communication. Without skills in this area, it is almost impossible to surmount the barriers of misunderstanding, jealousy, possessiveness, and insensitivity to the other person's needs. However, improving communication skills can lead to a vital marital relationship which promotes understanding, caring, and a deeper level of self-knowledge. Open marriage, then, is not a static agreement but a process which leads through several levels of interpersonal development. The basic assumption on which this process is based holds that personal growth increases when the marital pair works together. Thus, each can accomplish more by exploring his or her individual identity within the open marriage than either one could possibly achieve without it.

Another feature of the open-marriage model which has sparked considerable attention and controversy is the acceptance of extramarital sexual relations. The O'Neills did suggest that not everyone was ready for a marital pattern in which partners released each other from a vow of sexual fidelity. Some partners working within the open-marriage guidelines might be able to block their feelings of jealousy when their spouses develop close friendships with someone of the opposite sex; but they may not be able to countenance sexual intimacy. The O'Neills seem to imply, however, that the ultimate test of whether one has overcome the possessiveness of traditional marriage is the partner's willingness to accept his or her spouse's extramarital sexual affairs. Those who can, they suggest, have achieved the highest stage, from which they can view their marital relationship as a "nonbinding commitment."

Quite apart from the logical problems of "nonbinding commitments"—which Christopher Lasch (1979:139), for one, believes are enough to dismiss the idea as sheer foolishness running counter to a viable partnership—the problems of marital jealousy proved to be somewhat more troublesome than most proponents of open marriage expected. Ira Reiss (1980:292) realistically concludes that, while some might agree in principle with the idea of sexual freedom in marriage, very few actually would want their mate to become sexually involved with another person, even though they might have full knowledge of the affair so that it was not a secret episode. Others, meanwhile, have suggested that open marriage amounted to little more than justification for extramarital affairs. Thus far, no solid empirical evidence demonstrates that open marriage really improves the quality of marital life or fosters the personal growth of marriage partners. The O'Neills' (1972b) own research efforts, which they characterized as "open-minded" interviews, ascertained that many respondents simply could not cope with the sexual jealousy aroused by a partner's extramarital relations. Although most social scientists would not have found this reaction surprising, the O'Neills thought such disclosures revealed problems in the married partners' relationship. Apparently, from their perspective, the only way to manifest sexual maturity was to endorse openly and knowingly extramarital sexual involvements, both for oneself and for one's mate.

A social scientist, of course, has no business prescribing the marital life-style couples ought to pursue. However, one should not hesitate to point out that the normative guidelines for open marriage formulated by the O'Neills are not the result of sophisticated social research. From the social scientific point of view, about all that can be concluded is that the merits of the open-marriage approach, whatever they may be, have yet to be empirically established. Some persons were apparently attracted to the O'Neills' proposals in the 1970s, but the data are not yet in on how many couples may be pursuing the open-marriage program in the 1980s.

Swinging

Swinging is a more recent term for mate-swapping, a form of recreational sex which is based on an agreement between marriage partners to engage in sexual relations with another couple and usually at the same time. Little social research on this alternative life-style has actually been undertaken. Estimates of the number of couples who "swing" range rather widely from 2.5 million to 8 million couples (Danfield and Gordon, 1970). The secretive nature of the activity makes it somewhat difficult to gather accurate figures.

By and large, swingers view their extramarital sexual activity as complementing their marriage. They usually justify swinging by saying that extramarital sex occurs frequently, is usually secretive, and can lead to an emotional involvement which damages the primary marital relationship. Swinging, they contend, is set within a group and follows strict rules to help ensure impersonality (Reiss, 1980:298–9). Thus, the danger of disrupting a marital relationship is greatly reduced, according to swingers. Many people regard swinging as a way to revitalize a boring or monotonous marriage.

Initiation into swinging usually results from the husband's urging. However, couples who start swinging are already sexually permissive, have some premarital sexual experience, and often are in their second marriages. Apart from their unusual sexual practice, most swinging couples are otherwise typical suburbanites with families, respectable jobs, and surprisingly conservative social attitudes with respect to other patterns of their lives (Bartell, 1971). The typical age for swingers is between 25 and 35 years, although some researchers have found active participants 70 years old.

Swinging candidates are contacted in a variety of ways. One approach is to place an ad in a swinger's magazine seeking other interested couples. Or, contact can be made through personal reference or by personal recruitment (Denfeld and Gordon, 1970). Probably the most common location for a swinger's party is in the home of one of the couples. Sometimes couples separate into different rooms; sometimes they remain together. Generally, the rules of the game are spelled out quite clearly so that everyone has a good idea of what is permissible and what is not. Some swinging groups place tight restrictions on contacts between parties, banning meetings other than the group sessions.

Although the literature on swinging is not very extensive, most commentators tend to suggest that this activity does contribute to healthy marriage adjustment. However, Denfeld (1974) observes that many swinging researchers also have been "swinging" researchers, and they sometimes use their reports to advocate swinging, often quite zealously, as a positive activity. Accordingly, Denfeld pursued an alternative strategy of studying the dropouts from swinging to discover some of the possible problems. The major problems reported, in the order of frequency are: jealousy, guilt, threat to marriage, development of outside emotional attachments, boredom, loss of interest, disappointment, divorce or separation, wife's inability to "take it," and fear of discovery. Not all couples in the dropout sample reacted negatively toward their swinging experience. Some reported improvement in their marital relationship, but most discovered this improvement was only temporary. Denfeld (1974) concludes by noting that many couples "left swinging hurt and psychologically damaged." In his view, earlier reports may have contributed to this by portraying swinging in a positive light when many couples simply were not emotionally capable of handling the experience.

Communal Living and Group Marriage

Experiments in communal living arose initially out of the counterculture movements of the 1960s and early 1970s. Unlike the orientation of swingers, however, the thinking behind communal life-styles was aggressively hostile to dominant middle-class mores and values, at least in many instances (Melville, 1972). Not all communes, of course, embraced a doctrine of sexual freedom which tolerated relations among all the participants on an indiscriminate basis. However, sexual latitude was a major aspect of the new cultural styles which many commune members sought to introduce. Recently, the number of communes supporting a counterculture ideology has drastically declined. Most communes of this type have disappeared altogether, in fact.

Closely affiliated with the communal experiments was another alternative known as **group marriage.** In one sense, this was communal living on a small scale. The group marriage brought together three or more persons who shared the same household and treated each other as spouses on a more or less equal basis. Probably the most well-known piece of research on group marriage was the report published by Joan and Larry Constantine (1973). They traveled around the country interviewing people who were or had been partners in a group-marriage household. Almost all of the respondents reported that they entered a multilateral family arrangement, expecting the relationship would be permanent. Most were not, however. The Constantines estimated that probably no more than 1,000 group marriages exist in the entire country at any one time. Moreover, the average time span for keeping intact a group marriage is between 6 and 12 months. This suggests that the

A Season for Marriage

organizational difficulties, the issues of jealousy, and the problems of close interaction are extraordinarily hard matters to resolve permanently. In fact, many adjustments which partners mentioned remind one of the solutions often devised by polygymous marriage arrangements in traditional cultures. A fixed rotation schedule for bed partners, for example, is highly reminiscent of family systems in which there are several wives.

The complexities arising from an effort to integrate even two married couples—some group marriages try to include more—into a mutually bonded quartet of spouses appear almost insurmountable. No cultural system has succeeded in institutionalizing group marriage on a wide scale. This helps explain why the Constantines could find no more than 100 groups and why two thirds of them broke up before the interviews could be completed. The low numbers of such marriages and their extreme instability suggest that this alternative will never become a popular marital life-style in America. No doubt, many people will continue to be very interested in group-marriage arrangements. But the number who actually live in such households will just as surely remain extremely small in comparison to other marital styles.

Summary

Traditional marriage is now a pattern followed by a minority of American families. A traditional marriage is a partnership in which husband and wife have entered a life-long commitment of fidelity to one another, with the husband alone supporting the family while the wife supervises the household and the child rearing in a home that is apart from both relatives and friends, and within an emotionally bound unit in which love permeates both husband-wife and parent-child relationships.

The alternatives to a traditional marriage style are quite varied. Those which we discuss in this chapter include staying single—by conscious choice, by delaying marriage, or by being forced into singlehood through death, divorce, or separation from a spouse—cohabitation, childless marriage, dual-career and dual-worker marriages, and the liberated alternatives, such as open marriage, swinging, and communal and group marriage. The liberated alternatives in particular are likely to be justified by ideas hostile to traditional marriage. Each of these life-styles, then, will usually be viewed by its proponents as an improvement on the traditional marriage. Any criticism of the traditional model in the other alternatives is quite muted. Of course, some alternatives, such as unchosen singlehood, are not even implied criticisms of traditional marriage.

The more popular and commonplace alternatives—and we would include here singlehood, cohabitation, childless marriage, and dual-earner families—should be seen primarily as efforts to accommodate marital life to the social and personal needs of contemporary partners. Chosen childlessness or a dual-career marriage, for example, are often compromises between the desire to pursue a career and the desire for the satisfactions of marriage. For some people, traditional marriage simply does not afford enough latitude for them to pursue their full range of interests. Meanwhile, other alternatives are not so much an escape from traditional marriage, but a sort of prelude to it. Prolonged singlehood and cohabitation which eventually leads to marriage are examples of short-term alternatives. The number of women who remain in the work force after marriage or reenter after the birth of children has been steadily rising. No doubt, the need for increased income accounts for a great many dual-earner families. But it also appears that many women enjoy being gainfully employed. They derive considerable satisfaction, self-esteem, and personal reward from their occupations. Hence, among all the varied alternatives, one should expect the greatest increase to be registered in the trend toward more working wives and mothers with careers.

STUDY QUESTIONS

1. What are the various reasons for staying single and how is chosen single-hood different from unchosen singlehood?

2. How has recent social research corrected the myth that homosexuals follow a uniform life-style? What are the various types of homosexual living patterns?

3. How can one account for the increasing popularity of cohabitation over the last two decades and what are the different meanings which cohabitation can take on for participating couples?

4. What are the major differences between dual-career and dual-worker couples? Why have the numbers of both increased in recent years?

5. To what extent are the liberated alternatives in contemporary marriage relations—namely, open marriage, swinging, or communal or group marriage—likely to become widespread and to what extent are they likely to remain limited to a very small proportion of American marriages?

6. Why is the group marriage relationship so difficult to maintain over an extended period of time?

PART FOUR

A Season for Parents and Children

An increasing number of married couples in America are in the life-cycle stage designated here as a "Season for Parents and Children." Approximately 95 percent of all American couples desire children, and slightly less than that number actually become parents. At the same time, couples also are choosing to have fewer children. Thus, the trend among contemporary couples is to avoid the two extremes of childlessness and large families.

Parenthood and childhood are two complementary role patterns. Each requires the other for the definition of its status. The two chapters which comprise this section examine these linked relationships from both sides. Chapter 9 focuses on the parental point of view by discussing the value parents ascribe to children, recent trends in fertility rates, and the parental roles of the mother and father. Chapter 10 is more concerned with the child's participation in the family circle. It describes in detail the role of family members in socializing children, so that they can mature into fully independent members of society.

9

The Choice of Parenthood

This chapter begins with a grotesque and bizarre quotation from the Roman philosopher, Seneca, a humane, literate, and able statesman, who writes here in defense of the ancient Roman practice of blinding and mutilating children abandoned by their parents. The purpose of ripping off or crushing limbs, of twisting spines, and plucking out eyes was to provide objects at which the Romans could laugh and miserable creatures who could beg for money in the streets and marketplace of the city. In support of this practice, Seneca wrote:

> Look on the blind wandering about the streets leaning on their sticks, and those with crushed feet, and still again look on those with broken limbs. This one is without arms, that one has had its shoulders pulled down out of shape in order that his grotesqueries may excite laughter—Let us go to the origin of all those ills—a laboratory for the manufacture of human wrecks—a cavern filled with the limbs torn from living children. . . .What wrong has been done to the Republic? On the contrary, have not these children been done a service inasmuch as their parents had cast them out? (quoted in Greenleaf, 1979:19).

Today, people would recoil at the callousness of Seneca's argument. We find it difficult enough to understand how parents could abandon their children alongside the road to die. But for others to come along and disfigure these helpless babies for life, so that as beggars they might incite their fellow citizens to laughter is even more difficult for us to understand. However, this illustration dramatizes quite plainly that the valuation of children has not remained the same across the span of time and cultures.

Since the decision to become a parent coincides with the eventual process of birth, both processes will be treated in this chapter. In American society, all young couples who marry are expected to want to have children sooner or later. However, a wife and husband choose to become parents for some specific reasons. Accordingly, the value of children is the first topic to be considered. The decision to become a parent also will be set within a broader frame of reference by examining recent fertility rates. Family planning is relevant by virtue of its impact on the number of offspring parents decide to bring into the world. Following an examination of the social roles of mother and father, a brief analysis of the pains and gratifications of parenthood will be explored. In the following chapter, the process of socialization—in which a biological organism is transformed into a human self—will be detailed.

The Valuation of Children

All societies depend upon the procreation of children to replenish their ranks. Therefore, one might well assume that society would take special care to assure that the next generation is nurtured adequately. This assumption is only partially borne out in actual social practice. The rules of legitimacy do specify which adults, usually the parents, are responsible for the early physical care and social training of the newborn (Goode, 1964:10–30). In many cultures, however, children have been regarded as a renewal resource, and thus little value has been attached to the lives of individual children. Even in Western civilization, whose Judeo-Christian heritage used its considerable symbolic influence to attribute value to the personal integrity of the human being, children were often neglected or relegated to a position of relative unimportance in family and social affairs until the beginning of the modern era (Aries, 1962). Thus, the child-centered orientation of contemporary Western culture, which is taken for granted today, really emerged quite recently in human history. Moreover, this perspective has yet to spread to all the peoples of the world.

The Reasons for Desiring Children

The vast majority of married couples in America desire children. It is a fair assumption that few have ever considered why they found parenthood attractive. The common expectation that parenthood follows marriage is part of what the sociologist E. E. LeMasters (1977) calls the traditional "folklore of parenthood." However, few couples today, regard childbirth as an "act of God" over which they have no control. More and more parents are now delaying the birth of their first child so that the wife and husband can enjoy several years together and work out any personal adjustment problems before bringing children into their family circle. Parents also are limiting sharply the size of their families and they are spacing the births of their children according to their specific timetable of needs and family plans (*Social Indicators*, 1976:2–3,16–17,26).

While parents now expect fewer children and most wish to control the time of each birth, these changes have not greatly reduced the number of couples who want at least one child. Some earlier reasons for desiring children are no longer strong motives for them today. When America was an agricultural society, children were an economic asset whose labor could be put to good use in the fields and around the homestead. Altered economic circumstances created by industrialization have now completely realigned the cost/benefit ratio of children. Today, sons and daughters are substantial financial investments on which parents receive little economic return—although as we shall see shortly, they receive other noneconomic compensations (Espenshade, 1977). Similarly, with improvements in modern medicine, the infant mortality rate has plunged, and with it the parent's need to have large families. No longer must parents expect that at least half of their offspring will die before adulthood. Moreover, having children is not so critical to cultural identity as it was in the past. Especially in the middle and upper classes, husbands generally do not view their ability to procreate as a sign of masculinity, nor do wives see childbearing as absolutely necessary to their fulfillment.

What, then, are the main reasons why couples want to become parents? Bernard Berelson (1979:245–7) has compiled a list of several personal benefits which can arise from parenthood. Of course, not everyone would rate these gains as equally compelling. Some parents might find one or two of these benefits not at all relevant to their own outlook. Included among these factors are:

Personal Power Most people exercise little direct influence over others in their everyday lives. Parents, however, hold a great deal of power over the lives of their children. The exercise of parental power can, on occasion, be gratifying, even though it also carries with it considerable responsibility. Parents frequently enjoy the experience of having someone look up to and admire them, and for most parents their decisions for their offspring are often the most direct form of influence they will ever hold over the affairs of another person. The personal power wielded by parents is a necessary feature of the parent-child relationship, particularly when children are still very young. As young people grow up, parental power steadily decreases and is transformed from a direct control over behavior to an indirect form of influence which is based on respect, love, and psychological appeals.

Personal Competence For a variety of reasons, individuals may be frustrated in their attempt to demonstrate competence in economic, political, or other areas of social life. However, "mother" and "father" are two of the major social roles available to almost everyone. Competence in these roles may well be within the reach of persons who are determined to perform well, even when they lack the talent, opportunity, or social training to achieve in other social roles.

Personal Status Parenthood automatically confers status upon a couple. "Honor thy Father and Mother" is not only one of the Ten Commandments. It is also a general cultural norm that parents deserve respect simply because they are parents. Mother's Day and Father's Day are but two of the many ways we symbolize the social value attached to parenthood.

Personal Extension Parents tend to look upon their children as extensions of themselves, as persons who carry on their lineage, their flesh and blood. This is egoistic, without necessarily being selfish. For many parents, children are one way to answer their own need for immortality. Consequently, children often are named after their parents or another close relative so that family names continue to be passed down from generation to generation. Knowing that they will be remembered by their children, if by no one else, is one of parenthood's major psychological gratifications.

Personal Experience The experience of parenthood is unique among the many activities of life. Nothing quite compares to it or even comes close. Having children has many facets: the opportunity to love and be loved, the challenge of helping to shape a new life, the chance to relive one's own childhood, the deep anxiety of a seriously ill child, the thrill of watching your child learn to ride a bicycle, your deep curiosity about how the child will turn out,

Figure 9-1.
Many activities—such as taking a ride on a ferris wheel—are more exciting when done in the company of one's children. This excitement is often contagious. (© *Beryl Goldberg)*

the sense of pride at each of your child's achievements, and the hurts you share in the child's disappointments. Certainly, life without children can be satisfying, but the fulfillment of parenthood is different from all others.

Personal Pleasure   While children can be a drain on parental time, patience, money, and energy, they also can be a source of a great deal of fun and many good times. Going to the zoo, visiting relatives, watching a parade, catching a fish, flying in a plane, riding in a bus, decorating a Christmas tree, even baking a cake, all become different experiences when your children take part. Seeing the world through their eyes is often more adventuresome, exciting, and fun-filled than seeing it through a parent's adult eyes. Children are fre-

A Season for Parents and Children

quently a source of comic relief in a human drama that can be fraught with small but daily tensions. Indeed, parents most often cite the personal pleasures they derive from their children as the number-one reason for wanting them.

Berelson's list of reasons for desiring children may not be exhaustive, but it does include the major motives most parents mention. Of course, people can have unhealthy reasons for wanting to become a parent, and several of the reasons Berelson identifies can have their darker side as well. Personal power can be overextended until the parent stifles the child's development. Parents who try to relive their own childhood through a son or daughter may force them to engage in activities they deeply detest. Several other examples of unhealthy reasons for wanting children also spring readily to mind. Couples who are experiencing marital difficulties sometimes conclude that having a child will help cement their relationship and smooth over their problems. More often than not, this strategy fails and simply adds to an already stressful situation—the additional strains of rearing a child (Thornton, 1977). Having a child is occasionally seen by a husband as an excellent way to get his wife to leave the work force and stay home and play the homemaker role he prefers for her. Or, a wife with a boring, unsatisfying job may decide that pregnancy is the simplest way to escape that situation (Rubin, 1976:75). The problem in the last two examples is that the child is not chosen for his own sake, but to achieve another goal. When this occurs, a couple is probably not ready for parenthood.

The Declining Birth Rate and the Value of Having Children

As we have already noted, the birth rate has been declining in American society in recent years. Many people jump to the conclusion that this statistic suggests a similar decline in the value people see in having children—an idea that is clearly untrue for several reasons. Perhaps most telling is the fact that the number of childless couples also has been declining. For example, Glick (1977) found, in his examination of fertility data for the last 80 years, that between 21 to 26 percent of couples remained childless during the first 40 years of the study period, while only 9 to 14 percent had no children in the last 40 years. This sharp decline in childless Americans may very well result largely from better medical services which improve a woman's ability to conceive a child. Yet the decline in childless couples also indicates that a sizable share of the population still desire children (Bane, 1976:12). Thus, we really are witnessing two trends tending in somewhat different directions. On the one hand, parents are having fewer children than couples did in the past, while on the other hand, a larger percentage of couples are having one child. The overall result, therefore, is a decline in the fertility rate, but without a loss of interest in having children. The number of families with more than three children has dropped off sharply in the last 20 years, while families with one to three children have increased. These data clearly indicate a continuing desire to have children as a part of the family circle.

Over the past quarter century, the population explosion has been identified as a major world social problem—perhaps outweighing the problems of nuclear war and economic development. Doomsday prophets have been warning us of a time in the not-too-distant future when there will be standing room only on this planet, unless quick and decisive action is taken to curtail world population growth (Ehrlich, 1968). Such movements as Zero Population Growth have mounted a concerted effort to warn us of the dangers of overpopulation.

However, recent data indicate that the world population crisis may be easing, even though it is still not resolved and some areas of the world continue to experience almost runaway population growth. The turning point for the less-developed countries appears to have occurred between 1970 and 1975 (Tsui and Bogue, 1978:4). Moreover, the birth rate now appears to be declining more universally and at a faster pace than most experts expected. Some scholars are now guardedly optimistic about the idea that controlling population growth worldwide still may be possible, but this feat has not yet been accomplished.

Industrialization and Fertility Rates

Students of population processes have long been puzzled over what forces curb the birth rate. For several decades, the accepted wisdom was that industrialization of a nation seemed to lower fertility rates more than any other single factor. William Goode (1970) argued, for example, that a cross-cultural "fit" or link existed between the rise of an industrialized economy and the emergence of a small, isolated nuclear family unit with a low birth rate. However, Goode (1970:10–25) cautioned against too hastily concluding that industrialization caused the shift to smaller family structures and limited population in modern societies. All we can definitely show now, he concluded, is that the two factors are related.

Nonetheless, the idea was widely accepted that less-developed countries would continue to experience uncontrolled population increases until the forces of industrialization made deep inroads on traditional cultural practices and norms. The demographic transition theory emerged as the way to interpret how this process came about. According to this theory, societies move in a series of stages from a high birth rate, high death rate, and low standard of living to a low birth rate, low death rate, and high standard of living. The first step that results from economic progress is a lowering of the death rate due to better medical care, diets, and sanitation. For a while, the birth rate remains high, threatening overpopulation. Then modernization gradually erodes the institutional supports—such as the religious ideas, family ideals, and economic norms, which encourage high fertility rates. As the birth rate begins to decline, the standard of living begins to increase, and therefore a built-in social reward—the desire to keep that living standard—reinforces the trend toward smaller families.

This demographic transition theory supported the belief that no family-planning campaign could affect fertility rates in societies which were not progressing toward modernization. However, in the last few years that supposition has come under attack, and even the most conservative of these theorists are now beginning to revise their assumptions. In a careful analysis of world population data, Tsui and Bogue (1978:30–3) discovered that the level of family planning in any developing country greatly affected its birth rate, even when its other socioeconomic signs of modernization were few or almost entirely lacking. Apparently, family-planning programs do work on their own, and nations need not wait until modernization is under way before launching birth-control efforts. This finding is an important breakthrough for policy decisions on population-control programs.

Another recent study by van de Walle and Krodel (1980) has challenged a separate feature of the demographic transition theory. Using historical data from Western Europe, these two scholars demonstrated that the decline in fertility occurred before the decline in infant deaths, which was exactly the reverse of the demographic transition thesis. In the judgment of van de Walle and Krodel, it was not the overpopulation pressure triggered by a lower mortality rate among infants which caused the drop in fertility. Rather, it was the conscious decision to limit family size, influenced by new cultural factors and values, which caused the decline in the birth rate. Moreover, this occurred in many social settings; some were industrialized and urbanized while others were untouched by these modern social forces. Thus, the decline in fertility seems to be fairly independent of the modernization process.

Fertility Rates in American Society

The United States was among the first nations to pass through the demographic transition. Indeed, our fertility rate has decreased rather steadily since the 1850s, except for the brief period following World War II known as the "baby boom" (1947–1961). In the 1960s, the fertility rate started to drop off quite rapidly (Social Indicators, 1976:2–5). Our current fertility rate is approximately 15 births per 1,000 citizens (U.S. Bureau of the Census, 1979:11). This produces continued population growth, but at a declining rate of increase. However, if the rate of decline begun in the last 15 years continues, we could experience a net decline in population in the relatively near future.

Predicting future population growth is always risky. The U.S. Bureau of the Census has devised three projection series in population changes in American society up to the year 2040, with each series based on different fertility assumptions. Series I, for example, assumes an average of 2.7 births per woman in the population of childbearing age. This is considered the highest rate of population growth which falls within the range of probability, although few analysts actually believe we will ever see that high a fertility level

Figure 9-2
(Top) Population
Growth: 1790–2040;
(Bottom) Average An-
nual Rate of Popula-
tion Change between
Decennial Census
Years: 1790–2040.
(*Source:* Social Indicators
1976:4)

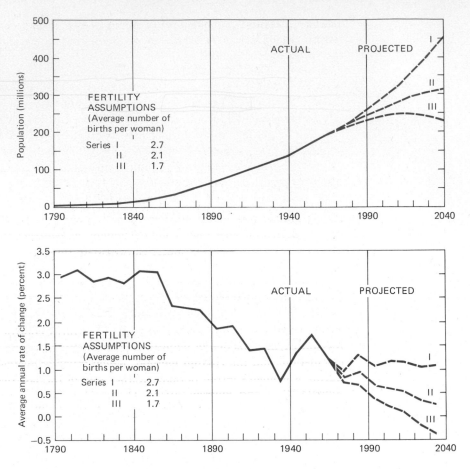

again. If population growth should follow the projection of Series I, then the United States would have a total population of 450 million by the year 2040, approximately double the present figure.

Series II assumes that women of childbearing age will, in the future, give birth to an average of 2.1 children. This would be very close to our current birth rate, and it would basically maintain the present population size. According to this projection, the national population in the year 2040 would be about 312 million (Social Indicators, 1976:22). Series III assumes a fertility rate only of 1.7 births per woman of childbearing age. Projections based on this figure would project a growth peak of 252 million persons in the year 2020, followed by a decline to 238 million in the year 2040. Interestingly, while Series I and III differ by only one average birth per woman of child-bearing age (2.7 compared to 1.7), the net difference in population size by the year 2040 is about 212 million people (450 million projected by Series I as opposed to 238 million by Series III). Therefore, even a slight change in the average fertility rate can make a great deal of difference in the nation's population growth over several decades. Barring major disruptions in our so-

A Season for Parents and Children

cial life, the most probable course may be assumed to lie somewhere between Series II and III.

The Increase in Family Planning

Family planning refers to a couple's effort to control the number and spacing of children born to them. Across the ages, couples have desired a means to prevent pregnancy. Most traditional cultures used exotic and bizarre practices based on magic, superstition, or folk medicine to limit fertility; their reliability, of course, was almost nil (Katchadourian and Lunde, 1980:163). Not until the modern era have safe, effective **means of contraception** (and **abortion**) become available, so that couples can regulate their family's size with relative ease.

A number of birth-control measures are available, some of which involve contraceptive devices and others which do not. The oldest form of birth control, for example, is simple **abstinence,** that is, the decision not to engage in sexual relations. Other "natural" methods of birth control include **coitus interruptus,** the practice of withdrawing the penis from the vagina just before ejaculation, and the **rhythm method**, which involves avoidance of intercourse during a woman's fertile period. Neither one of the last two methods is very reliable (Ross and Piotrow, 1974). The most common types of birth control today are contraceptives, which include the oral pill, the condom, the diaphragm, spermicidal foams, and the intrauterine device (IUD). And finally, birth control can also be achieved through sterilization or abortion. (The various types of birth control are discussed more fully in the Appendix).

Contemporary Attitudes toward Contraception

When Margaret Sanger led the fight for a birth-control movement that could freely disseminate its information to American women, she was confronted by fierce opposition and later imprisoned (Kennedy, 1970). Today, such information is readily available from Planned Parenthood, school sex-education classes, or other organizations. Not only has Sanger's central argument that women have a right to contraception information finally triumphed, but public policy also has recognized that birth control is in the nation's— and the world's—collective social interest. However, pockets of resistance still exist in some regions of the country, and in some places they are even increasing in strength under pressure from the Moral Majority. The battle over birth control is not yet over.

The major sources of organizational opposition to birth-control information and practices are the Roman Catholic Church (Murphy and Erhart, 1975) and Protestant conservatives. But not all birth-control practices violate Catholic teaching. Abstinence and the rhythm method are legitimate forms of preventing a new pregnancy when the couple has a serious reason for desiring not to procreate, such as the health of the mother or economic hardship. The crux of the matter, as Thomas (1965:114) points out, is not whether the means of contraception is natural or artificial, but whether the "means employed is in conformity with the nature and purpose of the conjugal act." Thus, coitus interruptus is condemned by the Church, just as is the use of the pill, condom, or diaphragm. In each case the possibility of intercourse leading to conception is disrupted so that the natural process of conception is made subject to human interference. By contrast, the rhythm method works with the regular processes of nature and therefore is not seen as a violation of natural law.

The official position of the Roman Catholic Church has not gone unchallenged, either by Church officials or by the faithful. In July 1968, Pope Paul VI issued the encyclical, *Humanae Vitae*, which immediately unleashed a fresh storm of protest against the traditional position of the Church on birth control. While the encyclical has reaffirmed the Church's ban on forms of birth control other than the rhythm method, many American Catholics dissented from this stand. Fifty-eight percent of American Catholics interviewed in a Gallup poll taken three years after the encyclical was promulgated stated that they could ignore the Vatican's prohibition on birth control and still be good Catholics (Rosten, 1975:393). The Roman Catholic sociologist, Father Andrew Greeley (1977:165), reported that 60 percent of the priests in America do not believe that all artificial contraception is wrong, and only 20 percent are sure that it is wrong. Indeed, the number of priests opposed to birth control even by artificial means has *decreased* since the 1968 encyclical restating traditional Catholic teaching. Similarly, the number of Catholic women under the age of 45 who used some form of birth control, including the rhythm method, increased by 4 percent between 1965 and 1970 (from 77 to 81 percent). However, during the same period, the number of women who used only the rhythm method declined by 14 percent, while use of the oral contraceptive pill increased by 14 percent (Greeley et al., 1976:140). John Scanzoni (1975) also found that, while some differences still exist between Catholic and non-Catholic wives in their attitudes toward contraceptive use (non-Catholic contraceptive use was higher) and in the number of expected children (Catholic women expected to have more children), these differences were narrowing rapidly, especially among younger women. Given the current trends in contraceptive attitudes, Ira Reiss (1980:361) predicts that even the small differences between Catholics and non-Catholics will almost vanish during the early 1980s.

The sheer size of the American Catholic Church makes its opposition to most forms of birth control a newsworthy item. However, Roman Catholicism is not the only faith in America to oppose birth control. John Wilson (1978:251) reminds us that "the various Orthodox churches and the Mormons also oppose contraception by any means other than periodic abstinence." Moreover, many Protestant sects continue to exhibit much higher fertility rates than the population average. But this is mostly because these groups are largely drawn from the lower classes which have had higher fertility rates.

On balance, then, positive attitudes toward family planning and contracep-

This case history was provided by a colleague who teaches in the Midwest. It shows how couples can switch from one contraceptive method to another as their needs and interests change over the course of their life cycle. It is reprinted here with permission from the author who requested to remain anonymous.

Both college educated, my wife and I have always been concerned about family planning. Over the years we developed a sequence of contraceptive methods that has worked fairly well for us.

When we were first married, we used condoms and foam. This method turned out to be too messy and inconvenient for us. Since we knew that we didn't want children for a few years, my wife started using the pill. After our third year of marriage, my wife stopped using the pill and we started trying to conceive. Her menstrual cycle had always been irregular, and it remained so at this point. Then, shortly before our fifth wedding anniversary, our first son was born.

After his birth, we decided to switch to the IUD (Lippies Loop). Our doctor had advised us that it works better after childbirth. Things worked well for about three years when, surprisingly, my wife's IUD came out. An accidental pregnancy occurred, but it ended in an early miscarriage. We switched to a diaphragm for about a year until we were ready to conceive again. Our second son was born 5½ years after the first one.

We now had two wonderful boys and decided to stop there; we were already well into our 30s and figured that we'd done enough to perpetuate the species. We went back to an IUD for about a year, long enough to see that our second child was developing normally. Then, I underwent an irreversible vasectomy. Although our doctor warned me about mild and temporary side effects in about a quarter of the cases, I've experienced none so far.

As a result of my operation, we've eliminated all worry and inconvenience about sexual intimacy, and we are both pleased about the way we organized our contraceptive strategy. By frequently switching methods, we've consciously tried to minimize the possible health problems associated with long term use of any method. Just as important, we've worked together in developing our approach, and we've shared equally the responsibility of being the primary contraceptive agent.

tives have grown stronger over the last two decades. The officialdom of various religious bodies still formally oppose these developments, but their influence on the faithful in these matters has been steadily decreasing. Some people do become agitated when Planned Parenthood or similar organizations discuss the policy of distributing contraceptives to single young people, especially when they are minors and are receiving contraceptives without their parents' knowledge. But most people no longer question contraceptive use by married couples.

Family Planning and Contraceptive Choice

Choosing a contraceptive sometimes leads to confusion. A bewildering array of different types is available and couples often are at a loss to know which one will best meet their individual needs. No one type is "just right" for

Figure 9-3
Modern technology has made available a wide variety of family planning options. Today, couples can choose which form of contraception best meets their family planning needs. *(Copyright © by Stock, Boston, Inc.)*

everyone. Several factors must be weighed before making a choice. Contraceptives differ in effectiveness, hazardous side effects, and convenience. If the various types were to be rated only for how well they prevent pregnancy, most experts would order them in this way: the pill, IUD, diaphragm, condom, and finally spermicidal foams (see Appendix). The order would be very nearly reversed when ranked by reference to health risks, with the condom and diaphragm least harmful, followed by spermicidal foams, the IUD, and finally the pill, whose hazard for certain women is quite high. Unfortunately, the safest forms of birth control are also the least convenient to use.

In balancing the factors of effectiveness and potential health risk, couples would be well advised to consult with their physician. The female partner's medical history will be especially relevant to this decision, since she alone would bear the risk of side effects from the pill or an IUD. A physician also might point out that the expected level of sexual activity is a factor in selection, as is the degree of marital disruption which an unexpected pregnancy might create. With these issues in mind, a couple can decide which form of contraception best fits their life-style, sexual behavior, and their normative point of view.

The Parenthood Roles

Few decisions are more far-reaching in their effects than the decision to become parents. Marriages can be dissolved when the relationship deteriorates, but the birth of a child is an irrevocable event. Today, of course, most couples are fully aware of the seriousness of the parental role. Childbearing is seldom taken lightly, or entered into without some preparation. However, no

A Season for Parents and Children

amount of planning and arrangements ever seem ample to prepare for all the new sorts of problems and anxieties which new parents typically encounter.

The Cultural Shock of Parenthood

Preparation for parenthood begins in earnest with pregnancy. The months prior to birth, especially for a first child, tend to be devoted to preparing for the delivery and the care of the newborn immediately afterward. In today's nuclear family, young parents cannot learn to care for infants from members of their extended family as easily as previous generations could. Physicians, friends, child-care classes, and "baby books," such as the 26 million copies of Dr. Spock's, *Baby and Child Care*, have all helped to fill the information gap. Despite their minimal or elaborate preparations, however, most new parents learn the bulk of their new tasks through on-the-job training.

The birth of a child requires a reordering of wife and husband roles, as well as changes in their life-style. Several social scientists have described the first child's appearance as a cultural shock (Rossi, 1968; Lopata, 1972; Le-Masters, 1977). The transition to parenthood is abrupt and all embracing. Few aspects of the domestic scene are untouched. No longer can parents pursue their own interests at will, such as dashing out at midnight to get a spur-of-the-moment pizza. Nor is such activity quite as attractive when at least one of them will have to get up for the 2 A.M. feeding. Indeed, every time they go out, logistical problems must be solved. If they go out alone, a baby-sitter must be found. And if they take the baby along, the crib, bottles, and diapers must be packed. No wonder couples frequently decide to avoid all the hassle and just stay home.

The amount of time a young infant requires is another aspect of the cultural shock of parenthood. A husband and wife are generally accustomed to spending a great deal of time together. After a baby arrives, however, free time is usually in very short supply, especially for the mother. Patterns of behavior that the husband and wife had worked out now must be changed to accommodate a third person. Moreover, new infants live on their own time-tables, pressing demands for food, clean diapers, or attention without regard for what the parents may be doing or planning to do. Parental routines, meal-time schedules, and even sexual activities are all subject to interruption at any time. Young couples are seldom prepared for the loss of sleep and privacy, and the restrictions on their social activities caused by the "little bundle" they brought home from the hospital.

Of course, these observations are not meant to place parenthood in a negative light. The point is considerably more modest. Just as marriage partners idealize their mates or romanticize marriage, they also tend to fantasize parenthood into an ideal situation. The Madison Avenue approach to parenthood portrays an adoring couple observing their smiling or sleeping child safely nestled in a sparkling clean crib. The reality is that babies get colic, cry unmercifully when they are teething, soil mounds of diapers which are no fun to change, require the expenditure of large sums of money, and completely demolish household routines (Duberman, 1977:143). Thus, the adjustment to

Figure 9-4
Motherhood today is
frequently a very de-
manding—and some-
times an anxiety-rid-
den—role. *(Courtesy of
Vincent Balduc.)*

parenthood is often as difficult as the adjustment to marriage, and for some couples it is more difficult.

This is not an argument against becoming a mother or father. Rather, it is a suggestion that parenthood is an extremely demanding role, probably far more demanding than most young couples realize. For this reason, it is generally not entered into lightly or without preparation. An infant cannot choose its parents, but parents can choose not to have children until they are reasonably well prepared for those responsibilities. To be sure, it is not easy to know when they have reached this point. Probably the best sign is that their own relationship is stable. Many couples are reluctant to even think about having children until they are convinced their marriage is secure enough to withstand the additional strains of parenthood.

Behavioral scientists do not agree about the extent to which the transition to parenthood disrupts a couple's lives. Hill (1949) and LeMasters (1957) pioneered the view that parenthood was a "crisis" in the family life cycle. Later researchers cautioned that the term "crisis" may be too strong. Rossi (1968) recommended "transition to parenthood" to suggest that, while the marriage was changing, especially with the birth of the first child, the change was not so disruptive as to threaten most family units. Russell (1974), Hobbs and Cole (1976), and Hobbs and Wimbish (1977) have all documented the limited character of the disruption caused by parenthood and suggested that "transition" rather than "crisis" more accurately reflects the experience of most couples. Generally speaking, mothers had to adjust more than fathers, and black parents had somewhat higher rates of adjustment difficulties than white parents. Overall, however, few couples reported "severe crisis." Thus, it seems safe to conclude that for most parents the cultural shock is real, but not overwhelming.

The Social Role of Mother

In American culture, the role of motherhood is adorned with a great deal of sentimentality. John Quincy Adams wrote, "All that I am my mother made me." His aphorism was later topped by the more famous quote of Abraham Lincoln: "All I am, or hope to be, I owe to my angel mother." Furthermore, everyone is familiar with the general feeling of respect and courtesy that is reserved for mothers by most of society. For example, Mother's Day, with all its commercial overtones, is nonetheless widely and enthusiastically observed in the United States. No doubt exists that motherhood is a critical social role in our culture. While the following chapter will focus on the influence of both mothers and fathers in the socialization of their children, our concern in this section is the parental side of the parent-child relationship. Unfortunately, almost all behavioral research has been confined to the child (Rossi, 1968). Consequently, we really know less about how parents relate to their roles as mothers and fathers than about how these roles affect their children.

In approaching the social role of motherhood from the mother's perspective, we must begin with the obvious observation that the role of mother is drastically different from the role of wife or other occupational roles women may assume. Skills in other role performances do not guarantee success as a mother. The vast majority of women who marry expect that eventually they will become mothers. Among young married women, only about 5 percent want to remain childless (Bane, 1976:9). This nearly universal desire for children should not be taken as evidence for the existence of a maternal instinct, however. The motherhood role is not an inherited behavior pattern, but a learned set of social skills. Indeed, motherhood today involves a complex combination of responsibilities which require skills in child care, emotional support, guidance, and discipline. Blending all of these tasks into a smooth performance is a delicate and demanding job which takes time to master. However, as maternal experience increases, most women become quite good at the maternal role; they also get more satisfaction from motherhood (Lopata, 1972:182–223). Understandably, then, the highest reports of feelings of inadequacy, anxiety, or dissatisfaction with motherhood usually come from new mothers. At this stage, the combination of a lack of experience, limited information about the task and total absorption in it, can create intense feelings of role ambiguity and deep frustration. In addition, young mothers keenly feel the loss of freedom that results from child rearing, especially with the first child. Seldom do young women enter motherhood fully prepared for the role ambiguity, insecurity, and apprehension which they can experience during their first years as mothers.

Of course, motherhood is not without its gratifications—if it were, women would simply refuse the role. The most important payoff is probably psychological. Mother-child contact produces an emotional bond of exceptional intensity, at least for mothers in our culture. The recent upsurge in incidents of child abuse (Fontana, 1976) and child neglect (Wooden, 1976) show that not all mothers are loving, caring persons. However, these acts of aggression reveal deep frustration with parental roles, or even mental illness. Unlike these unfortunate cases, most mothers experience a bond of love and solidarity with their children which is equaled only by the bond with their husbands. Much has been written about the child's absolute need to be loved, but much less has been said about the mother's need to give love, provide nurturing care, and receive in return the affection of her children (Parsons and Bales, 1955:67–88). Yet, of all the rewards of motherhood, the greatest appears to

---

TEST YOURSELF

On Support for Day Care Centers and Maternity Leaves

Each of the questions below has actually been used in a sample survey designed to test your opinion on the need for and funding of day care centers as well as the appropriateness of maternity leaves. After each statement, circle whether you agree strongly (AS), agree mildly (AM), disagree mildly (DM), or disagree strongly (DS). Under each choice is a number. Add up all your scores when you have completed the self-test. If your score is close to 6, then you have expressed a conservative opinion on day care and maternity leaves. A score close to 24 will indicate a liberal attitude on these issues.

There ought to be more day care institutions for children so that women can participate in work and public activities.

AS	AM	DM	DS
4	3	2	1

The University should provide free child care for students with children, even if this means cutting back elsewhere.

AS	AM	DM	DS
4	3	2	1

Cost for day care should be borne entirely by the mothers whose children are cared for.

AS	AM	DM	DS
1	2	3	4

Cost for day care should be borne entirely by the government.

AS	AM	DM	DS
4	3	2	1

A woman's job should be kept for her when she is having a baby.

AS	AM	DM	DS
4	3	2	1

Employers should be required by law to give women maternity leave with full pay.

AS	AM	DM	DS
4	3	2	1

Source: Karen Oppenheim Mason, with the assistance of Daniel R. Denison and Anita J. Schacht. *Sex-Role Attitude Items and Scales From U.S. Sample Surveys.* Rockville, Md.: National Institute of Mental Health. 1975, pp. 27–8.

A Season for Parents and Children

be the response of genuine love from offspring (Bernard, 1975a:75–6) who see their mothers as persons of unlimited importance and value, as well as persons concerned with their children's well-being.

While the affection bestowed on mothers is a crucial payoff for their role performance, a number of other gratifications also arise. Russell (1974) identified such positive responses as: a sense of pride in watching the baby grow and develop, less boredom, a closer relationship to relatives, a deeper purpose for living, the enjoyment of the baby's company, the fun of playing with the baby, a sense of "fulfillment," a new appreciation for one's own parents, a greater appreciation for family and religious ties, and a sense of feeling "closer" to one's spouse. Indeed, most adults are fascinated with the cute antics of babies of almost any species—kittens, puppies, or piglets—but human infants hold the greatest attraction of all. However, when that infant is your own, the product of your labor, your investment of time and care, the attraction is immensely intensified. To watch an uncoordinated baby grow through the creeper, toddler, and early childhood stages is one of life's great experiences. But to know, in addition, that you have been primarily responsible for this infant's distinctive human personality, as most mothers are, generates a unique pride and sense of accomplishment. Making money may have its own special pleasure, building a career may be self-fulfilling, but creating and then molding a life produces a gratification that, for many people, is without parallel in human experience.

To be sure, much of the mother's role is boring and menial. When a baby soils its diapers two minutes after being changed, spews strained beets all over the kitchen, or pulls all the books off the shelves for the tenth time, the mother is certainly to be permitted an occasional outburst of exasperation. But when mothers are asked if all the time, worry, and care are really worth it, the vast majority answer yes (Blood and Wolfe, 1965:138–41). Indeed among the "good things about having children" cited most often by the mothers in Blood and Wolfe's study were the pleasures and emotional satisfactions, companionship, the sense of purpose, and the strengthening of family life which offspring inspired. Very few mothers reported "nothing good" about having children.

No doubt, of course, the role of motherhood can be made easier. Greater social support from the husband and other family members, as well as from the school, church or synagogue, or community can lessen the burdens mothers carry. These support networks may well become more important as the nature of motherhood is redefined. Over the last several generations, motherhood has shifted from a concern with rearing children who were clean, neat, quiet, and well behaved (Lopata, 1972:212–3). Motherhood now tends to be oriented to relationships—at least among better-educated mothers—and concerned with the development of children's abilities and their overall growth process. Mothers using this approach recognize the importance of child-rearing techniques in molding the character and talents of their children (Duberman, 1975a:64–7). Thus, amid the plentiful advice from child-rearing specialists, mothers must sort out the practices that seem likely to help form happy, capable children. The orientation toward relationships can produce more problems and stress for mothers, but it also draws more heavily on the social facilities available to mothers in their role performance, and thus can help reduce their own burdens.

The Social Role of Father

Far less attention has been paid to the social role of fathers than mothers by social scientists (Fein, 1978). Indeed, Lamb (1976:28–29) is convinced this imbalance has contributed to a general devaluation of fatherhood in contemporary society. A flurry of research reports on fathering over the last decade gives promise that this situation is being corrected. The traditional point of view—generally shared by fathers and social scientists—has been that the father's relationship to his children takes a clear second-place position to the mother's. The mother is usually the one who drops out of the work force to care for the child during infancy. Meanwhile, as Duberman (1975a:67) observes, most American men "consider the paternal role peripheral to the provider role and feel that if they discharge their financial obligations to their children they are 'good' fathers."

The idea that a father can best help his children by providing for their material support and leaving the child rearing to their mother is now under attach from many quarters. Jessie Bernard (1975a), for example, argues that being a mother is too important a social function to be left to women alone. Fathers also should be involved in the nurturing activities of child care. Others suggest that inadequate father-child interaction denies men a source of pleasure and emotionally gratifying relationships with their offspring (Nash, 1976). Thus, it is now becoming more fashionable to regard parenting as suitable to fathers as well as mothers.

However, fatherhood is quite different in its makeup from the social role of motherhood. Based on the collective body of research undertaken by Benson (1968), Broderick (1978), and others, we can isolate three major aspects of the fathering role: material support, leadership, and nurturance. While fathers do share each of these aspects of parenting with mothers, fathers nonetheless tend to contribute to the child-rearing process in somewhat different ways than mothers.

1. The responsibility for providing material support normally is given primarily to the father by both custom and law, and only secondarily to the mother. Therefore, a father who views his parental role largely as that of a provider, merely reflects the assumption of his society. Recently, this assumption has begun to change since a greater proportion of women work outside the home and more working mothers are sharing the provider role with their husbands. But in most families the father still earns the higher income and assumes the major responsibility for meeting family needs or aspirations related to financial matters (Glick and Norton, 1977:10–13).

2. Leadership is another aspect of parenthood in which both husband and wife engage, although sometimes with differing degrees of power and authority. The traditional father role gave him far greater authority—to enforce behavior, establish values, and set the attitudinal patterns for the household. He was the final court of appeal in family decision making and the ultimate disciplinarian. Today, such a one-sided exercise of power is no longer seen as desirable in most middle-class families. The autocratic pattern of father dominance has given way to a more equalitarian leadership structure in which the mother takes part in decision making, discipline, and the framing of moral values for the family. Parental leadership is no longer a shorthand term for the father's authority.

Another aspect of the father's leadership function is to serve as a role model for his children. In this capacity, he demonstrates through his behavior and values the actions and attitudes he expects his children to adopt. They learn honesty, dedication to hard work, and reliability by imitating his example. Boys in particular acquire much of their first knowledge of basic elements of the masculine sex role by identifying with their father. Of course, their father is by no means the only source of such information for young boys. But interaction with him is certainly one of

Figure 9-5
Victorian fathers often looked quite uncomfortable when caring for their children. (*Courtesy of William Garrett.*)

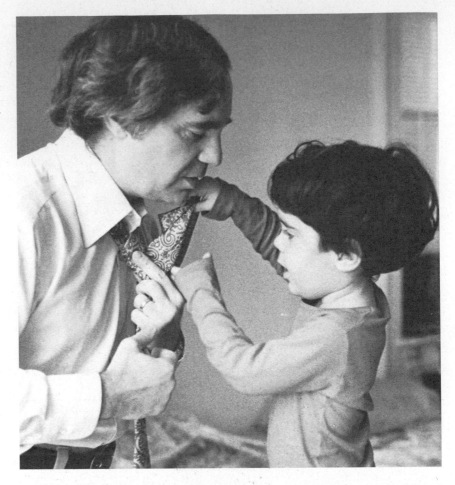

Figure 9-6
But today's fathers are taking a more active role in nurturing their children. They still remain important role models, however, especially for their sons. © *Alice Kandell, Photo Researchers, Inc.)*

the most important ways in which they learn. However, imitation of attitudes is not confined to male children. Girls also take on many of their fathers' views even though their sex-role cues tend to derive from their mothers.

3. And finally, the role of fatherhood is expanding to include expressive nurturing. Several generations ago, fathers were expected to be relatively aloof from their offspring. The mother was the parent to whom one turned for love, comfort, and emotional support. Today, however, more and more fathers are actively caring for their children by feeding, loving, and playing with their offspring. Fathers may not yet spend as much time with their children as mothers, but they are intervening more often at critical points to advise and encourage their children (Duberman, 1975a:69). Such expressions of love and concern can help a great deal to make a child feel secure. Moreover, such expressions from the father also help relieve the mother of some of the psychological burdens of child rearing. Thus, for mothers, children, and fathers, the re-

cent upsurge in fatherly nurturing can be expected to produce positive results. More than ever, children are turning to their fathers for the warm supportive guidance which once they could expect to receive only from their mothers.

The Costs and Gratifications of Parenthood

Birth is a biological process, but the decision to care for children and to accept the responsibilities of parenthood is a social process. As this chapter has made clear, there are alternatives to parenthood. Conception can be prevented today through various birth-control techniques—including abortion—or the infant can be put up for adoption, so that adults other than the parents assume the social roles of mother and father. These possibilities raise the question of the costs and rewards derived from parenthood. Why do marriage partners still insist on bringing children into the world, in spite of the problems involved? Examining these issues is the aim of this section.

The Costs of Children

Let us be frank: children are expensive. When America was an agricultural society, children provided labor around the homestead which more than offset what they consumed in food, clothing, shelter, and other basic necessities. For most middle-class youth today, this is no longer the case. Many young people hold jobs, of course, but few contribute to the family budget. Teenage earnings more frequently are spent on records, recreation, or such expensive items as cars which parents have refused to buy. An estimate based on 1977 data calculates that raising a child from birth through four years of college for an average middle-class family costs about $64,000 (Epenshade, 1977). When the inflation of the last few years is added, the figure swiftly draws near to $100,000. Before very long, a couple with five children can expect to invest almost half a million dollars in their offspring. No wonder, then, that couples are limiting their children to three or fewer.

CLOSE-UP

Costs of Being a Parent Keep Going Higher
The cost of raising children, like the cost of almost everything, continues to escalate.

From bunkbeds to braces, from potato chips to pop records, the amounts may be surprising. "If you ask a family what they think they're spending to raise children, they don't have the slightest idea," says Thomas J. Espenshade, a senior research associate at The Urban Institute in Washington.

(continued)

Mr. Espenshade created a stir in 1977 with a report called "The Value and Cost of Children." At that time, he figured it cost $64,215 (in 1977 prices) to raise a child to age 18 and send him or her to a public college.

He recently redid those calculations—again for the Population Reference Bureau Inc., a Washington educational concern. His new conclusions: The costs of raising a child have risen about 33% since his previous report. (Between June 1977 and June 1980 the consumer price index rose 36.2%.)

"Seeing a child through birth, 18 years under the parental roof, and four years at a public university now costs the average middle-income U.S. family about $85,000 in 1980 dollars in direct, out-of-pocket expenditures" Mr. Espenshade reports. For low-income families, the cost has risen about 32% to about $58,000 from his estimate of $44,000 three years ago.

(Middle-income family means a family with after-tax income in the $22,500 to $27,500 range. Low income means after-tax income of $14,000 to $18,000.)

The figures vary around the country, of course. Here are some regional figures on 18 years of child-rearing costs, excluding childbirth and college education, for a moderate-income family:

	Farm	Rural Nonfarm	Urban
North Central	$63,800	$64,246	$68,898
South	$71,478	$75,027	$74,568
Northeast	$62,328	$77,952	$72,878
West	Not Available	$79,215	$76,288

Those figures, however give only part of the picture, Mr. Espenshade stresses. There is a second kind of childbearing cost to be considered—the "lost" earnings of a mother who chooses to stay at home with her children. Economists call those "opportunity costs," or the money a woman might have made if she had worked instead of stayed home.

Cost of Raising One Child

Housing	$24,711
Food	17,931
Transportation	12,027
4 Years Public College	9,784
Clothing	5,686
Medical	3,718
Childbirth	2,485
Educational Materials	1,020
All Other	7,726
Total:	$85,088

Adding the two costs—direct and opportunities lost—in 1980 shows that the total cost per child "varies from slightly more than $100,000 at the low-income level to nearly $140,000 for middle-income families," up about 30% from 1977.

Many mothers are trying to make up "opportunity costs," of course, by working while they have young children. Thus, Mr. Espenshade observes, the labor force participation rate for mothers recently has moved much closer to that of women without children.

He also believes that greater awareness of the cost may be affecting the decision of couples to have children. Recent high levels of inflation "have taken the cost of children up quite substantially," he says.

If child-rearing costs have risen sharply in the past three years, a look several decades back shows alarming changes. Mr. Espenshade has in his files some estimates from the 1930s by two researchers at the Metropolitan Life Insurance Co.

Of course, the figures we have been citing are only the direct costs of nurturing and educating children. Additional costs are created by the loss of the mother's or father's earnings, if one parent provides at-home child care, thus foregoing earnings from outside employment. For instance, a parent who gives up a job paying $20,000 a year to care for a child from birth until kindergarten will sacrifice, over that five-year period, a total of $100,000. Loss of income, in other words, very nearly doubles the real cost of rearing a child. Thus, the total family investment is $200,000 or more. If it were invested in blue-chip stocks, treasury bills, or even a savings account, this sum would produce a handsome return over a 20-year period.

Admittedly, reducing the cost of a child to such raw economic terms is

Figure 9-7
Taking home a new supply of Pampers reminds us that, while the parenting role may vary drastically among cultures, there are some basic child-rearing tasks which parents everywhere hold in common. (© *Robert Azzi, 1981. All rights reserved.*)

The Choice of Parenthood

somewhat crass and perhaps even offensive to some. Stated in abstract terms, parents might be astounded by such figures. But if they were asked if their Kevin, Jennifer, Elizabeth, or Todd is worth it, they surely would respond: "Of course, my child is worth it, and much more besides." Current data tend to bear out a willingness of parents to incur the enormous expense of child rearing. We now have the lowest rates of childlessness of any period of our history (Bane, 1976:7–12). However, parents are accommodating to the high cost of having children, by reducing the size of their families rather than by having no children at all. Moreover, it is the case that subsequent children can be reared with less expense than the first child.

Financial expenditures are only one form of cost borne by parents, however. Beyond the dollars and cents lie the psychological and emotional burdens of parenthood. This broad category includes the physical energy and many hours expended to carry out the social instruction required to make an infant socially self-sufficient. No monetary figure can properly value these personal investments in children. Why, we might reasonably ask, are parents eager to invest so much money, time, and personal attention in their children? For some answers, we need to examine the gratifications of having children.

The Gratifications of Having Children

We probably shall never have a fully rational explanation of why people choose to become parents. The desire for children is an extremely complex drive. The value placed on children, which we discussed earlier in this chapter, is a partial answer—namely, that children are a source of pleasure and fulfillment, and are an extension of ourselves. Yet, the things we value in life may not necessarily be sources of personal gratification. For example, we may value a strong national defense and still not find our stint in military service a particularly gratifying experience. Therefore, in this discussion, we want to probe several of the more common reasons parents give for deriving personal gratification from children.

Perhaps the most common response is that children are a source of pleasure. Parents generally mean that not only are their children entertaining, but they also provide intense emotional satisfactions (Blood and Wolfe, 1965:138–9). Children often are described as bringing joy into family life. Their energy, antics, and enthusiasm, as well as their need for love and their ability to love in return, make parenthood extremely enjoyable. Indeed, the greatest pleasure of children is that they provide both the opportunity to give and receive love.

Children also are appreciated by their parents because they afford companionship. During the early years, the companionship is somewhat one-sided. That is to say, as infants children cannot respond with adult actions, thoughts, and expressions. Still, babies can smile, coo, and react in many other nonverbal ways to their mothers or fathers. As children grow older, of course, their ability to take part in companionable relationships increases steadily. Furthermore, the companionship of children persists even after they

A Season for Parents and Children

have grown up and left the family nest. Parents continue to rely on their offspring for help, security, and nonfinancial support in their later years.

And finally, children are often mentioned by their parents as giving their lives meaning and purpose. Some parents even assert that life would not be worth living without children. Offspring provide someone to work and plan for, and someone whose future is open-ended so that they need guidance and direction. In other words, children orient their parents to the future; they are a "cause" to which parents can dedicate themselves, a focus of loyalty beyond the immediate interests of the husband and wife. For this reason, couples frequently discover that their children make them more mature. Especially after the children themselves have begun to mature, parents usually can take a great deal of pride in a job well done. This sense of accomplishment in having nurtured happy and capable children also can prompt parental pride in having contributed to society. Thus, parenthood is not only a fulfilling experience in its own right; it is also an obligation which society rewards with honor and esteem.

Summary

The decision to become parents is one of the most important choices couples can make. The tasks of parenthood are also among the most demanding obligations which couples can assume. The birth of the first child, especially, is something of a cultural shock. It necessitates a complete realignment of parental routines, a reordering of their priorities, and a drastic limitation of their freedom. Parents are willing to accept these changes, by and large, because they value children. Indeed, over the past several decades, the rate of childlessness has declined to an all-time low for American society, even though couples today are having fewer children than people were, say, three generations ago.

The decrease in the birth rate has been accompanied by an increase in family planning. Couples today—in the United States and elsewhere—are interested in limiting family size and spacing births. Consequently, contraceptive use has increased quite sharply in the twentieth century, even among such groups as Roman Catholics whose church leaders officially oppose all artificial forms of birth control. The means of contraception most frequently used today include the oral contraceptive pill, the condom, the diaphragm, intrauterine devices, spermicidal foams, and in the last resort, abortion. No one method of birth control is "right" for everyone. Each couple must evaluate the relative risks of pregnancy and the danger of the birth-control methods to select the contraceptive that is best for them.

Birth bestows on spouses the new social roles of mother and father. Historically, the role of motherhood in American society has been more demanding than fatherhood. Mothers had the primary responsibility for care of the young, including the day-to-day feeding, cleaning, clothing, and training. Mothers often found their role emotionally rewarding, but also burdensome, physically tiresome, and often just downright tedious. In recent years, the father's role has expanded so that the husband no longer sees his primary task solely as breadwinner, but also as a partner in the expressive tasks of parenthood. Thus, child rearing is becoming a shared responsibility of husband and wife, much more than it was even a few decades ago.

Having children creates costs and gratifications. One can quantify economic costs more readily than the other investments in children. In 1977, the cost of raising a child from birth through four years of college was approximately $65,000. In the early 1980s, this figure rose to almost $100,000 per child. Therefore, in simple economic terms a child is a major investment. If loss of earnings during the years of child care are added in, the figure can double. Of course, the psychological and emotional costs of child rearing are not easily quantified. In spite of these demands, however, parents persist in believing that the experience of child rearing is worth the investment. The major gratifications of parenthood are the sheer pleasure of children in family life, the companionship they afford, and the sense of purpose which children bring to a couple's life. Apparently, these gratifications far outweigh the costs of being a parent for the rate of childlessness in America has reached an all-time low.

STUDY QUESTIONS

1. Given the declining birth rate in American society, how can one account for the value parents continue to place on having children?
2. What is the general trend of the fertility rate in industrialized societies? What is the evidence for and against industrialization as a cause of these changes in the fertility rate?
3. Which groups in American society are opposed to the use of birth control techniques and which groups support the use of family planning and contraception? What is the ground for their support or opposition?
4. Describe the meaning of "the cultural shock of parenthood." Should the birth of the first child be described more accurately as a "crisis" or "transition" in the life-style of parents?
5. What are the direct and indirect costs of having children?
6. What are the gratifications that parents report as the reasons for having children?

The Socialization of Children 10

One of the major responsibilities of parents is to provide the social training required to transform their children from biological organisms into functioning social selves. Except in rare instances, everyone is born with the learning capabilities, aptitudes, and neurological potential for acquiring a personality. However, the actual development of a personality structure and the formation of a self-image takes place through a learning process which social scientists call socialization. Through socialization one adopts the norms, values, ideas, and beliefs of one's culture, and the roles appropriate to one's social positions. Tracing the process of a child through this learning process and describing the role of parents—and other socializing agents—as they mold a child's self-image are the major concerns of this chapter. As the discussion unfolds, it will become clear that social scientists do not agree fully on how personality is formed. Primarily for this reason, no clear-cut stand has been taken on the best method of child rearing. Several alternatives are presented at the close of the chapter.

The Socialization Process: From Biological Organism to Social Self

Classical French sociologist Emile Durkheim was one of the pioneering figures in the development of the concept of socialization. From his point of view, each new generation confronts society with the need to reestablish itself by transmitting its culture to new members. Each infant represents an egoistic and asocial being to whom society must, as soon as possible, add a social character (Durkheim, 1956:24–25). Without a social nature implanted in us by parents, relatives, teachers, and religious and civic leaders, we would remain nothing more than human animals, incapable of acting cooperatively for the common good (Durkheim, 1961, 1965).

This view of the civilizing influence of socialization has been shared—with modifications—by most social scientists since Durkheim. For example, Peter Berger (1967:5) has observed that human beings are remarkably "unfinished" at birth. While many of the lower animals can survive on their own immediately after birth and most are behaviorally "programmed" by inborn biological drives, our species is thrust into a world of choices without well-developed instincts to guide our conduct. We must internalize a culture before our world takes on meaning and our ability to survive is assured. Culture becomes our "second nature" whose function is, in part, to equip us with a personality and a social framework in which our action can make sense to us and to our fellow human beings.

Like most social scientists, Durkheim and Berger are basically siding with the nurture advocates in the debate over whether a human personality is a product of our biological nature or of the nurturing which we receive during the socialization process. The nature-versus-nurture controversy is far from being resolved. Clearly, both factors are important in forming our personality and our identity. Socialization theories, however, tend to accent the ways in which individuals conform to social norms, meanings, and role expectations and are thereby nurtured to become social selves. Yet, the process also results in a unique individual. Children raised by the same parents often exhibit quite different personality characteristics—largely because no two individuals share identical genes, social experiences, and developmental sequences. Thus, while emphasizing the social forces in our nurturing (Elkin and Handel, 1972:7), socialization also tries to account for how each person also becomes a unique self (Stryker, 1980: 59–62).

Although most of the discussion of socialization in this chapter focuses on childhood experiences, the process is not confined to the youthful years. In the early years, it is called **primary socialization** because young persons are acquiring their first skills in language use, thought, and action within basic role patterns. Socialization actually continues throughout one's life, however, even though the most important period is during childhood when one's initial mastery of cultural norms and roles occurs. Our primary socialization in the family and other social groups where we experience intimate, face-to-face interaction produces our early self-image. At the start of the adolescent years or before, young people begin moving into the phase of **secondary socialization** where interaction is set within larger, less intimate groups and institutions. At this point, people learn to function within economic, educational, and political roles, as well as within other more formal social roles of major institutions. Even in adulthood, resocialization occurs with some regularity as individuals move into new social positions—whether at work, in the community, or in family life. Resocialization also is required when a person retires from the work force, or when a spouse dies and one mate must adjust to widowhood or widowerhood. In other words, socialization is a continuing process.

The Beginning of the Socialization Process

Infants begin to respond to the world about them very shortly after birth. Fresh from the controlled environment of the womb, they are thrust into a world that is a drastically different temperature and has bright lights, loud noises, and physicians who poke them to test their reflexes. Infants also are suddenly cut off from a constant food supply, so that they now experience hunger and thirst. The new food may cause colic, and the elimination of waste products invariably creates some degree of discomfort. Thus, birth ushers a child into a strange, new world with a succession of new problems. During this time, babies are totally dependent on adults for care and for help in meeting a broad range of physical and social needs.

Infant Dependence on the Mother and Other Family Members

In our culture, we often assume that the biological connection between mother and child also creates a strong emotional attachment. Maternal love often is regarded as a "natural" response bonding mother and child together. However, cross-cultural and historical evidence calls this assumption into question. In various times and places, parents have shown an indifference toward children which has allowed them to practice infanticide or to neglect the basic needs of their fragile offspring (Shorter, 1977; Greenleaf, 1979). Thus, it seems that maternal love is a learned response, like the skills of child care.

The attachment of child to mother also can be understood as a learned relationship. Since the mother in our society is the primary care provider, an infant soon learns to associate being fed, cuddled, and cleaned with the mother. Very quickly, a child begins to depend on the mother and looks to her for help whenever a need or threat arises. This means that even an infant begins to develop certain expectations early in life about what services ought to be provided and who ought to provide them (Parsons and Bales, 1955:63). Accordingly, the child's first meaningful social relationship is usually with the mother. She dominates the child's world, and represents security, need fulfillment, and concern for the child's well-being.

When the mother-child bond is first forming, the child is more passive than active. The mother cares for the newborn for quite awhile before the infant can understand the nature of his or her needs. Gradually, the child's passive dependency gives way to an active involvement with the mother. The child begins to recognize the mother's touch, voice, and physical features. Dependency becomes a positive attachment in which the child does more than react. The sight of the mother makes the child visibly happy. Thus, well before language communication is possible, a child signals the mother that her efforts have created a social bond.

Mother Attachment and Role Acquisition

The interaction between mother and child is critical for an infant's future development. From it, the child gains the social skills needed to form other human relationships. The child also learns how to respond to others' expectations by learning how to read and accept the mother's role demands. At first, of course, the role expectations imposed on the infant are extremely simple. Little more is demanded than that the child eat regularly, sleep long enough to avoid fussiness, and eliminate properly so that a stomachache does not produce pain and crying. Any child who performs these three behaviors is considered by the parents as fulfilling the role pattern of a "good baby."

A child who fails to conform to these expectations is subtly encouraged by the parents to change his or her behavior patterns. Waking parents at four in the morning for another feeding, after the child has been fed at midnight, for example, is likely to produce a quick meal without the cuddling typical of feedings at other times. The baby soon learns that parents favor sleeping longer at night, and that he or she will receive more attention before midnight and after six in the morning. Thus, even without language skills, a baby soon acquires the skill to adjust to parental expectations. The parents' body language, their tone of voice, and the reward of affection all help mold infant behavior in the desired direction.

As the bond between mother and child develops into a strong attachment, the child becomes even more responsive to the mother's attitudes. By six months of age or less, a child recognizes the mother as the primary care-giver and shows signs of attachment to other family members as well. These signals may include a desire for physical contact, crying for attention when left alone, smiles at a familiar face, and efforts to engage in baby talk. This stage of social development makes it easier for the mother to encourage the sort of behavior she wants from the child. By being stern and withholding warmth, she can encourage the baby to stop spitting out the strained peas. She can also follow the challenge of getting her infant to eat the vegetables with a reward of strained apricots, served with a smile and with ready praise for improved eating behavior. However, scolding and the threat of rejection alternated with praise and affection achieve social control only after the child has learned to value his or her attachment to the mother.

Soon, the child will be able to generalize from the mother attachment to other social situations and to a wider range of social role players. The father, brothers, sisters, grandparents, playmates, and others also expect the child to follow certain rules of conduct. Therefore, the role patterns internalized from contact with them, but especially with the mother, can serve as basic building blocks for other, more complex role behaviors. Mastering these social skills is absolutely necessary for all role development and for the formation of a distinct personality.

To succeed at this stage of development, however, the child must become actively involved as a socializing agent in relation to the mother and others. Thus, by the end of the early dependency stage, the child can begin imposing role demands on others while responding to their expectations (Aldous, 1978: 236–8). So we see that the passiveness of the child's early experience soon gives way to a relationship in which the child helps socialize the mother, while the mother is socializing the child.

The Emergence of Selfhood in the Socializing Process

Before proceeding into a discussion of how the self is formed in the socialization process, we must define several critical terms: **personality,** the **self,** and **self-image** or **identity.** Generally speaking, personality is a term employed most often by social scientists to mean a relatively fixed and organized structure of characteristics and dispositions, which are formed early in childhood and distinguish one individual from another. A personality structure, therefore, lies behind behavior, organizing and shaping an individual's pattern of action (Sanford, 1966). In contrast to the fixed set of personality traits, the concept of self tends to stress the dynamic process of personality formation.

Self is an organized set of attitudes based on the sum of those roles a person performs framed in response to others. Moreover, by performing within the roles one has internalized—such as boy or girl, son or daughter, brother or sister, student or playmate—one can develop an image of one's self. This self-image is called a personal identity. An identity is formed in part by feedback from other people. Their response helps us to see ourselves through their eyes and to compare our role performances to shared standards. Self differs from identity. The self is made up of the role patterns a person has internalized and through which action is channeled. On the other hand, an identity includes the evaluations one has developed—partly in relation to others—about the character of one's role performances.

The social scientists most instrumental in developing concepts of the "self" and "personal identity" are role theorists. George Herbert Mead (1863–1931) was the founder of this line of interpretation, and his early work has recently been extended by social psychologists and the symbolic interactionist school (Stryker, 1980). In this view, a **role pattern** is a set of behavioral expectations shared by the self and others about a certain social position within a group or institution. Role theorists assume that we are the roles which we enact (Parsons, 1964:78–82; Elms, 1969). For example, if a person behaves in a loud, boisterous, and extroverted fashion, that person is the extroverted individual which his or her behavior indicates. One can, of course, change one's role behavior and thereby modify one's self. Indeed, role theory assumes that the self is a dynamic process. By joining new groups, internalizing new roles, and rejecting earlier roles, we can change who we are at any point in our life cycle.

With these preliminary comments we now can consider how the self is formed in the socialization process. Having already observed how a child becomes attached to the mother and other socializing agents in his or her primary groups, we can explore the process in which a child begins to organize roles into a self-conscious structure.

Language, Symbols, and Socialization

A baby communicates with parents largely through gestures, facial expressions, and nonlanguage sounds like crying when mad and gurgling when happy. Toward the end of the first year, children usually begin imitating speech. Their first words are often the names of persons or objects they frequently encounter, such as "ma-ma" or "da-da" for their parents. The ability to link verbal symbols with particular persons, objects, or behaviors is a major breakthrough in the learning process. After this point, a child can be taught directly by the parents and others. Even with a limited number of words like yes, no, hush, and good baby, parents can convey their intentions to a child much more quickly. No longer must the child guess the parents' meanings from their tone and body language. The child also can communicate to the parents. While "me want cookie" is not perfect English, it communicates better than squealing and pounding on the tray of the highchair.

Mead (1962) argued, however, that language is more than just an efficient vehicle for exchanging meanings between persons. Language frees us to use symbolic reasoning, for language is the symbolic form in which our meanings arise in our consciousness (Pfuetze, 1961:72). When two persons converse, they use verbal symbols to trigger the same meaning in the mind of the listener as in the speaker. Indeed, the unique feature of talking is that the speaker and listener both are stimulated in the same way and at the same time. Furthermore, as we speak, we also listen to ourselves and respond to our own speech in the same way that others do. This means we are both subject (speaker) and object (listener) when we converse.

Conversing is important because it allows us to take the other person's point of view toward our own vocal language. By listening to ourselves, we can take part in and understand the response others make to our words. Thus, it is in vocal language, according to Mead's famous phrase, that we are able to see ourselves as others see us, and to respond to ourselves as others respond. Why is this important? The answer, Mead claims, is that our ability to become a self hinges on our ability to be both subject and object simultaneously. We possess at birth the subjective dimension of our self, which is the feeling, perceiving, and acting component. However, because as infants we lack an objective set of symbols with which to communicate, our behavior is not fully understandable to others nor can we understand their action. Gradually, as a child begins to link a verbal symbol or word with a particular person, object, or action, that symbol takes on a meaning. Then, a verbal expression will stimulate the same response in the child as in the person who is speaking. A mother can say to a child, for example, "where's da-da?" and the child immediately begins looking for the father because that word stands for him.

As the child internalizes the objective symbols used by others, the world begins to make sense. The call for "ma-ma" brings the attention of the mother; saying "wa wa" produces a drink. More important, the infant can now react to his or her conduct as the parents or others react to it. Some of the first signs of a child taking an objective stance toward his or her behavior appear in play. For example, a common episode in playtime is for the child to sit the teddy bear or a favorite doll down to be fed. The teddy "accidentally" spills his milk. The child immediately reacts like a parent by scolding the toy bear for the mess he created and perhaps by turning it over for a good spanking. Such play allows the child to assume the role of parent. By acting in a fashion similar to the parents, the child will be better equipped to understand and accept the parental point of view toward his or her own behaviors (Erikson, 1963:209–46).

As a general rule, Mead suggests that in most children the integration of subjective and objective dimensions of the self occurs between the ages of three and four. A child's use of pronouns can be a clue to whether an individual has fully developed a consciousness of herself or himself as a distinct self. When children first learn to speak, they often use pronouns incorrectly, especially the pronouns which refer to themselves. On seeing a playmate with a ball, for example, a child is likely to blurt out, "Me want ball." Such language usage is not merely a linguistic problem, but probably also reflects a conceptual difficulty at this stage—the inability to think of oneself as both subject and object. Later, when the child is able to sort out the correct pronouns and say, "*I* want you to give *me* the ball," the child now can see himself or herself as both subjective actor ("I want . . .") and object ("give me . . .") of the action. From such patterns of speech, therefore, we can trace the child's progress toward the fully conscious self.

The Stages of Socialization

Socialization can be thought of as a series of stages through which a child progresses as he or she acquires more and more social experience. Early socialization, according to Mead (1962:150–64), includes two major levels, which he labeled the "play" and the "game" stages. The development of a mother attachment, the casting of the child in elementary social roles, and an increasing knowledge of language all serve as minimal social experience which allow the child to enter the "play stage."

The Play Stage   Playtime is not simply devoted to having fun. The hours spent in play can be viewed as a laboratory for learning. Not only are motor skills mastered during play, but more importantly the child also learns important social skills. In cuddling a doll or serving tea to stuffed toys, a toddler usually engages in a steady stream of conversation. The toys, in their turn, are praised and corrected, instructed and questioned, loved and rejected. The expression of these various attitudes along with suitable behaviors helps a child understand the same attitudes when they are directed at the child in everyday life. At first, play actions tend to be imitations of the parents. However, in acting them out, the child begins to understand and take part in their meanings. Successful integration into the social world of attitudes and role behaviors requires a great deal of practice.

The most important aspect of the play stage is the development of the child's ability to play a role. Assuming a role in play is a relatively complex behavioral action. The first make-believe roles in which children perform are usually drawn from their immediate families, from television, or from their story books. Some of the roles may be those a child could fill when grown, such as the role of mother, father, or teacher. Trying on role patterns that are likely to be assumed in adult life is called anticipatory socialization (Merton, 1968).

Playing other roles helps a child to cope with some unpleasant realities that are part of growing up. For example, after returning from a visit to the pediatrician, a youngster may make that experience easier to accept by lining up all the dolls and stuffed toys and giving them shots. By assuming the role of nurse or doctor and assuring all the toys that the injections will not hurt or that it is for their own good, a child can deal with a painful experience. Thus, this sort of role playing has a therapeutic character (Erikson, 1963).

Other forms of role playing neither prepare a child for adult life nor help him to cope with life's problems; they are purely imaginative and escapist in character. By pinning a towel around his neck, for example, a young boy suddenly is transformed into Superman and is able to "leap tall buildings in a single bound." His sister, meanwhile, can throw a baby blanket over her head, pick up a basket, and become Little Red Riding Hood, hounded at every turn by the big bad wolf. These diversions, too, have their value. Not only do they stimulate a child's creative capabilities, but they also tend to foster a clear distinction between right and wrong, good and bad, proper and improper behavior. Superman is good; the wolf is bad. Playing such roles also helps develop a sex-role identity—as, of course, does playing other roles. Boys, for instance, learn they should be strong, brave, and protective like Superman. Girls are subtly told to be innocent and wary of the big, bad wolves of this world.

The roles acted out during the play stage of socialization allow a child to learn several extremely important lessons. First, they teach a child what a role includes. After all, role performance is governed by certain norms, and trying on several different roles gives a child experience in the necessary art of role playing. Second, a child discovers who he or she is in relation to the roles assumed. Being someone else in play leads one to learn who one is in real life. By playing mother or father, a child develops a clearer understanding of his or her own position as a child within the family circle. Taking on the role of teacher, nurse, or physician helps a child recognize how to play his or her role as student or patient. And finally, role playing gives a child a first glimpse of society and its various social positions. Most children understand very little about their parents' occupations. However, they are exposed

Figure 10-1
During the play stage, children invent their own scripts for the activities in which they engage. Play is open-ended but socially important. (© *Beryl Goldberg*)

to such roles as airline pilot, mail carrier, nurse, teacher, astronaut, police officer, and fire fighter. From a familiarity with these basic role patterns and the functions of each, a child can gain a fuller understanding of his or her society.

Two other traits typify the play stage, and thus require some explanation. The first trait is young children's tendency to play highly specific roles which require little or no integration with the roles of other playmates. If two children are playing together, for instance, and one is a police officer while the other is a fire fighter, each can perform his role without much need to coordinate their play. Such situations are altogether typical of the play stage. Role performance tends to be more of a solo act rather than several roles playing in concert.

A second distinctive feature of the play stage is that its activities usually are supervised rather closely by the parents. This is partly because the children are not mature enough to play unsupervised for long periods. Consequently, parents intervene considerably in their play. Parents set the basic ground rules for the play, provide occasional suggestions for role performances—"A good mother does not hold the baby's head under water when giving him a bath"—and try to encourage cooperative behavior while preventing hostilities among playmates. Moreover, and perhaps more importantly, parents usually are the basic role models for children, no matter which specific social role their child may act out in play. Parental influence—both by example and by direct instruction—is usually stronger during the play stage than in almost any other time in a son or daughter's life cycle.

Since the play stage involves the playing of individual roles, specific persons usually are the models children imitate. Those people are called "**significant others.**" For most children, parents are the most important significant others, but they are not the only ones. Older children in the neighborhood, relatives, teachers, indeed, anyone whom a child looks up to and admires can be a significant other. Furthermore, many persons who serve this function may not know of their importance to a young child. Without such other role models, however, children would find it hard to develop a clear picture of their goal in a given role performance. Particular models become somewhat less important when children move from the play stage into the game stage.

The Game Stage   While the play stage may span the years from two to eight and the game stage from eight to adolescence, no fixed time exists for either of these two periods of socialization. Indeed, the play stage gradually evolves into the game stage, starting some time after a child has begun school. The main feature of the game stage is that children now learn to play roles that relate to those of other persons in the game. In free play, children assume and play roles with a good deal of independence from the other players. The basic script for play is open-ended; children make up dialogue and activities as they proceed. Moreover, their play has no fixed goal which signals its end.

A particular activity or a role-playing episode is over when children tire or lose interest.

Mead considers game playing a different sort of activity. It consists of organized roles linked to specific positions in the structure of the game. For example, in a baseball game, each player must master not only his or her own role, but those of other team members, and, under certain circumstances, those of the opposing team. For instance, if the bases are empty and the batter hits a ground ball to the shortstop, that player should throw the ball to the first baseman to make the out. But, if the bases are loaded and the shortstop fields a ground ball, the ball should be thrown to home plate to make the out and prevent a run from being scored—unless, of course, two outs already have been made. Then the shortstop can force an out, by merely throwing the ball to the closest base before the runner gets there. Thus, games not only involve rules and specialized roles, but a complex strategy which players can use to decide what to do under certain conditions.

A game strategy has the chance to develop in the first place because the play has an ultimate goal as well as a specific end point in time. In baseball, the object is to score the most runs during the nine innings in which each team is allowed three outs. But after nine innings, the game is over and one side is declared the winner if the score is not tied. Thus, in the game stage children must have considerably more social sophistication than in the play stage. The social roles in games are determined not by a given player, but by the relationship of that role to others. Even in a very simple game like hide-and-seek, which has only two roles, each position is still defined in terms of the other. If everyone hides and no one seeks, the game cannot be played. Therefore, the structure of games, with their rules, fixed end points, strategies, and interdependent roles means players must understand the total situation in which the action takes place.

What do games really have to do with our social development and the emergence of an authentic self? A great deal, according to Mead. He regards the game situation as a miniature of community life. The social roles which make up our individual selves are defined in relation to others and played out very much like a position in a game. Furthermore, to understand our own social positions and our role performances, we must be able to grasp the larger scene in which we act and evaluate our own behavior from the point of view of others. Being able to assess the total situation and predict the reactions of others in different social positions is absolutely crucial to our participation in society.

In one sense, however, our role performances do differ from the game situation, as Mead clearly understood. Each of us occupies several social positions at once and our role behavior changes as the other role players vary. For example, we conduct ourselves differently around parents than we do in the company of peers who are close friends, and teachers normally see another facet of our behavior than do friends or parents. Furthermore, each of these separate "audiences" must be taken into account when we plot real-life strategies or consider a course of action.

Although socialization takes place in a wide variety of social settings and in relation to a large number of different social actors, each role we internalize links us with a specific social group. The more important groups for overseeing primary socialization include the family, the school, the play group, the neighborhood, and the church. We define these groups as the **agencies of socialization** because they impose the first highly specific roles on us and they actively see that we internalize them properly. Moreover, particular individuals tend to be given special responsibilities in preparing us for social life. These individuals are **agents of socialization.** Some—such as parents, teachers, and clergy—are fully aware that they mold our behavior. Others—such as playmates, siblings, neighbors, or distant relatives—may serve as important socializing agents, even though they are not conscious of doing so (Elkin and Handel, 1972:96–141).

The Family as an Agency of Socialization

No agency of socialization is more important than the family (Duberman, 1975a:24). Not only does a child spend more time in the family than in other social groups, but this social group contains the individuals who are most concerned about the child's welfare. The family is where we are first nurtured, loved, taught to speak, instructed in right and wrong, and urged to accept certain values as guides for our behavior (Group for the Advancement of Psychiatry, 1973:20–29). The family enjoys not only the first, but also the most extensive and emotionally powerful role in shaping our personalities.

TEST YOURSELF

On Whether Child Rearing Practices Should Be Different for Female and Male Offspring

The following questions have been selected from several sample surveys used by social scientists in testing opinions about whether female and male children should be treated differently. After each statement, circle whether you agree strongly (AS), agree mildly (AM), disagree mildly (DM), or disagree strongly (DS). Under each choice is a number. Add up all your number scores when you have completed the self-test on these seven items. A low number toward the 7 range will indicate a traditional orientation toward sex role socialization in child rearing, while a high score—toward 28—will indicate a strongly equalitarian attitude toward sex role socialization.

Child rearing should proceed without regard for traditional sex role stereotypes.

AS	AM	DM	DS
4	3	2	1

One of the most important things a mother can do for her daughter is prepare her for the duties of being a wife.

AS	AM	DM	DS
1	2	3	4

Parents should encourage just as much independence in their daughters as in their sons.

AS	AM	DM	DS
4	3	2	1

The modern girl is entitled to the same freedom from regulation and control that is given to the modern boy.

AS	AM	DM	DS
4	3	2	1

A son should have the use of the family car more often than a daughter.

AS	AM	DM	DS
1	2	3	4

Girls should have stricter curfew hours than boys in a family

AS	AM	DM	DS
1	2	3	4

Boys as well as girls ought to learn to take care of the home.

AS	AM	DM	DS
4	3	2	1

Source: Karen Oppenheim Mason, with the assistance of Daniel R. Denison and Anita J. Schacht. *Sex-Role Attitude Items and Scales From U.S. Sample Surveys.* Rockville, Md.: National Institute of Mental Health. 1975, pp. 19–20.

Within the family, the parents are the prime socializing agents. Legally, parents must provide minor children with the material necessities of life and keep their behavior within socially recognized norms. Parents also must train their children to become responsible and competent members of society. Of course, most parents willingly accept their roles as socializing agents because they want to influence their children as they grow up. Parents internalize their values, norms, and role expectations in their children because they believe this is best for the child and society. Thus parents are becoming increasingly protective about their right to mold their child's personality, refusing to give it up to other relatives, to outside agencies, and especially to persons or groups who represent the state (Bane, 1976:141–43).

Siblings and other close relatives—especially grandparents, followed by aunts, uncles, and cousins—influence socialization in various ways. By virtue of sheer opportunity and daily contact, siblings tend to be the most important socializing agents after the parents. Sibling contact leads to age-linked identification (Parsons, 1964:41–9). Through their daily involvement in family affairs, brothers and sisters become aware that they are part of a generation that is different from their parents'. They also see that the parental generation has certain decision-making powers and obligations which children do not

Figure 10-2
A second child often
develops more rapidly
because of the model
provided by an older
sibling. (© Alice Kan-
dell, Photo Researchers,
Inc.)

share. By the same token, children have freedoms and duties as a result of
their generational status. Siblings not only share a common identity as members of the same generation, but they also reinforce that identification when
a brother or sister forgets that fact. An older brother's command to a younger
sibling can be expected to prompt the remark, "You can't make me do that;
you're not my father." Behind this retort stands the assumption that the two
siblings are equal in authority because both belong to the same generation.

Of course, siblings contribute to each other's socialization in other cooperative ways (Aldous, 1978:307–13). An older brother frequently is a role
model for a younger brother. By imitating his older brother as well as his
father, a boy often can master his sex-role identification more quickly and
engage in certain behaviors at an earlier age than his older brother who lacked
a sibling model. The frequent lament of parents that their second child seems
to be growing up too quickly often reflects the socializing influence on an
older sibling. The additional effect of another socializing agent—both by direct instruction and by example—almost always produces a more rapid social
development in the younger child.

Compared to the influence of nuclear family members, other relatives do
little to socialize young people today. Only when extended family members
live with or near the nuclear family is their role likely to be important. Typically, grandparents maintain the closest ties to nuclear family members (Williams, 1970:83–87). This results in especially strong emotional bonds among
the three generations of grandparents, parents, and grandchildren. Today,
however, grandparents discipline their grandchildren less than grandparents
did several generations ago. Today, grandparents are far more inclined to fully

enjoy their role by loving and even "spoiling" their grandchildren. Indeed, Robertson (1977) found that 80 percent of grandmothers found the role enjoyable and 37 percent experienced more pleasure from being grandparents than parents, largely because grandparents had the joys and pleasures of children without their parents' socialization responsibilities. This does not mean, however, that grandparents are not needed in the socialization process. Instead, the grandparent role has become more specialized and less disciplinary. Grandparents now contribute a unique sense of family continuity and tradition which few grandchildren would find elsewhere. They also strengthen children's perception of the family as a source of love, care, and social support through the attention they lavish on their grandchildren. Thus, present-day grandparents influence the social development and identity of their grandchildren in ways which are often regarded as immensely gratifying to both generations.

The Play Group and the Neighborhood as Socializing Agencies

Most young children spend a good deal of their time with the play group. This time is important for the shaping of our social relationships and our personal identity. The play group is one social context where subtlety and tact are almost completely lacking. A playmate typically responds directly and honestly to our role behavior. An adult might try to mold or correct our misbehavior with a rhetorical question such as, "Are you sure you're playing by the rules and being fair?" A playmate is more likely to lay it right on the the line with a direct assertion like, "You're cheating!" More often than not, of course, the playmate is right. Such a less-than-tactful sanction immediately condemns our behavior. We swiftly learn from such experiences that rules are to be obeyed—and a price is to be paid if they are not. Members of play groups provide children with clear definitions of reality, so that we quickly learn which behavior is acceptable and which is not.

By contrast, family members may tolerate our bending the rules of a game. Parents, in particular, may allow us to win—sometimes through dubious means just so we can have the thrill of victory. But with playmates, it is different. They tend to be legalists. They stick to the rules and do not give one member an unfair advantage; playmates typically enforce social norms very strictly. The opinions of our peers, however, are important contributions to our social development. They make very clear that we should not expect the same latitude and tolerance from playmates that we ordinarily receive from family members. Playmates underscore the fact that the world is made of groups less forgiving and patient than one's family.

The neighborhood also contributes to the formation of our self-image through the way others view our behavior and respond to it. A neighborhood's adult members tend to evaluate our conduct against an objective set of community norms. In this way, they form judgments that we are "a good kid," "a real troublemaker," "a shy child," "exceptionally bright for her age," "the neighborhood bully," or "a child who was never any problem." These descriptions not only tell us how others view us, but they also influence how we view ourselves, and—more importantly—they affect how we actually behave. A child known as "good" in the neighborhood is encouraged to behave in that way to satisfy adult expectations. On the other hand, a child labeled "a real troublemaker" is likely to live up to that reputation. This is not to suggest that all labels imposed on us become self-fulfilling prophecies. But we do tend to act very much as others expect us to act. Thus, members of the neighborhood provide a response that helps us locate our social identity in relation to a framework that is larger than the nuclear family.

Neighborhood reactions are especially potent forces in socialization because they come from persons who are usually familiar with our family background and our parents' expectations. For example, one often hears an adult member of the community say something like, "Why, Johnny, I know your mother and father and they would just die if they saw you doing that." Because neighbors really do know our parents, they can put greater pressure on us than can total strangers. Depending on our conduct, our reaction of mortification, fear, or pride is more important when it is expressed toward persons we encounter regularly in community life.

Moreover, we also learn soon enough that quite often neighbors truly are concerned about our well-being. While strangers may be indifferent to our behavior, neighbors form an interpersonal network which creates a mutual sense of care, interest, and feeling for one another. Thus, most neighborhood adults correct our misbehavior because they care enough about us to be concerned about the kind of person we are becoming. Likewise, most neighbors are genuinely happy for us when we exhibit the qualities that are valued in the community. In short, then, neighbors represent a personal support network whose promptings we can trust and those judgments of us we usually can accept as well intentioned.

The School and Church as Socializing Agents

Children usually spend more time in school than in any other institution outside the family. Indeed, the school has long been recognized as a critical socializing agency (Durkheim, 1956, 1961; Mead, 1964:114–22). We gain more than formal knowledge from the classroom experience. Together, teachers and classmates mold our social character as well. For students in the earlier grades, the teacher is probably the strongest influence on daily behavior. He or she also helps us to internalize the basic values and norms of our culture (Parsons, 1964:143–8). In addition to increasing our basic competence in reading, writing, spelling, and arithmetic teachers also give us a knowledge and appreciation of our normative cultural heritage. Often, they also instill in us a personal commitment to such social values as achievement, equality, freedom, discipline, self-expression, creativity, and honesty.

For most middle-class children, the school simply reinforces the values and social norms first introduced in the family. Home and school tend to support each other as institutions, since they share a view of the social norms and behaviors suitable for children. However, cooperation between school and home often takes very subtle forms. For example, a common technique

Figure 10-3
As a socializing agency, the school teaches children more than reading, writing, and other academic skills. In the early grades, especially, children become familiar with the basic roles that people play in society. (© Sepp Seitz, 1980/ Woodfin Camp & Associates.)

of first-grade teachers is to give their young charges a blank sheet of paper and a box of crayons and encourage them to draw a picture of their house and family. Usually, the result is quite primitive by artistic standards. But the teacher will praise the student's drawing as though it were a masterpiece. When the child takes the picture home, the parents usually praise the work again. Moreover, it is taped to the refrigerator door as a reminder to all family members that the child has done something important. The combined effect of both home and school is to reward the child for his or her achievement. It really does not matter that the mother could not tell the difference between the dog and the baby brother in the picture. It matters only that the child tried and was rewarded for that effort. The next time, the first-grader will try harder, because the lesson has been implanted that the parents and teacher alike are impressed by the drive for achievement. From such simple experiences a young child also learns to respect achievement.

Teachers of younger children, especially, are likely to spend a great deal of their time helping with the social adjustment of their students. If a shy child is left out of group games, they try to see that he or she is included. If one child has trouble relating to another classmate, the teacher sees that they work together on a project and learn to relate to someone who at first did not interest them. Similarly, the teacher acts as an agent of social control who disciplines antisocial behavior and stresses the need for a pupil to adjust to his or her class (Clark, 1962:20–25).

Finally, teachers are role models for pupil behavior (Goslin, 1965:69–71). Apart from parents, young people probably imitate the attitudes of their teachers and conform to their behavioral expectations more than those of any other adult they see frequently. Thus, by example and by formal instruction, teachers can influence the conduct of young people tremendously.

We should also note that teachers are not miracle workers. They cannot undo many of the harmful effects of improper family socialization and antisocial forces in the community. More and more, as the inequalities created by racial discrimination and poverty have emerged, American society has looked to its schools to foster not only opportunities for less priviledged children but also actual achievement. However, as the research of Coleman (1965, 1971) Banfield (1974), and others has demonstrated, the socializing influence of the educational institution cannot possibly compensate for all the failures of the family, the community, and government social-service agencies. The school works best when it reinforces the social norms children have acquired in the family. But if familial and communal shaping of a pupil's personality is inadequate, the school cannot by itself overcome such social deprivation, at least in most instances (Sexton, 1967:117–8). This is not because our educational system is inadequate or unconcerned about children, but because problems created by disorganization in the family or community are simply too pervasive in their effects for educators to solve.

CLOSE-UP

Jimmy is in the second grade and he likes school. He pays attention in class and does well. He has an above average I.Q. and is reading slightly above grade level.

Bobby is a second grader too. Like Jimmy, he is attentive in class, which he enjoys. His I.Q. and reading skills are comparable to Jimmy's

But Bobby is the son of a successful lawyer whose annual salary of more than $35,000 puts him within the top percentages of income distribution in this country. Jimmy's father, on the other hand, works from time to time as a messenger or a custodial assistant, and earns $4,800 a year.

Despite the similarities in ability between the two boys, the difference in the circumstances to which they were born makes it 27 times more likely that Bobby will get a job that, by the time he is in his late 40's, will pay him an income in the top tenth of all incomes in this country. Jimmy has only about one chance in eight of earning even a median income. And Bobby will probably have at least four years more schooling than Jimmy.

Although being born poor does not guarantee that one will remain poor, it makes it far more likely. "Class, race and sex are the most important factors in determining a child's future"—Horatio Alger notwithstanding. Given the compounding penalties of being born poor, or a member of a racial minority, or to parents with little education and with intermittent or dead-end employment, or—a further disadvantage—female, a particular child will be unlikely to advance significantly above the socioeconomic status of his parents.

Although the standard of living for all Americans, including the poor, has risen during the last generation, claims Richard de Lone in "Small Futures," a

A Season for Parents and Children

recently published report originated by the Carnegie Commission, Mr. de Lone also charges that the distributional inequities in American society—and hence the opportunities for those at the bottom of the scale—have changed little throughout American history.

In his view, one conceptual flaw that has helped perpetuate those inequities is the emphasis on programs predicated on the mistaken assumption that helping children today will equalize their opportunities in the future. Without equality in the present, de Lone says, that is simply not true. "Confronted with unacceptable economic and social inequalities, we Americans have reflexively channeled our moral indignation into efforts to improve the morality, character, skills and intelligence of children—especially those who are poor, immigrant or nonwhite."

Creating such equality, de Lone acknowledges, is a formidable task. The top 20 percent of American families currently receive over 40 percent of the country's net income, and families in the bottom 20 percent receive less than 6 percent. The top 4 percent of families own 37 percent of personal wealth, while the net worth of the average family in the bottom 20 percent is zero. Only one man in five exceeds his father's social status through individual effort and achievement—and that figure may drop as the post-World War II boom years dissolve into the shrinking economy forecast for the coming decades. And finally, according to Mr. de Lone, the employment, earnings and social mobility gaps separating blacks and whites in this country have scarcely changed in a century.

The report, which traces the sources of inequality to a "basic tension between the democratic and capitalist strands of our heritage," argues that Americans have generally failed to perceive that the ultimate penalty of poverty is the pervasive influence on one's adult future of "growing up unequal," with all the developmental limits that may entail. The material hardships of poverty may finally be less damaging than the permanent narrowing of a child's sense of possibilities in the world.

De Lone quotes one child of a migrant worker as saying, "Once a policeman asked me if I liked school and I said sometimes I did and then he said I was wasting my time there, because you don't need a lot of reading and writing to pick the crops, and if you get too much of schooling, he said, you start getting too big for your shoes, and cause a lot of trouble, and then you'll end up in jail pretty fast and never get out if you don't watch your step—never get out."

What is needed, de Lone suggests, are far deeper structural changes to reduce economic distance between classes, including public policies of full employment, targeted economic and investment development, aggressive affirmative action and income-tax reform to lighten tax burdens on the poor and transfer them to the wealthy.

—Leslie Bennetts,
adapted from *The New York Times*

The church or synagogue is another significant socializing agency for many young Americans. Its influence is somewhat less than the schools, however, because school is compulsory while attending worship is not. Thus, some Americans do not receive any formal religious instruction. For those who do, the church or synagogue tends to be linked to the family. Religious teachings typically support the nuclear family's moral values and behavioral expectations. Furthermore, very much like teachers, religious leaders often act as role models for young people. A priest, pastor, or rabbi can frequently influence the moral attitudes and conduct of impressionable youngsters by their own examples as faithful followers of their belief. Moreover, the religious institution also has on its side a supernatural authority to legitimate the particular role expectations of believers. Thus, especially in American society where religious participation is higher than in other industrialized nations, the church or synagogue seeks to train children in ways suitable to that faith (Wilson, 1978:262–4). The result is to add further social support to the social character that parents want to see nurtured in their children.

The Influence of the Primary Socializing Agencies

The family, play group, neighborhood, school, and church or synagogue are usually called our **primary groups** for two reasons. First, they are intimate groups in which we meet face-to-face with others, and second, they are the initial social settings in which our characters, attitudes, role patterns, and values are shaped (Cooley, 1909). Most primary groups confront a child with a more or less uniform image of reality and a common set of social expectations. For example, the correct behavior for children in the family is usually the behavior that is also expected in the school, community, or religious organization. By taking part in the various primary groups we learn who we are and what we must do to sustain our social identity. While our dependence on primary groups lessens as we grow older, we still need their intimacy, personal contact, and social support.

The Psychoanalytic Perspective on Socialization

Socialization has been described thus far largely as it was seen by George Herbert Mead and the social psychologists influenced by his ideas. With their concept of psychosexual development, Sigmund Freud and his followers presented a major alternative to Mead's theory of socialization. The ideas of Freud and the Freudians on how our personality is formed have spread throughout our culture in the twentieth century. For example, the belief that the first six years of life are the critical period for personality development is taken from Freud. Moreover, many child-rearing techniques—which we shall consider at the end of this chapter—also are based on Freudian ideas. For these reasons, we need to be familiar with the central themes of psychoanalysis, the name for Freudian psychological theories.

The Stages of Psychosexual Development

Freud taught that personality developed as we matured through three basic stages. The dynamic force which motivates our action is **libido** or the dynamic display of sexuality (Freud, 1959:106). However, our libido or sex drive can be expressed in many actions other than sexual relations. This idea is the key to understanding Freud's theory of personality development. The three major stages through which we all are said to pass are the **infantile stage,** the **latent stage,** and finally the **genital stage** (Hall and Lindzey, 1957:51–7).

The Infantile Stage This first stage is the most important, in Freud's view, because during it our basic personality structure is framed. Disorders which develop in this stage can appear in our adult years. The infantile stage spans roughly the first six years of life. It is divided further by Freud into three different phases (Freud, 1965:97–9). The first is the **oral phase** which lasts from birth to about one year. During this time, a child's major source of pleasure is manipulation of the oral cavity. Sucking, biting, and eating are all ways of getting what is essentially sexual pleasure. Frustration in this phase can produce an adult fixation, or "oral personality," as Freud phrased it. Such a person overeats or enjoys placing objects like cigarettes or a pipe in the mouth (Freud himself was a heavy cigar smoker).

The **anal phase,** extending from about age one to three, is the time when children gain their greatest pleasure from bowel movements. During the same period children usually are being toilet trained. Freud takes this to mean that children are called upon to restain and control the one activity from which they gain the greatest pleasure. Toilet training is the first major intrusion of reality upon the child. Bowel control is one area in which children conflict with external authorities, such as the parents, and where they first learn to adjust their behavior to social demands (Hall, 1954:107–9). During the anal phase, an overly demanding parent can influence a child to develop a personality structure which in later life resists authority, is stingy, or is too concerned with neatness. Indeed, Freud regarded all hobbies which involved collecting objects—such as coins and stamps—as basically "anal" activities. He believed that an adult substitutes the socially acceptable practice of hoarding stamps for an unfulfilled childhood desire to retain feces. Freud's own hobby was to collect objects of Greek or Roman antiquity.

The **phallic phase,** spanning the years from three to six, is the most important in the infantile stage for structuring the personality. During this time, the child's genital organs provide the greatest pleasure. More important, however, is the emergence of the **Oedipal complex,** named after Oedipus, the mythological figure of Greek tragedy who unknowingly killed his father and married his mother. According to Freud, every child falls in love with the parent of the opposite sex, desires to kill the parent of the same sex, and then marry the beloved parent. However, a child soon discovers that these wishes cannot be fulfilled because the parents are so much larger and stronger. Thus, a child identifies with the parent of his or her sex, accepts the moral norms of the parents—which include the incest taboo—and represses the early erotic desires into the unconscious (Freud, 1960:46–53; Becker, 1962). Thereafter, the child possesses the basis for a moral conscience as the **superego,** the personality's moral agency, arises from the resolution of the Oedipal complex (Rieff, 1961:63).

The Latent Stage   Passage through the Oedipal complex caps the infantile stage. Internalized moral norms press sexual desires into the unconscious and the child enters a relatively calm period which Freud labels the latency stage (Freud, 1962b:25). From six years to the onset of adolescence, a young person develops physically, socially, intellectually, and morally, while sexual drives lie dormant. This period allows a child to catch up in other important dimensions with his or her early sexual development.

The Genital Stage   With the onset of puberty and the approach of physical maturity, the sexual drives of childhood are rekindled once again. The libidinal drive first attaches itself to one's own body, thereby producing the narcissistic phase, which is named after Narcissus, of Greek mythology, who fell in love with his own reflection in a pool of water. In this period of our life cycle, we are egoistic and self-centered. This phase gradually gives way to a homosexual period, when the love object is a person of of the same sex. Freud is not contending that actual homosexual behavior occurs during this period, but only that boys enjoy the company of boys, while girls prefer being with other girls. However, if psychosexual development is arrested at this phase, a permanent homosexual orientation may result. The final transition of the genital stage is described by Freud as the heterosexual phase in which the love object is a person of the opposite sex. Movement into this final phase means that a young person is now prepared to select a spouse and assume adult responsibilities. Thus, by age 16 or 18, the personality is essentially formed, according to the Freudians. A mature "ego"—Freud's label for the rational, conscious portion of an individual's personality—is now fully developed, as is a superego. Any major changes that later occur in one's personality structure—such as those required by the development of neurotic symptoms—will normally require psychoanalytic treatment. In this therapy, an individual must work through with a psychiatrist the events that caused the neurosis, events that probably occurred during childhood or early adolescence.

Two Approaches to Understanding Personality Development

Freud's psychosexual interpretation and Mead's concept of socialization are two quite strikingly different viewpoints on personality development. For example, Freud's conviction that personality structures are largely set by the end of the infantile stage is thoroughly rejected by socialization theorists. The Meadian school argues that personality can be changed at any number of major points in the life cycle. This difference is due largely to the Meadian's view of personality as an ongoing "process." In addition, Freud's sexual emphasis and concept of the Oedipal complex are wholly lacking in the Meadian interpretation of socialization.

Of course, to say that one view is correct and the other is wrong is impossible. Both theories deal with different aspects of personality development. Freud's analysis has been accepted by many people because his view seems to illuminate their experience. Moreover, his psychoanalytic theory is more widely accepted in medical circles—psychiatrists must become physicians before beginning their psychoanalytic training. Among academic social scientists, Mead's view tends to be somewhat more widespread because he points to social interaction which can be observed more concretely.

Also, more than Mead, Freud's thought has been popularized in versions that barely resemble his actual ideas. Child-rearing "experts," writing in popular magazines on Freudian ideas they only partly understand, have scared many a young mother by implying that one slap on the backside of her mischievous four-year-old son may make him a homosexual or a neurotic personality. Of course, Freud would find such a notion laughable. Frued's view on sexuality has also been frequently misunderstood. Although he favored lessening sexual repression in society, this stance must be understood against the backdrop of his time—namely, the rigid sexual morality of the Victorian period. Yet, Freud did not promote free love and unrestrained eroticism (Reiff, 1961:370–79). Above all, Freud stressed the need for self-mastery, firmly opposing surrender to one's passion, including sexual passions. Civilization is only possible, he believed, when members of society can discipline themselves by reason and by adhering to moral norms (Freud, 1962a). Indeed, it is quite revealing to note that one of Freud's ego-ideals was the Puritan leader of the English Civil War, after whom he named his second son, Oliver Cromwell Freud (Jones, 1963:19). Freud admired Oliver Cromwell for his self-discipline, his strong leadership, and his moral integrity. Indeed, the Puritan commitment to discipline lived on in Freud himself. Given the basic thrust of his thought, Freud undoubtedly would have disapproved of linking his name to the permissiveness of the sexual revolution that began in the late 1960s. We would do well to remember, Philip Reiff (1961) suggests, that the mind of Freud was first and foremost the mind of a moralist.

Approaches to Child Rearing

While scholars are interested in theories of personality development, parents and many students of family life are more interested in the practical aspects of child rearing. Parents want to know, for example, how to raise their child to be a happy, successful, and well-adjusted adult. They ask, "What traits should I encourage in my child and how can I screen out bad traits which I see developing?" Unfortunately, these are not simple questions. Nor does any one child-rearing technique guarantee parents instant success and the kind of adult personalities they want their children to possess. Child rearing may well be one of life's most difficult tasks, and certainly it is one of the most imprecise arts adults can practice.

Most child-rearing strategies are based on a set of psychological or social-psychological principles. Sometimes the assumptions behind a technique are clearly spelled out; other times they are not. Some child-rearing techniques appeal to common sense, while others suggest that common sense is a poor guide in matters as complex as the raising of children. Indeed, common sense

The Idea of Children

I've had enough. Not that I have anything much against children per se—after all, who could blame children for being children? But I do have something against adults, for it is adults who have sentimentalized children and fostered a variety of misconceptions about childhood—misconceptions that have had serious consequences in both our homes and our schools.

Foremost among these misconceptions is the idea that children are imaginative and creative. Can anyone who has taken the trouble to think about it really believe that children are imaginative? They certainly have little respect for diversity, the average child being as desperate as any executive at IBM to conform to the ways of his peers. And most children are hopelessly dependent upon adults for direction.

What we rush to label as "imagination" is at best a degree of spontaneity. Prolonged conversation with a 9-year-old is unlikely to be very stimulating. The truth of the matter is that children are relatively predictable. Despite much evidence to the contrary, we also like to believe that children are sensitive. Never mind the idiotic television programs that engage them for hours. Or their fascination with violence and all the paraphernalia of violence from water pistols to BB guns. Never mind the shrieks of delight that are likely to accompany the magic cinematic moment when a car goes tumbling over a California cliff, and the adults inside (who look suspiciously like parents) are presumable burned to a crisp.

Another myth has it that children are somehow "purer" than you or I. Few advocates of "children rights" would go so far as to demand sexual rights for children. Nearly everyone agrees that children deserve the protection of law, since they are vulnerable to abuse.

But is it wise to assume that if you protect children from adults, you need not worry about protecting them from other children? Children may indeed be "born innocent," but complete innocence is seldom likely to survive the first grade. The realization that children are interested in their own bodies and that they are not beyond sexual experimentation makes many adults extremely uncomfortable. Apparently, we prefer to think of our children as Victorian gentlemen thought of their wives: attractively ornamental but blissfully sexless. The alternative is disturbing. It is to recognize that while not necessarily more sensitive or more creative than adults, children can be every bit as complex.

But what has happened to our memories? Children can be appallingly cruel to one another. We knew this when we were young, and we were constantly on guard lest some other kid got to us before we got to him. But somehow or other we manage to forget all this when we have children of our own—it's so much more satisfying to believe that children are happier than we are.

We need to recognize that ideas have consequences. By granting a special status to children, we go far toward ensuring that they will be self-occupied and, all too often, irresponsible. If children are fundamentally different from you and me, how could we possibly expect them even to begin to measure up to the same standards? How can you discipline them when, by definition, they are supposed to be creative natural and free?

Consider also the dubious results of progressive education, which is based in part on the idea that children are intrinsically good and that if they are free to be themselves, they will respond by learning and growing. I've always thought that a positively lovely notion—but it's hard to believe in its practicality when we look at the serious decline in reading and math abilities over the last ten years.

Of course, I am speaking here of an extreme. And it is only fair to admit that there are many delightful children who represent everything that we like to believe is the norm—imagination, sensitivity and honor. On the other hand, many adults have precisely the same virtues. I do not wish to argue that children are any worse than adults, only to assert that they are not fundamentally better simply by virtue of being children. It's time that we recognized that children are not some marvelously enlightened minority group from which we all need to learn. Children can be clever, but they can also be dull—and a callous child is no more extraordinary than a callous adult. Children are, in short, only human. We should see them as they are, not as we wish we were.

—R. Keith Miller,
excerpted from
Newsweek

often is cited as the cause of many problems among young people. In discussing several techniques we shall concentrate on some of the most popular ones. In addition, we have tried to assess each technique objectively for its strengths and weaknesses.

Piaget and the Cognitive-Development Approach

Jean Piaget (1896–1980), the Swiss structural psychologist, based his approach to personality development on stages of physical maturation. In each stage a particular type of thought process or cognitive development occurs. Intellectual capacity, Piaget (1926, 1932, 1952) suggests, cannot proceed faster than a child's physiological ability to register experiences and understand them. Thus, Piaget (1963) structures cognitive development into four basic stages: the sensorimotor, the preoperational, the concrete-operational, and the formal-operational stage.

The sensorimotor stage extends from birth to about two years of age. During this time, it is extremely difficult to teach a child to follow specific rules, and the reasoning which stands behind parental rules is, of course, entirely beyond their grasp. Hence, the demands of parents must be extremely simple. Children simply cannot distinguish between "good" and "bad" behaviors, nor can they retain parental instructions for very long.

By the stage of preoperational thought, which extends from age two to seven, children have acquired some language proficiency. Now parents can spell out in some detail the rules they impose. However, children can understand only a small part of the parent's motives for demanding certain behavior. Toward the end of this stage, children may comprehend that certain parental requirements are for their own good, but they still do not understand the potentially harmful effects of some conduct. Furthermore, during this period, children also begin to use some symbols. They can understand that certain things stand for other actions or objects. This intellectual skill is crucial for their later development.

Piaget's third level of development, the concrete-operational stage, generally spans the ages from seven to eleven. The formal capacity for reasoning now begins to emerge. The first sign of logical deduction occurs when the child distinguishes between classes of objects. More importantly, the child can begin to appreciate why the parents demand certain behavior (Elkind, 1979:65–79). However, young people of this age still have difficulty changing frames of reference. They need experience in social interaction to perfect this skill and to comprehend the moral reasoning that governs parental actions.

In the final stage, which Piaget labels the formal-operational period, young persons from about 12 to 15 years of age become good enough at social skills and symbolizing to understand the spirit as well as the letter of the law which parents insist upon. A child is no longer a literalist; he or she now can grasp irony, metaphors, and even hypocrisy without becoming confused. Parents with children at this stage find themselves relating to young persons who now have mental processes comparable to their own even though children do not yet have their parents' backlog of social experience.

The major use of Piaget's research in child rearing has been to warn parents that they should not expect more of their children than their current developmental stage will permit (Elkind, 1979:3–16). Children are not miniature adults. Their thought processes, symbolic thinking, and their ability to understand reasons as well as rules are related directly to their level of physiological maturity. Attempting to impose demands and expectations on children before they can meet them will only frustrate parents and children. Hence, parents must adjust their expectations to the abilities of their children, which will result in happier children and more competent parenting.

Piaget's influence probably has been most pronounced among educators, who extended it to child-rearing techniques (Wadsworth, 1971). The major criticism of Piaget's ideas is that they create too rigid a developmental model. His critics claim that individuals vary much more in their acquisition of intellectual and social skills than Piaget recognized. Consequently, some children can accept parental guidance much earlier than Piaget suggested. Parents' failure to understand this fact can deny a child certain social training when she or he most needs it. Indeed, the late use of parental guidance may be as serious a problem as the imposition of parental demands too early in a child's experience.

Adler and Dreikurs' Approach to Child Rearing

Alfred Adler (1870–1937) was a member of the Freudian circle in Vienna, who later broke with psychoanalytic tradition over its view of personality. His "individual psychology" was far less complex than Freud's (Hall and Lindzey, 1957:116–9). Adler's early research interest in medicine was focused on human compensation for physical disability. For example, an individual who suffers from blindness often develops the senses of touch, smell, and hearing to compensate for the loss of vision. Such dynamics also occur, Adler claimed, in the psychological realm (Brown, 1964:38–40). Every child begins to take part in family life with a sense of inferiority. A child is a small member of a social group dominated by large parents. Many of the child's desires are frustrated. Children try to overcome their inferiority feelings by developing a strategy that allows them some mastery over their situation. The attitudes that make up this social strategy form the basis of what later becomes an adult personality. Thus, our style of overcoming our sense of inferiority in the family context gradually evolves into our adult character structure (Ansbacher, 1956; Adler, 1957). Adler called this the **"creative self,"** because an individual creates a distinctive personality out of the basic materials of heredity and social experience.

Adler's major contribution to child-rearing practices was the insight that children need understanding parents who can correctly "read" their behavior. A child who seeks attention through misbehavior or withdrawal from social contact really is expressing a basic insecurity. Therefore, parents need to help the child develop a sense that he or she belongs to the family circle so that the need for these behaviors is eliminated. Rudolf Dreikurs (1964) sought to translate Adler's basic personality theory into a full-blown technique for nurturing children. Dreikurs' main concern was to urge that parents try to integrate their children into the family network where children could receive encouragement, rather than ego-destroying criticism, from family members. Toward this end, Dreikurs recommended a democratic family council which would allow children to take part in the family decision-making process with their parents. Moreover, parents were advised to take every chance to reward their children's accomplishments and to give them enough freedom to allow them to carry out their decisions, even when they make mistakes. Above all, parents were urged to understand fully that their child's basic motive in the countless situations of family life is to find security, approval, and a sense of belonging.

A whole series of criticisms have been leveled at the Adler-Dreikurs' approach to child rearing. Academic social scientists have frequently pointed out that little hard evidence supports the claim that a life-style developed to respond to childhood inferiority feelings is the basis for adult character. Furthermore, Dreikurs is commonly rebuked for suggesting that children can or should take part in family decision making as equals to their parents. The family is not a democracy, critics reply, nor are parents and children equal in social responsibilities, experience, or cultural wisdom. Finally, the Dreikurs' approach of letting children learn by suffering the natural consequences of their actions is regarded by many as a clumsy and potentially harmful way to gain experience. It is simply impractical to let a child learn that he or she will catch a nasty head cold by going outside in the winter without a coat or boots. Thus, while Dreikurs' method is praised for good intentions, many fault its impracticality.

B. F. Skinner and the Behavior-Modification Approach

B. F. Skinner is a behavioral psychologist who introduced the idea of **operant conditioning.** According to Skinner (1953), children are constantly responding, reacting to a specific set of events. Those actions that parents wish to see repeated should be rewarded, while behaviors that parents do not want repeated should be punished. Soon, the rewarded behaviors will become habits, and the punished behaviors will gradually decline and then disappear altogether. In short, behavior can be modified by alternating reward and punishment. For example, if a child cries to get attention, and the mother or father comforts the child because the crying is distressing, the end result will be to reward the child's crying. The parental response has increased the likelihood the child will cry again simply to gain attention. To break this pattern of behavior, the parent must disregard crying when the child is simply seeking attention. Soon, this means of gaining attention will disappear from the child's repertoire of behaviors. Thus, a child's behavior can be readily molded by parents who follow the rules of positive reward and negative reinforcement.

Skinner's proposals have won over some educators and parents who find behavior modification a simple technique to employ in training children. Yet, the enterprise also has found some critics. The most frequent argument against Skinner's program is that it treats children like objects to be manipulated. Moreover, those who favor behavior modification tend to play down the importance of thought processes. Skinner claims that consciousness is not a necessary assumption, since conduct can be controlled solely with reward and punishment. His critics are not so sure. They claim that people can be so clever that others may not always perceive what their behavior means. Parents may mistake a child's vigorous and alarming cry for attention for a real cry of pain. While Skinner's techniques may work on simple problems of child rearing, some professional child-care experts doubt that behavior modification will work as a full-blown theory of child rearing.

Gordon and the Parent-Effectiveness Training Approach

Among the more recent efforts to inform parents how to raise their children is the program launched by Thomas Gordon (1970) called PET (Parent-Effectiveness Training). Underlying this program is the psychological thought of Carl Rogers, the person-centered therapist. Gordon's approach concentrates on improving a child's self-image and the realization of his or her full potential. He attempts to achieve these aims without parental punishments to discipline children. To accomplish this, Gordon recommends "active listening" by the parents. An active listener enters into the communication process between parent and child by recognizing that children have a need which they are trying to express. By responding to the needs as well as to the actual messages parents can decode the "signals" of children and help them fulfill those needs. In this manner, both children and parents can become self-actualizing persons. Moreover, in the inevitable conflicts between parents and children, Gordon insists that a solution must portray neither side as the winner or loser. In authoritarian households, the parent always wins; in permissive households, the child frequently wins. In both cases, he insists, everybody really loses. For a truly equitable solution to the contests between parents and children, both sides must feel satisfied with the outcome. When this happens, both sides really win.

In the Parent-Effectiveness Training programs offered around the country, Gordon and his followers provide a great deal of specific advice for parents in particular child-rearing situations. As with the other alternatives, however, some critics question this method. For example, let us assume that a 16-year-old has begun taking drugs. What kind of compromise is likely to be acceptable to both parents and the youngster? The "no-lose" method does not appear likely to resolve conflicts in which parents and older children seriously disagree, as they might on such important matters as drug use, sexual relations, and alcohol consumption. Young people are likely to see negotiation in these areas as parental permissiveness. Thus, while Gordon's goal of protecting the personality integrity of both parents and children is clear, it is much less clear how he could achieve this goal and still protect young people from activities with which they would not be able to cope.

The Enduring Problem of Child Rearing

Arnold Gesell (1946), Haim Ginott (1965), and John Holt (1974) are three more quite popular child-rearing specialists—and there are many more. For all their good advice, however, the problems of parenthood persist. Unfortunately, no one approach can magically make these difficulties go away.

Many parents are puzzled about how to raise their children properly, but little evidence suggests that parents are ready to give up their child-rearing functions to youngsters who have less social experience than they do. Meanwhile, the search continues for better techniques. Perhaps the most optimistic aspect of the child-rearing process is that young people today still recognize their parents' concern, effort, and love for them (Keniston, 1965:200–16; 1968:44–76). They seem to understand that parents do make mistakes and that they must not be faulted too much when they make the wrong move as they try to nurture their daughters and sons. More importantly, however, youngsters also seem to comprehend the deeper message that parents are doing their best. Indeed, the parents' efforts to show their children that they love them appears to be the most important factor in parent-child relations, probably far more important in the long run than any particular technique employed in the day-to-day process of child rearing.

Summary

A major responsibility of parenthood is child rearing. A mother and father are called upon to transform a biological organism into a fully functioning social self. In this chapter, the process of developing a child's personality structure and self-image is thoroughly explored. Our point of departure is the concept of socialization first introduced by George Herbert Mead and now widely accepted by social psychologists, sociologists, and other social scientists. Mead's view stresses the importance of family members in shaping the initial role patterns, the language use, and the social norms which a child internalizes. However, while the family is the main social group in the socialization process, it is not the only one. Children soon move into the play group, the neighborhood, the school, and often the church or synagogue where their personality development continues. All of these groups—called primary socializing agencies—contribute to the process launched within the family circle by bringing the children to an objective awareness of their unique selves. Only when they can see themselves as others see them and respond to their own behavior as others respond to it do their selves really come into full existence. Thus, our personality development is basically a social process, just as the maintenance of our personal identity is also a social process.

An alternative view is provided by Freud's psychosexual theory of personality formation. Freud's model lays heavier emphasis on the personality structures erected as we pass through three developmental stages in the course of individual maturation. The infantile stage is the most critical, for in its three phases (oral, anal, and phallic) we lay the basic foundations for our personality in response to internal sexual compulsions and external social demands. The Oedipal complex at the end of the infantile stage marks the beginning of our moral development. The latency stage begins around age six and persists until puberty. During this time, sexual drives lie dormant as we develop physically, socially, intellectually, and morally. The genital stage completes the process of our psychosexual development. With sexual drives now reactivated, we progress toward a state in which our love object is a person of the opposite sex. By late adolescence, we are far enough along in our personality development to allow us to assume adult responsibilities and enter marriage. In Freud's view, therefore, personality is by and large completed by the end of the genital stage.

The differences between Mead's social-psychological theory of socialization and Freud's idea of psychosexual development are quite striking. Social psychologists propose a dynamic understanding of the self in which personality change can occur rather readily at any point in the life cycle. The Freudians, by contrast, embrace a structural model in which basic personality characteristics are set in early childhood. Neither view can be declared obviously correct. But both illuminate aspects of the process by which we acquire our personality and identity. Moreover, the influence of both traditions is apparent in the various techniques suggested by child-rearing experts.

Our final section in this chapter explores various proposals for child rearing. We examine the approach of Piaget and his cognitive development model, the alternative recommended by Adler and Dreikurs, the approach of B. F. Skinner with his concept of behavior modification, and the program of Gordon called Parent-Effectiveness Training. Each viewpoint provides insights, yet each one also has certain weaknesses which we identify. The fail-safe technique of child rearing is yet to be invented. Meanwhile, parents must rely on their own resources, performing as best they can with all the information, social skills, and love at their command. Thus far, most children seem to appreciate their parents' concerned efforts on their behalf.

STUDY QUESTIONS

1. Why does the human infant require such a lengthy socialization process in order to become a self-sufficient and responsible member of society?
2. Why is an infant's attachment to the mother considered so critical for the formation of later social relationships?
3. What are the characteristics of the play stage and how does it differ from the game stage of socialization?

A Season for Parents and Children

4. How do such social agencies as the play group, neighborhood, church, and school contribute to the socialization process and help mold our personalities?

5. Compare and contrast George Herbert Mead's view of socialization with Freud's theory of psychosexual development. Which is more adequate? Why?

6. What are the differing emphases in child-rearing strategies which arise from the conceptual orientations of Piaget, Adler, and Skinner?

PART FIVE

A Season for Husbands and Wives

In a sense, this part is the center of gravity for this survey on marriage and family living. Husband-and-wife interactions are the hub around which the rest of family life revolves. Children may be added to the union, but they soon grow up and leave. Husband-and-wife relationships persist—at least in most cases. The initial adjustments of husbands and wives were discussed in Chapter 7. The first chapter of this section examines marriage relationships during the mature family years. Surveying the various roles included in the social positions of husband and wife and describing the typical marital conflicts and their management sets the stage for the discovery that successful adjustment to married life can be achieved in many ways.

Not all marriage partners manage to cope with the pressures that bear on romantic love. In the second chapter of this section, we deal with the process of "reconsidering," that is, with the social patterns of separation and divorce. A central theme of this chapter is that the quality of American marriages cannot be directly "read" from the divorce rate. A high divorce rate does not necessarily mean that the institution of marriage is crumbling, nor does a low divorce rate necessarily indicate happy marriages. Thus, this chapter is designed to place the social process of marriage dissolution in a fuller context that will permit us to assess its importance for family life in contemporary American society.

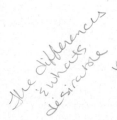

11 *Husband-and-Wife Interactions in a Full Family Setting*

The Family as a Small Group

Leadership Roles in the Family
 The Instrumental Leader
 The Expressive Leader
 Instrumental and Expressive Orientations and Sex Roles
 Critical Responses to the Instrumental-Expressive Leader Distinction

The Housewife Role:
 The Six Stages of the Housewife Role: The Interpretation of Helena Z. Lopata
 Three Variations on the Housewife Role
  The Restricted Housewife
  The Uncrystallized Housewife
  The Multidimensional Housewife
 An Evaluation of the Housewife Role

Sexual Role Patterns of Married Couples
 Trends in Attitudes toward Sexual Relations in Marriage
 Trends in Sexual Behavior in Marriage
 Extramarital Sexual Behavior

The Companionship Role in Marriage
 The Content of the Companionship Role
 The Companionship Role and the Quality of Married Life

Strategies of Conflict Management in Marriage
 The Major Causes of Marital Conflict

Summary

When John Demos (1971) set out to describe family life in Plymouth Colony, he titled his essay *A Little Commonwealth*. Implied in this title was one of his central themes that the family in Colonial times was a miniature society. In fact, the family was at once a business, a school, a vocational institute, a church, a house of correction, and a welfare institution. Because all of these functions were carried on within the domestic household, the family assumed enormous responsibilities and the very welfare of the colony rested on the smooth performance of its several tasks.

Today, of course, such a characterization of our family life as a miniature society would be wholly inaccurate. No longer is the family a little commonwealth; instead, it is a highly specialized institution. Many of its earlier functions have been transferred to other institutions. Household and business tend to be physically separated. Education takes place in a school with professionally trained teachers. Even vocational education occurs in specialized schools or departments, and the system of household apprenticeship has long since vanished. Religious instruction and worship may find reinforcement in the family, but formal instruction usually is handled by religious experts. Likewise, the correctional and welfare functions have been assumed largely by social service agencies, the courts, and government officials.

Some contemporary commentators on American life have jumped to the conclusion that few activities remain for the family to perform. In this view, all the truly important tasks seem to have been assigned elsewhere. The "loss of family functions" theme can be traced back at least as far as William F. Ogburn (1938), who saw in these changes a sign of the decline of the family's social importance. Although Ogburn's interpretation was accepted widely at first, it has since been subjected to a great deal of criticism. Parsons (Parsons and Bales, 1955) pointed out that change in family functions did not necessarily mean decline—only that the family was acquiring more specialized responsibilities. Vincent (1966) stressed the adaptive function of the family as it responded to new social demands created by changes in other institutions like the economy and school. More recently, Nye (1974) has proposed that as some functions are transferred from the family others take their place as a focus for family activities.

On balance, then, many social scientists believe that the loss of some functions has freed the family to handle new tasks. In the previous chapter, for

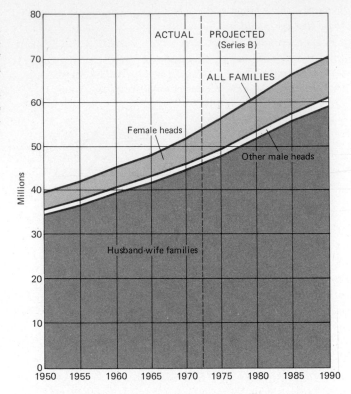

Figure 11-1
Families, by Type: 1950–1990. This figure shows the variety of forms a family as a small group may take. Note that the projections go through the year 1990. *(Source: Social Indicators 1976, p. 44.)*

example, we noted the family's critical responsibility to oversee the socialization process and child rearing. This chapter focuses more directly on the marital pair and the tasks they perform in addition to socialization. These activities are organized around several major roles, namely, the leadership roles, the homemaker role, and the sexual and companionship roles. The parents perform some of these roles—such as leadership—for the family as a group, while others are designed to meet the needs of husband and wife, such as the sexual and companionship roles. Husband-and-wife interactions inevitably produce disagreements and strains. Some strategies for conflict management and some ways to assess marital success will be surveyed at the end of the chapter.

This chapter should help lay to rest the myth that the family is declining as a social institution. As we shall see, the loss of some family functions is counterbalanced by the increasing importance of several other role functions.

The Family as a Small Group

A distinguishing trait of the modern family is its small size. Behavioral scientists have recognized for some time that small groups differ in their social

A Season for Husbands and Wives

dynamics and have different needs than large groups or mass institutions. Accordingly, a number of family analysts have used some concepts taken from small-group research to analyze the family. Results have been promising, illuminating, and in some instances, highly controversial. In one of the more interesting developments, Robert Bales, Talcott Parsons, and their colleagues have advanced an interpretation of leadership roles. We shall examine their proposals after making some observations about family leadership in general.

Leadership Roles in the Family

The wife and husband have the major leadership roles within the American nuclear family. Not only are husbands and wives equipped with more social experience and practical knowledge, but they also have the legal responsibility to make decisions for their minor children. The American family has been described—and quite rightly so—as a **child-centered family unit.** This means that parents typically take into account the needs of their children, even though children lack the ability and wisdom to take part fully in the family decision-making process.

Husband and wife are expected to exercise their power to keep the group operating in an orderly and socially acceptable fashion. They must make decisions, assign household tasks, and see that these tasks are performed. When parents assign tasks, like washing the dishes or mowing the lawn, they also must try to build into their family relations enough motivation to encourage members to do their jobs. Thus, a parent does not issue commands like a drill sergeant. Rather, he or she usually tries to assign tasks in a way that leads the child to cooperate.

Because of the intimate emotional relations among family members, leaders can be manipulated subtly by those who have less power, namely their children. A youngster with a paying job would think twice before asking the boss to be excused from work to go to the movies with "the gang." Parents, by contrast, are frequently asked for such privileges. More often than not, the parents end up clearing away the dinner dishes while their children dash off to the movies. Of course, such behavior does not mean that the parents are not the true leaders of the family. Instead, it shows that they can be manipulated by their children because, out of their commitment to a child-centered family, they allow themselves to respond to their children's emotional appeals.

Despite the emotional character of the husband and wife's leadership roles, aspects of their role performances compare with leaders of other small groups. For example, a husband-and-wife team must deal with the administrative and emotional problems common to almost all small groups. Parents must make sure certain activities are performed while ensuring the family's emotional solidarity. The discovery of these two distinct role functions in other small groups led Parsons and Bales (1955) to suggest that the instrumental (administrative) and expressive (emotional) types of leaders also are found within the family.

The Instrumental Leader

Since **the instrumental leader** is usually the family's breadwinner (Zelditch, 1955:339), this person is likely to have a broad range of social contacts beyond other family members and neighborhood friendship networks. This leader's main concern is with those daily activities which are necessary to maintain the family group. The instrumental leader not only assigns specific tasks, but also provides the necessary information, motivation, and household organization to ensure that the tasks are completed in a socially acceptable manner. Furthermore, the instrumental leader has the main responsibility for integrating the family with society. In other words, this person is the family's major link with the outside world.

The Expressive Leader

The **expressive leader** usually is attached to the home and provides the warmth, affection, and sympathy needed to achieve the psychological balance of the nuclear family unit. The expressive leader responds to the emotional needs of family members by resolving some of the tensions that are created by the instrumental leader's demands for certain behaviors. Thus, the household, which is the domain of the expressive leader, usually is associated symbolically with security, love, and personal support.

Instrumental and Expressive Orientations and Sex Roles

In most societies, the two leadership roles are divided between the sexes. The typical pattern in American society is for the husband and father to take the instrumental role, while the wife and mother assumes the expressive role. Of course, no real mother or father is expected to fully meet the rather idealized roles defined for each type; rather, these models are simply meant to identify basic orientations. Instrumental actions are related to task or administrative goals. They include such behaviors as earning an adequate family income, socially placing the family within the community status system, and efficiently organizing the family unit. Expressive leaders try to establish emotional solidarity, maintain motivation, and dispel tensions among family members.

While men can and do perform some expressive behaviors and women can and do exhibit some instrumental behaviors, each gender's sex-role socialization tends to promote a stronger instrumental orientation in men and a stronger expressive orientation in women (Weitz, 1977:127–30). While Parsons and Bales (1955) agree that, in principle, both kinds of action are possible for each sex, our culture does socialize women to develop emotional skills and men to develop instrumental skills. Yet, one should not conclude that one leader is incapable of performing the tasks usually assigned to the other. Kanter (1977), for example, has shown clearly that women can be highly efficient corporate executives, which certainly requires well-honed instrumental skills. Similarly, women executives can assume the expressive leader role when they shift from work to family.

Instrumental and expressive orientations are not only encouraged by sex-role socialization and cultural norms. They also are chosen by people because of the rewards for each type of performance. Instrumental action tends to be rewarded with the recognition of achievement and personal approval, such as income, social honor, and high grades (as in education). Expressive leadership is rewarded by such personal gratifications as affection, social approval, love and concern (Stockard and Johnson, 1980:173–6). While each sex can respond to both types of rewards, men tend to find greater social support in their striving for instrumental rewards and women in expressive gratifications. These preferences are, of course, socially learned, but that fact does not make either one any less gratifying to the people involved.

Critical Responses to the Instrumental-Expressive Leader Distinction

Some social scientists have criticized Parsons and Bales' instrumental-expressive distinction because they think it supports those who assign women to passive, dependent, home-based roles. Ann Oakley (1976:181–3), for example, characterizes the distinction as a sociological myth which 'condemns women to servitude in the homemaker role. Forisha (1978:60–61) similarly objects to this model's tendency to attribute to men the role capacity to *do* things and to women the role capacity to *feel* things. In her view, such a distinction makes women socially subordinate to men. Her argument recalls Philip Slater's (1961) earlier claim that separate persons are not needed to perform the instrumental and expressive roles.

From a different perspective, Leik's (1963) research findings supported the view that while husbands played the instrumental role *outside* the family, *within* the family husbands generally shared expressive functions with the wife. George Levinger (1964) subsequently produced data that generally supported this position. He found that a wife who is expressive toward her husband expects him to be emotionally expressive in return. Moreover, both partners found expressiveness more rewarding than task performance. Thus, a husband and father may well exhibit instrumental behavior in his breadwinner role, expressive behavior with his wife, and both types of behavior with his children.

A more critical response to the Parsons and Bales' theory emerged from two studies by Aronoff and Crano (Crano and Aronoff, 1975, 1978). The first study of 862 societies revealed no major tendency to allocate family tasks to a male leader. A second study, based on data from 186 societies, examined how much the roles of the instrumental and expressive leaders complement each other. They found that mothers were slightly more expressive than fathers during their children's infancy. After the children matured, however, these differences between mothers and fathers disappeared completely. This led Aronoff and Crano to conclude that the separation of task and expressive roles between the parents was simplistic and unsupported by hard evidence.

However, other studies of family life have shown that the distinction—in American society, at least—is not simply a figment of theoretical imagination. Scanzoni (1975) discovered in his research that men and women do define their self-concepts in terms which can be understood as instrumental actions. Similarly, Johnson and others (reported in Stockard and Johnson, 1980:175) found that women in their sample showed their independence through expressiveness, while men tended to demonstrate their independence through instrumental actions. Hence, these researchers concluded that, whereas women could relate positively to both expressive and instrumental traits, men could relate positively only to instrumental forms of action. They also noted that some working women hesitate to show their expressiveness, fearing that in the job market it would place them in supportive or low-level occupations. Johnson urged that women not be encouraged to reject expressiveness, but that society recognize its value. In other words, women should not allow the masculine bias against expressiveness to influence their own positive feelings about it, especially since expressiveness need not imply passivity, incompetence, or dependency.

On balance, it appears that the instrumental and expressive leader roles do exist in the nuclear family. We do not yet know whether these roles must be segregated by sex or whether segregation promotes role performance. Perhaps American society promotes more leadership role segregation than traditional cultures—some of the data clearly appear to point in that direction. At present, however, the conflicting evidence suggests that while the task and expressive roles may provide a useful division of family leadership, these concepts should not be applied too mechanically to American family life.

The Housewife Role

The long treatment of the homemaker role in this chapter, without a comparable discussion of the male role within the household, may seem to create an imbalance in coverage. The reasons for this one-sided treatment are actually quite simple. The male counterpart to the homemaker role is the role of breadwinner, whose major activities occur outside the domestic unit. Furthermore, in the field of family analysis, far more investigations have been undertaken on women's roles than on men's. Studies of motherhood abound, for example, but research on fathers is very slight (Lamb, 1976:1–34). Similarly, a number of excellent studies probe the homemaker role and its changes throughout the female life cycle, while very little such research has been done on the male life cycle. For the moment, then, this survey will concentrate on the available research pertaining to the homemaker role.

The Six Stages of the Housewife Role: The Interpretation of Helena Z. Lopata

Among the more thorough treatments of the homemaker role is the research of Helena Z. Lopata (1972). She sets the role into the larger framework of the feminine life cycle. As a result, six basic stages are identified as typical developmental patterns for American women:

1. *From home-based infant to single, young woman.* This stage covers the period when personality formation begins in the home, in primary groups, the school, and finally in the work roles within a wider community. In these first 20 years or so, females are not only socialized to their sex role, but they also come to take part in secondary social networks in which their performance is evaluated by rational standards based on competence and achievement. Hence, the woman moves from home-bound roles to several social roles outside the home.

2. *From the young woman's multidimensional, nonfamily roles to wife and homemaker roles.* During this stage, some freedom is lost as the homemaker role supplements or replaces the career or student role. However, women usually continue working until the first child is born, and sometimes afterward as well.

3. *From young wife to new mother.* The change in this period is from the external participating role of an active wife to the physically confining role of mother. She now must give her attention to small children who demand considerable time and energy. Many women watch their adult social life disintegrate, which can produce one of the most stressful periods of the female life cycle.

4. *From immersion in the motherhood role to increasing competence in the homemaker, wife, and community roles.* This stage is marked by fewer demands from children and an increase in the skills needed to manage children, the home, and community affairs. Frequently, women return to the work force, taking up careers suspended with their first child was born.

5. *From full participation in family life to the departure of children and the death of her spouse.* The "shrinking circle" stage, as this period is often called, frees the homemaker to explore new interests and community involvements, to work outside the home, and to spend more time with her husband. His death ushers in the final stage.

6. *From sole surviving member of the household to the death of the homemaker.* In this period of widowhood a number of role variations are possible. She may wish to travel, take part in community affairs, develop new interests, or perhaps remarry. These options vary according to her psychological outlook, financial resources, health, and friendship networks. Of course, this period also may be a time of forced isolation, loneliness, and dependency during which she simply marks time until she dies.

Naturally, this general model for the female life cycle is not a blueprint which every woman follows to the last detail. Each individual performs somewhat differently—either by choice or by force of circumstances. However, Lopata does identify three major variations on the housewife role which are significantly affected by an individual woman's skill, creativity, outlook, and education. Class standing is the major factor determining which of the three role variations a woman is likely to choose. Briefly summarized, those three variations to the housewife role are:

The Restricted Housewife The **restricted housewife** is generally a woman of the lower classes who has completed four years or less of high school, who depends on her husband, and is homebound as well as task oriented in her homemaker activities. Moreover, she often feels incompetent or ineffective in social relationships outside the home and immediate neighborhood.

The Uncrystallized Housewife By contrast, the **uncrystallized housewife** model includes women of the lower middle classes who have high school educations and often a year or two more. Women in this category accept the homemaker role less passively, establish social relationships with greater ease, share power more equally with their husbands, and generally are happier with their lives. Homemakers of this type also can organize life rather than simply adjusting to it.

The Multidimensional Housewife Lopata regards the third type as the most competent and satisfying role variation. Usually, women in this category have completed college and enjoy an upper-middle class status. Their home is not shut off from the outside world, but is instead a place for entertaining and—due to her artistic and decorating skills—the world of culture is introduced into the family living space. Such women also relate to their husbands in a companionable fashion, taking an interest in his vocational endeavors and supporting his career advancement. Similarly, the husband tends to share authority equally with his wife so that decision making is a joint enterprise. The multidimensional pattern is the most competent, satisfying, and creative of the three variations on the housewife role.

CLOSE-UP   The Emergence of the Housewife Role: Two Interpretations
The housewife role has recently been severely criticized, especially be women's liberationists. Opponents charge that this role is assigned automatically on the basis of sex, that it is a menial social role, and that it frustrates women's self-fulfillment because it is unpaid, nonstatus work. In *Woman's Work*, the British sociologist, Ann Oakley, explains how the housewife role emerged after the Industrial Revolution. Here is her basic argument, followed by a counter-interpretation.

Women in preindustrial England were very active in the labor force. They also enjoyed the same rights as men to own property, make business contracts, and earn profits. Most businesses were centered in the home—such as baking bread, brewing beer, spinning wool, or operating a farm or small business. A wife typically shared decision-making power with her husband, and the children from an early age contributed to earning the family livelihood.

The Industrial Revolution introduced sharp changes. Workplace and home were separated as the center of economic activity shifted to the great factories. At first, women were employed as well as men by factory owners. Indeed whole families were hired, so that children were not separated from their parents during the day and parents could oversee the factory training of their offspring. Child labor laws enacted in the 1820s, however, forced children out of the work force. Mothers and fathers then faced the modern problem of how to care for their children if both parents worked. The usual decision was for the mother to stay home and provide child care, run the household, and meet her husband's needs.

The practical adjustment to industrial life, Oakley continues, soon acquired ideological support. By the 1840s, upper- and middle-class wives were not expected to work outside the home. Only working class women were still employed in the mines and factories. A series of Government Commissions reported in the 1840s that the working conditions of women were horrible, shocking, and "not favorable to the development of the female character." Legislators quickly enacted protective labor bills restricting the role of women in the economy. Much of this legislation, Oakley argues, was based on the "domestic ideology" that a woman's proper place was in the home. Thus, by the turn of the twentieth century, the vast majority of even working-class women were effectively excluded from productive labor outside the home.

The emergence of the housewife role with its supporting "domestic ideology" had several important consequences. First, Oakley suggests, women were tied down to family roles and confined to the household. Whereas formerly women had found companionship in the factories and shops, housework took place in isolation from other adults, so that loneliness became a serious problem. Also, the housework ascribed to women was routine, low status, and generally viewed an nonproductive labor. More distressful from Oakley's point of view was the dependency of the housewife role. Since housework is unpaid, the wife is financially dependent on her husband. Finally, the doctrine of feminine domesticity was primarily a product of male status striving. In Victorian England, the symbol of middle-class success was the ability of a husband to support his wife and daughters as "leisured ladies." A wife who worked outside the home was considered "a misfortune and disgrace," especially for the husband.

In this manner, then, the forces of industrialization, legislative action, and the status goals of husbands conspired to create the housewife role and force it upon women. Today, however, women are again returning to the labor force outside the home. Oakley contends that this fact, by itself, will not eliminate the burdens of the housewife role. To abolish this role, she urges, it will be necessary to abolish the family and gender roles as well.

Oakley's historical thesis is only one among several possible interpretations. Using her data, in fact, a quite different explanation of the events which led to the rise of the housewife role can be proposed. This counter-interpretation is *not* claiming, of course, that women should be dependent, that child care is

(continued)

easy, or that housework is fun. Rather, at stake in this debate is whether women were forced out of other jobs and into the housewife role against their will during the Victorian era. Our thesis proposes that women initially chose the housewife role because it was more attractive than employment in the mines, factories, and sweatshops. Only in this century did that decision lose luster as outside employment came to offer better working conditions, higher status, and personal fulfillment. If our interpretation is correct, then the emergence of the housewife role is not to be credited to the blind force of industrialization and male chauvinism, but it also entailed the active participation of women. Consider, then, this alternative view.

We have no quarrel with Oakley's claim that women in preindustrial England engaged in numerous economic activities or that their labor was enlisted by factory owners during the early days of industrialization. We would lay greater stress on the fact that the housewife role emerged initially among the ranks of the upper classes. Yet, these first housewives were far from idle, since they were responsible for organizing and overseeing the household servants. Upper status housewives did not do housework, but they did direct the domestic labor force.

As industrialization expanded—increasing the standard of living—more women were afforded the opportunity to withdraw from paid employment. Middle-and then working-class women gradually swelled the ranks of housewives. The model of housewife provided by upper status women could not be replicated in their lower class counterparts, however, since these families could not afford household servants and the menial tasks of housework had to be performed by the lower status housewife herself. Why, then, would lower status women accept the housewife role, if they could not imitate the managerial style of upper status women? The answer, we can suggest, lies in the kind of jobs women were fleeing. Work outside the home for lower status women was typically dirty, hard, tedious, and often dangerous. Women in the coal mines, for example, had to work in damp, dark, and cramped conditions for long hours with minimal pay. Factory employment meant long hours in the routine operation of machines. Sweatshops placed enormous production pressures on their employees. Therefore, even though housework was menial, it did offer more freedom, lighter labor, and fewer demands than outside employment. Thus, women whose families could afford to have them stay at home found that option more attractive than hard labor in the mines, factories, and sweatshops.

By the 1970s, however, the appeal of the housewife role was rapidly declining. The return of housewives to paid employment in large numbers coincided with an erosion of the ideological support for the housewife role. Reversing the legitimation process of a century before, scholars like Oakley and her colleagues reinterpreted history to show that the whole notion of the "housewife" was flawed from the beginning and forced upon women against their will. While this argument may now be politically useful in liberating women from the expectation that housework and child care constitute their primary occupation, Victorian women were clearly of an entirely different mind. From their historical vantage point, the emergence of the housewife role was precisely what offered them liberation from the drudgery of the factory system.

Thus, the social meaning of the housewife role has been drastically transformed over the last century. While the emergence of the housewife role was originally regarded as a great step forward in the liberation of women, it had

A Season for Husbands and Wives

been reinterpreted by the 1970s as a great curse which burdened women with the thankless task of maintaining a household. Perhaps each interpretation was appropriate for its own historical period and prevailing social conditions in society at large. Yet, it would be historically inaccurate for us to impose our current anxieties about the housewife role on women in the Victorian era who viewed the housewife in an altogether different—and much more favorable—frame of reference.

An Evaluation of the Housewife Role

Not all recent assessments of the housewife role have been as favorable as Lopata about the multidimensional pattern. In the popular culture, the homemaker role has been portrayed as a mindless, menial, and unrewarding role in which women simply serve their husbands and children. Feminists like Betty Friedan (1963) and Germaine Greer (1971) have not only reinforced this image, but they also have launched a protest against its imposition on women.

From a social scientific point of view, Ann Oakley (1974, 1976) agrees and has developed a supportive argument. Using both historical and contemporary data, Oakley (1976:222–33) contends that the housewife role cannot promote self-actualization and therefore cannot be truly rewarding. Even though some women may say they enjoy the homemaker role, Oakley argues, they still need to be liberated from this demeaning social position.

Perhaps the most important result of Lopata's analysis is the questioning of the accuracy of the homemaker stereotype. Lopata's position suggests that Oakley and others really are reacting against the restricted housewife role of the lower classes, and not the other variations achieved by the middle and upper-middle classes. Lopata's research indicates that as competence in homemaking and child rearing increases, creativity, role variation, and—perhaps most important of all—personal satisfaction with the housewife role also increases. In short, lower-class women more often feel locked into a rigid homemaker role which they see as one of unfulfilling drudgery, while women who possess greater social skills usually approach the role as a creative opportunity, managing to find happiness and fulfillment in it. With such different points of view, one suspects that this social role will be a subject of considerable research and political interest in the decades ahead.

TEST YOURSELF

On the Conditions of Women's or Men's Happiness or Satisfaction with Life. The questions below have been used in social scientific surveys to sample attitudes about those social conditions which contribute to the happiness or life satisfaction of women and men. Read each question, and then circle the response—agree strongly (AS), agree mildly (AM), disagree mildly (DM), or disagree strongly (DS)—which best represents your point of view. Scoring instructions can be found at the bottom of this questionnaire.

(continued)

Women are happiest when they are taking care of a home and looking after children.

AS	AM	DM	DS
1	2	3	4

A woman can live a full and happy life without marrying.

AS	AM	DM	DS
4	3	2	1

A man can live a full and happy life without marrying.

AS	AM	DM	DS
4	3	2	1

Women are better off married to public leaders than holding political office themselves; then they get all the pleasure and few of the problems of public life.

AS	AM	DM	DS
1	2	3	4

Most women need and want the kind of protection and support that men have traditionally given them.

AS	AM	DM	DS
1	2	3	4

Economic and social freedom is worth far more to women than acceptance of the ideal of feminity which has been set by men.

AS	AM	DM	DS
4	3	2	1

If a woman is not satisfied being a wife and mother, it is a sign she has emotional difficulties.

AS	AM	DM	DS
1	2	3	4

Giving birth to a child is a wonderful thing that all women should experience.

AS	AM	DM	DS
1	2	3	4

Taking care of a home and raising children is more rewarding for a woman than having a job.

AS	AM	DM	DS
1	2	3	4

The housewife/mother role does not really provide women with enough opportunity for self-fulfillment.

AS	AM	DM	DS
4	3	2	1

Scoring: Total your numerical scores for the questions above. A high score indicates that you believe that happiness and life satisfaction can occur best when equality of sex role relations prevail, while a low score indicates that you believe that fulfilling traditional male and female sex roles promises greater happiness and life satisfaction.

Source: Karen Oppenheim Mason, with the assistance of Daniel R. Denison and Anita J. Schacht. *Sex-Role Attitude Items and Scales From U.S. Sample Surveys.* Rockville, Md: National Institute of Mental Health. 1975, pp. 46–7.

A Season for Husbands and Wives

Chapter 7 discussed some of the married couple's first adjustments to sexual life. In this section, the focus is on the partner's mature sexual relations. Several trends in sexual attitudes and behavior have developed. Before surveying the behavior changes, we shall examine changing sexual attitudes.

Trends in Attitudes toward Sexual Relations in Marriage

The Victorian Age, which ended shortly after 1900, was marked by a stern sexual repressiveness that can serve as a baseline against which to measure contemporary attitudes toward marital sexuality. The standard Victorian view toward men was that they had strong sexual urges which they should control through manly discipline. However, the attitude toward feminine sexuality, was marked by ambivalence, inconsistency, and an effort to keep women in their traditional roles as wives and mothers. On the one hand, women were regarded as basically asexual, and were not expected to enjoy sexual relations. On the other hand, the Victorians believed the female reproductive system unleashed powerful forces which women often found difficult to control. Between puberty and menopause, therefore, a woman's most demanding task was to restrain her periodic sexual crises (Smith-Rosenberg, 1974:23–37).

Among the Victorians, the purpose of marital sexual intercourse was the procreation of children and the reduction of male tensions. Husbands were not encouraged to spend time arousing their mates during sexual relations. A double standard also emerged which permitted men to enjoy sexual relations secretly in premarital and extramarital affairs and legitimately in marital life.

When the Kinsey (1948, 1953) studies were published, they showed that a great deal of change had taken place already. No longer was sexual pleasure seen as for the husband only. While the double standard had not been wholly overcome, the gap between the sexual rights of the husband and the wife was clearly narrowing. Moreover, marriage manuals from the 1900s to the 1950s encouraged new expectations in both partners. Perhaps the most decisive development was what Michael Gordon (1978) labeled the "cult of mutual orgasm." T. H. Van de Velde's, *Ideal Marriage* (1930), was one of the first and most influential sex manuals which showed concern for the wife's gratification. He instructed husbands that they should not only arouse their wives so as to achieve simultaneous orgasm, but he also described a wide variety of techniques for improving sexual relations.

The underlying assumption in this and other such marriage manuals was that erotic love strengthened marriage bonds. Marital sexuality was coming to be viewed as a legitimate means of expressing love between husband and wife. The assumption also surfaced, perhaps naively, that because wives had more difficulty coping with marital sensuality, husbands probably should be the teacher of new sexual techniques. Indeed, most instruction on erotic fore-play described how to awaken the female sexual response. Perhaps the lingering remnants of the double standard had convinced marital experts that male efforts still held the key to sexual success.

The mid-1960s were a benchmark period when sexual attitudes registered one of their most abrupt changes. Edward Shorter (1977:108–19) noted a dramatic change in attitudes toward premarital, marital, and extramarital sexual relations. Permissiveness—the word most often used to describe the post-1960s era—included increased frequency of sexual intercourse, experimentation with sexual techniques, and a stronger emphasis on recreational sex. With widespread availability of contraceptives, the fear of pregnancy all but vanished. In addition, the sexual revolution nearly eliminated the double standard.

Thorough acceptance of an active sex life as an integral part of marriage has left some marriage experts uneasy for two reasons. First, some feel sexual technique is being overemphasized to the exclusion of the total marital relationship (Lasswell and Lobsenz, 1978). They fear that some couples may forget that marriage is more than good sex. Some contemporary marriage manuals assert that if partners have not tried at least six coital positions, or had intercourse at the average national weekly rate and always achieved orgasm together, they have a less than fulfilling sex life. Derek Wright (1975) warns, for example, that sexual liberation may become a new form of tyranny under which we rate our partners by the standards of sex "experts."

A second, and related concern is that sexual satisfaction may be taken for the basic factor determining marital success. No one disputes, of course, that the two affect each other. Ira Reiss (1980:282–3) argues, however, that while marital satisfaction and a fulfilling sex life are a two-way street, marital satisfaction is the more important factor behind sexual enjoyment in marriage.

Trends in Sexual Behavior in Marriage

Attitudes and behavior do not always coincide in a neat one-to-one relationship. Undoubtedly, marital or extramarital sexual attitudes vary more than sexual behaviors from one generation to the next. Before Kinsey's studies, social scientists had underestimated the sexual behavior of married couples. This is quite understandable, since no one before Kinsey had studied sexual behavior with the same scientific rigor and scope. Kinsey's landmark research enables scientists to estimate the trends on such matters as the frequency of marital intercourse, the types of physical arousal, and the variety of coital positions. Since the data on sexual practices are limited and often are based on volunteer, nonrepresentative samples, one cannot be sure that the data are wholly accurate. However, because the trends arising from the available research do point in the same direction, one may assume that these data reasonably reflect actual behavior patterns of married people.

On the question of the frequency of marital intercourse, the basic trend that emerged between the time of the Kinsey studies and the research in the 1970s shows an increase in coitus for both husbands and wives in all age groups. A comparison of Kinsey's findings for 1938 to 1949 with Hunt's (1974) findings, which reported weekly coitus on the average, reveals a significant rise in intercourse rates. Moreover, in two studies conducted by Charles F. Westhoff (1974) on coital frequency of women during four-week periods in 1965 and 1970, the subjects showed an increase from 6.8 times in 1965 to 8.2 coital times in 1970. Thus, these data do reflect a real increase in sexual intercourse within the general population.

Frequency of sexual relations helps account for the rise in the rate of orgasm. Because males have less difficulty achieving orgasm (Pierson and D'Antonio, 1974:17), the rates for orgasmic response are tabulated for the female partner only. Again, Kinsey provides the baseline for measuring these changes in behavior. From his (1953:408) sample, Kinsey reported that 25 percent of married women did not experience orgasm during their first year of marriage, and 12 percent had not achieved orgasm by their fifteenth year of marriage. By contrast, the Hunt (1974) study found that only 7 percent of his subjects had never experienced orgasm. A questionnaire published in *Redbook* magazine in 1974 and answered by 100,000 women also indicated that 7 percent of the women in that nonrandom sample had never achieved orgasm (Tavris and Sadd, 1977:74), the same figure as in the Hunt study. These data seem to indicate that the percentage of women who achieve orgasm has increased substantially since Kinsey's studies. Moreover, the frequency of orgasmic response also has risen proportionately.

As might be expected, higher orgasmic rates correlate with longer periods of foreplay. While about half of the couples in Kinsey's (1953:364) study on female sexual behavior devoted only 10 minutes or less to arousal, Hunt and later studies indicate that couples today typically spend much longer in foreplay. Not only does this produce higher rates of female orgasm, but it also provides more opportunity to experiment with different sexual techniques (Pierson and D'Antonio, 1974:73–84). The variety of sexual behaviors—touching, caressing, fondling, kissing—with both partners actively engaged in love making, indicates a new sexual permissiveness which would not have been common between a husband and wife even a generation ago. The growth of sexual equality also has increased the likelihood that the wife will begin lovemaking, rather than waiting for the husband to make the first overtures.

An important factor in determining sexual behavior between married couples is social class standing. The popular belief is that the lower classes have sexual relations more often and experiment more than couples from the better educated, higher income groups. Kinsey's data were among the first to show that just the opposite was true. Later studies have borne out the essential accuracy of Kinsey's conclusions. Although lower-class people may begin their sexual life somewhat earlier than upper-class people, lower-class marital behavior tends to be much more traditional, with less frequent coital behavior and less fulfilling overall sexual experience—especially for the wives (Howell, 1973). Upper or middle-class spouses apparently are more willing to discuss their sexual relations openly and be more sensitive to their partner's needs than lower-class couples (Reiss, 1980:275–85). Furthermore, a greater sense of closeness exists between better educated couples, and this factor correlates strongly with a higher frequency of sexual intercourse.

Extramarital Sexual Behavior

"Extramarital relations," Gerhard Neubeck (1969:1) observes, "have existed as long as has marriage itself." In some societies, extramarital liaisons have not been considered troublesome (Rodman, 1971). However, this has not been true as a general rule; more often, an extramarital involvement has been regarded as a breach of marriage vows. Roman law, for example, gave a husband the right to execute a wife found guilty of adultery (Queen and Habenstein, 1967:169), although a wife was not given a similar right. Today, extramarital affairs occur with some frequency. While they often create jealousy and a sense of betrayal, they appear to play a less important role in decisions to divorce than might be expected. Two factors help account for this. The first is that many extramarital affairs occur without the knowledge of the spouse. And second, once detected, many spouses choose to forgive unfaithfulness rather than dissolve the marriage.

Gathering reliable data on extramarital relations is an extremely difficult undertaking. The Kinsey (1953:416) study of female sexual behavior found that 26 percent of the women had been involved in an extramarital affair by age 40. However, the *Redbook* data analyzed by Tavris and Sadd (1977:116) revealed that 40 percent of women aged 40 and older had had extramarital intercourse. Kinsey (1948:585) estimated that approximately 50 percent of all married men have intercourse with women other than their wives at some time during their married lives. Adequate current data are not available to determine whether this estimate still holds true today. However, the percentage of men who have extramarital relations probably has not declined over the last 30 years.

Among the factors likely to increase extramarital involvements are long marriages, full-time employment, which increases the opportunity for sexual involvements, lack of religious affiliation or a low level of participation, and an unsatisfying marital sex life or relationship (Tavris and Sadd, 1977:114–34). Indeed, in a study of 2,262 married women, Robert Bell and others (1975) found that the single most important predictor of extramarital involvements was the rating of the marriage. Women who rated their marriages as happy and satisfying were less than half as likely to have had an extramarital experience than women who rated their marriages low on happiness and satisfaction. Furthermore, when women from highly rated marriages were also sexually conservative and followed a conventional life-style, their commitment to marital fidelity was increased.

From these data, it appears relatively clear that most women who engage in extramarital affairs do so because they are disappointed with their marriages. This is not, of course, the case in all instances. Some women—and we should assume men as well—do find it possible to enjoy their marriage and carry on an affair with a lover. However, the percentage who can maintain such relationships, does not seem to be very large. Tavris and Sadd (1977:129)

A Season for Husbands and Wives

believe on the basis of their data that only about 6 percent can be simultaneously happy in marriage and in extramarital involvements. No doubt, this low percentage reflects the emotional and social difficulties of maintaining two love relationships at the same time.

The Companionship Role in Marriage

Although social attention is firmly fixed on the sexual compatibility of marriage partners, companionship repeatedly appears in the research data as more important to marital satisfaction. When Reiss (1980:280–85) argues, for example, that affectional closeness tends to determine the quality of a couple's sexual relations, he really is pointing to the overriding importance of the companionship role in creating an emotional environment in which sexual compatibility can be achieved. Similarly, Marini (1976) reports that companionship plays a key role in marital happiness and in reducing tensions between partners.

The emergence of romantic love as the basis of marriage and the rise of the companionship ideal are, in fact, two of the distinguishing features of the modern family. Burgess and Locke (1953) were among the first students of family life to emphasize the importance of the compionship role. Since then its pervasiveness has been documented in numerous studies. Blood and Wolfe (1965) found, for example, that roughly 50 percent of the wives in their study chose "companionship in doing things together with the husband" as the most valuable aspect of their marriage, outpacing such factors as understanding, standard of living, and the opportunity to have children.

The Content of the Companionship Role

Why do partners stress the companionship role more than love, money, children, or other factors? To answer satisfactorily, we first must define the companionship role. It means more than simply spending a large part of one's leisure time in the company of the spouse, although this is certainly important. Companionship implies a certain quality of relationship binding partners together. Sharing experiences with a mate is complemented in the companionship role with caring, a sense of attachment, trust, confidence, and commitment to the other person.

In the distant historical past, the family was held together by several external social forces. These included the extended kin group, tradition, community mores, the power and authority of the male family head, law, and public opinion. These social forces continue today, but their role is reduced a good deal. Now, the major unifying force in the family is the relationship of husband and wife. Community pressures contribute less to family solidarity than the mutual affection, understanding, and companionate bonding between partners.

The companionate relationship alters other aspects of husband-and-wife interactions. Partners are encouraged to support each other emotionally, to share equally in decision making, to perform tasks, and generally to advise, nurture, praise, confide in, and share with the other person. The companionate relationship usually leads to equality between spouses. When a husband and wife depend on one another for security and affection and when each responds to the other's whole personality, inequality is almost impossible to maintain in a marriage. Put somewhat differently, a person one loves, confides in, leans on for emotional support, identifies with, cherishes, and interacts with daily simply cannot be treated as a social inferior (Williams, 1970:70). Thus, the very dynamics of the companionship role encourage marriage partners to treat one another as equals.

The Companionship Role and the Quality of Married Life

One important feature of the companionship role is its sheer length in years. The major responsibilities of parenting are completed within a relatively few years, but companionship starts during the mating process and continues until death or divorce. Moreover, with increasing life expectancy, couples have more time to develop close bonds of affection.

A major benefit of the companionate relationship is that it allows marriage partners to find a haven from the tensions and pressures of normal social interaction. In the security of the marital relationship, a spouse can blow off

Figure 11-2
Contemporary couples tend to rate companionship as the most important aspect of their life together.
(© *Jim Anderson, 1979/ Woodfin Camp & Associates.*)

A Season for Husbands and Wives

steam or express feelings without being penalized, sanctioned, or criticized. When everyone else appears indifferent to our needs, a spouse can be ready to lend a sympathetic ear to our problems, offer a word of encouragement, and be an understanding friend.

This sort of refuge from the pressures of the external world is tremendously important; it helps introduce a sense of balance into adult personalities. While companionate relationships probably would help all marriages, they are more easily accomplished in middle and upper-class marriages than in working-class unions. A number of studies (Komarovsky, 1967; Lopata, 1972; Howell, 1973; Rubin, 1976) have shown clearly that in the blue-collar class the husband tends to be oriented primarily toward his "breadwinner" role and the wife toward her "mothering and housewife" role. In this strict division of labor, the companionship role is generally underdeveloped. The husband and father typically comes home after work, eats dinner, watches television, or putters around the house, but he spends little time conversing with his wife. Consequently, neither shares much of their daily experience with the other, nor can they openly communicate their feelings toward one another. For this reason, working-class partners tend to be less satisfied with their husband and wife role performances than higher-status couples who see companionship as the focus of their marriage.

As a general rule, working-class couples encounter more adjustment problems because they cannot enter fully into the companionate role. Working-class husbands are more likely to share their problems with male relatives or buddies at work than with their wives. By the same token, a wife with problems will normally turn to female friends or relatives for advice and support. The most convincing explanation social scientists have developed for these behaviors is that working-class spouses adhere to more rigid sex-role stereotypes than couples who are better educated and enjoy a higher social status (Komarovsky, 1967:148–75).

Thus, while husband and wife in the working class share the same household, they often live in two different mental worlds with little overlap between them. His world is largely confined to work and leisure-time male friends; hers is comprised of children, household, and female friends or relatives. Friendship between husband and wife is simply not part of their marital expectations. For example, among the working-class women whom she interviewed, Rubin (1976:93) found that their image of an ideal husband was one who "worked hard, didn't drink, and doesn't hit me." Yet, having married a man who lives up to these standards, Rubin also found a number of women dissatisfied with their marital relationships. Most indirectly expressed a desire for companionship. Their comments indicate that while companionship is not a formal part of working-class expectations, many couples do regret not being able to share their feelings, worries, hopes, and dreams. Moreover, they also seem to recognize intuitively that much of the anxiety in their lives could be relieved if they could overcome the barriers to marital communication and establish companionable relationships with their spouses.

Even among middle and upper-class couples, of course, companionship is not a cure for every problem. However, couples who can sustain a marital dialogue—which conveys affection, concern, and interest—rate their marriages higher in happiness and personal satisfaction. More importantly, these marriages also reveal that the companionate relationship has a therapeutic effect on both partners. A husband and wife who talk about their feelings express fewer anxieties and worries because they can share problems with their mates. Thus, middle-class couples place a high value on companionship not simply because of the happiness it produces, but also because it stabilizes their lives.

CLOSE-UP

"I want you to meet my live-in lover"

It was easy back in Eden, living together and not having to introduce each other to friends and relations. Eve hardly had to tell the viper, "This is the man I share a garden with."

For the modern unmarried, however, language has not kept pace with reality and there's still no word in English, at least, that quite says it all.

It's not difficult to write about the nation's 1.4 million cohabitees. Living Together was always hot copy, and it became even newsier since the flower children of the 1960s planted the label "old lady" and "old man" on their lovers. It was a far cry from the days of Leo Gorcey and the Dead End Kinds, who used the phrases simply to mean mom and dad.

In print, it's always been easy to slip into the jargon of "co-habiting couples" and "live-in lovers." A few years ago, for instance, *Newsweek* did not hesitate to cite examples of public folks who "casually shack up," including unwed couples such as Woody and Diane Keaton.

But in real life, when a mysterious new couple enters the arena of a dinner party, thrown to the social lions, it's different.

It is proper to inform total strangers. "We're live-in lovers" or "We co-habit, you know" or with pride, "I'd like to meet my shack-up"? Hardly.

What's really needed is one new word that will capture all the elements of blissful unmarried co-habitation. The word must at least blend a reference to residency, a suggestion of sexuality, a shading of emotional care, a hint of permanence and a dash, perhaps, of economic sharing. It's a tough order and too many words and phrases in current use are flawed or phony or fatuous.

The Census Bureau came up with the acronym POSSLQ, thought up by the bureau's family expert, Arthur Norton, who used it to denote "Persons of the Opposite Sex Sharing Living Quarters," but while it's been printed in a more humanized version—posselque—it's hardly an icebreaker over martinis.

Even more stuffy is modern psychology's entry, "significant other"—that is, people in significant relationships who are not related by blood, marriage or adoption. As one psychologist with the Veterans Administration explained, "It's simply a way of saying 'the lady you're living with.' " As in, "And now, I'd like you to say hello to my significant other." Another conversation stopper.

Elizabeth Post recognized the problem a few years back and allowed that the new etiquette permitted a two-edged approach. The use of the word "friend" might be used when introducing a live-in lover to elders. With peers, she advised, the phrase, "This is the person I live with," could be used without embarrassment. But it is clearly a choice of understatement or overstatement.

There are many other words and phrases lovers and live-ins have tested:

"I used to just say, "This is my honey," one young co-habitee recalled. Her

A Season for Husbands and Wives

parents, however, referred to her live-in boyfriend as "the son-out-law." She ended the war of words simply—last year she married her honey.

She had also tried another approach. He's my LT . . . for Living Together." But the shortcut never caught on somehow, perhaps because it sounded too much like a gas-guzzling car.

Other choices are also problematic.

"Boon companion" is vague, even though it suggests an exchange of favors, chummy and sexual.

"Good friend" depends on voice tone.

"Very good friend" sounds like a wink.

"Old lady," sound either affected or tasteless, hardly the handle a middle-aged lawyer, for instance, would grasp in introducing his live-in lover to business associates.

"Lover" is too intimate and possibly non-residential, and boyfriend" or "girl-friend" sounds a trifle adolescent.

"Paramour" is a bit old-fashioned, with a dash of pretense, unless the para-mour in question was Greta Garbo, or Doug Fairbanks.

"Roommate" suffers also—too cute or too casual—and "husband or wife-to-be" sounds like a business arrangement.

Something always seems to be missing. "Fiancé," for instance, says nothing about living arrangements and "housemate" hedges on sex.

There are, of course, a heap of old-fashioned niceties such as sweetheart, pal and companion, playmate, steady, heartthrob, darling, inamorata, one and only, beau and even bosom buddy. And there are some new but silly phrases like "important person" or "meaningful relationship." But the problem is always clarity.

"Yes, we are living together," you might let it be known at a cocktail party, gesturing to some unseen mate across the room. The listener, however, might not be sure if you're talking about a lover, an uncle or a parrot.

It does seem to be a problem of viewpoint. For instance, when a spouse says, "This is my husband," or "This is my wife," there is no question raised about sexuality, even if the listener assumes the married couple aren't sleeping to-gether.

Wife-husband phrasing clearly implies a legal and possessive relationship and an emotional connection, even if it's not necessarily healthy, happy, wise, or even interesting.

But if an unknown, role-free couple enters the scene, the unspoken question is often inquisitorial. "Are you or have you ever been a sexual couple?" In other words, "Are you sleeping together or did you meet in the elevator?"

—David Behrens, *Newsday*

Strategies of Conflict Management in Marriage

All marriages have some tension, misunderstanding, and disagreement. In-deed, a marriage free from conflict might well be a cause for concern, for this probably would signal a highly submissive partner who allows the other to make all the decisions, or a dull relationship in which both partners are indifferent to each other, or perhaps a marital bond so fragile that disagreements might shatter it. Thus, the absence of conflict cannot be taken at face value as a sign of a healthy marriage.

Social scientists have long recognized that conflict also can draw partners closer together (Cuber and Harroff, 1965). In fact, one approach to family therapy is based on the conviction that couples who fight together are couples who stay together, provided their conflicts follow certain rules (Bach and Wyden, 1968). The **"therapeutic aggression"** suggested by Bach and his followers is designed to help couples vent their hostility through verbal abuse, making physical violence unnecessary. Sociologist Murray Straus (1974) cautions that the procedure may be dangerous in actual practice. Although Bach and Wyden do not recommend personal insults which are designed only to hurt, they do urge a strategy which they call "leveling." This means the partners tell each other honestly exactly how they feel, "letting it all hang out," even though feelings may be offended. Using results from a study of 385 married couples, Straus (1974:27) criticized the Bach approach on two counts. First, the data indicated that "expressing aggression against others probably tends to increase subsequent aggression," and second, the results showed that "the greater the amount of verbal aggression, the greater the amount of physical aggression." Thus, Straus concluded that while openness and honesty are generally desirable in marital communication, a certain degree of "civility" also should be maintained as a check on the escalation of violence from verbal to physical forms.

The research findings of Straus are a sober warning that one needs to evaluate strategies for conflict management carefully to ensure that a strategy will not worsen problems rather than resolve them. Several strategies also exist which, while they do not worsen matters between partners, also do not hold much promise of solving deep-seated conflicts. Marital conflict research is, unfortunately, still in its infancy (Glick and Gross, 1975:511). Thus, many strategies for conflict resolution exist, but we have little hard evidence on how well they work. We shall begin to sort out the issues of marital conflict with a look at the major causes of strife, followed by an examination of two popular self-help strategies, and finally conclude with some general guidelines for conflict management in mature marriages.

The Major Causes of Marital Conflict Management

Chapter 7 explored the sorts of marital strains newly wedded couples encounter. Problems with money, sexual adjustment, in-laws, communication, and expectations persist into later married life and therefore continue to create conflict. One additional problem, not common in the early adjustment to marriage, is conflict connected with rearing children. Some of these issues, of course, are more likely than others to prompt marital strain. Scanzoni (1972), for example, distinguishes between what he calls basic and nonbasic conflicts. Basic conflicts threaten the marriage itself. Nonbasic conflicts are simply disagreements over issues, producing a temporary irritation. A spouse who drinks too much or attacks the other partner would create basic conflicts. By contrast, mates who watch too much television, are untidy, or never want to go out to dinner are only chronic irritations who are unlikely to break up a marriage.

Research on marital troubles reveals a fairly consistent pattern of major problems between husbands and wives. In their study of suburban Detroit, Blood and Wolfe (1965:244–9) ranked the sources of trouble, listing the most frequent irritation first: money, children, leisure time, in-laws, family roles, and religion-politics-sex. Money's top place on the list is not surprising, but the finding that sexual problems were reported so seldom that they fell into the final, catchall category was unexpected. John Scanzoni (1970:157) discovered that respondents in his sample indicated similar types of disagreements. The specific breakdown of his data revealed the following: "38 percent indicated conflict over the production and consumption of money, 19 percent responded in terms of issues connected with children, 10 percent said friends, 3 percent referred to kin, 21 percent were combined in the miscellaneous category." Curiously, the number of respondents who said sex was their first area of disagreement was only .07 percent, an even smaller number than in the Blood and Wolfe study. Interestingly, 9 percent of Scanzoni's sample reported "nothing" as their most serious cause of conflict.

Issues which most frequently cause conflict between husband and wife are not necessarily the issues cited most frequently in marital disruption and divorce. For example, while husbands and wives regularly clash over how they will spend their money, spending patterns are not often a central factor in divorces. However, nonsupport often is as a major complaint among those who divorce (Goode, 1965:123; Levinger, 1966). Thus, money problems pertaining to spending may be the chief cause of marital conflict without leading directly to divorce. In other words, most money problems are nonbasic, while such problems as infidelity may be serious enough to be basic sources of conflict. Of course, this does not mean that conflict over nonbasic issues should be routinely ignored. Even minor problems, if left to accumulate and escalate tensions, eventually can damage a relationship. Furthermore, social scientists cannot always predict which issues will take on greater importance for a given couple. One couple might well regard sexual incompatibility as rather unimportant, while another couple might find that different sexual expectations are an enduring source of tension which affects their total relationship. Thus, as we shall see more clearly in the next chapter, social science cannot do more than identify the factors which are likely to create marital strife. Whether these sources of conflict lead to serious marital problems hinges very largely on how important the disputed issues are to the couples and how effectively they deal with them to discharge tensions.

Two Popular Strategies for Conflict Management

The process of conflict management is nearly always the same, whatever the cause of the disagreement. In recent years, the number of different approaches recommended in popular and technical journals has risen sharply.

Two common strategies outlined by Lloyd Saxton (1980:359–63) have been selected as representative of the field. Both are self-help models, designed to allow couples to work through their own problems without professional help from marriage counselors or other experts.

Role Taking   This strategy appears to be an adaptation of the encounter group techniques popularized by Bach and his associates. In role taking, partners try to understand the conflict from the spouse's point of view. Both must agree at the outset that they will attack the conflict and not one another. The strategy normally takes about two or three hours to complete, so preparations must be made to prevent any interruptions. The process itself proceeds through four steps:

1. The session begins with one partner—let us say the wife—presenting her point of view on the problem(s) confronting the couple. She would include a statement of her feelings as well as the logical reasons for seeing the issue(s) as she does. The husband must not interrupt her during the statement. He should listen carefully and attempt to understand fully what she is saying. When she feels that she has outlined her position to her own satisfaction, step one is over.
2. In step two, the husband restates her position and plays her role. This is not only a test of his ability to listen, but it is also a way to measure his ability to share her feelings and logic. If he misrepresents her stance, leaves out a critical point, or clearly misinterprets what she was saying, the wife may interrupt him to clarify her position. When he has adequately played the wife's role, and identified, to her satisfaction, why she feels as she does the second step is competed.
3. The third stage of the process is like the opening step except that this time the husband presents his view on the issues. Now, the wife must listen and try to understand his perspective.
4. In the final step, she takes his role and seeks to express his feelings. He, then, is free to correct any errors which she might make in repeating his position. The process is completed when she has presented his point of view to his satisfaction.

    The underlying assumption in this process is that role taking will allow each partner to understand better the other's feelings and attitudes. Out of this understanding, a couple can work toward resolving the problems which have grown up between them. Perhaps not all differences can be resolved in this fashion, but at least the lines of communication will have been opened so that disagreements may no longer possess the destructive consequences which they had before.

Examining Mutual Goals   The second strategy is an adaptation of the technique for marriage enrichment devised by David and Vera Mace. The procedure is relatively simple. Each partner is asked to rate their marriage on 10 items. These include:

1. Common goals and values

A Season for Husbands and Wives

2. Commitment to growth
3. Communication skills
4. Creative use of conflict
5. Appreciation and affection
6. Agreement on gender roles
7. Cooperation and teamwork
8. Sexual fulfillment
9. Money management
10. Parent effectiveness

With this list of items, each partner retires to a quiet place to score their marriage. A perfect score on each item is 10, while 0 represents the lowest possible rating. Each partner goes through the list first and records his or her first reaction to each item. Then, each goes back over the list and carefully reflects on the final score for each category. When the two have completed their rating process, they exchange papers and discuss agreements and discrepancies between their scores. If the total score is low, they probably will have a great deal to discuss, especially about the items which produced the most dissatisfaction. A low score, however, does not necessarily mean that their marriage is on the verge of breaking up. Nor does a high score mean that no improvements can be made in the relationship. Furthermore, this strategy allows couples to pinpoint those items on which one partner rates the marriage high and the other gives it a low rating. A striking difference in their scores for an item indicates an area to be explored to find out why one feels dissatisfaction. Moreover, this instrument can be used in a follow-up assessment to see whether the couple's later efforts to improve the marriage have succeeded. It also can warn of an emerging problem, if a high-scored item on a previous assessment suddenly earns a lower rating. Because marriage is a dynamic relationship and process, some fluctuation over time should be expected.

An Evaluation of the Strategies Although Saxton regards these two strategies as creative approaches to resolving marital conflict, some questions about their practicality immediately come to mind. Couples who are not engaged in conflict might find either technique useful. But couples who are sharply divided over an issue, who already have had heated verbal exhanges and felt the sting of insult, are not likely to sit down rationally to work through either of these two processes. Moreover, couples who have the social skills and personality resources to disengage themselves from a conflict to discuss their mutual problem(s) probably do not need the elaborate techniques of role taking or mutual goal evaluation. In short, we can conclude that both strategies for conflict resolution probably would work better when couples are not in a heated argument. Similarly, both strategies would seem to work better for couples who really do not need either strategy, but less well for couples who cannot handle conflicts and need a technique to help them resolve their problems.

These criticisms underscore the complexities of marital conflict and the difficulties of any strategy for its resolution. Regardless of strategy, more than enough help with marital problems is always available to those who need it least, and the least help is available to those who need it most. Social scientists can do very little to alter this situation. Nevertheless, some processes do have a better chance of succeeding than others, and no one strategy is likely to meet the complex needs of all couples.

Guidelines for Conflict Management in Marriage

The set of general guidelines for conflict management presented in this discussion is something less than a formal strategy for resolving husband and wife disputes. It is more like a series of helpful hints which partners might do well to remember when they confront the inevitable marital strains. These guidelines have been gleaned from a wide survey of writings on marriage conflict and its resolution. Their intent is not to banish conflict altogether—a wholly unrealistic goal—but to help couples deal constructively with marital disagreements. Toward this end, then, we offer the following guidelines.

Listening to one another. In modern society, couples are constantly bombarded with messages. As a defense mechanism, all of us learn to tune out certain communications and listen to others. This social skill can have disas-

Figure 11-3
Conflicts in marriage cannot be resolved if couples refuse to communicate with each other. *(Copyright © by Stock, Boston, Inc., 1981.)*

A Season for Husbands and Wives

trous results in our relationships. We cannot begin to resolve a conflict until we are sure that we have understood accurately the meanings which the other person is conveying to us. Thus, couples need not only pay close attention to what their marriage partner is saying, but they also need to check on the accuracy of what they have heard. A simple repetition, "Here's what I heard you saying . . ." is enough to confirm you have gotten the speaker's point. Many conflicts rapidly escalate because of faulty communication in which partners talk past one another. Good listening allows a couple to get at the real conflict rather than chasing after lesser misunderstandingings.

Empathize. Listening only assures the clear reception of a meaning intended by the other. Empathy involves more than listening. It is the willingness to put yourself in the place of the other person and to view the disagreement through the other's eyes. Empathy accomplishes two desirable goals. First, it enhances your ability to understand the other's feelings and perspective; and second, it fosters some sympathy for the other's position as you see the logic behind their complaint. Empathy does not eliminate differences in personal interests, but it is a major step toward a compromise.

Avoid destructive quarrels. Disagreements between spouses can quickly degenerate into vicious personal attacks. Since spouses know each other intimately, they are keenly aware of the vulnerable points in the other person's defenses. Bitter quarrels sometimes draw out the worst in us, so that we

Figure 11-4
One form of "fighting dirty" has been labeled the "Virginia Woolf" conflict, after the film of the same name. *(Museum of Modern Art Film Archives)*

inflict more injury than we intended. In the heat of anger, we may be tempted to fight "dirty" by attacking the character or deameaning the integrity of our mate. Such destructive verbal combat is what Bach and Wyden call **"Virginia Woolf" conflict**—a reference to Edward Albee's sharp and biting play about a dissolving marriage, called "Who's Afraid of Virginia Woolf?" The longer this kind of marital warfare continues, the more difficult a conciliation will be. Moreover, when spouses are determined to harm one another, they are doing little to resolve the underlying problems.

Be prepared to bargain and compromise. Serious conflicts seldom are the fault of only one partner. Indeed, the effort of one spouse to force the other to take full responsibility for the conflict probably will prevent a swift resolution. Therefore, couples are well advised not to fix blame on one another but to seek a compromise. Such a settlement is easier when both parties recognize that the other's position holds some merit (Turner, 1970: 147–50). Moreover, a compromise gives each partner a face-saving maneuver. However, a bargained solution cannot occur until both sides want to end the dispute.

Define conciliation in concrete behavior. A real and lasting settlement almost always requires behavior changes. Apologies and expressions of love may relieve immediate tensions, but modified conduct almost always is required to ensure marital peace. Marriage partners should agree on what each actually will do to prevent the same problem from creating conflict again. The nature of the problem will help define the behavior changes that are needed. For example, a wife who feels neglected may find that her husband's offer to take her along to his Friday night bowling meet will suffice. If the husband feels neglected, the wife might suggest that they get a baby-sitter at least once a week so that they can go out to dinner, dancing, or a movie. Obviously, other problems will require different types of behavioral changes. Yet, some concrete alteration of behavioral patterns should be explored as both a constructive and symbolic attack on the problem(s) which sparked the conflict.

Seek professional help if necessary. Americans tend to value family life and marital relationships more than any other social bonds. Yet, we are an achievement-oriented people; we regard self-reliance as a mark of individual success. For this reason, many Americans see the use of professional help in dealing with our marital problems as an admission of failure. The unfortunate result is that many of us seek help only after marital bonds have deteriorated almost hopelessly. When it first becomes clear that couples are not handling their problems adequately, they should seek outside help before matters get worse.

Many varieties of external help are available. The most frequently used marriage advisors are clergymen and physicians. Usually, these persons are helpful professionals. If the problem is not terribly serious, their practical counsel often can resolve the difficulty without further professional help. Moreover, most clergy and physicians quickly recognize when a couple's problems are complex enough to need someone of greater competence. Therefore, they may suggest that a couple see a marriage counselor, social worker, sociologist, or family psychologist. Such recommendations should be

A Season for Husbands and Wives

taken seriously, since they come from an observer who has some professional objectivity.

Selecting a marriage counselor is not easy. There are many varieties of marriage counselors using different socio-psychological theories and techniques. Moreover, marriage counseling tends to be expensive. Fees may run as high as $50 for 50 minutes and some times even higher. The major accrediting organization is the American Association of Marriage and Family Counselors. Couples contemplating professional counseling services should first check out the counselor's credentials. However, checking for certification by a responsible national organization is only the first step. References also should be requested from local friends or referral agencies. These will yield more information on the quality and the type of the counselor's skills. Some counselors, for example, are excellent with parent-child difficulties, but work less well on problems related to alcoholism, family violence, or sexual maladjustment. Couples must make sure that the counselor they select is competent in their area of marital conflict.

Physical Violence between Marriage Partners

Another important aspect of marital conflict is physical violence between the partners. More physical abuse is being reported to authorities today than ever before. Does this mean that physical conflict between spouses is increasing? Probably not. More likely, "wife beating" (or less frequently, "husband battering") simply used to be regarded as a routine part of married life. No completely accurate data documents the extent of physical violence in marriage. Steinmetz (1978) estimates that, nationally, 7 percent of wives and about .5 percent of husbands receive "severe beatings" from their spouses during their marriages. Laura Meyes (1980:334) notes that estimates of the number of American families that experience wife abuse range from 3 to 40 million. Many of these incidents eventually lead to the death of the battered wife or the offending male. Moreover, physical violence appears to cross both economic and racial lines (Tavris and Offir, 1977:20).

One can readily understand why physical abuse might lead to separation or divorce. Indeed, what probably needs to be explained is why abused mates continue to live with their violent partners, since many spouses apparently do remain in violent family situations. Richard Gelles (1976), a social scientist, has attempted to discover why abused wives remain with their husbands. Previous research had shown that abused wives were more likely to stay with their husbands if they had negative self-images; believed their husbands would reform; feared the economic hardship of separation; believed the children needed the father's material support; thought they could not get along on their own; or regarded divorcées as social outcasts. Gelles discovered several additional factors. First, the less frequent and the less severe the abuse, the more likely a wife was to remain with her husband. Second, women who took abuse usually had been exposed to violence in their own families. Victimized children had a much greater tendency to tolerate abuse as adult mates.

Figure 11-5
Physical violence between spouses is now regarded as a major social problem. Today, many people wonder why abused spouses stay with their mates. *(© Arthur Tress, 1981/Woodfin Camp & Associates.)*

And finally, less educated and unemployed wives were more likely to feel trapped and not seek outside help or divorce.

Another major difficulty for abused spouses is the reluctance of legal authorities to enter into a family dispute, even when evidence of physical violence exists. Many abused wives do not seek outside help because they fear they will be beaten again if they bring charges against their husbands and are not helped by the authorities. Thus, many abused wives find themselves in a vicious circle. In many urban centers, women's groups have begun to establish shelters to protect abused wives. In the long run, however, more concerted action by public authorities probably will be needed to assure family members a reasonable degree of safety within the household. As the tolerance for physical violence between spouses declines, wife abuse probably will lead to divorce more frequently.

Assessing Marital Success

Assessing marital success presents a number of rather unique problems. First, such success has no universal measure or standard. Indeed, no universal vocabulary even exists to define a successful marriage. Marriages frequently are evaluated as "good" if they are stable, well-adjusted, satisfying, happy, or integrated. But a "happy" marriage may not be the same as an "integrated" marriage. Nor is happiness the same for all married couples. One must recognize that marital success takes several different forms and varies in a number of qualitative aspects (Duberman, 1977:106–7).

The Varieties of Marital Adjustment

Most Americans probably equate marital adjustment with fulfillment of the romantic ideal. The establishment of an intimate relationship based on love, companionship, and loyalty is, however, only one style of marital adjustment. Moreover, as Janet Askham (1976) has shown in a pilot study on marital intimacy, the underlying search in this sort of relationship is for identity and stability. Thus, romantic attachment is itself a complex relationship which breaks down into more specialized types of adjustment between marriage partners. But Askham recognizes that the guest for identity and stability may well be important for only one type of relationship, and not at all common to those marriages in which intimacy is a lesser interest of the partners.

Other social scientists also have recognized how marital adjustment can vary. A well-known study conducted by Cuber and Haroff (1965—see box on pages 316-17) developed a broad spectrum of marital types. They ranged from the "conflict-habituated marriage" of constant tension and confrontation through the "devitalized" and "passive-congenial" marriages to two types of close bonding in the styles of "vital" and "total" marriages. Each type is a different concept of marriage. Partners in each one can be viewed as "adjusted," at least in the sense that most are contented with their marital arrangement.

More recently, John Scanzoni (1981) has developed a slightly different model for categorizing various marital styles. He divides contemporary marriages into three patterns which he calls **husband and wife as equal partners; husband as senior partner and wife as junior partner;** and **husband as head and wife as complement.** Each type varies in how much power is allocated to husband and wife, in the ways tasks are divided, and how the breadwinner role is shared or allocated. The complementary and junior-partner types tend more toward traditional marital styles, while the equal-partner model is more modern. However, Scanzoni cautions that all three types can produce adjusted relationships, and no evidence suggests that equal-partner marriages are less viable than the more traditional models.

#19 From this survey of marital styles, it appears that the first step in assessing a particular marital relationship is for a couple to decide upon their marriage style. Only then can they decide whether their union is successful, happy, and adequately adjusted.

Formal Means of Marriage Assessment and Enrichment

Many services are available to couples dissatisfied with their marriages. Although partners usually seek out a professional counselor only when the threat of a divorce or a serious crisis looms, counselors also can help assess an otherwise stable relationship which marriage partners would like to improve.

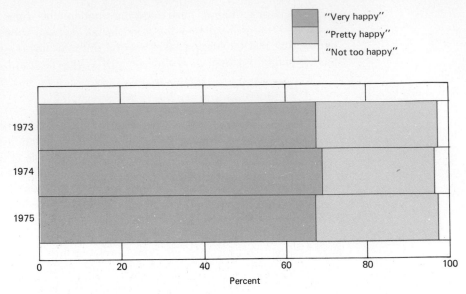

Figure 11-6
Marital Happiness: 1973–1975. This figure clearly demonstrates the high levels of reported marital happiness in American society. Note the very low percentage who describe their marriage as "not too happy." *(Source:* Social Indicators *1976, p. 58.)*

Legend:
"Very happy"
"Pretty happy"
"Not too happy"

Pencil-and-paper diagnostic tests as well as counseling sessions can help evaluate specific areas for improvement.

In addition, most communities offer family-life and marriage-enrichment programs through community centers, churches and synagogues, as well as through university extension or public school organizations. These programs tend to vary widely in their quality, length, and formal instruction. The many programs sponsored by religious organizations and community agencies often are based on an encounter-group format, such as the weekend marriage retreat. Typically, marriage-enrichment sessions concentrate on such problem areas as communication, sex-role adjustments, problem-solving techniques, child rearing, improving sexual relations, and defining marriage goals.

Improving the quality of marriage-enrichment programs has been a major interest of the Association of Couples for Marriage Enrichment which now has chapters in all 50 states. Moreover, particular individuals—like David and Vera Mace (1974, 1975)—have worked through this association to develop preventive programs aimed at training partners to handle problems on their own. In this way, they hope to lessen the danger of broken marriages. The trend to more widespread participation in marriage-enrichment programs has yet to be fully assessed. Some are convinced that marriage enrichment may well improve communication between spouses without dramatically affecting the divorce rate or permanently improving the quality of family life.

For most family-life and marriage-enrichment programs, the assessment

---

CLOSE-UP   **Five Types of Marital Adjustment—An Interpretation of Cuber and Harroff (1965)**
Not all marriages that stay together are patterned in the same fashion. Cuber and Harroff devised the following five types to organize data collected from 211

A Season for Husbands and Wives

married persons who had never seriously considered divorce or separation and who had achieved some measure of contentment, if not overwhelming happiness, in their marriage relationship. These types included:

The Conflict-Habituated Marriage: In this style of marital interaction, husband and wife are constantly in a state of tension and conflict. Much of the fighting is petty nagging which tends to take genteel forms. Yet, it goes on continually in private and even periodically breaks out into the open in public gatherings. The need to keep conflict within controlled bounds is the dominant activity in the lives of those couples who are habituated to the psychological battle their marriages have become. Apparently for some, however, marital struggles can persist over the whole lifetime of their union, and yet marital bonds remain unbroken.

The Devitalized Marriage: The distinguishing feature of the devitalized style is the sharp contrast between the early years and the middle-age routine. Whereas couples in this type began their marriage "deeply in love," when they spent a great deal of time together, enjoyed sex, and formed a close, companionate relationship, they have now drifted apart into a routine of daily life which has little or none of the former closeness they once shared. The husband typically devotes almost all of his energy to his career, while the wife cares for the children, the house, or her own vocation. Some accept this situation gracefully by convincing themselves that the pattern is normal for middle age. Others are less accepting and yearn for the excitement of their youth. Few seem to believe, however, that their marriage will ever be any different than it is now.

The Passive-Congenial Marriage: This type differs from the devitalized marriage in the sense that there were no experiences of an early period of emotional excitement and closeness to remember fondly. From the outset, the marriage has been one of a convenient arrangement with mild involvement by both partners. Since most couples participating in this marital style give little evidence that they ever expected anything different, there is no real expression of disillusionment.

The Vital Marriage: Although externally the vital marriage might well resemble any of the other three types, a sharp contrast does emerge when the relationship between partners is examined more closely. Couples in a vital relationship exhibit a genuine togetherness and sharing. They are intensely bound together psychologically, and the essence of life is found in time spent with each other. Activities in which the mate is not involved are considered uninteresting and dull. Couples in a vital relationship do not lose their separate identities, however, and they occasionally quarrel like other marriage partners—but their quarrels are quickly settled as a general rule so that the couple can again find their basic satisfaction in the life they live with and through one another.

The Total Marriage: This final type is really something of an intensification of the vital relationship. A total marriage is one in which almost everything is shared—work, home life, recreation, child rearing, hobbies, community participation, and so forth. They typically experience little tension, because almost every problem is dealt with before it arises. This form of marital relationship tends to be rare. It is so encompassing that it virtually rules out the possibility of a private existence apart from one's mate.

standards usually are modeled on what Cuber and Haroff called the "vital-marriage" style. The goal is to bring couples closer together through better communication, sexual relationships, sharing, joint decision making, conflict management, and personal growth. The tendency among many popular enrichment programs, therefore, is to define a successful, happy, and well-adjusted marriage by rather narrow standards. By implication, those who follow any other style often are encouraged to assess their marriages as less than satisfactory. In the long run, this approach may be less than fair. Even worse, it may well lead some couples who have developed another marital style to conclude that they are maladjusted. Thus, in assessing marital success a marriage is not to be labeled inferior simply because it differs from the model which seems to us, or to a school of marriage enrichment, to be the best type of relationship.

Summary

The focus of this chapter is on the relationship between husband and wife in a full family household. As the family engages in a number of specialized functions, partners are called upon to perform within a series of important social roles. We examine, first, the leadership roles which fall logically (and legally) to the husband and wife team. Small-group research has suggested the need for two complementary leaders. The instrumental leader—usually the husband and father in American society—serves as the chief executive of the household, while the expressive leader—usually the wife and mother—promotes emotional solidarity among family members. Both types of leaders are essential for the maintenance of the family.

The housewife role pertains, of course, to women only. Using Lopata's penetrating analysis, the six-stage life cycle of the housewife is presented. Three variations of the housewife role which Lopata links to social class standing also are introduced. These include the upper lower-class pattern of the restricted housewife, the working-to-middle-class style of the uncrystallized housewife, and the multidimensional housewife of the upper middle class. Note was also taken of the fact that satisfaction with the homemaker role increases as one moves from the restricted to the multidimensional type.

Husband and wife meet one another's needs as sexual partners, and hence sexual relations is the next role pattern which is considered in this discussion. We discuss trends in both attitudes toward sexual behavior and in actual sexual conduct. Generally speaking, sexual attitudes are becoming more liberal and sexual behavior more permissive in American marriages. Closely allied with the role of sexual partners is the companionship role. Since the rise of the modern family, companionship has become an increasingly important role function. Indeed, most couples rate companionship as the most important aspect of marriage. This importance arises from the fact that spouses contribute greatly to their mate's psychological stability.

All marriages, no matter how satisfying, create tensions and occasionally erupt in conflict. After briefly setting forth some of the major causes of marital strife, we introduce several strategies for conflict management in marriage. Our final topic concerns the difficult matter of assessing marital success. Since no universal standard exists for determining a happy, well-adjusted, and successful marriage, several types of contemporary marriage styles are presented, each of which has the potential for successful adjustment. While reporting on the trend toward increased use of marriage-enrichment programs, we warned against settling for too narrow a definition of what constitutes a satisfying, successful, and happy marriage.

A Season for Husbands and Wives

STUDY QUESTIONS

1. What are the differing role orientations that distinguish the expressive from the instrumental leader? How essential is it that these two leadership types be divided between the sexes?
2. Lopata describes three variations on the homemaker role. Which one is the most satisfying and why?
3. How do the current trends in attitudes toward sexual relations in marriage correspond to sexual behavior between marriage partners?
4. What do social scientists mean by the companionship role in marriage, and why do they regard this relationship so critical in the contemporary dynamics between marriage partners?
5. Why is an absence of conflict not necessarily an indication of a stable marriage partnership?
6. What are some of the typical strategies for conflict management in marriage, and how can one assess marital success?

12

Reconsidering: Separation and Divorce

Current trends · No fault Divorce

Various Ways a Marriage is Dissolved
 * Death of a Spouse *problems. who handles it better*
 Annulment
 Divorce *Rise of Rates related to norms, attitudes & beliefs*
 Factors contributing to Divorce : age, children, ed. social class

The Process of Marriage Partner Disengagement
 The Growth toward Incompatibility between Marriage Partners
 The Tendency to Reach Unresolved Conflicts
 stages & adjusting to·

The Meaning of Divorce in Contemporary American Society
 The Liberalization of Divorce Laws
 The Recent Rise in the Divorce Rate
 * Social Factors Contributing to Divorce
   Age at First Marriage
   The Presence of Children
   Divergent Social Backgrounds
   Religious Affiliation
   Employment of the Wife
   Social Class Standing
 Continued Support for the Institution of Marriage
 Sociologist point of view

Divorce as an Internal Adjustment within the Marriage System
 The Process of Divorce
   The Decision to Separate
   The Initiation of Divorce Proceedings
   Postdivorce Adjustment

The Tendency to Remarry After Divorce *more than 70%*
 * The Rates of Remarriage
 Stability and Happiness in Remarriage after Divorce

Probably the most commonly expressed worry about the American family is the relatively high separation and divorce rate. The dissolving of a marriage is almost always a traumatic event for immediate family members—husband and wife, children, and in-laws on both sides. Marriage dissolution also tends to be perceived as a symbol of the decline of family life, an important sign that something is terribly wrong with the institution of marriage. This occurs because the divorce rate is regarded as a direct barometer of the state of marriage. In this chapter, we attempt to look beyond such conventional interpretations and explore more thoroughly the complex meanings of divorce and separation in American society. In addition, we shall examine the social factors behind the tendency to divorce, as well as the divorce process itself, the rate of remarriage, and the impact of divorce on children. Finally, this chapter poses the question of whether serial monogamy—the practice of being married several times during one's life, but to only one spouse at a time—is becoming the norm in American social life.

Various Ways a Marriage Is Dissolved

Just as a marriage can be formed in several ways—a religious wedding, a civil service before a judge or justice of the peace, a common law relationship—it also can be dissolved by a variety of events. The possibilities include the death of a spouse, annulment, and divorce.

Death of a Spouse

Most marriages that end by the death of a spouse are involuntarily terminated. Many problems associated with divorce—such as income for the remaining family members, child care, and psychological trauma—also occur when a mate dies, especially if the children have not yet reached maturity. Some marriages, of course, are voluntarily ended when one spouse murders the other—a possibility that is not so remote as one might expect. A little over 15 percent of all murders each year are committed by spouses against their mates, with victims about equally divided between the two sexes (see the Uniform Crime Reports for the United States, issued each year by the FBI).

The number of marriages prematurely ended by the death of a spouse has steadily declined in this century. Yet, the percentage of women living with their first husbands was almost the same in 1970 as in 1910. The difference is that at the turn of the century, families were more commonly disrupted through the death of a spouse, while today a family is more commonly fragmented by divorce. Thus, as the death rate declined, the divorce rate increased, with the result that the family-disruption rate is now almost identical to the rate in the early 1900s (Bane, 1976:29–31).

Annulment

An **annulment** is a court declaration which states that a marriage was invalid from the start. In other words, an annulment ends a marriage which technically never existed (Dille, 1971:50). A declaration of annulment may be sought on several grounds. Marriages are automatically void before the law, if the newly created marital union is either incestuous or bigamous. Judicial action also can void a marriage in many states under four circumstances:

1. An underage partner. When either partner is underage at the time of the wedding, parents often bring suit to terminate the union. A court may decide, however, that the couple was mature and responsible enough to make the marriage valid.
2. Sexual impotence in either partner from the start of the marriage. Generally, one partner must be proven psychologically or physically incapable of intercourse.
3. Absence of "true consent." This may occur when a person is forced to marry against her or his will—as in the case of a "shotgun wedding"—or when a partner is mentally unsound, or again when the couple marries frivolously without intending to form a lasting union.
4. Fraud is committed by one partner. This means that one partner concealed from the other information which could disrupt the marital relationship, such as a history of serious mental illness, the circumstances of a previous marriage, or the fact of having parented a child with another partner. Courts are not very willing to grant an annulment for slight exaggerations, such as the wealth of a partner or the inability to provide a promised lifestyle. In borderline cases, the court frequently must decide whether the misrepresentation was serious enough to constitute fraud injurious to the relationship (Dille, 1971:50–51).

Divorce

We may define **divorce** as a court decree which dissolves a valid marriage and allows both partners to remarry. The rules for granting a divorce changed a good deal in the 1970s, after California introduced the first **"no-fault" divorce.** Today, divorce is the most common way in which a marriage is dissolved. Annulments account for only about 3 percent of all divorces, and hence annulments usually are included in divorce statistics for tabulation purposes (Reiss, 1980:316).

Most divorces are preceded by a separation which serves as a halfway step toward dissolving a marriage (Goode, 1965:173–88). No reliable data on the number of couples who are separated exists since legal proceedings to establish a separation are less important than they were before the "no-fault" divorce. Glick and Norton (1977:15) estimate that the number of separated partners is nearly half as large today as the number of divorced individuals. This probably results from the new ability to move directly to a divorce decree without the previous long waiting period. Separation does tend to create a new social status, accompanied in many cases by social disorientation, trauma, and role ambiguity. A separated person lacks the normal opportunities of married persons, while retaining the married person's obligations and limitations. Technically speaking, sexual relations with another person is adultery, and the separated husband is still responsible for his wife's financial support (Dille, 1971:52). In practice, however, separated persons are setting new behavior patterns. Many conduct themselves as though the marriage already were terminated and they are single. Others suffer through guilt and depression as they slowly readjust to the single life (Weiss, 1975:69–82). The movement from separation to divorce is by no means automatic. Apparently, some couples can work out their problems during the time they live apart. Because reliable data are lacking, we cannot accurately predict how many separations lead to divorce and how many to reconciliation. Moreover, some couples who separate, never divorce nor do they become reconciled; they simply live apart for the rest of their lives—often referred to as the "poor man's divorce" (Glick and Norton, 1977:15). With the recent easing of divorce laws and the decline in the cost of a divorce, the number of couples who have been forced to settle for this sort of relationship has been reduced notably.

The Process of Marriage Partner Disengagement

When courtship patterns were described, falling in love was suggested as a process which moved through a series of stages. Falling out of love, even after marriage, is basically a reversal of the process. Disengagement between partners does not happen overnight. It is the result of an accumulation of negative experiences which extinguish the partner's feelings of intimacy, love, and affection. Seldom is detachment pleasant, even when it brings some relief from the couple's hostilities. Disengagement often entails psychological pain, distress, embarrassment, and self-doubt (Brown, Perry, and Harburg, 1977:

549–51). Moreover, detachment forces partners to reassess their lives together. Sometimes they find they still have enough feelings for one another to rekindle a sense of commitment. In other cases, they see the effort as hopeless; the marriage, they believe, is dead.

The Growth Toward Incompatibility Between Marriage Partners

Almost all marriages begin with the wife and husband convinced that they love one another. Marriage failure is something which happens to other people. It will not happen to us, most confidently assure themselves. But people who marry today face more than a 50 percent likelihood that they will separate for some time during their married lives due to husband-wife conflicts, and almost 40 percent are likely to divorce (Glick and Norton, 1977:36–7). Thus, for a large segment of the population, separation and divorce are not things that "happen to someone else." The really interesting question behind the high divorce rate is: How do couples who began by loving one another arrive at an impasse to which divorce is the probable solution?

Of course, not everyone arrives at the decision to divorce in the same way. Many separated or divorced couples acknowledge that they just grew apart gradually. In his wheel theory of love, Ira Reiss (1980:126–32) helps to explain how this occurs. Generally speaking, the first aspect of the marital relationship to erode is the sense of intimacy. Wife and husband slowly cease to reveal to one another their innermost confidences. This does not necessarily mean they stop having sexual relations, but their psychological support for one another declines. The next barrier to fall is a sense of mutual dependency. One or both partners find that they can live without the other. Their life-styles and habits begin to move in opposite directions, and they become accustomed to doing things their own way without help or interference from their partners. This, in turn, leads to a loss of self-disclosure. One's feelings are shielded from the other, so that the partner no longer knows exactly what you think or how you are reacting to daily events. And finally, rapport is lost. People in this last stage feel they have little or nothing in common with their mates. The "chemistry" between the man and woman is gone, and so is the desire to accompany, to share, to relate to the other person. In its place has arisen a sense that the mate is a "stranger," with whom one no longer feels comfortable for a sustained period. When the final stage is reached, little usually remains to be salvaged. Couples driven to this point are likely to want release from the tension created by their constant conflict. Those who now feel nothing but profound indifference toward their mate usually seek a deep personal attachment to another person.

Couples who can recognize the early stages of disengagement often can take corrective action. Yet many partners slip into a routine that allows them to drift apart. The husband, or both spouses, may be concerned about a career, or the wife may be devoting most of her time to the children and household. They only realize what is happening when the companionship they possessed is all but gone. Indeed, the more a husband and wife grow apart from one another, the more difficult it is to rebuild their relationship. This is especially the case when they have become openly hostile.

The Tendency to Reach Unresolved Conflicts

Couples who cannot form the emotionally close, companionate relationship that is today's ideal marriage become frustrated and frequently grow hostile to each other. Neither seems to do anything that pleases the other. In-law problems, financial crises, or child-rearing differences which they once could resolve are now sources of bitter conflict. A married couple often will be quite unaware that the problem they are arguing about really is not the root of their hostility. More likely, the underlying cause of their conflict is their disappointment and despair at failing to find fulfillment or satisfaction in their companionship role.

Moreover, once conflicts arise regularly and are resolved inadequately they cause further hostility. As anger and insults mount, partners tend to be forced apart. At some point, if they do not strike a truce or simply resign themselves to constant strife, couples are likely to decide that the tension is more than they can endure. Of course, the amount of disappointment which couples can bear varies considerably from one couple to another. When couples expect less companionship in marriage—as in the working class, for example (Komarovsky, 1967; Rubin, 1976)—they generally tolerate more conflict than when companionship is the norm for husband-wife relations. Thus, the amount of conflict is not as critical as spouses' expectations, as well as the meaning they assign to conflicts in their relationships.

Whatever the threshold for considering divorce, the build-up of unresolved conflicts can make couples conclude that their marriage was a mistake. But not all couples who entertain the idea actually divorce. Sometimes, facing failure is enough to awaken interest in solving their problems. Even after a separation, many couples decide they want to make their marriage last. However, the divorce statistics clearly indicate that others draw the opposite conclusion. For them, the conflicts appear too deep, the bitterness too intense, or the lack of rapport too great to rebuild the relationship.

(handwritten margin note: Conflict + spouses Expectations concerning conflict)

The Meaning of Divorce in Contemporary American Society

Divorce is far more complex than most people realize. One cannot conclude much about the health and stability of the institution of marriage or the quality of family life directly from the divorce rate. For example, in pre-Communist China, where wives often lived in tense situations, the divorce rate was very low, but the suicide rate for wives was very high. Wives were advised by the old adage, "Good women should hang themselves; only bad women seek divorce" (Yang, 1965:81). Most Americans would agree that divorce is a more humane way than suicide to reduce family tensions. But if a society's low divorce rate does not ensure a harmonious family life, what does America's high divorce rate mean?

The Liberalization of Divorce Laws

Today's high divorce rate may not result wholly from marital unhappiness. It also could reflect the relative ease with which a divorce can be obtained. This would mean that some of the higher divorce rate in the 1970s is due to the easing of divorce laws when many states enacted no-fault statutes. Laws on divorce do provide some insight into how society views marriage. Indeed, by examining traditional divorce laws, we can see quite readily how the legal system reinforced the conventional division of labor between spouses. While the law did not establish marital roles, it did legitimate and help perpetuate traditional role expectations.

In a careful study of the history of divorce law, Weitzman and Dixon (1980) identified four major elements in traditional American divorce statutes which almost all the states had adopted by 1900. These elements were:

1. "Traditional divorce law perpetuated the sex-based division of roles and responsibilities in traditional legal marriage" (Weitzman and Dixon, 1980:358). In other words, traditional family law allocated the breadwinner role to the husband, while the wife was expected to perform household tasks and raise the children.
2. "Traditional divorce law required grounds for divorce." The underlying assumption was that a legal marriage could be terminated only when one partner's misbehavior was demonstrated clearly in court. Moreover, the offense would have to be serious, such as adultery, mental or physical cruelty, or desertion.
3. "Traditional legal divorce was based on adversary proceedings." This meant no divorce until a partner was found at fault in disrupting marital happiness and tranquility. In this situation, divorce was a means of punishing the "guilty" partner and vindicating the "innocent" spouse. If both parties were proved to be at fault, a divorce might be withheld to punish both parties.
4. "Traditional divorce law linked the financial terms of the divorce to the determination of fault." Being found "guilty" or "innocent" had an immediate bearing on alimony payments, child support, and property settlements. A husband who was found at fault could expect financial punishment for his misbehavior. Similarly, if the wife were found to be at fault, she could lose alimony, property, and sometimes even custody of the children.

Clearly, traditional divorce law was written to approve conventional expectations for husband-and-wife role performance. Weitzman and Dixon (1980:361) point out that, on the positive side, family law did guarantee support to the spouse who performed marital obligations satisfactorily. Justice was considered a reward for the partner who observed traditional task allocations. However, the law did not recognize that each partner might be fulfilling their marital expectations, and not be fulfilled in their interpersonal relations. Most states did not recognize imcompatibility—or the failure to achieve a companionate relationship—as grounds for divorce.

In the last decade, more than half of the states have reformed their statutes to embrace "no-fault" divorce law. This modern form of divorce regulation is based on the principle of "marital breakdown" (Wright and Stetson, 1978:575). As the name for the reform law suggests, the need to determine fault—declaring one party guilty and the other innocent—was eliminated from the proceedings. In its place, the law established "irreconcilable differences" as the sole ground for divorce (Weitzman and Dixon, 1980:361–2). This system strives to avoid moral condemnation and hostile recriminations. The court's central interest is the fact of marital breakdown, rather than the reasons for it. Moreover, the monetary settlements in no-fault divorces typically are based on economic need and equality between the former partners. No longer are property divisions and alimony payments regarded as a means of punishing the guilty and rewarding the innocent.

The primary reasons states endorsed no-fault divorce were to align the law with the actual grounds for seeking a divorce (Weitzman and Dixon, 1980:361), to eliminate the deception and hypocrisy which flourished under the old system (Stetson and Wright, 1975:537), and to avoid an adversary relationship which heightened the trauma, hostility, and moral condemnation of divorce proceedings under the old system (Dille, 1971:61). When the grounds for divorce were strictly limited to adultery, physical or mental cruelty, or desertion, many couples who wanted a divorce because of their incompatibility found that they had to exaggerate their basic problems and deceive the court to gain a divorce. Such maneuvers undermined respect for the law itself and led to recriminations between divorcing partners. The no-fault system sought to make divorce more amicable, especially when neither partner contested the decision to dissolve their marriage.

Has the no-fault system increased the rate of divorce? Stetson and Wright (1975), two social scientists who did some of the most convincing research on the law's effect on the divorce rate, concluded that the no-fault system does not appear to have increased the divorce rate very much through the 1970s (Wright and Stetson, 1978). As far as they could determine, the increasing divorce rate during the period did not result from liberalization of the no-fault system, but from the increasing demand for divorce. Moreover, in their view, demand is a variable which is relatively independent of the strictness or permissiveness of divorce law.

The Recent Rise in the Divorce Rate

Although data on divorce in American society reach back to this nation's founding, the information is far from perfect—including some collected during the twentieth century. Not until the 1930s did accurate birth and death statistics become available, and only more recently have divorce statistics been assembled (Reiss, 1980:319–20). Generally speaking, however, the

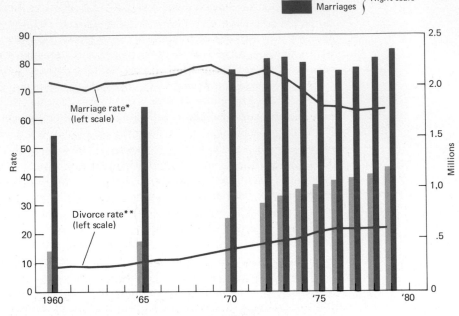

Divorces } Right scale
Marriages }

* Rate per 1,000 unmarried women, 15 years old and over.
** Rate per 1,000 married women, 15 years old and over.
Source: Chart prepared by U.S. Bureau of the Census.

trend since the 1900s has been an increasing number of divorces in each new generation. Since the population has been steadily growing during this century, the divorce numbers also have increased. More revealing than the sheer number of divorces within the population is the rate of divorce per 1,000 married women over 15 years of age. Three periods of marked increase stand out sharply during the twentieth century. The first occurred when the figure jumped from 4.7 in 1910 to 8.0 in 1920 (Kephart, 1966:579). Another sharp rise appeared in the mid-1940s, when World War II prompted many hasty marriages and the long separations of soldiers from their spouses took a heavy toll on marital solidarity (U.S. Bureau of the Census, Social Indicators, 1977:53, 65). The 1950s saw a drop in the divorce rate, only to be followed in the mid-1960s and through the 1970s by a sharp rise (U.S. Bureau of the Census, 1979:xx). While in 1960, the divorce rate stood at 9.0, the figure had more than doubled to 21.0 by 1977.

The divorce rate also tends to vary according to religious, regional, and age-specific factors. Roman Catholics—because of their church's strong stand against divorce—have lower divorce rates than most other major denominations (Stetson and Wright, 1975:538–9). In addition, as one moves from the East to the West, the divorce rate increases, a trend which may well relate to the general stability of the population and the institutionalization of traditional norms (Reiss, 1980:320). The divorce rate also increases for younger people. This reflects not only a greater tolerance of divorce, but also the fact that divorce brings fewer complications for younger women. They can more readily support themselves and they have fewer children—due to the declining birth rate and the delay of the first child—to hinder their return to the single life (Glick and Norton, 1977:5). These factors and others have pushed up our divorce rate over the last 20 years. Suggestions have been made that the divorce rate may be leveling off in the early years of the 1980s. If this is the case, it may well result from the recession and high inflation of 1980, since during economic hardships the divorce rate is known to decline (Goode, 1965:39).

Viewed cross-culturally, the U.S. divorce rate is notable in two important respects. First, this country has typically had a higher divorce rate than most other Western nations (U.S. Bureau of the Census, *Social Indicators*, 1977:61). However, ours is not the highest rate ever recorded. Before industrialization, Japan had an exceptionally high rate of divorce (Goode, 1965:11; 1970:358–65), as did Russia during the 1930s (Burgess and Locke, 1953:158–63). The second notable factor about the U.S. divorce rate is that the gap between ours and the rates of other industrialized nations has been narrowing steadily (Glick and Norton, 1977:4). This trend may be due, in part, to the fact that youth in other countries are gaining more autonomy in mate selection and are sharing in the rising prosperity of an industrialized economic order. The one major exception is Japan, which, because of its traditionally high divorce rate, actually has recorded a decline as a result of industrialization (Vogel, 1971:256). Across the industrialized world,

Figure 12-2
Divorce Rates, Selected Countries: 1955–1975. *(Source: Social Indicators 1976, p. 61.)*

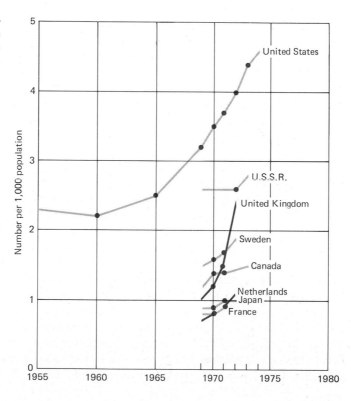

then, similar processes may be at work in setting the rate of marital dissolution.

Social Factors Contributing to Divorce

To get at the meaning of divorce in contemporary American society, we shall consider the social factors that contribute to the tendency to end marriage by divorce. We are specifically *not* trying to spell out the causes of divorce. As William Goode (1965:113) has wisely observed, looking for the "cause(s)" of divorce, as though one factor or even a set of factors triggered marital disruption, is really a hopeless enterprise. All marriage breakdowns do not result from the same kinds of individual or social forces. Thus, we cannot say that if people were more religious, mastered a few sexual techniques, or even learned to communicate better, the divorce rate would drop off drastically. However, social scientists can identify several characteristic social factors which tend to increase the likelihood of divorce. Among the more important variables are age at first marriage, the presence of children, different social backgrounds, religious affiliation, employment of the wife, and social class standing.

Age at First Marriage   According to Mary Jo Bane (1976:32), age at first marriage is the best predictor of divorce. Considerable evidence suggests that teenage marriages are far more likely to break down than later marriages. Indeed, the rate of divorce for teenage marriages is twice as high as the rate for couples married in their twenties (Glick and Norton, 1977:15–6). Several aspects of teenage relationships can account for the instability of teenage marriages. For example, teenage brides are far more likely to be pregnant than older brides, and couples who are premaritally pregnant have greater instability (Reiss, 1980:323). Also, teenage spouses frequently have more serious financial problems, which create tensions in their relationship. We know, too, that lower-class couples are inclined to marry earlier, so financial problems may be a result of class standing as well as age at first marriage. And finally, the lack of maturity may well lead some young people to choose their mates unwisely (Bane, 1976:32).

We also might point out that late age at first marriage correlates strongly with the tendency to divorce. Women who marry beyond their twenties are half again as likely to end their first marriages in three to five years as women who marry before age 30. Glick and Norton (1977:16) try to explain this fact by suggesting that many older brides may have some graduate school training, and this group is known to have a higher divorce rate. Furthermore, older women who marry are likely to have well-established independent life-styles which may make it hard for them to adjust to the routine of married life. Statistically, then, marriage in the early twenties is most likely to produce a stable union.

The Presence of Children   Almost 40 percent of all divorces occur in childless marriages (U.S. Bureau of the Census, *Social Indicators*, 1977:67). The

A Season for Husbands and Wives

vast majority of these divorces happen during the early years of marriage. However, this does not mean that children hold marriages together. More couples probably postpone having children until they believe their marriage is stable enough to justify bringing a new life into their family circle (Parsons and Bales, 1955:4; Goode,1965:109–10). Therefore, the decision to bear children affirms that they believe their marriage will endure, providing an adequate home for offspring. Other couples may prefer to divorce and remarry in the hope of finding a better partner with whom to have children. Ironically, then, their desire for a quality family life may actually be a powerful influence prompting them to seek a divorce, and thus this concern helps elevate the divorce rate.

Divergent Social Backgrounds   Divorce appears more common in marriages whose partners are drawn from dissimilar age brackets, religious traditions, racial groups, rural-urban backgrounds, ethnic communities, or educational levels (Goode, 1965:33–111). With greater emphasis on companionship, similar backgrounds make compatibility easier in marriage, since attitudes, values, outlooks, and marital expectations tend to be similar. Marital stability is one of the payoffs of homogamy in mate selection.

Religious Affiliation   The religious factor affects the divorce process in two different respects. First, the Roman Catholic Church's firm commitment to the indissolubility of marriage (Thomas, 1965:71–100) has depressed the divorce rate for Catholics in comparison to Protestants and those not affiliated with a religious organization (Greeley, 1977: 187–9). More important than the religious organization itself is religious participation. Regular attendance at religious services decreases the likelihood of divorce (Goode, 1965:104–5) and generally supports the synagogue or church's attitude toward divorce, and thus creates in the couple a greater commitment to staying together.

Employment of the Wife   The number of working wives has dramatically increased during the twentieth century. While only one in 40 wives was employed outside the home in 1890 (Smith, 1974:120), one in two wives was working by 1980. Marriages in which the wife works are much less stable than marriages in which the husband is the sole breadwinner (Bane, 1976:28–33). Economic independence not only increases a wife's decision-making power within the household—which may create greater tensions between a traditionally oriented husband and a working wife—but it also gives a woman the freedom to end an unhappy marriage, since she has already demonstrated that she can support herself.

Social Class Standing   A number of excellent social scientific studies demonstrate that an inverse relationship exists between social class standing and the tendency to divorce. For example, William Goode (1965), in a classic investigation of divorced women, found that lower-status persons had a much higher divorce rate than persons in the higher classes. The popular image of lower-class marriages as warm, easygoing, but stable relationships was swiftly dismissed. Lower-class persons not only have a larger share of social problems, but they also have fewer social skills to deal with them. One result is a higher divorce rate than is found among persons with higher class standings.

These predictors of divorce need to be understood very clearly for what they are—factors contributing to the likelihood of marital dissolution and breakdown. For example, then, a woman who married in her teens, who has no children, whose spouse comes from a vastly different social background, who is not affiliated with a religious organization and does not attend services regularly, who works outside the home, and is set within the lower class, has a statistically greater chance of going through a divorce. However, many individuals in this situation beat the odds and create a happy, enduring marriage. Thus, these factors are not predictors of success for particular couples, but are only probability measures for classes of marital partners.

Continued Support for the Institution of Marriage

Social concern over divorce in American society expresses a deep-rooted anxiety that the increase in marital dissolution may signal an erosion of collective support for the institution of marriage. At first glance, divorcing couples may seem to be rejecting the importance of marriage or denying the institution's value. But we can state firmly that to draw this conclusion is to misread almost wholly the intentions of most divorced persons. As the divorce rate has climbed over the last two decades, so has the remarriage rate. This strongly suggests that divorcing partners are not rejecting the institution of marriage, but only the partners they chose (Bane, 1976:34).

Indeed, the qualitative information gathered from divorcing persons suggests that a number of couples seek a dissolution of their union *because* they value marriage. Their present marriage falls far short of their ideal expectations. The decisions made during their youth now appear to have been dreadful mistakes. Rather than live with those errors of judgment for the rest of their lives, they prefer to divorce and try again to find a mate with whom they can share their lives, raise children, and spend their mature years. Therefore, remarriage rates are not only a testimony to the popularity of marriage, but they also show a commitment to a quality union.

Divorce as an Internal Adjustment within the Marriage System

We have discussed the legal changes pertaining to marital dissolution, the social factors affecting the divorce rate, and the strong commitment still made to the institution of marriage. In light of all this information, how are we to understand the meaning of divorce in contemporary American life?

Perhaps the first thing to be said is that as long as young persons can select their own partners, we should expect a number of mistakes to be made. This is not said to criticize young persons or scorn their judgment. It is simply a stubborn fact that wherever preferential mating and intimate relationships between spouses are the norm, errors will occur in the decision-making process. Moreover, even couples who start out deeply in love can falter. Or, over several years, a man and woman gradually can become quite different persons than they were when they exchanged their marriage vows. For spouses today, love is the cornerstone of their life together. When love dies, the basis for the relationship is lost.

Some persons might well suggest that no marriage really need break down. They might argue that with proper counseling, motivation, and commitment, any marital union can be saved. Unfortunately, we have yet to uncover any substantial research findings which support this claim. More and more, social scientists are coming to regard divorce as an internal adjustment going on within the institution of marriage. That is, divorce is a mechanism for correcting marriages in which the emotional strain undermines the very quality of family life (Parsons and Bales, 1955:24–5). This is by no means a recommendation for divorce. At best, it merely suggests that divorce may not be the worst thing to happen to a marriage. A conflict-ridden marital relationship may produce far more unhappiness in the long run than divorce and remarriage.

While this view of divorce is likely to help clarify the meaning and role of marital breakdown in our society, it does not answer the important question of what ought to be done about the issues surrounding divorce. Policy makers and such spokesmen for public opinion as legislators, religious leaders, and family specialists generally recognize that makers of divorce policy face a real dilemma. If, in the effort to lend social support to marriage, divorce laws limit the opportunity to dissolve unhappy unions, many couples may be condemned to a miserable existence. Yet, if the laws and public opinion toward divorce are relaxed, couples may find it so easy to end their marriages that they will do so without facing up to their problems and working them out in a mature fashion. Therefore, much public controversy over divorce is really a dispute about the proper balance between social leniency and restrictiveness. No-fault divorce is not aimed at devaluing marriage, but at adjusting to the needs of spouses to encourage a more healthy marriage system.

Finally, viewing divorce as an internal adjustment within the institution of marriage may help us understand why our divorce rate is, and probably will remain, relatively high. But this point of view is not likely to comfort partners caught up in the turmoil and psychological pain of divorce. Given our autonomous mating system with its inevitable mismatches, divorce may be needed to uncouple partners who cannot achieve a happy companionate relationship. But any divorce, no matter how amicable, exacts a social cost from the partners, their relatives, and friends. Indeed, divorce may advance marriage in general; it may even improve the quality of family life by eliminating unhappy marriages. Yet, the painful consequences for family members cannot be overlooked. In the years ahead, policy makers may well need to focus their attention less on divorce as a social phenomenon and more on helping family members cope with the trauma it creates.

The Process of Divorce

Few decisions to separate or divorce are made quickly or lightly. Generally, as we mentioned earlier, couples drift apart or consistently reach unresolved conflicts. During this disengagement period, their life together is filled with bickering, misery, and disappointment. But couples who eventually separate and divorce reach a point at which they decide that the personal cost of holding their marriage together outweighs the price to be paid for ending it. In this section, we focus on the stages of disengagement.

The Decision to Separate   For most adults in American society, their personal identity as well as the social organization of their daily lives pivot on their marital roles. Even if careers are going well, a couple has enough friends, and they are regarded as pillars of the community, the decision to separate can be a dislocating experience. When a marital relationship goes awry, all else matters little. Disruption in one's homelife overwhelms all other successes in the outside world, especially when the disruption threatens the marital bond itself. At stake is one of the most critical relationships of adult life. The breakdown of a marriage is unlike any other type of social experience, for it touches our most personal attachments and feelings.

When a marriage begins to deteriorate, couples usually begin by separating. Yet, as Robert Weiss (1975:83) correctly observes, the decision to separate is best understood as a critical event between spouses, but not as an end of their marriage. When a husband or (less often) a wife moves out of the family home, interaction with the spouse and children—if there are children—is interrupted, even though the marriage bond remains. Generally, both are very anxious because the final outcome of the separation—either reconciliation or divorce—has not been decided. This uncertainty and the inability to make definite plans leaves both spouses in a state of limbo.

Indeed, contrary to conventional wisdom, which holds that the greatest distress and anxiety arises after divorce, William Goode (1965) demonstrated that the most traumatic period in the whole divorce process extends from separation until the divorce is finally granted. To be divorced, he argued, is a definite status. One is returned to the single status and dating, remarriage, and one's relationship to a former spouse is clearly understood. But the period of separation, even when a divorce petition is pending in the courts, suspends a husband and wife between two social positions. They are married, but not living together as husband and wife. Role behavior for separated couples is not socially defined. Thus, they must work out their role behavior without specific guidelines to direct them. Is it proper, for example, for a separated person to date? Should either one search for a new partner or is this behavior premature since they are still married? Questions like these plague separated couples because no definitive answers are readily available.

Social scientists have long been aware that being without norms of conduct is one of the most frightening and difficult social experiences. Generally speaking, people can handle distasteful social expectations better than uncertainty about how to behave. The lack of suitable and well-defined behavioral roles for separated marriage partners is a form of social pressure that subtly encourages reconciliation. The trauma of being in the separated status is enough to convince some couples that assuming the full role of husband or wife again, even with continuing strife, would be preferable.

We should quickly point out that the experience of separation is not the same for all couples who are contemplating divorce. One's response to the decision to separate is greatly affected by the length of time a couple has been married, the degree of their intimacy, which partner was left and which chose to leave, and whether the partners already have established new love relationships with others (Weiss, 1975:47–68). But even those who welcome separation usually cannot avoid paying some social price. Telling the children that their parents are separating, informing relatives and friends, and bearing the social stigma of having failed in this highly personal relationship is often very difficult. In addition, they face the personal adjustment—coping with loneliness, enduring the loss of someone in whom to confide and the almost inevitable loss of a certain number of friends. The experience of most partners is that separation is very hard, even though they may remain convinced that it is the best course of action for both of them.

Over time, the sense of loss, guilt, or rejection created by separation may begin to diminish. However, when divorce proceedings are near, some animosity or bitterness may arise, if it was not already there. Ending a marriage brings to the surface the conflicting vested interests of marriage partners. The property must be divided; the questions of child custody, visitation rights, and financial support must be settled. These issues can be major points of contention under the best of circumstances, and even more troublesome when one partner tries to use the settlement as a ploy to block the divorce or punish the other person. Thus, forces are at work which can increase the sense of alienation during separation, and thereby hurry them toward the ultimate solution of divorce.

The Initiation of Divorce Proceedings William Goode (1965:137) identifies four obvious steps toward divorce. The process includes serious consideration of divorce, the final decision to seek a divorce, filing a suit in court for marital dissolution, and the actual obtaining of the divorce decree. Separation may occur almost anywhere in this process. Some couples separate before giving any serious thought to divorce, while others separate only after the divorce is granted. Occasionally, as a couple moves toward divorce, separation is followed by a brief reconciliation, and then reseparation once a final decision to file suit is reached. Thus, each couple tends to work out their own timetable as marital disengagement proceeds.

Procedures for filing a divorce suit vary according to the legal requirements of the state in which the divorce decree is being sought. The introduction of the no-fault system has made filing easier, since the need to prove one party the offender has been eliminated. Indeed, some couples file under this system without the services of a lawyer (handling all legal matters yourself is called a **pro se divorce**). This pattern can generate problems when a good deal of property must be divided or child custody arrangements must be worked out (Adam and Adam, 1979:117–23). Even couples obtaining an amicable divorce frequently can benefit from legal counsel.

The shift toward the no-fault system also has affected filing patterns. Under the traditional adversary system, the wife usually filed for a divorce, even though the husband was usually the one who first wanted to end the marriage. However, after the introduction of the no-fault system, the behavior and filing patterns have almost been reversed in some respects. In regard to behavior, William Goode (1965:133–7) discovered that the husband was more often the one who first desired a divorce. His decision to seek a dissolution often resulted in the adoption of a "strategy," consciously or not, which led him to follow a line of behavior that eventually prompted his wife to suggest that they ought to consider a divorce. As for filing patterns, Gunter (1977) found, for example, that while 38 percent of males and 62 percent of females filed for divorce under the traditional system, 64 percent of all divorce filings were begun by males and 36 percent by females under the no-fault arrangement in his Florida sample. Gunter further suggested that a notable change in male-female role behavior appears to be occurring in other no-fault states. The person first desiring the divorce is now also more likely to be the person who files for one.

Indeed, the no-fault system has changed almost every legal aspect of the divorce process. In California, for example, partners are no longer plaintiffs and defendants, but petitioners and respondents. Alimony has been renamed spousal support, and is awarded only when fairness and equity demand it (Weitzman and Dixon, 1980:363). In most states, the period of residence in the state required before filing has been reduced sharply, as has the legal waiting period between filing and the decree itself. Not only have these changes simplified the legal process, but they also have lessened the psychological trauma created during that transitional period.

Postdivorce Adjustment Recovery after divorce is rarely easy. But research does indicate that starting over in the newly gained single status may be easier than living through the tumultuous and chaotic time between the separation and the divorce. While the awarding of a divorce decree may bring to the surface some feelings of depression, regret, and sorrow, it also puts behind the couple a difficult period of uncertainty. Now they can set their lives on a new course. Robert Weiss (1975:235–6) observes that a stable recovery is marked by the reestablishment of a coherent personal identity and a stable life pattern. They tend to occur at the same time. A series of problems must be confronted when a formerly married person begins to establish a new identity as a single individual. The marital habit of thinking in terms of "we" must be broken so that one starts to think automatically in terms of "I" once again. In almost all instances, the formerly married person also must develop new friendships and new patterns of socializing. Most married couples interact socially with other married couples, because they have similar interests and experiences. Divorcées often find the role of the single person in a social world of married couples quite difficult. Moreover, many people come out of their divorce experience feeling that their old friends deserted them during their hour of need by withholding support, consolation, and companionship. Contact with former friends often is lost as divorcées move to a new residence, making old patterns difficult to continue. On the positive side, for most divorced persons, social life presents an opportunity to seek a new marriage partner.

Before a formerly married person can successfully move into the mainstream of social life and form new friendships, he or she first must rebuild a sense of self-confidence and personal esteem. The negative images of failure, worthlessness, and embarrassment often associated with divorce must be replaced. Different strategies are used. Some people prefer a time alone to sort out their feelings. Others turn to old friends whom they can trust to help them nurture their self-confidence. Some seek professional help, and still others launch immediately into a new social life, rebuilding their battered egos as they develop new friendships in the social world of other singles. Whichever strategy they choose, it usually takes some time, and often some disappointments along the way before they successfully establish a new identity.

While one's ego is being refortified, a new pattern of social life typically emerges as well. Living alone is thrust upon the formerly married—unless, of course, one has custody of children. Yet, one can integrate oneself back into a network of community relationships if one is prepared to work at it. Employment normally offers a number of social contacts and the work place is frequently a source of new friendships. But other outlets for social activities also are available. Since divorcées are at first searching for friends more than new lovers or mates (Adam and Adam, 1979:154), such activities as taking courses at the local community college, joining special interest clubs, entering political groups, and signing up for tennis lessons are all likely to enable one to meet persons with interests similar to one's own. If there are children, one can take an active role in the PTA or such groups as Parents Without Partners. Many religious organizations also have programs specially designed for single adults. Although the size of communities affects the number of opportunities to return to social life, the crucial element is not how many activities are available, but how willing the formerly married are to make new contacts. Ultimately, a new pattern of social involvement can be established only when the divorced person decides to rebuild the network of community relationships severed by the divorce. Once this hurdle has been overcome, a new life is possible.

CLOSE-UP   Divorce Talk
As with any profound fact of life, discussions of divorce are conducted in a rich, constantly evolving vocabulary. Below, a glossary of some current terms.
No-fault divorce: *To get a divorce it is no longer necessary for one spouse to prove the other was at fault—no more love nests invaded by flash-popping photographers. Incompatability, irreconcilable difference or an irretrievable breakdown of the marriage are cited instead of grounds like adultery or mental cruelty. The grounds are liberally interpreted. One judge defined an irreconcilable difference as one person wanting a divorce and the other not wanting one.*
Dissolution: *Divorce, in no-fault states.*
Spousal support: *Used to be called alimony.*
Rehabilitative maintenance: *Spousal support given for a short time to allow the recipient to become self-supporting. Learn a trade, for example.*
Peace of mind surveillance: *Hiring a private detective to spy on your spouse to determine whether you should be considering a divorce. The peace of mind comes from knowing that your spouse was working late when he said he was.*

A Season for Husbands and Wives

Modification of spousal support: *Request by one spouse either to reduce or to augment the spousal support set at the time of the divorce.*

Marvinizing: *"In" term for what used to be called living in sin; after the Lee Marvin case.*

Bombers: *Top divorce lawyers who can convert your anger with your ex into assets. Instruments of revenge as well as of defense.*

Childnapping: *When parents take their children and run rather than face losing custody. Often used by a parent as leverage to force the other parent into making a better deal in a divorce settlement.*

Community property: *In community property states, that property which belongs to both husband and wife and must be split evenly at the time of divorce. Earnings, for example, are community property, as is anything bought with those earnings.*

Pro se: *Legal term for someone representing himself without benefit of a lawyer. People filing their own no-fault divorce do so "pro se." Also called do-it-yourself divorce.*

—Kathleen K. Wiegner
Forbes Magazine

The Tendency to Remarry After Divorce

Few social patterns tell us as much about how Americans see the value and importance of marriage as their rate of remarriage after divorce. If a genuine disaffection with marriage as an institution were mounting in our culture, far more divorces without remarriage would appear in our vital statistics. So far, however, this is far from being the case. Apparently, divorcing spouses are not rejecting marriage, but a particular partner (Bane, 1976:34). Thus, the rate of remarriage among divorced persons holds special interest for us as we try to understand the meaning of divorce in contemporary society.

The Rates of Remarriage

According to Glick and Norton (1977:36–7), of each 100 first marriages, 38 will end in divorce. Of the 38 divorcees, 29 or 75 percent, will remarry. Of the 29 who remarry, 13 (or 44 percent) eventually will divorce again. This yields a divorce rate of about 40 percent of all marriages contracted. However, these raw figures do not disclose the deeper meaning of the divorce and remarriage rate. Nor do they indicate the quality of second marriages and the degree of happiness which couples achieve "the second time around."

Remarriage is not new in American society. In Colonial times, the remarriage rate was relatively high, but this was due mostly to the death of a spouse (Morgan, 1966; Demos, 1971). Indeed, Cherlin (1978) reports that as late as 1920, more people were remarrying after widowhood than after divorce. This

Figure 12-4
First Marriages, Di-
vorces, and Remar-
riages of Women:
1950–1977. *Source:* So-
cial Indicators *1980, p.*
28.)

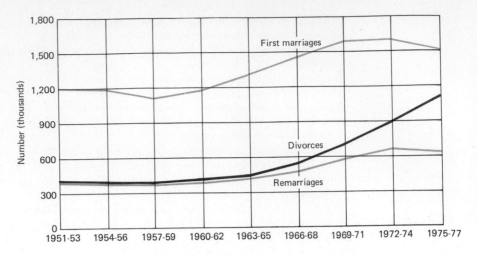

pattern had changed dramatically by 1975 when 84 percent of women and 86 percent of men who were remarrying had been divorced previously. Similarly, only 3 percent of all brides had been divorced in 1900, while the figure had risen to 25 percent in 1975. Clearly, remarriage after divorce has become more common than remarriage after the loss of a spouse.

Stability and Happiness in Remarriage after Divorce

More data are available on the stability than on the quality of second marriages after divorce. This is true partly because stability is much easier to detect and measure than happiness or other qualitative factors. Of course, the stability and quality of second marriages are related. Lately, social scientists have been puzzled over the slightly higher divorce rate among the remarried (44 percent) than among first marriages (38 percent). Those who remarry after divorce tend to be older, presumably more mature, and experienced in marriage. They should bring to their new unions a more realistic set of marital expectations. All of these features should increase the likelihood of marital stability. Moreover, as Lucile Duberman (1975b) points out, **reconstituted families**—or those that include at least one child from a previous marriage— typically try harder to achieve the norms of an ideal family group.

Cherlin (1978) contends that part of the problem of maintaining marital solidarity in remarriages is the incomplete institutionalization of the second marriage. He suggests that few guidelines exist to inform the behavior and help resolve the daily conflicts which are often unique to second marriages. For example, between 1950 and 1974, the number of divorces involving children rose from 46 to 60 percent. More and more, remarriage involves step-child-stepparent relationships. Glick (1980) further reports that 90 to 95 percent of stepchildren are living with their natural mother and a stepfather, while only 5 to 10 percent are living with their natural father and a step-mother. In the United States, roughly 3.5 million households, or one in seven, now include one parent who has remarried and at least one child from a previous marriage (Norman, 1980).

Disciplining a stepchild is immensely more complicated than correcting one's own child. And this is not all. Frequently, stepsibling interactions can produce troublesome rivalries, jealousies, and competitiveness. In addition, problems can arise in relations with the former in-laws, the new in-laws, and the former spouse who still has visitation rights with his or her children. Duberman (1973) found, however, that stepfathers were somewhat more apt to achieve excellent relations with their stepchildren than stepmothers, although adjustment was easier if both stepfathers and stepmothers were young. Somewhat surprisingly, stepfathers who had never been married before scored the highest adjustment ratings.

Thus, the reconstituted family is considerably more complex and the relationships more extensive than they are in the typical family formed by a first marriage. Futhermore, the rights and duties, the norms and expectations, the customs and conventions are ill-defined so that partners in a reconstituted family must work out their own strategies as problems arise.

Limited institutional support and guidance for the second marriage account for its precariousness, according to Cherlin (1978). Further evidence for this argument is the fact that, when no children are involved from a previous marriage, the stability of second marriages increases a good deal. Moreover, if the couple forming the second marriage have a child of their own, the union has a still better chance of lasting.

For women, the tendency to remarry is influenced by age and whether they have children. In analyzing data on white women, Koo and Suchindran (1980) discovered that among women divorcing before age 25, being childless increased the likelihood of remarriage. Among women divorcing between the ages of 25 and 34, neither having children nor the number of children influenced remarriage chances. For women divorcing at age 35 or older, however, having no children *decreased* the likelihood of remarriage. The authors concluded that older women with children apparently felt more pressure to seek a husband to gain material, social, and emotional security.

In spite of the incomplete institutionalization of remarriage, evidence shows that many second marriages produce happy unions and emotional well-being (Weingarten, 1980). Although twice-married women appear to select mates less like themselves the second time around (Dean and Gurak, 1978), over half of all second marriages do avoid divorce. Glenn and Weaver (1977) attempted to assess the happiness in second unions by examining data from three national surveys. They discovered that never-divorced women tend to report slightly more marital happiness than divorced women who have remarried. However, the chances are somewhat better for divorced males to remarry happily. The overall difference between the happiness scores of never-divorced and remarried persons, however, is not very large. Thus, Glenn and Weaver (1977:336) conclude that remarriage apparently remains a satisfactory "solution" to divorce for a large percentage of divorced persons. This prompts them to suggest further that divorce and remarriage seem to be rather effective ways to replace poor marriages with good ones and to keep the national level of marital happiness fairly high.

Perhaps we should remind ourselves again that this is not a recommendation for divorce. But it does suggest that worse things can happen to a marriage. A marriage filled with bitterness and hostility may well be more painful than dissolution. Also, the high remarriage rate after divorce and the relatively high degrees of marital happiness achieved in second marriages do support the notion that divorce and remarriage are an internal adjustment within the institution of marriage. Thus, the present divorce rate in American society does not signal a mass rejection of marriage and family life, even though divorce does create a great deal of trauma in the lives of persons caught up in the process.

The Children of Divorce

Mary Jo Bane (1976:3) has observed that worry about the family is very largely worry about the next generation. Certainly, how children are affected when their parents divorce is a major cause of public concern. When spouses choose to end their relationship, their children are seldom consulted. Without question, divorce strains children severely. But parents must decide whether the tension of keeping the marriage together would not be more harmful to themselves and their children. Unfortunately, social science can offer no easy answer which will cover all family situations. However, we can explore certain social results of divorce which affect children.

Telling the Children about the Parental Decision to Divorce

One of the most difficult times in the divorce process occurs when the parents have to tell their children of the decision to separate or to end their marriage. Especially if home life has been happy and relatively free from conflict, the news that their mother and father are splitting up will come as a severe shock. Apparently, some parents think seriously about staying together to avoid hurting their children. But if parents decide that a divorce is the only realistic solution, children must be informed. Even so, it is not an easy task.

Rita Turow (1978:5–7) provides a few suggestions to lessen anxiety among the children. She suggests, first, that the parents should jointly tell the children of their decision. Parents need to decide in advance what they will say and remain as calm as possible. Because the children are likely to get upset, the parents will need to provide as much composure, comfort, and reassurance of their love as they can under the circumstances. Parents should avoid blaming each other. The reasons for the divorce are best explained to the children honestly and with as much detail as they can understand. Above all,

children need to be assured that they had nothing to do with the marriage splitting up; the problems exist only between the mother and father, and not between parents and children. And finally, the children need to be told what the divorce means for them. They will want to know with which parent they will be living, whether they will have to leave their neighborhood, how often they will see the other parent, and what other arrangements have been made for their future.

While these guidelines do not eliminate the children's pain, they can provide some order and stability to an experience that surely will distress and confuse them. Indeed, John and Nancy Adam (1979:107) suggest that the major effect of divorce on children is determined less by the event itself than it is by how parents explain and handle the process. If one parent tries to enlist the children as allies against the other parent, the offspring probably will suffer a great deal of unnecessary pain. The child's feelings about a divorce are likely to be confusing enough without having to take sides in the parental conflict.

The Problems Children Encounter in Accepting Divorce

A child's ability to understand and accept the parents' decision to divorce varies greatly with age. Children from 18 months through 7 years probably will not be able to comprehend the reasons for the separation. Although they may have detected some hostility between their parents, young children are not likely to foresee the serious implications of such conflict. Thus, they will need to be assured that, even though the mother and father will no longer be together, they will still have a family that loves and cares for them. Surprisingly, children in the latency years (roughly ages 7 to 14) can cope quite maturely. In their study of children in the later latency years, Wallerstein and Kelly (1980) observed as typical responses fears of being forgotten or abandoned by parents, a shaken sense of identity, some guilt that they may have caused the divorce, loneliness, and loyalty conflicts in their relationships to both mother and father. Yet, through all the trauma, young people in this sample showed considerable social skill in handling the family disruption. A follow-up study done one year after the divorce also indicated that many of the children's early fears and worries had abated, even though some feelings of bitterness and regret still remained.

The Behavioral Consequences of Divorce on Children

Most people believe that divorce is harmful to children, and that partners with children should hesitate to divorce. Sorting out the moral and social bases for this judgment is extraordinarily difficult (Goode, 1965:307). We cannot be certain how much damage children might suffer by growing up in a conflict-ridden home as opposed to a divorced-family situation. Social scientists generally agree that some divorces are better for the children than intact marriages in which continued hostility holds the possibility of psychological or physical abuse (Nye, 1957).

Two major questions loom large when assessing the behavioral impact of divorce on children. First, are children of divorce more likely to become juvenile delinquents, have trouble at school, or be more hostile than other young people? Second, does growing up in a single-parent family increase the chances of personality disorders or identity crises? The limited research available may not answer these two questions absolutely, but we note certain important findings and considerations which do apply.

The issue of whether a divorce contributes to juvenile delinquency and other forms of antisocial behavior was addressed some time ago in research undertaken by the Gluecks (1950). Although they found slightly higher rates of juvenile delinquency among such youth, delinquency correlated most strongly with widowed families, followed next by separated households. They interpreted these surprising findings to mean that while divorced parents may not be living together, they still are available for guidance, discipline, and counsel. On the other hand, a dead parent is, of course, totally removed from the life of a youngster and cannot control his or her behavior in any way. Separated households, however, are likely to be somewhat disorganized be-

cause of the unresolved family situation. Children frequently manifest this disorganization—which actually is anger, frustration, and disappointment—in antisocial behavior. Subsequent studies have supported the Gluecks' initial findings.

However, we need to be a little cautious in taking these data at face value. While family disruption probably would increase the likelihood of youthful antisocial behavior, we also know that both divorce and juvenile delinquency correlate strongly with the behavioral patterns of the lower classes in American society (Leslie, 1979:555). Divorce and delinquency both may be results of class influences. A clear cause-and-effect link between divorce and juvenile delinquency has yet to be proven.

CLOSE-UP

A Son Divided

My son, 10 years and one day old, waves gamely as the Greyhound pulls out. He is bound 150 miles south to spend the long Fourth of July weekend with his mother. I stand in the hot parking lot, waving back until the bus fades far down into the stream of traffic. My son has made this strange shuttle many times before. He is one of the new legion of suddenly old children, paying in part for their parents' failures.

I have stood here before and should not be too upset. Only this trip is different: His mother has remarried in the past month, and my son is going to live for the first time in a new house with a new, part-time surrogate father. The man is a complete stranger to me.

My situation is better than most. Unlike nearly all divorced fathers, I enjoy joint custody: All major decisions regarding my son must be made by mutual

(continued)

agreement, and each parent is legally entitled to physical custody for half of each year. Because of school, the year is not split evenly: My son spends about 160 days each year with me, 200 with his mother. The summer, however, is nearly all mine, and the summer is the best of times. We have a good beach on Lake Champlain, a healthy garden, and my son plays centerfield for a baseball team of eight-to-10-year-olds that I coach. I should be satisfied, but I am not.

The 200 days away are 200 too many. More than half his year, more than half mine. And now there is this new man. Who is he? What is he like? Does that make any difference? By what right does he shelter my son under his roof more nights of the year than I do?

The Government statisticians measure everything relentlessly. They tell us that one of two children born today will spend at least part of his life in a single-parent home. Most of these children will be reared by their mothers, since the courts still almost automatically, and unthinkingly, grant child custody in divorce to women. The fathers often become phantoms. They are limited to weekend visits, cut off from any role in vital choices, of schooling, community and religion, vulnerable to termination of their visitation rights. Are the men of Greece, India, Japan, Brazil also so quick to yield their children? Why is the father's role and responsibility so diminished in America?

My immediate problem is that both his mother and I love our son.

I should be grateful that my son and I are together as much as we are. We are not strangers to each other, nor, I hope, will we ever be. We are involved in each other's lives, and we have many fine times together. I shouldn't mind that he now lives with another man. After all this will give him a new "relationship" to develop. Learning to develop relationships is a vital survival skill in the new world a-building in America. I shouldn't mind.

But the thing still seems wrong.

—William Colgan,
excerpted from *The New York Times*

A Note about the Author: William Colgan is 35 years old. He has been separated and divorced for a total of three years.

Moreover, research findings also have not shown an increase in personality disorders among the children of divorce. Most families in which divorce occurs become single-parent households, with about 90 percent headed by women (Brandwein, *et. al.*, 1974:510). Even many social scientists assumed that fatherless families often lacked discipline and a male role image, a particularly critical problem for young men. The suggestion was that improper socialization might well occur when children are reared in a single-parent family system. The growing file of research on single-parent households has by and large laid to rest the fear of inadequate socialization for the children of divorce. Boys in fatherless homes have ample masculine role models in the community about them to foster a healthy sex-role identity. Indeed, the major problems for female-headed households is not maintaining discipline over children or nurturing stable personalities, but in providing income for the family (Brandwein, *et al.*, 1974; Bould, 1977). Thus while divorce may be expected to introduce some strain into the lives of children, it does not appear to leave a permanent mark on their personalities, nor create serious emotional problems, particularly when the family enjoys economic stability.

Serial Monogamy: A Rising Pattern?

Polygamy, as noted in Chapter 2, is the practice of having several spouses at the same time. United States law permits a woman or man to have several spouses over the course of a lifetime, as long as a legal divorce precedes each marriage. This has prompted some social scientists to question whether we are not legitimating a system of **serial monogamy.** Behind this question is a basic concern that America may be entering a period when persons will drift in and out of marriage in a casual fashion. The evidence on divorce and remarriage does not seem to support that interpretation, however, as we have noted. Mary Jo Bane (1976:36) argues that the divorce rate currently falls short of indicating that marriage in American society is becoming a series of casual liaisons rather than permanent families. Americans today do tend to end bad marriages through divorce and try to form others which are better. This does increase the divorce rate. But to label such a pattern serial monogamy runs the danger of demeaning divorcées' motivations and creating unwarranted doubts about the value Americans place on the institution of marriage.

Summary

American society has embraced two norms for the institution of marriage which all but guarantee a relatively high divorce rate. First, Americans have endorsed a mating system which allows individuals to select their own marriage partners. Such a practice inevitably produces a number of mistakes and a higher divorce rate than in traditional societies where mates are selected by parents or extended family members. In addition, when love is the basis for partner commitment, maintaining marital solidarity becomes a more intense problem. The loss of romantic attachment can be expected in a fair number of cases, even when two people began a marriage deeply in love. Given these two patterns, divorce is a predictable feature of American family life.

At present the U.S. has a relatively high divorce rate. Of every 100 first marriages, 38 end in divorce. Amost 80 percent of those who divorce eventually remarry. Of all remarriages, 44 percent end in divorce. This gives us a divorce rate for all marriages of about 40 percent. These raw figures do not tell us the whole story of divorce in American society, however. The value attributed to the marital institution and the relative well-being of family life cannot be directly deduced from the divorce rate. Accordingly, in this chapter we suggest that divorce should be regarded as an adjustment internal to the marriage institution whereby a sizable number of people choose to dissolve unhappy unions and remarry to create better ones. Thus, many Americans choose divorce because they want a quality marriage.

To be sure, a succession of social factors increase the likelihood of divorce. For example, marriage prior to age 20 or after 30 produces statistically less stable marital relationships. The absence of children, dissimilar socail backgrounds, different religious affiliations, employment of the wife, and lower social class standing all correlate with increased marital instability. The actual decision to divorce, however, typically follows a social process in which marriage partners drift apart. The period of gradual disengagement may stretch over years, but it often culminates in unresolved conflicts and eventually in the decision to separate.

For most couples, the most traumatic period in the whole process of marital dissolution extends from the time when divorce is first seriously contemplated until the final granting of the divorce decree. The uncertainty of separation and the inability to plan one's future during divorce proceedings thrusts marriage partners into a situation without norms. Role patterns, relations with former in-laws, and patterns of friendship all tend to be ill-defined while a divorce is in process. Thus, both the person getting the divorce and the others involved find it difficult to interact normally. Postdivorce adjustment affords the divorcée an opportunity to rebuild friendships and make plans for the future—which, in many instances, involve a search for a new marriage partner.

Just as America's divorce rate has risen over the past few years, our remarriage rate has also grown. Persons under 30 who divorce are especially likely to remarry. Second marriages are somewhat less stable than first marriages. Cherlin contends that this is due to the incomplete institutionalization of remarriage. In other words, many second marriages contain children from previous marital unions, and thus a complex pattern of family relationships emerges, creating problems for many couples. Despite stepparent-stepchild problems, however, most second marriages do result in happy and stable unions.

Finally, this chapter considered the children of divorce. Almost everyone agrees that divorce is harmful to children. However, many conflict-ridden marriages also are harmful. Ultimately, parents must decide whether divorce will disrupt their children's lives more than a home filled with hostility and bitterness. We do know that while divorce is psychologically painful to children, young people from divorced homes are somewhat less inclined toward delinquent behavior than those from widowed homes. Moreover, the children of divorce who grow up in single-parent families apparently can develop normal personalities and escape the serious emotional problems which many people have regarded as a permanent result of divorce.

Overall, then, we may conclude that even though divorce is almost always a stressful, emotional experience for individual family members, it may not be the worst thing that can happen to a family. Indeed, the remarriage rate signifies that many persons value marriage so highly that they prefer to try again to form a happy union rather than to live the single life. Americans do not appear to be drifting toward "serial monogamy," however, if one means by that term, a series of casual liaisons rather than permanent marriages.

STUDY QUESTIONS

1. What are the different ways in which a marriage partnership can be dissolved and what are the individual and social ramifications of each one?
2. Just as falling in love is a social process, what are some of the typical dynamics of the process leading toward marriage partner disengagement?
3. What are the major social factors that contribute to the likelihood that a marriage will end in divorce?
4. When social scientists speak of divorce as "an internal adjustment within the marriage system," what precisely do they mean?

A Season for Husbands and Wives

5. What is the remarriage rate after divorce in contemporary American society and what does this rate have to say about the way Americans view the institution of marriage in our society?
6. How damaging is the divorce process on children? Are there instances when keeping a marriage together for the sake of the children might not serve the best interests of the children involved?

PART
SIX

A Season for Family Interaction with the Wider Society

Family members live in a complex world and are part of the major institutions and social groups which make up a society. Part VI illuminates some of the linkages through which family members and other groups interact. These exchanges help both parties. That is to say, the family as a small group contributes to other social institutions, while it receives certain social benefits and rewards. Chapter 13 spells out the nature of those exchanges by which the family and other social institutions improve each other's performance.

Chapter 14 deals with the variations in family life produced by different ethnic and class patterns. The diversity of American family life is a reminder that not all families are middle class or fully blended into the dominant American culture. Moreover, our review of these differences is not based on the idea that all families should be alike. Familiarity with ethnic and class variations is simply essential if one is to understand how complex are the family systems in America and how they contribute in different ways to our total social life.

13

The Family and Its Community Involvements

trends self-sufficient
less self-sufficient
Dependent on ect. for
schools ect.
socialization

How religion
affects marriage
socialization of kids.
Divorce

Poet John Donne's famous line, "No man is an island" has survived because it is very largely true. While no man is an island, neither is any social group or basic institution. No social institution can function well in isolation from a society's other major institutional bodies. Nor, by the same token, can we thoroughly understand an institution like the family unless we appreciate how it interacts with, contributes to, and depends upon the other institutions. Accordingly, this chapter treats the critical link between the family and the economy, the community, the governmental system, the religious institution, and the educational system. The concluding section examines the important issue of the family's role in promoting a sense of civic responsibility in its members.

Figure 13-1
The Interchanges between the Nuclear Family and the Functional Subsystems of Society. *(Source: Bell and Vogel,* The Family, *p. 10)*

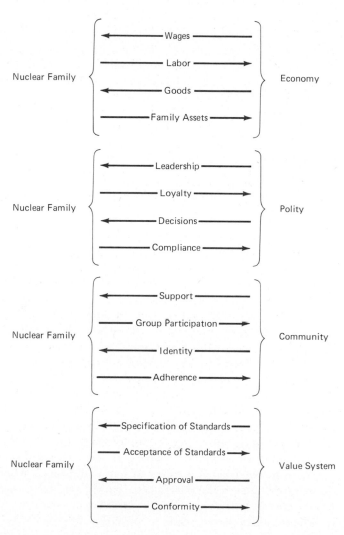

"Money is not the root of all evil," asserted the Irish playwright G. B. Shaw. "The lack of money is the root of all evil." Few among us could fault his logic. For example, money is cited typically as the chief trouble spot and the number-one cause of disagreements in marriage (Blood and Wolfe, 1965:241). However, when couples say money problems are their chief source of conflict, it is not simply the shortage of money which bothers them, but opposing viewpoints on how to spend their limited resources. "Enough money," after all, is a relative term. Families earning $100,000 a year can suffer from a lack of money as easily as couples earning $15,000, if they do not manage their money wisely.

Indeed, while a great deal of concern is expressed about couples' lack of information on sexual matters, the information gap on money matters probably is more serious. Many young people marry today with very little thought about the cost of setting up housekeeping or how much money they will need to assure a stable financial future. Rubin (1976:71) quotes one working-class wife who describes in a typical fashion the problems many newly wed couples encounter when they finally face the stark economic realities of married life:

> I don't know how we survived that period. The first thing that hit us was all those financial problems. We were dirt poor. Here I'd gotten married with all those dreams and then I got stuck right away trying to manage on $1.50 an hour—and a lot of days he didn't work very many hours.

Like many others in the working class, this couple was so anxious to get married, so elated by the prospect of being on their own, that they failed to figure out how much money they would need to pay the rent, buy food, keep up the car, furnish their home or apartment, and cover all the other normal family expenses which their parents had paid for them. In many instances, of course, both husband and wife were working when they married. Two incomes often can create a false sense of financial security. Because they need so many expensive items right after they are married, such as furniture, kitchen appliances, clothes, housing and insurance, the temptation is to go heavily into debt in the first year or two of marriage. This may not be a serious problem while both incomes continue. But if the wife becomes pregnant or if the husband loses his job, they may swiftly discover that one salary simply cannot buy all the things they purchased when both were working. Overspending and poor handling of financial assets are fairly common experiences among young married couples, and often among couples who have been married for a number of years. Indeed, one of the most difficult adjustments in married life is learning to live within one's means, especially when those means may well be reduced sharply through pregnancy or the lesser job security of younger workers in business and industry.

Since money never seem to be adequate—whatever a family's income level—to purchase all the items which couples desire, they must have some way of managing the family's disposable income. Especially when budgets are tight, extravagant purchases by one spouse, without consulting the other, can produce accusations of selfishness, irresponsibility, and bad faith. Indeed, few actions can produce more tensions and family strain than unwise spending. Talking over financial problems, making joint economic decisions, and settling on some form of family financial planning does not produce more income, but it does help reduce conflicts, which might otherwise throw the relationship into deep jeopardy (For a discussions of a family budget and other economic matters, see the Appendix).

The Relationship between the Family and the External Economic Institution

A distinguishing mark of the modern family is that it has almost completely exchanged its role as a producing unit for a special role as a consuming unit. No longer are residence and work place combined. Today, labor is rewarded with wages earned outside the home, and it is a major concern of one or both parents (Shorter, 1977). But the sharp distinction between traditional family affairs and economic activities has not completely isolated the modern family life from economics. Critical points remain at which the family performs functions for the economy, and the economy, in turn, performs functions for the nuclear family. In this section, our major interest is to explore the exchange relationship between the economy and the modern family. Norman Bell and Ezra Vogel (1968) have supplied a model that helps us to understand the interaction between the family and the economy. Their analysis provides a basis for the following discussion.

The Provision of Workers for the Economy

The economy is that institution of society which produces goods and services. To function, the economy must have workers. The family provides replacements for members of society as a whole and for the economy as an institution, both of which would soon wither without young blood. As we noted earlier, the family is the only institution legitimately charged with the responsibility of procreation. But the family controls not only the quantity of new workers, but also the quality. Through the socialization process, the family imparts to each individual a basic orientation toward the value of productive labor as well as the fundamental skills needed to enter the labor market and perform well. A poorly socialized person may be an unreliable, irresponsible, or incompetent worker. By contrast, the traits which spell success in economic endeavors—such as honesty, dependability, self-discipline, and commitment to the meaningfulness of labor—are all instilled in a person by the family. Thus, the family, and not the economic system itself, determines the quality of the labor force. If the family fails to produce workers with these social skills, the economy can do very little to change the situation. Usually, this fact is most visible in lower-income families which are beset by many problems, and whose children often do not internalize the discipline and other social skills needed to function in the labor market (Rainwater and Yancey, 1967). By the same token, upper-status families transmit to their children personal skills as well as educational expectations which later mean better jobs and higher incomes (Jencks, 1973:213–6). While the family is not the sole influence on the quality of a worker, it is clearly one of the most important forces shaping a worker's eventual performance on the job.

The Return of Wages from the Economy

In return for the labor of family members, the economy supplies the family with an income. As a general rule, higher wages are awarded to those persons who perform better, who have invested more time and money acquiring the skills required for their jobs, and who hold positions of greater responsibility. For example, we find it relatively easy to justify a high income for a physician, with long years of expensive training, who has just saved our life because of his or her knowledge and ability. A similar income paid to a service station attendant or to a plumber would strike us as unwarranted. Of course, this is not to suggest that income levels are entirely fair for all occupational groups.

The Exchange of Family Resources for Goods and Services

The family's monetary resources are returned to the economy through the purchase of goods and services. One family, of course, does not affect the balance between supply and demand for goods and services, but the collective demand of many families certainly can exert considerable influence. When Detroit lagged behind the demand of families for small, fuel-efficient cars, foreign models displaced the American cars, selling in large numbers. Detroit finally was forced to develop competitive models. Similarly, when concern for the natural environment led many women and men to stop buying phosphate detergents, soap manufacturers soon began making products that were compatible with nature. The exchange of family income for consumer goods, on a large scale at least, still has an important impact.

These are the major interactions between the nuclear family and the economy in the highly industrialized American society. Of course, the patterns are quite different in less-developed nations where economic roles tend to be patterned on family roles (Bell and Vogel, 1968:13). Moreover, in the United States and other modern nations, the family is expected to help its members meet the demands of the economic order. For example, the wives of professional men and corporate executives can be important aids to their husbands, often contributing decisively to their success (Lopata, 1972; Kanter, 1977:194–226). Increasingly, however, women are choosing to assist their families economically by entering the job market themselves rather than by simply supporting their husbands' careers (Chafe, 1974; Bernard, 1975a).

Families support their working members in other ways as well. Often, a family must move from one city to another to meet the demands of the labor market or to accommodate a family member whose firm has assigned him or her to a new position. This may create severe complications if both partners are working and they cannot arrange to change jobs at the same time. Without a willingness to make this kind of adjustment, family life or the work experience, or both, may be disrupted seriously. Furthermore, families also assist their working members by reinforcing the motivation of those members to establish a good attendance record on the job; frequent absences jeopardize the family income. And finally, the family must allow its wage earners some independence as they seek to fulfill an employer's expectations (Bell and Vogel, 1968:13). Some jobs require the worker to travel, or to take work home at night, or to put in extra hours during seasons of heavy business activity. The failure of family members to understand these demands could weaken a wage earner's overall job performance, and endanger promotions, higher income, and personal satisfactions which might otherwise arise from a job well done.

For most Americans, family and occupation are the two major elements around which personal identity is organized. If one element goes well, it helps our performance in the other. A person's stable, secure, and happy family life increases the probability of a rewarding occupation or career. Conversely, problems at work, or worse, the loss of one's job, can produce enormous strains in family relations. Thus, the link between the family and the economy is a complex, interdependent relationship. Neither institution can work well for very long without the other's contribution.

The Relationship of Economic Achievement to Status Aspirations

American society often has been called a materialistic social order (Lipset, 1963:122–9). While the drive for hard work and success have been major themes of American life (de Tocqueville, 1954, II:161–2) bequeathed to us by our Puritan heritage, we have good reason to ask whether it is money and material things which really motivate Americans to work. Indeed, one cannot fully understand why families are so supportive of their wage earners in our society unless one first appreciates the subtle links between achievement and economic success down through the centuries of American social history.

Economic Success in an Achievement-Oriented Society

One of the root values of Americans since the creation of the nation is **achievement** (Williams, 1970:454–8). We speak of it in everyday language as the "desire to get ahead."

What is the measure of success? What are the symbols of getting ahead? How does one know that gains have been registered? The conventional mea-

sure of success for family members in American society is the amount of their income. Higher income means greater success, while lower income indicates less achievement—unless payoffs come in other forms, such as social status or political power (Weber, 1958a:18–95). Many college and university professors who study long years to attain the doctoral degree receive a lower start-

A Season for Family Interaction with the Wider Society

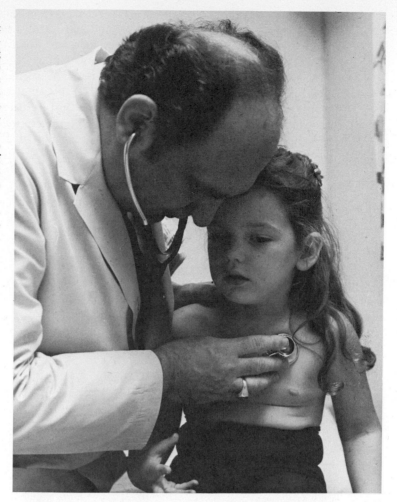

Figure 13-2
Members of different occupations are rewarded by varying levels of both income and status. Physicians and sanitation workers, for example, are divided not only by wide income differences, but also by the prestige ratings of their respective occupations. *(Copyright © Stock, Boston, Inc., Anestis Kiakopoulos, photographer; © Suzanne Szasz, Photo Researchers, Inc.)*

ing salary, for example, than starting sanitation workers in San Francisco. Yet professors enjoy a higher occupational status which helps compensate for their lower income. Similarly, many officials in all three branches of government could make more money in the private sector, but they choose to work for lower incomes to gain political power, and with it the respect and symbols of achievement which political power yields. For the majority of working Americans, meanwhile, the size of their income is the standard measure of success.

We need to be cautious, however, about jumping to the conclusion that money is the chief motive impelling Americans to engage in economic activity. We must distinguish carefully between the goal of success and the measure of success (McClelland, 1967:233–7). Moreover, we can suggest on the basis of this distinction that Americans work primarily for the goal of achievement and not simply for money, which is the measure of success. If making money were the exclusive motivating factor, people would work until they had all they could possibly use and then retire from the work force. This has rarely happened in the past, and it rarely occurs today. Those who have made money typically reinvest it to try to build up a larger fortune or financial empire. Furthermore, if money were the sole aim, then one would have to assume that to offer people a higher income would lead them to work harder. But as economist John Kenneth Galbraith (1967:138) correctly observes, many executives would be insulted by the suggestion that they are not making their best effort, and that paying them more would inspire them to be more productive. The same can be said, of course, for persons in many professions and occupations. Indeed, after reviewing studies on how well money motivates workers to perform better, McClelland (1967:236–7) discovered that only very low achievers actually responded to offers of higher pay by working harder. For most wage earners and all high achievers, the offer of more money did not increase their job performance at all. This is not to suggest that achievers were not interested in money. In fact, they were keenly inter-

Figure 13-3
Purchasing a home involves more than simply securing a dwelling for family members; it also serves to identify a family's status position in the community. *(Monkmeyer Press Photo Service. Mimi Forsyth, photographer.)*

A Season for Family Interaction with the Wider Society

ested in money and profit, but not for its own sake. To them, McClelland contends, money was a measure of their success, a concrete symbol of their achievement.

The essence of McClelland's conclusion is supported by a sizable number of social scientists (Lipset, 1963; Galbraith, 1967; Williams, 1970; Bell, 1976). They refute the stereotype that Americans are basically a materialistic people. But money in the bank does not symbolize our success to others. Income must be exchanged for material objects suitable to our income level. Thus, we buy homes, cars, furniture, and we pursue a life-style that tells people where we stand in the social class and status structure of society. For example, couples who have experienced a sizable increase in their income commonly sell their first home and move to a higher-status neighborhood. Although the new home may be more attractive or comfortable, the major payoff of the residential move is likely to be that it allows them to register their upward mobility gains. The real gratification arising from the accumulation of material possessions, therefore, often lies less in the objects themselves than in the status level they symbolize.

The Social Pressure to Spend beyond Family Means

The American social system lacks rigid boundary lines between classes. For this reason, social-class identity tends to express itself in consumption patterns and life-styles. Members of a class not only have similar income levels, but they also tend to share tastes in consumer goods, belong to similar social organizations, achieve similar levels of education, and take part in similar recreations (Warner, 1960). Thus, the class placement of a nuclear family is based on its income and how that income is expended through comsumption and life-style patterns.

Because American society is an achievement-oriented social order, family members feel pressure to attain upward social mobility. This involves more than simply earning more money. Family members must, in addition, adopt the consumption patterns, manners, tastes, and life-styles of the **status group** to which they aspire. Clearly, when status drives are extremely strong, family members may be tempted to consume more than they really can afford in the effort to be accepted by those in the higher-status group. "Easy credit" offers from many firms supplying goods and services to American consumers add to the temptation to overextend one's financial resources while striving for status. The irony is that many family members really may not want all the material possessions which they feel compelled to buy. They simply want the status level which these items symbolize.

Over the last two decades, American college youth have become increasingly critical of status striving and the pursuit of money as an end in itself. Yankelovich (1974:60) found in his 1973 survey of college students that 80 percent would welcome less emphasis on money. This compared with 76 percent taking that point of view in 1971 and 65 percent in 1968. Regardless of whether status striving is overemphasized in American society, the often unrecognized pressure on Americans to spend more than they can afford in the status race can lead to severe problems in family money management. Unfortunately, no simple "cure" can be applied to this problem other than a sober warning against the widespread temptation to live beyond our means in an effort to symbolize our success.

The Interaction of the Family and the Community

When we use the concept of community in everyday language, it brings to mind several different images and meanings. Frequently, we use the term in a strictly metaphorical sense, as, for example, when we speak of the scientific community, the college community, or the business community. To avoid confusion in our social scientific analysis, we need to define the concept of a community as exactly as possible. Accordingly, **community** is a type of social organization that provides a territorially based setting for most of the needs and problems of daily living, and in which primary, face-to-face relationships are the rule (Martin, 1970:11–2). Community generally provides its members with a sense of belonging. Thus, community refers to a unit of social organization which is larger than the immediate neighborhood, but with many of the traits—the cooperation, sympathy, mutual helpfulness, and social support—that usually are part of the neighborhood concept.

The community plays a critical role in the total structure of social life by helping to integrate various local institutions, social groups, and individuals into a working unit (Parsons, 1960:250–79). This is accomplished, in part, through formal and informal communication networks; a transportation system that links home to work place, schools, churches, recreational and retail outlets; and a complex of social controls with enough legal authority and force to maintain public order and attain common political goals. The community also promotes social bonds through the creation and enforcement of normative rules and standards which are the guidelines for the conduct of family members. In this manner, the community regulates as well as integrates its population. By identifying with the norms of a social class and status group within the community, individuals and family members can find their place in the structures of the local stratification system. This is especially critical in an open-ended class system, such as we possess in the United States, because no sharp boundaries separate one class from another.

The Exchange of Family Participation for Community Support

In this section we begin to trace some of the linkages between the nuclear family and the local community. Bell and Vogel (1968:10) provide a particularly useful model for understanding the interaction patterns between the family and community. The first sequence includes the family's participation in community life, and the community's response of social support for family affairs. Each aspect of this interaction process can be explained briefly.

A family can become so absorbed in its own activities that its members find themselves taking very little part in day-to-day community life. Such withdrawal from community affairs is especially acute today as we emphasize the need for family privacy and regard the home as a refuge from the tensions of the outside social world (Shorter, 1977; Lasch, 1979). But community well-being depends upon the willingness of its members to actively engage in its various activities. Accordingly, the community must encourage family members to lay aside their other concerns to devote ample time and energy to the achievement of social goals. Every community relies heavily on family members to enter formally into its necessary activities—such as voting, serving on the school board, going to PTA meetings, joining civic and professional groups dedicated to community improvement, aiding charity drives, serving in the volunteer fire department, leading a girl or boy scout troop, and taking an active part in church or synagogue affairs.

TEST YOURSELF

On Whether Women Should Assume Political or Leadership Roles
The questions below have been designed to sample opinions on whether women should take a larger role in political and leadership positions in American society. Read each question and circle the response—agree strongly (AS), agree mildly (AM), disagree mildly (DM), or disagree strongly (DS),—which best represents your point of view. Scoring instructions are included at the bottom of this questionnaire.

It is the woman's duty as well as the man's to participate in leading and taking care of things in society.

AS	AM	DM	DS
(1)	2	3	4

We need more women in politics.

AS	AM	DM	DS
1	(2)	3	4

The intellectual leadership of a community should be largely in the hands of men.

AS	AM	DM	DS
4	3	(2)	1

There won't be a woman President of the U.S. for a long time and that's probably just as well.

AS	AM	DM	DS
4	3	2	(1)

(continued)

One half of the delegates at national nominating conventions for the two major political parties should be women, in order to represent their half of the U.S. population.

AS	AM	DM	DS
1	(2)	3	4

Politics is too dirty a business for women to become involved in.

AS	AM	DM	DS
4	3	2	(1)

When it comes to politics, women don't have a mind of their own and tend to vote the way their husbands tell them to.

AS	AM	DM	DS
4	3	2	(1)

Most men are better suited emotionally for politics than are most women.

AS	AM	DM	DS
4	3	2	(1)

Feminine charm and diplomacy can be a woman's greatest asset in getting ahead in politics.

AS	AM	DM	DS
4	(3)	2	1

Women are more attentive to detail and therefore can be better administrators in high office than men.

AS	AM	DM	DS
4	(3)	2	1

In actual fact, men generally do make better leaders than women.

AS	AM	DM	DS
4	3	(2)	1

Scoring: Total up your numerical score from the questions above. A high score—out of a possible 44—would indicate that you have strong objections to women assuming political and leadership roles, while a low score would indicate a strong commitment to the need for more women in leadership positions.

Source: Karen Oppenheim Mason, with the assistance of Daniel R. Denison and Anita J. Schacht. *Sex-Role Attitude Items and Scales From U.S. Sample Surveys.* Rockville, Md. National Institute of Mental Health. 1975, pp. 30–33.

Not all such forms of participation are channeled through formal organizations. Just as important and certainly more frequent is informal community involvement, such as carpooling to the commuter train or nursery school, lending your neighbor a tool, providing helpful hints on home repairs, buying a raffle ticket to support the high school band's drive to buy new uniforms, helping your neighbor start his car when the battery's power is low, or even just talking over the back fence.

The commitment of family members to formal and informal types of community participation brings a wide variety of social rewards. Generally speaking, the repayment is communal support as the family strives to fulfill social norms, maintain its self-image, and rear its offspring. Moreover, a family that helps neighbors also can expect to receive a helping hand from community

Figure 13-4
Participating in neighborhood improvement drives is generally rewarded by community support for family members. *(Monkmeyer Press Photo Service. Paul Conklin, photographer.)*

members when it is in need. In short, reciprocity is a basic part of community affairs. A family unit is treated much as it treats others in the neighborhood.

The Exchange of Family Identity for Adherence to Community Norms

At least as important as the exchange of economic benefits by the family and the community is the exchange of family indentity for adherence to the norms of the community. In exchange for the family's obedience to a set of guidelines, the community bestows an identity on the family. That identity often is expressed in such evaluative phrases as, "They're a hardworking family," "They're rich folks, but they aren't snobbish," "They're a good, Catholic family," "They're a very artistic family, always into weird things," "They're an absolute disgrace to our whole neighborhood," "They're a very close-knit family, constantly doing something with their kids." Behind these ordinary descriptions stands a fairly elaborate stratification system into which a family is placed on the basis of such variables as income, consumption patterns, and styles of behavior (Warner, 1963). Each class and status group has its own set of behavioral norms, and the community awards status identity on the basis of whether the family's social performance meets those norms. For example, a college professor with a middle-class income is likely to be identified with a lower-class status position if he stores his battered 1965 Chevy on cement blocks on his front lawn. For a middle-class neighborhood, such behavior is clearly deviant, while in a lower-class neighborhood it might not even raise an eyebrow. Hence, the status standards to which a family conforms largely determine the identity which the community bestows (Bottomore, 1968).

The importance of this status-placement function is hard to overestimate (Parsons, 1951:414–27). Family members need to know where they stand in the levels of the stratification system. Not only does a family's class-and-status identity prevent a feeling of "normlessness" and produce a sense of belonging; it also provides the social bearings necessary to tell which behavior the family is to perform and which to avoid to achieve upward social mobility. A family lacking a social identity would literally be lost in community affairs, devoid of any sense of direction and unable to distinguish between normal and deviant behavior.

The Interaction between the Nuclear Family and the Government

Every society must construct an administrative system to organize its movement toward collective social goals. This administrative structure is the government (Parsons, 1967:300). The government's first important obligation is to set the social goals for members of society, such as providing a strong national defense, eliminating poverty, ending racial discrimination, controlling inflation, and conserving energy. Spelling out these goals for society and then marshaling the necessary manpower and money to attain them falls under the general heading of providing political leadership (Giddens, 1975:118–27).

The Exchange of Family Loyalty for Political Leadership

At the conceptual level, family members direct their loyalty toward government as a whole. No one is born with a commitment to democratic practices; we acquire it largely through our family training (Shostak, 1969:216). Indeed, it is primarily through our political socialization in the family that we receive our first political attitudes and our preference for a particular political party. Furthermore, the family affects our level of participation in political affairs as well (Hyman, 1969:64–6). Even in the chaotic 1960s, social scientists discovered a continuity of political attitudes which spanned the generations. Radical young people, it turned out, were offspring of politically liberal or radical parents (Keniston, 1968; Yankelovich, 1974).

At a lower level within the political system, families express loyalty to particular political leaders and their ideals or programs. But because political leaders make policies for the entire community, individual families do not have the opportunity to select from among the policy options when they choose political leaders in quite the same manner as they can select among different consumer goods. When they vote for a politician because he says he wants to lower taxes, they are also voting for a politician who may favor other policies they completely oppose. Yet, shifting loyalty from one party or administration to another during elections allows families to register their opinion of leadership policies, and thereby influence the course of political affairs. Thus, loyalty is something no politician, not even a president, can take for granted. If leadership has not been exercised in the eyes of the general public, their loyalty will swiftly fade away.

A Season for Family Interaction with the Wider Society

The Exchange of Political Decisions for Family Compliance

On the second level of exchange, the family complies with government in return for political decisions. While single families have little control over specific decisions made by politicians, leaders nonetheless must be concerned that people may not abide by government decisions.

In most cases, of course, the state is hard pressed to enforce decisions which large portions of society regard as improper. Yet, noncompliance can take forms other than the simple refusal to obey. The taxpayer's revolt signaled by California's passage of Proposition 13 is one type of tactic for rejecting the decisions of leadership. The family is the smallest social unit engaged in the evaluation of political decisions and one of the most crucial in determining whether a law will be obeyed. Families are important units for the review of policy decisions. Family evaluations can mold the opinion of two or more voters. While two voters cannot affect public policy, the combined effect of similar discussions in other households can mushroom into a sizable segment of the voters. Moreover, parents' political attitudes and viewpoints are transmitted to the next generation through the socialization of their children to a specific political orientation. In the long run, the nuclear family's political influence has a good deal of social impact.

The Family and the Religious Institution

The intimate connection between religious organizations and the family has been discussed and written about a great deal in America. The once-popular slogan, "The family that prays together stays together," revealed the widespread belief in American culture that religion promotes family solidarity. Indeed, families that were members of religious denominations were more integrated as a unit. Among families whose husband and wife actively take part in the same mainline denomination, the couple is less likely to divorce or separate, or to have deep marital conflicts, adolescent rebellion, or juvenile delinquency (Moberg, 1962:357–66). Moreover, religiously active couples typically report higher levels of marital satisfaction that nonreligious couples (Wilson, 1978:257–8). We do not know whether the religious factor causes marital satisfaction or whether it simply results from other factors in the partners' backgrounds. However, the strong correlation between religious involvement and family stability is striking. Especially in the modern world, people tend to turn to their families and religious communities for the experiences which shape their lives and give meaning to their existence (Luckmann, 1967:97–106). Perhaps the most obvious connection between religion and the family is in the marking of life-cycle events. For many individuals, the church or synagogue actively symbolizes their move from one status or social position to another. In our society, such rituals, or rites of passage, include baptism, confirmation, bar mitzvah or bat mitzvah, marriage, and a

Figure 13.5
Religious affiliation affects members' behavior in a number of distinct ways across the life cycle, from the very young to the very old. *(Monkmeyer Press Photo Service. Paul Conklin, photographer.)*

funeral. Of course, not everyone celebrates life-cycle events by taking part in a religious ceremony, but many family members do make a serious effort to secure these minimal religious services, even if they do not otherwise take part in a religious community.

The family enormously influences the growth of piety and religious devotion. Especially during America's Puritan era, the family worked with the church to instill religious belief and a commitment to the church (Morgan, 1966; Illick, 1975:323–31). Religious themes ran though all of Puritan family life. Bible reading before bedtime, prayers at meals, and discussion of the sermon on Sunday afternoon were standard practices in many homes (Greven, 1977). Over the course of American social experience, however, this sort of devotion has steadily declined. Today, private family worship is relatively rare, even though the practice of saying grace before meals does persist as the most common religious ritual in the home (Moberg, 1962:353–4).

Moreover, the religious instruction of children, once shared by the home and church, now has been transferred almost entirely outside the household. Parents rely on religious educators or qualified lay personnel teaching in Sunday schools, catechism classes, or Hebrew schools to instruct their children in the specific teachings of their faith. Many religious leaders lament the family's decline as a center of religious education. But the low level of knowledge about religious affairs that is typical among American worshippers strongly suggests that most parents are not well enough informed to help instruct their children. Among American adults who claimed a religious affiliation, Stark and Glock (1970:141–62) discovered levels of ignorance that they considered astounding. For example, 6 percent of those who claimed to be Catholic could not correctly identify the mother of Jesus, 79 percent of Protestants and 86 percent of Catholics could not name one Old Testament prophet, 41 percent of Protestants and 81 percent of Catholics did not know the name of the first book in the Bible, and 79 percent of Protestants and 94 percent of Catholics could not identify St. Paul as the author of the most books in the New Testament. These data suggest that parents' simple ignorance prevents them from passing along much religious information to their children.

We should not conclude, however, that parents are unconcerned about the religious education of their children. Some 2.2 million Catholic families continue to send their children to parochial schools with the expectation that, along with their secular education, they also will receive a better religious education (Greeley, 1977:145). Similarly, Protestants and Jews spend large sums on their Sunday schools and other religious training programs, even though these groups have not developed the large-scale parochial school systems typical of American Catholicism. Parents also encourage their youth to take advantage of the educational opportunities within their church or synagogue. Especially when younger children are involved, who probably could not take a very active role in religious activities without the cooperation of parents, it is the mother or father who drives them to such events and motivates them to attend.

This fact prompted Nash and Berger to develop a theory on the influence of child rearing on church participation. Their research (1962) indicated that a large number of suburban parents joined churches for the sake of their children. Parents clearly seemed to regard church attendance as good for family life and the well-being of their school-age youth. But later studies detected no higher level of religious participation among couples with school-age children. Roof and Hoge (1980) conclude from their analysis of data collected in a 1978 Gallup survey of "unchurched Americans" that only Catholic couples with children have a slightly higher rate of participation. Overall, then, little support emerges for the child-rearing theory as an explanation for church attendance. While parents who already belong to religious organizations enroll their children in educational programs and want them socialized into their religious tradition, few couples actually seem to join a denomination solely to give their children religious training. But since 62 to 65 percent of American adults belong to a religious organization (Roof and Hoge, 1980), a large number of young Americans have the opportunity for formal religious instruction.

The Religious Impact on Family Life

Religious influence on family life is often difficult to separate from such factors as social class, ethnic identity, educational level, race, and region of residence. Despite the problems in gathering reliable data, religious affiliation and the degree of religious participation seem to affect family behavior in distinct areas. For example, social scientists have demonstrated that religious participation influences mate selection, the tendency to divorce, family size, attitudes toward contraception and abortion, patterns of sexual behavior, and the degree of marital satisfaction and adjustment.

As we observed in Chapter 5, religious affiliation is very important in mate selection. Almost all religious communities encourage their young people, formally or informally, to marry someone of their own faith. Moreover, most worshippers believe that it is wiser to marry someone who belongs to their group. For example, in his classic study on the role of religion, Lenski (1963:54) found that 92 percent of the Jews, 81 percent of the Catholics, and 75 percent of the Protestants in his sample supported **religious endogamy** or marrying a person who belongs to one's religious community. Furthermore, 85 percent of white Protestants and Catholics reported that they and their spouses belonged to the same major faith. Yet, a closer examination of marriage partner backgrounds revealed that only 68 percent were reared in the same faith. Obviously, a sizable number had converted to another faith when they married. Following this line of analysis, Lenski (1963:55) further discovered a stronger probability now than previously that one partner in a **religiously mixed marriage** will convert to the religious affiliation of his or her spouse. Thus, the actual rate of intermarriage is not clear if we examine only the present religious homogamy of couples.

Efforts by religious leaders to prevent intermarriage have grown less effective over the last several decades (Yinger, 1970:240–41, 494–5, 504). More and more young people are willing to marry across religious lines, a pattern no doubt created in part by the cultural assimilation of immigrant ethnic groups into the mainstream of American life (Gordon, 1964). However, not all religious groups intermarry at the same rate. Catholics are most likely to enter an interfaith marriage, followed by Protestants, and then Jews (Alston, *et al.*, 1976:262). Moreover, as one might expect, religiously mixed couples attend church less often than homogamous couples. A possible explanation is that couples in mixed marriages reduce the strain of having different religious views by curtailing church attendance.

All the major religious communities in America regard marriage as a permanent commitment. However, they tolerate varying degrees of permissiveness toward divorce. The Roman Catholic Church opposes divorce most strongly, while Protestants and Jews reluctantly concede that sometimes spouses cannot fulfill their original intention to establish a union "until death do us part." Meanwhile, the data have consistently revealed that people who do identify with Protestant, Catholic, or Jewish communities do have notably lower divorce rates than those who do not (Moberg, 1962:363; Salisbury, 1964:424; Wilson, 1978:252). But no clear pattern suggesting "proneness to divorce" exists for the major religious communities, except that Jews generally have a much lower divorce rate than either Protestants or Catholics. Thus, the stern Catholic Church opposition to divorce apparently does not result in a much lower Catholic divorce rate.

On the other hand, religious affiliation clearly is related to fertility and family size. The historical stance of the Catholic Church is that procreation is a primary reason for marriage. Accordingly, not only do Catholics have higher fertility rates than Protestants and Jews, but devout Catholics also have considerably higher birth rates than less committed Catholics (Scanzoni, 1975:87). Jewish couples have had the lowest birth rates and smallest families among American religious communities for some decades (Sklare, 1971:40–44, 79–85). Some social scientists contend that this results from Jewish minority status while others believe the cause is the Jewish drive for upward social mobility. Neither interpretation is entirely convincing. Protestant fertility rates, both historically and currently, fall between the Catholic and Jewish levels.

One decisive influence on fertility rates is a religious group's attitude toward contraception and abortion. The official Catholic position holds that artifical means of birth control are immoral. Abstinence and the rhythm method are the only allowable birth-control practices. In fact, however, Catholic couples use birth-control measures almost as readily as the statistically average American (Wakin and Scheuer, 1966:46–51). Church teaching seems to have limited birth-control methods among Catholics to the less reliable ones. The "pill" is not, for example, as favorably regarded as less successful means, and thus many Catholic couples exceed their desired family size (Bouvier, 1972:520–21).

Roman Catholics also have been among the most articulate spokesmen against abortion. The "right to life" campaign, however, has long been a position approved by many conservative and fundamentalists Protestants as well (Peterson and Mauss, 1976). Indeed, one study (Hartel, *et al.*, 1974:32) concluded that not only conservative Christians, but also liberals who attended church frequently tended to disapprove of abortion. A later investigation using a nationwide sample came to a different conclusion (Ebaugh and Haney,

1978:407–13). The data, in this instance, indicated that members of liberal denominations who frequently attended church also remained quite a bit more liberal in their attitudes toward abortion than conservative Christians. Two conclusions seem suitable. Religion does profoundly influence attitudes toward abortion, and Catholic as well as conservative Protestant groups oppose abortion more strongly than other more liberal religious bodies.

A long tradition of research indicates that religious participation and marital happiness, success, and adjustment correlate closely. Several earlier studies were unable to confirm that religious affiliation itself caused marital success. The possibility was left open that both religiousness and marital adjustment were the result of a "conventionalized" style of life which led to religious and marital well-being. But in a recent investigation, Hunt and King (1978) controlled for exactly this possibility and they found that religious participation did, indeed, correlate positively with greater satisfaction, happiness, and adjustment in marriage. Thus, the "hunch" of the earlier pieces of research was finally demonstrated. William D'Antonio (1980: 100–03) has suggested why religious affiliation should exert this sort of influence on married life. After surveying some 60 texts on the sociology of marriage and the family, he discovered that none mentioned an obvious, yet important fact about religion and the family: religious organizations universally teach the need that love prevail in family relationships. Because couples today view love and companionship as the primary basis of their marriage, the stress on love by religious groups can be expected to nurture both marital happiness and family solidarity.

The Family and the School

In a technological society, such as the one in the United States today, the family can no longer impart to its youth the type of social training and skills necessary for their success in our social order (Sexton, 1967:1–8). The resulting need for formal education outside the family has caused a massive expansion of the school's role and a longer period of time in which young people prepare to play occupational and social roles. Moreover, the educational process took on a wide range of goals in this century, including instruction in the basic cognitive skills of writing, reading, and simple arithmetic, which are essential to full participation in a modern, industrialized society; instruction in specific subjects—the sciences, business, vocational courses—which will help students to decide whether to seek further preparation for a particular occupation; the instilling of attitudes which will help the student become a more active and well-adjusted citizen with a respect for law and the national culture; and the provision for physical and psychological help through such programs as health clinics, counseling services, and physical education (Armor, 1972:171). Thus, the school now teaches many skills once acquired in the home. However, the loss of family functions to the school has not put

A Season for Family Interaction with the Wider Society

home life outside the educational process. On the contrary, a vital link still connects the two institutions of family and school.

The Family and School as Socializing Agencies

The socialization process begins in the home under the supervision of parents. Since we discussed that process extensively in Chapter 10, we need say little more except to highlight the importance of socialization at school and its relationship to family life. When a child enters school, it is usually the first formal institution beyond the family—with the possible exception of the religious institution—in which the child takes part. Immediately, the child is swept into a number of new social relationships and roles which differ sharply from those prevailing in the family (Clark, 1962; Goslin, 1965). School is more impersonal, more structured, and one must quickly learn how to respond to the expectations of teachers and schoolmates. By presenting the child with a new set of loyalties and social involvements, the school helps a great deal to lessen the child's emotional dependence on his or her family (Elkin and Handel, 1972:111). New ties formed at school help the child to move from a relatively closed circle of kinship relationships into a broader involvement with others in the world outside the home.

The Influence of the Family on School Achievement

Education cannot be carried on by the school alone. Family and community support is essential for individual scholastic achievement. Indeed, we are only beginning to understand the full effect that family background has on academic performance. One major breakthrough was the research led by James Coleman (1966) on the equality of educational opportunity. This survey, which was undertaken to fulfill a provision of the Civil Rights Act of 1964, was a massive study of the American educational system. The investigation focussed not only on educational factors, such as per-pupil costs, the quality of facilities, teacher training, and experience for certain school systems, but also on the actual academic achievement of students who attended these schools.

Two major findings of the Coleman report are of particular interest to us. The first is that the facilities of mostly black schools are not especially inferior. This discovery surprised many social scientists and citizens who shared the popular view that blacks were largely taught in substandard schools. The second finding was in many ways more startling. Coleman found that the school staff and educational facilities did not have a major effect on achievement. Far more important was family background, over which the school had little control and for which it could not really compensate.

The Coleman Report created almost instant controversy. Both his methods and his findings have been subjected to widespread scrutiny and criticism. For the most part, the findings have held up rather well. One careful reappraisal undertaken by David Armor did more than simply confirm the essential soundness of Coleman's conclusions. He (1972:225) also proceeded to draw out several policy implications, one of which merits being quoted at length:

> One clear implication is that government programs concerned with improving academic performance of blacks or other minority groups should give as much attention, if not more, to the environment—both family and neighborhood—in which the minority child lives. There does not seem to be any way for blacks to catch up with whites if family factors are ignored. Also, if school programs are to be initiated, they will probably be more effective as they approach the younger, preschool ages. Since blacks are just about as disadvantaged in the 1st as in later grades, and since they do not seem to be able to overcome this disadvantage, it is clear that special programs will have to concentrate on the early years, possibly even the infancy period.

For our purposes, the most significant insight of the original Coleman Report and the research it prompted is the importance which these investigations gave to family life in promoting academic achievement. Before a child enters school, the family provides the cultural background and skill preparation upon which the school can then build through its academic program. If preschool training is culturally disadvantaged, then the school can produce less by way of scholastic achievement. Furthermore, once a young person enters school, the home is an important force urging that student to do his or her best. This is not to suggest that, if students fail, it is their parents' fault. Rather, we merely are suggesting that the school, like the economy in a previous section, cannot control the quality of the students sent to it. The family, then, is a critical institution for preparing youth to use the opportunities afforded by the school.

The Family and the Value System

The family is a value-carrying institution. It is the smallest social unit responsible for overseeing the internalization of value standards. Values are general orienting principles, and therefore they are more basic guidelines than the specific patterns of behavior which are the object of community interest. Accordingly, the family relates to the society's value system by accepting the standards of the value system. Thus, the value system furnishes the standards by which patterns of behavior are judged as proper or desirable. For example, the American norms for family relations legitimate the practices of treating in-laws as the equals of blood relations and treating offspring without favoritism because of sex or order of birth. Both of these normative rules spring from our society's commitment to the value called equality.

In the second set of exchanges, meanwhile, the value system gives approval and the family responds with conformity. This underscores the fact that not only does the value system set standards, but there are also social rewards for those who conform to them. As a general rule, values are internalized so that family members feel either guilt or esteem whenever they measure their behavior against the values of the larger society. Usually, no external agency is necessary to interpret whether family members' patterns of conduct are really acceptable. But alongside these internal judgments, the community often stands as an external source of reinforcement. Together, these internal and external judgments give family members an adequate understanding of the degree of approval due them on the basis of their society's value system.

The Family and Civic Responsibility

Most Americans are well aware that the family meets many individual needs—such as those for companionship, sexual gratification, love between spouses, and the need for child socialization and material support. Yet, it is less commonly recognized that the family plays a vital role in determining the quality of our society. Indeed, the importance of the family to the proper working of all other institutions of social life is so obvious that it often is overlooked. In an uncritical fashion, political and religious leaders frequently reaffirm the commonly held view that a strong family institution is crucial to our societal order. But rarely do they explain why this is true. The answer goes beyond the family's task of replenishing the ranks of society through procreation. Far more important is the role of the family in producing quality members of society. As we have seen in this chapter, the level of productivity achieved in the economy, the loyalty extended to the government, the commitment to religious organizations, and the success of the educational institution, all depend on the quality of the people supplied to these social institutions by the family. If the family fails to train, socialize, and motivate its members adequately, the other institutions can do little to overcome these shortcomings.

This should not be taken to mean, of course, that the family is the only basic social institution. Without a viable economy or government, a society also would not work smoothly. Instead, the point is somewhat more modest. We need to be aware that, behind its obligations to individuals and their well-being, the family also is allocated a unique set of tasks and duties to discharge for society. Moreover, the civic responsibilities entrusted to the family as a social group bear directly on the ability of other institutions to perform their tasks within the wider social order. Thus, when social scientists speak about the isolated nuclear family as the norm for the modern world, when individual self-fulfillment is held forth as a leading family goal, we also should recognize that the isolation and individual orientation have not eliminated the family's specialized task of socially orienting its members. In short, the family and its wider community involvements are relationships of mutual interdependence.

Summary The family does not exist in isolation from the other institutional structures of society. It is linked to the community and the wider social order through a number of critical interchanges. In this chapter, we examine the interaction of the family with the economy, the government, the local community, the religious institution, the school, and the societal value system. In each instance, our focus is centered on both what was done for the family and what the family does for the other institutions.

The relation of the economy to the family is discussed on two levels. A brief consideration of internal money management of nuclear families precedes a consideration of the major link between the family and the economy: The family, for example, provides workers to the economy, and receives wages. In turn, family assets are invested in the economy, and the family buys goods and services.

The government provides leadership in return for family loyalty, and political decisions for family compliance with government rules. The community gives support and identity to the family in return for group participation and family adherence to community norms. The religious institution provides religious instruction and socialization for family members, while the family responds by motivating its members to maintain their affiliation with that particular religious organization. The school transmits a broader range of cultural knowledge to youth than the family could possibly provide, and the family prepares its young people—to the best of its ability—to assimilate the academic knowledge presented by the schools. The value system of the wider society supplies the family with an ultimate set of evaluative standards and bestows approval on families which accept and conform to its values.

Identifying the patterns of interaction between the family and other community institutions helps underscore the mutual dependency of the family and other social structures in community life. This shows that the family has not, as some argue, withdrawn from social involvements to serve primarily its own individual needs. Instead, the isolated nuclear family of modern life has developed specialized social functions. The family continues to enjoy—and perform—roles and responsibilities of a strictly social nature.

STUDY QUESTIONS

1. What are the activities that the nuclear family performs for the economy which the economy cannot perform for itself?
2. American society has long been described as an achievement-oriented social order. What are the positive and negative ramifications of this achievement orientation on the American family?
3. How is family identity shaped by its participation in community affairs, and what are the typical forms of community support a family can expect by virtue of its participation in community life?
4. In what ways can a group such as the family exert its influence on and benefit from the political institution?
5. How does a family's social background affect school performance for youngsters, and how effectively can the school compensate for patterns of disorganization in the family and community?
6. What is the civic responsibility which nuclear families are called upon to discharge? How do families influence the quality of our social life?

Ethnic and Social Class Variations in Family Life

14

Up to this point, we have used the phrase, "the American family," as short-hand for the dominant, middle-class family. If a white-collar job is the sign of middle-class status, then more than 50 percent of American families are in the middle class. The United States is, however, a nation of immigrants. We live in a pluralistic society composed of many ethnic, racial, religious, and social-class groups. Patterns of family life vary a great deal among these groups. In other words, ethnic and class groups show their individuality through their different family organizations, beliefs, customs, and behavior patterns. Moreover, each subgroup tends to bring to the contemporary scene dissimilar social histories and cultural traditions which reflect their social experience or national origin.

This chapter explores the family patterns represented in several important American ethnic and social-class groups. Our discussion had to be somewhat selective. Each group was chosen on the basis of its historical or contemporary prominence in American life, and its contrast to the dominant pattern of the middle-class family. The family types we describe are the immigrant family of the 1800s and early 1900s, the black family, the Jewish family, and the Spanish-American family. In examining family life by social class, we shall consider the family of poverty, the working-class family, and the white-collar family.

Before going further, a few general remarks and basic definitions may help put the subject matter in perspective. The nature of the role which ethnic groups have played historically in American life and which they play today is highly debatable (Gordon, 1964; Newman, 1973). Social scientists have put forth a variety of theories to explain the **assimilation** processes by which ethnic groups were taken into the dominant culture and the reasons why they remain distinct social groups. We will try to avoid unnecessary complications in this social analysis, but we should recognize that this matter is still fiercely debated by scholars. Glazer and Moynihan (1970:16) probably speak for many social scientists when they suggest that the ethnic group in American society today is not a remnant from the age of mass immigration, but a wholly new social form.

In this connection, a clear definition of an **ethnic group** will be useful. An ethnic group may be defined as a population socially identified according to cultural criteria, such as language, religion, or national origin. Ethnic identity may be either imposed on a group by a dominant culture or created by persons who see themselves as a distinct cultural group with a common heritage. For example, many peasant immigrants who came to America identified only with their village, and not with their nation of origin. Only in American society did they recognize themselves as Italian, Greek, Hungarian, or Swedish (Herberg, 1960:12–4). Dominant American culture had imposed upon these immigrants an identification with a national-language group. At first, the ethnic identity had little meaning for many peasants, and only gradually did they come to see themselves in the social category to which the dominant culture assigned them.

Today, of course, the situation is quite different. Most ethnics take considerable pride in their national heritage and identify with their country of origin voluntarily. Indeed, Americans feel strong social pressure to take on an ethnic

A Season for Family Interaction with the Wider Society

identity because we are an immigrant nation. There is no such category as "just American." We are all Native American, or white Anglo-Saxon, Protestant American (WASP, for short), Irish American, black American, German American, Polish American, Italian American, Japanese American, and so forth. Our ethnic heritage, therefore, is a crucial way in which we acknowledge our "Americanness."

Only among certain ethnic groups today does the traditional Old-World family persist. The large waves of immigrants who flooded into American society before 1924 have now been almost fully assimilated, and their cultural traditions, including family structures and processes, have been transformed to conform to the prevailing norms of American life. Our discussion will open with a description of the classic family type among the early immigrants, then examine changes in family life prompted by the assimilation process, and conclude with an assessment of some of the lingering heritage of immigrant family patterns among contemporary ethnic groups.

The Immigrant Family of the Nineteenth and Early Twentieth Centuries

Before 1820, most immigrants to the new American nation were English, Dutch, French, or Scandinavian. The century between 1820 and the early 1920s was the period of greatest influx. More than 33 million persons entered American society before immigration was sharply cut back in 1924 (Ward, 1971:52–3). Historians and social scientists distinguish between two distinct periods of immigrant expansion. The **"old immigrants"** arrived between 1820 and 1880, and were largely from the United Kingdom, Canada, and northern Europe. The **"new immigrants,"** who entered American society between 1880 and 1920, included poorer and culturally less sophisticated newcomers primarily from southern and eastern Europe (Handlin, 1957:75). Although the old immigrants were subjected to a generous amount of prejudice and discrimination—such as the shopkeepers' signs in Boston which advertised, "Help wanted, no Irish need apply"—the immigrants entering after 1880 were considered far less desirable by the native population. They were seen as much more difficult to "Americanize" because of their peasant status, language barriers, and cultural differences, especially since the new immigrants included large numbers of Catholics and Jews. Indeed, it was the established Americans' fear of the foreign-born element which led to the restrictive legislation that in 1924 closed our borders to "the tired, the poor, the huddled masses yearning to breathe free."

Family Patterns among the "Old Immigrants"

Of the four major ethnic groups that make up the bulk of the "old immigrants," the English had family patterns most similar to those already estab-

Figure 14-1
The arrival of an Ital-
ian mother and her
three children at Ellis
Island in New York
marked the start of a
new life in America.
Immigrants such as
these confronted enor-
mous hardships along
with their new oppor-
tunities. (The Bettman
Archives, Inc.)

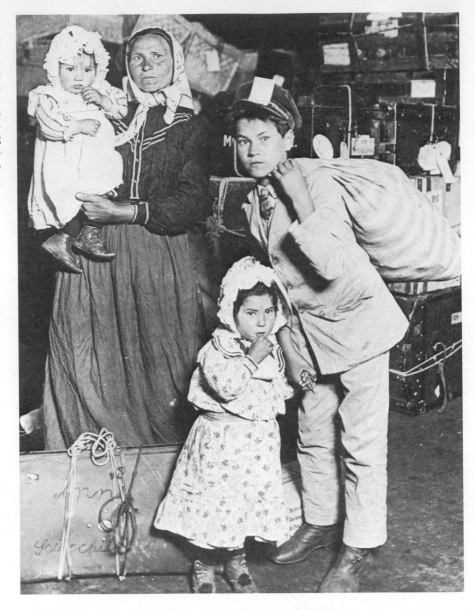

lished in America. Many of the English were poor yeoman farmers, artisans, or proprietors of small businesses. The native population in the New World did not see them as troublesome. Along with the English came the Scots and Scots-Irish. The Highlander Scots and Scots-Irish were more distant from the cultural center than the Scottish Lowlanders and the English. Hence, the Highlanders and Scots-Irish took longer to assimilate fully into American life. They quickly swept across the Allegheny Mountains into western Pennsylvania, and many finally settled in the hill country of the Appalachian range (Boorstin, 1958:67). A major pillar of Scots-Irish identity was commitment to

A Season for Family Interaction with the Wider Society

their "clan," basically an extended family network which kept alive cultural, social, and religious (Protestant) loyalties (Anderson, 1970:33–42). Even today in the back country of the Appalachian hills, one still hears references to "my clan" as a designation for blood relatives. For some, it is still a rallying point for personal identity and the source of fierce loyalty.

The Irish settlers who came to the New World in massive numbers during the early nineteenth century were largely driven from their homeland by poverty and the great potato famine of the 1840s (Robertson, 1960:407–11). Many who left Ireland were single men and women. Their intention was to work in American society and send home money so the rest of their families could join them. The more fortunate Irish sailed together as whole families, though often one or more members died en route. Most immigrants could afford only the most uncomfortable accommodations on leaky lumber ships. Housed three or four decks below the main deck in windowless, cramped, and poorly ventilated quarters, fed poor food, and limited in medical services, "ship fever" (typhus) quickly decimated immigrant ranks and brought many more ashore weak and with permanently injured health. Often between the 1820s and 1860s, 20 to 50 percent of the steerage passengers coming from Ireland were lost to disease during the voyage (Feldstein and Costello, 1974:24–8). Those who survived the ordeal found a harsh environment awaiting them. Although most of the Irish were peasant-farmers, the majority settled in the urban areas along the East Coast (Ward, 1971:55–6). They had low-paying jobs, poor housing, and few social services. At first, the Irish immigrant community achieved integration primarily through their sense of commitment to the family and religion (Greeley, 1972b). Extended family relations generally were severed by the move to the New World. When nuclear families encountered crises which they could not handle on their own, their church was often the first—and frequently the only—source of aid (Ahlstrom, 1972:540–43). Moreover, the rapid growth of the Irish-Catholic population triggered a vigorous "**Protestant Crusade**" by nativist Americans against the Roman Catholic minority, culminating in the formation of the "**Know-Nothing**" **political party** prior to the Civil War (Billington, 1964). But an immediate result of the outpouring of nativist hostility was to increase Irish attachment to family and church, and somewhat later, to spark their interest in ethnic politics.

The situation of German immigrants in the United States was much different. Political unrest rather than poverty encouraged many Germans to come to America (Feldstein and Costello, 1974:10–14). The average German immigrant had much greater financial resources than the Irish. Consequently, many could afford to travel far beyond their port of entry and buy land in the Midwest. By 1850, 48 percent of all German immigrants lived in the north-central states (Ward, 1971:64). Some German Catholic communities immigrated as a unit, bringing with them their parish priest and even the paintings from the walls of their church (Cogley, 1974:44–5). Protestant Germans tended to leave their homeland as single families, but they generally settled in German communities in the New World where they could maintain traditional life-styles. For the most part, German family life retained the patriarchal structure of the homeland. Only gradually did Americanization erode the father's authoritarian role and promote a more egalitarian pattern consistent with U.S. cultural norms.

Scandinavian immigrants, especially the Swedes and the Norwegians, behaved much like the Germans. In large numbers, they settled in homogenous communities in the northern Midwest (Anderson, 1970:43–78). Mainly Lutheran farmers, they preserved much of their cultural identity for a long while, even though they met enormous hardships on the frontier. The Swedish and Norwegian newcomers tried to confine their primary group life to their own ethnic communities. Especially during the late nineteenth and early twentieth centuries, almost 70 percent of the young people from these two ethnic groups married someone of their own national background (Anderson, 1970:51–5, 67–9). These patterns tended to be self-imposed, however, since Scandinavian Americans generally have not been subjected to the harsh discrimination faced by other ethnic groups. In large part, their treatment can be explained by noting that the Scandinavians shared many values with American society, maintained strong family-ethnic ties, worked hard, adhered to a Protestant religious tradition, followed a highly civil life-style which posed no threat to public order, and remained for many years in relatively self-contained ethnic communities.

Family Patterns among the "New Immigrants"

The American Civil War drastically cut back the influx of immigrants. Foreigners are less attracted to a society split by an internal war. When peace returned, immigrants began to be admitted in much larger numbers than before to provide the manpower needed by our emerging industrial society. Moreover, the new surge of immigrants brought peoples from different regions of the Old World. After 1880, Irish and German newcomers gradually were replaced by immigrants from southern and eastern Europe, including Italians, Poles, Greeks, Russians, Hungarians, and members of several Slavic groups (Ward, 1971:53–7). The native population saw these folk as drawn from peasant ranks, more illiterate, less skilled, and both culturally and religiously incompatible with the dominant social norms of American life (Handlin, 1957:75–110). These assumptions, often shared by high government officials, gradually led to a series of actions designed to reduce immigration. The most dramatic step was the National Origins Quota Act of 1924 which set an annual allotment of 127,000 for immigrants from western and northern Europe and only 24,000 from eastern and southern Europe (Newman, 1973:62). These restrictions were justified by a lengthy report of the Dillingham Commission of 1907 which used then current social theories and statistics—information that by today's standards is biased and misguided—to demonstrate that the "new immigrants" were undesirable.

The family structure of the new immigrants will be discussed collectively, except for the Jewish family which we will examine later in this chapter under a separate heading. Most new immigrants came from peasant, village backgrounds and settled in urban, industrialized areas in the United States. Thus, while they had different languages and national traditions, the majority of new immigrants followed the same pattern of fleeing from rural poverty and un-employment and entering a vastly different world of industrialized, city life. They soon discovered that the traditional order of peasant family life could not be sustained in their new environment. The resulting assimilation had its effects on the family.

The Patriarchal Pattern of Peasant Family Traditions   Social scientists commonly describe the new immigrants' family structure as patriarchal (Blood and Wolfe, 1965:24–5; Lopreato, 1970:57–74). But this term needs to be qualified carefully. Although fathers enjoyed considerable privileges in most peasant households, they did not possess the full decision-making power of a patriarch. Family governance in the Old World village was determined largely by the needs of the nuclear group and limited by the pressures from the extended family, in-law families, and the community at large. Consequently, parents enjoyed more respect than formal power. Lopreato (1970:58–9) describes the situation for most new immigrants accurately when he suggests that for the Italians the patriarchal pattern was more fiction than fact. A woman readily acknowledged her husband as head of the household, but she also had a firm voice in family decisions, in the rearing of children, in the maintenance of social relations, and in controlling the relations between father and children.

In the New World, however, the peasant community's support for the myth of patriarchal power was thoroughly undercut. While ethnic ghettos in the cities protected and kept alive some Old World cultural traditions, the unquestioned authority of the father was diminished within the more equalitarian and increasingly child-centered culture of American society. The children of the new immigrants quickly learned to love their father, but not to fear him. When the time came to choose a mate, the offspring of immigrant parents were clearly unwilling to have this choice made for them, even though they still valued parental consent highly (Lopreato, 1970:63). Yet, the weakening of parental authority, especially the father's, was but one of many changes the families of the new immigrants would experience in the urban culture of the New World.

The Split between Generations   In almost all societies, parents are responsible for introducing their children to the language, norms, and customs of their culture. For immigrants, however, this normal state of affairs very often is reversed. To give some continuity to their lives, parents tend to cling to their old language and cultural traditions in the new environment. By contrast, their children adapt more swiftly to the new culture because it is thrust upon them in the streets and the classroom (Herberg, 1960:16–9). Immigrant youth often emerged as culturally more sophisticated and knowledgeable than their parents. Elders frequently depended on their children to translate messages sent to them in English or to explain subjects their sons and daughters had studied in school. In this way, the proper relation between the generations was reversed; the parental leaders became the "led" (Handlin, 1951:252–5).

The most difficult generational tensions arose between maturing second-generation youth and their immigrant parents. The children knew they were more attuned than their parents to the dominant themes of the new society. So even well-intentioned parental advice and direction often fell on deaf ears. Perhaps worse, parents were frequently an embarrassment to their children, a reminder of the family's foreignness and their outsider status in American life. To gain acceptance and achieve upward social mobility in the wider social order, many young people felt they had to break off relations with their parents, the old ethnic neighborhood, and all those cultural trappings which identified them with their ethnic heritage. The loss of their children in so thorough a sense was a bitter experience for immigrant parents who nonetheless wanted the best for their sons and daughters. Of course, not all second-generation youth shed their ethnic identity. Those who did not often played a critical mediating role by bridging the cultural gulf between their parents at home and the social life of society at large. But in many respects the tension between these two cultural worlds was harder on the members of the second generation.

The Movement toward Full Assimilation Many in the second generation felt trapped in a "no-man's land." They could not, or would not, identify with the ethnic culture of their parents, but neither could they fully and easily take part in the social life of their new country, for they still bore the mark of a foreigner. But their children, the third generation, enjoyed the fruits of their tribulations. To be perfectly accurate, it was the actions of the second generation which made the world seem brighter to their offspring. By and large, the second generation broke ties with the old ethnic background. They moved out of the ethnic ghetto in large numbers, ceased speaking the Old World language, adopted American foods, dress, and customs, moved into better-paying and higher-status jobs, formed primary group relations in the wider society's cliques and institutions, and sometimes even Americanized their names to erase the mark of ethnicity (Herberg, 1960:18–36). Thus, the second generation set in motion the processes of assimilation on two levels. On the behavioral level, they absorbed the American cultural life-style; and on the structural level, they penetrated into the community organizations and institutional structures of civic life (Gordon, 1978:203).

The gains in upward mobility and social acceptance placed the third generation in an odd position. While the second generation tried to forget their ethnic roots, the third generation wanted to remember them. Since the third generation was born and socialized in America, they no longer felt the intense inferiority of the immigrants and their children. The third generation was not interested in giving up American culture by returning to their forefathers' traditions, but they were searching for their "place" in contemporary culture, a place defined in part by their ethnic heritage. Thus, full assimilation into American life is not necessarily marked by a waning of ethnic-group identification. Indeed, for many descendants of America's new—and old—immigrants, full assimilation is marked partly by a renewed attachment to their ethnic identity. They see that identity as a way to define who they are, reinforcing such identity symbols as occupation, religion, race, political party affiliation, and class standing.

Several conclusions may be drawn from this brief survey of the social experience of immigrant families. The first is that family life underwent tremendous strains as the newcomers went through the trauma of coping with different economic, social, cultural, and housing conditions. The old structural patterns of rural peasant family life that had developed over the centuries did not fit the social environment of America. Since children usually assimilated faster than their elders, a split between the generations commonly emerged, producing varying degrees of conflict and misunderstanding. By the second generation, the structural patterns of immigrant descendants generally had embraced the nuclear model and personal mate selection was the preferred arrangement. The crucial role of the family in personal identity was to link a person to his or her ethnic heritage. Family lineage can locate one in the present, because it provides a vital connection to the rich heritage of one's past. Perhaps this is why we have been experiencing a "rediscovery of ethnicity" (TeSelle, 1973), or perhaps ethnic communities never lost the loyalty of many of the descendants of immigrants. At any rate, for the immediate future, ethnic subcultures will continue to flourish as strategic points that symbolize the social interests, mobilize the political action, and frame the cultural identities of the various national groups that have entered into the mainstream of American life (Glazer and Moynihan, 1970). In all of this, of course, the family remains the crucial institution, for the family carries the ethnic-group identity.

The Black Family in America

The social experience of black Americans is unique in American life. Black American history has become a much-debated field of interpretation over the last two decades. At the center of this controversy is the nature of the black family, both in slavery and in freedom. The issues at stake in this scholarly debate are far too complex and important for us to attempt an easy resolution. Accordingly, our discussion will present the view which prevailed until the last decade, and then indicate where recent scholarship has introduced critical questions about that view.

The Impact of Slavery on the Black Family

Black Americans were introduced into this society one year before the Pilgrims landed at Plymouth Rock in 1620 (Pinkney, 1969:1). These blacks were slaves, and with them the "peculiar institution" of slavery was introduced into American life. The orthodox view of American slavery is best described by Daniel Patrick Moynihan in his famous report, "The Negro Family in America." He (Rainwater and Yancey, 1967:61) claimed that slavery in the United States was the worst form of bondage ever known. Nowhere else did the slavery system deny the slave's very humanity. Where the tradition of Catholicism prevailed, slaves did receive a series of rights and protections, as they did, for example, in Brazil. The United States, however, was founded on English Common Law and Protestant theological principles, both of which had never known slavery, and they consequently had no provisions for how human bondage should be regulated. In the absence of safeguards, slaves were swiftly reduced to the status of **chattel**—that is, property without any basic rights as human beings.

For families, the effects of this point of view were profound and devastating. It meant, above all else, that slaveholders could split up families at will. Children of any age could be sold to another plantation and husbands and wives could be separated according to the whims of the white master. Indeed, technically speaking, since slaves could not enter into binding contract agreements, their marriages actually were not recognized by law (Frazier, 1966).

The fragile character of slave marriages, the freedom of masters to sell

Figure 14-2
In recent years, historians and social scientists have begun to revise the traditional interpretation of family life among slaves, such as those pictured here. Apparently black families in slavery were far more stable than was previously believed. *(Photo Researchers, Inc.)*

A Season for Family Interaction with the Wider Society

spouses to separate buyers, and the nonlegal status of slave unions, all undermined the black husband's role. In the white culture, the male leader of the family was expected to protect his wife and children; the black slave husband was denied this function. The master took over the role of protector, and in the process the black father's image during slavery was greatly weakened (Genovese, 1976:492–4). From this fact, according to Frazier (1966:33–49), flowed the matriarchal black family that was common in the black experience in America. Unable to play the traditional role, the father often lost interest in his family, and sometimes he deserted or was forced to leave them, so that they had to fend for themselves. Thus, the family life of black Americans under slavery frequently took place in a female-dominated household.

The Free Black Family after the Civil War

For most black families, the Emancipation Proclamation of 1863 brought the appearance of liberty rather than actual freedom. Indeed, the free status of blacks in the South was soon degraded into another type of economic bondage (Clark, 1968:57–60). In place of slavery, the sharecropper-tenancy system arose, a system which eventually was little more than legal slavery.

Not only did the **sharecropper-tenancy system** exploit blacks economically, but it also psychologically crippled them, especially the males (Rainwater and Yancey, 1967:62–4). Very much as they were under the slavery system, black fathers again became entrapped by a tangled web of social relations in which they could not provide adequately for their families or protect their wives and children from the abuse of the white landowners. The result was to reinforce the old sense of inferiority and black powerlessness that began under slavery (Bernard, 1966:73–7).

The closed social system of post-Civil War segregation in the South imposed a highly specific role pattern on black men which Stanley Elkins (1968:115–39) has described as the "Sambo" model. Of course, black males did not willingly accept this role as the norm for their race, but through the alternating use of terror and force, the image was nonetheless imposed on many of them. The specific traits of the "Sambo" image were docility, obedience, faithfulness, humility, cheerfulness, and similar childlike characteristics. Moreover, it also was assumed, without actually being taught, that blacks were basically lazy, irresponsible, playful, silly, in need of supervision to work diligently; they were thought to love to dance and sing, and it was believed that lying and stealing came easily to them.

Once black males were socialized into this role image, Elkins concluded, the Sambo character traits were an important means of social control. Clearly, the most damaging injury inflicted on black fathers and their sons was to convince them of their own powerlessness and innate inferiority. Recovery from that sort of psychological wound—the ability to assert "Black is beautiful"—has not only taken several generations, but it also has aroused an understandable bitterness. The realization that the mark of the Sambo image imposed on black males was wholly a product of racial discrimination and that the suffering it caused black families was deliberate and unnecessary cannot help but create profound resentment, not only on the part of black Americans but white as well.

The Emergence of the Black Bourgeoisie

Not all blacks succumbed to, or were forced into, the Sambo image. Even before the Civil War, a number of freed blacks established a stable family life and carved out careers for themselves in the South, especially in the cities (Genovese, 1976:398–413). In this century, a growing segment of the black population has risen above the masses and achieved fame, wealth, and a considerable degree of "social security." E. Franklin Frazier was the first to study this new class of affluent blacks in some depth. He (1957; 1966:190–205) described them as the "black Puritans" or the **"black bourgeoisie."** Frazier found much to praise, and criticize, in this group's behavior.

Most members of the black bourgeoisie had worked hard to overcome the drawback of race. They had made the most of meager opportunities, and by sheer determination—and perhaps more luck than some would admit—they had managed to achieve economic or educational success. To preserve their gains and pass them on to their children, family life was strict. Parents insisted on high moral standards, which were one cause of their success and a symbol of their achievement. This behavior won them Frazier's label the "black Puritans." The distressing feature of the black bourgeoisie's life-style was their self-conscious social isolation from lower-status members of the black community. Their basic motive Frazier identifies as a fear of jeopardizing their own status position by being associated with a disfavored social group.

The Urbanization of Black Americans

Billingsley (1968:72–3) remarks that a little over a century ago 90 percent of black Americans lived in the rural South. Now only 20 percent reside there, while almost 30 percent live in the urban South, and the remaining 50 percent live in the urban North and West. The migration of blacks from the rural South to the industrialized North was one of the largest population movements in U.S. history.

First Frazier (1966) and then Moynihan (Rainwater and Yancey, 1967) argued that urbanization, especially in the North, devastated the black family. The matriarchal pattern established in slavery grew stronger under the economic and social conditions prevailing in the city ghettos. For example, black women tended to find employment more readily than black men. This was due, in part, to the demand for domestic help and black women's generally higher levels of education (Rainwater and Yancey, 1967:65–73). As a result, black males found it hard to assume the traditional breadwinner role.

Indeed, many black families developed what Moynihan described as a "tangle of pathology." Because black men had little education and few skills, they could not find adequate employment to support their families. Frustrated and demoralized, many deserted their families, which almost immedi-

TABLE 14.1
Marital Status of the Black Population: 1960 to 1978

Sex and Year	Number of Persons (1,000)					Percent Distribution				
	Total	Single	Married	Widowed	Divorced		Single	Married	Widowed	Divorced
MALE										
1960	5,713	1,692	3,619	264	139	100.0	29.6	63.3	4.6	2.4
1965	6,211	1,980	3,795	245	191	100.0	31.9	61.1	3.9	3.1
1970	5,898	1,435	3,944	307	212	100.0	24.3	66.9	5.2	3.6
1973	6,115	1,699	3,829	335	252	100.0	27.8	62.6	5.5	4.1
1974	6,284	1,712	3,959	308	305	100.0	27.2	63.0	4.9	4.9
1975	6,368	1,733	3,990	319	327	100.0	27.2	62.7	5.0	5.1
1976	6,560	1,861	4,042	271	386	100.0	28.4	61.6	4.1	5.9
1977	6,756	2,039	4,024	327	367	100.0	30.2	59.6	4.8	5.4
1978	6,894	2,160	3,970	285	478	100.0	31.3	57.6	4.1	6.9
FEMALE										
1960	6,375	1,386	3,842	910	237	100.0	21.7	60.3	14.3	3.7
1965	7,062	1,621	4,201	949	291	100.0	23.0	59.5	13.4	4.1
1970	7,074	1,233	4,366	1,120	355	100.0	17.4	61.7	15.8	5.0
1973	7,514	1,522	4,295	1,210	486	100.0	20.3	57.2	16.1	6.5
1974	7,702	1,556	4,429	1,209	508	100.0	20.2	57.5	15.7	6.6
1975	7,894	1,716	4,383	1,202	593	100.0	21.7	55.5	15.2	7.5
1976	8,108	1,882	4,416	1,181	631	100.0	23.2	54.5	14.6	7.8
1977	8,320	1,963	4,452	1,170	734	100.0	23.6	53.5	14.1	8.8
1978	8,520	2,274	4,285	1,166	795	100.0	26.7	50.3	13.7	9.3

[1960 and 1965, persons 14 years old and over; thereafter, 18 and over, 1960 as of April, based on 25-percent sample; other years, as of March, and based on Current Population Survey.]
Source: U.S. Bureau of the Census, *U.S. Census of Population, 1960,* PC(2)1C, *Nonwhite Population by Race;* and *Current Population Reports,* series P–20, No. 338, and earlier issues. Reprinted from: *Statistical Abstracts 1979,* p. 41.

ately qualified the families for welfare aid. Male children growing up in a fatherless home often were deprived of the father's socialization and discipline. They tended to drop out of school after doing poorly and entered the work force with no skills or adequate education. When they married, many encountered unemployment problems similar to their fathers' and repeated their behaviors (Liebow, 1967). Thus, their sons, too, lacked the role model, discipline, and the socializing influence of a father, and the cycle began again.

With this interpretation, Frazier, Moynihan, and a whole succession of other social scientists gave shape to what became the dominant point of view about the plight of black Americans. This interpretation held that, while slavery, racism, segregated housing, minimal education, and a lack of job skills contributed to poverty, the best way to break the tangle of pathology was to address the question of black family structure. If family life could be strengthened and fathers retained, boys would be socialized to acquire the education and job skills they needed to escape from the ranks of poverty and move into stable, middle-class life. Thus, government programs should be designed to increase the stability of the black family so that these Americans could take a full and equal part in the life of the nation.

Counter-Interpretations of the Black Family in America

The "Moynihan Report" triggered a passionate controversy almost overnight, an exchange fully documented by Rainwater and Yancey (1967). The opponents of Moynihan's analysis felt that he was "blaming the victim" rather than isolating the real causes of black inequality (Ryan, 1971:61–85). In other words, blacks were being condemned for family problems caused by racism, poverty, and oppression. Within a relatively short time, a whole series of studies on the black family appeared which sought to set the record straight (Ladner, 1973).

Perhaps the most ambitious historical study was undertaken by Herbert Gutman (1977). He acknowledged that his research was a direct result of the questions raised by Moynihan. Gutman's historical data on slave families, however, convinced him that Frazier, Elkin, and a number of other scholars had mistakenly portrayed the black family as matriarchal. Although slavery was clearly a brutal institution, Gutman discovered that blacks were able to sustain their families against enormous odds and that fathers took a large, important, and persistent role in family affairs. Similarly, his data on Northern blacks up until 1925 showed that they were poor, but steadily employed and that two-parent households accounted for 82 to 92 percent of his sample. Thus, Gutman concluded that Moynihan's historical thesis about the matriarchal pattern of the black family simply was not borne out by the historical facts.

Andrew Billingsley developed a somewhat different line of criticism in his study of the black family. Like many other social scientists, Billingsley faulted Moynihan for not considering seriously enough the factor of social class when he framed his interpretation of the black family. Taking issue with the 1968 Presidential Commission on Civil Disorders' warning, Billingsley argued that the United States is *not* moving toward two societies, one white and one black, separate and unequal. Rather, he said, we have had this sort of society for three centuries. Furthermore, the argument between Moynihan and his critics over whether slavery or current discrimination harmed the black family falsely poses the problem for these, as well as other social factors, block achievement by black families (Billingsley, 1968:195). However, if one considers the social disorganization in white families below the poverty line, one discovers that they are almost identical to those of poor black families. Indeed, what impresses Billingsley is not that 25 percent of black families are headed by women, but that 75 percent meet Moynihan's criteria for stability, despite the racial prejudice, job and housing discrimination, inferior education, and debilitating levels of poverty. Billingsley concludes, therefore, that the black family is not falling apart, nor is it the cause of the difficulties blacks face in white society. The central problem remains racial discrimination which keeps blacks in the run-down neighborhoods, poor schools, and lower-paying jobs. Thus, the elimination of these conditions should be the first national priority. Once that is accomplished, black families can use their own inner strength to achieve the quality of social life they wish to enjoy in American society.

The debate over the black family is far from resolved. The problems many black families encounter are also as pressing today as they were when Moynihan issued his report. The civil rights movement and the legislation that

Figure 14-3
Many black families have overcome numerous social obstacles to become firmly established now within the ranks of the middle class, where they enjoy material comforts as well as a stable family life. *(Monkmeyer Press Photo Service. Mimi Forsyth, photographer.)*

followed have opened up the social structure to allow blacks to take a fuller part in American society. Yet, job discrimination, unfair housing practices, and racial prejudice still persist. The barriers to black families clearly are not fully dismantled. As long as they stand, these barriers do violence to black and white families alike, and to American society as a whole.

The Jewish Family

Jewish immigration to America usually is divided into three distinct waves. The first wave, which occurred during the Colonial period, brought **Sephardic Jews** to the New World. The "Sephardim" were the Jews of Spanish and Portuguese background. They had achieved considerable education and cultural sophistication before they were forced to immigrate from southern to northern Europe, and from there to Brazil and the American colonies (Sklare, 1972:20–25). The second and larger wave arrived between 1820 and 1870. This group was comprised largely of German Jews who were known as the "**Ashkenazim**" (Glazer, 1957:20–42). They were economically less well off than their Sephardic predecessors, but they came in much larger numbers. The final wave brought almost 2.5 million **eastern European Jews** to America. This was by far the largest and poorest single group since most of them came from the peasant villages of eastern Europe where they recently had suffered from vicious anti-Semitic pogroms. The stopping of mass immigration in 1924 markedly slowed the growth of the American Jewish community. Future increases would result from procreation rather than immigration.

Each of the three waves created its own distinctive communities and religious subcultures within the American social order. However, in all three instances the family played a major role. Historically, American Jews have been identified as a religious community and as an ethnic group. Membership in each is defined by family membership. Consequently, in Jewish culture, the obligation of marriage and family life is binding on all its members (Sklare, 1971:74). This Jewish tradition helps explain why American Jews have the fewest single individuals among all U.S. ethnic groups.

Other aspects of the Jewish family also are worth noting. The first is that American Jews have very low fertility rates. Although Jewish tradition emphasizes the desirability of large families, the size of second-generation American Jewish families has always been below the national average. For some time, Jewish leaders have expressed concern that fertility rates are steadily reducing the size of the Jewish population in American society. In 1937, for example, the Jewish population reached a high point of 3.7 percent of the total population, but by 1967 it had declined to 2.92 percent (Sklare, 1971:37–8). With lower fertility rates, this downward trend has continued.

Smaller family size for Jewish couples is related to the strong achievement drives which Jews have shown since they arrived on American shores. The Jewish family has been a critical institution reinforcing the thirst for knowl-

A Season for Family Interaction with the Wider Society

edge and the desire to attain formal education. A primary reason for the limitation of family size was to permit children to receive "everything" from their parents, including an opportunity to go as far in education as their motivation and intelligence would take them (Sklare, 1971:88–93). As a result, the family among native-born members of the Jewish community has become starkly child-centered. The image of the overly protective Jewish mother with the ever-present bowl of chicken soup reflects in a mildly humorous way the level of attention Jewish parents have lavished on their children. The payoff for such behavior has not only been high levels of achievement among Jewish youth, but an exceptionally cohesive family life.

Traditional Jewish values stress the overriding importance of family solidarity. Goldstein and Goldscheider (1968:102–6) have gathered evidence to show that this value commitment also has been translated into behavior. For

CLOSE-UP

Anzia Yezierska (1885–1970), for a time a well-known novelist, was locked in a struggle with her father that lasted for years. Her story, quite typical in its beginnings, turned at its end into an American legend:

She arrived in New York in 1901, sixteen years old. Her first job was as a servant in an Americanized Jewish family "so successful they were ashamed to remember their mother tongue." She scrubbed floors, scoured pots, washed clothes. At the end of a month she asked for her wages, and was turned out of doors: "Not a dollar for all my work." Her second job was in a Delancey Street sweatshop kept by "an old wrinkled woman that looked like a black witch." Anzia sewed buttons from sunup to sundown. One night she rebelled against working late and was thrown out: "I want no clockwatchers in my shop," said the old witch.

Her third job was in a factory where she learned a skill and, luxury of luxuries, "the whole evening was mine." She started to study English. "I could almost think with English words in my head. I burned to do something, be something. The dead work with my hands was killing me."

She began to write stories with heroines—Hannahs and Sophies—who were clearly projections of her own yearnings. They were not really good stories, but some streak of sincerity and desperation caught the fancy of a few editors and they were published in magazines. By now, she was no longer young—a woman in her mid-thirties, trying to make up for years of wasted youth.

A first novel, *Hungry Hearts*, won some critical praise. . . . All the while, in the forefront of her imagination, loomed the figure of her father, a stern pietist who regarded her literary efforts with contempt. . . .

Her first book published, Anzia confronted her father. "What is it I hear? You wrote a book about me? How could you write about someone you don't know?" Words of wrath flew back and forth, but Anzia, staring at her father in his prayer shawl and phylacteries, "was struck by the radiance that the evils of the world could not mar." He again threw up the fact that she had not married: "A woman alone, not a wife and not a mother, has no existence." They had no meeting ground but anger. . . .

Source: Irving Howe, *World of Our Fathers* (New York: A Touchstone Book/Simon & Schuster, 1976), pp. 268–9.

example, not only are marriage rates high, but the divorce rate tends to be lower than in other religious, ethnic groups (Lenski, 1963:218–9). The low separation and divorce rate for Jewish family members may result, in part, from the fact that Jews generally marry later than the average person in the U.S. population. Later marriage usually correlates with lower divorce rates. Similarly, Jewish concentrations in social groups with higher-level educations and occupations may account for some of the Jewish family's stability. In spite of these other factors, however, Goldstein and Goldscheider (1968:104) believe that the data indicate that much of Jewish family cohesion is a direct result of the Jewish cultural tradition's emphasis on marriage and family life.

Today, Jewish identity and family solidarity find a major source of support in the Jewish subcommunity which preserves a sense of group distinctiveness among the fully assimilated, postimmigrant generations. The subcommunity has helped buffer the hostility of a predominantly Christian culture. Three types of Jewish organizations make up the subculture: the congregation in which formal religious worship is conducted, the Jewish community center, and a wide variety of social service agencies, such as hospitals, child-care agencies, and retirement homes (Sklare, 1971:110). In its own way, each of these organizations has helped to strengthen personal and familial identity bonds with Jewish culture, bonds which otherwise might have been strained severely by assimilation, upward social mobility, and wide-scale participation in the secular institutions of American life.

The Spanish-American Family

The category of Spanish American includes several distinct nationality groups and the white and black races. The largest group of persons of Spanish origin is made up of Mexican Americans (or Chicanos) who reside mostly in the southwestern states. The second largest group includes Cubans and immigrants from South and Central America. The third group is made up of Puerto Ricans, most of whom live along the East Coast in densely populated urban areas (U.S. Bureau of the Census, 1979:33). The Puerto Rican community differs from the other ethnic communities of Spanish origin in that Puerto Ricans entered American society with full citizenship, a right conferred on the island's residents in 1917 (LeMasters, 1977:96). However, Puerto Ricans share with other Spanish-American immigrants the language barrier and the problems that flow from it as well as lower socioeconomic status, widespread poverty, high fertility rates, and scant educational-vocational skills. All of these problems place severe strains on much of Spanish-American family life.

The Mexican-American Family

No single model can represent all the Mexican-American families of today (Simpson and Yinger, 1965:356). The traditional peasant family of rural Mexico was dominated by a patriarchal father figure, had a large number of offspring and strong extended family ties, and was characterized by poverty, overwork, violence, and misery (Lewis, 1961). This family type has existed for some time in the farming communities of the southern and western United States, but its numbers are diminishing steadily. Migratory farm laborers—which is the occupation in which many Mexican-American family members make their living—have difficulty keeping up ties with extended kin. Urbanization and "Anglicization" also have prompted the development of the nuclear family model typical of American culture.

With the emergence of the nuclear family as the norm for a large portion of Mexican Americans, other related changes also are visible. Among second-generation youth, the power of parents, and especially the authority of the father, has declined a good deal (Stoddard, 1973:102–4). Especially in urban settings, the father's role has been weakened by the children's participation in formal schooling where, like earlier immigrant generations, the youngsters acquire a better command of the language, knowledge of the culture, and support from their peer group in dropping the old ways. Americanization also has produced greater equality between spouses. Thus, it is not only young people but women as well who have found freedom from the traditional culture's male dominance.

Among lower-class members of the Mexican-American community, however, a number of traditional traits persist. A prominent one is the practice of "consensual unions" rather than legal marriages. The desertion rate—the "poor man's divorce"—is also unusually high among lower-class Mexican Americans, while the legal divorce rate is somewhat lower than the national average and the rates of other ethnic groups (Stoddard, 1973:105). Given the "macho" emphasis in this cultural tradition, the female-headed households are surprisingly numerous. This can be explained by the fact that desertion, widowhood, and divorce create single-woman or female-headed households, and by the fact that Mexican-American women are less likely to remarry when they lose a mate than Anglo-women. Thus, almost 16 percent of Mexican-American households are headed by females (U.S. Bureau of the Census, 1979:33), a factor which indicates that the patriarchal image does not apply to a large number of families in this ethnic group.

Meanwhile, cultural assimilation is occurring at an accelerating pace (Dyer, 1979:308–9). Chicanos are not only moving into higher education, better-paying jobs, and more desirable communities, but they also are intermarrying with Anglo-Americans at an increasing rate and organizing into effective political and economic lobbying groups (Steiner, 1970). Intermarriage occurs primarily among urban, socially mobile young people whose education or occupation brings them into regular contact with persons outside their minority group (Stoddard, 1973:240). Undoubtedly, this pattern will continue. Moreover, while intermarriage will hasten the assimilation of individual Mexican Americans into the American culture, it will just as surely threaten a self-conscious Chicano culture. To date, no major ethnic group has been able to sustain a bilingual subculture in America, while also gaining the full acceptance of the wider culture. Spanish Americans may well have the best opportunity to do just that, but they must overcome enormous obstacles in the process.

The Puerto Rican Family

Among Spanish-speaking Americans, the Puerto Rican community is relatively small. Mexican Americans number over seven million (not counting perhaps one or two million illegal aliens). Puerto Ricans, on the other hand, account for somewhat less than two million persons out of the total U.S. population (U.S. Bureau of the Census, 1979:33).

The Puerto Rican family had developed under the same patriarchal tradition of Latin culture as the Mexican-American family. Among the poorer classes, however, the "macho" ideal for males may well be the only remaining legacy of this heritage. Most Puerto Rican families in America emphasize more the mother's side of the family. The mother is regarded as the loving, caring parent to whom children may turn in time of trouble (Simpson and Yinger, 1965:357–8). The father, in turn, is expected to provide for his own family, and then for any of his kin who may be in need. A father's relationship to his children tends to be more distant than the mother's.

One major cause of children's dependency on their mother is the high rate of consensual unions among lower-class Puerto Ricans, and the equally high rate of desertion when these relationships encounter difficulties. Lewis (1966:xxxviii–xxxix) found the number of free unions increased in New York City when compared to behavior in the Puerto Rican slums. His New York sample revealed that women who were separated from their husbands or consensual partners headed 26 percent of the households. The bond between mother and children was far stronger than the bond between man and woman. The ease of making and breaking consensual unions both caused and reflected a great deal of sexual adventurism (Glazer and Moynihan, 1970:89). This resulted in confused family settings for a large number of children.

The Puerto Rican family also has a remarkably high fertility rate. This can be attributed to a variety of distinct factors in the Puerto Rican life-style and social customs. The first is a strong preference for early marriage or cohabitation (Glazer and Moynihan, 1970:89–91, 117–9). Moreover, when several marriages and consensual unions are entered, and when children are desired by each male partner, the number of children is readily explained. And finally, most Puerto Ricans subscribe to no form of family planning (Simpson and Yinger, 1965:358). This probably is due less to Puerto Ricans' nominal Catholic religious affiliation (LeMasters, 1977:97) than to the high value that children have in the ethnic culture.

Despite the poverty, unstable marriages, free unions, large family size, and miserable living conditions for many Puerto Ricans, the family remains one of the more stabilizing influences. Even though the children of one mother might have several different fathers, each one is assured equal love and attention from the mother and other relatives who might help oversee the child's social development. The lack of adequate economic resources does not produce resentment toward children nor are they neglected.

Persons of Spanish Origin—Selected Characteristics: 1978

Characteristic	Total	Mexican	Puerto Rican	Other[1]
Total ....1,000.	12,046	7,151	1,823	3,071
Male ....1,000.	5,850	3,528	825	1,496
Female ....1,000.	6,196	3,623	997	1,575
Percent Distribution				
Age (in years):				
Under 5	12.6	13.9	11.3	10.5
5–13	20.5	20.5	25.4	17.4
14–17	8.7	8.6	9.3	8.5
18–21	8.0	8.6	6.4	7.7
22–24	5.9	6.4	5.0	5.2
25–34	15.7	16.1	16.4	14.6
35–44	11.0	10.2	11.5	12.8
45–54	8.4	7.8	8.2	10.0
55–64	4.8	4.2	4.4	6.4
65 and over	4.3	3.7	2.3	6.9
Marital status:[2]				
Single	31.2	30.8	32.2	31.5
Married	59.9	61.6	55.9	58.2
Widowed	3.9	3.6	3.9	4.4
Divorced	5.1	4.0	7.9	5.9
Years of school completed:[3]				
Male:				
Less than 5 yr	16.4	21.9	14.0	6.2
High school, 4 or more yr	42.2	36.6	36.0	56.9
College, 4 or more yr	8.6	4.8	5.1	18.0
Female:				
Less than 5 yr	17.9	24.4	15.7	7.4
High school, 4 or more yr	39.6	32.1	36.0	55.1
College, 4 or more yr	5.7	3.9	3.6	10.3
Residence of families:				
Metro. areas (SMSA's)[4]	85.4	81.0	95.2	89.2
Central cities	51.1	46.3	79.0	44.7
Nonmetro areas	14.6	19.0	4.8	10.8

Characteristic	Total	Mexican	Puerto Rican	Other[1]
Persons 16 yr. old and over ....1,000.	7,544	4,394	1,064	2,087
In civilian labor force 1,000.	4,653	2,828	528	1,297
Percent of total	61.7	64.4	49.6	62.1
Percent unemployed	9.5	9.6	11.7	8.5
Male:				
Employed ....1,000.	2,597	1,619	293	684
Percent distrib'n	100.0	100.0	100.0	100.0
White-collar workers	24.1	18.5	26.2	36.4
Blue-collar workers	57.8	63.1	52.3	47.8
Service workers	13.3	11.5	19.8	14.9
Farm workers	4.8	6.9	1.7	1.2
Female:				
Employed ....1,000.	1,613	938	173	502
Percent distrib'n	100.0	100.0	100.0	100.0
White-collar workers	48.0	44.8	56.3	51.4
Blue-collar workers	28.2	29.1	30.9	25.9
Service workers	22.6	24.5	11.9	22.7
Farm workers	1.1	1.6	.9	.4
Families, total ....1,000.	2,764	1,623	437	704
Percent headed by—				
Husband and wife	76.1	80.5	56.1	78.6
Female[5]	20.3	15.5	41.0	18.6
Family money income, 1977:				
Percent with income of—				
Under $3,000	5.4	5.2	7.3	4.8
$3,000–$5,999	16.3	13.4	30.6	13.7
$6,000–$9,999	20.7	21.1	21.5	19.4
$10,000–$14,999	22.8	25.3	16.2	21.3
$15,000–$19,999	15.4	15.9	12.8	16.2
$20,000–$24,999	9.6	10.1	5.3	11.1
$25,000 and over	9.7	8.9	6.3	13.4
Median income $1,000	11.4	11.7	8.0	12.7
Percent below poverty level[6]	21.4	18.9	38.9	16.3
Percent below 125% of poverty level[6]	28.8	26.8	46.4	22.4

[1]See footnote 3, table 35. [2]Persons 14 years old and over. [3]Persons 25 years old and over. [4]Standard metropolitan statistical area (243) as defined for the 1970 Census of Population. See Appendix II. [5]No spouse present. [6]For poverty levels, see table 758.

Source: U.S. Bureau of the Census, *Current Population Reports,* series P-20, No. 328, and unpublished data. Reprinted from: *Statistical Abstracts 1979,* p. 33.

Of course, not all Puerto Ricans have remained within Lewis's **"culture of poverty."** The opportunities for steady employment and higher-paying jobs have allowed some families to escape the ghetto and enter the ranks of the middle class. For the most part, however, mobile Puerto Ricans are less apt to be identified with their ethnic group of origin. Many simply are no longer seen as Puerto Ricans, but as middle-class persons with Spanish surnames. Others in the professions, such as politicians, social workers, and teachers, retain a strong sense of ethnic-group identity (Glazer and Moynihan, 1970:110–16). The new leaders emerging in the Puerto Rican community are making a concerted effort to secure the sort of social resources needed by family members in their ethnic group (Rogler, 1972).

Social-Class Variations in American Family Life

American society is not only a mosaic of varying racial, ethnic, and religious groups, but it also includes class variations as well. Family patterns are different in different classes. Rather than discussing upper, middle, and lower-class families, we shall concentrate on the somewhat broader categories of the family of poverty, the working-class family, and the white-collar family.

The Family of Poverty

The family within the culture of poverty normally is categorized with the lower-lower class. Frequently social workers describe them as **multiproblem families.** They are distinct from the stable poor who have limited income but solid family structures. The stable poor are normally considered a part of the upper-lower class because they can keep up their social lives without regular help from social service agencies.

By one calculation, the family of poverty in the lower-lower class is about 15 percent of the total population, although other estimates say the numbers are slightly higher or lower (Rainwater, 1967:4). For the most part, family members in this group see themselves at the bottom of the social structure. They share in few of society's benefits. Most work as unskilled laborers, experiencing chronic scarcity of work or complete unemployment. However, a lack of financial resources is more of a result than a cause of the culture of poverty. That is to say, low income is in many respects created by the life-style and family problems of people in this class.

Almost all major traits of social disorganization appear in lower-lower class families. Often, their educational level is less than the eighth grade; so they bring few skills to the job market. Typically, they have high birth and divorce rates (LeMasters, 1977:17–21). Thus, it is very hard to keep family life stable. Alcoholism, drug abuse, and petty crimes are chronic in this group, creating more problems for family members. They often are confined to slums whose streets offer many unwholesome and sometimes dangerous activities for

A Season for Family Interaction with the Wider Society

lower-class youth. Amid all this, it is little wonder that members of the lower-lower class suffer many more mental disorders than the average American (Hollingshead and Redlich, 1964). Finally, the life-style of this class tends to be oriented to the present. They seek adventure, release from boredom, and immediate gratification of their basic needs and special wants.

The cultural orientation and life-style of the family of poverty is transmitted to the next generation through socialization, as it is in other social classes. However, lower-class families are thought to be fully aware of middle-class values, and to approve of many of them, such as independence, discipline, and orderliness. Nor, by the same token, do parents in this class try to instill in their offspring values which would keep them in the lower class (Bronfenbrenner, 1966:375). But children often do acquire from their lower-class parents a behavioral style destined to block their exit out of the lower class as they repeat that behavior in their own lives. Children learn early to be oriented to the present like their parents, to quit school early, to enter marriage in their teens, take a low-paying job now rather than waiting and acquiring vocational skills, and to escape through drugs, alcohol, or sex from an otherwise miserable life. Thus, the cycle is renewed in the next generation. The miracle is that, in spite of all these obstacles, some persons from this social background do manage to escape and carve out for themselves satisfying lives in stable families, jobs, and neighborhoods.

The Working-Class Family

Working-class or blue-collar families include persons from the upper-lower class to the lower-middle class. Working-class families are generally stable, even though they do not have much financial security to fall back on during hard times. Many recently assimilated ethnic groups fit within the working-class category (Kornblum, 1974). These working-class people take great pride in their families and their jobs, which normally entail difficult, manual labor. Although working-class wages and educational training still trail those of white-collar workers, blue-collar families have enjoyed a real gain in their standard of living over the last three decades (Weinberg and Williams, 1980). However, an improved material situation with more cars, better homes, and color televisions does not necessarily mean that the working class has changed its values and family patterns. In recent years, social scientists have vigorously debated the persistence and change in working-class life-styles. We can review some of the more important conclusions drawn thus far.

Before World War II, American working-class parents were viewed as more permissive in their child-rearing techniques than white-collar parents. Today, this view is almost completely reversed (Bronfenbrenner, 1966). The working class now is seen as following conservative practices in child rearing by enforcing stricter discipline, using more physical forms of punishment, and reasoning less with their offspring than parents in the upper classes. But most studies supporting this conclusion suggested that the differences between working-class and white-collar parents were narrowing steadily. In an examination of 10 surveys of punishment practices, Erlanger (1974) concluded that

In this selection from her study of working-class families, Lillian Rubin reports on the dream and the reality of marriage from the point of view of working-class wives—which she then contrasts with the perspective of middle-class wives. Note the sharp differences between the two.

I guess I can't complain. He's a steady worker; he doesn't drink; he doesn't hit me. That's a lot more than my mother had, and she didn't sit around complaining and feeling sorry for herself, so I sure haven't got the right.

[Thirty-three-year-old housewife, mother of three, married thirteen years.]

"He's a steady worker; he doesn't drink; he doesn't hit me"—these are the three attributes working-class women tick off most readily when asked what they value most in their husbands. Not a surprising response when one recalls their familiarity with unemployment, alcoholism, and violence, whether in their own families or in those around them. That this response is class-related is evident from the fact that not one woman in the professional middle-class families mentioned any of these qualities when answering the same question. Although there was no response that was consistently heard from the middle-class wives, they tended to focus on such issues as intimacy, sharing, and communication and, while expressed in subtle ways, on the comforts, status, and prestige that their husbands' occupation affords. Janet Harris, writing about middle-class women at forty, also comments that she never heard a women list her husband's ability to provide or the fact that he is "good to the children" as valued primary traits. "The security and financial support that a husband provides are taken for granted," she argues; "it is the emotional sustainment which is the barometer of a marriage."

Does this mean, then, that working-class women are unconcerned about the emotional side of the marriage relationship? Emphatically, it does not. It says first that when the material aspects of life are problematic, they become dominant as issues requiring solutions; and second, that even when men are earning a reasonably good living, it is *never* "taken for granted" when financial insecurity and marginality are woven into the fabric of life. These crucial differences in the definition of a good life, a good husband, a good marriage—and the reasons for them—often are obscured in studies of marriage and the family because students of the subject rarely even mention class, let alone analyze class differences.

Still, it is a mixed message that these working-class women send; for while many remind themselves regularly that they have no right to complain, their feelings of discontent with the emotional aspects of the marriage are not so easily denied. Indeed, once the immediate problems and preoccupations of the early years subside, once the young husband is "housebroken," an interesting switch occurs. Before the marriage and in the first years, it is the wife who seems more eager to be married; the husband, more reluctant. Marriage brings her more immediate gains since being unmarried is a highly stigmatized status for a woman, especially in the working-class world. Both husband and wife subscribe to the "I-chased-her-until-she-caught-me" myth about courtship in America; both believe that somehow, using some mysterious feminine wiles, she contrived to ensnare him. It is no surprise, then, that it is he who has more trouble in settling down at the beginning—feeling hemmed in, oppressed by the contours and confines of marriage, by its responsibilities.

Source: Lillian Breslow Rubin *Worlds of Pain: Life in the Working-Class Family* (New York: Basic Books, Inc., 1976), pp. 93–4.

when additional scientific controls are applied to investigative studies, the difference between social classes in the use of physical punishment is not, and has never been, large. Consequently, to suggest that working-class youth and young adults are more aggressive, violent, prone to child abuse, or authoritarian (Lipset, 1960) because of the physical punishment they received as children is, from Erlanger's point of view, completely wrong. Nathan Hurvitz (1964:100) may well have provided a partial clarification for why the findings of most studies have been so mixed and inconclusive with respect to working-class child-rearing practices. He (1964:100) notes that working-class fathers typically believe they must raise their children to be tough. Thus, they are more likely to use physical forms of punishment. The working-class mother, however, tends to favor reasoning and instruction tempered with love to control the children. Thus, a common complaint in working-class households is that the father is too severe on the children while the mother is too lenient. Hurvitz's findings suggest that the traditional forms of punishment associated with the working class are actually only employed by the father while the mother uses the child-rearing techniques of middle-class parents.

Another area in which a conservative pattern has been said to prevail in blue-collar life is in husband-and-wife relations. A number of studies have indicated that the traditional roles of breadwinner for the man and homemaker and mother for the woman are preferred more by working-class couples than by their white-collar counterparts (Komarovsky, 1967; Rubin, 1976). Again, however, we must qualify this portrayal of blue-collar spouses in light of trends which now are being revealed by social scientific studies. Handel and Rainwater (1964), for example, divide the working class into two main groups which they characterize as the traditional and modern working-class groups. In the traditional working class, the wife defines her role in terms of what she does *for* the family, such as cooking, cleaning, and child rearing. The modern working-class mother thinks in terms of what she does *with* the family. She is more concerned with social relationships than household tasks. Similarly, in the traditional working class, a great deal of nuclear family interaction occurs as well as dependence on the extended family. But members of the modern working class give greater importance to the nuclear family alone, and this influences a wide variety of family attitudes and behaviors, including place of residence, occupation, social participation, leisure-time activities, and family roles. In other words, the modern working class is tending toward the cultural life-style of the middle class, while the traditional working class is retaining the old cultural patterns which social scientists historically have associated with blue-collar family life.

The White-Collar Family

The white-collar work force has expanded notably in our postindustrial society. The expansion of the service sector of the economy, the vast increase in office workers, educational personnel, and government-related occupations has meant that, since 1970, white-collar workers have outnumbered blue-collar workers by a ratio of five to four (Bell, 1976:17). In terms of income, white-collar workers now are found from the lower middle class to the upper class.

Thus, the white-collar family pattern is even more diverse and varied than family patterns in the blue-collar segment of society.

Several features and problems of the white-collar or middle-class family can be summarized fairly readily. First, white-collar families usually enjoy stable incomes which are adequate to meet their major aspirations and secure enough to allow for long-range planning. White-collar parents generally can provide their children with the physical necessities of life and with many of the luxuries such as cars, spending money, private rooms, and stereos, which, a couple of generations ago only the wealthy could afford. Most white-collar parents, especially in the upper-middle class, have attained their social level through personal effort and achievement (LeMasters, 1977:81–3). In the professions, they generally had to acquire advanced education to gain access to a vocational position with substantial income. These parents can provide their children with many cultural and social advantages, but they cannot pass along a similar class position to their offspring. Children of the upper-middle class must either attain the skills to secure an occupational position through their own efforts or lose their class position. Lawyers, accountants, or corporate executives cannot assure their offspring that they will automatically retain this status position in their own adult work experience. Consequently, upper-middle-class parents are quite concerned about the future of their children.

Another widely employed trait that distinguishes the white-collar family is

Figure 14-4
Even former "flower children" must eventually grow older. This young couple has made the transition to middle-class family life, parenthood, and a mortgage, and, of course, has acquired the standard equipment of suburban living, complete with a dog. *(Copyright © Stock, Boston, Inc. Owen Franklin, photographer.)*

A Season for Family Interaction with the Wider Society

its isolation from other kin. Working-class families tend to live close to, and organize much of their social life around, visiting relatives. This is especially the case for recently assimilated ethnic families (Gans, 1965). But white-collar families are often compelled by labor-market forces to leave their community and relatives to make the most of career opportunities (Parsons and Bales, 1955:8–9; Lenski, 1963:213–20). Their willingness to leave their relatives has earned the white-collar family its designation as an "isolated, nuclear family."

That label needs to be used cautiously, however, for it may imply more separation among relatives than actually exists. Isolation should not be taken to mean that no contact occurs via telephone, letters, and visits, or that the extended family provides no social support to the nuclear family in white-collar kinship networks. In two important studies, Litwak (1960a, 1960b) demonstrated that extended family contacts are maintained in both occupationally and geographically mobile families. Indeed, nuclear families which are mobile are exactly the ones who are more likely to need and receive either economic or social support from relatives, especially parents and siblings. Thus, Litwak suggests that the term **"modified extended family"** be applied to white-collar families that gain upward social mobility and yet retain family ties. A new term in our technical vocabulary may not be necessary as long as we keep in mind the basic point of Litwak's research—that physical distance should not be taken to mean that all contacts with relatives are severed.

A final, important trait of white-collar families is found in their pattern of child rearing. The socialization techniques of middle-class parents tend to be quite unlike those of traditional working-class mothers and fathers. White-collar parents try to internalize social norms in their children at a very early age, so that their youngsters will become self-regulating persons (Parsons, 1964:95–103). Working-class families rely more heavily on external controls, such as the use of force, fear, and punishment, to regulate the behavior of their children. Thus, though white-collar parents often may appear to be permissive toward their children, they actually are only relying on those inner controls which a child has internalized (Williams, 1970:77–83). Furthermore, rather than simple conformity to external rules, middle-class parents tend to value more highly their children's development of a sense of individuality, responsibility, freedom, and self-expression.

Interest in nurturing unique personalities in their children also prompts white-collar parents to seek the latest "expert" advice on child rearing. Parents want to create a child independent enough of the nuclear family to experience freedom, make responsible adult choices about a career and a spouse, and be psychologically prepared to found a new family (Seeley, Sim, Loosley, 1963:164–7). White-collar parents no longer find it enough to merely rely on traditional child-rearing techniques. They seek scientific information about child development as well as more progressive techniques which take into account contemporary personality theories. Unfortunately, much of the available information tends to be pseudoscientific theories of child rearing concocted by self-proclaimed "experts." Christopher Lasch (1979) may have been right to warn that parents need to be wary of too much dependence on child-rearing fads.

Nonetheless, the eagerness with which middle-class parents search for expert advice is a measure of their interest in nurturing quality children. From the point of view of middle-class youth, probably the most important message communicated by parents—quite apart from the specific child-rearing technique employed—is that children of the middle class are deeply loved, cared for, and occupy a great deal of their parents' attention. Indeed, Kenneth Keniston (1968:60–67) was somewhat surprised to discover in his study of radical youth during the 1960s that all his subjects reported excellent relationships with their parents. Radical students did believe the generation gap between parents and youth existed, but it was always a gap experienced by others in their group and not by the person speaking to the researcher. Individual students expressed praise and affection for their parents, and a willingness to forgive parental failures. Conflict over values and behavior patterns do emerge regularly between parents and their children, whose views are formed by the peer group as well as the family. But these conflicts do not appear to be breaking the bonds of affection between middle-class parents and their offspring.

Summary

The United States is a pluralistic society that includes several classes. This chapter explores the variety of family patterns in several important ethnic and social-class groups. The chapter provides some insight into the various ways in which American families have adjusted to the New World and its social stratification system.

The discussion opens with a consideration of the immigrant family of the nineteenth and early twentieth centuries. Immigration into American society usually is divided into two separate waves. The "old immigrants" who entered between 1820 and 1870 were largely of English, Irish, German, or Scandanavian background. Most were from poor rural regions; they brought with them a family structure in which fathers had the decision-making power. Assimilation into American life was often a trying experience for these groups, but it was marked by only moderate discriminatory practices rather than by the full brunt of hostilities that later groups would encounter.

The "new immigrants" entered the United States between 1880 and 1924. Drawn primarily from eastern and southern Europe, most were extremely poor and often unskilled peasants who were considered less desirable for a variety of religious, racial, and social reasons. For these groups, assimilation was somewhat more difficult and accompanied by family strain which tended to divide parents and children.

No other family system in American life has suffered as long and completely as the black family. Moreover, the effects of the black family's experience are still being debated by historians and social scientists. One view, which Frazier and Moynihan helped greatly to develop, held that slavery, emancipation, the sharecropper system, and later urbanization, all tended to promote a matriarchal system in American black families. A countering viewpoint, presented by Billingsley and Gutman, claims that the matriarchal pattern did not emerge until later in the twentieth century, when blacks moved to Northern cities in large numbers. Moreover, they insist that matriarchy arises from the conditions of poverty and is no more common among poor blacks than among the poor of any other ethnic group.

The Jewish family adapted quite well to American society. Although the last wave of Jewish immigrants was made up mostly of poor peasants from eastern Europe, their family structure proved to be very helpful to those who sought upward social mobility.

The Spanish-American family is made up of those from Mexican and Puerto Rican backgrounds. Most Chicanos first entered the United States as farm workers, and many still work on farms today. Although Latin family culture generally supports a strong father's role, the processes of assimilation and upward social mobility have produced more equalitarian forms. The Puerto Rican immigrants in East Coast cities also brought with them a strong male role, but nonetheless the mother has long been the dominant figure in most lower-class households. Family life remains unstable among Puerto Ricans below the poverty line, but the family still remains the critical institution for extending child care and personal support to individual Puerto Ricans.

Social-class variations have been divided into three broad categories. *The family of poverty* is characterized by instability, unemployment, and a series of other disabling problems. Still, persons from this background do regularly manage to reach the stability of the working class. *The working-class family* is generally stable, employed, and able to manage its own affairs without aid from society. The traditional family among the working class is conservative and endorses the customary breadwinner role for the father and the homemaker role for the mother. The modern working-class subgroup is more equalitarian. Its patterns are moving closer and closer to the middle-class norm. *The white-collar family* is expanding more rapidly than any other social-class group as we move into the postindustrial era. This family group is organized around the isolated nuclear pattern, although all contacts with relatives have by no means been terminated. The white-collar family enjoys a secure income, supports educational achievement, and is seriously concerned with nurturing quality children by employing the most modern and effective child-rearing techniques.

STUDY QUESTIONS

1. Explain the differences between the "old" and the "new" immigrants in terms of their social characteristics and family structures. Why were the "old" immigrants better received by Americans of the time than were the "new" immigrants?
2. Contrast the two major interpretive schools of thought on the history of black family life in America. Which interpretation appears more sound? Why?
3. In what ways has the Jewish community in America managed to promote family solidarity within its religious subculture?
4. What are the differing family characteristics displayed in the separate groups which comprise Spanish Americans?
5. Why are the family units in the culture of poverty often described as "multiproblems" families? What are the major problems these families encounter?
6. What are the outstanding differences that distinguish blue-collar from white-collar families? How can one account for these differences?

PART SEVEN

A Season for Growing Old

Speaking through Hamlet's mother, Shakespeare reminds us: "Thou know'st tis common—all that live must die." Although Americans recognize that the aging process cannot be stopped, our culture tends to glorify youth and its physical well-being, mental alertness, and active social life. But any thorough consideration of the family life cycle must give some attention to the dynamics of aging. The two chapters in this section focus on the later stages of family life.

After the family has reached the full-household stage, the period from middle age on is a time of shrinkage for the family circle. Chapter 15 examines that social process. The family is a self-liquidating group. It must send forth its younger members to form their own new families. This produces the "empty nest," and the need for parents to readjust their interpersonal dynamics to themselves, the original conjugal pair. The launching of children signals the completion of the woman's career as a mother, just as retirement generally symbolizes the completion of the father's major social role.

The following chapter addresses the social experiences of death, widowhood, and living alone. The loss of a spouse is one of the most traumatic events in the course of the life cycle. Surviving spouses must come to grips with the problem of reconstructing their role patterns in a single-member household. This adjustment falls more often to the wife than to the husband—for the male is usually the first spouse to die. By the time the second spouse dies, however, the next generation is normally well into the process of forming new families. And so the cycle of life continues.

15

The Shrinking Family Circle
from Middle Age to Retirement

The Family as a Self-Liquidating Group

Changing Relationships Between Parents and Their Maturing Children
  The Developing Autonomy of Children
  The Need for Parents to Relinquish Control
  The Attitudes of Young Adults toward Their Parents
  Parents relinquishing control

Launching Children and the Completion of the Mother's Career
  Psychological Adjustment of Mothers to the "Empty Nest"
  The Empty Nest as a New Beginning
  who has difficulty w/ this - problems

Retirement and the Completion of the Father's Career
  Economic factor
  The Psychological Adjustment to Retirement
  The Meaning of Retirement in an Achievement-Oriented Society
  Social class differences

Husband and Wife Together at Middle Age and Beyond
  The Process of Getting Reacquainted   *Companionship*
  Divorce and Remarriage in the Middle and Later Years

The Role of Grandparents
  The Joys of Being a Grandparent
  The Characteristics of the Grandparent's Role
  How this role changes

Summary

Almost every parent who reaches middle age has remarked at one time or another, "It seems like only yesterday that the children were mere babies, and today they're all grown up and out on their own." Comments like this are nearly universal because the parents' experience of finding themselves once again alone after the children have left home is nearly universal. For the parents, this experience generally produces a bittersweet feeling. On the one hand, parents feel the inevitable pride at having seen their children begin in the world as helpless infants and develop under their care into mature, self-sufficient adults who are independent. Yet, on the other hand, they also feel the pain of losing the daily contact with children they love.

When children grow up and strike out on their own, parents find life drastically altered. They have more time for themselves, more privacy in which to enjoy one another's company, and frequently—once the children are through college or launched in their careers—more money to devote to their own interests. Thus, the last child's leave-taking is a major symbolic event for parents, though unmarked by such rites of passage as those that celebrate the young person's graduation or marriage. One major episode in the parental life cycle has been completed. The ideal presented to most young people—and an ideal to which most aspire—is to grow up, get married, have children, and raise them to become young adults. Once they have done this, parents look to the future in full awareness that many of their life's ambitions are now a part of their past—a history of cherished memories, no doubt, but behind them all the same. When children leave home to go to college, work, or military service, they never again return as children. It is a time, as one mother described it, of "sad joyfulness" (Rubin, 1981:33).

In this chapter, we examine the family from the viewpoint of parents who are in midlife and immediately beyond. In this period, the family circle is shrinking. The hustle and bustle of a full family life no longer surrounds the parents. No more must Mom or Dad drive the kids to the junior high dance, attend the high school band concert, go to PTA meetings, force the children to practice the piano, schedule appointments for the orthodontist, make sure everyone's homework is done, and attend to a thousand and one other details which children always forget, such as brushing their teeth, changing

---

CLOSE-UP

Measuring and Relating Life Stress to Physical and Mental Disorders
This Social Readjustment Rating Scale (SRRS) was developed by T. H. Holmes as an objective method for measuring the cumulative stress to which an individual has been exposed over a period of time. The scale measures life stress in terms of "life change units" (LCU) involving the following events.

Events	Scale of Impact
Death of spouse	100
Divorce	73
Marital separation	65
Jail term	63

(continued)

Death of close family member	63
Personal injury or illness	53
Marriage	50
Fired at work	47
Marital reconciliation	45
Retirement	45
Change in health of family member	44
Pregnancy	40
Sex difficulties	39
Gain of new family member	39
Business readjustment	39
Change in financial state	38
Death of close friend	37
Change to different line of work	36
Change in number of arguments with spouse	35
Mortgage over $10,000	31
Foreclosure of mortgage or loan	30
Change in responsibilities at work	29
Son or daughter leaving home	29
Trouble with in-laws	29
Outstanding personal achievement	28
Wife begins or stops work	26
Begin or end school	26
Change in living conditions	25
Revision of personal habits	24
Trouble with boss	23
Change in work hours or conditions	20
Change in residence	20
Change in schools	20
Change in recreation	19
Change in church activities	19
Change in social activities	18
Mortgage or loan less than $10,000	17
Change in sleeping habits	16
Change in number of family get-togethers	15
Change in eating habits	15
Vacation	13
Christmas	12
Minor violations of the law	11

For persons who had been exposed in recent months to stressful events that added up to an LCU score of 300 or above, these investigators found the risk of developing a major illness within the next two years to be very high, approximating 80 percent.

Source: Holmes T. S. and T. H. Holmes, "Short Term Intrusions into the Life-Style Routine," Journal of Psychosomatic Research, June 1970, pp. 121–32.

their socks, and cleaning up their rooms. Thus, launching children from the nuclear family has a number of effects on the parents, but its impact most affects the mother. Meanwhile, a father also realizes that he has reached the peak of his career. Before him, in a few short years, lies retirement. After retirement, husband and wife usually can expect to have a number of years together, a period which can be filled with fresh experiences and renewed companionship or plagued by anxiety about declining health, incompatible interests, or coming old age. And finally, husband and wife often can assume a new role during this period, the role of grandparents. While most young people are inclined to regard middle age and beyond as a staid, unexciting stage when little change occurs, this period is actually a time of successive and far-reaching adjustments for parents.

The Family as a Self-Liquidating Group

Among the five basic institutions of advanced societies, the nuclear family is unique in that it is the only institution which is comprised of social groups whose normal life cycle leads to their own liquidation (Parsons, 1964:61). That is to say, after the man and woman marry, the usual pattern is for the nuclear household to expand through the procreation of children. Childbearing, in turn, leads to the socialization of the young. Eventually, however, children must be encouraged to establish a family unit of their own and leave the parental family. Once again reduced to its original size, the parental family finally ceases to exist altogether as a unit after the death of the second spouse.

The persistence of the family as a social institution is directly related to the birth and eventual death of particular family groups. As long as children remain within the household, they cannot create new families of their own in the culturally acceptable manner. Thus, the **launching of children** is more than culturally desirable; it is socially necessary for the very survival of society. A great deal of parental training is specifically directed toward the day when children depart from the family nest. Parents may well see themselves as failures if their offspring cannot leave the family of orientation and, in most instances, create a new and independent family of procreation.

Changing Relationships between Parents and Their Maturing Children

Often, the experience of launching children is traumatic for parents, even though they have socialized their children for the time when each one could leave the nuclear family circle as a self-sufficient person. Generally speaking, however, a young person does not leave in one, abrupt moment, and this helps somewhat to lessen its impact. Rather, the offspring begin a period of disengagement from their family of orientation well before they finally leave the family nest.

Quite early in their lives, American youth today begin taking part in activities outside the home. Scout programs, religious youth activities, and community athletic programs all provide an organizational outlet for young people still in grammar school. By junior high, youngsters usually make their first contacts with the youth peer culture as they acquire familiarity with the current language, dress codes, and behavior styles (Kett, 1977:266–72). As young people move into their high school years, they typically take in an ever-widening circle of peer-group activities and friendship networks which takes them away from the close confines of the nuclear family. Thus, for several years, parents experience their maturing children's steady withdrawal from family affairs, before one day they leave the household permanently (Duvall, 1967:335–6).

Young people also demonstrate their developing autonomy by taking on responsibilities and making decisions. The first signs of independence usually occur in their choice of clothes, followed by an insistence on selecting their own friends, choosing whom they will date, deciding whether they will take part in extracurricular activities, and determining how they will spend their money. Later, however, the decisions they will make will have a greater and longer influence on the course of their overall development. These decisions

Figure 15-1
As young people grow older, they develop an ever-widening network of friends within the peer culture, which draws them away from the close confines of the nuclear family circle. *(Monkmeyer Press Photo Service. Paul S. Conklin, photographer)*

include a large number of choices about college or work, about which vocation to select, whom to marry, and when to leave the single life and assume the responsibilities of marriage. None of these latter decisions can be made by the child's parents. Nor, similarly, will parents have to live with the consequences as directly and intimately as their children.

The Need for Parents to Relinquish Control

When social scientists speak of parents launching their offspring from the family nest, the mental image may be one of a young adult being forced out of the family home. Often, of course, just the opposite situation exists. Frequently, parents hesitate to cut the apron strings and let their children begin to manage their own affairs. Various motives may prompt this parental behavior. Mothers and fathers may worry that their children are too young to make responsible decisions. They may fear that the decisions will not be in their child's best interests, as the parents understand it. Or, it may simply be that parents do not want to admit that their children have grown up and no longer need their guidance.

However, even the best of intentions, such as the desire to save their children from unnecessary pain and hardship, cannot erase the fact that young people can only become responsible when they begin to exercise their freedom and make their own choices. Parents who pressure their grown children too much in the effort to continue controlling their behavior are likely to encounter all sorts of disappointments. Most children can easily torpedo parental plans which they oppose vehemently. For example, parents who coerce their child to go to college, when the young person had other aims and objectives in mind, may soon find their son or daughter has managed to fail enough courses to prompt the school authorities to politely ask the student not to return next semester.

Although there are real limits to parents' power to impose their will on their children, more compelling reasons suggest parents should willingly give up their control over maturing youth. Assuming more and more autonomy in decision making can be a sobering, sometimes frightening, experience for young people. Parents can increase their self-confidence by honoring the choices they make. Moreover, if parents clearly show that they are not trying to control their children's lives, they are far more likely to be able to offer a word of advice or suggest a course of action that their child will consider seriously.

This does not mean, of course, that parents should abandon their children to the whims and norms of the peer group once they enter high school. Christopher Lasch (1979:172–8) may well be right when he suggests that parents who give up their authority early in the child's adolescence make it more difficult for maturing offspring to accept the rules laid down by other social authorities outside the family. Yet, the effort to control the lives of young adults and keep them dependent on the parents also may be harmful. In this regard, the peer group is important in that it removes young people from the parents' exclusive control and helps to thrust them out into the wider social world.

The Attitudes of Young Adults toward Their Parents

Mark Twain once said that when he was in his teens, his father seemed to be so dumb he could scarcely stand to have the old man around. But when Twain became a young man, he was amazed at how much his father had learned in just a few short years. Apparently, this attitude is not unusual. Grown children tend to reproduce the parental culture in their own attitudes when those children and their parents have had a close relationship resulting in the children's identification with their parents. Conversely, weak parent-child interaction and inadequate socialization make young adults less likely to agree with parental values and more likely to embrace radical attitudes toward family life (Yost and Adamek, 1974). Thus, the quality of parent-child interaction markedly affects the attitudes which grown children will hold toward their parents and their values.

Similarly, several studies on parental power indicate that the influence of parents continues, even after their children have left the family nest. In this context, parental power obviously does not mean the physical coercion of children. Rather, parents exercise their power through a young person's identification with them and their point of view, through the recognition of the parent's legitimate right to exercise control, and through the belief that parents possess expert knowledge or social experience in an area the young adult views as difficult (Smith, 1970; McDonald, 1977). Several important studies have disclosed that young adults continue to use their parents as resources in decision making. To be sure, children also gain advice from others, but parents do retain considerable influence, both directly and indirectly, over their children.

Launching Children and the Completion of the Mother's Career

The social role of motherhood is extraordinarily demanding, as we have noted several times. The reduction of family size with falling fertility rates has not done much to ease the anxieties of modern motherhood (Bernard, 1975; A:77–9). Indeed, the distance between the nuclear family and kin has tended to intensify the responsibilities of mothers. Just as the mother's competence in her role is reaching its peak, the time approaches when children begin to leave the family nest (Lopata, 1972:36–44; 222–3). Technically speaking, of course, motherhood does not cease with the loss of children to adulthood. Yet, the approaching end of the role's daily activities often does make a mother feel ambivalent, especially when motherhood has been the primary occupational endeavor.

Psychological Adjustment of Mothers to the "Empty Nest"

The frustrating task that many mothers encounter during the **empty-nest** phase is that of finding a new meaning for their lives and other social roles around which to establish their identities. For many mothers, this psychological adjustment is far from easy. For much of their early lives, they were socialized to the wife and mother roles. In many instances, the ideal image of their future lives never reached beyond the stage of motherhood, except perhaps for an occasional thought about the joys of becoming a grandmother. Consequently, women who internalize such expectations often find the transition to **postparenthood** is a time of loneliness, restlessness, and discontent. Because they had not given much thought to how they would spend their lives after the children were gone, the shrinking household often provokes a sense of anxiety and a concern for their future.

Against this backdrop, the departure of children symbolizes the completion of an important and socially acknowledged role for mothers. To be sure, she will receive visits, telephone calls, and letters from her children. Yet for many married women who put their motherhood role first in terms of their personal identity, their lives will never be quite the same again (Duberman, 1977:151). In earlier centuries, adjustment to the postparental period was a somewhat smaller problem for mothers and fathers. Parents were lucky to launch their last child before one or both of them died. Today, however, with lengthening life expectancy rates, mothers especially can go through the transition to postparenthood with at least half of their life span still ahead of them.

Moreover, many of the options mothers have at this time in their lives are not seen as terribly attractive. Since housework is now reduced to a minimum with only the husband to care for, filling one's hours with satisfying activities

Figure 15-2
Graduation is a public event which symbolically marks the growing autonomy of a young person and an increasing independence from parental control. *(Woodfin Camp & Associates. Rick Winsor, photographer)*

is likely to become a problem. What does one do with the rest of the day? Postparenthood women could reenter the labor force, but most of the available work is low-paying, offers very little challenge, requires minimal intelligence, and holds few opportunities for advancement. They can choose the outlets of club meetings, volunteer work, or socializing with the neighbors, yet for active women this, too, can become boring in a short while. When the opportunities exist, some mothers of grown children may enter college or pursue advanced degrees, for their own fulfillment or as a means of launching a new career. But most women will not be interested in pursuing educational enrichment indefinitely. Wives of business managers may spend more time helping advance their husbands' careers, and find this a socially productive role (Kanter, 1977:104–26). Not only is the number of women in this category small, but they are also the most likely individuals to have the educational skills and training needed to pursue a career of their own, rather than playing a supporting role in their husbands' careers. Still others may decide to follow previously neglected hobbies, to read, garden, and thoroughly enjoy the life of retirement. Some postparental mothers may stagnate by simply falling into the dull routine of housework, watching television game shows and soap operas, and losing their sense of identity and purpose.

Clearly, the options available to women in the postparental stage are many and varied. Unfortunately, the existing social scientific data are inadequate for us to state definitively which options are the most popular. Documenting the loss of the motherhood role is far easier than specifying which new roles women acquire during the transition period. Moreover, on the basis of the limited evidence, many women appear to find the need to select new roles a bewildering experience. For this reason, it has become rather common for social scientists to characterize this transition period as a **"mid-life crisis"** (Lowenthal, Thurner, Chiriboga, 1975; Handelman, 1978; Whitbourne and Weinstock, 1979).

But calling this stage of adult development a crisis can create some misunderstandings. We should not think that the trauma at the loss of the motherhood role is abnormal. Nor should one assume that all mothers go through this period disoriented and filled with anxiety (As we shall see in the next section, many mothers feel liberated when their children leave home. This is the other side of the coin which often fosters the mother's ambivalence.) The crisis label does emphasize that adult experience changes dramatically at certain stages in the life cycle. These changes are both psychological and behavioral. Most women undergo a transformation of their personal identity and a transition to a new set of social roles with their own patterns of behavior.

As social scientists acquire more detailed information about how mothers cope with this transition, "mid-life crisis" may seem to be too strong a term to describe the changes that actually occur. Furthermore, we also are likely to discover that women use a wide range of responses and coping mechanisms to confront the "empty nest" period. Those whose identities are deeply intertwined with child rearing are likely to experience the most disruption of their self-image and role behavior. Those who can formulate clear personal goals for the postparental period and can see the empty nest as a chance for self-

A Season for Growing Old

renewal are most likely to have a healthy outlook and a satisfactory adjustment (Handelman, 1978:214–5).

The Empty Nest as a New Beginning

Much research on the transition of mothers to the postparental phase has stressed the depression and social dislocation caused by the empty nest. In a recent study of women at midlife, Lillian Rubin (1981:14–5) has suggested that this stereotype is strong because most research has focused on hospitalized women. However, in her sample of 160 women who completed in-depth interviews, the major traits of the empty-nest syndrome simply did not appear. Some women were sad, depressed, at loose ends, lacking in confidence, and uncertain about their futures, but they were not overwhelmed at beginning a new phase of their lives. The differences between the reactions of the women were determined largely by how well they thought they had raised their children, how much they had prepared for the transition period, and how they felt about their marriages. The one major similarity in the whole group was a decided "sense of relief" now that the time actually had come for the children to depart.

Since Rubin herself was surprised by these expressions of relief, she probed further into its causes. Time and again, her respondents spoke of the enormous burden of child rearing. It was not so much the time, the physical tasks, or even the demands for love or affection which took their greatest toll on mothers. It was the psychological pressure created by the fact that mothers are held responsible for how children turn out. While husbands are under social pressure to make money, the mothers are under pressure to produce quality children. Her perception is that if the children she has nurtured are psychologically or socially deviant, she will be blamed.

Thus, the launching of children is an escape from these social pressures and responsibilities. Easing out of the motherhood role is by no means a simple process, however. Rubin also found that many women felt quite guilty because they looked forward to the time when the children would be gone. All said that they loved their children, but they also were pleased to see them reach an age when they could manage on their own. Now mothers could begin to look forward to the fulfillment of their own dreams and aspirations, dreams they had sidelined to care for the children.

Although Rubin's study is largely descriptive, her analysis includes a number of insights into how the mother's transition to postparenthood might be eased. Like many other social scientists, she hints that the pressures of motherhood are too intense. Mothers who take upon themselves the total responsibility for their children's fate are likely to approach the empty nest period filled with anxiety that they have not done enough or that they have done the wrong things for their children. Sharing child-rearing responsibilities with their husbands may help reduce some of these tensions. In addition, women must prepare for their children's absence by developing outside interests, career goals, or planning more extensively for mid-life and beyond. Mothers also need to be assured that it is perfectly normal to feel relieved that the children have departed and they may now spend time on their own interests. Finally, Rubin proposes that all talk about the empty nest, which implies that a mother's main life goal is completed, should be replaced with language which suggests that mid-life is a new beginning. If revised cultural expectations allowed women to approach mid-life as a time of opportunities, the adjustment would be more likely to proceed smoothly and create greater personal satisfaction later on.

Retirement and the Completion of the Father's Career

Although most husbands and fathers realize that they reached their career peak at about the same time that their wives are facing the end of the daily motherhood role, retirement remains more of a cultural shock for a father than most other events he will confront in his later years—except, of course, for the loss of his mate. The meaning of retirement varies considerably (Mass and Kuypers, 1974). This is true largely because the meaning of work varies markedly between class groups and individual men. However, almost every retired man feels some disruption as he adjusts to his new status and works out a self-image that fits his position in the nonworking segment of the population.

The Psychological Adjustment to Retirement

The completion of one's formal work experience is a major event in the male life cycle. Most men's identities are intimately tied up in their work. Blue-collar husbands and fathers are more inclined to be prouder of their general breadwinner role than of the specific job they perform (Rubin, 1976:155–84). Work in general is regarded as a necessarily masculine area, but the unskilled or semiskilled nature of the job prevents many blue-collar workers from attaching any meaning to what they do to provide for their families (Shostak, 1969:57–9). For this reason, blue-collar workers look forward to retirement more readily than their white-collar counterparts, but blue-collar workers also adjust to retirement less well (Loether, 1964).

White-collar employees usually have more positive feelings toward their jobs. For them, work is more than simply a means of making money to fulfill the breadwinner role. It is a career and they usually see their specific economic activity as having a basic meaning. Despite this seemingly greater attachment to his work, the white-collar worker's adjustment to retirement is generally smoother, even though he may dread leaving a job whose status he sees as important to his self-esteem. The white-collar worker brings greater role flexibility to his retirement (Loether, 1964:532). He is better prepared to shift into other roles. For many blue-collar workers, by contrast, work is the

A Season for Growing Old

Figure 15-3
Postparenthood cou-
ples looking toward
retirement can begin
to plan a new phase of
their life together
when they are free to
do things like travel
abroad. (© Alice Kan-
dell, Photo Researchers,
Inc.)

primary link to the larger social system. Therefore, retirement is more likely to cut the blue-collar worker off from personal contacts with others in his social world.

To be sure, common concerns appear to cut across blue- and white-collar groups. For men in particular, the drop in income at retirement is a major fear (Rapoport and Rapoport, 1980:104). Morever, they also must fill a great deal of leisure time. Men who have anchored their identity in their occupations cannot easily walk away from their work at some arbitrary retirement age. If other outside pursuits have not been developed, retirement is probably going to be a burden and an unhappy stage in the life cycle.

CLOSE-UP

Retirement means new challenging and creative activities for some.

In our society, it has usually been the male who retires. Few women have had careers in the past—here is a daugher's account of her mother's "retirement," which led to an active life of social involvement.

We welcomed the phone call that told us of Mom's retirement. Who else deserved it more? Acting as sole provider for four growing and often demanding daughters meant that she had spent years of self-sacrificing.

The retirement dinner which was given for her suggested that, as important as her work had been, it was now finished.

But, she wasn't listening. She merely clipped the article on her retirement from the paper, put it into a drawer, and proceeded to become even more active.

"Retirement" has brought Mom a new career. Her organization of the senior citizens in her city amazes us, and it is here that she has found her greatest challenge and reward.

On a prominent hill stands a three-story Victorian home dedicated to the senior citizens of her city. With Mom's determination and ceaseless efforts, she convinced the city fathers that senior citizens needed a recreation center. It is here they gather, in this, *their* home, with pride and satisfaction. And it is to this house that she regularly goes to help organize dances as well as trips to the farthest corners of the state. My mom—organizing dances? Yes, she, and many like her. She is alive, doing well, and loving every minute!

It is summer in Vermont and I called last week to ask if she would be able to come up soon. I was surprised, though why I do not know, to hear her say,

"I really can't say. You see, I am in charge of the kiln at the pottery three days a week, and, in return any yard work and minor house repairs are done free. I also have a few other commitments that make it difficult to get away right now."

I didn't dare ask who organized this barter of services and who undoubtedly would keep it going, because in my foolish way I still like to think of her sleeping late and drinking morning coffee on a lazy veranda. This I verbalize, but inwardly I cheer her on.

—Courtesy of Linda Henry Garrett

The Meaning of Retirement in an Achievement-Oriented Society

Retirement is a peculiarly modern problem. Not so long ago, men did not live long enough to retire, just as many women did not survive to see their last child leave the family circle. Industrial societies with high standards of living, modern health services, and social benefits, have managed to assure a substantial portion of the population that they will live for some time in retirement. But one major factor contributing to the economy's enormous success in our society is the average American's orientation toward work (Lipset, 1963). Yet, a work-oriented culture also complicates the adjustment to retirement, for people quickly begin to measure their worth by their ability to produce.

By definition, persons in retirement are cut off from this source of self-esteem. Males, in particular, lose a primary role involvement. Several researchers have noted people's tendency to continue working after 65 or to come back into the work force a few months or years after retirement. They often say that they need something to keep themselves busy or that they will simply "go crazy" hanging around the house (Shostak, 1969:226). But more recent studies have tended to play down the psychological problems of adjustment to leisure time. Robert Atchley (1976) found, for example, that less than a third of retiring persons had major difficulties accepting their new status; of these, only 7 percent were distressed by the loss of their jobs. Limited income was a more important frustration to retirement, whether the income loss resulted from leaving the work force, ill health, or the loss of a spouse.

While some research findings of the last 10 to 15 years do suggest that the level of income rather than attitudes toward role loss best predicts the ease of retirement (Johnson and Williamson, 1980:68–9), this major event cannot be reduced to a simple matter of economics. Those with greater financial security in retirement are also the ones with more education, as a general rule (Rapoport and Rapoport, 1980:105–6). Thus, income actually may mask the more important factor of being educationally prepared to shift to other roles. Unfortunately, the available studies on retirement and aging are too limited to determine with certainty the importance of income or education in the transition to a satisfactory life as a senior citizen.

Figure 15-4
Retirement does not
necessarily have to be
an inactive period in
a person's life. Some
couples are drawn
close together and
have new beginnings.
*(Woodfin Camp & Asso-
ciates. Timothy Egan,
photographer)*

Impending or actual retirement also is more attractive when husband and
wife share an interest in some common activities. Indeed, the quality of the
partners' relationship greatly affects how they evaluate the quality of the retirement period.

Husband and Wife Together at Middle Age and Beyond

Often, the coincidence of the wife closing out her mothering career while the
husband is "peaking" in his vocation can force spouses to reevaluate their
relationship. A husband and wife frequently will drift apart during the years
when she is investing her time heavily in the children and he is devoted to
advancing his career. Between the ages of 40 and 50, they may discover that
they have been moving in different orbits for the last 20 years. With the
children gone and the husband's career well established, each has more time
to spend with the other.

The Process of Getting Reacquainted

Of course, not all couples grow apart during the child-rearing years. But this
pattern does occur often enough to merit some concern (Duvall, 1967:401–3).
The relationship between husband and wife in American families is built
around basic tension between parenting and mating demands. Thus, when
parenting responsibilities are reduced, a renewed emphasis can be placed on
husband-wife companionship. Indeed, this is exactly what appears to happen
in many marriages. A growing number of studies on marital satisfaction have

Figure 15-5
Shown in this figure are the average standard scores on marital satisfaction over eight stages of the family life cycle, as indicated by three separate studies. Note that all three record a sharp decline in marital satisfaction around the time of the birth of children and a sharp increase in marital satisfaction when children leave home. *(Source: Boyd C. Rollins and Kenneth L. Cannon, 1974:275.)*

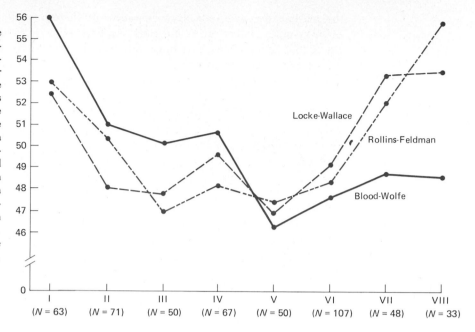

shown a marked increase in happiness in the years after the children have been raised.

Although measuring marital happiness presents a series of difficulties, we can see some broad patterns of marital reactions. Cross-sectional studies of life-cycle rates of marital happiness show, by and large, that newlyweds score high in the happiness category. The first child signals a decline in marital satisfaction; while the drop is more pronounced for mothers, it is also apparent in fathers. After the children grow up and leave, happiness scores climb to at least the level of the "honeymoon period" and sometimes higher (Stinnett, et al., 1972; Campbell, 1975; Troll, Miller, and Atchley, 1979:45–60).

Like many social patterns, these data are not self-interpreting. Does happiness increase among couples who are married longer in these studies because unhappy couples divorce? This may well be a factor. Do couples who are older settle for less in their marital relationship, and thus report more marital satisfaction? Again, this may be occurring in some postparenthood relationships. Overall, however, the rise in happiness is so clear in such a wide variety of studies that it does seem reasonable to conclude that real gains in marital satisfaction are achieved during this stage. Moreover, happiness scores also appear to be directly related to the amount of companionship, the leisure activities pattern, and the quality of communication between husband and wife (Orthner, 1975).

Troll and Smith (1976) suggest, however, that the companionship developed in the later years of marriage differs a great deal from the companionship of the "honeymoon period." At the beginning of marriage when the experience is still novel, attraction is higher than attachment. Over the course of the marital life cycle, attraction becomes routinized, while attachment grows as the couple shares more and more experiences—joys, crises, and memories. Thus, while companionship and marital happiness are high early and late in marriage, companionship and the components of happiness are structured differently during these two periods in the life span.

Divorce and Remarriage in the Middle and Later Years

Over the past several decades, the divorce rate has steadily increased. However, the proportion of divorces which occur after age 45 has not shown a large increase (Troll, Miller, Atchley, 1979:54). Some social scientists had been concerned that the departure of the children would provoke a sharp bulge in the divorce rate as couples who had stayed together for the children's sake finally parted rather than spend another 20 years or more in an unsatisfying relationship. But, apparently, this pattern has not emerged. Divorce among older couples has increased at about the same rate as in the overall population.

Moreover, the remarriage rate also has kept pace among older persons. However, almost 75 percent of those who remarry at a later age are widows or widowers, and about 25 percent are persons who had been divorced (Troll, Miller, Atchley, 1979:65–7). The major reason people cited for remarrying during their later years is companionship. In addition, older couples also desire the love, respect, and sexual outlets which marriage provides. But since men die at an earlier age, fewer men are available, which no doubt makes it hard for many middle-aged and older women to find a new partner.

The Role of Grandparents

When Parsons and others were formulating the notion of the nuclear family, the fear was rather commonly expressed that older parents would have little contact with their children because of the distance separating their residences and the psychological need for privacy. Since the grandparent-grandchild relationship is channeled through the parents, observers thought the pattern of isolation might hinder interaction between the grandparents and grandchild. While few older Americans do live with their married children, grandparents were actually far less isolated from their grandchildren (and children) than they were believed to be (Spark and Brody, 1970). Seventy-five percent of parents who are 65 years or older live within an hour's drive of their nearest child (Glick and Norton, 1977:21). Furthermore, the contacts, visits, and other ties by which grandparents are related to their grandchildren are not only frequent but also quite varied. Such contacts range from giving gifts or babysitting to telling stories, relating family history, providing advice on personal problems, and many other activities (Robertson, 1977:171).

To be sure, grandparents play their roles in a great many ways. We can see this variety as we look at the reported joys of grandparenthood and the major traits of this social role.

The Joys of Being a Grandparent

One common theme in interviews with grandparents is how much they enjoy playing with, entertaining, and loving their grandchildren, especially since they know that at the end of their visit they can go home and leave the children's diapers, feeding, discipline, and supervision to the parents. Grandparenting affords all the pleasures of children without the worry or the mess. For this reason, grandparents often can feel somewhat freer in "spoiling" their grandchildren than they could with their own children.

Most studies have focused on grandmothers rather than on both grandparents. However, Robertson (1977) found in her sample of grandmothers that 80 percent were elated, proud, excited, and happy when they learned that one of their children was expecting a child. Presumably, the other 20 percent found the news less than thrilling because they thought themselves either too young or—less likely—too old for their new position. Moreover, 37 percent of the grandmothers interviewed by Robertson preferred grandparenting to parenting—with only 32 percent favoring parenting over grandparenting and 25 percent enjoying both roles equally.

Figure 15-6
The joys of being a grandparent include sharing your favorite activities with your grandchild. *(Gloria Karlson, photographer)*

Judging from the limited studies on grandfathers, this new role does not seem to make much of an impact until after retirement (Leslie, 1979:614). Prior to that time, grandfathers apparently find their jobs too demanding to invest in their grandchildren the time and concern their wives can extend. But after retirement both grandmothers and grandfathers often come to regard their grandchildren as persons who can help keep them young, give them welcome relief from exclusive contact with older persons, and help break up their routines or loneliness by introducing something different into their lives. For all these reasons, most older parents see grandparenting as desirable and intensely pleasurable.

The Characteristics of the Grandparent's Role

Major changes have occurred in the grandparent's role over the past few years, largely because grandparents are younger today (Duberman, 1977:153). Younger grandparents can engage in a much wider variety of activities with their grandchildren since they are less likely to suffer from ill health, low physical stamina, and a shortage of patience in dealing with the antics of young children. Today, however, women are marrying in their late teens or early twenties, and may well become grandmothers before they are 40 years old. Men are becoming grandparents earlier too, though they are slightly older than their wives.

Early grandparenthood can create problems for persons who do not feel they are old enough for that status. Grandchildren are a reminder that one is middle-aged or older. Moreover, young grandparents will not be very far beyond their own child-rearing experience. These problems, however, apparently are offset somewhat by the chance to enjoy one's grandchildren while still fully active.

In addition to beginning earlier, the grandparent role has expanded from its scope in earlier generations. Grandmothers still come to care for the family when a child is born. Immediately after the birth, someone needs to look after the new mother, her baby, and the husband who usually has a job that takes him away from the household during the day. This responsibility usually is taken on by one of the grandmothers. But this is only one task which grandparents perform. They also baby-sit periodically, if they live close enough to the parents. They may help out in emergencies, take the grandchildren on vacations, give advice when requested to both grandchildren and their parents, teach practical skills, entertain, and inform grandchildren about their heritage.

All of these activities tend to be organized into a behavioral type. In her research on grandmothers, Robertson (1977) outlined the patterns of four different approaches to the grandmother role. These included the symbolic, individualized, apportioned, and remote types. Grandmothers in the symbolic behavioral style took the normative social expectations very seriously and tried to do what was morally good or right for their grandchildren. Individualized grandmothers showed little concern for social expectations, being almost totally interested in the joys and pleasures of their grandmother role for

426

themselves and their grandchildren. Grandmothers playing the apportioned role tried to blend normative and personal meanings. Included in the remote type were grandmothers who found little meaning or satisfaction in their roles.

Although grandfathers have not been studied in a similar way, we probably can assume that these patterns also would fit their role behaviors fairly well. However, we might find a striking difference in the percentage of grandfathers in each category. For example, we probably could assume that more grandfathers than grandmothers would fall into the remote category. One also might expect to find more grandfathers in the individualized category than in the symbolic or remote groups. However, these are only hunches; it remains for future studies to confirm or deny them.

Summary

This chapter explores the transitions which parents undergo from middle age to the onset of retirement. Paul Glick (1977) has argued that no period in the life cycle has experienced more drastic change than the time after the launching of children.

The family group is unique in that its normal course of development in American society requires self-liquidation. For new families to be formed, children must leave the nuclear family. Preparation for this event begins during adolescence as children acquire more and more autonomy. Changes in parent-child relationships affect both parties. Adults begin to look at their maturing children differently and allow them more behavioral leeway, while youth also begin to see their parents in a new way.

The "middle-age crises"—as the transition to postparenthood often is labeled—is different for wives and husbands. Entrance into the empty nest period for mothers marks the completion of what many women consider their primary career role. The adjustment of mothers to this period reveals some ambivalence, ranging from some loss of identity to relief that she has been freed from child-rearing responsibilities. Launching children is less traumatic for the father. His major adjustment occurs when he confronts his retirement. Though transition to retirement can be difficult for all, it is generally easier for white-collar fathers than for working-class fathers.

The departure of children gives the parents more time to get reacquainted. Although this companionship is different than it was during the first years of marriage, it again becomes an important feature in the lives of middle-aged couples. Their marital happiness also tends to increase throughout this period.

Most parents in middle age and beyond take on a new role with the birth of new family members in the third generation, namely, the role of grandparents. Many in this age group see grandparenting as more satisfying than parenting. Grandparents have all the joys and pleasures of having young children without the responsibilities of caring for and socializing them. Since grandparents tend to be younger today, they now share more activities with their grandchildren.

STUDY QUESTIONS

1. What do social scientists mean when they speak of the family as "a self-liquidating institution"?
2. How do the relationships between parents and children change as the children grow older and become independent adults?

3. In what sense can the launching of children be seen by mothers as a completion of their career? What are the alternatives to this view for mothers?
4. How is a father's retirement from his occupation similar to the launching of children for many mothers?
5. Why is it often necessary for a husband and wife to get reacquainted after middle age and beyond?
6. What are the various styles of fulfilling the grandmother role identified by social scientists? Which one do you find the most satisfying? Why?

Being Alone: The Dynamics of Aging, Widowhood, and Death

the Disengagement theory

Life has been the central subject matter of this book. More precisely, we have tried to understand how people organize their lives and live them within the institutions of marriage and the family. Death is the final rite of passage. Moreover, it is a reality with which all families must meet at some point. Our discussion in this chapter will consider the meaning of death in contemporary Western culture, then discuss the experience of being alone in widowhood and widowerhood, the dynamics of aging, the use of one's leisure time in old age, the psychological problems of facing death, the symbolic meaning of the funeral, and finally the various ways to cope with grief.

The Meaning of Death in Western Civilization

The master sociologist, Max Weber (1958a:356), once said about the death of Abraham, the Old Testament patriarch, that death no longer means for us what it meant for ancient people. About Abraham, it was said that he died "full of years and satiated with life." Weber remarked that Abraham could be "satiated with life" because he lived in a world where history was viewed as a cycle. The goal of life was to complete the circle, that is, to be born, grow up with parental favor, marry, have children, acquire property, enjoy one's grandchildren, and then die having experienced all that life has to offer. Today, however, we view history as a continuing straight line. Our cultural values stress the importance of future achievement, so that one can never really accomplish everything one desires. No matter how much power, money, or knowledge one may amass, we always could do more. The great enemy confronting those of modern sensibilities is not the scarcity of material luxuries, but the scarcity of time. Furthermore, because life can never be "completed" in the same sense that it was for the ancients, Weber concludes that death has ceased to possess a firm meaning for contemporary men and women. Every death tends to be viewed as a premature foreclosure on life. The end comes before one's goals can be achieved. Thus, Weber suggests that death has become a disturbing event in Western culture. The recent explosion of interest in death and dying—as evidenced by the increasing number of college courses, books, and organizations concerned with this human experience—indicates its troublesome nature for many people today.

We are not raising issues associated with the meaning of death as a way to introduce some glib "solution." The complexity and importance of these matters is much too great for simple-minded responses. One does need to be aware, however, that the meaning of death is intimately tied up with a person's ability to see meaning in life. Moreover, widowhood, aging, and the reality of death may mean more when they are seen against the transformation of the ultimate meaning of death in contemporary Western culture.

When a young couple marries, the partners seldom think about the likelihood that one of them will outlive the other by several years. In most cases, the wife is the survivor. Reentry into the single life is often a painful and difficult experience, especially for those older couples who have been married for a long time before one or the other spouse dies. Typically, men find it harder to adjust to a spouse's death than women. As a rule, however, widowers are much more likely to have the opportunity to remarry than widows (Kastenbaum, 1979:84). In part, this fact is explained by the different life expectancy rates for men and women.

CLOSE-UP

Charlie and Josephine were so devoted that they had been inseparable for nearly 10 years. Then one midwinter day, in a senseless act of violence so typical of our times, Charlie was fatally shot in a melee with the police.

Josephine saw it all and, horror-stricken, sank to her knees beside Charlie's still body, placing her head at the site of his mortal wound. Fifteen minutes later, she, too, was dead.

Charlie and Josephine were llamas who lived at the Lollipop Farm Zoo in Rochester. Josephine, who had been healthy until Charlie's sudden demise, apparently died of a broken heart, a phenomenon well known in poetry and folklore but rarely acknowledged by modern medicine.

Yet numerous studies in recent years have emphasized the high toll that bereavement and loneliness can take on human life and health. With divorce and widowhood on the increase, marriage on the decline and the extended family all but gone, growing numbers of Americans are living alone.

A British study of the close relatives of 488 persons who died showed that in the first year after becoming widowed, the death rate among surviving spouses was 10 times higher than among married people of comparable age and sex.

Another study at Montefiore Medical Center in the Bronx disclosed that in the first 15 months after being widowed, older persons with such major medical problems as heart disease or diabetes became much worse and were more likely to seek medical help than those of the same age who were not bereaved.

The author of the report, Dr. Anne R. Somers, a specialist in family and community medicine at Rutgers Medical School in Piscataway, N.J., says the statistics from 1940 through 1961 show that among men and women at every age, married people on the average live longer than the single, widowed or divorced.

Although data relating death rates to marital status are not available for the 1970's, recent national health statistics show that, except for persons who never married, married people make the least demand on the health care system.

The data on admissions to mental hospitals are far more striking. In 1975, according to the National Institute for Mental Health, among married persons

(continued)

89.9 per 100,000 Americans 14 and older were admitted to a state or community psychiatric hospital. In each marital category the rates for men were much higher than those for women.

Similarly, among residents of nursing homes in the United States in the mid-1970's, only 12 percent were married, 64 percent were widowed, 19 percent had never been married and 5 percent were divorced or separated (divorce being uncommon among this older generation). A main reason for these statistics is obvious, Dr. Somers said in an interview. Elderly, ill persons who live alone often cannot care for themselves. She noted that 30 to 40 percent of nursing home residents are there not strictly for medical reasons. But factors like loneliness and despair as a precipitant of illness also play a largely neglected role, she and others believe.

Lynch, a psychologist at the University of Maryland School of Medicine in Baltimore, notes that unmarried persons not only visit physicians more often but also stay in hospitals longer than do married people with similar illnesses. Illness, he points out, is a legitimate means for lonely people to get others to pay attention to them.

"Individuals who live alone—widows and widowers, divorced and single people—may be particularly vulnerable to stress and anxiety," Dr. Lynch believes, because they "continuously lack the tranquilizing influence of human companionship during life's stresses." This increased vulnerability to stress, in turn, makes them more susceptible to physical as well as emotional illnesses, numerous studies have suggested.

Dr. Thomas Holmes and his colleagues at the University of Washington in Seattle have established through studies of thousands of persons a clear-cut relationship between the stresses of various "life events" and the onset of illness. At the top of their list is death of a spouse, followed by divorce and marital separation.

Rather than avoiding discussion of the deceased with the bereaved and trying to "take their minds off" grief, the researchers suggest, friends and relatives should do just the opposite. As part of preventive medical care, they urge hospitals to establish "bereavement clinics" to assist the survivors.

The stresses of remaining single or becoming divorced may be easing as these states become socially more acceptable, Dr. Somers said. There has also been a recent about-face—in the declining rate of marriage and a slowing of the increase in the divorce rate.

According to Dr. Somers, it is too soon to know the permanence of these trends or what effect they may have on health. But if Dr. Holmes's data are any indication, the effect of changing marriage and divorce rates will be minimal. His data show that "happy" life events can be as stressful as unhappy ones.

—Jane E. Brody,
excerpted from *The New York Times*

Differential Death Rates for Men and Women

Although life-expectancy rates have been increasing steadily for the total population over the last century (Social Indicators, 1976:146–56), women continue to outlive their husbands by a number of years. About 12 percent of

American men between the ages of 65 and 74 are widowers, but the rate of widowhood is considerably higher. Between the ages of 65 and 74, almost 45 percent of all previously married women are widows, and at 75 years of age, almost 71 percent of married women have lost their husbands to death. The higher death rate for men is partially a function of their less hardy biological constitution—men die sooner at all age levels than women. To compound this problem, as we noted in Chapter 5, the cultural norm in American society encourages men to marry women who are an average of two years younger. This ensures that more husbands will die before their wives. If the pattern simply were reversed, the rate of widowhood might be reduced considerably.

The Experience of Widowerhood

While relatively few husbands outlive their wives, being a widower is generally seen by family members and by widowers themselves as more troublesome than being a widow (Berardo, 1970:13). Grief over the loss of a spouse is divided equally between the sexes, so far as we know, but men often are thrust into a number of household functions which are new to them. A widower is more likely than a widow to need outside help to cook his meals, clean the living quarters, and look after his general welfare.

Moreover, widowers usually feel more social isolation than widows. Among kinship relations, grandfathers usually find their role somewhat less meaningful and gratifying than grandmothers. Widowers are also somewhat less likely to move in with their married children than widows, presumably because mothers can be more useful by contributing to household maintenance. Furthermore, men commonly engage in outdoor social activities—fishing, hunting, sports of one sort or another. With advancing age, these activities become less and less possible.

Thus, widowers often have more problems adjusting to the single life than widows. This is especially the case if they are beyond the retirement age—which eliminates their occupational status as a major source of personal satisfaction—and if their health is declining. In fact, under such conditions, widowerhood may be devastating (Berardo, 1970:17). Without these personal resources to fall back upon, older men can, in effect, give in to death because they have nothing to live for.

The Experience of Widowhood

Most wives expect to outlive their husbands. This probably cushions the impact of widowhood to some extent. Certainly, the loss of a mate with whom a woman had established an intimate relationship cannot be accepted easily. Yet, maintaining a separate residence, performing household tasks, continuing kinship relationships, and avoiding social isolation are all easier for widows than widowers.

The major problem of widows does not appear to be the trauma over losing a husband, nor ill health, nor even the loss of social contacts with friends and relatives. Instead, women, far more than single men, face a shortage of income (Harvey and Bahr, 1974). Many women who are becoming widows today have never worked outside the home or have such limited retirement benefits that they can barely live above the poverty line. Sustaining an adequate life-style is almost beyond their means, in more than a few instances.

However, widows do have a number of social factors decidedly in their favor. Women typically develop more extensive and intricate social networks than men. These can be an important defense against loneliness and social isolation. Moreover, women are more likely to engage in quiet social activities which they can share with others, such as knitting and handicrafts.

Widows also keep up family ties and friendship patterns more readily than widowers. However, without her husband, a single woman may find it harder to keep up her friendships with other couples. Couple activities tend to be quite different from those friendships in which single persons engage. Often, a widow can find some continuity with the past in the routine maintenance of her home, and sometimes, such activity can moderate the shock of her sudden widowhood. Yet, the absence of her husband may make these tasks less gratifying because no one else appreciates the fact that they have been done.

The loss of social relations and functions among widows, especially, is reflected in dramatically higher mortality rates. In a recent survey of important research on death rates among widows, as opposed to elderly couples, Berardo (1970:17–9) reported that in some studies recent widows had death rates as much as seven times the normal rate. Other researchers did not report quite as strong a link between bereavement and mortality. Yet, the relationship was clear enough to conclude that grief, identity disorientation, and a loss of the "will to live" often followed a spouse's death. The combination of all of these factors hastened the death of the last survivor of the original pair.

Part of the difficulty of "grief work," according to Hiltz (1978), is that **widowhood** is a **"roleless role."** This means that widowhood tends to be defined negatively as a loss of role functions. The lack of clear directions for redefining one's identity, for rebuilding morale, and for reconstructing one's life in the single status makes recovery from bereavement all the more complicated and difficult. Thus, Hiltz targets the overcoming of the roleless role of widowhood as an important step toward lessening the harmful effects of widowhood.

Remarriage in the December Years

A person whose spouse dies is once again in a position to marry. **December marriages** are becoming increasingly common, partly because of a growing social acceptance of the practice and partly because of increased life expectancy. The major reason given for marrying after the retirement years is the desire for companionship (Troll, Miller, Atchley, 1979:66). Just as the loneli-

Figure 16-1
The major reason for December marriages is the desire for companionship, which not only dispels loneliness but also raises morale and often gives a couple a renewed zest for living in their senior years. *(Monkmeyer Press Photo Service. David Striczler, photographer)*

ness of the previously married can lower morale, marriage can raise morale and provide a new reason for living. Moreover, since male and female sexual drives persist into the senior years—though the appetitie for sexual activity frequently diminishes after age 70 (Koller, 1968:45)—an outlet for the sexual drive is not an uncommon reason for remarriage in later life.

The number of December marriages might well be larger, if such a number of obstacles did not stand in the way for many senior citizens. For various reasons, children discourage their parents from remarrying by suggesting that "You are simply too old for that sort of thing" (Kastenbaum, 1979:88). Although this attitude is changing, it probably still does condemn a number of postretirement singles to live in more loneliness than necessary. Another formidable obstacle is purely economic. In some instances, Social Security laws reduce payments to the married. Thus, remarriage is often a larger burden than many older folks can afford. As a result, a fair number of older Americans are cohabiting without a marriage license, but with their full retirement incomes (Schwartz and Peterson, 1979:109).

Not all widows and widowers, of course, want to remarry. This does not necessarily mean that they had endured unhappy marriages and do not want to repeat the experience (Lopata, 1973). Some who were extremely happy simply cannot envision being married to another person. Others feel their kinship bonds with their children and other relatives are strong enough to support them through their remaining years, and still others are hampered with declining health, which could make remarriage unattractive to themselves and to a potential mate.

Despite the complications and obstacles, however, many couples in their senior years decide to remarry. Although the data are limited on late marriages, we may conclude from the rate of divorce and from the studies of marital happiness that most find that remarriage helps their morale, their psychological well-being, and their outlook on life.

Aging and the Problem of Declining Health

One sign of advancing age is the limitation of activities caused by declining health. Government statistics for 1977 indicate that 43 percent of Americans over the age of 65 were forced to limit their activities due to a chronic health condition (U.S. Bureau of the Census, 1979:122). The degree of disability varies a good deal according to the type of health problem. For example, chronic diabetes usually can be controlled with medication and proper diet, while a severe loss of vision may be considerably more confining. Moreover, people vary in their capacities to cope with the failure to carry on their daily activities. Most elderly persons can compensate for the loss of one skill or ability by developing other skills within their physical competence.

Successful adjustment to increasing age requires a resocialization process which both realigns one's self-concept and reorganizes the activities of one's daily routine. Of course, no set life-style exists into which all elderly persons automatically are socialized. In some instances, individuals adopt the popular image of an old person and act as though they were passive, frail, and incompetent, even though they may enjoy relatively good health. Others accept the physical limitations and retain their psychological vitality by developing their social roles selectively. They pour new energy into doing the things they can with their limited physical abilities. Social well-being among the aged is not solely a matter of the absence of disease or chronic disability. Well-being also includes a mental outlook which allows a senior citizen to establish a life-style with purpose and meaning.

Maladjustment to the aging process and forced isolation because of ill health are more common problems among the impoverished elderly (Social Indicators, 1976:144–5, 209–11). Low-income, older Americans are confined more often to their homes, have a lower calorie intake, receive less dental care, and generally cope less adequately with the problems of age than persons with higher retirement incomes and more education. Thus, the ability to adapt to the limitations imposed by age is not determined by one's psychological outlook alone, but also by one's position within the social class system.

In several critical respects, American culture works against the elderly person's need to develop a positive self-image. The popular culture tends to glorify youth and disparage old age. Cosmetic commercials promise that women can look 22 when they reach the "ancient" age of 30. Our work ethic implies that those who are not producing are socially worthless. Modern medicine has brought us the surgical "face-lift" which partially removes the signs of age. Running through all these examples is the common theme: To be young is good, to be old is unfortunate. The popular culture finds little to value in age. Instead, the old are encouraged to "age gracefully, " which often means to step aside and allow themselves to be shelved while younger persons assume the important business of living.

Faced with such cultural attitudes, it is difficult to be resocialized into the role of senior citizen and find the status gratifying. Men are especially likely to regret the loss of physical stamina. Women are somewhat more inclined to regret the loss of their physical appearance. But the most difficult adjustment of all may be the forced isolation which so often follows illness or incapacitation. Elderly persons who are confined to their homes or a home for the aged become dependent on others, not only for their basic services but also for the vital influence of human contact. Those who can no longer maintain relationships may withdraw involuntarily from social affairs.

One group of scholars has developed a "**disengagement theory**" to account for gradual withdrawal from social life, even before ill health or reduced income begin to restrict the elderly person (Cumming and Henry, 1961). According to this view, both individuals and society prepare for the time when physical disability and eventually death remove older persons from social life by encouraging a process of steady disengagement from relationships within the wider society. Disengagement lessens the disruption of social life caused by the loss of one of its members, and it allows old persons to confront death without fear that their departure will disturb those social groups in which they previously participated.

Disengagement theory has been subjected to a considerable amount of criticism (Koller, 1968:151–3). Its critics claim that people have not voluntarily retreated from social involvement; more often, they have been forced to retreat by circumstances beyond their control. Thus, disengagement is not inevitable, nor should it be tolerated. Many senior citizens can make important contributions to friends, neighbors, relatives, and social groups. But, to do so, they may need a system of social engagement, new roles to assume after retirement. Reengagement strategies could be introduced by voluntary agencies, religious and community service agencies, or other types of civic organizations. Or, they could be developed by individuals. But the major thrust of **reengagement programs** must be to change the attitude that old age is a kind of holding pattern until death.

Ultimately, of course, the normal aging process must take its toll on health endurance. However, reengagement theorists and social service workers try to stress that aging has an important mental aspect. People who feel that they are old, useless, and socially unproductive will have a hard time keeping up their morale, and their physical strength as well. Such a mental outlook may hasten death. On the other hand, a positive attitude toward aging, coupled with a realistic appraisal of remaining skills may be both socially and person-

Figure 16-2
Senior citizens may use their leisure time to engage in new or exciting activities and make new friends, or they may be forced by reason of declining health into long periods of isolation with only an occasional visit by family or friends to break up their boredom. *(Copyright © by Stock, Boston. Peter Menzel, photographer; Michael Weisbert, photographer)*

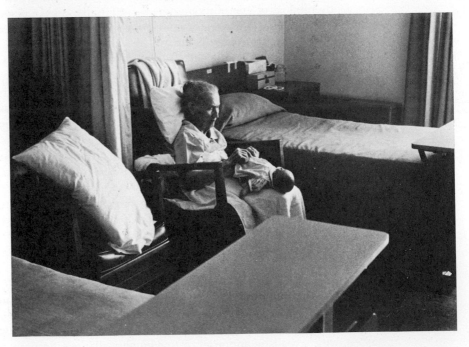

438

A Season for Growing Old

ally productive. Old age is not a time we can calculate exactly. Nor, by the same token, can the potential of older Americans be defined neatly across the whole population. Successful adjustment and a vital life-style include more than simply an absence of disease or physical disability. Much depends as well on how the elderly approach aging and make the most of the possibilities of later life.

The journals of **social gerontology**—a relatively new field which studies the process of aging and the problems of the elderly—are filled with reminders that age is both a physically determined condition and a social position or status. Thus, the social roles the elderly adopt are determined in large part as much by self-image as by age and physical abilities. A zest for life can prevail among the elderly and chronically disabled, despite the popular culture's tendency to write them off as socially useless. One aim of social gerontologists is to devise means to tap the knowledge and skills of the elderly, not only because these skills are a valuable social resource, but also because their use can help bring elderly persons back into the dynamics of social life.

The Creative Use of Free Time in Later Years

Many American cultural analysts believe that our strong achievement orientation and work ethic make the enjoyment of leisure activities a problem for younger and older Americans. Persons who have devoted most of their lives to work often find it difficult to enjoy recreation without the guilty feeling that they should be doing something productive. Moreover, greater longevity provides senior citizens with more years of leisure which can weigh heavily on those who cannot enjoy activities that are not related to work.

The activities of the elderly vary according to their health and income. Those with good health and enough money often travel, frequently on tours that are designed specifically for the elderly. Many older persons join associations to enjoy social activities, such as luncheons, card games, participation in sports, and outings to the movies, the theater, or museums. Others keep up active social lives through informal means. They design their own schedules for visiting neighbors or relatives, inviting guests in for dinner, or helping others in the neighborhood.

Of course, many activities of the elderly are passive in nature, even among those in good health. Among the more popular solitary activities are watching television, reading, sewing, gardening, and individual hobbies (Schwartz and Peterson, 1979:124–6). In their recreational outlets, the elderly seek goals similar to those of other age groups, namely activities which provide new experiences, pleasure, and entertainment. In addition, many elderly people seek various nonrecreational activities in which they can serve others through counseling, direct aid, or simply by filling otherwise lonely hours with companionship and conversation.

Figure 16-3
A foster grandmother can bring joy and love to a child's life, even as her foster grandchildren can help her stay active and socially involved. (© Rapho/Photo Researchers, Inc.)

Living With One's Children

Over the past few decades, the living arrangements of older Americans have been discussed widely in our society. The main concern has been whether children would assume responsibility for their aging parents when they become too old to live by themselves. Indeed, a number of social commentators have charged children with a callous disregard for their elderly parents. They see a rising trend among children to pay for their parents' care in a nursing home or to relegate them to a senior citizens' apartment house, rather than take them into their own household.

At first glance, the data seem to suport the idea that children are shirking the duty of caring for their aging parents. In 1955, for example, 80 percent of all men over 65 were living as head of the household (either as heads of primary households or as single individuals). By 1975, however, almost 95 percent of all men over 65 were living in their own households. Similarly, the number of older women living as primary individuals jumped from 23 percent in 1955 to 39 percent in 1975 (*Social Indicators*, 1976:42, 64). Also during the 1970s, a dramatic rise occurred in federal spending for subsidized public

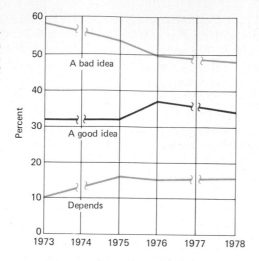

Figure 16-4
Older Persons Sharing Home with Their Grown Children. (Source: *Social Indicators 1980, p. 11*)

housing for the elderly, rising from $0.2 billion in 1971 to $1.1 billion in 1978 (U.S. Bureau of the Census, 1979:330).

These data do not explain why older persons are living apart from their children and in government-subsidized housing. Have their children abandoned them or do they choose to maintain a separate household for as long as possible? Almost all of the available studies point toward the second option. Today, an average male at age 65 has almost 14 more years to live, and a woman almost 19 years. Both are generally quite active, healthy, and capable of caring for themselves. Indeed, many persons who reach age 75 still handle their own personal affairs. Healthy and financially secure senior citizens generally prefer to live on their own and manage their own households.

When living alone no longer is possible because of declining health or finances, about three times more elderly persons live with their children or other relatives than enter nursing homes, hospitals, or other institutions. Mary Jo Bane (1976:46–9) reports, for example, that only 2 percent of the elderly between the ages of 65 and 74 are living in homes for the aged, and of those 75 and older only 7 percent of all males and 11 percent of all females are receiving some form of institutional care. These low figures are especially impressive since today's elderly were born around the first decade of this century when marriage and fertility rates reached an all-time low. Almost 10 percent of this generation never married and between 15 and 20 percent of those who married did not have children. Consequently, about 25 percent of today's elderly have no children to care for them. The rise in the number of elderly people seeking public housing and help as well as the rise in nursing home residents seems to result not so much from abandonment of the elderly by their children, as from the fact that many elderly simply have no children to care for them.

We can draw two conclusions about the living arrangements of elderly persons in America. The first is that older Americans prefer to live independently on their own for as long as possible. Increased prosperity and government assistance have made this arrangement realistic for a growing proportion of the aged in this society. The second conclusion is that, when family support is necessary, children and other relatives do not appear reluctant to provide it. Many elderly people who can no longer live alone, of course, require more health care than their children can provide in their homes. Thus, a nursing home is the only adequate solution for many aged persons who fall within this category. But from what we know, it is probably unfair to suggest that middle-aged children are turning their backs on their aged parents. Although this may occur in isolated instances, it does not appear to be widespread.

CLOSE-UP

Rose was a successful woman—and very resourceful. At the age of 19, she had traveled alone from Russia to the United States via Canada. Her early years of marriage were hard; she and Sam were poor. To supplement their income, she took in laundry and raised several foster children along with her own two sons and daughters. But despite the difficulty they had in making ends meet, her home was always immaculate and her family well groomed.

She and Sam had a full life together, yet he died 20 years before her, leaving her a widow at age 69. Her pride and inner strength kept her in her second-floor apartment. Then, at the age of 82, her arthritis became severe enough to make the climb up and down the stairs too difficult. Until then, she had been able to cook and clean for herself, albeit slowly, but in the manner she liked. Now, the proud woman admitted that she could no longer stay in her apartment. She had to find a place where her needs could be more easily met.

Rose talked with her daughter about coming to live with her daughter's family. They both agreed that that wouldn't be a comfortable situation for either of them. So her daughter took her to a number of senior citizen hotels and she chose one where she felt she would be most comfortable. After dividing her possessions and treasures among her family and keeping only a few momentos for herself, she moved in.

She now began a new phase of her life. The first few years were okay. Her children and grandchildren visited her as often as they could—they only lived 45 minutes away—and life was made easier by the service in a dining room and a maid service to keep the room clean, though she still preferred to dust and do some cleaning herself. Her arthritis left her in constant pain, but her pride prevented her from complaining. Only she knew how much she really suffered.

Then one day she fell and broke her hip—the nemesis of aging people. She was in the hospital for several weeks and was then moved to a nursing home for rehabilitation. Her daughter visited her almost every day. Rose was determined to leave that nursing home on her two feet—she would show them what "stuff" she was made of. After several months, she returned to the senior citizen hotel.

At 86, age really began to take its toll. Although she could still clean and groom herself, she needed more regular medical care than could be provided where she was living. Her daughter and son located a facility that was similar to a hotel, but also provided additional medical services. Once again, Rose was uprooted. And, to further complicate her life, she had to share a room with another woman—sicker and older than she. "I hate old people," she said with a mischievous glimmer in her eye. "I'm not old, am I?" She enjoyed being around young people and felt rejuvenated by them. People often commented that she was very sharp for her 86 years.

In the December of her eighty-ninth year, Rose entered the hospital with a problem resulting from her arthritis. After a four-month stay, it was clear that she would never leave again. Bringing the great-grandchildren with them her children and grandchildren came to see her during her last few days. The babies were too young to be permitted to her room, but they smiled at her through the window and she waved to them. As one of the babies gurgled at her one bright day in late March, she asked, "Why isn't the baby wearing a hat?" The pride, the sharpness, the family commitment were all still there. Two days later she died, still a proud woman.

Planning One's Estate

In planning their estates, most persons want to see that their financial resources are passed on to their dependents and other close relatives. This does not happen automatically. One must clearly designate in an appropriate legal manner who should receive the estate and under what conditions. When properly written and filed, a will is a fairly simple device to assure that one's family will receive their fair share of one's property and estate.

One's will should be reviewed regularly and changed when the circumstances require a revision. Most wills are prepared when a couple is relatively young. A number of changes may be needed during the course of a couple's life cycle. Certainly, when the death of one's spouse seems likely to occur soon, a final review is in order so that the surviving spouse will be assured of swift access to the funds he or she will need during the bereavement period. This time of grief is difficult enough, without also having to worry about one's financial situation.

Psychological Preparation for Death

The American attitude toward death has changed a number of times in the course of our brief national history. In his study of the Puritan "way of death," David Stannard (1979) has pointed out that the early inhabitants of New England confronted death with a marked ambivalence. On one hand, their sense of human sinfulness made death a terrifying "day of reckoning." On the other hand, death served as a release from this world of striving and held forth the promise of a better world without sin, pain, or disease. By the nineteenth century, Stannard continues, the somber reminders of Hell had fallen away and Americans tended to romanticize death as a glorious time when loved ones were united in heaven. In the twentieth century, the dominant attitude toward death has moved toward a denial and avoidance of this final stage in the life cycle. Death has been socially relegated to hospitals and nursing homes where it touches only the dying person's closest relatives. The process of dying has been shrouded from all but a few medical personnel and next of kin; it also has been depersonalized through the use of sedatives and complex life-support equipment so that the dying person often is reduced to being only a functioning body.

Stannard concludes that contemporary Americans try to avoid the reality of death because we are bewildered by its awesome finality and irrevocable character. Our conceptual resources are no longer enough to give death a meaning. Thus, we are intrigued by death as a universal human experience and yet eager to escape when it draws near.

Similar observations on the American way of death appear frequently in the literature on dying written by workers in the medical, theological, and social sciences. One unfortunate result of the avoidance attitude toward death is that it greatly complicates people's efforts to deal with their own deaths. When death is perceived as emptiness, it becomes a frightening and lonely experience. If family members withdraw from contact with the dying, refuse to speak of death, and act as though nothing extraordinary is happening, the experience for the dying person may well become more difficult and painful than necessary.

It probably would be unfair to suggest that family members consciously abandon loved ones when death approaches. A more plausible view is that family members simply do not know the needs of a dying person and how they can help satisfy these needs. Robert Kastenbaum (1979:116–8) proposes that, as death approaches, an elderly person is likely to be flooded with many feelings and needs. These can best be met if we keep in mind that the dying person is a specific individual who deserves consideration on his or her own unique terms. Some may simply need to talk—either as a way to confront their coming death or to maintain for as long as possible a vital contact. Others may want help in putting their personal affairs in order. Still others may wish to pass along instructions for their funerals or make final decisions about who is to receive their personal property. Frequently, elderly persons simply want companionship as they face their deaths. Conversation is likely to focus on common memories, on accomplishments, or on things left undone. Sometimes, the dying wish to explain some previous behavior or tell secrets which they feel the living ought to know. And for some, this is a chance to share their fears and receive comfort from those whose love they depend upon.

Since death is the final event of a life cycle, most persons confront this last rite of passage in the way they lived their lives. Elisabeth Kubler-Ross (1969) proposed that most persons pass through five stages as they adjust psychologically to the knowledge of their approaching deaths. While people may generally adjust in some such sequence, subsequent research has largely failed to confirm her theory. More likely, people adapt to death through a number of personal strategies shaped by their own character structure and life experiences (Johnson and Williamson, 1980:157–60). Just as each of us works out our own life-style, each person appears to work out his or her own style of dying. The individuality achieved over a lifetime prevails in that life's last event.

The Symbolic Significance of the Funeral

The major turning points of life, such as baptism, confirmation, marriage, and twenty-fifth wedding anniversaries, are marked by public ceremonial events which signal our movement from one status to another. The funeral is also a public commemorative event, symbolizing the end of a life. Its purpose is both to show respect for the dead person and to comfort those who mourn the loss of that loved one. Burial ceremonies are among the most ancient of human rites, extending well back into the Paleolithic era (Smart, 1976:39).

American funeral practices have been criticized a great deal in recent years. Beginning with Jessica Mitford's (1963) expose of the commercialization of funeral rituals in her book, *The American Way of Death*, the American funeral industry has been accused with using hard-sell techniques on grief-stricken survivors, with gross exploitation, and with widespread misrepresentation of the value and usefulness of the services provided by funeral directors. Industry spokesmen, of course, have responded with a defense of their charges and services. They contend that the specialized training of funeral directors makes them skilled professionals who can help survivors deal with death in a responsible and therapeutic fashion (Johnson and Williamson, 1980:164–71). Moreover, industry supporters contend that the high cost of dying is simply an extension of the high cost of living.

The U.S. Bureau of Consumer Affairs has arrived at a different conclusion. Their investigation revealed industry-wide deceptive and unfair practices which need government control and regulation (U.S. Bureau of Consumer Protection, 1978). But government action to control abuses will not address the more pervasive fact that contemporary funeral customs support lavish ceremonies with expensive flowers, caskets, embalming techniques, burial vaults, cemetery plots, and long-term maintenance charges. Moreover, it is primarily those who can least afford expensive funerals, namely, the lower and working classes, that are least critical of the funeral industry (Johnson and Williamson, 1980:164).

In a practical vein, several measures may help restrain the high cost of dying. If at all possible, it is much better to make funeral arrangements well in advance, providing, of course, that death does not occur prematurely. Prior arrangements enable the person for whom the funeral will be performed or the survivors to make rational decisions without the complicating factors of grief and sorrow. Many, of course, will find such a suggestion too ghoulish, but an increasing number of elderly persons and their children are choosing this alternative. Costs also can be kept down by being aware of the pressures, subtle and unsubtle, of greedy funeral directors who want to sell the bereaved their most expensive casket. Burial vaults designed to maintain a constant humidity, temperature, and air-tight seal are also pointless extravagances, since bodies will decompose despite these frills. Families also can request that instead of sending perishable flowers, friends and relatives contribute to an enduring memorial, perhaps a scholarship fund or charitable organization. And finally, funeral home services can be reduced. Families can drive their own cars to the cemetery or church instead of renting limousines. They can ask friends or relatives to serve as pallbearers rather than hiring strangers, and they can limit other use of the funeral home to a bare minimum. Above all, family members need to avoid the common psychological pitfall of trying to show how much they loved their deceased relative by spending a lavish sum of money on the funeral.

Beyond the sheer waste of money, the larger danger of an over-commercialized funeral is that it may obscure the real meaning and purpose of burial rites. A funeral should be designed to celebrate the life of the person who has just died. The beauty of the casket, the quality of the make-up on the deceased, and the number of floral wreaths are all secondary to the heartfelt sentiments of the survivors. It is appropriate that funerals are somber occasions, for the loss of any life is a sad event. Yet, there is also something to be said for the New Orleans style of jazz funeral in which the burial party returns from the cemetery accompanied by the joyful sounds of "When the Saints Go Marching In." This celebrates the goodness, the joy, and the unique personal qualities almost everyone manages to share with a select company of relatives and friends. Properly conducted, a funeral should remind those who attend how much their lives have been enriched simply by knowing the deceased.

Coping with Grief and Bereavement

Death is a traumatic experience for the survivors. The sense of loss, permanent absence, and longing for the deceased lingers on in the living (Pincus, 1976). Even if one is prepared for death, it is often difficult to accept. The loss of a parent in advanced old age is still the loss of a parent, and the sorrow is just as intense as it would have been had they died earlier. Indeed, a major result of the emotional closeness of nuclear family members is that they feel keener pain over the loss of a loved one than earlier generations when family bonds were functionally, but not as emotionally, integrated.

Bereavement, especially when a spouse dies, usually shows itself in several forms. These include psychological problems, such as distress and depression, physiological problems such as shortness of breath, lack of energy, or digestive malfunctions, and intellectual difficulties, such as idealizing the deceased and finding it difficult to make decisions on one's own (Troll, Miller, Atchley, 1979:71–81). Coping with bereavement is harder than identifying it. Some persons never quite recover from the loss of a loved one; others require long periods before they can resume their normal routines and reestablish their lives. Grief rehabilitation is seldom scheduled to provide an immediate recovery. Gradually, however, individuals must come to accept the reality of the loved one's death and recognize that their own lives must go on.

One major element that can help survivors move through the bereavement is the support group. Such groups can provide understanding, counseling, and psychological assistance to the bereaved. In England, an organization known as CRUSE aids widows in surviving the mourning period. In the United States, a few groups follow a similar model, pioneered primarily by the Association of Retired Persons (Schwartz and Peterson, 1979:252–3). For the most part, however, families must help individuals in this society cope with grief, since other types of social programs are limited severely in personnel and scope.

The feelings of bereaved persons range across a broad spectrum. A relatively common feeling is guilt at having survived the spouse. Men often feel a profound sense of loss and disorientation because they have lost their wives, on whom they depended for many personal services. Women, by contrast, report a sense of abandonment and desertion (Troll, Miller, Atchley, 1979:71). Moreover, although men find it more difficult to express their grief in emotionally therapeutic forms, most can accept the reality of death more swiftly than women.

The central concern for persons swept up in bereavement is that they recapture the ability to sustain their own lives in a satisfying fashion. Time

Figure 16-5
Loss of a spouse is usually the most traumatic event in a person's life. Expressing one's grief is, however, often the first step toward recovery from bereavement and the realization that one's own life must go on. *(Woodfin Camp & Associates. Julian Calder, photographer)*

alone may help lessen the sense of loss, but if individuals confront their grief, recovery may occur much sooner. Unfortunately, outsiders cannot do this for an individual. Grieving persons must face the fact and resolve within their own minds that a loved one has been lost to death. Only then can they begin to recover and chart a new course. Families and other support groups may be helpful to a bereaved person, but they cannot force someone in the grip of grief to start living his or her own life afresh. If this were possible, the number of incapacitated widows and widowers would be markedly reduced.

Death and the Completion of the Family Life Cycle

Just like individuals, families mark their progress by movement through a life cycle. A family is "born" at the marriage of a man and a woman who create a new nuclear unit. Most marriages result in children, expanding the group. The nuclear unit begins to shrink when children leave to create new families of their own. The death of a spouse reduces the original nuclear family to the slender number of one. Eventually, that parent too will keep his or her rendezvous with death, and the nuclear family of that generation will become extinct. But before this happens, at least one and sometimes two generations of heirs usually are well along in the process of perpetuating the family lineage. The ultimate destiny of a marital pair is death, but the family as a social institution endures into the next generation, and the next, and the next.

Summary

Death is the final experience of life. The two are inextricably bound together, however, for the meanings of life and death intertwine. Western culture has in recent centuries found it more and more difficult to accord meaning to death, and so, too, to life. In an achievement-oriented culture, death arrives too swiftly for us to complete all that we wish to experience; it is the scarcity of time, not material possessions, which most bewilders us.

In the retirement years, the loss of a spouse through death can bring with it a deep loneliness. Widowhood and widowerhood occur at different rates, however. Men die on the average about seven years earlier than women. Consequently, the number of widows is about four times higher than the number of widowers. Moreover, family members tend to regard widowerhood as more troublesome than widowhood. Various studies seem to confirm that men do have a more difficult time adjusting to life alone than do widows their age.

One increasingly attractive choice of single elderly people is the decision to remarry in the December years. Most who choose this option seek companionship. But a number of obstacles may block remarriage, such as financial problems, opposition from other family members, poor health, and the lack of available marriage partners.

Resocialization to the status of senior citizen also includes adjustment to declining health and physical vitality. Many senior citizens have to sharply reduce the activities in which they can engage. American culture's youth orientation does not make the adjustment process any easier. Yet most elderly people do eventually fashion a new

A Season for Growing Old

self-image and accept their physical limitations. Learning to be creative in the use of their free time is one major component in the adjustment process. Persons accustomed to working hard all their lives do sometimes find leisure difficult to enjoy. Usually, this problem can be solved, if the elderly person has good health and is not overburdened with financial worries.

Lately, many social analysts have expressed the fear that children are abandoning their aged parents. The number of elderly living alone has increased sharply over the last two decades. But social scientists are inclined increasingly to suggest that this pattern does not result from callous children leaving their parents, but from a conscious decision of the parents to remain independent for as long as they can. The fact that a senior citizen can live alone also reflects the improved health and financial security of America's older persons.

Preparing for death involves a number of specific adjustments and decisions. People should plan their estates early by drawing up a will and specifying who will care for their children and receive their possessions. One also needs to prepare for death psychologically. Family support and other types of social help may be quite crucial in fostering an acceptance of one's own death or in moving through the grief which accompanies the death of a loved one. The funeral is the symbolic event which marks the passing of a person from this world. Properly designed, it should celebrate the life of the deceased and remind those who attend how much their lives have been enriched by the simple fact of having known the deceased.

The death of the last surviving spouse marks the end of a particular marital union. In the end of one generation, the life cycle completes one revolution, but the family as a social institution endures through the next generation. Indeed, by the time of death, the family has usually already begun the process of recreating itself.

STUDY QUESTIONS

1. How has the meaning of death changed over the centuries, from the time of the ancient Hebrews to today?
2. In what ways does the experience of widowhood differ from the experience of widowerhood?
3. What are some of the more creative ways in which free time can be used in the later years of the life cycle?
4. The number of elderly persons living with their children has been declining over the last few decades. Is this social pattern a reflection of the callousness of children or a result of the preference of older persons to maintain their own household as long as possible.?
5. What are the various symbolic forms bound up in the funeral ceremony to which family members can respond?
6. In what sense does the emotional closeness of contemporary family members contribute to a heightened sense of loss and bereavement when a family member dies?

PART EIGHT

Chapter 17   *Evaluating the Status of Marriage and the Family: Trends and Forecasts*

Reflections on the Seasons of Marriage and Family Life

In the previous sections devoted to specific "Seasons of the Family" at various stages in the life cycle, we emphasized description and analysis. The basic concern in this final section is at once more reflective, speculative, and future-oriented. Several of the major themes introduced earlier in the book are reconsidered here in terms of their present meaning and future effects on American family life. This chapter is not simply an exercise in "idle speculation." If we are to control our future—rather than be controlled by it—we must attempt to anticipate what lies ahead. Seasons invariably come and go. Whether they will be "good" or "bad" seasons in family life is a matter over which we have some control. Our choices are in part shaped by what is going on in the present, and in part by those decisions by which we collectively chart our future.

17

Evaluating the Status of Marriage and the Family: Trends and Forecasts

look at how things are changing for the family;
spouses talk to each other for therapy.

The Family as a Specialized Institution
   Socialization of Children
   Promoting Psychological Balance in Adults

The Decline-of-the-American-Family Thesis: A Review of the Evidence
   Divorce
   Sexual Freedom
   ✳Geographic Mobility positive & negitable
   ✳ Family Size - for the future
   ✳Loss of Family Functions - what it doesn't do now that it did in the past
   ✳The Generation Gap
   The Contemporary Status of the American Family

✳Keeping the Family Responsive to Individual and Societal Needs
   The Role of the Family in Meeting Individual Needs
   The Role of the Family in Meeting Societal Needs
   Decreased - family relyes on friends moe now.

Summary
   will the family continue as a social unit.

The aim of this book has been to piece together a wide range of studies, research reports, and interpretive essays so that students might gain a better insight into marriage and family life today. But in this chapter, we have an opportunity to move beyond mere description. Now we can direct our attention to an assessment of the larger meaning of several of the major patterns introduced earlier in this book.

The evaluation of current trends also lends itself to the formulation of a few modest forecasts. Predicting the future is always a risky business, and no less so for social scientists. Yet, the enterprise is worth undertaking. Undoubtedly, some truth exists in the axiom that those who fail to anticipate the future are condemned to relive the past. Perhaps these forecasts can best be described as "informed hunches," since they are based on scientifically measured patterns of the present which simply have been extended into the next few decades. But considering the complex materials with which we are dealing, no one can guarantee that current social trends will continue as we approach the twenty-first century. Changes in family patterns can be more quickly recognized, however, if we possess some basic expectations about what the future ought to hold.

The Family as a Specialized Institution

Social change is a clear hallmark of modern life. No institution is immune to its transforming influence, nor can any escape its turbulence. The family is no exception. Already it has been modified a good deal since the dawning of the modern era. Curiously, however, the family has tended to move against the mainstream of those trends typical of the other basic institutions. While the economy, government, religion, and education all have grown larger, more bureaucratic, complex, and specialized, the size and social functions of the family in industrial societies have shrunk.

Like other institutions, the family has become more specialized. Yet, the loss of several social roles traditionally assigned to the family has not reduced the family's social importance. Rather, with fewer tasks to perform, family members have had the opportunity to perfect those tasks which are still assigned to them. Various forms of practical training once conducted in the household, for example, have now been thoroughly integrated into the school's curriculum. Most religious instruction has been reassigned to specialists within the churches. Domestic and economic activities have been largely separated from one another, so that the household is no longer a center of economic production.

Yet, the loss of these and other family functions has merely emphasized those tasks still under family supervision. In this category are such responsibilities as procreation, the socialization of the young, providing for the material support of family members, status placement, and the balancing of adult personalities. Two of these activities merit further comment, for they are the areas in which the family has become more specialized. One function is carried out on behalf of younger family members—socialization—while the other is conducted on behalf of parental leaders—developing psychological balance in adult personalities. Both require well-developed social skills.

Socialization of Children

Not only does the family create and physically maintain children, but it also assumes the serious responsibility of socializing each child. In Chapter 10, we defined socialization as the process, beginning at birth, through which one eventually adopts as one's own the norms, values, and beliefs of one's culture, and the roles appropriate to one's social position. Parents, who are the two major socializing agents in the immediate family, bring to this process two rather different concerns. First, they wish to see their child develop a unique, independent, and self-reliant personality. And second, they try to nurture their child so that he or she will behave in socially approved patterns. Nurturing children so that they can become both individualists and conformists is not a simple undertaking.

Parents today are making a more concerted effort to socialize their children effectively than did parents several generations ago. This includes

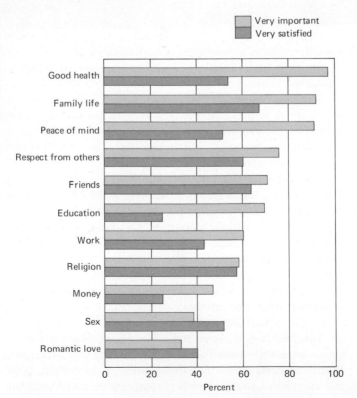

Figure 17-1
This figure shows that Americans are more satisfied with family life than with any other major concern in their experience. *(Source: Social Indicators 1980, p. xxxv)*

Reflections on the Seasons of Marriage and Family Life

spending more time and devoting more attention to their offsprings' social development. For many, it also involves keeping pace with the latest child-rearing techniques and selecting those practices which promise to instill the traits the parents desire. While parents have become more skilled and specialized as socializing agents, they also have come to appreciate more than earlier generations the pitfalls of parenthood. Accordingly, parents today are somewhat more anxious about their children and willing to take the blame if the children fail to become the persons they had envisioned.

This situation may not be altogether fair for parents, nor, in the end, healthy for parents or children. Once a young person enters adolescence, the influence of the parental family is reduced a good deal by the youth's participation in the peer culture. In the final analysis, then, who each of us becomes is largely a product of our own choices—many of which are made after we achieve some independence from parental guidance. But in a positive vein, it can be said that the evidence accumulated by social scientists tends to reveal that young people criticize their parents' socialization efforts less than do the parents themselves. While mothers and fathers worry about having done enough or having done the right things for their children, young people are much more tolerant. They do not expect their parents to be perfect, nor do they always agree with parental behaviors, but they do seem to appreciate and respect their parents' efforts, concern, and sacrifices.

Parenting probably will not become easier in the years ahead. Indeed, parents may well put more pressure on themselves to perform at higher levels of efficiency in the socializing role. However, part of the difficulty which parents encounter in this area is that they have no universal standards for parental effectiveness in socializing their young. Expectations, techniques, and definitions of proper behaviors for young people vary across social class, religious, ethnic, racial, and regional groups. Thus we should expect that parents will continue to try to bring up fine children and yet feel a fair amount of anxiety about the outcome of their efforts. If the past is any guide, most parents will look back on their role with a sense of pride and accomplishment.

Promoting Psychological Balance in Adults

Children's dependence on the family was widely recognized by the general public well before social scientists documented the fact. Without the family— or some equally competent substitute—children could neither survive physically nor be adequately trained to assume their adult roles. Less obvious were the fundamental needs of adults which are met through the intimate dynamics of family life. Indeed, not so long ago, gratification of the sexual drive was considered the primary purpose of marriage for the adult family members, especially the males.

Today, a satisfactory sexual relationship is only one part of the companionate bond linking spouses. The emergence of the modern family changed marital relations more than almost any other aspect of family life. Previously husband and wife attended to their traditional functions; now, each is expected to share fully in the life of the other. Each looks to the other to bolster individual feelings of self-worth, importance, and respect. Spouses also rely on their mates to sympathize with them when they are treated unfairly, to serve as a sounding board when they are angry or frustrated, and to share in their sense of accomplishment and joy when they achieve a major goal. In a quite profound sense, the marital relationship has taken on a therapeutic dimension.

The pressures adults experience in contemporary society increase their need for a place where they can restore their psychological balance. In the world of less intimate relationships outside the home, adults have to be concerned constantly about the image they project. Role management takes a great deal of psychological energy and creates anxiety as well as frustration. Thus, the modern nuclear family has become an important refuge from the pressures of contemporary life. Of course, the extent to which a home can be a "haven in a heartless world" depends on the quality of spouses' relations. Psychological balance requires more than privacy; it also requires love, companionship, and sensitivity.

Most evidence suggests that the importance of the companionate relationship between partners certainly will not decline over the next several decades. It may well come to play an even larger role in marriage, since psychological pressures on adults are more likely to increase than diminish. Curiously, however, as spouses rely more and more on one another for psychological support, additional stress is placed on the marriage bond itself. Partners who are unable to sustain love for one another, or who find their partner cannot fulfill their emotional needs, are more likely to seek divorce. Therefore, in those marriages which do remain intact, the trend is toward greater satisfaction. The upward spiral in the divorce rate partly reflects the difficulties many couples have attaining the emotional gratification which they have come to regard as desirable. A relatively high divorce rate is the price of failing to maintain strong emotional ties between husband and wife.

Socialization and the promotion of psychological balance are not, as we indicated earlier, the only lasting functions of marriage and family life. But these two forms of social relations will probably be the focus of greater attention in the future. Thus, we can expect the effort to nurture fine children and to improve husband-and-wife relations to proceed indefinitely.

The Decline-of-the-American-Family Thesis: A Review of the Evidence

The conviction that the family is a declining institution enjoys wide popularity. Such varied voices of public opinion as *Redbook* magazine, the Reverend Billy Graham, and the FBI have warned of the imminent collapse of the American family. Let us examine the evidence critically to see whether this alleged decline is social myth or empirical fact.

The prophets of doom for the American family cite a number of factors as signs of deep-seated crisis. Included are the rising divorce rate; greater sexual freedom (the new morality, the increased rate of illegitimate births, and a higher incidence of unmarried couples living together); the rapid geographic movement of families creating a sense of rootlessness; a decline in the number of offspring per nuclear family; the family's loss of certain functions; and the generation gap. Some of these factors are clearly more important than others. Moreover, because we have discussed many of them in earlier chapters, we can summarize several of these topics in this section. A brief forecast also is included after each topic.

Divorce

A low divorce rate does not necessarily mean that a harmonious family life prevails, nor does a high divorce rate indicate that the family is falling apart. This rate must be examined in relation to several other factors. First, almost half of all divorces occur in the early years of marriage before children are born. Teenage marriages are among the most likely to end in divorce. The rate is also high among couples who are drawn from different social backgrounds. Currently, 75 to 80 percent of those who divorce will eventually remarry. All this suggests that divorce is an adjustment within the marriage system. As such, it still testifies to the value Americans attach to marriage and not to a denial of marriage's importance, as many assume.

The current divorce rate stands at 38 out of every 100 marriages. This rate has been increasing steadily since 1955, with a sharp jump after 1965. But the remarriage rate has kept pace with the divorce rate. And what of the future? No one is predicting a sharp decline in divorces in the near future. Nor, on the other hand, do most students of family life expect a sharp increase either, like the one of the last 15 years. It appears that the 1980s may well be a period of consolidation, a time of only minimal change upward, or less likely, downward. The time between divorce and remarriage also may be stretched out by a few months on the average, a pattern which we already began to see in the last decade. The divorce rate does not yet signify a disenchantment with the institution of marriage, nor should we expect such a meaning to become apparent in the near future.

Sexual Freedom

Many Americans associate the rising divorce rate with the increased sexual freedom that has emerged since the mid-1960s. But no direct connection between the sexual revolution and divorce has yet been established. Many family life analysts are troubled because the sexual revolution may signal a move toward greater hedonism and pleasure-seeking among both youth and adults, and this could undercut the discipline needed to achieve a quality family life.

One obvious result of the sexual revolution is that more unmarried couples are living together. This once lower-class phenomenon has spread into the middle and upper classes, and especially into the ranks of the college population. Glick and Norton (1977) first predicted that considerably less than 10 percent of the total adult population would ever live together like husband and wife without being married. Glick and Spanier (1980) soon revised these projections upward as cohabitation quickly became more widespread. Reiss (1980:460) suggests that cohabitation is rapidly becoming a form of institutionalized courtship, and predicts that as many as half of the unmarried young people will cohabit in the late 1980s.

Because the acceptance of cohabitation is located more solidly among younger members of American society, this practice probably will increase as younger generations mature. The larger questions, however, concern the impact of cohabitation on the inclination to marry and on marital stability. Are couples who cohabit likely to avoid marriage altogether? Are they more likely to separate and divorce later on, or does cohabitation improve marital adjustment?

Almost all studies of cohabitation point to the same conclusion—living together is a temporary, not a permanent, alternative to marriage. While cohabitation should be expected to delay the age of first marriage, and the time before remarriage among divorced persons, it does not appear to be an important influence on the national marriage rate. Furthermore, no information yet has established a causal relationship between cohabitation and later marital stability.

Thus, cohabitation is one aspect of a larger social pattern of increased liberalization of sexual attitudes and practices. Love is still regarded as a precondition for most sexual relationships, however. Permissiveness without love—or purely recreational, pleasure-oriented sex—has not yet emerged as the norm for younger Americans. Current trends in sexual behavior do point toward more casual relationships, and solid evidence suggests that the sexual revolution is still underway.

Geographic Mobility positive? neg.

A third issue considered troublesome by many interpreters of our family system is increased geographic mobility which they fear helps break up the American nuclear family as a residential unit, and thereby creates a sense of rootlessness. Like the divorce rate, this single piece of data must be examined carefully. While one of every three or four families does move each year, this figure can be misleading. Mary Jo Bane (1976:59–61) points out, for example, that 39 percent of men 20 to 24 years old move every year, while families who move across a state line are only 4 percent of the population. Furthermore, the patterns of geographic mobility in nineteenth-century America were very nearly the same as they are today. If geographic mobility were a destructive force with respect to the American family, its impact should have been felt years ago.

Since residential moves for complete families, rather than single individuals, are largely produced by economic forces, we should not expect a decline in mobility. Families will continue to move, as long as job opportunities open up in other parts of the country, making a change of residence desirable. Behind the concern over family mobility lie the practical questions of whether family leaders will continue to be interested in where and how the family is housed, and whether the family will remain part of community life. On neither issue does compelling evidence suggest that slippage has begun. The isolated nuclear family, cut off from kinsfolk and neighbors, is not the wave of the future any more than it was the family of the past.

Family Size *For future*

A decrease in the number of children in each nuclear family also has been cited as a measure of social disenchantment with family life. As we noted earlier, a decline in the birth rate is a response to the reduced need for large numbers of children to work the family farm, repopulate society, and care for aged parents. In recent decades, a major shift has occurred, with families desiring fewer children and being more concerned about raising them well. More time, money, and emotional support can be invested in children if the number is two or three instead of ten.

Predicting population trends is one of the most risky forms of forecasting in which social scientists engage. A slight change in the average fertility rate can add millions of persons to the total population of a society as large as the United States. Nonetheless, the number of children per married woman does not seem likely to increase much over the next several decades. Indeed, a real population decline may occur in the United States around the year 2020. This coincides with the U.S. Bureau of the Census Series III projection of population growth based on an average of 1.7 children per married woman (Social Indicators, 1976:2–4). As more women enter the work force and opt for careers rather than simply second-income jobs, the number of families of less than two children probably will increase. The number of childless couples also may increase slightly, but this probably will not affect the fertility rate. In the last few years, the number of couples who have chosen a childless marriage has actually declined. This trend is not likely to reverse itself sharply. Most couples still regard at least one child as essential for the full experience of family life.

Loss of Family Functions *past & present*

Without question, many activities once undertaken by the family have been transferred to other institutions. It is plausible to argue, however, that this has not lessened the family's value as a social group. Rather, relinquishing some tasks has permitted the family to do a better job on those tasks which it retains, such as socialization and the balancing of adult personalities.

Two consequences have arisen from this change in family functions. The first is that the family has adapted itself to its new functions by enlarging the social importance of the tasks. For example, while the family has always been a socializing agency, this function has now become more specialized, with parents intensifying their efforts and consciously honing their skills in this area. The second result is that other institutions which picked up former family functions, particularly education and government, now seem to be somewhat overloaded. Thus, the family has been freed to perform better but at the cost of an overburdened educational institution. However, we should not expect a significant return to the family of those tasks which are now conducted by the schools, government, and other social institutions.

The Generation Gap

A final issue associated with the decline-of-the-American-family debate is the much-celebrated generation gap. Initially developed in the 1960s, this view held that a widening division had opened up between parents and their children on such matters as basic value commitments, political attitudes, and sexual norms. The generation-gap concept was accepted widely in the popular culture well before it was tested by social scientists. When research was undertaken, it tended to reveal that more continuity existed between generations than this slogan implied. More importantly, the data showed that the real gap in American life was not between generations but between college and noncollege segments of the population. On several issues, this gap also appears to be closing (Yankelovich, 1974:23). It is reasonable to conclude that the division in American society was never just a family problem; it was an issue that more directly affected the political, economic, and cultural spheres of American social life.

The Contemporary Status of the American Family

Families, like all social groups, encounter difficulties, face periods of severe social strain, and sometimes function poorly. Personal failures or poor adjustments by family members account for some of these difficulties. But other problems result directly from social forces too overwhelming for a person to cope with adequately. For example, the pressure on families to fulfill the social goal of achievement, often encourages parents to spend beyond their income to attain a higher status position. This can swiftly cause severe strains in family relations. The ideal of companionship in marriage creates keen expectations of sensitivity, self-disclosure, and psychological support which some spouses simply cannot realize in their marriages. The growing influence of the youth peer culture threatens to liberate some young people from parental influence and guidance, often before many parents think their offspring are socially prepared to make critical decisions on their own. Masculine and feminine sex roles are being redefined, and some measure of social tension inevitably results from such basic transformations. And always, parents face the stresses and strains of organizing the family household and assigning tasks so that the group performs within the boundaries of current social norms. But these are only a few of the more obvious pressures affecting family life today.

On balance, however, and in spite of the social demands placed upon it, the American family appears to be one of our most stable social institutions. Of course, such a positive evaluation is open to the charge that critical evidence has been overlooked, resulting in this naively optimistic view. That charge would be justified if we had suggested that all stresses, problems, and

Reflections on the Seasons of Marriage and Family Life

conflicts have been eliminated from marital relations and family affairs. We did not, nor is such a utopian situation likely to emerge in the near future. But we can say that current data shows that marriage and the family have been neither overwhelmed nor thrust into desperate disorganization by the problems surrounding them.

If this overall assessment is basically accurate, we must ask how the widespread concern about the state of American marital and family affairs can be explained. Perhaps the concern reflects more the value Americans attach to these institutions than a well-informed evaluation of their organizational strengths and operating efficiency. Ironically, one can even go so far as to suggest that as long as Americans worry over the decline of the family, it probably will remain a relatively healthy institution. Such a claim is admittedly a kind of catch-22. That is to say, when Americans stop feeling concerned about a decline in the quality of their family life, that decline probably will have already begun in earnest.

Keeping the Family Responsive to Individual and Societal Needs

The institutions of marriage and the family are strategically located between two different sets of interests. From the point of view of societal interests, family life is widely regarded as a basic pillar of our social structure. A weakening of the family institution or a degrading of marital responsibilities bodes ill. From the individual point of view, marriage and the family afford certain gratifications and meet a variety of personal needs. Unfortunately, however, societal and individual expectations are not always compatible. When they clash, family members often are thrust into tension-filled situations. Coping with that problem of opposing expectations is an enduring dilemma for family members.

The Role of the Family in Meeting Individual Needs

For almost every person today, the family is the first social group in which one takes part. This experience nurtures our ability to become a social being. In the family, we learn how to develop social relations, how to use language, how to acquire and act within the behavioral patterns of social roles, and how to view ourselves as distinct personalities interacting with parents, siblings, playmates, relatives, neighbors, and other persons. In overseeing our development from infant dependency to adult self-sufficiency, the family of orientation does far more than meet our basic needs for protection, food, clothing, and shelter. It also instills in us the necessary social skills for eventually surviving on our own and charting our own course.

By and large, a different set of personal needs is satisfied when we select a mate and form our own families. Although even newborn infants desire affection and can respond to it, young adults seek affection which goes beyond parental love when they assume husband and wife roles. Companionship, sexual intimacy, emotional self-disclosure, mutual dependency, sympathetic understanding, and someone in whom to confide are some of the benefits of the love relationship which spouses need and desire. The degree to which these needs are met in the relationship influences an individual's outlook, self-image, and the likelihood that the person will report a high level of happiness in life generally.

On the other hand, it is at least possible that the role of the marital relationship in personal gratification has been overemphasized. Over the last decade, some family analysts and marriage counselors have promoted the idea that self-fulfillment is the primary goal of marriage and family life. Traditional marriage has been characterized as a set of arbitrary social norms imposed by a society whose demands often frustrate individual growth. Accordingly, couples were urged to experiment with new forms of married life-styles, sexual practices, and communal living to gain new experiences and put some excitement back into their lives.

While no one is likely to argue in favor of a dull marital relationship, the "personal fulfillment" concept of marriage creates expectations that can be destructive. The assumption that marriage vows should be approached as a contingency agreement—to be honored only as long as one feels that marriage fulfills one's needs—places the institution on quite a slippery footing. In the so-called traditional marriage pattern, marital fulfillment was not defined only in individualistic terms. That is to say, a husband and wife typically regarded his or her own happiness and personal fulfillment as part of the fulfillment of the other partner. Mutual satisfaction was the measure of marital success.

Advocates of the personal-fulfillment concept urge that modern couples must learn to kick the "togetherness habit," or marriage will become a shackling institution that inhibits personal growth and prevents an identity independent of one's spouse. However, this view appears to be based on the faulty psychological principle that individuality is attained outside of one's social relationships. Who we are is defined through those social roles which we enact in relation to other persons. To be sure, one's personal identity can be shaped by subordinating individual needs, interests, and preferences to the demands of roles primarily devoted to serving others.

Without doubt, Americans, in particular, find this self-fulfillment view to be quite appealing. Who, for example, is not committed to the values of individual growth and development? Yet, in our more reflective moments, we also might admit that the self-fulfillment views can easily be a noble justification for selfishness. Indeed, a number of contemporary social scientists, including Daniel Bell, Edward Shorter, and Christopher Lasch have detected a recent critical turn in American cultural life toward greater pleasure-seeking, hedonism, rejection of self-discipline, privatization of values, and stress on "feelings" in place of reason. The self-fulfillment ideal in marriage readily fits within this broader trend to make the self the measure of all things.

Thus, it does seem likely that a major challenge to couples in the 1980s will be to balance personal interests and the demands of other role obligations arising from marriage and the family. Reiss (1980:462), for example, believes that the period of intense experimentation with alternative marriage styles is probably ending. Accordingly, he sees ahead a time of greater satisfaction with conventional marital patterns. Though this may be the case the ferment of the last two decades has also left a permanent mark on the institution. Today, couples are more thoroughly sensitized than couples were even a generation ago to the role of the marital relationship in meeting spouses' personal needs. If a consensus is emerging, it appears to be that self-fulfillment is one goal, but not the only goal of marriage.

The Role of the Family in Meeting Societal Needs

Society has a profound stake in the quality of family life. More than any other basic institution, the family determines the motivation and competence of society's new members. If the family fails to socialize youth to the skills and sense of commitment they will need in the educational system, the economy, and the political system, the other institutions of society can do little to compensate for their lack of social training.

More specifically, every society relies on the family to instill within the next generation a sense of allegiance to that society's norms, values, and institutional structures. This commitment must be carefully nurtured as children mature into active members of society. While other institutions—most notably, the school, church, and community—help cultivate our social consciousness, the family is still the primary social group through which we internalize our sense of obligation to social norms and institutions.

Because societies are organized around different cultural traditions, the freedom people enjoy in the pursuit of their private needs and interests varies dramatically. Typically, traditional societies, more than modern social orders, require that individuals subordinate more of their prerogatives to collective demands and goals. But no society can endure for very long without its citizens' willingness to sacrifice for the common good. Paying taxes, voting, serving in the armed forces, curbing our energy consumption, and behaving in a law-abiding manner are some of the more obvious ways in which family members fulfill their obligation to society.

One of the major debates likely to develop in the 1980s will focus on the extent to which families are willing to shoulder the burdens, including taxes and community participation, which are required to maintain public services and achieve the goal of "the good society." The dilemma we confront is whether the quality of social life in general will improve with reduced social services and an increase in the disposable income of many families? The Reagan administration seems to signal a swing toward the elimination of some public programs in the interest of reduced taxes and private consumption. If this trend also includes a scaling down of commitment to "public needs" in favor of private "wants," the long-term results could seriously affect the quality of our social life.

Whether choices made during the first part of the 1980s were in the best interests of family members and society probably cannot be adequately assessed until we approach the 1990s. In the meantime, the seasons of family life will continue along their developmental course. No doubt the American family will survive in the decades ahead. However, the larger question is whether the American family will be able to tap its considerable societal and individual resources to become all that it can be. We will all take part in the social process which answers that question.

Summary

Rather than present new material, this chapter is concerned with evaluating the state of American marriage and family life. Several forecasts of the future of these two institutions also are included. Basically, these projections were the extension of present trends into the next few decades.

The family, like other aspects of our lives, has undergone social change. Since the beginning of the modern era, the overriding trend in family life has been toward increased institutional specialization. This has been accompanied by a reduction in the size of the nuclear family and a loss of several social functions. However, the family has not declined in social value in the wake of these changes. The two major areas of specialization continue to be the socialization of children and the maintenance of psychological balance in the personalities of adult family members.

The conviction that our family system is in crisis and heading into a period of decline enjoys wide popularity. Our second major focus was on the evidence gathered to support this thesis. The most frequently cited signs of deep-seated crisis for American families include the rising divorce rate; greater sexual freedom; the frequent residential moves of families; a decline in the number of offspring per nuclear family; the loss of family functions; and the generation gap. On balance the evidence in each of these areas does not appear to signal a decline in the overall stability of the American marriage and family systems. Problems, strains, and conflicts still persist. Yet, spouses and family members have not been overwhelmed with numerous difficulties which they could not handle reasonably well.

The final issue to command our attention was the need to balance the demands of individuals and societal interests as they come together in marital relations and family decision making. Clearly, a trend has developed over the last two decades that emphasizes personal self-fulfillment as a primary goal of marital life. Although extensive experimentation with alternative marital styles may not continue as intensely as in the last decade, the concern with meeting individual needs can be expected to remain a high priority among spouses in the immediate future. Furthermore, we may expect to face throughout the 1980s the troublesome question of whether the quality of family life can be improved through more communal services and higher taxes or by reducing social services and taxes so that families will have more disposable income. Unfortunately, because we lack an adequate means of calculating the relative costs and benefits of public services versus private consumption, it may well be late in the decade before we can discern whether our choices have contributed to the enduring solidarity of marriage and family life in America.

Reflections on the Seasons of Marriage and Family Life

Means of Birth Control and Abortion

The Means of Contraception

Modern technology has made available a large variety of contraceptive methods based upon differing strategies for preventing pregnancy. However, there are specific advantages and problems with each method. Some produce potentially harmful or disagreeable side effects that must be measured against degrees of reliability or the dangers of conception itself. No contraceptive method is absolutely effective, of course, although failure rates are often a result of carelessness or error on the user's part rather than a problem with the contraceptive method. Among the more common contraceptive methods are the oral contraceptive pill, condom, diaphragm, intrauterine devices, and spermicidal preparations.

The Oral Contraceptive Pill Few drugs have been so immediately and widely accepted by the public as the pill. The purpose of the pill is to prevent ovulation during the menstrual cycle and thus make conception impossible. This is accomplished through the ingestion of synthetic steroids called progestens (Katchadourian and Lunde, 1980:168). Contraceptive pills vary in strength and chemical compounds, and therefore they are available only with a physician's prescription. Most doctors recommend periodic checkups to make sure the dosage is adequate and no harmful side effects are apparent. A woman usually takes one pill a day for 20 to 21 days, starting on the fifth day of menstruation. Reliable estimates now place the number of women using contraceptive pills at 94 million throughout the world (Rinehart and Piotrow, 1979).

Oral contraceptives can generate a variety of side effects, ranging from mild psychological distress to serious physiological ailments. So much has been said in the mass media concerning the dangers associated with the pill that most developed nations actually have registered a decline in pill users (Rinehart and Piotrow, 1979). The most serious hazards linked to oral contraceptive use are the increased risk of thromboembolism (blood clotting, especially in the legs), stroke and circulatory disease, and a possible carcinogenic (cancer producing) effect (Piotrow and Lee, 1974). Less serious complaints attributed to use of the pill include headaches, bleeding, dizziness, nausea, weight gain, and a general feeling of discomfort. To counteract these side effects, the newer pills have substantially reduced the steroid dosages. Medical and population experts are now attempting to assess whether this has reduced the risks of pills (Rinehart and Raveholt, 1977), and whether multiple pregnancies constitute a greater danger to maternal health. In less developed countries, the pill still remains the most popular form of birth control.

The Condom   The condom is the most reliable and oldest of male contraceptive devices. Recently, too, it has been making a comeback as a more popular means of birth control (Dalsimer et al., 1973). The condom is a sheath of very thin rubber that fits over the erect penis to prevent sperm released during intercourse from entering the vagina. Several features of the condom make it attractive as a birth control method. It is cheap, readily available without prescription, easy to use, effective, and it removes the responsibility of birth control from the female partner. The condom also provides protection against venereal disease. On the negative side, however, some users complain that it reduces sensitivity and that its use interrupts the free flow of sexual activity, since it must be put on after arousal and before genital contact is made. Also, there is the danger of the sheath bursting or coming off during intercourse. Manufacturing improvements, however, have greatly reduced the technical flaws which were common a few decades ago. Used in conjunction with a spermicidal foam, condoms are now almost completely reliable birth control devices.

The Diaphragm   Like the condom, the diaphragm is another barrier method that prevents sperm from reaching the ovum and thereby prevents fertilization. The diaphragm is a thin rubber dome that is mounted on a flexible metal ring. It is inserted in the vagina so as to cover the cervical opening through which sperm must pass if conception is to occur. A doctor's visit is required to make sure that a woman is properly fitted and to receive instruction about its proper use. The diaphragm is inserted with a coat of spermicidal jelly before intercourse occurs. It may be left in for up to 24 hours, but then it must be removed and cleaned before it is stored. When the diaphragm is properly fitted, neither partner is likely to be aware of its presence during intercourse.

While the diaphragm declined in popularity between 1965 and 1974 when use of the pill was increasing, recent studies made in the United States reveal an upswing in its use (Wortman, 1976). The disadvantages of the diaphragm are by and large matters of convenience, but it does not pose any health hazard to the user such as those that may be associated with the pill or intrauterine device. But, it does require a high degree of motivation to prevent conception; for this reason primarily, the diaphragm has not been a popular alternative for women in less-developed countries. Properly fitted and used correctly, however, it is a highly effective method of birth control.

Intrauterine Devices   The first IUD was introduced into American society a little over two decades ago. The idea, however, is of ancient origin. Arab camel drivers implanted pebbles in the uterus of their female stock to prevent pregnancy during the long trek through the desert. We still do not understand precisely how the IUD works, but it has proven to be an effective means of preventing pregnancy. The procedure of implanting the IUD— which comes in a variety of shapes and sizes—must be performed by a physician or someone trained in the procedure. The second generation of IUDs, which is currently available, is not simply a plastic coil of varying configurations—it also contains metallic copper or progestational steroids that are gradually released in the uterine cavity (Piotrow, Rinehart, and Schmidt, 1979). The foreign object in the uterus along with the chemical compounds appear to be doubly effective in preventing pregnancy.

Despite recent improvements, however, IUDs have consistently been plagued with a number of disquieting problems. Among the more common complications are increased menstrual bleeding, expulsion soon after insertion, pelvic pain, infection, and damage to the uterine wall. Especially during the first year of use, between 5 and 20 percent of all IUDs are expelled, most frequently during the menstrual cycle. Only in a very small number of cases have complications from an IUD proved fatal. Moreover, there is no evidence that an IUD increases the likelihood of cancer or birth complications, should a user later decide to become pregnant.

The most common IUD is the Lippes loop which is stretched into a linear form during insertion and then springs back to its original coiled position once it is in place within the uterine cavity. As with most IUDs, several threads are attached which drop down into the vagina. This makes it possible for the user to determine whether the device is properly in place before intercourse. Thus, frequent checks are essential to ensure the user of continued protection against unwanted pregnancy. When conception is desired, a physician can remove the IUD and reinsert another a few months after the mother has delivered her child. The IUD does not appear to decrease fertility once the device is removed.

Spermicidal Preparations   A variety of substances are readily available which contain sperm-killing chemical compounds. They come in the forms of jellies, foam, creams, and suppositories. Many are effective when used with the diaphragm or condom, but by themselves they are often difficult to apply and less effective than most other birth control methods. Moreover, the preparations often contain agents that irritate the vaginal area, at least temporarily. Therefore, many couples are forced to stop using them after a few applications. The failure rate of many spermicidal substances is considerably higher than most of their advertisements claim, because couples either wait too long or not long enough after application for the best results. Hence, couples who

really do not want to get pregnant should not place all their faith in spermicidal preparations.

Abortion

The political, moral, and social controversy that continues to swirl around the
issue of abortion can sometimes lull us into believing that the question of
abortion has only sprung to life in the modern era. In point of fact, abortion
has served as a means of birth control for centuries (Rosen, 1967). Many techniques practiced in ancient and traditional cultures were either ineffective or
extremely dangerous to the life of the mother. Modern medicine has produced safer and more efficient procedures, but it has not stilled the religious
and political debate about the morality of abortion. Almost everyone would
agree, however, that the best form of birth control is one that prevents conception, rather than one that waits until later and then terminates an unwanted pregnancy.

Technically speaking, there are two types of abortions. Spontaneous abortions (or miscarriages) occur very frequently throughout the world's population, especially among young women who have never been pregnant before.
They are not a form of birth control, of course, since they are not the result
of willful action. Induced abortions refer to intentional actions, usually by a
physician, to end a pregnancy. In America, most abortions prior to 1973 were
illegally performed, even though several states had enacted liberalized abortion laws after 1967. The Supreme Court ruled in January 1973 that the Four-
teenth Amendment grants women the right to seek an abortion, that any state
law that allows abortion only to save the life of the mother is unconstitutional,
and, in a further ruling, that all requirements stating abortions can only be
performed in accredited hospitals, or with other physicians concurring, or that
specify residency requirements before women are eligible are also unconstitutional (Alexander, 1975:83–91). The net effect was to overturn almost all
state laws that prohibited abortion on request. Most states, however, have
retained abortion laws within their legal codes, which remain unconstitutional
in terms of these U.S. Supreme Court guidelines. Quite predictably, meanwhile, one consequence of these rulings has been a sharp increase in the
number of legal abortions performed in America since 1973. In 1977, for example, 1,320,300 abortions were recorded. This produced a ratio of 400 abortions to every 1,000 live births, or, in other words, there were two abortions
for every five children delivered live during that year (U.S. Bureau of the
Census, 1979:69).

Methods of Abortion As a general rule, the method of abortion is determined by the length of the pregnancy. Indeed, the Supreme Court ruling of
1973 stipulated that only during the first trimester is the decision to abort a

matter between a physician and the patient. After that, the state may introduce limitations in the interest of the health and well-being of the mother. This decision recognizes that the dangers of abortion increase very rapidly with the growth of the fetus. Approximately 90 percent of all abortions performed in the United States occur during the first trimester. For those performed during the second trimester, the death rate for the mother is 12.2 per 100,000, which is slightly higher than the 11.2 death rate for mothers who experience complications during childbirth (Katchadourian and Lunde, 1980:186). If an abortion is to be performed, sooner is clearly safer.

Vacuum Aspiration   One of the more popular techniques for performing abortions during the first trimester is vacuum aspiration of the uterus. This rather simple procedure involves the insertion of a suction instrument through the cervical opening and into the uterus. When slight suction is applied it is possible to vacuum out all tissue which is essential to sustain conception. If a fertilized ovum should be present, then it too would be removed. This procedures offers several advantages: it is relatively safe, it can be performed by a paraprofessional as well as a physician, the determination of pregnancy is not necessary, the physiological side effects are minimal, the whole procedure takes but a few minutes and can be provided on an out-patient basis, no general anesthesia is required, the equipment is inexpensive, the cost low, and the procedure almost ensures that a pregnancy has been avoided (Van der Vlugt and Piotrow, 1973). As with all techniques that involve inserting an instrument into the uterus, there is some possibility of damage to the uterine wall, infection, or subsequent abdominal pain.

Dilation and Curretage   This procedure (often called a D and C) is very similar to the vacuum aspiration. In this instance, however, the cervical opening is expanded so that an instrument (the curette) can be inserted into the uterus. The lining of the uterine wall is gently scraped so as to remove the fetus and the supportive tissues. Like the vacuum technique, a D and C is usually performed only during the first trimester and rarely beyond the twelfth week of pregnancy.

Saline Solutions   Abortions with the use of saline solutions are most common during the second trimester of pregnancy and they involve considerably higher risk to the mother than the other two techniques we have just outlined. The procedure for saline abortions is to insert a needle into the amniotic sac in which the fetus is suspended and withdraw approximately seven ounces of fluid. This is replaced with a 20 percent salt solution. Even though the exact mechanism for this technique's effectiveness is not yet understood, contractions and the eventual abortion of the fetus usually is accomplished within 12 to 24 hours (Chaudry et al., 1976).

A variation of the saline technique is the insertion of prostaglandins—a group of biologically related fatty acids—or urea into the amniotic sac. Prostaglandins work somewhat more quickly than saline solutions, but they also may produce uncomfortable side effects, such as nausea, vomiting, or diarrhea. Urea is still somewhat more experimental. Some researchers claim it is safer than saline solutions and that it does not produce the gastrointestinal side effects of prostaglandins (Chaudry et al., 1976). The maternal mortality rates for each of these three procedures remains relatively high, however, with saline solutions and urea producing about 15.2 deaths per 100,000 and the projected rate for prostaglandins of 10.5 per 100,000.

Abortion as a Birth Control Procedure   Most authorities from the medical and social sciences seem to agree almost universally that abortion should not take the place of contraceptives as a means of birth control. Often, this stand is not solely a result of moral arguments against the practice. Indeed, the sociologist Amitai Etzioni (1975:173–75) enunciates a more compelling reason when he reports a medical fact little known outside the circle of experts and seldom reported in abortion debates, which focus largely on moral issues— namely, that vaginal abortions greatly increase (some studies showed tenfold) the likelihood of premature births in subsequent desired pregnancies. Moreover, premature infants have a much higher incidence of abnormalities. The obvious conclusion is that women who select abortion as a birth control method may well be jeopardizing their ability to have a baby when they want one, especially when the abortion occurs during the second trimester. Thus, quite apart from the moral issues involved in the abortion question, we may conclude on strictly technical grounds that the risk to future childbearing, as well as the risk to the mother, suggests that abortion is one of the less advisable forms of birth control.

Sterilization

A final means of birth control is sterilization. This term applies to a range of surgical procedures that render either the male or female partner incapable of reproduction. The overriding goal of medical research in this area has been to develop a technique that is safe, effective, simple enough to be performed by paramedical personnel, sufficiently free from pain so that only local anaesthesia is required, and reversible should a couple decide later that they wish to have a baby. (Hulka and Omran, 1972:57). Thus far, no procedure has been developed that meets all these criteria—although a number of important advances have been made in recent years.

Over the last decade, sterilization has become increasingly popular, both in the United States and elsewhere. By 1973, in fact, it had become the leading birth control technique employed around the world in developing as well as economically developed countries (McCary, 1979:142). Older couples who have attained their desired number of children are especially likely to opt for the sterilization of one partner as a birth control solution. Sterilization methods differ not only for men and women, of course, but also in terms of the complexity of procedures available to each sex.

Male Sterilization

The most common form of male sterilization is the procedure known as vasectomy. Today, this is a relatively simple surgical procedure, which can easily be performed in a physician's office using only local anesthesia. The purpose of this technique is to sever the two vas deferens, or the two tubes which carry sperm from the testicles to the base of the penis, so that a discharge of sperm during ejaculation is rendered impossible. A small incision is made on each side of the scrotum, the vas tubes are cut, tied off, and usually a small portion of the vas is removed to further reduce the chances that sperm will be able to find their way into the uretha canal of the penis. The ease with which the procedure can be performed as well as its high rate of effectiveness makes it singularly attractive as a form of birth control.

The major disadvantage of vasectomy is its relative irreversibility. Although some attempts at reconstructive surgery rejoining the two segments of the vas have been successful, a fully effective technique resulting in almost complete reversibility is not currently available. Indeed, since nerve tissue in the vas are invariably damaged when the tubes are cut, there are major physiological complications to be overcome in reconstructive surgery—although research in this area is still underway (Population Reports, 1976B). One means available to men who elect this operation and yet wish to preserve their reproductive capacity is to place their sperm in a sperm bank prior to surgery. Thus, someone with a vasectomy who finds himself in a drastically changed situation—through remarriage after divorce or the death of his wife, or because of improved economic circumstances, or after the loss of one or more children—can still produce offspring through the artificial insemination of his sperm into his female partner.

In addition to the problem of reversibility, some men are reluctant to seek a vasectomy because they fear the psychological ill effects associated with their loss of fertility. In point of fact, a vasectomy does not physiologically impair a man's sexual response. Pre- or postoperative counseling may be required, however, to deal with the potential injury to a man's masculine self-image. For some men, the emotional risk simply outweighs the possible benefits associated with a vasectomy.

A more radical, and less popular, surgical procedure of sterilization in males is castration. This involves the removal of both testicles so that sperm can no longer be produced (Pierson and D'Antonio, 1974:325). Castration is employed today usually only in those instances when the testicles have become diseased. This operation does not directly reduce a man's ability to engage in sexual relations, but it may create some hormonal imbalance as a result of the loss of those male hormones produced by the testicles. Over time, a reduction of the sex drive can occur, unless hormonal treatment is instituted.

All of the sterilization techniques for women are more complicated than the relatively simple vasectomy operation for men. Among the more common procedures employed today are: tubal ligation, laparoscopic sterilization, oophorectomy, and hysterectomy. The last two procedures are usually performed when there is some compelling medical reason and not for the purpose of sterilization alone.

Tubal ligation (popularly known as "tying the tubes") is one of the more common sterilization techniques available to women. Similar to a vasectomy in men, this procedure involves cutting the fallopian tubes, removing a small segment, and then tying both ends so that an egg discharged by an ovary cannot reach the uterus. The fallopian tubes can be reached either through the vagina or through an incision made in the abdominal wall. Recovery from this operation generally entails several days of hospitalization. To have the tubes "untied" is a major surgical procedure (Pierson and D'Antonio, 1974:216). Often, a skilled surgeon can reconnect the tubes, but even if they remain open, there is no assurance that fertility will have been restored.

A more recently developed technique is laparoscopic sterilization. A laparoscope is a long, slender instrument with a cold light at the end which can be inserted into the abdominal cavity through a small incision under the navel or through two small incisions in the abdomen. A physician can either cut the fallopian tubes or put small clips into place so that the passage of the egg is blocked with the laparoscope (Population Reports, 1973a, 1973b, 1974a, 1974b, 1976a). The procedure can be performed under general or local anesthesia—and if only local anesthesia is used, it can be performed on an outpatient basis. Because of the small incisions, this operation is often called "Band-aid surgery" (Population Reports, 1973a). Moreover, compared to tubal ligation, a laparotomy is quicker, less painful, inexpensive, and an easier technique from which to recover.

An oophorectomy is the female counterpart to the operation of castration for men. In an oophorectomy, the ovaries are surgically removed so that no more eggs can be released for fertilization. Since this procedure entails major surgery, a long recovery period, and permanently ends the ovulation process, it is not favored as a sterilization technique when other, equally effective methods are available. Thus, an oophorectomy is usually called for only when there is some abnormality in the ovaries themselves which warrant removal.

A hysterectomy also produces sterilization, but it too represents radical surgery that should be justified on grounds other than fertility control. In a hysterectomy, the uterus is removed surgically, often along with the ovaries and fallopian tubes. It produces permanent sterility, and women must often receive some form of hormone treatment as well to correct any imbalance created by the loss of the ovaries and the hormones they introduce into the metabolism process.

Although both the oophorectomy and hysterectomy procedures can trigger emotional trauma, Pierson and D'Antonio (1974:216) suggest that women are generally more receptive to tubal ligation or laparoscopic sterilization than are men to vasectomy. This may result, in part, from the fact that women bear the larger emotional and physical burdens with the addition of children to the family unit, and hence, they also have more to gain from sterilization. At any rate, sterilization is becoming an increasingly popular alternative for birth control, especially among older couples who have reached their desired number of children and who wish to put their reproductive years behind them.

APPENDIX II: The Biological Basis of Human Development

The social roles of mother and father are contingent on one important factor—the birth of a baby. Preparation for parenthood begins with pregnancy—or the onset of adoption proceedings—so that there is always some lead time before the full assumption of mothering and fathering roles. Both the parenting roles and the eventual development of selfhood, however, are rooted in certain biological processes. Before we can fully understand the social-psychological aspects of human develpment, we must possess some familiarity with the physiological processes that underlie our growth from conception to biological maturity.

Prenatal Development from Conception to Birth

Our unique individuality originates from the combination of genes that we acquire from our parents. Genes include the codes that determine a wide variety of physical characteristics, such as eye color, physical size, facial features, skin pigmentation, and intelligence aptitudes. Genes are arranged in chromosomes. Each cell in our body contains 46 chromosomes formed into 23 pairs. One chromosome in each pair is contributed by our mother and the other by our father (Hambley, 1972:115). Our sex is determined by which types of chromosomes are formed at conception. Females have two XX chromosomes, while males are characterized by an XY chromosomal structure. Thus, the mother will always contribute an X chromosome to the new organism. To form a male embryo, the father must contribute a Y chromosome. If the father contributes an X chromosome, the embryo will develop into a female. For this reason, we popularly credit the father with the ability to determine the sex of a child. Although this may bolster the male ego, it can be misleading unless properly qualified. Fathers have no control—at least as yet—over whether a sperm carrying an X or a Y chromosome will form the initial pair at conception. There is research underway attempting to develop the technology for allowing parents to select the sex of their child, but it is still not perfected (Etzioni, 1975:223–139). Moreover, some social analysts are strongly opposed to the whole idea on the grounds that it would seriously disrupt the sex ratio between men and women in society. For the time being, however, it is still the lottery of nature, rather than parental choice, which determines our sex.

The uniting of chromosomal pairs is accomplished in the course of fertilization. This actually begins when an egg is discharged from the ovary during the female menstrual cycle. Normally, only one egg is released per menstrual cycle, but occasionally two or more eggs may be ovulated, especially if a woman has recently taken fertility drugs. If all the eggs are fertilized, multiple births can result. In any case, once the egg is emitted from the ovary, it starts the journey down through the fallopian tube toward the uterus. Fertilization occurs when sperm ejaculated into the uterus by the male during intercourse travels up the fallopian tube to penetrate the egg and provide the second half of the chromosomal pair. Shortly thereafter, cell division commences in the

Figure 1
Schematic drawing of the internal male reproductive organs, showing the route followed by sperm from the testis to the urethra.

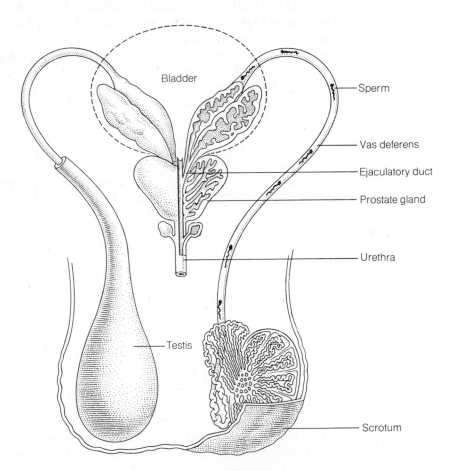

Bladder

Sperm

Vas deferens

Ejaculatory duct

Prostate gland

Urethra

Testis

Scrotum

474

Appendix II

ovum and a new organism has begun its process of development toward what may eventually become self-sustaining life.

The period of prenatal growth and development is called gestation. For the human species, this process takes approximately 266 to 280 days from fertilization to birth. The time period can vary for a wide variety of reasons. Three rather distinct stages comprise gestation (McCary, 1979:69). The *ovum stage* covers the first two weeks when cell division is occurring to produce identical replicas of the original cell with its 23 chromosomal pairs. During this time, the cell mass is first referred to as a zygote. When the cells begin to cluster into layers, however, the organism is known as a blastocyst. It achieves implantation in the wall of the mother's uterus between 8 and 14 days after conception. A firm attachment to the mother's womb marks the beginning of the embryo stage (Ambron, 1978:26).

The embryo stage roughly spans the second through the eighth week of the gestation cycle. The three layers of the blastocyst now begin taking on special functions to form the embryo. The outer layer develops into the nervous system, sense organs, and skin. The middle layer forms into the bone and muscle structures as well as the excretory, sexual, and circulatory systems. The inner layer gradually evolves into the respiratory and digestive systems (McCary, 1979:70). As these structures are growing, a sac forms around the embryo containing a fluid in which it is suspended. This is attached to the mother's body by the placenta, a tissue composed of a mass of blood vessels which provides nourishment to the embryo and carries away its waste products. At no time, however, do the systems of the mother and embryo intermingle. By the end of the embryonic stage, the development of males and females is identical and the sex of the organism is still not discernible (Oakley, 1972:19–23).

The fetal stage commences around the ninth week of gestation and continues until birth. Most of the systems of the body have begun to take shape in elementary form at least by the beginning of the fetal period. The one exception is the formation of the organism's sexual organs. Between the third and fourth months, if the fetus is to become male, the Y chromosome must trigger the release of the male hormone—androgen—which causes the sexual structures of males to develop. The exact links in this chain reaction from the Y chromosome to androgen production to genital development as a male fetus are not completely understood. Apparently, however, female hormones are not necessary for the fetus to develop into a girl. Only boys require something additional to alter the course of development to produce their sex (Oakley, 1972:22–23).

Hormonal influence appears to drop off dramatically after the sex of the fetus has been established. The most rapid period of growth occurs during the fourth month. By the sixth month, almost all features of the newborn child have been developed. The heartbeat is audible, the fetus sleeps and awakens, the eyes open and shut, and movement can clearly be felt by the mother. An infant born during the seventh month has at least a slim chance of surviving, even though respiratory complications are to be expected for infants born so prematurely. The ninth month is essentially a time for gaining weight and strength to live in the world outside the controlled environment of the womb.

Postnatal Development of Children: Sexual Differences and Similarities

Apart from the differences in genital organs, boy and girl babies evince several other dissimilar characteristics at birth. In the first instance, girls are often born from 5 to 9 days earlier than boys (McCary, 1978:73). Also, newborn males are usually larger, longer, and more active than female babies. Boys tend to cry more frequently, to require less sleep, and to crave more attention than their female counterparts in the nursery (Leslie and Leslie, 1980:25). The greater strength and the larger size of males does not seem to translate into a higher survival rate, however. Both prenatal and postnatal risks are higher for boys than for girls. Again, the reasons for this differing mortality rate between the sexes is not very clearly understood.

The biological-physical variation between girl and boy babies undoubtedly exerts some influence on their respective temperaments and early behavior patterns. Yet, we should not overlook how swiftly cultural influences are set in motion to mold infant conduct. The social definitions of appropriate behavior for boys and girls are introduced almost immediately after the birth of a child. For example, we tend to handle, speak differently to, and admire a differing set of traits in girl babies than we do in boys. For this reason, it is

Figure 2
Cross-section of male pelvic region, showing the major organs of reproduction.

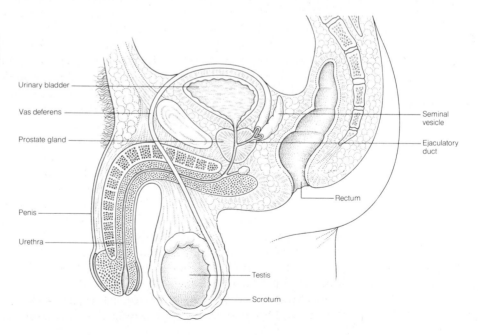

Urinary bladder

Vas deferens

Prostate gland

Penis

Urethra

Seminal vesicle

Ejaculatory duct

Rectum

Testis

Scrotum

difficult to separate sexually innate characteristics from our culturally informed perceptions and expectations. Perhaps the behavioral patterns for the two sexes that we observe in the nursery are already a reflection of cultural conditioning, even among infants who are only a few days old.

During the first few years of a child's life, at any rate, as he or she progresses from the infant into the toddler stage, it is quite clear that a great deal of attention is directed toward both acquiring the proper gender identity and fitting into the appropriate sex roles established by society. The development of motor, cognitive, and language skills is subtly interlaced with the internalization of sex-specific behavioral patterns.

Female Development from Puberty to Adulthood

Puberty is often a time when youth find their bodies changing in a variety of ways that they do not fully understand. It is at once one of the most exciting, frightening, and awkward periods of our life cycle. Properly speaking, puberty refers to that two-to-four-year period in which an individual matures physically so that she or he is capable of the sexual functions essential for reproduction (Bohannan, 1970:95). We often use puberty and adolescence interchangeably in everyday conversation. This can lead to confusion, however, for each term focuses attention on a different aspect of the maturation process. Adolescence covers a much longer span of time, stretching from the beginning of puberty to the full attainment of adulthood. Moreover, adolescence points more directly to the social-psychological dimensions of the experience of youth rather than to the physiological changes with which puberty is more immediately concerned (Eisenstadt, 1965).

The age at which puberty begins varies widely, even within the same sex. Some girls may be almost completely through the process, for example, before others begin. This may be a cause for some anxiety among those who develop later. Between the sexes, girls tend to enter puberty from one to two years earlier than boys on the average. Thus, the frequently heard comment that girls seem to mature sooner than boys has its basis in biological fact.

The first visible signs of puberty occur in what are called the secondary sex characteristics. For girls, this includes a change in the hip size as the pelvic bone becomes wider, and a layer of fatty tissue increases around the buttocks. This change has the effect of making the waist look smaller in comparison to the shoulders and hips. Soon afterwords, breast development also begins. Auxiliary hair starts to develop, along with pubic hair around the genitals. Sweat glands under the armpits are activated and other glands under the facial skin release an oily fluid which can, and often does, cause acne, perhaps the most bothersome physical condition of the teenage years (Ambron, 1978:418–20).

All these secondary characteristics are triggered by the increased level of the female hormone estrogen. Its production, can begin to increase as much as a year before any outward changes become apparent. The internal sex organs, including the vagina, uterus, fallopian tubes, and ovaries, also respond to the elevated level of estrogen by entering a phase of rapid growth. This is accompanied by a similar enlargement of the external genitalia. Internally, the ovaries, in particular, soon begin to secrete hormones which affect the state of the menstrual cycle and help stimulate the development of secondary sex characteristics. Menarche, or the first menstruation, normally occurs between the ages of 11 and 15. The age of menarche has been dropping steadily over the past several decades at a rate of about four months per decade, although in recent years this appears to be leveling off (McCary, 1979:26–27). Girls may be maturing earlier because of an improvement in diet or perhaps because increased body weight and size affects the release of estrogen. At present, the trend is far clearer than the cause that underlies it.

Early menstruation tends to be somewhat irregular. Over a year or so, however, it usually achieves stabilization into 28-day cycle, although variation from 21 to 34 days is still considered normal. The menstrual cycle, of course, is a sequence of events designed to prepare the female reproductive organs for pregnancy. This entails the growth of the lining of the uterus to receive a fertilized egg, the discharge of an ovum from the ovaries, and finally the shedding of the lining of the uterus, if pregnancy has not occurred (Katchadourian, Lunde, and Turner, 1979:78). Conception is possible for many girls as early as 14 or 15 years of age, with the earliest documented case of conception being a young Peruvian girl of 5 years and 7 months. The complete development of the sex organs is not attained by the age of menarche, however. The

Figure 3
External view of female genitalia.

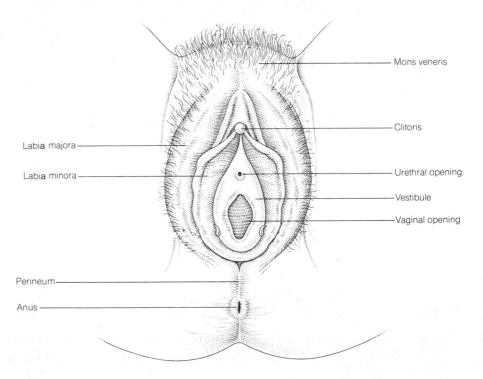

Mons veneris

Clitoris

Labia majora

Labia minora

Urethral opening

Vestibule

Vaginal opening

Perineum

Anus

Cross-section of female pelvic region, showing the major organs of reproduction.

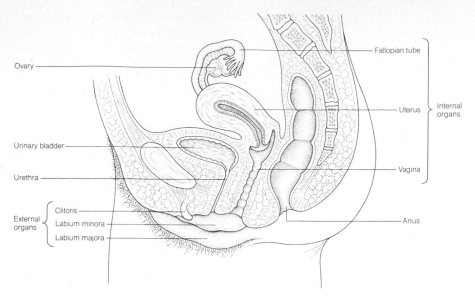

Ovary

Fallopian tube

Uterus — Internal organs

Urinary bladder

Vagina

Urethra

External organs { Clitoris / Labium minora / Labium majora

Anus

ovaries, for example, do not reach their mature size as a general rule until around the ages of 21 or 22.

The menstrual cycle is controlled by the variation of hormone levels in the body. The assumption has long been held that the chemical changes caused by hormones also create mood changes in women as well. Recently, a number of feminist social scientists (for example, Oakley, 1972; Weitz, 1977; Forisha, 1978) have launched a full-scale assault on this inherited wisdom. The research on which such claims are based, they jointly claim, was almost universally very poorly conceived, methodologically flawed, and hence the findings are inconclusive and untrustworthy. To their mind, no causal link between changing hormone levels and variations in the mood of women has been clearly demonstrated. In addition, no control studies on men have been undertaken to determine whether male hormone levels vary in a similar fashion. Hormonal fluctuations in men as well as women would be an important discovery, especially if the degree of male variation were pronounced. Such a finding would undercut the notion that women are biologically ill-suited for top positions in business management and government because of the hormonal and mood changes associated with the menstrual cycle. Thus, it may well take a long time to unravel the complex interrelations among hormones, temperament, and learned behavior that are typical for the two sexes.

Male Development from Puberty to Adulthood

One or two years before the outward signs of puberty become evident, young men begin generating androgen, the male hormonal counterpart to the estrogen in females. Androgen causes the internal and external sex organs to begin their growth process. The seminal ducts, prostrate gland, and testes start to enlarge and function. The penis also increases in length and becomes capable of erection by means of physical or visual stimulation. If not at first ejaculation, then shortly thereafter sperm are present in the seminal fluid, even though full maturity has not yet been achieved (Pierson and D'Antonio, 1974:245).

Many of the secondary sex characteristics of young women at puberty are also seen in men, despite the fact that they occur about a year or so later in men. These include growth spurts, the appearance of pubic and auxiliary hair, sweat-gland secretions, and acne. Some changes in secondary sex characteristics, of course, are unique to men. For example, the voice drops in pitch by approximately an octave, after an awkward period when the teenager's speaking voice is plagued by uncontrollable fluctuations and embarrassing squeaks. Somewhat later, the beard begins to grow, and shaving often becomes necessary from age 16 on. Moreover, the physical structure and size of young men undergo rapid changes toward the end of the puberty period. The shoulders and rib cage expand, in sharp contrast to the enlargening of the pelvic region in women. Muscle masses also begin to form around the shoulders, upper arms and legs, and body weight increases proportionately. The long bones in the skeleton continue growing until signaled to stop by male hormones at roughly the age of 22 (Katchadourian, Lunde, and Trotter, 1979:84). Meanwhile, particularly during the rapid growth spurts, parents are often constantly struggling to keep their sons in shirts and pants that fit reasonably well.

While the process of physical and sexual maturation in males starts somewhat later, their period of growth does last longer than similar processes in females. This accounts in part for the larger size of males on the average in comparison to females. Male physical-sexual development also may be regarded as somewhat less complex. To be sure, growth spurts may create periods of awkwardness and nocturnal emissions may cause some embarrassment, especially for boys who have not been given adequate information about their sexual development. Yet, generally speaking, boys do not experience anything quite so dramatic as the onset of the menstrual cycle in girls. Most of the serious problems encountered by adolescent boys tend to be products of cultural rather than biological forces.

APPENDIX III: The Family and Its Finances

Planning a Family Budget

The ability to manage money effectively varies quite considerably among people. Even those with a real talent in handling money matters, however, can probably benefit from the discipline of establishing a family budget and learning to live within it. Good budget planning will need to take into account two major considerations. The most basic is the amount of income available to the family. Couples with limited financial resources obviously will have fewer choices open to them, and less leeway for error in the manner they spend their scarce resources. The second variable concerns personal priorities. One couple, for example, might decide they want to live in an attractive home and scrimp in other areas. Another couple might choose to enjoy a full social life with frequent dining out, movies, and recreational weekends at ski resorts or the beach rather than investing money in a house or well-furnished apartment. Still another couple might prefer to forego the house or recreational diversions to invest in private schools for their children or in savings to help them finance four years of college tuition payments. Thus, the budget process must take into account the long-term goals that a couple have set for their life together. How a couple use their money is, in large measure, an important expression of their individuality. Expenditures chosen by one couple, therefore, might not be appropriate for another couple. Hence, budget preparation should reflect the unique interests and goals marriage partners have adopted for their family.

The first concrete step in drawing up a family budget is to identify the amount of income generated by the working members of the family. Although a budget may be based on weekly, monthly, or yearly figures, most couples find monthly budgeting periods the most practical with which to work, even though they may be paid weekly. Income should be calculated on the actual take-home pay (after taxes, social security, retirement, and/or health and other forms of insurance are deducted). One should also include along with regular wages the amount of income from other sources, such as interest from savings accounts, stock dividends, bonuses, and part-time employment. As nearly as possible, however, one should include only the net earnings on these other sources, after additional taxes have been deducted.

Once monthly income is established, the next step is to list all fixed expenses. This includes such items as rent or house payments, home maintenance costs, food, taxes, utilities, transportation expenses (automobile loan payments, gas, and service), insurance, loan repayments, personal supplies (toilet articles, barber and beauty-care expenses, major clothing items, and medical supplies), medical and dental expenses, and household maintenance supplies, which include such diverse necessities as light bulbs, stamps, laundry and cleaning supplies, and kitchen utensils.

Most items in the fixed-expenditure column represent costs over which people have little or no control. One might elect to use public transportation if it is available, and thus eliminate the cost of an automobile, but some form of transportation expense is likely to figure prominently in any budget. One can also opt for hamburger and tuna fish rather than steak and lobster to keep food costs down. There are limits, however, to the amount of economizing one can effect in such basic fixed expenses as housing, fuel, food, clothing, utilities, insurance, and transportation.

After totaling all the costs from the various categories that comprise the fixed expenses column, the next step is to subtract this figure from the spendable income of the family. The amount left over is the money available to cover discretionary or variable expenses. Here is where one's priorities may make a considerable difference. Among the more common discretionary expenditures are such items as money reserved for savings and investment, personal allowances (pocket money), additional clothing, recreation and entertainment, replacement of worn out household possessions (such as linens, major appliances and furniture), charitable contributions, expenses associated with special events like birthdays, Christmas, anniversaries, graduations, and weddings, and miscellaneous expenses, such as books, records, pets, newspapers, and hobbies.

The number of decisions necessary to establish an adequate budget for discretionary expenses varies in terms of the amount of money left over after fixed expenses are met. Some discretionary funds, of course, may be added to fixed-budget items to improve the family housing, or purchase a better car, or to allow for greater dining pleasure at mealtime. Some discretionary items, however, are quite important. Most consultants on money matters insist that couples need to set aside a percentage of their income each month in savings to cover unexpected expenses. The water heater may break down a month after the warranty has run out, or the car may need a major repair, or one of the breadwinners may be forced to go out on strike. Without an adequate savings to fall back on during these times, an unexpected event can quickly mushroom into a major financial crisis. Saxton (1980:554–55) recommends that savings ought not to be viewed as removing money from spendable income altogether, for couples will then be less inclined to save. Rather, savings should be considered as deferred spending which family members can use to meet a crisis, or take advantage of a bargain, or even avoid high finance charges when they make a major purchase. Similarly, a modest amount reserved for long-term investment should also receive a high priority in the discretionary expenses column. Not only do couples need something substantial to symbolize their long hours of labor, but long-term investments also provide a monetary reserve to be tapped when couples want to make a major purchase—such as a home—or a nest-egg for when they retire.

Alongside the responsible use of their earnings, individual family members also need some percentage of the family income as a personal allowance. Each person should feel free to spend "their" money on whatever they wish—their own interests and desires. Deferring all gratifications until retirement can produce forty years of drudgery before a couple finally feel able to spend money on things that are not essential, but nonetheless add zest to life. In short, then, there is something to be said for marriage partners counterbalancing long-term savings and investments with immediate gratifications of special interests. The stress on one extreme to the exclusion of the other may produce unwholesome consequences in family relations by leading to charges that one member is too miserly and the countercharge that the other is too wasteful of family resources.

Indeed, it is over discretionary expenditures that married couples are likely to experience their most serious disagreements in setting up a budget. Whereas husband and wife will tend to stand together in regarding the telephone and electric company's charges as excessive, they really have no alternative but to pay the going utility rates. With respect to discretionary items, however, it is they who set the priorities and determine how their money will be allocated, rather than agencies and market forces beyond the control of family members. As husband and wife become more responsible for making economic decisions, so too does the potential for conflict increase. Consensus on discretionary priorities, therefore, becomes not only desirable, but necessary between marriage partners, if serious disagreements are to be avoided.

For most households, however, the task of setting up a family budget is not overly complex. Probably the major reason families fail to create a budget for their household is not because they lack the technical skill to do so, but because they lack the motivation. Framing a budget and living within it requires some social discipline. Couples sometimes prefer simply to muddle through their financial affairs in the hope that fewer worries will arise from their failure to engage in rational planning. Money management is one area, however, where muddling through is not a very sound policy. Ignorance of one's financial situation does not make money matters go away; it simply makes economic decision making more troubling and the danger of mismanagement more likely.

By the same token, one can overdo the budget process of rational planning. A budget should be kept reasonably simple. Attempting to account for every penny can become so tedious that couples are tempted to scrap the whole process. Moreover, a budget should be recognized for what it is, namely, a basic guideline for how family members will spend their monetary resources. If a budget is approached legalistically and without some degree of flexibility, it can create unnecessary hardship. When the money allocated for the food budget runs out five days before the end of the month, for example, it is simply unrealistic to expect everyone to eat peanut butter sandwiches until the new budget period begins. In other words, adhering too strictly to budgetary guidelines may undercut its effectiveness as quickly as being too lenient.

And finally, family members need to remember that budgets ought to be periodically reviewed and amended. As the family's economic situation changes, or as inflation makes some allocations in particular categories unrealistic, or as the needs of the family shift, the budget ought to reflect these changes. Most families try to plan their budgets approximately a year in advance. By the end of this period, however, any number of unexpected factors may have intervened. A failure to readjust budgetary allocations to take into account the altered reality confronting the family will only reduce the budget's effectiveness as a planning instrument.

Making Economic Decisions Together

In American society, a surprising number of wives pay the bills and handle the family's financial affairs. This might seem to suggest at first that women must already share an almost equal amount of power with their husbands in money matters. The data appear to indicate, however, that such a conclusion is not really warranted. Rubin (1976:107–13) points out, for example, that in those blue-collar households where there are virtually no funds left over for discretionary items, almost three-fourths of the wives are entrusted with managing the family's financial affairs. But as soon as the financial structure of the family improves, a significant discretionary pool of money begins to accumulate, and so does the husband's control over the family's finances. Almost three quarters of the husbands in upper-middle-class households manage the money. Indeed, several researchers have demonstrated a persistent trend for the husband's decision-making power to increase with his income, occupational prestige, and social status (Komarovsky, 1967; Gillespie, 1971; Rubin, 1976; Blood and Wolfe, 1965). Since we know that higher status marriage partners are more deeply committed to equalitarianism, how can we explain the fact that women have less decision-making power in financial affairs as social class standing increases? William Goode (1970:21–22) has offered the following interpretation:

> Lower-class men concede fewer rights ideologically than their women in fact *obtain,* and the more educated men are likely to concede *more* rights ideologically than they in fact grant. One partial resolution of the latter tension is to be found in the frequent assertion from families of professional men that they should not make demands which would interfere with his *work:* He takes precedence as *professional, not* as family head or as male; nevertheless, the precedence is his. By contrast, lower-class men demand deference as *men,* as heads of families.

Thus, it would appear that real equality in marital decision making is far from an accomplished fact, even though lower- and middle-class husbands employ somewhat different rationales to justify their superiority.

There are sound reasons for why husbands and wives should share in the budget-setting operation of the family, and some family analysts argue that children should be involved as well (Saxton, 1980:556–57). Perhaps the first reason is that shared decision making gives both parents a realistic sense of having contributed to the family's well-being. Solidarity and commitment to the family unit is enhanced when both feel that they are actively engaged in shaping the family's future. Second, most families need all the expertise they can muster to make their limited financial resources go as far as possible. And finally, both parents have a legitimate right to decide how family funds will be spent. Even if the wife does not work outside the home, her contribution to family life as homemaker, mother, and wife is a significant asset. But whether there are two salaries or one to be budgeted, family members should make a concerted effort to regard total income as an economic asset that belongs to the family as whole, and not to one or the other parent.

Because each family member is likely to bring to the budgeting process distinctly different interests, expectations, and goals for the family unit, some delicate negotiations and compromises will usually be necessary to achieve harmony among family members. Often, the most difficult choices will be between two items both husband and wife desire but cannot afford at the same time. The major problem in this instance is to reconcile the differing timetables. While it might seem that timetable conflicts should be more easily reconciled than disagreements over basic goals, this is not always the case. One partner, for example, might hold to the view that they should start their family and have a baby, while the other is convinced that they should purchase a house first. Both decisions are costly and represent long-term economic commitments. Furthermore, strong feelings are likely to be associated with the decision as to which item ought to come first.

Indeed, facing the fact that everything a couple wants cannot be obtained at once is one of the most troublesome realities that a husband and wife must confront. The consumer orientation of our economy tends to encourage couples "to buy now and pay later." For some major items and with moderation, many financial advisors agree that this strategy can be a sound economic policy. The key, however, is moderation and knowing the limits of the amount of debt a family can comfortably handle. Otherwise, this strategy can lead to financial ruin. Young couples, in particular, may be tempted to try to accumulate in their first few years of marriage all those material possessions that their parents may have worked for 25 years to acquire. Making good budgetary decisions, then, requires patience as well as rational planning to attain a clear set of family goals.

Family Debt, Savings, and Major Purchases

At several points in our discussion, we have touched upon the issues of family debt, savings, and major purchases. However, these three aspects of the family economy are so important they deserve independent consideration. Because the economic situation of specific families is so varied, we are not attempting to give explicit financial advice here. Rather, our intent is to set these three major concerns in perspective and define some general principles by which family members can deal with them.

Perhaps the first rule of family finance to remember is that debt is much easier to accumulate than to eliminate. This does not mean that all indebtedness should be avoided, but couples should be careful about what kind of items and how many they buy on credit. Moreover, there are a number of ways in which indebtedness can be incurred. Probably the most common way Americans borrow money—although it is often not perceived as a personal loan—is through the use of credit cards. Today, almost 550 million credit cards are in use (Leslie and Leslie, 1980:247), issued by retail stores (such as Sears, Roebuck and J.C. Penney), banks (Visa and Master Card), oil companies, and general purpose credit card companies (such as Carte Blanche, Diner's Club, and American Express). Credit may also be obtained through charge accounts at retail stores; from banks in the form of home mortgages, automobile loans, or personal loans; from credit unions; or from finance companies, which usually lend only small amounts of money (usually $1,500 or less) to high-risk individuals at exceptionally high rates of interest. Which form of credit is best for a couple depends on what is being purchased, the rate of interest, and the schedule of repayment.

When used skillfully, some charge accounts and credit cards can provide family members with a 30-day, interest-free loan. This applies in those instances where no interest charges are added to the bill if the full amount on the statement is repaid within 30 days of the billing date. Let us say, for example, that you are going to make a purchase that costs $1,000. If you put it on a 30-day charge, rather than pay for the item immediately, you could retain your money in a savings account for another money earning (at say, 6 percent per year) an additinal $5.00. The gain on this one item is not substantial but when this pattern is repeated over many items, the savings begin to mount up. The danger, of course, is that one will charge too many other items, so that it is impossible to pay everything before the 30-day limit. The normal charge for the unpaid balance is 1.5 percent a month, or a total interest charge of 18 percent a year. In other words, carrying a $1,000 balance for a full year would cost $180 in finance charges. This form of installment buying is clearly quite expensive, and people would be well advised to avoid it, if they possibly can.

Loans from commercial or savings banks are usually taken to purchase major items only. This would include home mortgages, automobile, home-improvement, and education loans, to cite but a few of the more typical examples. Generally speaking, mortgages represent fairly sound financial investments, because the home appreciates over the 25- or 30-year payment period. A car loan, however, is usually for no more than three years, and during this time the value of the car is depreciating. Furthermore, automobile loans tend to carry higher interest rates than home mortgages. As a rule of thumb, couples should try to borrow as little as possible for automobiles, furniture, and other goods. There are exceptions, however. Let us say a husband and wife find a dining-room set on sale for 25 percent off its list price of $3,000. If they take advantage of the sale and borrow the full amount ($2,250 with the 25 percent reduction) to cover the purchase with a personal loan at the bank at a rate of 14 percent interest per year, they could still pay off the loan in two years and save $120. The interest on their loan would cost them $630 over two years, while the sale savings would be $750. In instances such as these, it might make more sense to borrow the money than save for two years and miss the sale price. A better alternative, however, is to have already saved the money so that one can take advantage of the sale price and not incur any indebtedness. Few couples can avoid entering into some type of credit arrangements during their marital career, however.

The opposite of going into debt is the amassing of savings and long-term investments. Saving money is infinitely harder than spending it, for almost all of us. Almost every married couple recognizes the need to save, however, even if they do not manage to do so very well. Young couples often find savings the hardest part of their budget to meet. So many other needs seem to demand their dollars that not much is left over to put away for a rainy day. Financial advisors insist that systematic saving is probably more important than the amount a couple saves. One good way to launch a program of systematic saving is to have your employer automatically deposit a small amount of your paycheck in a savings account each payday. Money set aside in this fashion can provide a financial resource for buying such expensive items as furniture or cars without having to pay high interest charges.

Investment differs from savings in the sense that the former represents an attempt to achieve long-term financial growth. A savings account which pays 6 percent interest during a time when the inflation rate is 10 percent a year means that you suffer a net loss of around 4 percent a year. Investments are designed to make money. Wise investments, where a couple depends on more than luck, require considerable knowledge of the economy. Therefore, a professional investment counselor may well be a good source of advice for how a couple can make their money work for them. Several relatively safe options exist, such as putting one's money in stocks, bonds, treasury bills, or real estate. Investing in gold or commodities, however, is considerably more risky. Couples who feel quite unsure about trusting their own judgment in these matters can buy stock in a mutual fund company whose professional brokers buy and sell the fund's stocks. As one's income grows, most financial advisors recommend diversifying one's economic assets, with some life insurance, immediate-access savings, real estate, stocks, and securities.

Purchasing major items or incurring major expenses such as having a child should also be integrated into a family's long-term investment and credit-use strategies. A home and automobile are two major purchases which couples generally consider very carefully. Apart from children, a home is the most expensive item a married couple purchase. The American ideal has been, for some time, that every couple should have a "home of their own" (Parsons and

Bales, 1955:7). Over the course of the twentieth century, the percentage of couples living in their own home has risen gradually from almost 45 percent in 1920 to 60 percent in 1970 (Gieseman, 1978:565). The question of whether a couple should meet their shelter needs through renting or buying really involves several questions. It includes, for example, concerns such as, Can we afford to buy a home at this time? Is renting more economically beneficial than buying a home? Do we want the maintenance headaches of home ownership?

For many couples, the first question is as far as they get. Housing prices and interest rates have soared in recent years, forcing many marginal buyers out of the housing market. At one time, the rules of thumb were that a couple could afford to spend 25 percent of their take-home pay on mortgage, taxes, and home insurance or that couples could afford a home which was two and a half times their annual net income. Gieseman (1978:539) argues, however, that the data on actual spending reveal that these rules have been relatively meaningless in the past, and probably will have even less value in the future. From his point of view, there simply are no rules that are suitable for most families. But he does provide a number of factors that couples need to consider in deciding whether to rent or buy. Included in his (1978:541) analysis of shelter costs are such issues as the terms of purchase for shelter that meets your needs; the monthly outlays required to retain and maintain your home; the tax savings you experience as a homeowner; your estimate of net proceeds from the sale of your home after a given number of years; and the plans you make for alternative use of your money. Of course, these factors must be balanced against the current state of the local housing market, the size of the downpayment and the current rates being charged by the banks. Moreover, if a couple plan to move (or regard it as likely they will move) within three years, the closing costs on buying a home might well wipe out all capital gains realized during that period. Over the long run, however, most couples have found home ownership a sound economic investment as the equity in their house increases. The appreciated value of residential dwellings has, to date, more than offset the downpayment, interest, taxes, and maintenance costs, making ownership of a home cheaper shelter for most couples than renting.

The purchase of an automobile, however, is an altogether different proposition than buying a home. A new car rapidly depreciates in value during the first year, often losing as much as one-third of the purchase price. Only by the third year does the rate of depreciation begin to slacken considerably. To compensate for this loss of value new cars have a warranty. Some buyers feel safer with a new car under warranty than with a cheaper, used car for which they must assume the full cost of keeping the car in good running order. Again, no rules of thumb in buying a car are applicable to all couples. However, a wise shopper will attempt to calculate roughly how much a particular automobile will cost in the long run, including not only the purchase price but also maintenance and repairs, fuel, insurance, taxes, and registration fees. And for most of us without mechanical skills and aptitude, a mechanic's inspection of a used car being considered for purchase is a wise and readily available safeguard which can often save a great deal of time, money, and headaches later on.

Consumer Rights and Consumer Resources

Until very recently, American business tended to operate on the tacit principle of "buyer beware." In the last couple of decades, however, a movement to affirm and enforce consumer rights has been growing rapidly, especially in those sectors of the economy in which the most serious abuses were occurring. Still, a smart consumer will take some time to familiarize him or herself with the rights and responsibilities that an individual enjoys in today's marketplace. For example, the tangled mess of credit cards and lending transactions improved greatly by the enactment of the 1969 Consumer Credit Reporting Act (Dille, 1971:194). These laws prohibited the issuing of unsolicited credit cards, required a clear statement of finance charges for all credit transactions, limited a credit-card holder's liability in the event that the card was stolen or lost, and provided an opportunity for individuals to examine and correct the information held on them by credit bureaus. In addition, further protection against credit discrimination was provided for women in the 1974 Federal Equal Credit Opportunity Act (Brown et al., 1977:270–78). This Act prohibited discrimination on the basis of sex and marital status in any credit transaction. The Fair Housing Act of 1974 also included provisions that prohibited discrimination on the basis of sex in the selling, financing, and renting of housing. Since many states have enacted laws pertaining to all these consumer rights and issues, anyone who feels they have been the victim of unfair practices might well be advised to seek more information from representatives of a consumer agency or legal counsel.

Becoming a wise consumer, however, entails more than simply acquiring some knowledge of one's legal rights and responsibilities. Many Americans waste money by buying unnecessary or poorly made items. Protection against this sort of exploitation must largely be self-provided. But, a few helpful rules will undoubtedly help. First, avoid impulse buying whenever possible. Before you make a purchase, always question whether you can get along comfortably without this item. Second, comparison-shop before you spend your money. Often, this can be done over the telephone without wasting expensive gas to go to several stores. Third, if you are unsure of the quality or performance of a particular brand of item, consult an independent testing bureau. For major items, *Consumer Reports* magazine is a helpful place to begin, and most local libraries are subscribers. Finally, consult friends who have used a particular product you are considering or who have dealt with a particular firm with whom you are considering doing business. If their experience has been less than satisfactory, you should probably avoid the repetition of their mistake. These rules cannot prevent all the unwise choices and unfortunate experiences which consumers will normally experience in the marketplace, but they can help reduce the amount of family resources that are wasted in unwise purchases of goods and services. The fact is that "buyer beware" is not an attitude wholly applicable to the past; it is still sound advice today in many of the financial transactions that Americans undertake.

GLOSSARY

abortion an expulsion of an embryo or fetus from the uterus prior to the completion of the full gestation period. A miscarriage (or spontaneous abortion) occurs naturally, whereas medical intervention to terminate a pregnancy is called an induced abortion.

abstinence refraining from sexual relations; used as a means of birth control. Although highly effective, this means enjoys little popularity.

achievement orientation a value orientation of both individuals and societies that is characterized by a strong desire to get ahead.

affinal kin those persons to whom one is related by marriage—in American society, affinal kin are known as "in-laws."

agencies of socialization groups that oversee our socialization process through the internalization of specific roles pertinent to their social organization.

agents of socialization specific individuals—such as parents, teachers, clergy, playmates, siblings, neighbors, and so forth—who mold our role behavior.

anal phase the second phase of the infantile stage in which a child receives sexual gratification from the manipulation of the anal cavity.

androgyny a single social role for men and women in place of the present-day sex roles of masculinity and femininity.

annulment a court declaration that states that a marriage was invalid from the start.

anticipatory socialization the acquiring of attitudes and learning of behaviors appropriate to statuses in which one is not yet engaged, but in which one is likely to enter later.

asexual homosexual a person who identifies as homosexual, but who has little experience, interest, or participation in sexual affairs.

Ashkenazim Jews of largely German background who immigrated to America between 1820 and 1970.

assimilation the process by which a minority group gradually gives up its own cultural patterns and acquires those of the dominant culture.

autonomic marriage an equilitarian pattern in which each spouse has specific spheres of decision-making power for the family unit.

autonomic model an egalitarian form of family decision making in which each spouse has separate spheres of decision making allocated on the basis of special skills, interests, or expertise.

bilaterality the practice of tracing kinship through both female and male lines.

black bourgeoisie a descriptive title given the black, urban middle class by E. Franklin Frazier.

body language nonverbal gestures that express our feelings and attitudes.

bundling a courtship practice in colonial New England (and several northern European countries) in which a young man and woman considering marriage were allowed to share the same bed for the evening, although sexual relations were strictly forbidden.

career work that requires a high degree of commitment, specialized training, and in which a person follows a developmental sequence by moving through a series of stages.

casual dating dating for fun and recreation, but without any expectations of seeking a mate.

chattel an article of personal or movable

property, in contrast to real property such as land.

child-centered family unit an orientation, typical of modern family units, in which parents do not relinquish decision-making power but do give high priority to the needs of their children in family affairs.

close-coupled homosexuals a quasi-marriage relationship in which two partners live together, are faithful to one another, and rely on each other for sexual and interpersonal satisfactions.

cohabitation the practice of an unmarried man and woman living together. This arrangement may be an alternative to marriage or a courtship pattern, according to the meaning assigned to it by the participating couple.

cohabitation contract a document signed by partners who are living together that specifies obligations, rights, and property arrangements. These instruments are not regarded as legally binding in all states, however.

coitus interruptus the practice of withdrawing the penis from the vagina just before ejaculation.

common-law marriages a legal term whereby a cohabiting couple is regarded as married if they meet certain requirements, such as the intent to be viewed as married, cohabitation for a specified length of time (usually seven years), and so forth.

community a type of social organization that provides a territorially based setting for most of the needs and problems of daily living, and in which primary, face-to-face relationships are the rule.

companionate relationship a style of marital interaction in which both husband and wife look to one another for their most intimate, fulfilling, and intense social relationship. Thus, interaction with one's mate as someone to do things with, talk to, and love is regarded as more important than the traditional breadwinner and housewife roles insofar as marital success and satisfaction is concerned.

complementary needs theory a thesis introduced by Robert Winch that asserts that, once couples have narrowed the field through a homogamy of background factors, they select a mate from among those whose psychological needs differ from and complement their own.

comprehensive marriage contracts a recent innovation in which a man and woman spell out in detail the rights and obligations that they assume in the institution of marriage. These contracts could probably not be enforced in a court of law if one partner fails to live up to its specific provisions.

conjugal family a family unit comprised of wife and husband (the conjugal pair) and any children who are their offspring.

conjugal rights a common legal term for expressing the legitimacy of married persons to engage in sexual intercourse. The term is little used in social science literature today because it carries historical connotations of a husband's right of sexual access to his wife.

consanguineal kin those persons with whom one shares a "blood" lineage by virtue of descent from a common ancestor.

counter-culture a subculture whose ideas and normative behavior patterns conflict directly with those of the majority of a culture, and whose members oppose actively—and sometimes violently—the dominant ideas and behaviors of the dominant culture.

creative self Adler's concept of personality that an individual creates out of the basic materials of heredity and social experience, especially the social experience of attempting to compensate for our original sense of inferiority.

culture of poverty the hypothesis that the very poor establish behavior patterns to accommodate to the difficulties and insecurities of their lives, behavior patterns that vary considerably from those practiced or considered desirable by higher class groups.

December marriages a marriage in which both partners are in their senior years.

demographic transition theory a model of population changes that suggests that societies move, in a series of stages, from a high birthrate, high death rate, low standard of living to a low birthrate, low death rate, and high standard of living.

descent system a system of social rules that define who will be related to whom and in what manner.

developmental approach an approach to the study of family life that organizes its analysis around the major events of the life cycle of family members and units.

disengagement theory a hypothesis that suggests that older persons, even before ill health or reduced income restrict their activities, begin a process of social withdrawal from activities and relationships in the wider society. This lessens the disruption of social life caused by the loss of one of its members and allows older persons to confront death without fear that their departure will disturb those social groups in which they previously participated.

divorce a court decree that dissolves a marriage and allows both partners to remarry.

double standard the belief that premarital intercourse is more acceptable for men than for women.

dual-breadwinner families a nuclear unit in which both the husband and wife hold jobs outside the home.

dual-career families a nuclear family in which both husband and wife are actively engaged in the pursuit of a career outside the home. Dual-worker families are those in which both husband and wife hold a noncareer job.

dysfunctional homosexual a person who is troubled by his or her homosexuality and who has difficulty in sexual relationships.

Eastern European Jews the last wave of Jews to enter America during the era of mass immigration, who were drawn largely from Poland, Russia, and other eastern European countries.

the economy the institution of society that organizes land, labor, and technology for the production of goods and services.

empty nest a term used to describe the postparental household, after adult children have left to establish independent lives of their own.

endogamy rule a requirement that one must marry within a specific social group.

engagement a public announcement of a couple of their intentions to marry. Usually, this commitment is symbolized by the giving of an engagement ring to the girl by her fiancé.

equalitarian marriage the form of family authority structure in which power and decision making are shared equally between spouses.

ethnic group a population socially identified according to cultural criteria, such as language, religion, or national origin.

exogamy rule a requirement that one must marry outside a particular social group.

the expressive leader according to Parsons and Bales, the emotional leader of the family who provides love, sympathy, and solidarity to the unit and functions within the environment of the home.

extended family three or more generations included in a single, functional family unit consisting of grandparents, parents, and grandchildren, brothers, sisters, and their spouses and children, and so on.

the family a kinship-structured institution, found in many different forms, but normally composed of an adult male and female along with their children who live together in a more or less permanent relationship approved by society as marriage, the minimal functions of which entail procreation, affectional intimacy including sexual relations, status placement, and the socialization of children.

family of orientation the family unit into which a person is born and from which one receives his or her primary socialization.

family of procreation the family unit established by one's marriage and in which the reference individual is one of the parental leaders.

family planning a married couple's effort to control the number and spacing of children born to them

foreplay physical contact between a couple that leads to sexual arousal.

"free-choice" mate selection a system in which a married pair is responsible for making their own selection of a mate.

functional definitions of the family this approach to defining the family focuses on essential family *activities* that serve to distinguish this institution from others.

functional homosexuals a person who lives as a "single" homosexual and organizes his or her sexual life around a number of partners.

the game stage in Meadian social theory, a later stage of socialization in which a child learns to play particular roles that are organized in relation to the total situation (the game) and whose performance requirements change according to the immediate circumstances.

gender identity the psychological identification with one of the two biological sexes.

genital stage the final stage of personality development in Freudian theory that begins after the onset of puberty. This stage is divided into the narcissistic, homosexual, and heterosexual phases. With the attainment of the final phase, psychosexual development is completed.

group marriage an alternative life-style (nowhere recognized by legal authorities as a legitimate marriage) in which three or more persons live together and treat each person as a spouse on a more or less equal basis.

heavy petting mutual stimulation of one's sexual partner through kissing, touching, and fondling that may or may not lead to sexual intercourse.

heterogamy the practice of selecting a marriage partner who is dissimilar to you in certain social aspects or personality type.

homogamy the practice of selecting a marriage partner who is similar to you in certain social aspects or personality type.

homosexual a person whose choice of a sexual partner is someone of the same sex.

husband and wife as equal partners a marriage type defined by Scanzoni in which husband and wife regard themselves as coproviders and equal in power on issues such as decision making.

husband as head and wife as complement a marital style defined by Scanzoni in which a nonworking wife views her husband as provider and head of the household. She assumes a role as subservient to and complementary with his leadership.

husband as senior and wife as junior partner a marriage style defined by Scanzoni in which a working wife regards her husband as primary breadwinner and as endowed with more power and authority in family decision making.

the husband-dominant pattern a power relationship within the family that allocates the major decision-making responsibility to the husband. This pattern is on the decline today with the shift toward more equality in husband and wife power relations.

idealization the tendency of an individual to perceive his or her loved one in an unrealistically favorable light, and thereby overlook that person's faults.

illegitimacy the birth of a child to a couple who are not married.

incest taboo a prohibition against marrying immediate family members or closely related relatives.

the infantile stage in Freudian psychology, this comprises roughly the first six years of life and includes the oral, anal, and phallic phases.

infant mortality rate the ratio of children who die between the time of birth and, usually, the first year of life.

informal marriage contract a term, often used by marriage counselors, to identify the assumed conditions that one marriage partner believes his or her spouse has agreed to simply by entering into marriage.

instrumental leader according to Parsons and Bales, the administrative leader of the family who allocates tasks, provides information and motivation to see that tasks are performed, and integrates the family unit with the external society.

kibbutz an Israeli commune in which the social training of youth is a collectivised process.

kinship system a complex of social relationships established by marriage or descent from a common ancestor.

"Know-Nothing" political party a nativist political party that was swept to prominence in the 1840s and declined after the mid-1850s.

latency stage that period in a young person's psychosexual development, according to Freud, when sexual drives lay dormant and one's physical, social, intellectual, and moral development continues.

launching of children the time in the life cycle of the family when children leave the parental household to establish a separate residence of their own either as a single adult or as a member of a new married pair.

legitimate procreation the right to reproduce children accorded by society to a married pair.

legitimate sexual relations the social right accorded to spouses to engage in sexual intercourse.

Levirate duty a Hebrew requirement that a woman widowed without children was to marry her dead husband's brother.

libido the dynamic manifestation of sexuality.

liking a social relationship between a man and a woman that entails affection and respect.

loving a social relationship between a man and a woman that entails affection, respect, and such additional characteristics as caring, attachment, the desire for intimacy and physical closeness. Loving, then, is an intense emotional bond.

marriage a stable set of socially recognized relationships between husband and wife including, but not limited to, sexual relations.

marriage contract the legal obligations that a man and woman assume when they become husband and wife in a marriage ceremony.

mating the process of selecting a marriage partner and the dynamics of their paired relationship.

matriarchy the form of family authority structure in which the mother or oldest female exercises greatest power and holds title to all family assets.

matriliny the practice of tracing kinship through the female line.

means of contraception various devices and techniques for preventing pregnancy.

midlife crisis a term used by some social sci-entists to describe the personal identity problems that occur to persons in the postparent-hood stage. Other social scientists believe that "crisis" is too strong a term to describe this transition period.

modeling the learning of role behavior through imitation.

modified extended family a term suggested by Litwak to be applied to families that experience upward social mobility or geographic mobility, and yet retain important contacts with relatives on whom they depend for social, financial, and emotional support.

monogamy the marriage of one man to one woman.

multidimensional housewife usually a woman of upper middle-class status who uses the home as a place for entertaining and—through art and decorating skills—brings the world of culture into the family living space. She establishes a companionate relationship with her husband, takes an interest in his vocational endeavors, and shares equal authority with him in decision making.

multiple roles a term that applies to persons who simultaneously occupy several social positions, each in a different institution and requiring a different role performance, such as one person who is simultaneously a mother, wife, lawyer, Methodist, Democrat, and so forth.

multiproblem families a designation for low-er-lower-class families that experience simultaneously problems in the areas of health, income, education, and often conflicts with legal authorities.

Natural Law a philosophical school originating with the Stoics that urges that persons, through the exercise of reason, can discern the proper order of society.

"new immigrants" persons who immigrated into American society between 1880 and 1920, largely from southern and eastern Europe.

no-fault divorce the form of marriage dissolution in which neither partner must prove "grounds" for divorce and thereby place one spouse at fault. Irreconcilable differences are the basis for divorce in this situation. Most states have now adopted no-fault divorce laws.

nuclear family a married couple and their children who reside together.

Oedipal complex according to Freud, this is a universal experience in which a child falls in love with the parent of the opposite sex and desires to kill the parent of the same sex and marry the beloved parent.

"old immigrants" persons who immigrated into American society between 1820 and 1880, largely from the United Kingdom, Canada, and northern Europe.

open-coupled homosexuals homosexual pairs who live together, but who also seek sexual relationships outside this partnership.

open marriage a marital style in which both partners agree to encourage their own and their partner's growth as a person by giving them considerable freedom from traditional expectations, often including the freedom to engage in extramarital sexual relationships.

operant conditioning a learning theory of B. F. Skinner that urges that, as a person emits a response to a particular situation or stimulus, positively rewarded behavior will be encouraged while negatively reinforced behavior will decline in frequency and gradually be eliminated altogether.

oral phase the first phase of the infantile stage in which a child receives sexual gratification from the manipulation of the oral cavity.

"parallel pattern" of development a relationship in which the social roles of husband and wife are sharply segregated on the basis of sex, so that the husband is primarily oriented toward the breadwinner role and his wife toward the homemaker and mother roles.

pater familias the male head of the household who held extensive powers in Roman society.

paternalism a milder form of the husband-dominant pattern in which the husband-father is viewed as the family's protector, breadwinner, disciplinarian, and final authority in all family disputes.

patriarchy the form of family authority structure in which the father or eldest male exer-

cises greatest power and holds title to all family assets.

patriliny the practice of tracing kinship through the male line.

personality a relative fixed and organized structure of characteristics and dispositions that are formed early in childhood and distinguish one individual from another.

phallic phase the final phase of the infantile stage in which a child receives sexual pleasure from the manipulation of his or her genital organs. During this phase the Oedipal transition occurs.

the play stage in Meadian social theory, an early stage of socialization in which a child learns to "play a role," but in relative isolation to what other playmates are doing.

polyandry the marriage of one woman to two or more men.

polygamy the marriage of three or more persons.

polygyny the marriage of one man to two or more women.

postchild-rearing marriages a husband and wife unit after the launching of their last child.

postindustrial society a recent concept meant to capture the essence of advanced societies in which there occurs a growth in the service and technological sectors economically; an increase in citizen participation and a demand for social justice politically; and culturally an emphasis on self-expression, pleasure-seeking, and creativity in the realm of values and meaning.

the postmodern family a description of the family system in the postindustrial society that emphasizes the self-fulfillment notion of marriage, a greater dominance of the youth peer culture in the activities of young persons, and a lessening of family solidarity.

postparenthood the stage in the life cycle of a married couple after their children have grown up and left the family of orientation.

power the ability of an individual to impose his or her will on another.

preferential mate selection a system in which a person may select a mate from among a socially defined pool of eligibles.

prescribed mate selection a system in which a marriage partner is selected by someone other than the nuptial couple.

present-orientation the desire for immediate gratification of one's needs and wants; the opposite of achievement orientation in which a person exercises discipline and immediate rewards in order to achieve future goals.

primary group a small group such as a family or play group in which interaction among members is frequent, usually face to face, and characterized by a high degree of intimacy. In early socialization such groups are important for shaping our attitudes and role patterns.

primary socialization early socialization set within primary groups where our initial personality is formed through intimate, face-to-face interaction.

propinquity a term used by social scientists to describe the fact that couples live geographically close to one another.

pro se divorce a divorce proceeding in which one or both partners handle all legal matters without the aid of an attorney.

"Protestant Crusade" an anti-Catholic movement that reached its high point of influence between 1830 and 1850.

"rating and dating complex" a type of dating first identified by Willard Waller in which the goal is to date the highest ranking member of the opposite sex as determined by certain materialistic criteria such as fraternity or sorority membership, money, access to a car, dance skill, personality, and so forth. Waller regarded this system as a hedonistic, exploitive arrangement that fostered antagonism between the sexes.

reconstituted family a nuclear family in which at least one of the spouses has been married before and brings to the new union one or more children from a previous marriage.

recreational sex engaging in sexual activities for the physical pleasure derived, but without any pretext of loving one's partner.

reengagement programs various strategies designed to bring senior citizens back into meaningful social activities and relationships so that old age becomes something more than a kind of holding pattern until death.

reference group any group that helps to define one or more social roles, and which helps in the evaluation of one's role performance or otherwise contributes to attitude formation.

religious endogamy the practice of marrying someone who belongs to your religious group.

restricted housewife usually a woman of lower-class standing who depends on her husband for economic support, is home-bound, task-oriented, and feels ineffective in dealing with many social relationships outside the family and immediate neighborhood.

rhythm method the avoidance of sexual intercourse during a woman's fertile period.

"the rise of domesticity" a modern trend identified by Philippe Aries in which the family unit withdraws into a private living space, the workplace is separated from the home, and intimacy and affection characterize the relations among family members.

rites of passage ceremonial events in the life cycle that typically mark movement from one important status to the next, including such events as birth, baptism, confirmation, and Bar or Bat Mitzvah; marriage; retirement; and death.

role ambiguity the lack of clear behavioral guidelines for persons holding a particular status with its attached social role.

role pattern a set of behavioral expectations shared by the self and others about a certain social position set within a group or institution.

role strain the conflict that arises between two roles we are called on to play at the same time, or the tension that occurs when we must switch from one role performance to another.

"romantic love complex" a value perspective operative in many advanced societies—including the United States—that prescribes falling in love as the legitimate basis for courtship and especially marriage.

secondary socialization later socialization set within secondary groups where we learn to function in the role patterns appropriate to statuses of larger, less intimate social institutions.

self an organized set of attitudes based on the sum of those roles an individual performs framed in response to others.

self-image or identity the perceptions, feelings, and beliefs one has about one's personality formed in relation to the evaluations we receive from others.

Sephardic Jews members of the Jewish faith of Spanish or Portuguese background.

serial monogamy the practice of being married to several spouses over the course of one's life cycle, with a legal divorce preceding each marriage.

serious dating dating in which there is at least some expectation that the relationship will lead to marriage.

sex the biological differences between males and females, including genetic, hormonal, and anatomical differences.

sex roles the expectations shared by members of society about those behaviors appropriate to men and women.

sharecropper-tenancy system a pattern of land cultivation developed by white plantation owners in the South in which a black sharecropper was extended on credit at the start of the growing season such items as seed, food stuffs, and other household essentials. After planting, tending, and harvesting his crop, the tenant sold his yield to the plantation owner who could deduct the amount of credit owed to him from the value of the crop. Typically, because the plantation owner kept the books, the value of the crop was rarely sufficient to cover the original debt. Each year, then, the sharecropper went deeper and deeper into debt to the plantation owner.

significant others the role models that children imitate as they learn how to perform within particular role patterns.

single-parent families a family unit with only one parent residing with the children. Single-parent families may result from a child born out of wedlock, divorce, separation, or the death of one of the spouses.

social gerontology a relatively recent field that studies the process of aging and the problems of the elderly.

socialization the learning process that begins shortly after birth by which one adopts as his or her own the norms, values, and beliefs of a given culture, and the roles appropriate to one's social position.

social placement the assignment of a position within the stratification system for a newly born child, which also has the effect of designating which adults are responsible for the child's care and social training.

social role a mutually recognized set of behavioral expectations for a person of a particular status position.

sociobiology a recent theory pioneered by Edward Wilson that claims that our genes determine much of our social behavior, such as aggression, love, and parental care.

status group a group of people granted a similar level of prestige by others in the community on the basis of such characteristics as property, income, education, race, religion, and life-style, who interact with one another as equals and are set apart from others.

status identity an individual's recognition of the status position that he or she occupies in society.

structural-functional theory a conceptual perspective (often called simply functionalism) that concentrates on the structural arrangement of social organizations and the dynamic activities (functions) resulting from these social forms. Structural functionalism tends to view society as a social system comprised of interdependent parts whose basic order and stability is controlled by cultural values.

substantive definitions of the family this approach to defining the family focuses on the patterns of social organization that distinguishes this social group from others.

superego the moral agency in an individual's personality, according to Freud.

swaddling children the practice of wrapping infants in cloth strips that strapped them to a board so as to restrict their movement.

swinging an alternative to monogamous marriage (often called mate swapping) in which partners switch sexual partners with another couple, but agree to keep these sexual encounters on an impersonal, recreational level so as not to harm the emotional attachment between a husband and wife.

symbolic interactionism a theoretical perspective with a micro-sociological emphasis that views interaction among selves as the basis in social life for forming symbolic meanings, roles, and orienting behavior.

syncratic marriage an equalitarian pattern in which all decisions are made by both spouses.

syncratic model an egalitarian form of family decision making in which both husband and wife share equally in all major decisions.

task allocation the assigning of particular tasks—such as cooking, mowing the lawn, painting the house, and so forth—to the husband, wife, or children.

therapeutic aggression a conflict management technique suggested by Bach and his associates in which couples are encouraged to vent their hostility through verbal abuse, thereby making physical violence unnecessary.

transsexualism the identification with the gender that is opposite to one's biological sex.

uncrystallized housewife usually a woman of lower- middle-class status who is less passive than the restricted housewife in her daily functions, shares power more equally with her husband, and establishes social relationships more easily. The uncrystallized housewife is able to organize life rather than simply adjusting to it.

"Virginia Woolf" conflict destructive verbal combat between spouses in which an intimate knowledge of the other is used to attack his or her character and demean his or her integrity.

widowerhood the status of a married man whose spouse has died.

widowhood the status of a married woman whose spouse has died.

widowhood as a roleless role the tendency to define widowhood as the loss of something, rather than in terms of actual behavioral guidelines.

wife-dominant the form of family authority structure in which the female spouse makes the major decisions as a matter of cultural tradition.

Abramson, Joan. 1979. *Old Boys, New Women: The Politics of Sex Discrimination*. New York: Praeger.

Adam, John, and Nancy Adam. 1979. *Divorce: How and When to Let Go*. Englewood Cliffs, N.J.: Prentice-Hall.

Adler, Alfred. 1957. *Understanding Human Nature*. New York: Premier Books.

Ahlstrom, Sydney E. 1972. *A Religious History of the American People*. New Haven, Conn.: Yale University Press.

Aldous, Joan. 1978. *Family Careers: Developmental Change in Families*. New York: Wiley.

Aldridge, Delores P. 1973. "The Changing Nature of Interracial Marriage in Georgia: A Research Note." *Journal of Marriage and the Family* 35:641–642.

Alexander, Shana. 1975. *State-by-State Guide to Women's Legal Rights*. Los Angeles, Ca: Wollstonecraft.

Alston, Jon P., William A. McIntosh, and Louise M. Wright. 1976. "Extent of Interfaith Marriages Among White Americans." *Sociological Analysis* 37:261–264.

Ambron, Sueann Robinson. 1978. Child Development. 2d ed. New York: Holt, Rinehart and Winston.

Anderson, Charles H. 1970. *White Protestant Americans*. Englewood Cliffs, N.J.: Prentice-Hall.

Andrae, Tor. 1960. *Mohammed: The Man and His Faith*. New York: Harper & Row.

Ansbacher, H. L., and Rowena R., eds. 1956. *The Individual-Psychology of Alfred Adler*. New York: Basic Books.

Arafat, Ibtiha, and Betty Yorburg. 1973. "On Living Together Without Marriage." *Journal of Sex Research* 9:21–30.

Aries, Phillippe. 1962. *Centuries of Childhood: A Social History of Family Life*. New York: Vintage Books.

Armor, David J. 1972. "School and Family Effects on Black and White Achievement: A Reexamination of the USOE Data." In Frederick Mosteller and Daniel P. Moyorihan, eds., *On Equality of Educational Opportunity*, pp. 168–229. New York: Vintage Books.

Aronoff, Joel, and William D. Crano. 1975. "A Re-examination of the Cross-Cultural Principles of Task Segregation and Sex Role Differentiation in the Family." *American Sociological Review* 40:12–20.

Askham, Janet. 1976. "Identity and Stability Within the Marriage Relationship." *Journal of Marriage and the Family* 38:535–547.

Atchley, Robert C. 1976. *The Sociology of Retirement*. New York: Halsted Press.

Baber, Ray E. 1953. *Marriage and the Family*. 2d ed. New York: McGraw-Hill.

Bach, George R., and Peter Wyden. 1968. *The Intimate Enemy*. New York: Avon Books.

Bailey, Derrick Sherwin. 1959. *Sexual Relation in Christian Thought*. New York: Harper & Bro.

Balswick, Jack, and Charles Peck. 1971. "The Inexpressive Male: A Tragedy of American Society." *The Family Coordinator* 20:363–368.

Bane, Mary Jo. 1976. *Here to Stay: American Families in the Twentieth Century*. New York: Basic Books.

Banfield, Edward C. 1974. *The Unheavenly City Revisited*. Boston: Little, Brown.

Bardwick, Judith M., and Elizabeth Douvan. 1971. "Ambivalence: The Socialization of Women." In Vivian Gornick and Barvara K. Moran, eds., *Woman in Sexist Society*, pp. 225–241. New York: New American Library.

Bartell, Gilbert. 1971. *Group Sex*. New York: Wyden Books.

Bebbington, A. C. 1973. "The Function of Stress in the Establishment of the Dual-Career Family." *Journal of Marriage and the Family* 35:530–537.

Becker, Ernest. 1962. *The Birth and Death of Meaning*. New York: Free Press.

Belkin, Gary S., and Norman Goodman. 1980. *Marriage, Family, and Intimate Relationships*. Chicago: Rand McNally.

Bell, Alan P., and Martin S. Weinberg. 1978. *Homosexualities: A Study of Diversity Among Men and Women*. New York: Simon & Schuster.

Bell, Daniel. 1976. *The Coming of Post-Industrial Society*. New York: Basic Books.

———. 1978. *The Cultural Contradictions of Capitalism*. New York: Basic Books.

Bell, Norman W., and Ezra F. Vogel. 1968. "Toward a Framework for Functional Analysis of Family Behavior." In Norman W. Bell and Ezra F. Vogel, eds., *A Modern Introduction to the Family*, pp. 1–34. New York: Free Press.

Bell, Robert R., Stanley Turner, and Lawrence Rosen. 1975. "A Multivariate Analysis of Female Extramarital Coitus." *Journal of Marriage and the Family*, 37:375–384.

Bem, Sandra Lipsitz. 1974. "The Measurement of Psychological Androgyny." *Journal of Consulting and Clinical Psychology*. 42:155–162.

Benson, Leonard. 1968. *Fatherhood: A Sociological Perspective*. New York: Random House.

Berardo, Felix M. 1970. "Survivorship and Social Isolation: The Case of the Aged Widower." *The Family Coordinator* 19:11–25.

Berelson, Bernard. 1979, "The Value of Children: A Taxonomical Essay." In J. Gipson Wells, ed., *Current Issues in Marriage and the Family*, 2d ed., pp. 241–249. New York: Macmillan.

Berger, David G., and Morton G. Wenger. 1973. "The Ideology of Virginity." *Journal of Marriage and the Family* 35:666–676.

Berger, Peter L. 1967. *The Sacred Canopy*. Garden City, N.Y.: Doubleday.

———. 1976. *Pyramids of Sacrifice*. Garden City, N.Y.: Doubleday.

———. 1977. *Facing Up to Modernity*. New York: Basic Books.

———. and Brigitte Berger. 1972. *Sociology: A Biographical Approach*. New York: Basic Books.

Bernard, Jessie. 1964. "The Adjustment of Married Mates." In Harold T. Christensen, ed. *Handbook of Marriage and the Family*, pp. 675–739. Chicago: Rand McNally.

———. 1966. *Marriage and Family Among Negroes*. Englewood Cliffs, N.J.: Prentice-Hall.

———. 1975a. *The Future of Motherhood*. New York: Penguin Books.

———. 1975b. "Note on Changing Life Styles, 1970–1974." *Journal of Marriage and the Family* 37:582–593.

Berne, Eric. 1970. *Sex in Human Loving*. New York: Simon & Schuster.

Bernstein, Barton E. 1980. "Legal Problems of Cohabitation." In James M. Henslin, ed., *Marriage and Family in a Changing Society*, pp. 116–127. New York: Free Press.

Bettelheim, Bruno. 1965. "The Problem of Generations." In Erik K. Erikson, ed., *The Challenge of Youth*, pp. 76–109. Garden City, N.Y.: Doubleday.

Bienvenu, Millard J., Sr. 1970. "Measurement of Marital Communication." *The Family Coordinator* 19:26–31.

Billingsley, Andrew. 1968. *Black Families in White America*. Englewood Cliffs, N.J.: Prentice-Hall.

Billington, Ray Allen. 1964. *The Protestant Crusade, 1800–1860*. Chicago: Quadrangle Books.

Binstock, Jeannie. 1978. "Motherhood: An Occupation Facing Decline." In Jerald Savells and Lawrence J. Cross, eds, *The Changing Family*, pp. 298–305. New York: Holt, Rinehart and Winston.

Blood, Robert, O., Jr. 1955. "A Re-test of Waller's Rating Complex." *Marriage and Family Living* 17:41–47.

———, and Donald M. Wolfe. 1965 (1960). *Husbands and Wives: The Dynamics of Married Living*. New York: Free Press.

Blumer, Herbert. 1969. *Symbolic Interactionism: Perspective and Method*. Englewood Cliffs, N.J.: Prentice-Hall.

Boatright, Mody C. 1968. "The Myth of Frontier Individualism." In Richard Hofstadter and Seymour Martin Lipset, eds., *Turner and the Sociology of the Frontier*. New York: Basic Books.

Bohannan, Paul. 1970. *Love, Sex, and Being Human*. Garden City, N.Y.: Doubleday.

Boorstin, Daniel J. 1958. *The Americans*. 2 vols. New York: Random House.

Bottomore, T. B. 1968. *Classes in Modern Society*. New York: Random House.

Bould, Sally. 1977. "Female-Headed Families: Personal Fate Control and the Provider Role." *Journal of Marriage and the Family* 39:339–349.

Bouvier, Leon F. 1972. "Catholics and Contraception." *Journal of Marriage and the Family* 34:514–522.

Bower, Donald W., and Victor A. Christopherson. 1977. "University Student Cohabitation: A Regional Comparison of Selected Attitudes and Behavior." *Journal of Marriage and the Family* 39:447–453.

Brandwein, Ruth A., and Carol A. Brown, and Elizabeth Maury Fox. 1974. "Women and Children Last: The Social Situation of Divorced Mothers and Their Families." *Journal of Marriage and the Family* 36:498–514.

Brisset, Dennis, and Lionel S. Lewis. 1970. "Guidelines for Marital Sex: An Analysis of Fifteen Popular Marriage Manuals." *The Family Coordinator* 19:41–48.

Broderick, Carlfred B. 1978. "Fathers." In H. Z. Lopata, ed., *Family Factbook*, pp. 106–112. Chicago: Marquis Academic Media.

Bronfenbrenner, Urie. 1966. "Socialization and Social Class Through Time and Space." In Reinhard Bendix and Seymour Martin Lipset, eds., *Class, Status, and Power*. 2d ed., pp. 362–377. New York: Free Press.

Brown, Barbara A., Ann E. Freedman, Harriet N. Katz, and Alice M. Price. 1977. *Women's Rights and the Law*. New York: Praeger.

Brown, J. A. C. 1964. *Freud and the Post-Freudians*. Baltimore: Penguin Books.

Brown, Prudence, Lorraine Perry, and Ernest Harburg. 1977. "Sex Role Attitudes and Psychological Outcomes for Black and White Women Experiencing Marital Dissolution." *Journal of Marriage and the Family* 39:549–561.

Buchanan, Scott. 1966. "Natural Law and Teleology." In John Cogley et al., *Natural Law and Modern Society*, pp. 82–153. New York: Meridian Books.

Burgess, Ernest W., and Harvey J. Locke. 1953. *The Family*. 2d ed. New York: American Book.

———. and Paul Wallin. 1965. "Factors in Broken Engagements." In Ruth S. Cavan, ed., *Marriage and Family in the Modern World: A Book of Readings*. 2d ed. pp. 172–184. New York: Crowell.

Burgess-Kohn, James. 1979. *Straight Talk About Love and Sex for Teenagers*. Boston: Beacon Press.

Burke, Ronald J., and Tamara Weir. 1976. "Relation of Wives' Employment Status to Husband, Wife and Pair Satisfaction and Employment." *Journal of Marriage and the Family* 38:279–287.

Cadwallader, Mervyn. 1975. "Marriage as a Wretched Institution." In Jack R. Delora and Joann S. Delora, eds., *Intimate Life Styles*, 2d ed. pp. 133–138. Pacific Palisades, Ca: Goodyear.

Calvin, John. 1960. *Institutes of the Christian Religion*, 2 vols. John T. McNeill, ed. Philadelphia: Westminster Press.

Campbell, Angus. 1975. "The American Way of Mating: Marriage Si, Children Only Maybe." *Psychology Today* 8:37–43.

Caplin, Arthur L., ed. 1978. *The Sociobiology Debate.* New York: Harper & Row.

Carey, James T. 1968. *The College Drug Scene.* Englewood-Cliffs, N.J.: Prentice-Hall.

Carns, Donald E. 1973. "Talking About Sex: Notes on First Coitus and the Double Sexual Standard." *Journal of Marriage and the Family* 35:677–688.

Cavan, Ruth Shonle. 1964. "Subcultural Variations and Mobility." In Harold T. Christensen, ed., *Handbook on Marriage and the Family*, pp. 535–581. Chicago: Rand McNally.

Centers, Richard, Bertram H. Raven, and Arolodo Rodriques. 1971. "Conjugal Power Structure: A Re-Examination." *American Sociological Review* 36:264–278.

Chafe, William H. 1972. *The American Woman: Her Changing Social, Economic, and Political Roles, 1920–1970.* New York: Oxford University Press.

Chaudry, Susan L. et al. 1976. "Pregnancy Termination in Midtrimester—Review of Major Methods." Population Reports, Dept. of Medical and Public Affairs. George Washington University. Series F, no. 5.

Cherlin, Andrew. 1978. "Remarriage as an Incomplete Institution." *American Journal of Sociology* 84:634–650.

Christensen, Harold T. 1964. "Development of the Family Field of Study." In Harold T. Christensen, ed., *Handbook of Marriage and the Family.* pp. 3–32. Rand McNally.

Clark, Burton R. 1962. *Educating the Expert Society.* San Francisco: Chandler.

Clark, Elizabeth, and Herbert Richardson, eds., 1977. *Women and Religion: A Feminist's Sourcebook of Christian Thought.* New York: Harper & Row.

Clark, Thomas D. 1968. *The Emerging South.* 2d ed. New York: Oxford University Press.

Clayton, Richard R. 1979. *The Family, Marriage, and Social change.* 2d ed. Lexington, Mass.: D. C. Heath.

—— and Harwin L. Voss. 1977. "Shacking Up: Cohabitation in the 1970's." *Journal of Marriage and the Family* 39:273–283.

Cogley, John. 1974. *Catholic America.* Garden City, N.Y.: Doubleday.

Coleman, James. 1961. *The Adolescent Society.* New York: Free Press.

——. 1965. *Adolescents and the Schools.* New York: Basic Books.

—— et al. 1966. *Equality of Educational Opportunity.* Washington, D.C.: U.S. Government Printing Office.

Constantine, Larry L., and Joan H. Constantine. 1973. *Group Marriage: A Study of Contemporary Multilateral Marriage.* New York: Macmillan.

Cooley, Charles Horton. 1909. *Social Organization.* New York: Scribner's.

Coser, Lewis. 1964. *The Functions of Social Conflict.* New York: Free Press.

——. 1977. *Masters of Sociological Thought.* 2d ed. New York: Harcourt Brace Jovanovich.

Coser, Rose Laub, ed. 1969. *Life Cycle and Achievement in America.* New York: Harper & Row.

Coulance, Fustel de. 1873. *The Ancient City.* Garden City, N.Y.: Doubleday.

Cox, Harvey. 1966. The Secular City. rev. ed. New York: Macmillan.

Crano, William D., and Joel Aronoff. 1978. "A Cross-Cultural Study of Expressive and Instrumental Role Complementarity in the Family." *American Sociological Review* 43:463–471.

Cronkite, Ruth C. 1977. "The Determinants of Spouse's Normative Preferences for Family Roles. *Journal of Marriage and the Family.* 39:575–585.

Cuber, John, and Peggy Harroff. 1965. *The Significant Americans.* New York: Penguin Books.

Cumming, Elaine, and William E. Henry. 1961. *Growing Old.* New York: Basic Books.

Cummins, Marvin. 1978. "Police and Petting: Informal Enforcement of Sexual Standards." In James M. Henslin and Edward Segarin, eds., *The Sociology of Sex*, pp. 123–139. New York: Schocken Books.

Dalsimer, Isabel et al. 1973. "Condom—An Old Method Meets a New Social Need." *Population Reports.* Dept of Medical and Public Affairs. George Washington University. Series H, no. 1.

D'Antonio, William V. 1980. "The Family and Religion: Exploring a Changing Relationship." *Journal for the Scientifc Study of Religion* 19:89–104.

David, Deborah S., and Robert Brannon, eds. 1976. *The Forty-Nine Percent Majority: The Male Sex Role.* Reading, Mass.: Addison-Wesley.

Dean, Gillian, and Douglas T. Gurak. 1978. "Marital Homogamy the Second Time Around." *Journal of Marriage and the Family* 40:559–570.

Delissovoy, Vladimir. 1973. "High School Marriages: A Longitudinal Study." *Journal of Marriage and the Family* 35:245–255.

Demos, John. 1971. *A Little Commonwealth: Family Life in Plymouth Colony.* New York: Oxford University Press.

Denfield, Duane. 1974. "Dropouts from Swinging." *The Family Coordinator* 23:45–49.

——, and Michael Gordon. 1970. "The Sociology of Mate-Swapping: Or the Family That Swings Together Clings Together." *Journal of Sex Research* 6:85–100.

De Vaux, Roland. 1965. *Ancient Israel.* 2 vols. New York: McGraw-Hill.

Dille, John, ed. 1971. *The Time-Life Family Legal Guide.* New York: Time-Life Books.

Dreikurs, Rudolf. 1964. *Children: The Challenge.* New

York: Hawthorne Books.

Duberman, Lucile. 1973. "Step-Kin Relationships." *Journal of Marriage and the Family* 35:283–292.

———. 1975a. *Gender and Sex in Society.* New York: Praeger.

———. 1975b. *The Reconstituted Family: A Study of Remarried Couples and Their Children.* Chicago: Nelson-Hall.

———. 1977. *Marriage and Its Alternatives.* New York: Praeger.

Durkheim, Emile. 1933 (1893). *The Division of Labor in Society.* New York: Free Press.

———. 1956. *Education and Sociology.* New York: Free Press.

———. 1961. *Moral Education.* New York: Free Press.

———. 1965 (1912). *The Elementary Forms of the Religious Life.* New York: Free Press.

Duvall, Evelyn M. 1954. *In-Laws: Pro and Con.* New York: Association Press.

———. 1967. *Family Development.* 3d ed. Philadelphia: Lippincott.

Duvall, Sylvanus. 1969. "The New Morality's Challenge to the American Family." *The Family Coordinator* 18:282–283.

Dyer, Everett D. 1979. *The American Family: Variety and Change.* New York: McGraw-Hill.

Ebaugh, Helen Rose Ruchs, and C. Allen Haney. 1978. "Church Attendance and Attitudes Toward Abortion: Differentials in Liberal and Conservative Churches." *Journal for the Scientific Study of Religion* 17:407–413.

Eckland, Bruce K. 1980. "Theories of Mate Selection" In James M. Henslin, ed, *Marriage and Family in a Changing Society*, pp. 132–140. New York: Free Press.

Eder, Donna, and Maureen T. Hallihan. 1978. "Sex Differences in Children's Friendships." *American Sociological Review* 43:237–250.

Edwards, G. Franklin. 1967. "Community and Class Realities: The Ordeal of Change. In Talcott Parsons and Kenneth B. Clark, eds., *The Negro American*, pp. 280–302. Boston: Beacon Press.

Ehrlich, Paul. 1968. *The Population Bomb.* New York: Ballentine Books.

Ehrmann, Winston. 1964. "Marital and Nonmarital Sexual Behavior." In Harold T. Christensen, ed. *Handbook of Marriage and the Family*, pp. 585–622. Chicago: Rand McNally.

Eisenstadt, S. N. 1965. "Archtypal Patterns of Youth," In Erik K. Erikson, ed. *The Challenge of Youth.* Garden City, N.Y.: Doubleday.

Elkin, Frederick, and Gerald Handel. 1972. *The Child and Society: The Process of Socialization.* 2d ed. New York: Random House.

Elkind, David. 1979. *The Child and Society.* New York: Oxford University Press.

Elkins, Stanley M. 1968. *Slavery.* 2d ed., Chicago: University of Chicago Press.

Elms, Alan C., ed. 1969. *Role Playing, Reward, and Attitude Change.* New York: Van Nostrand Reinhold.

Engles, Frederick. 1942. *The Origin of the Family, Private Property, and the State.* New York: International.

Erikson, Erik K. 1963. *Childhood and Society.* 2d ed. New York: Norton.

———. ed. 1965. *The Challenge of Youth.* Garden City, N.Y.: Doubleday.

———. 1968. *Identity: Youth and Crisis.* New York: Norton.

Erlanger, Howard S. 1974. "Social Class and Corporal Punishment in Childrearing: A Reassessment." *American Sociological Review* 39:68–85.

Espenshade, Thomas J. 1977. "The Value and Cost of Children." *Population Bulletin*, vol 32, no. 1. Washington, D.C.: Population Reference Bureau.

Etzioni, Amitai. 1975. *Genetic Fix.* New York: Harper & Row.

Farley, Reynolds. 1977. "Trends in Racial Inequalities: Have the Gains of the 1960's Disappeared in the 1970's?" *American Sociological Review* 42:189–208.

Fein, Robert A. 1978. "Research on Fathering: Social Policy and an Emergent Perspective." *Journal of Social Issues* 34:122–135.

Feldstein, Stanley, and Lawrence Costello, eds. 1974. *The Ordeal of Assimilation.* Garden City, N.Y.: Doubleday.

Filene, Peter Gabriel. 1975. *Him Her Self: Sex Roles in Modern America.* New York: New American Library.

Fontana, Vincent J. 1976. *Somewhere a Child Is Crying: Maltreatment—Causes and Prevention.* New York: New American Library.

Forisha, Barbara Lusk. 1978. *Sex Roles and Personal Awareness.* Morristown, N.J.: General Learning Press.

Franklin, Benjamin. 1950. *The Autobiography and Selected Writings.* New York: Random House.

Frazier, E. Franklin. 1957. *Black Bourgeoisie.* New York: Free Press.

———. 1966. *The Negro Family in the United States.* Chicago: University of Chicago Press.

Freedman, Maurice. 1964. "Kinship and Kinship Systems." In Juline Gould and William L. Kolb, eds., *A Dictionary of the Social Sciences.* New York: Free Press.

Freud, Sigmond. 1959. *Beyond the Pleasure Principle.* New York: Bantam Books.

———. 1960. *Group Psychology and the Analysis of the Ego.* New York: Bantam Books.

———. 1962a. *Civilization and Its Discontents.* Trans. and ed. by James Strachey. New York: Norton.

———. 1962b. *The Ego and the Id.* New York: Norton.

———. 1965 (1933). *New Introductory Lectures on Psychoanalysis.* New York: Norton.

Friedan, Betty. 1973. *The Feminine Mystique.* New York: Norton.

Fromm, Erich. 1956. *The Art of Loving.* New York: Harper & Bros.

Furstenberg, Frank F. 1976. *Unplanned Parenthood: The Social Consequences of Teenage Childbearing.* New York: Macmillan.

Gagnon, John, and Bruce Henderson. 1980. "The Social Psychology of Sexual Development." In James M. Henslin, ed., *Marriage and Family in a Changing Society.* New York: Free Press.

Galbraith, John Kenneth. 1967. *The New Industrial State.* Boston: Houghton Mifflin.

Galligan, Richard J., and Stephen J. Bahr. 1978. "Economic Well-Being and Marital Stability: Implications for Income Maintenance Programs." *Journal of Marriage and the Family* 40:283–290.

Gans, Herbert J. 1965. *The Urban Villagers.* New York: Free Press.

Geertz, Clifford. 1973. *The Interpretation of Cultures.* New York: Basic Books.

Gelles, Richard J. 1976. "Abused Wives: Why Do They Stay?" *Journal of Marriage and the Family* 38:659–668.

———. 1980. "Power, Sex, and Violence: The Case of Marital Rape." In James M. Henslin, ed., *Marriage and Family in a Changing Society,* pp. 389–402. New York: Free Press.

Genovese, Eugene D. 1976. *Roll, Jordon, Roll: The World the Slaves Made.* New York: Random House.

Gersuny, Carl. 1970. "The Honeymoon Industry: Rhetoric and Bureaucratization of Status Passage." *The Family Coordinator* 19:260–266.

Gesell, Arnold, and F. L. Ilg. 1946. *The Child from Five to Ten.* New York: Harper & Row.

Giddens, Anthony. 1975. *The Class Structure of Advanced Societies.* New York: Harper & Row.

Gieseman, Raymond W. 1980. "Rent or Buy? Evaluating Alternatives in the Shelter Market." In Helena Z. Lopata, ed., *Family Factbook,* pp. 537–565. Chicago: Marquis Academic Media.

Gillespie, Dair B. 1971. "Who Has the Power? The Marital Struggle." *Journal of Marriage and the Family* 33:445–458.

Ginott, Haim G. 1965. *Between Parent and Child.* New York: Avon Books.

Glak, Bruce R., and Steven Jay Gross. 1975. "Marital Interaction and Marital Conflict: A Critical Evaluation of Current Research Strategies." *Journal of Marriage and the Family* 37:505–512.

Glazer, Nathan. 1957. *American Judaism.* Chicago: University of Chicago Press.

———. and Daniel Patrick Moynihan. 1971. *Beyond the Melting Pot.* 2d ed. Boston: MIT Press.

Glenn, Norval D., and Charles N. Weaver. 1977. "The Marital Happiness of Remarried Divorced Persons." *Journal of Marriage and the Family* 39:331–337.

Glick, Paul C. 1975. "A Demographer Looks at American Families." *Journal of Marriage and the Family* 37:15–26.

———. 1977. "Updating the Life Cycle of the Family." *Journal of Marriage and the Family* 39:5–13.

———. 1980. "Remarriage: Some Recent Changes and Variations." *Journal of Family Issues* 1:455–478.

———, and Emmanuel Landau. 1950. "Age as a Factor in Marriage." *American Sociological Review* 15:517–529.

———, and Arthur J. Norton. 1977. "Marrying, Divorcing, and Living Together in the U.S. Today." *Population Bulletin,* vol. 32, no. 5 Washington, D.C.: Population Reference Bureau.

———, and Graham B. Spanier. 1980. "Cohabitation in the United States." *Journal of Marriage and the Family* 42:19–30.

Glock, Charles Y., and Rodney Stark. 1969. *Christian Beliefs and Anti-Semitism.* New York: Harper & Row.

Glueck, Sheldon, and Eleanor Glueck. 1950. *Unraveling Juvenile Delinquency.* Cambridge, Mass.: Harvard University Press.

Goffman, Erving. 1959. *The Presentation of Self in Everyday Life.* Garden City, N.Y.: Doubleday.

———. 1979. *Gender Advertisements.* New York: Harper & Row.

Goldberg, Steven. 1973. *The Inevitability of Patriarchy.* New York: Morrow.

Goldberg, S., and M. Lewis. 1969. "Play Behavior in the Year-Old Infant: Early Sex Differences." *Child Development* 40:21–31.

Goldstein, Sidney, and Calvin Goldscheider. 1968. *Jewish Americans: Three Generations in a Jewish Community.* Englewood Cliffs, N.J.: Prentice-Hall.

Goode, William J. 1964. *The Family.* Englewood Cliffs, N.J.: Prentice-Hall.

———. 1965. *Women in Divorce.* New York: Free Press.

———. 1966. "Family and Mobility." In Reinhard Bendix and Seymour Martin Lipset, eds., *Class, Status, and Power,* pp. 582–601. New York: Free Press.

———. 1970. *World Revolutions and Family Patterns.* New York: Free Press.

———. 1973. *Explorations in Social Theory.* New York: Oxford University Press.

Gordon, Michael. 1978. "From an Unfortunate Necessity to a Cult of Mutual Orgasm: Sex in American Marital Education Literature, 1830–1940." In James M. Henslin and Edward Sagarin eds., *The Sociology of Sex.* rev. ed., pp. 59–83. New York: Schocken Books.

Gordon, Milton M. 1964. *Assimilation in American Life.* New York: Oxford University Press.

———. 1978. *Human Nature, Class, and Ethnicity.* New York: Oxford University Press.

Gordon, Suzanne. 1976. *Lonely in America.* New York: Simon & Schuster.

Gordon, Thomas. 1970. *Parent Effectiveness Training: The*

Tested New Way to Raise Responsible Children. New York: Peter H. Wyden.

Goslin, David A. 1965. *The School in Contemporary Society.* Glenview, Ill.: Scott, Foresman.

Gould, Robert E. 1979. "What We Don't Know About Homosexuality." In Martin P. Levine, ed., *Gay Men: A Sociology of Male Homosexuality*, pp. 36–50. New York: Harper & Row.

Greeley, Andrew M. 1972. *That Most Distressful Nation: The Taming of the American Irish.* Chicago: Quadrangle Books.

———. 1977. *The American Catholic: A Social Portrait.* New York: Basic Books.

——— et al. 1976. *Catholic Education in a Declining Church.* Kansas City, Mo.: Sheed and Ward.

Greenleaf, Barbara Kay. 1979. *Children Through the Ages: A History of Childhood.* New York: Barnes & Noble Books.

Greer, Germaine. 1971. *The Female Eunuch.* New York: McGraw-Hill.

Greven, Philip. 1977. *The Protestant Temperament: Patterns of Child-Rearing, Religious Experience, and the Self in Early America.* New York: Knopf.

Group for the Advancement of Psychiatry. 1973. *Humane Reproduction.* New York: Scribner's.

Gunter, B. G. 1977. "Notes on Divorce Filing as Role Behavior." *Journal of Marriage and the Family* 39:95–98.

Gutman, Herbert G. 1977. *The Black Family in Slavery and Freedom, 1750–1925.* New York: Random House.

Haley, Jay. 1970. "Whither Family Therapy" In Paul H. Glasser and Lois N. Glasser, eds., *Families in Crisis*, pp. 181–216. New York: Harper & Row.

Hall, Calvin S. 1954. *A Primer of Freudian Psychology.* New York: New American Library.

———, and Gardner Lindzey. 1957. *Theories of Personality.* New York: Wiley.

Hambley, John. 1972. "Diversity: A Developmental Perspective." In Ken Richardson and David Spears, eds., *Race and Intelligence*, pp. 114–127. Baltimore, Md.: Penguin Books.

Handel, Gerald, and Lee Reinwater. 1964. "Persistence and Change in Working-Class Life Style." In Arthur B. Shostak and William Gomberg, eds., *Blue-Collar World: Studies of the American Worker*, pp. 36–41. Englewood Cliffs, N.J.: Prentice-Hall.

Handelman, Phyllis. 1978. "Midlife Transition and Contextual Change." In Helena Z. Lopata, ed, *Family Factbook*, pp. 212–216. Chicago: Marquis Academic Media.

Handlin, Oscar. 1951. *The Uprooted.* New York: Grosset and Dunlap.

———. 1957. *Race and Nationality in American Life.* Garden City, N.Y.: Doubleday.

———, and Mary F. Handlin. 1971. *Facing Life. Youth and the Family in American History.* Boston: Little, Brown.

Hareven, Tamara K. 1978. "The Dynamics of Kin in an Industrial Community." John Demos and Sarane S. Boocock, eds., *Turning Points: Historical and Sociological Essays on the Family*, pp. 151–182. Chicago: University of Chicago Press.

Hartel, Bradley, Gary E. Henderskot, and James W. Grimm. 1974. "Religion and Attitudes Toward Abortion: A Study of Nurses and Social Workers." *Journal for the Scientific Study of Religion* 13:23–34.

Harvey, Carol D., and Howard M. Bahr. 1974. "Widowhood, Morale, and Affiliation." *Journal of Marriage and the Family* 36:97–106.

Hatch, Edwin. 1957. *The Influence of Greek Ideas on Christianity.* New York: Harper & Bros.

Havighurst, Robert J., and Hilda Taba. 1963. *Adolescent Character and Personality.* New York: Wiley.

Heer, David M. 1974. "The Prevalence of Black-White Marriage in the United States, 1960 and 1970." *Journal of Marriage and the Family* 36:246–258.

Henslin, James M. 1978. "Toward the Sociology of Sex." In James M. Henslin and Edward Sagarin, eds., *The Sociology of Sex.* rev. ed., pp. 1–25. New York. Schocken Books.

———, ed. 1980. *Marriage and Family in a Changing Society.* New York: Free Press.

Henze, Lura F., and John W. Hudson. 1974. "Personal and Family Characteristics of Cohabiting and Noncohabiting College Students." *Journal of Marriage and the Family* 36:722–727.

Herberg, Will. 1960. *Protestant, Catholic., Jew.* rev. ed. Garden City, N.Y.: Doubleday.

Hettlinger, Richard. 1974. *Sex Isn't That Simple.* New York: Seabury Press.

Hill, Reubin, 1949. *Families Under Stress.* New York: Harper.

———, and Roy H. Rodgers. 1964. "The Developmental Approach." In Harold T. Christensen, ed, *Handbook of Marriage and the Family*, pp. 171–211. Chicago: Rand McNally.

Hiltz, Starr Roxanne. 1978. "Widowhood: A Roleless Role." *Marriage and Family Review* 1:1–10.

Hobbs, Daniel F., Jr., and Sue Peck Cole. 1976. "Transition to Parenthood: A Decade Replication." *Journal of Marriage and the Family* 38:723–731.

———, and James Maynard Wimbish. 1977. "Transition to Parenthood by Black Couples." *Journal of Marriage and the Family* 39:677–689.

Hodgson, Marshall G. S. 1974. *The Venture of Islam.* 3 vols. Chicago: Univerity of Chicago Press.

Hofstadter, Richard. 1963. *Anti-Intellectualism in American Life.* New York: Random House.

Hogan, Dennis P. 1978. "The Variable Order of Events in the Life Course." *American Sociological Review* 43:573–586.

———. 1980. "The Transition to Adulthood as a Career

Contingency." *American Sociological Review* 45:261–276.

Hollingshead, August B. 1975. *Elmtown's Youth and Elmtown Revisited.* New York: Wiley.

———, and Frederick C. Redlich. 1964. *Social Class and Mental Illness.* New York: Wiley.

Holt, John. 1974. *Escape from Childhood.* New York: Ballantine Books.

Homans, George C. 1950. *The Human Group.* New York: Harcourt, Brace & World.

Houseknecht, Sharon K. 1977. "Reference Group Support for Voluntary Childlessness, Evidence for Conformity." *Journal of Marriage and the Family* 39:285–292.

Howell, Joseph T. 1973. *Hard Living on Clay Street.* Garden City, N.Y.: Doubleday.

Hulka, J.F., and K. F. Omran. 1972. "New Methods of Female Sterilisation." In Malcolm Potts and Clive Wood, eds., *New Concepts in Contraception*, pp. 57–67. Oxford: Medical and Technical Publishing.

Humphreys, Laud. 1979. "Exodus and Identity: The Emerging Gay Culture." In Martin P. Levine, ed., *Gay Men: The Sociology of Male Homosexualtiy*, pp. 134–147. New York: Harper & Row.

Hunt, Morton M. 1964. "The Married Mistress." In Henry Anatole Grunwald, ed, *Sex in America.* pp. 166–188. New York: Bantam Books.

———. 1974. *Sexual Behavior in the Seventies.* Chicago: Playboy Press.

———. 1975. "The Future of Marriage." In Jack R. Delora and Joann S. DeLora, eds., *Intimate Life Styles*, pp. 410–423. Pacific Palisades, Ca. Goodyear.

Hunt, Richard A., and Morton B. King. 1978. "Religiosity and Marriage." *Journal for the Scientific Study of Religion* 17:399–406.

Hurvitz, Nathan. 1964. "Marital Strain in the Blue Collar Family." In Arthur B. Shostak and William Gomberg, eds., *Blue Collar World: Studies of the American Worker*, pp. 92–109. Englewood Cliffs, N.J. Prentice-Hall.

———. 1975. "Courtship and Arranged Marriages Among Eastern European Jews Prior to World War I as Depicted in a *Briefenshteller.*" *Journal of Marriage and the Family* 37:422–430.

Hyman, Herbert H. 1969. *Political Socialization: A Study in the Psychology of Political Behavior.* New York: Free Press.

Illick, Joseph E. 1975. "Child-Rearing in Seventeenth Century England and America." In Lloyd DeMause, ed., *The History of Childhood*, pp. 303–350. New York: Harper & Row.

Jencks, Christopher et al. 1973. *Inequality: A Reassessment of the Effect of Family and Schooling in America.* New York: Harper & Row.

Johnson, Elizabeth S., and John B. Williamson. 1980. *Growing Old: The Social Problems of Aging.* New York: Holt, Rinehart and Winston.

Jones, Ernest. 1963. *The Life and Work of Sigmund Freud.* Abridged ed. Garden City, N.Y.: Doubleday.

Jorgensen, Stephen R. 1977. "Social Class Heterogamy, Status Striving and Perceptions of Marital Conflict: A Partial Replication and Revision of Pearlin's Contingency Hypotheses." *Journal of Marriage and the Family* 39:653–661.

Kaats, Gilbert, and Keith E. Davis. 1975. "The Dynamics of Sexual Behavior of College Students." In Jack R. DeLora and Joann S. DeLora, eds., *Intimate Life Styles: Marriage and Its Alternatives*, pp. 32–45. Pacific Palisades, Ca.: Goodyear.

Kagan, Jerone. 1964. "Acquisition and Significance of Sex Typing and Sex Role Identity." In Martin L. Hoffman and Lois W. Hoffman, eds., *Review of Child Development Research*, vol. 1. New York: Russell Sage.

Kahn, Malcolm. 1970. "Non-Verbal Communication and Marital Satisfaction." *Family Process* 9:449–456.

Kanter, Rosabeth Moss. 1977. *Men and Women of The Corporation.* New York: Basic Books.

Kantor, David, and William Lehr. 1975. *Inside the Family: Toward a Theory of Family Process.* New York: Harper & Row.

Karlen, Arlo. 1980. "Homosexuality: The Scene and Its Students." In James M. Henslin and Edward Sagarin, eds., *The Sociology of Sex*, pp. 223–248. New York: Schocken Books.

Kastenbaum, Robert. 1979. *Growing Old: Years of Fulfillment.* New York: Harper & Row.

Katchadourian, Herant A., and Donald Lunde. 1980. *Fundamentals of Human Sexuality.* 3d ed. New York: Holt, Rinehart and Winston.

———, and Robert J. Trotter. 1979. *Human Sexuality.* Brief ed. New York: Holt, Rinehart and Winston.

Katz, A. M., and Reuben Hill. 1958. "Residential Propinquity and Marital Selection: A Review of Theory, Method, and Fact." *Marriage and Family Living* 20:27–34.

Keniston, Kenneth. 1965. *The Uncommitted: Alienated Youth in American Society.* New York: Dell.

———. 1968. *Young Radicals: Notes on Committed Youth.* New York: Harcourt, Brace & World.

Kenkel, William L. 1966. *The Family in Perspective.* New York: Appleton-Century-Crofts.

Kennedy, David M. 1970. *Birth Control in America: The Career of Margaret Sanger.* New Haven, Conn.: Yale University Press.

Kephart, William M. 1966. *The Family, Society, and the Individual.* 2d ed. Boston: Houghton Mifflin.

Kerckhoff, Alan C., and Keith E. Davis. 1962. "Value Consensus and Need Complementarity in Mate Selection." *American Sociological Review* 27:295–303.

Kett, Joseph F. 1977. *Rites of Passage: Adolescence in America 1790 to the Present.* New York: Basic Books.

Keyes, Ralph. 1975. "Singled Out." In Jack R. DeLora and Joann S. DeLora, eds, *Intimate Life Styles: Marriage and Its Alternatives,* pp. 328–337. Pacific Palisades, Ca.: Goodyear.

Kiernan, Diane, and Irving Tallman. 1972. "Spousal Adaptability: An Assessment of Marital Competence." *Journal of Marriage and the Family* 34:247–256.

Kim, Choong Soon. 1974. "The Yon'jul-hon or Chain-String Form of Marriage Arrangement in Korea." *Journal of Marriage and the Family* 36:575–579.

King, Karl, Jack O. Balswock, and Ira E. Robinson. 1977. "The Continuing Premarital Sexual Revolution Among College Females." *Journal of Marriage and the Family* 39:455–459.

Kinsey, Alfred C., and Paul Gebhard. 1953. *Sexual Behavior in the Human Female.* Philadelphia: Saunders.

———, Wardell Pomeroy, and Clyde Martin. 1948. *Sexual Behavior in the Human Male.* Philadelphia: Saunders.

Kirkendall, Lester A. 1961. *Premarital Intercourse and Interpersonal Relations.* New York: Julian Press.

———, and Roger W. Libby. 1966. "Interpersonal Relationships—Crux of the Sexual Renaissance." *Journal of Social Issues* 22:45–59.

Knox, David. 1979. *Exploring Marriage and the Family.* Glenview, Ill. Scott, Foresman.

Kobrin, Frances E. 1976. "The Primary Individual and the Family: Changes in Living Arrangements in the United States Since 1940." *Journal of Marriage and the Family* 38:233–239.

Koller, Marvin R. 1968. *Social Gerontology.* New York: Random House.

Komarorsky, Mirra. 1967. *Blue Collar Marriage.* New York: Random House.

———. 1976. *Dilemmas of Masculinity: A Study of College Youth.* New York: Norton.

Koo, Helen P., and C. M. Suchindran. 1980. "Effects of Children on Women's Remarriage Prospects." *Journal of Family Issues* 1:497–515.

Koran, The. 1974. 4th rev. ed. Trans and ed. by N. J. Dawood. Baltimore, Md: Penguin Books.

Kornblum, William. 1974. *Blue Collar Community.* Chicago: University of Chicago Press.

Kübler-Ross, Elisabeth. 1969. *On Death and Dying.* New York: Macmillan.

Ladner, Joyce A., ed. 1973. *The Death of White Sociology.* New York: Random House.

Lamb, Michael E., ed. 1976. *The Role of the Father in Child Development.* New York: Wiley.

Larkin, Ralph W. 1979. *Suburban Youth in Cultural Crisis.* New York: Oxford University Press.

Lasch, Christopher. 1979. *Haven in a Heartless World: The Family Besieged.* New York: Basic Books.

Laslett, Barbara. 1977. "Social Change and the Family: Los Angeles, California, 1850–1870." *American Sociological Review* 42:268–291.

Laslett, Peter. 1965. *The World We Have Lost.* New York: Scribner's.

Laswell, Marcia, and Norman M. Lobsonz. 1978. "The Intimacy That Goes Beyond Sex." In Jerald Sarvells and Lawrence J. Cross, eds., *The Changing Family,* pp. 347–354. New York: Holt, Rinehart and Winston.

Lazareth, William H. 1960. *Luther on the Christian Home.* Philadelphia: Muhlenberg Press.

Leik, Robert K. 1963. "Instrumentality and Emotionality in Family Interaction." *Sociometry* 26:131–145.

LeMasters, E. E. 1957. "Parenthood as Crisis." *Marriage and Family Living* 19:352–355.

———. 1977. *Parents in Modern America.* 3d ed. Homewood, Ill. Dorsey Press.

Lenski, Gerhard. 1963. *The Religious Factor.* rev. ed. Garden City, N.Y.: Doubleday.

Leslie, Gerald R. 1979. *The Family in Social Context.* New York: Oxford University Press.

———, and Elizabeth M. Leslie. 1980. *Marriage in a Changing World.* 2d ed. New York: Wiley.

Lever, Janet. 1968. "Sex Differences in the Complexity of Children's Play and Games." *American Sociological Review* 43:471–483.

Levine, Martin P., ed. 1978. *Gay Men: The Sociology of Male Homosexuality.* New York: Harper & Row.

Levinger, George. 1964. "Task and Social Behavior in Marriage." *Sociometry* 27:433–446.

———. 1966. "Sources of Marital Dissatisfaction Among Applicants for Divorce." *American Journal of Orthopsychiatry* 36:803–807.

———. 1970. "Marital Cohesiveness and Dissolution: An Integrative Review." In Paul H. Glasser and Lois N. Glasser, eds., *Families in Crisis,* pp. 107–125. New York: Harper & Row.

Levitt, Eugene E., and Albert D. Klasson, Jr. 1979. "Public Attitudes Toward Homosexuality." In Martin P. Levine, ed., *Gay Men: The Sociology of Male Homosexuality,* pp. 19–35. New York: Harper & Row.

Lewinsohn, Richard. 1958. *A History of Sexual Customs.* Greenwich, Conn.: Fawcett.

Lewis, Oscar. 1961. *The Children of Sanchez.* New York: Random House.

———. 1966. *La Vida: A Puerto Rican Family in the Culture of Poverty—San Juan and New York.* New York: Random House.

Libby, Roger W. 1979. "Creative Singlehood as a Sexual Life Style: Beyond Marriage as a Rite of Passage." In J. Gibson Wells, ed., *Current Issues in Marriage and the Family.* 2d ed., pp. 36–64. New York: Macmillan.

Liebow, Elliot. 1967. *Tally's Corner: A Study of Negro Streetcorner Men.* Boston: Little, Brown.

Lipset, Seymour Martin. 1960. *Political Man.* Garden City, N.Y.: Doubleday.

———. 1963. *The First New Nation.* New York: Basic Books.

———, and Reinhard Bendix. 1959. *Social Mobility in Industrial Society.* Berkeley, Ca.: University of California Press.

Litwak, Eugene. 1960a. "Occupational Mobility and Extended Family Cohesion." *American Sociological Review* 25:9–21.

———. 1960b. "Geographical Mobility and Extended Family Cohesion." *American Sociological Review* 25:385–394.

Loether, Herman J. 1964. "The Meaning of Work and Adjustment to Retirement." In Arthur B. Shostak and William Gomberg, eds., *Blue-Collar World*, pp. 525–533. Englewood Cliffs, N.J.: Prentice-Hall.

Lopata, Helena Z. 1972. *Occupation: Housewife*. New York: Oxford University Press.

———. 1973. *Widowhood in an American City*. Cambridge, Mass.: Schenkman.

Lopreato, Joseph. 1970. *Italian Americans*. New York: Random House.

Lowenthal, M.F., M. Thurner, and D. Chiriboga. 1975. *Four Stages of Life*. San Francisco: Jossey-Bass.

Luckmann, Thomas. 1967. *The Invisible Religion*. New York: Macmillan.

Luther, Martin. 1962. *Luther's Works*. vol 45. *The Christian in Society*. Philadelphia: Muhlenberg Press.

Lyness, Judith L., Milton E. Lipetz, and Keith E. Davis. 1972. "Living Together: An Alternative to Marriage." *Journal of Marriage and the Family*. 34:305–311.

Mace, David, and Vera Mace. 1960. *Marriage East and West*. Garden City, N.Y.: Doubleday.

———. 1974. *We Can Have Better Marriages If We Really Want Them*. Nashville, Tenn: Abingdom Press.

———. 1975. "Marriage Enrichment—Wave of the Future?" *The Family Coordinator* 24:131–135.

Macklin, Eleanor D. 1972. "Heterosexual Cohabitation Among Unmarried College Students." *The Family Coordinator* 21:463–473.

———. 1980. "Nonmarital Heterosexual Cohabitation." In Arlene Skolnick and Jerome H. Skolnick, eds., *Family in Transition*. 3d ed., pp. 285–307. Boston: Little, Brown.

Malinowsk, Bronislaw. 1960 (1944). *A Scientific Theory of Culture and Other Essays*. New York: Oxford University Press.

Mallowe, Mile. 1978. "Quick, Name Three Virgins." In Jerald Savells and Lawrence J. Cross, eds., *The Changing Family: Making Way for Tomorrow*, pp. 153–158. New York: Holt, Rinehart and Winston.

Mandelbaum, David G. 1972. *Society in India*, 2 vols. Berkeley, Ca.: University of California Press.

Marciano, Teresa Donati 1975. "Variant Family Forms in a World Perspective." *The Family Coordinator* 24.

Marini, Margaret Mooney. 1976. "Dimensions of Marriage Happiness: A Research Note." *Journal of Marriage and the Family* 38:443–448.

Marshall, Donald S. 1971. "Sexual Behavior in Mangaia." In Donald S. Marshall and Robert C. Suggs, eds., *Human Sexual Behavior: Variations in Ethnographic Spectrum*, pp. 103–162. New York: Basic Books.

Martin, David, ed. 1970. *50 Key Words: Sociology*. Richmond. Va: John Knox Press.

Martin, Thomas W., Kenneth J. Berry, and R. Brooke Jacobsen. 1975. "The Impact of Dual-Career Marriages on Female Professional Careers: An Empirical Test of a Parsonian Hypotheses." *Journal of Marriage and the Family* 37:734–742.

Marx, Karl. 1974. *The Revolutions of 1848*. Edited and introduced by David Fernbach. New York: Vintage Books.

Mason, Karen Oppenheim, John L. Czajka, and Sara Arber. 1976. "Change in U.S. Women's Sex-Role Attitudes, 1967–1974." *American Sociological Review* 41:573–596.

Mass, Henry D., and Joseph A. Kuypers. 1974. *From Thirty to Seventy: A Forty Year Longitudinal Study of Adult Life Style and Personality*. San Francisco: Jossey-Bass.

Masters, William H., and Virginia F. Johnson. 1966. *Human Sexual Response*. Boston: Little, Brown.

———. 1970. *Human Sexual Inadequacy*. Boston: Little, Brown.

May, Rollo. 1969. *Love and Will*. New York: Norton.

McCary, James Leslie. 1979. *Human Sexuality*. 2d brief ed. New York: D. Van Nostrand.

———. 1980. *Freedom and Growth in Marriage*. 2d ed. New York: Wiley.

McClelland, David C. 1967. *The Achieving Society*. New York: Free Press.

McDonald, Gerald W. 1977. "Parental Identification by the Adolescent: A Social Power Approach." *Journal of Marriage and the Family* 39:705–719.

McKenzie, John L. 1971. *The Roman Catholic Church*. Garden City, N.Y.: Doubleday.

McLaughlin, Steven D. 1978. "Occupational Sex Identification and the Assessment of Male and Female Earnings Inequality." *American Sociological Review* 43:909–921.

McLaughlin, Virginia Yans. 1973. "Patterns of Work and Family Organization: Buffalo's Italians." In Theodore K. Raab and Robert I. Rotberg, eds. The Family in History: Interdisciplinary Essays, pp. 111–126. New York: Harper & Row.

Mead, George Herbert. 1934. *Mind, Self, and Society*. Chicago: University of Chicago Press.

———. 1964. *Selected Writings*. New York: Bobbs-Merrill.

Mead, Margaret. 1963. *Sex and Temperament in Three Primitive Societies*. New York: Morrow.

Melville, Keith. 1972. *Communes in the Counter-Culture*. New York: Morrow.

Merton, Robert K. 1968. *Social Theory and Social Structure*. Enlarged ed. New York: Free Press.

Meyers, Laura. 1980. "Battered Wives, Dead Husbands" In Arlene Skolnick and Jerome Skolnick, eds., *The*

Family in Transition. 3d ed., pp. 333–340. Boston: Little, Brown.

Michel, Andre. 1974. *The Modernization of North African Families in the Paris Region.* The Hague: Mouton.

Miller, Brent C., and David M. Klein. 1981. "A Survey of Recent Marriage and Family Texts." *Contemporary Sociology* 10:8–21.

Miller, Perry. 1961. *The New England Mind.* 2 vols. Boston: Beacon Press.

———. 1970. *Orthodoxy in Massachusetts, 1630–1650.* New York: Harper & Row.

Mitford, Jessica. 1963. *The American Way of Death.* New York: Simon & Schuster.

Moberg, David O. 1962. *The Church as a Social Institution.* Englewood Cliffs, N.J. Prentice-Hall.

Money, John, and Anke Ehrhardt. 1972. *Man and Woman: Boy and Girl.* Baltimore, Md.: Johns Hopkins University Press.

Moneymaker, James, and Fred Montanino. 1978. "The New Sexual Morality: A Society Comes of Age." In James H. Henslin and Edward Sagarin, eds., *The Sociology of Sex*, pp. 27–40. New York: Schocken Books.

Morgan, Edmond S. 1958. *The Puritan Dilemma: The Story of John Winthrop.* Boston: Little, Brown.

———. 1966. *The Puritan Family.* New York: Harper & Row.

Movius, Margaret. 1978. "Voluntary Childlessness—The Ultimate Liberation." In Jerald Savells and Lawrence J. Cross, eds., *The Changing Family*, pp. 306–315. New York: Holt, Rinehart and Winston.

Murdock, George P. 1949. *Social Structure.* New York: Macmillan.

Murphy, Francis X, C.S.S.R., and Joseph F. Erhart. 1975. *Catholic Perspectives on Population Issues. Population Bulletin.* Vol 30., no. 6, Washington, D.C.: Population Reference Bureau.

Nash, Dennison, and Peter L. Berger. 1962. "The Child, the Family, and 'The Religious Revival' in Suburbia." *Journal for the Scientific Study of Religion* 2:85–93.

Nash, John. 1976. "Historical and Social Changes in the Perception of the Role of the Father." In Michael E. Lanb, ed., *The Role of the Father in Child Development*, pp. 65–87. New York: Wiley.

Needleman, Jacob, and George Baker, eds., 1978. *Understanding the New Religions.* New York: Seabury Press.

Nemerowicz, Gloria Morris. 1979. *Children's Perceptions of Gender and Work Roles.* New York: Praeger.

Neubeck, Gerhard. 1969. *Extra-Marital Relations.* Englewood Cliffs, N.J.: Prentice-Hall.

Newcomb, Paul R. 1979. "Cohabitation in America: An Assessment of Consequences." *Journal of Marriage and the Family* 41:597–603.

Newman, William M. 1973. *American Pluralism: A Study of Minority Groups and Social Theory.* New York: Harper & Row.

Newsweek, editors of. 1979. "How Men Are Changing." In J. Gipson Wells, ed., *Current Issues in Marriage and the Family.* 2d ed. pp. 201–211. New York: Macmillan.

Nilsson, Martin P. 1940. *Greek Popular Religion.* New York: Columbia University Press.

Nimkoff, M. F., ed. 1965. *Comparative Family Systems.* Boston: Houghton Mifflin.

Nixon, Robert E. 1964. "Sex or Guilt." In Henry Anatole Gronwald, ed., *Sex in America*, pp. 126–139. New York: Bantam Books.

Norman, Michael. 1980. "Extended Family Relationships Created by Divorce, Remarriage, and Child Custody Arrangements." *New York Times Magazine*, November 23.

Nye, F. Ivan. 1957. "Child Adjustment in Broken and in Unhappy Unbroken Homes." *Journal of Marriage and Family Living* 19:356–361.

———. 1974. "Emerging and Declining Family Roles." *Journal of Marriage and the Family* 36:238–245.

Oakley, Ann. 1972. *Sex, Gender, and Society.* New York: Harper & Row.

———. 1974. *The Sociology of Housework.* New York: Pantheon Books.

———. 1976. *Women's Work.* New York: Random House.

Oesterley, W. O. E., and Theodore H. Robinson. 1962. *An Introduction to the Books of the Old Testament.* New York: Meridian Books.

Ogburn, William F. 1938. "The Changing Family." *The Family Coordinator* 19:139–143.

O'Neill, George, and Nena O'Neill. 1972a. *Open Marriage: A New Life Style for Couples.* New York: M. Evans.

———. 1972b. "Open Marriage: A Synergic Model." *The Family Coordinator* 21:403–409.

Oppenheimer, Valerie Kincade. 1977. "The Sociology of Women's Economic Role in the Family." *American Sociological Review* 42:387–406.

Orthner, Dennis K. 1975. "Leisure Activity Patterns and Marital Satisfaction over the Marital Career." *Journal of Marriage and the Family* 37:91–102.

Ory, Marcia G. 1978. "The Decision to Parent or Not: Normative and Structural Components." *Journal of Marriage and the Family* 40:531–539.

Osmond, Marie Withers, and Patricia Yancey Martin. 1975. "Sex and Sexism: A Comparison of Male and Female Sex-Role Attitudes." *Journal of Marriage and the Family* 37:744–758.

Otto, Luther B. 1975. "Class and Status in Family Research." *Journal of Marriage and the Family* 37:315–332.

Parsons, Talcott. 1951. *The Social System.* New York: Free Press.

———. 1954. (1964). *Essays in Sociological Theory.* rev. ed. New York: Free Press.

———. 1960. *Structure and Process in Modern Society.* New York: Free Press.

———. 1964. *Social Structure and Personality*. New York: Free Press.

———. 1965. "Youth in the Context of American Society." In Erik K. Erikson, ed., *The Challenge of Youth*, pp. 110–142. Garden City, N.Y.: Doubleday.

———. 1967. *Sociological Theory and Modern Society*. New York: Free Press.

———. 1977. *Social Systems and the Evolution of Action Theory*. New York: Free Press.

———, and Robert F. Bales. 1955. *Family, Socialization and Interaction Process*. New York: Free Press.

Paul VI. 1968. *Humanae Vitae, Encyclical of Pope Paul VI*. New York: Paulist Press.

Peterman, Dan J., Carl A. Ridley, and Scott M. Anderson. 1974. "A Comparison of Cohabiting and Noncohabiting College Students." *Journal of Marriage and the Family* 36:344–354.

Peterson, Larry R., and Armand L. Mauss. 1976. "Religion and the "Right to Life": Correlates of Opposition to Abortion." *Sociological Analysis* 37:243–254.

Pfuetze, Paul E. 1961. *Self, Society, Existence*. New York: Harper & Bros.

Piaget, Jean. 1926. *The Language and Thought of the Child*. New York: Harcourt, Brace & World.

———. 1932. *The Moral Judgment of the Child*. New York: Harcourt, Brace & World.

———. 1952. *The Origins of Intelligence in Children*. New York: International Universities Press.

———. 1963. *The Psychology of Intelligence*. Paterson, N.J.: Littlefield, Adams.

Pierson, Elaine C., and William V. D'Antonio. 1974. *Female and Male*. New York: Lippincott.

Pincus, Lily. 1976. *Death and the Family*. New York: Random House.

Pinkney, Alphonso. 1969. *Black Americans*. Englewood Cliffs, N.J.: Prentice-Hall.

Piotrow, Phyllis T., and Calvin M. Lee. 1974. "Oral Contraceptives—50 Million Users." *Population Report*. Dept. of Medical and Public Affairs. George Washington University. Series A, no. 1

———, Ward Rinehart, and John C. Schmidt. 1979. "IUDs—Update on Effectiveness, Safety, and Research. *Population Reports*. Population Information Program. Johns Hopkins University. Series B no. 3

Population Reports. 1973a. "Laparoscopic Sterilization—A New Technique." Series C, no. 1. Dept. of Medical and Public Affairs. Washington, D.C.: George Washington University Medical Center.

———. 1973b. "Laparoscopic Sterilization II: What Are the Problems?" Series C, no. 2. Dept. of Medical and Public Affairs. Washington, D.C.: George Washington University Medical Center.

———. 1974a. "Laparoscopic Sterilization with Clips." Series C, no. 4. Dept. of Medical and Public Affairs, Washington, D.C.: George Washington University Medical Center.

———. 1974b. "Female Sterilization by Mini-Laparotomy." Series C, no. 5. Dept. of Medical and Public Affairs. Washington, D.C.: George Washington University Medical Center.

———. 1976a. "Tubal Sterilization—Review of Methods." Series C, no. 7. Dept. of Medical and Public Affairs. Washington, D.C.: George Washington University Medical Center.

———. 1976b. "Vasectomy Reversibility—A Status Report." Series D, no. 3. Dept. of Medical and Public Affairs. Washington, D.C.: George Washington University Medical Center.

Queen, Stuart A., and Robert W. Habenstein. 1967. *The Family in Various Cultures*. 3d ed. New York: Lippincott.

Rainwater, Lee. 1967. *And the Poor Get Children*. Chicago: Quadrangle Books.

———, and William L. Yancey. 1967. *The Moynihan Report and the Politics of Controversy*. Cambridge, Mass.: M.I.T. Press.

Rallings, E. M. 1969. "Problems of Communication in Family Living." *The Family Coordinator* 18:289–291.

Ramey, James. 1978. "Experimental Family Forms—The Family of the Future." *Marriage and Family Review* 1:1–9.

Rao, S. L. N. 1974. "A Comparative Study of Childlessness and Never-Pregnant Status." *Journal of Marriage and the Family* 36:149–157.

Rapoport, Rhona, and Robert Rapoport. 1971. *Dual-Career Families*. Baltimore, Md.: Penguin Books.

———. 1977. *Dual-Career Families Re-examined*. New York: Harper & Row.

———. 1980. *Crowing Through Life*. New York: Harper & Row.

Rapoport, Robert, and Rhona Rapoport, eds. 1978. *Working Couples*. New York: Harper & Row.

Redfield, Robert. 1953. *The Primitive World and Its Transformations*. Ithaca, N.Y.: Cornell University Press.

Reiss, Ira L. 1960/1964. *Premarital Sexual Standards in America*. New York: Free Press.

———. 1961. "Sexual Codes in Teen-Age Culture." *Annals of the American Academy of Political and Social Science* 338:52–61.

———. 1967. *The Social Context of Premarital Sexual Permissiveness*. New York: Holt, Rinehart and Winston.

———. 1980. *Family Systems in America*. 3d ed. New York: Holt, Rinehart and Winston.

Reubin, David. 1969. *Everything You Wanted to Know About Sex—But Were Afraid to Ask*. New York: David McKay.

———. 1971. *Any Woman Can*. New York: David McKay.

Ridley, Carl A., Dan J. Peterman, and Arthus W. Avery. 1978. "Cohabitation: Does It Make for a Better Marriage?" *The Family Coordinator* 27:129–136.

Rieff, Philip. 1961. *Freud: The Mind of the Moralist*. Garden City, N.Y.: Doubleday.

Rinehart, Ward, and Phyllis T. Piotrow. 1979. "OCS— Update on Usage Safety, and Side-Effects." *Population Reports.* Population Information Program. Johns Hopkins University. Series A. no. 5.

————, and R. T. Ravenholt. 1977. "Oral Contraceptives." *Population Reports.* Dept. of Medical and Public Affairs. George Washington University. Series A, no. 4.

Robertson, Joan F. 1977. "Grandmotherhood: A Study of Role Conceptions." *Journal of Marriage and the Family* 39:165–174.

Robertson, Priscilla. 1960. *Revolutions of 1848: A Social History.* New York: Harper & Row.

Rockwell, Richard C. 1976. "Historical Trends and Variations in Educational Homogamy." *Journal of Marriage and the Family* 38:83–95.

Rodgers, Roy H. 1962. *Improvements in the Construction and Analysis of Family Life Cycle Categories.* Kalamazoo: Western Michigan University Press.

Rodman, Hyman 1969. "Fidelity and Forms of Marriage: The Consensual Union in the Caribbean." In Gerhard Neubeck, ed., *Extra Marital Relations,* pp. 94–107. Englewood Cliffs, N.J.: Prentice-Hall.

————. 1971. *Lower-Class Families: The Culture of Poverty in Negro Trinidad.* New York: Oxford University Press.

Roglen, Lloyd H. 1972. *Migrant in the City: The Life of a Puerto Rican Action Group.* New York: Basic Books.

Rollins, Boyd, C., and Stephen J. Bahr. 1976. "A Theory of Power Relations in Marriage." *Journal of Marriage and the Family.* 38:619–627.

————, and Kenneth L. Cannon. 1974. "Marital Satisfaction over the Family Life Cycle: A Reevaluation." *Journal of Marriage and the Family* 36:271–282.

Roof, Wade Clark, and Dean R. Hage. 1980. "Church Involvement in Americas Social Factors Affecting Membership and Participation." *Review of Religious Research* 21:405–426.

Rosen, Benson, Thomas H. Jerdee, and Thomas L. Prestwich. 1975. "Dual-Career Marital Adjustment: Potential Effects of Discrimatory Managerial Attitudes." *Journal of Marriage and the Family* 37:565–572.

Rosen, Harold, ed. 1967. *Abortion in America.* Boston: Beacon Press.

Rosenblatt, Paul C., and Paul C. Cozby. 1972. "Courtship Patterns Associated with Freedom of Choice of Spouse." *Journal of Marriage and the Family* 34:689–695.

Ross, Clara, and P. T. Piotrow. 1974. "Periodic Abstinence: Birth Control Without Contraceptives." *Population Report.* Dept. of Medical and Public Affairs. George Washington University. Series I, no. I.

Rossi, Alice S. 1968. "Transition to Parenthood." *Journal of Marriage and the Family* 30:26–39.

Roston, Leo. 1975. *Religion in America: Ferment and Faith in an Age of Crisis: A New Guide and Almanac.*

New York: Simon & Schuster.

Roszak, Theodore. 1969. *The Making of a Counter Culture.* Garden City, N.Y.: Doubleday.

Roy, Rustum, and Della Roy. 1979. "Is Monogamy Outmoded?" In J. Gipson Wells, ed., *Current Issues in Marriage and the Family.* 2d ed., pp. 125–138. New York: Macmillan.

Rubin, Jeffery Z., Frank J. Provenzano, and Zella Luria. 1974. "The Eye of the Beholder: Parent's Views on Sex of Newborns." *American Journal of Orthopsychiatry* 44:512–519.

Rubin, Lillian Breslow. 1976. *Worlds of Pain: Life in the Working Class Family.* New York: Basic Books.

————. 1981. *Women of a Certain Age: The Midlife Search for Self.* New York: Harper & Row.

Rubin, Zick. 1973. *Living and Loving: An Introduction to Social Psychology.* New York: Holt, Rinehart and Winston.

Russell, Candyce Smith. 1974. "Transition to Parenthood: Problems and Gratifications." *Journal of Marriage and the Family* 36:294–302.

Ryan, William. 1971. *Blaming the Victim.* New York: Vintage Books.

Sager, Clifford J. et al. 1971. "The Marriage Contract." *Family Process* 10:311–326.

Salisbury, W. Seward. 1964. *Religion in American Culture: A Sociological Interpretation.* Homewood, Ill. Dorsey Press.

Sanford, Nevitt. 1966. *Self and Society.* New York: Atherton Press.

Saxton, Lloyd. 1980. *The Individual, Marriage and the Family.* 4th ed. Belmont, Ca.: Wadsworth.

Scanzoni, John. H. 1970. *Opportunity and the Family.* New York: Free Press.

————. 1972. *Sexual Bargaining: Power Politics in American Marriage.* Englewood Cliffs, N.J.: Prentice-Hall.

————. 1975. *Sex Roles, Life Styles, and Child Bearing.* New York: Free Press.

————. 1981. "Contemporary Marriage Types: A Research Note." *Journal of Family Issues* 1:125–140.

Scheflen, Albert E. 1970. "Communicational Arrangements Which Further Specify a Meaning." *Family Process* 9:457–472.

Schoen, Robert 1975. "California Divorce Rates by Age at First Marriage and Duration of First Marriage." *Journal of Marriage and the Family* 37:548–555.

Schulman, Marion L. 1974. "Idealization in Engaged Couples." *Journal of Marriage and the Family* 36:139–147.

Schultz, David A. 1969. *Coming Up Black: Patterns of Ghetto Socialization.* Englewood Cliffs, N.J.: Prentice-Hall.

————, and Stanley F. Rodgers. 1975. *Marriage, the Family, and Personal Fulfillment.* Englewood Cliffs, N.J.: Prentice-Hall.

Schur, Edwin M. 1965. *Crimes Without Victims.* Englewood Cliffs, N.J.: Prentice-Hall.

Schurmann, Franz. 1966. *Ideology and Organization in Communist China*. Berkeley: Ca.: University of California Press.

Schwartz, Arthur N, and James A. Peterson. 1979. *Introduction to Gerontology*. New York: Holt, Rinehart and Winston.

Seeley, J. R., R. A. Sim, and E. W. Loosley. 1973. *Crestwood Heights: A Study of the Culture of Suburban Life*. New York: Wiley.

Sennett, Richard. 1980. *Authority*. New York: Knopf.

Sexton, Patricia Cayo. 1967. *The American School: A Sociological Analysis*. Englewood Cliffs, N.J.: Prentice-Hall.

Shorter, Edward. 1977. *The Making of the Modern Family*. New York: Basic Books.

Shostak, Arthur B. 1969. *Blue-Collar Life*. New York: Random House.

Simmel Georg. 1964. *The Sociology of Georg Simmel*. Trans. and ed. by Kurt H. Wolff., New York: Free Press.

Simpson, George Eaton, and J. Milton Yinger. 1965. *Racial and Cultural Minorities*. 3d ed. New York: Harper & Row.

Singer, June. 1977. *Androgyny: A New Theory of Sexuality*. Garden City, N.Y.: Doubleday.

Skinner, B. F. 1953. *Science and Human Behavior*. New York: Macmillan.

Sklare, Marshall 1971. *America's Jew*. New York: Random House.

———. 1972, *Conservative Judaism: An American Religious Movement*. New York: Schocken Books.

Slater, Philip. 1961. "Parental Role Differentiation." *American Journal of Sociology* 67:296–311.

Smart, Ninian. 1976. *The Religious Experience of Mankind*. 2d ed. New York: Scribner's.

Smelser, Neil J., and Sidney Halpern. 1978. "The Historical Triangulation of Family, Economy, and Education." In John Demos and Sarane S. Boocock, eds. *Turning Points: Historical and Sociological Essays on the Family*, pp. 288–313. Chicago: University of Chicago Press.

Smith, Donald Scott. 1975. "Family Limitation, Sexual Control, and Domestic Feminism in Victorian America." In Mary Hartman and Lois W. Banner, eds., *Clio's Consciousness Raised*, pp. 119–136. New York, Harper & Row.

Smith, Thomas Ewin. 1970. "Foundations of Parental Influence upon Adolescents: An Application of Social Power Theory." *American Sociological Review* 35:860–873.

Smith-Rosenberg, Carroll. 1978. "Sex as Symbol in Victorian Purity: An Ethnohistorical Analysis of Jacksonian America." In John Demos and Sarane S. Boocock, eds., *Turning Points: Historical and Sociological Essays on the Family*, pp. 212–247. Chicago: University

of Chicago Press.

Social Indicators, 1976. 1977. U.S. Department of Commerce Bureau of the Census. Washington, D.C.: U.S. Government Printing Office.

Spark, Geraldine M., and Elaine M. Brady. 1970. "The Aged Are Family Members." *Family Process* 9:195–210.

Spiro, Melford E. 1965. *Children of the Kibbutz*. New York: Schocken Books.

Stafford, Rebecca, Elaine Backman, and Pamela DiBona. 1977. "The Division of Labor Among Cohabiting and Married Couples." *Journal of Marriage and the Family* 39:43–57.

Stannard, David E. 1979. *The Puritan Way of Death*. New York: Oxford University Press.

Stark, Rodney, and Charles Y. Glock. 1970. *American Piety: The Nature of Religious Commitment*. Berkeley, Ca.: University of California Press.

Stein, Maurice R. 1964. *The Eclipse of Community*. New York: Harper & Row.

Stein, Peter J. 1976. *Single*. Englewood Cliffs. N.J.: Prentice-Hall.

———. 1980. "Singlehood: An Alternative to Marriage." In James M. Henslin ed., *Marriage and the Family in a Changing Society*, pp. 150–156. New York: Free Press.

———, ed. 1981. *Single Life: Unmarried Adults in Social Context*. New York: St. Martin's Press.

Steiner, Stan. 1970. La Raza: The Mexican Americans. New York: Harper & Row.

Steinmetz, Suzanne K. 1978. "Violence Between Family Members." *Marriage and Family Review*. 1:1–16.

Stetson, Dorothy M., and Gerald C. Wright, Jr. 1975. "The Effects of Laws on Divorce in American States." *Journal of Marriage and the Family*. 37:537–547.

Stevens, Emma, and Stephen Holmes. 1979. "Cohabitation: The Tender Trap." In J. Gipson Wells, ed., *Current Issues in Marriage and the Family*. 2d ed, pp. 97–108. New York: Macmillan.

Stinnett, Nick, Linda M. Carter, and James E, Montgomery. 1972. "Older Person's Perceptions of Their Marriages." *Journal of Marriage and the Family* 34:665–670.

Stockard, Jean, and Miriam M. Johnson. 1980. *Sex Roles: Sex Inequality and Sex Role Development*. Englewood Cliffs, N.J.: Prentice-Hall.

Stoddard, Ellwyn R. 1973. *Mexican Americans*. New York: Random House.

Stone, Lawrence. 1979 (1977). *The Family, Sex and Marriage* in England 1500–1800. Abridged ed. New York: Harper & Row.

Straus, Murray A. 1974. "Leveling, Civility, and Violence in the Family." *Journal of Marriage and the Family* 36:13–29.

Strong, Bryan, Rebecca Reynolds, Murray Suid, and Jane Dabaghian. 1979. *The Marriage and Family Experi-*

ence: *A Text with Readings.* St. Paul, Minn.: West.

Styryker, Sheldon. 1964. "The Interactional and Situational Approaches." In Harold T. Christensen, ed., *Handbook of Marriage and the Family,* pp. 125–170. Chicago: Rand McNally.

———. 1980. Symbolic–Interactionalism. Menlo Park. Ca.: Benjamin/Cummings.

Stuart, Richard B. 1970. "Token Reinforcement in Marital Treatment." In Paul H. Glasser and Lois N. Glasser, eds., *Families in Crises,* pp. 172–181. New York,: Harper & Row.

Suter, Larry E., and Herman P. Miller. 1973. "Income Differentials Between Men and Career Women." *American Journal of Sociology* 78:962–974.

Tavris, Carol, and Carole Offir. 1977. *The Longest War: Sex Differences in Perspective.* New York: Harcourt Brace Jovanovich.

———, and Susan Sadd. 1977. *The Redbook Report on Female Sexuality.* New York: Delacorte.

Taylor, Patricia Ann, and Norval D. Glenn. 1976. "The Utility of Education and Attractiveness for Females' Status Attainment Through Marriage." *American Sociological Review* 41:484–498.

TeSelle, Sallie. 1973. *The Rediscovery of Ethnicity.* New York: Harper & Row.

Thomas, John L. S. J. 1965. *Catholic Viewpoint on Marriage and the Family.* Rev. ed. Garden City, N.Y.: Image Books, division of Doubleday.

Thompson, Mary Lou, ed. 1970. *Voices of the New Feminism.* Boston: Beacon Press.

Thorton, Arland. 1977. "Children and Marital Stability." *Journal of Marriage and the Family* 39:531–540.

Tocqueville, Alexis de. 1954. *Democracy in America.* 2 vols. New York: Vintage Books.

Toffler, Alvin. 1970. *Future Shock.* New York: Bantam Books.

Tomassen, Richard F. 1970. *Sweden: Prototype of Modern Society.* New York: Random House.

Troeltsch, Ernst. 1931. *The Social Teachings of the Christian Churches.* London: Allen & Unwin.

Troll, Lillian E., Sheila J. Miller, and Robert C. Atchley. 1979. *Families in Later Life.* Belmont, Ca.: Wadsworth.

———, and Jean Smith. 1976. "Attachment Through the Life Span: Some Questions About Dyadic Relations in Later Life." *Human Development* 3:156–171.

Trost, Jan. 1978. "Attitudes Toward and Occurrence of Cohabitation Without Marriage." *Journal of Marriage and the Family* 40:393–400.

Tsui, Amy Org, and Donald J. Bogue. 1978. Declining World Fertility: Trends, Causes, Implications." *Population Bulletin.* Vol. 33, no. 4. Washington, D.C. Population Reference Bureau.

Turner, Jonathan H, and Alexandria Maryansll. 1979. *Functionalism.* Menlo Park, Ca.: Benjamin/Cummings.

Turner, Ralph H. 1970. *Family Interaction.* New York: Wiley.

Turow, Rita. 1978. *Daddy Doesn't Live Here Anymore.* Garden City, N.Y.: Doubleday.

U.S. Bureau of Consumer Protection. 1978. Funeral Industry Practices: Final Staff Report to the Federal Trade Commission and Proposed Trade Regulation View. Washington, D.C.: U.S. Government Printing Office.

U.S. Bureau of the Census. 1977. Statistical Abstracts No. 730. Washington, D.C.: U.S. Government Printing Office.

———. 1978. Department of Commerce. "Percent of Population Ever Married. 1900–1977." Marriage Statistics. Washington, D.C.: U.S. Government Printing Office

———. 1979. Statistical Abstract of the United States. 100th ed. Department of Commerce. Washington, D.C.: U.S. Government Printing Office.

U.S. News and World Report. 1975. "The American Family: Can It Survive the Shocks?" Vol. LXXIX, no. 17 (Oct. 27):30–46.

van der Berghe, Pierre L. 1978. *Man in Society: A Biosocial View.* 2d ed. New York: Elsevier.

———. 1979. *Human Family Systems: An Evolutionary View.* New York: Elsevier.

Van der Vlught, Theresa, and P. T. Piotrow. 1973. "Menstrual Regulation—What Is It?" *Population Reports.* Dept. of Medical and Public Affairs. George Washington University Series, F. no. 2.

van de Walle, Etienne, and John Krodel. 1980. "Europe's Fertility Transition: New Evidence and Lessons for Today's Developing World." *Population Bulletin.* Vol. 34, no. 6. Washington, D.C.: Population Reference Bureau.

Veerers, Jean E. 1973. "Voluntarily Childless Wives." An Exploratory Study." *Sociology and Social Research* 57:356–366.

Vener, Arthur M., and Cyrus S. Steward. 1974. "Adolescent Sexual Behavior in Middle America Revisited. 1970–1973." *Journal of Marriage and the Family.* 36:728–735.

Vincent, Clark E. 1966. "Family Spongia: The Adaptive Function." *Journal of Marriage and the Family* 28:29–36.

———. 1969. *Unmarried Mothers.* New York: Free Press.

———. 1970. "Mental Health and the Family." In Paul H. Glasser and Lois N. Glasser, eds., *Families in Crisis,* pp. 319–360. New York: Harper & Row.

Vogel, Ezra F. 1971. *Japan's New Middle Class.* 2d ed. Berkeley, Ca.: University of California Press.

Wadsworth, Barry J. 1971. *Piaget's Theory of Cognitive Development.* New York: David McKay.

Waite, Linda J. 1976. "Working Wives: 1940–1960." *American Sociological Review* 41:65–80.

Wakin, Edward, and Father Joseph F. Scherer. 1966. *The*

De-Romanization of the American Catholic Church. New York: Macmillan.

Wallace, Ronald S. 1961. *Calvin's Doctrine of the Christian Life.* Grand Rapids, Mich.: Eerdmans.

Waller, Willard. 1937. "The Rating and Dating Complex." *American Sociological Review* 2:727–734.

Wallerstein, Judith S., and Joan B. Kelly. 1980. "The Effects of Parental Divorce: Experiences of the Child in Later Latency." In Arlene Skolnick and Jerome H. Skolnick, eds., *Family in Transition.* 3d ed., pp. 438–452. Boston: Little, Brown.

Ward, David. 1971. *Cities and Immigrants: A Geography of Change in Nineteenth Century America.* New York: Oxford University Press.

Warner, W. Lloyd. 1960. *Social Class in America.* New York: Harper & Row.

———. 1963. *Yankee City.* Abridged ed. New Haven, Conn.: Yale University Press.

———. 1964a. *A Black Civilization: A Study of an Australian Tribe.* New York: Harper & Row.

———. 1964b. *Democracy in Jonesville.* New York: Harper & Row.

Weber, Max. 1952. *Ancient Judaism.* New York: Free Press.

———. 1958a. *From Max Weber.* Hans Gerth and C. Wright Mills, eds., New York: Oxford University Press.

———. 1958b. *The Religion of India.* New York: Free Press.

———. 1976. *The Agrarian Sociology of Ancient Civilizations.* London: NLB Press.

Weinberg, Martin S., and Colin J. Williams. 1980. "Sexual Embourgeoisement? Social Class and Sexual Activity: 1938–1970." *American Sociological Review* 45:33–48.

Weingarten, Helen. 1980. "Remarriage and Well-Being." *Journal of Family Issues* 1:533–559.

Weingarten, Kathy. 1978. "Interdependence." In Robert Rapoport and Rhona Rapoport, eds., *Working Couples,* New York: Harper & Row.

Weiss, Robert S. 1975. *Marital Separation.* New York: Basic Books.

Weitz, Shirley. 1977. *Sex Roles: Biological, Psychological, and Social Foundations.* New York: Oxford University Press.

Weitzman, Lenore J., and Ruth B. Dixon. 1980. "The Transformation of Legal Marriage Through No-Fault Divorce." In Arlene Skolnick and Jerome H. Skolnick, eds., *Family in Transition,* pp. 354–367. Boston: Little, Brown.

Wells, J. Gipson, ed. 1979. *Current Issues in Marriage and the Family.* 2d ed. New York: Macmillan.

Westoff, Charles F. 1974. "Coital Frequency and Contraception." *Family Planning Perspectives* 6:136–141.

Whitbourne, Susan Krauss, and Comilda S. Weinstock. 1979. *Adult Development: The Differentiation of Experience.* New York: Holt, Rinehart, and Winston.

White, Lynn K. 1979. "The Correlates of Urban Illegitimacy in the United States, 1960–1970." *Journal of Marriage and the Family* 41:715–726.

Wilkes, Paul. 1977. *Six American Families.* New York: Seabury/Parthenon Press.

Williams, Robin M. Jr. 1970. *American Society.* 3d. ed. New York: Knopf.

Wilson, Edward O. 1975. *Sociobiology. The New Synthesis.* Cambridge, Mass: Harvard University Press.

Wilson, John. 1978. *Religion in American Society: The Effective Presence.* Englewood Cliffs, N.J.: Prentice-Hall.

Winch, Robert F. 1958. *Mate Selection: A Study of Complementary Needs.* New York: Harper & Row.

Wooden, Kenneth. 1976. *Weeping in the Playtime of Others.* New York: McGraw-Hill.

Wortman, Judith. 1976. "The Diaphragm and Other Intravaginal Barriers—A Review." *Population Reports.* Dept. of Medical and Public Affairs. George Washington University. Series H, no. 4.

Wright, Derek. 1975. "The New Tyranny of Sexual Liberation." In Jack R. DeLora and Joann S. DeLora, eds., *Intimate Life Styles.* 2d ed., pp. 87–89. Pacific Palisades, Ca.: Goodyear.

Wright, Gerald C., Jr., and Dorothy M. Stetson. 1978. "The Impact of No-Fault Divorce Law Reform on Divorce in American States." *Journal of Marriage and the Family* 40:575–580.

Yang, C. K. 1965. *Chinese Communist Society: The Family and the Village.* Cambridge, Mass.: MIT Press.

Yankelvich, Daniel. 1974. *The New Morality; A Profile of American Youth in the 70's.* New York: McGraw-Hill.

Yinger, J. Milton. 1970. *The Scientific Study of Religion.* New York: Macmillan.

Yost, E. D., and R. J. Adamek. 1974. "Parent-child Interaction and Changing Family Values: A Multivariate Analysis." *Journal of Marriage and the Family* 36:115–121.

Zelditch, Morris, Jr. 1955. "Role Differentiation in the Nuclear Family: A Comparative Study." In T. Parsons and R. F. Bales, eds., *Family, Socialization, and Interaction Process,* pp. 307–352. New York: Free Press.

———. 1964. "Family, Marriage, and Kinship." "In R. E. L. Faris, ed., *Handbook of Modern Sociology.* Chicago: Rand McNally.

Zelnick, Melvin, and John F. Kantner. 1977. "Sexual and Contraceptive Experience of Young Unmarried Women in the U.S. 1976 and 1971." *Family Planning Perspectives* 9:55–71.

Name Index

Abramson, J., 72
Adam, J., 336, 338, 343
Adam, N., 336, 338, 343
Adams, J. Q., 239
Adler, A., 276–277, 491
Ahlstrom, S. E., 34, 381
al-Awsiyeh, F., 148
Albee, E., 312
Aldou, J., 255, 264
Aldridge, D. P., 112
Alexander, S., 468
al-Owssiy, B., 149
Alston, J. P., 371
Ambron, S. R., 475
Anderson, C. H., 381, 382
Anderson, J., *302*
Anderson, S. M., 200
Andes, J., 165
Andre, T., 34
Ansbacher, H. L., 277
Aquinas, Saint Thomas, 42
Arafat, I., 200, 202, 203, 204
Arber, S., 57
Aries, P., 44, 496
Armor, D. J., 372, 373–374
Armstrong, D., *83*
Aronoff, J., 289–290
Askham, J., 315
Atchley, R. C., 421, 423, 424, 434, 447
Augustine, Saint, 42

Avery, A. W., 203
Azzi, R., *247*

Baber, R. E., 170
Bach, G. R., 306, 308, 312, 498
Backman, E., 203
Bahr, H. M., 195
Bahr, S. J., 170, 177
Bailey, D. S., 42
Baker, G., 105, 165
Bales, R. F., 21, 141, 240, 254, 285, 331, 333, 403, 498, 492, 493
Balswick, J., 69, 70, 96, 97, 99
Bane, M. J., 5, 6, 73, 75, 107, 143, 145, 150, 229, 239, 248, 263, 322, 330, 331, 332, 342, 347, 441, 458
Banfield, E., 104, 268
Bardwich, J. M., 58, 69
Bast, G., 165, 166
Bast, P., 165, 166
Bebbington, A. C., 163, 210
Becker, E., 271
Behrens, D., 304–305
Belkin, G. S., 85
Bell, A. P., 196–200
Bell, B., 462
Bell, D., 50, 106, 361, 401
Bell, N. W., 8, 13, *353*, *355*, *356*, *357*, 362–363
Bell, R., 300
Bem, S. L., 71, 73, 74–75

Italicized numbers refer to illustrations.

Bendix, R., 150
Bennetts, L., 268–269
Benson, L., 242
Berardo, F. M., 195, 433, 434
Berelson, B., 2226–29
Berger, B., 49
Berger, D. G., 97
Berger, I., *104*
Berger, P. L., 19, 28, 49, 111, 252, 369–370
Bernard, J., 69, 73, 75, 166–167, 192, 207, 209, 213, 241, 242, 356, 387, 414
Berne, E., 179, 185
Bernstein, B. E., 205, 206
Berry, K. J., 212
Bettelheim, B., 82
Bienvenu, M. J., 183
Billingsley, A., 388, 390–391
Billington, R. A., 381
Binstock, J., 208–209
Blood, R. O., Jr., 17, 49, 87, 153, 167, 169, 170, 241, 248, 301, 307, 354, 383, 484
Blumer, H., 9
Boatright, M. C., 48
Bogue, D. J., 230, 231
Bohannan, P., 58, 477
Boorstin, D. J., 380
Bottomore, T. B., 149, 365
Bould, S., 346
Bouvier, L. F., 371
Bower, D. W., 201, 202, 204
Brandwein, R. A., 346
Brannon, R., 58, 65, 70
Brisset, D., 144
Broderick, C. B., 242
Brody, E. M., 424
Brody, J. E., 431–432
Bronfenbrenner, U., 399
Brown, J. A. C., 277
Brown, P., 323
Bruck, C., 74–75
Buchanan, S., 20
Burgess, E. W., 114, 167, 301, 329
Burgess-Kohn, J., 89, 90, 97, 98
Burke, R. J., 213

Cadwallader, M., 143
Calder, J., *447*
Calvin, J., 42; photo of, *45*
Campbell, A., 153, 423
Cannon, K. L., 153, *423*
Caplan, A. L., 20
Carey, J. T., 89
Carns, D. E., 96
Cavan, R. S., 118
Centers, R., 170

Chafe, W. H., 69, 76, 356
Chaudry, S. L., 469, 470
Cherlin, A., 339, 340, 341
Chiriboga, D., 416
Christiansen, H. T., 10
Christopherson, V. A., 201, 202, 204
Clark, B. R., 268, 373
Clark, E., 41
Clark, T. D., 387
Clayton, R. R., 32, 200, 202
Cogley, J., 381
Cole, S. P., 238
Coleman, J., 65, 66, 86, 268, 373–374
Colgan, W., 345–346
Comte, A., 11
Conklin, P. S., *365*, *412*
Constantine, J. H., 35, 218–219
Constantine, L. L., 35, 218–219
Cooley, C. H., 270
Coser, R. L., 177
Costello, L., 381
Coulanges, F. de, 40
Cox, H., 96
Cozby, P. C., 113
Crano, W. D., 289–290
Cromwell, O., 273
Cronkite, R. C., 186–187
Cuber, J., 159, 186, 306, 315, 316–317, 318
Cumming, E., 437
Cummins, M., 82
Czajka, J. L., 57

Dalsimer, I., 466
D'Antonio, W. V., 90, 179, 299, 471, 472, 480
David, D. S., 58, 65, 70
Davis, K. E., 89, 130, 201
Dean, G., 341
Delissovoy, V., 141
della Grotta, V., *71*
de Lone, R., 268–269
Demos, J., 47, 80, 285, 339
Denfield, D., 217, 218
Denison, D. R., *67, 143, 175, 210, 240, 263, 296, 364*
de Vaux, R., 39
Di Bona, P., 203
Dickens, C., 6
Dille, J., 158, 322, 323, 489
Dixon, R. B., 326, 327, 337
Donne, J., 353
Douvan, E., 58, 69
Dreikurs, 277
Duberman, L., 59, 113, 125, 237, 241, 242, 244, 262, 315, 340, 341, 426
Dullea, G., 164–166
Durkheim, E., 11, 146, 252, 266

Duvall, E. M., 10–11, 182, 183, 412, 422
Duvall, S., 94
Dyer, E. D., 171, 395

Ebaugh, H. R. R., 371–372
Eckland, B. K., 119, 122
Eder, D., 63
Egan, T., *422*
Ehrhardt, A., 61
Ehrlich, P., 230
Eisenstadt, S. N., 49, 477
Elkin, F., 147, 253, 262, 373, 390
Elkind, D., 276
Elkins, S., 387
Ellis, H., 181
Elms, A. C., 256
Engels, F., 44; photo of, *45*
Erhart, J. F., 233
Erhmann, W., 99
Erikson, E. 88, 103, 257, 258
Erlanger, H. S., 399–401
Espenshade, T. J., 146, 208, 226, 245–246
Etzioni, A., 470, 474

Farley, R., 169
Fein, R. A., 242
Feldstein, S., 381
Filene, P. G., 71
Fontana, V. J., 240
Forisha, B. L., 73, 289, 479
Forsyth, M., *360, 391*
Franklin, B., 92
Franklin, O., *402*
Frazier, E. F., 386, 387, 388, 390, 490
Freedman, M., 31
Freud, S., 74, 176, 270–273, 495, 497
Friedan, B., 295
Fromm, E., 89
Furstenberg, F. F., 121

Gagnon, J., 58
Galbraith, J. K., 360, 361
Galligan, R. J., 177
Gans, H. J., 403
Garrett, L. H., 420–421
Garrett, W., *238, 243*
Geertz, C., 13, 146
Gelles, R. J., 144, 313
Genovese, E. D., 387, 388
Gersuny, C., 157
Gesell, A., 279
Gieseman, R. W., 488
Gillespie, D. B., 484
Ginott, H., 279
Glazer, N., 125, 378, 385, 392, 396, 398

Glenn, N. D., 177, 195, 341
Glick, P. C., 84, 105, 113, 120, 121, 151, 152, 193, 194, *201*, 206–207, 229, 242, 306, 323, 324, 329, 330, 339, 340, 424, 457, 458
Glock, C. Y., 123, 369
Glueck, E., 344
Glueck, S., 344
Goffman, E., 9, 62
Goldberg, B., *228, 259*
Goldberg, S., 63, 76
Goldblatt, S., *115*
Goldscheider, C., 393, 394
Goldstein, S., 393, 394
Goode, W. J., 11, 13, 27, 36, 80, 112, 113, 116, 126, 139, 142, 145, 177, 194, 225, 307, 323, 329, 330, 331, 334, 335, 336, 344, 484
Goodman, N., 85
Gordon, Michael, 93–94, 181–182, 217, 297, 384
Gordon, Milton, 114, 370, 378
Gordon, S., 91
Gordon, T., 278–279
Goslin, D. A., 268, 373
Gould, R. E., 195
Grace, M., 165
Grace, R., 165
Graham, B., 456
Greeley, A. M., 123, 125, 234, 331, 369, 381
Greenleaf, B. K., 40, 44, 51, 57, 93, 225, 254
Greer, G., 144, 295
Greven, P., 48, 82, 191
Grunzweig, F. B., *17*
Gunter, B. G., 337
Gupte, P. B., 148–149
Gurak, D. T., 341
Gutman, H., 390

Habenstein, R. W., 40, 41, 97, 300
Hakim, W., 148–149
Haley, A., 38
Haley, J., 184
Hall, C. S., 271, 276
Hallihan, M. T., 63
Halpern, S., 46
Hambley, J., 474
Hamlin, E., *156*
Handel, G., 147, 253, 262, 373, 401
Handelman, P., 416, 417
Handlin, M. F., 82
Handlin, O., 82, 379, 382, 383
Haney, C. A., 371–372
Harburg, E., 323
Harris, J., 400
Harroff, P., 159, 186, 306, 315, 316–317, 318
Hartel, B., 371
Harvey, C. D., 195

Lenski, G., 370, 394, 403
Leonard, J., *59*
Leslie, E. M., 476, 486
Leslie, G. R., 122, 182, 345, 426, 476, 486
Lever, J., 63
Levine, M. P., 200
Levinger, G., 186, 289, 307
Levitt, E. E., 93
Lewinsohn, R., 118
Lewis, L. S., 144
Lewis, M., 63
Lewis, O., 104, 395, 396, 398
Libby, R. W., 94, 192, 193
Liebow, E., 390
Lincoln, A., 239
Lindzey, G., 271, 276
Lipset, S. M., 49, 73, 149, 150, 177, 357, 361, 401, 421
Lipsetz, M. E., 201
Litwak, E., 46, 403, 494
Lobsenz, N. M., 298
Locke, H. J., 167, 301, 329
Loether, H. J., 418
Loosley, E. W., 49, 403
Lopata, H. Z., 70, 163, 195, 237, 239, 241, 291−292, 295, 303, 356, 414, 435
Lopreato, J., 383
Lowenthal, M. F., 68, 416
Luckmann, T., 367
Lunde, D., 233, 465, 469, 478, 480
Luther, M., 42; photo of, *45*
Lyness, J. L., 201

Mace, D., 156, 185, 308, 316
Mace, V., 156, 308, 316
Macklin, E. D., 152, 201, 202, 203−204
Malinowski, B., 8
Mallowe, M., 96
Mandelbaum, D. G., 32, 116
Marchall, D., 98
Marini, M. M., 301
Martin, D., 362
Martin, P. Y., 71
Martin, T. W., 212
Marvin, L., 205
Marx, K., 44; photo of, *45*
Maryanski, A., 11
Maslow, A., 215
Mason, K. O., *57, 67, 143, 175, 210, 240, 263, 296, 364*
Mass, H. D., 418
Masters, W. H., 22, 181
Mauss, A. L., 371
May, R., 184, 215
Mazzaschi, M., *121*

McCary, J. L., 90, 168, 470, 475, 478
McClelland, D. C., 359, 360−361
McDonald, G. W., 414
McHugh, T., *196*
McKenzie, J. L., 123
McLaughlin, S. D., 68, 72
McLaughlin, V. Y., 169
Mead, G. H., 9, 62, 256−257, 258, 261, 266, 270, 272−273, 493, 495
Mead, M., 60
Melville, K., 218
Menzel, P., *438*
Merton, R. K., 11, 63, 68, 258
Meyes, L., 313
Michel, A., 112
Miller, B. C., 10
Miller, H. P., 72
Miller, P., 46
Miller, R. K., 274−275
Miller, S. J., 423, 424, 434, 447
Mitford, J., 445
Moberg, D. O., 367, 369, 371
Money, J., 61
Moneymakee, J., 89, 93, 179
Montanino, F., 89, 93, 179
Morgan, E. S., 35, 47, 191, 339
Moring, Jerry, 164, 166
Movius, M., 208
Moynihan, D. P., 125, 378, 385−386, 388, 390, 396, 398
Murdock, G. P., 8, 146
Murphy, F. X., CSSR, 233

Nash, D., 369−370
Nash, J., 242
Needleman, J., 105
Nemerowicz, G. M., 61
Neubeck, G., 181, 300
Newcomb, P. R., 85
Newman, W. N., 378
Nilsson, M. P., 40
Nimkoff, M. F., 32, 34
Nixon, R. E., 179
Norman, M., 341
Norton, A. J., 84, 105, 113, 120, 151, 152, 194, *201*, 206, 242, 323, 324, 329, 330, 339, 424, 457
Nye, F. I., 285, 344

Oakley, A., 58, 72, 75, 76−7, 163, 289, 292−295, 475, 479
Oesterley, W. O. E., 39
Offir, C., 313
Ogburn, W. F., 285
Omran, K. F., 470
O'Neill, G., 25, 215−217

Subject Index

Abortion, 233, 468
  as birth control, 470
  defined, 490
  methods of, 469–470
  religious objections to, 371–372
  spontaneous versus induced, 468
Absence of "true consent," 322
Abstinence, as birth control measure, 233
  defined, 490
Achievement orientation, 177
  among Jews, 392–393
  defined, 490
  and economic success, 357–361
  motivations for, 359–361
  and retirement, 421–422
  and status, 357–362
Active listening, 278
Adolescence, marriage in, 121–122
  marriage, and divorce rate, 330
  peer group and sex roles, 64–66
  versus puberty, 477
Affinal kin, 31, 490
Age, of children, and accepting divorce, 344
  at first marriage, and divorce, 330
  homogamy of, 120–122
Agencies of socialization, 262–270
  church, 269–270
  defined, 490
  family, 262–265
  play group and neighborhood, 265–266
  school, 266–268
Agents of socialization, 262, 490
Aging, and American culture, 436–437

Aging (cont.)
  and declining health, 436–439
  and estate planning, 443
  and living with one's children, 440–442
  and use of free time, 439
Anal phase, 271, 490
Androgen, 475, 480
Androgyny, 73–75, 490
Annulment, 322, 490
Anticipatory socialization, 63, 258, 490
Apportioned grandmother, 427
Arranged marriage, 112, 116–118
  Puritans, 47
Asexual homosexual, 196, 490
Ashkenazim, 392, 490
Assimilation, cultural, 378
  defined, 490
  Mexican-Americans, 395
  "new immigrants," 384–385
Association of Couples for Marriage Enrichment, 316
Authority, in family, 36–37
  See also Power relations
Autonomic marriage, 35, 490
Autonomic pattern, 170–171, 490
Available income, 481

"Band-aid surgery," 472
Bank loans, 486–487
Basic conflicts, 306
Behavior modification, 278
Bem Sex-Role Inventory (BSRI), 74–75
Bilaterality, 36, 490
Biological development, 473–480

523

Equality, in in-law relations, 182–183
  patterns of, 170–171
  as social value, 374
  and socialization, 268–269
Estrogen, 477–478
Ethnic group, 378, 492
Ethnic identity, and cultural assimilation, 384–385
  and mate selection, 125
Evolution, and the family, 13
Exogamy, 118–119, 492
Experience of parenthood, 227–228
Expertise, and tasks, 172
Expressive leader, 288–290, 492
Extended family, 31–32, 492
Extramarital sexual relations, 300–301
  and open marriage, 216

Family, as agency of socialization, 262–265
  American, history of, 46–51
  American frontier, 48–49
  benefits of, 24–28
  and biological necessity, 19–20
  change in functions of, 285–286
  Chinese, 14–15
  and church, 367–372
  contemporary status of, 460–461
  decline theory, reviewed, 456–461
  definitions of, 7–9, 492
  early Christian, 41
  eight stages of (Duvall), 10–11
  extended, 31–32, 492
  forms of, 286
  functional definitions of, 7–8
  future of, 18
  in Greco-Roman culture, 40–41
  Hebrew, before Christ, 39–40
  impact of research on, 23–24
  and Industrial Revolution, 42–46
  interaction with community, 362–366
  leadership roles in, 287–290
  loss of functions of, 459–460
  in medieval and Reformation doctrine, 42
  meeting individual needs within, 461–463
  meeting societal needs, 463–464
  modern, middle-class, 49–50
  modern, traits of, 42–43
  and natural law, 20–21
  nuclear, 31–32; See also Nuclear family
  participation versus analysis, 21–24
  postmodern, 50–51
  of poverty, 398–399
  power relations in, 168–171
  present status of, 6–7
  research on (see Research)
  and the school, 372–374

Family (cont.)
  seasons of, 2–3
  shrinking of, 409–411
  size of, 459
  as small group, 286–287
  social contributions of, 13–18
  and social convention, 21
  social importance of, 13–21, 25–27
  as specialized institution, 453–456
  substantive definitions of, 8
  types of, 31–32
  universal presence of, 13
  versus peer group, 106–107
  Western, history of, 38–46
  working definition of, 8–9
Family of orientation, 32, 492
Family of procreation, 32, 492
Family planning, 492
  and choice of contraception, 235–236
  increase in, 233–236
Fatherhood, and retirement, 418–422
  social role of, 242–245
Female sterilization, 472–473
Feminine roles, ambiguity in, 69–70
  young adult, 66–69
Feminist movement, 58
  and childbearing, 208–209
  and conjugal rights, 144
  and housewife role, 295
  See also Women's liberation
Fertilization, 474
Fertility rate (see Birth rate)
Fetal stage of development, 475
Fixed expenses, 481–482
Foreplay, 179, 299, 492
Formal operations stage, 276
Fraud, as cause for annulment, 322
Free-choice mating system, 112–113, 492
Frontier family, 48–49
Functional definitions of the family, 492
Functional homosexual, 196, 493
Funeral, significance of, 445–446

Game stage, of socialization, 260–261, 493
Gender identity, 58, 493
  and friendship and games, 63–64
Generation gap, 460
Genes, 473
Genital stage, 272, 493
Geographic mobility, 458–459
Gestation, 475
Go-between, 118
Government, and family, 366–367
Grandparents, enjoyment of role of, 425–426
  social role of, 424–427

Serious dating, 497
Sex, 58, 497
Sex roles, 58—59
   and adolescent peer group, 64—66
   defined, 497
   and leadership, 288—289
   learning of, 259
   masculine, adult, 70—71
   modeling, 64
   modern opposition to, 73—76
   modern support of, 76—77
   patterns of, in marriage, 297—301
   and social equality, 71—77
   socialization to, 59—71
   women, young adult, 66—69
   and work roles, 66—67
Sex-typed toys and play, 62—63
Sexual behavior, extramarital, 300—301
   marital, trends in, 298—300
Sexual freedom, 457—458
Sexual relations, contemporary norms, 94
   legitimate, and marriage, 144—145
   marital, attitudes toward, 297—298
   and marital strife, 179—182
   traditional norms, 92—94
   and youth culture, 105
Sexual stereotypes, male, 70—71
   in toys and play, 62—63
Sexual revolution, 94
   and dating, 89
   first and second, 101
Shakers, 37—38
Sharecropper-tenancy system, 387, 497
Siblings, and socialization, 263—264
Significant others, 260, 497
Single life, 191—195
   reasons for choosing, 192—193
   services available, 193—194
   through postponing marriage, 193—194
   unchosen, 194—195
Single-parent families, 497
Social class, and companionship in marriage, 303
   and consumption patterns, 361—362
   and dating, 86—87
   and divorce rate, 331—332
   and juvenile delinquency, 347
   lower-lower, 398—399
   and mate selection, 125—126
   and permissiveness, 99
   and sexual behavior, 299
   variations in, 398—404
   white-collar, 401—404
   working-class, 399—401
Social control, by family, 27
   by teacher, 267—268

Social convention, 21
   and task allocation, 173—174
Social equality, and sex roles, 71—77
Social gerontology, 439, 497
Social mobility, 149—150, 177
   and ethnic ties, 384
Social norms, 27
   and functionalism, 12
   and mating process, 113—116
Social placement, 145, 497
Social roles, 9—10, 497
   in family, 8
   of father, 242—245
   of husband, 166—167
   of mother, 239—242
   and mother-child attachment, 254—255
   in play of children, 258—260
   of wife, 167—168
Socialization, 15—17, 146—147, 454—455
   agents of, 262—270
   beginning of, 253—255
   concept of, 252—253
   defined, 146, 497
   and divorce, 346—347
   and emergence of selfhood, 255—261
   to labor, 355—356
   language and symbols, 256—258
   psychoanalytic view of, 270—273
   to sex roles, 59—71
   sex-typed toys and play, 62—63
   stages of, 258—261
Society, basic institutions of, 13—15
   needs of, and family, 25—27, 463—464
   pressure to marry, 150—151
   and romantic love, 141—143
Sociobiology, 19—20, 497
Spanish-American family, 394—398
   Mexican, 394—396
   Puerto Rican, 396—398
   selected characteristics of, 397
Spermicidal preparations, 467—468
Sports, and youth culture, 105
Spousal support, 338
   modification of, 339
Status group, 361, 497
Status identity, 497
   and marriage, 147—150
   and parenthood, 227
Steady date, 82
Stepchild-stepparent relations, 340—342
Sterilization, 470—473
Straight-life monogamy, 34
Stress, in dual-career marriage, 211—212
   in dual-worker marriage, 213
   and physical and mental disorders, 409—410